P9-CBI-803

*For Kathy,
Daniel, and Adam*

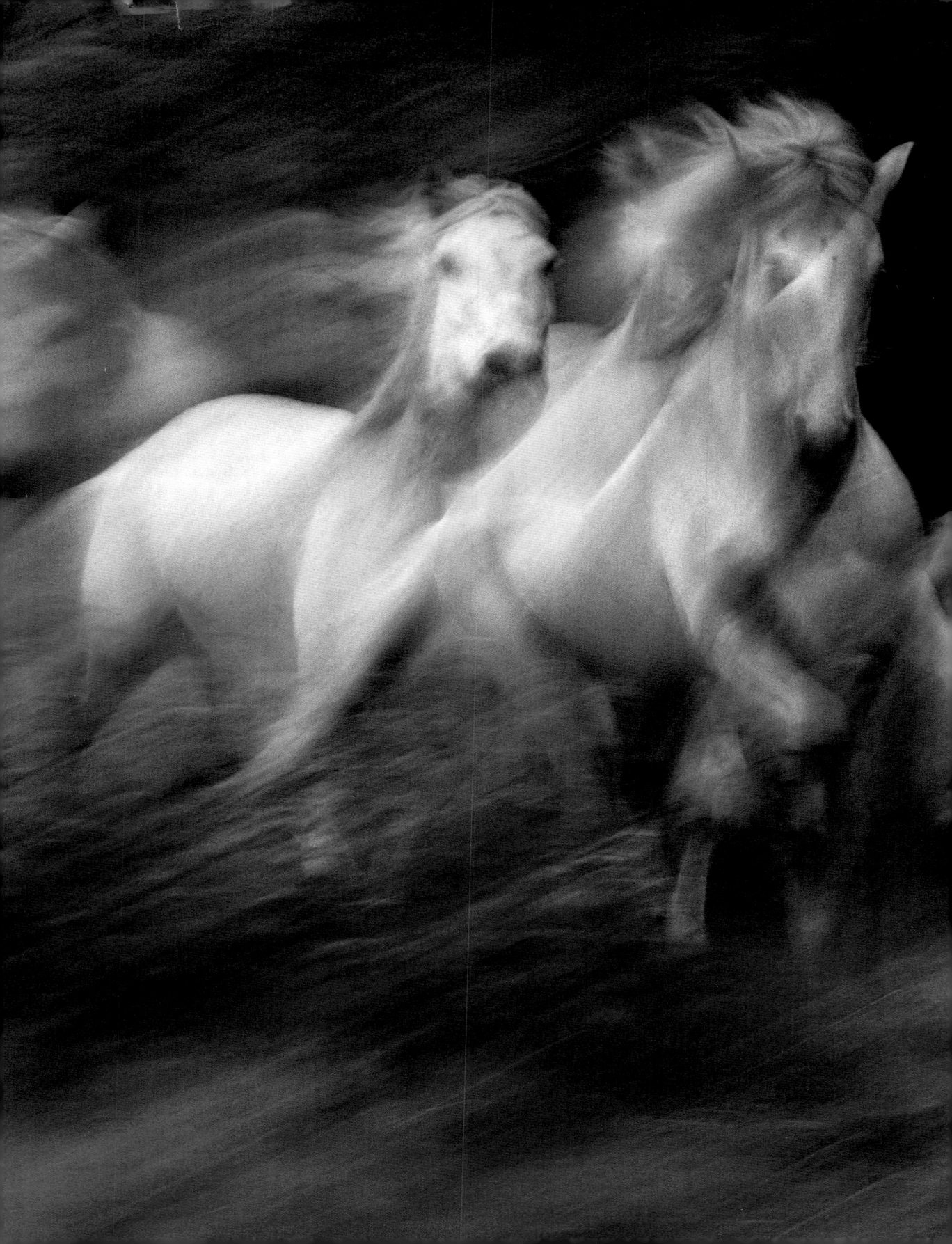

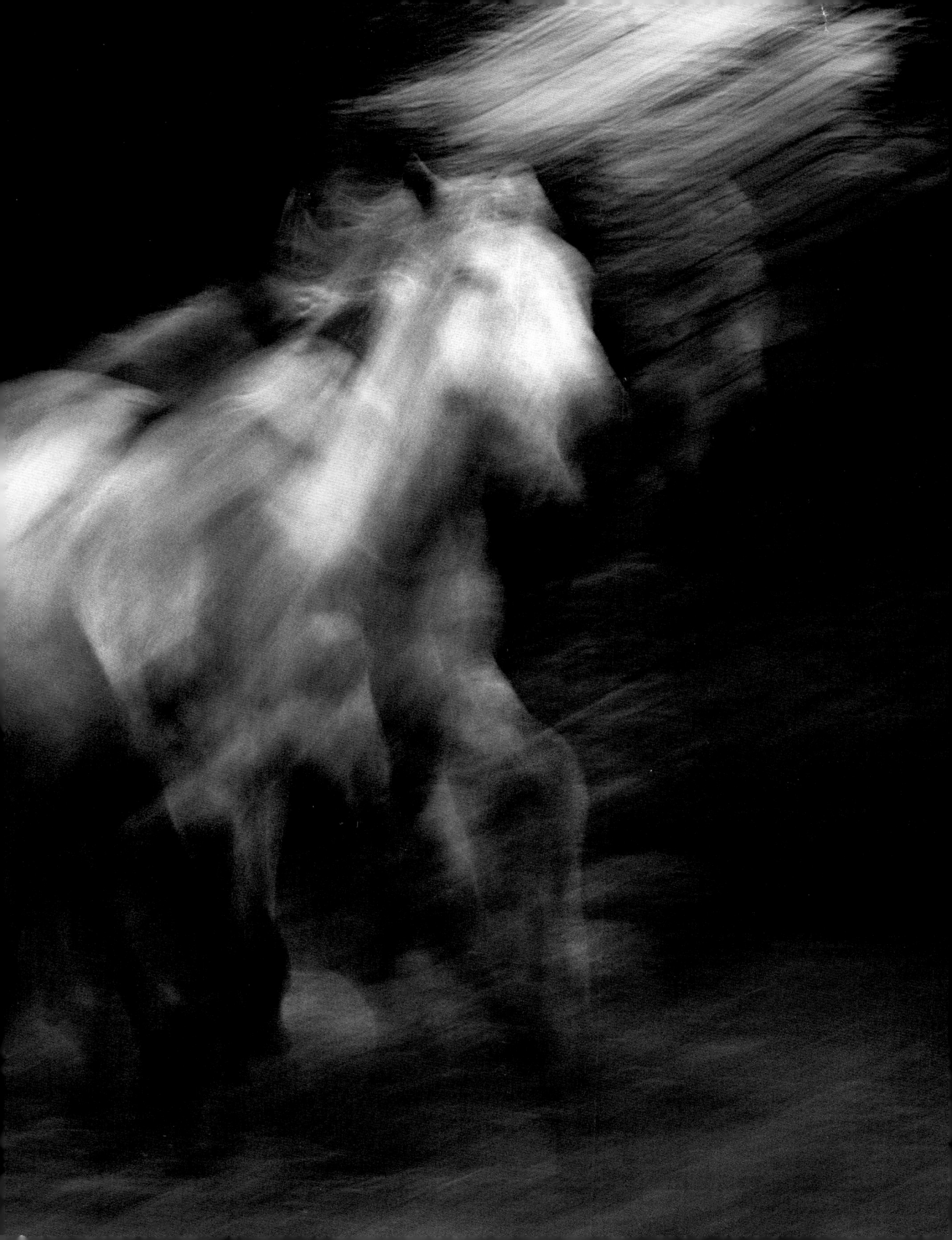

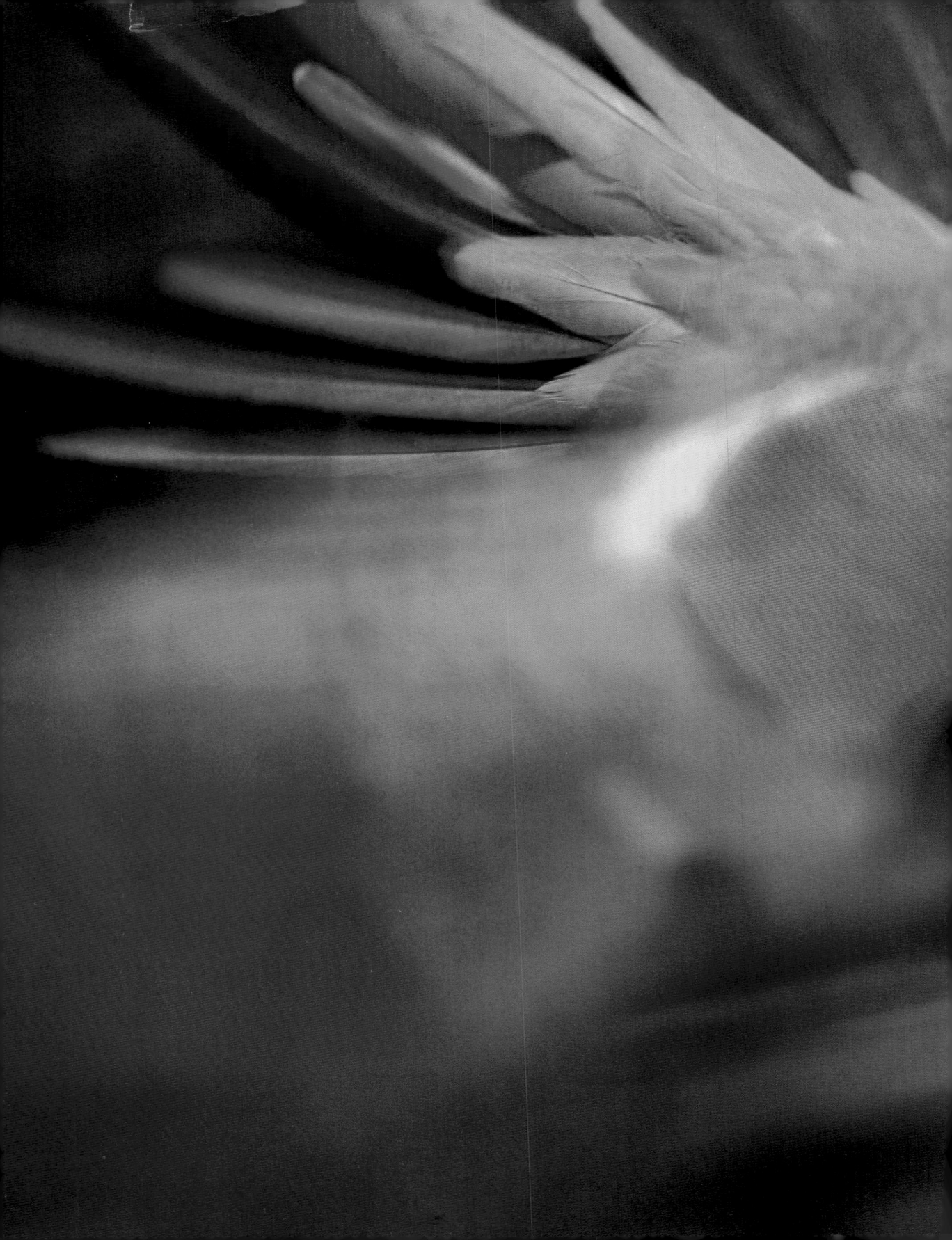

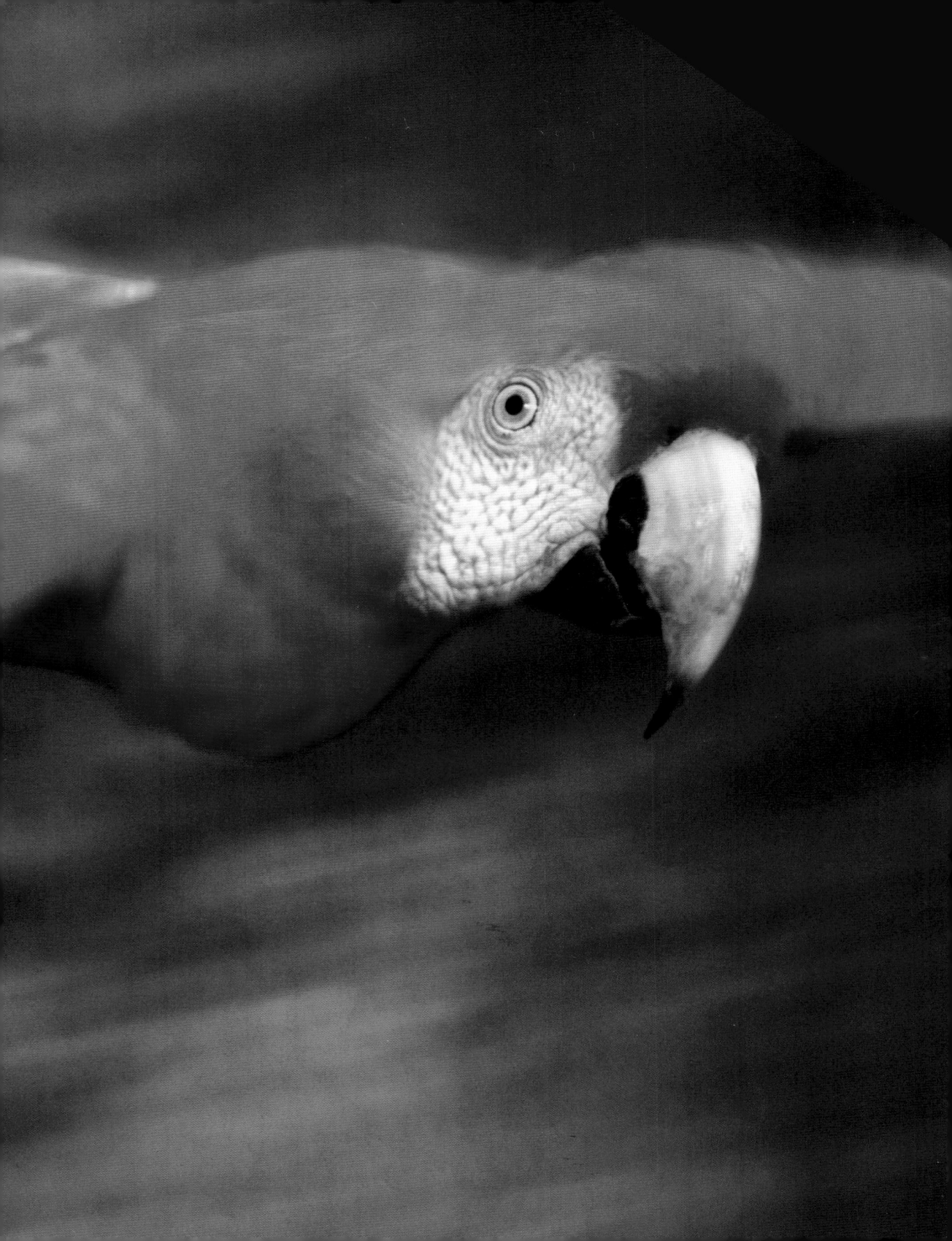

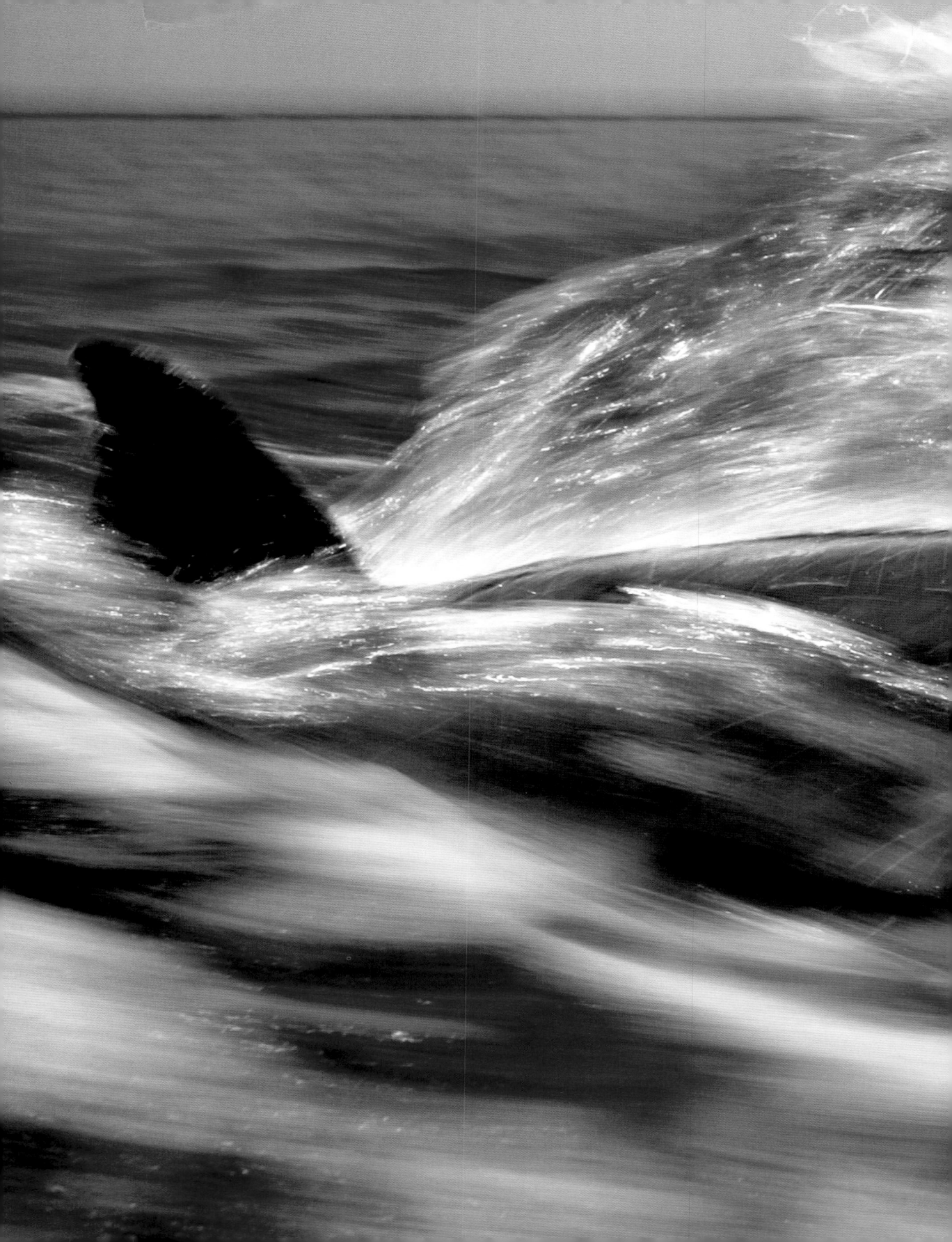

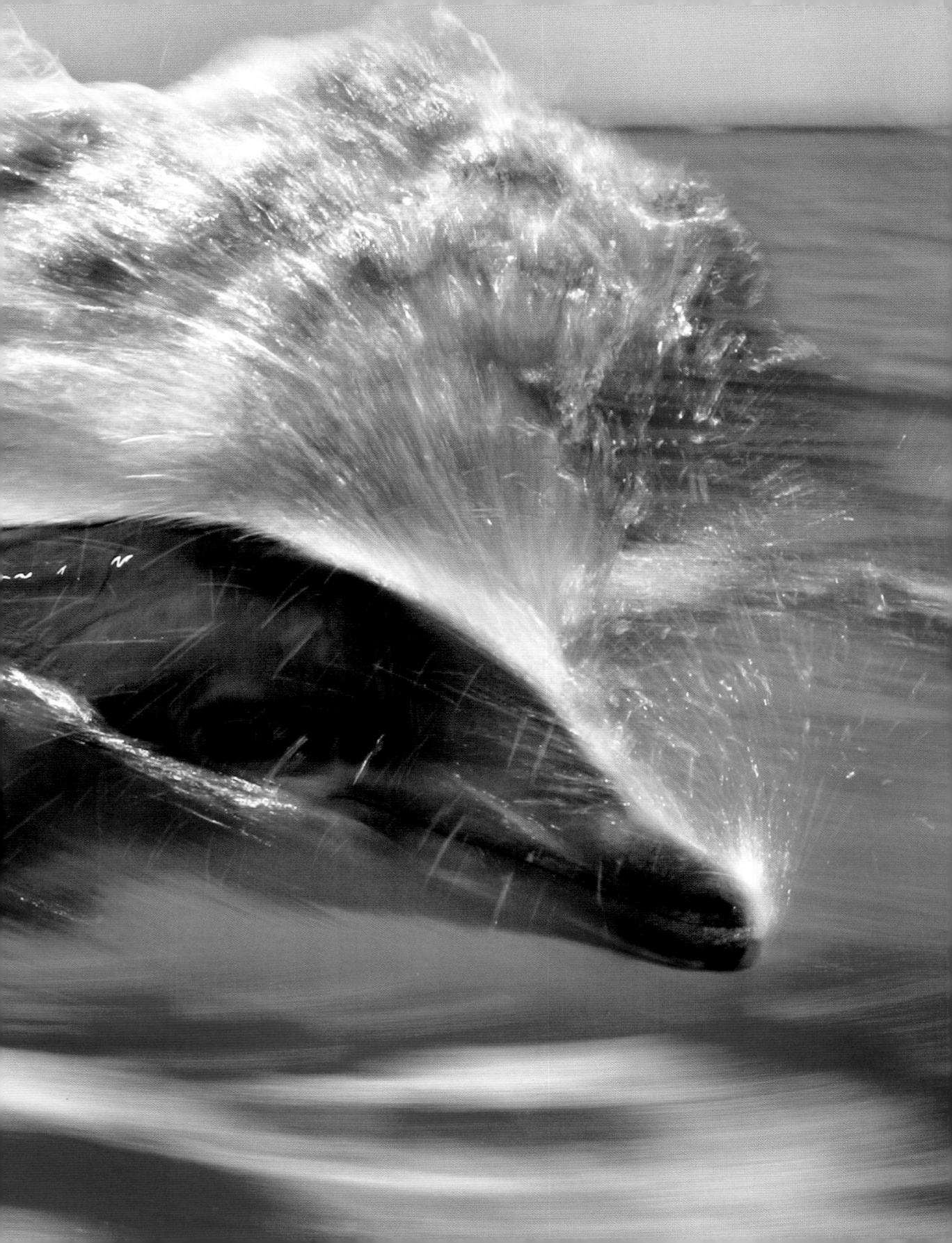

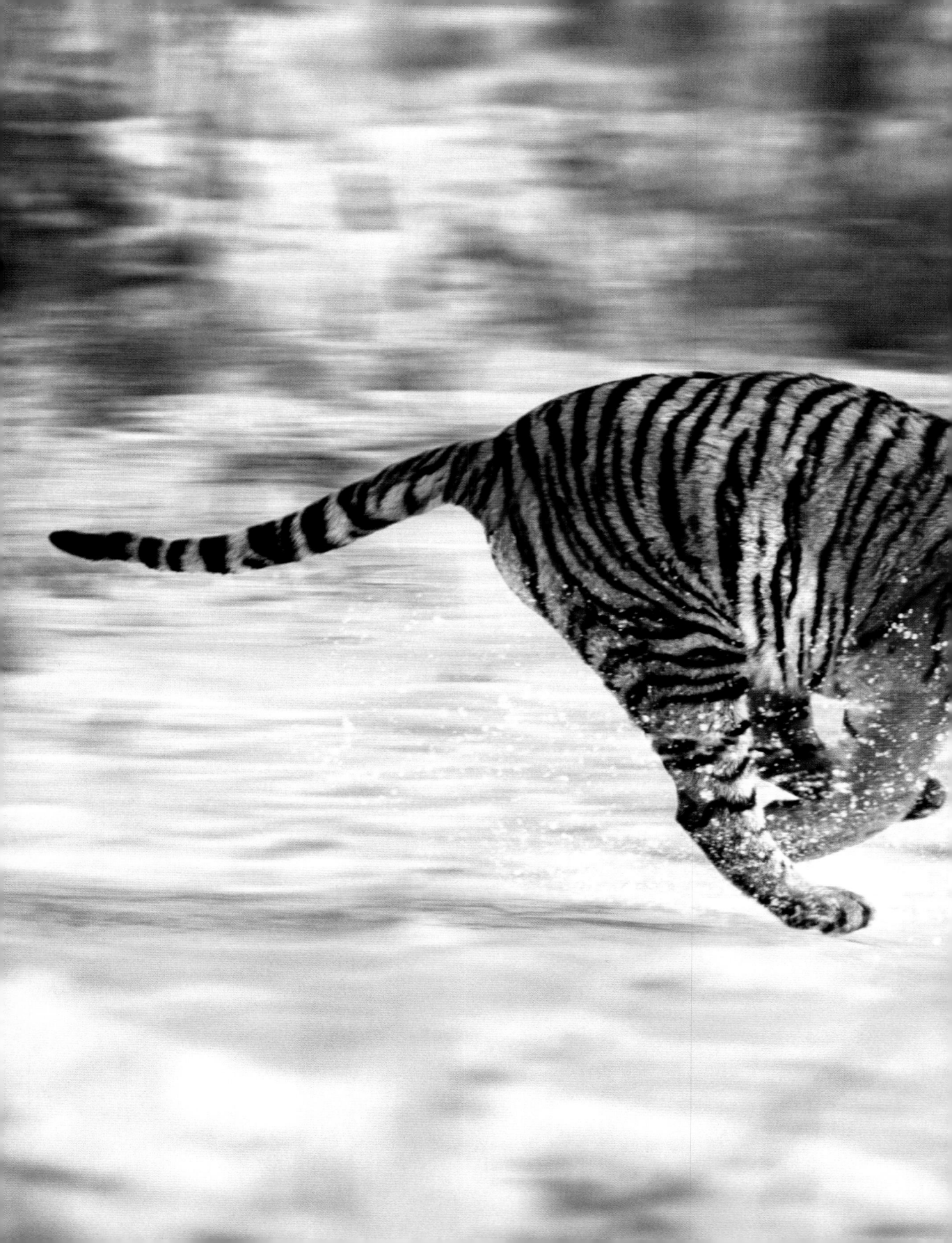

UNTAMED

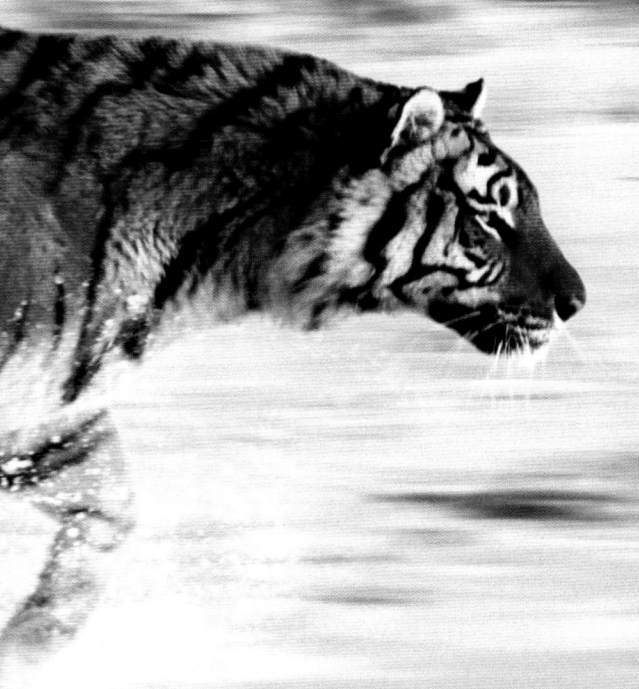

STEVE BLOOM

ABRAMS, NEW YORK

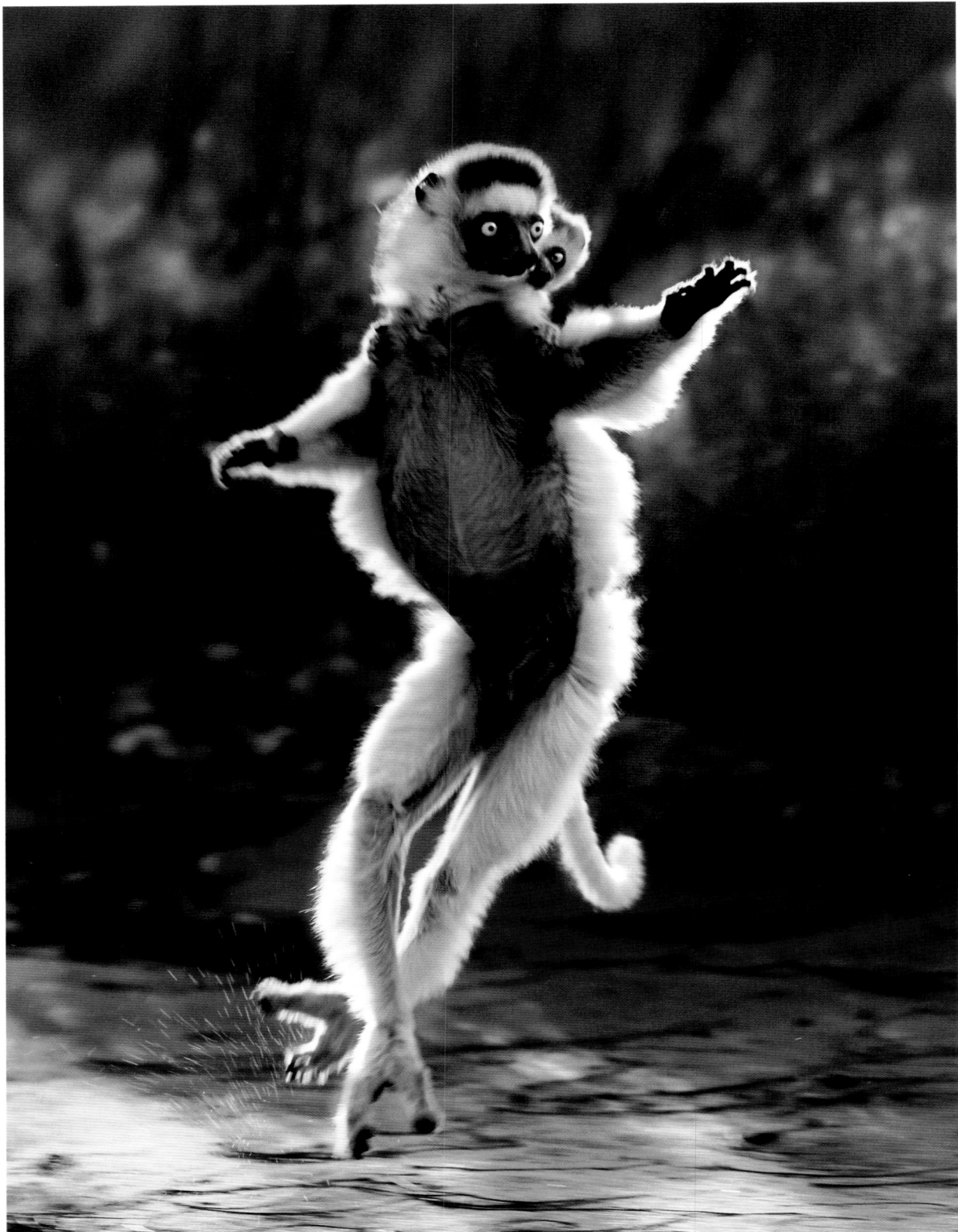

INTRODUCTION

When I first began photographing wildlife, I adopted a somewhat relaxed approach, naively believing that there was plenty of time to visit the world's wild places. How wrong I was. Environmental destruction is accelerating at an alarming rate, resulting in a major negative impact on the natural world. My determination to take photographs soon became dominated by a mixed sense of urgency and foreboding.

I now visit many places with profound feelings of concern. Shortly after my first trip to Borneo, forest fires ravaged the region, causing widespread destruction to the plants and wildlife. On a journey to Kenya, an area that I had visited the previous year had become so devastated by drought that I hardly recognized it. An albatross colony in the Falklands was accidentally destroyed by fire, only days after my departure. In Canada, extremes of temperature upset the migratory habits of polar bears; in Antarctica the ice is melting. We are witnessing tangible evidence of the fragility of ecosystems, brought about largely by the indifference humans have towards the earth and its resources. We have become dangerously complacent, believing that the world can sustain endless plundering. Yet we are all interdependent, and the preservation of animal cultures is essential to the balance and perhaps the ultimate survival of our fragile planet.

Some animals, such as dolphins and albatrosses, are renowned for the uplifting effect they can have on people. I have seen myself reflected in the eye of an albatross. While sitting alone on a hill one day, an albatross landed beside me. We sat together for a while, sharing the wind that buffeted our bodies, both looking down into the same valley. At close quarters I realized how large the albatross was, and how potentially lethal her enormous beak could be, yet she emitted an aura of peace and instilled in me a deep sense of calm. How safe these endangered birds should be, living far from human habitation and not normally hunted by man. Sadly, each year many birds die horrifically as a result of large-scale commercial line fishing. Caught on hooks, the albatrosses are dragged underwater where they drown. Simple adaptations to the fishing system could alleviate the problem without impacting the livelihood of the fishermen.

While all living creatures need the earth's resources to survive, many of today's problems stem largely from commercial greed. Logging companies that devastate large areas of forest solely for commercial profit cause considerably more damage than indigenous people working the land to survive. All those unnecessary car journeys we make and the senseless waste of electricity exacerbate the continuing decline in the quality of the world's air—the very air that sustains all our lives. If the earth were the size of an apple, then its atmosphere would be roughly the thickness of the skin. Pictures of the earth from space bear witness to this often overlooked reality.

We do not have the ability to master nature. We are all part of and dependent on it. Burning fossil fuels increases carbon dioxide and so raises the world's temperatures. Melting ice caps would raise sea levels with disastrous consequences. Summer heat waves take their toll on humans and animals alike. Kangaroos, for example, abandon their joeys when the heat becomes intolerable. Animals have become victims of events that are not of their making. Abuse undermines the very foundations on which the future is built.

Complacency is the easy option. I write these words while inside a pressurized metal tube, over 36,000 feet (11,000 meters) above a wintry Siberia. I sit in shirtsleeves, listening to music while tapping on my laptop computer. Half an arm's length away is a 466 mph (750 kph) wind and a temperature of -94°F (-70°C). In a day and night I shall have traveled from New Zealand to my home in England, exactly half the circumference of our small earth. Behind us, we leave a stream of pollutants half way around the world. Along with my fellow passengers, our major concerns might well be stiff limbs and jetlag. It is as if the ecological outcome of our actions is not a problem of our making—it is as remote as the deadly space outside my window, so enchanting above the clouds. Life is fragile and delicate—a critical balance which may be crushed at any moment. Unable to abandon our compulsion to maintain our lifestyles, we tear at the fabric of the natural world, making recovery harder and harder as each day goes by. We will recover from our jetlag long before the effect of our imprint fades from the atmosphere.

A personal perspective can be revealed in remote locations. Antarctica has shifted my values. There we can discover the futility of war among our collective madness. Self-importance evaporates when surrounded by the vast icy seascape and icebergs dotted with Adélie penguins. It never rains in some parts of this cold, dry world where the sun doesn't set for months. Frenzied activities of city life and scurrilous gossip belong to another time, another reality. While rubbing SPF 60 sunblock on my skin before venturing onto the ice, I am reminded how we have reached this place too, with our airborne pollutants. The lost ozone is an open wound in the sky, a seeping laceration through which the melting ice drips and drips. I visited the world's largest iceberg, the size of a small country, one summer day shortly after it broke in two. Looking up at it in awe, I found it difficult to comprehend that something so large could be free floating. While opinions differ over whether its break from the mainland is a consequence of global warming, the separation has disrupted the breeding habits of penguins and other wildlife dramatically. Higher than normal mortality rates are the result of abruptly damaged food chains. The wildlife strives to survive, unaware of the ominous threat whose menace is deepening.

When I visit places of profound beauty, I am filled with hope. Like a relationship with a sick lover, inner splendor promotes optimism, and reinforces the will to make all efforts for recovery. The world *is* capable of revival. I discovered this in Australia where I saw a small but noble attempt to return a few acres of farmland to rainforest. Thirty-year-old trees towered high above my head and marsupials foraged in the undergrowth. While the canopy of the young forest was not fully developed, it was growing healthily. Although it is a small sign, like the planting of a single seed, such moments fill me with delight. The harmony of nature nourishes the soul.

The ability to comprehend the consequences of our actions is one of our most precious strengths. By acting responsibly, we have already seen populations of elephants increase as a result of the ban on the ivory trade. But we are only touching the surface, with so much more to be done. Perhaps a starting point would be to understand how different life forms are made up of individuals, and not dispassionate groups. When we acquire such awareness, we can begin to feel compassion, and thus lay good foundations for responsible action.

The images in this book are a response to the notion that humans are central to everything. While it may be that such things as written words set us apart from other life forms, an intellectual brain is not a prerequisite for understanding. Living creatures are by their very nature cognitive. Certain trees sense the presence of gypsy moths and release substances that alert other trees of imminent attack. I sense, from the process of seeing with my camera, that chimpanzees are probably contemplative. By observing the natural world we can comprehend the threads that link humans with nature and appreciate that sentience and individuality are not unique human characteristics. People who have companion animals generally understand this.

Through the lens of the camera I have learned much about the nature of individual animals. Although animal groups display common behavioral characteristics, within many of those groups are sensitive individuals with unique personalities. Each has his own special place on this earth—his own role to play in the wider network of the ecosystem. My photographic approach is aesthetic rather than scientific. I believe aesthetics enable the objective viewer to reach an intuitive understanding. The interplay of light, color, and movement in nature can make us feel more alive and at one with the world. The photographs I produce hopefully offer an alternative viewpoint. The glint in an eye can touch us where textbooks cannot, and it is the artist's role to capture such feelings. We all know the immense power vested in the quirkiness of a human smile, and the feelings it can evoke.

The most innocuous event can have great influence on the wider world. A gorilla looked into my eyes in a zoo and this spurred me to photograph the great apes in the wild. When my images of wild gorillas were published, students wrote, telling of the influence the pictures had on them, and how they became inspired to work in conservation. Such is the power in a look. I am not suggesting that the gorilla's eyes alone were responsible for influencing people's lives, but somewhere along the way they had a valid role to play.

It seems very easy to reach solipsistic conclusions about our assumed place in the universe. We presuppose we have the monopoly on language, yet elephants use infrasound to communicate with each other over vast distances. The low frequencies of these sounds are imperceptible to humans and cover distances greater than that of any sound we can make. We have made great advances in medicine, yet animals too have discovered the medicinal properties of substances found in nature. Macaws eat clay, which neutralizes the acids from fruits, and chimpanzees have discovered that certain plants can alleviate digestive problems. Our navigational abilities have taken us as far as the moon, with unmanned probes leaving the solar system. Tiny starlings use sophisticated navigational methods too. In experiments, when let loose in a planetarium, they have been known to become disorientated by the apparent movement of the stars.

Naked and vulnerable, we depend heavily on technology for our physical survival. By contrast, emperor penguins are most adept when it comes to survival against natural adversity. They are the least accessible of the birds, and I was privileged to visit them during a month-long voyage on a Russian icebreaker. They lay their eggs in the depths of the Antarctic winter, where daylight is absent and temperatures plummet to -130°F (-90°C). In howling, freezing gales they huddle together to ward off the worst ravages of the cold. In such conditions the males suffer without food for two months, enduring near starvation in order to incubate the eggs. In this frozen bleakness, the most enchanting of chicks are hatched, tiny fragile creatures that are nurtured into adulthood by

parents most responsible. From the most adverse of circumstances emerges new life—light coming from darkness. We too, are sometimes capable of endurance beyond comprehension. The forces in our hearts motivate us to perform the most extraordinary feats of achievement, and help us survive against the odds.

The natural world is dominated by turbulence in the ongoing struggle for survival. I do not intend to portray a utopian viewpoint where suffering in nature is absent. I have witnessed African hunting dogs as they tore an impala to shreds in seconds, with brutal and heart-wrenching savagery. Yet the impala died with greater speed than many farmed animals that pass through our slaughterhouses. The dogs were hunting for food. Despite the constant tensions of surviving in the wild, the impala had experienced the smell of the morning air and had seen the sunrise. In the cruelest forms of intensive farming, factory animals, locked in their suffering, never know what it feels like to run free. I find it hard to imagine what it would be like never to experience a walk through the woods or wander down the street.

When a pride of young lions ganged up on a defenseless juvenile hippo in Kenya's Masai Mara Reserve, they taunted him all morning, taking turns to leap onto his back and rip into his flesh. He wearily tried to ward them off, as white tears of fear and pain streamed down his face. Then, as quickly as the lions appeared, they abandoned him. For a whole day he vainly crawled in agony towards the water where he lay down to die near its edge. The lions were not hungry, and they do not normally eat hippos. Humans do not have the monopoly on gratuitous violence.

We don't have the monopoly on compassion either. There are countless stories about companion animals caring for humans, often saving lives. Dolphins have been known to rescue distressed and injured people on numerous occasions. Dolphins cry when being butchered by fishermen. Different species share a whole gamut of states of being that we also experience.

I recall seeing a lost and frightened baby elephant become separated from his mother in the long grass. He ran after an egret, just like one of the small children

I have seen chasing pigeons in city parks. When the egret flew away, he noticed that his mother had gone. He ran back and forth, paused, went into a state of shock, and began to cry. His cry was soft at first, and then built into a resonating wail of terror. Such sounds of abandonment touch us all—a common language that helps to shatter the barriers separating living beings. During moments such as these, I find it difficult to comprehend how we can be so indifferent to suffering—moments that give us a greater, intuitive lesson about our shared world. Mercifully, mother and child were quickly reunited, and soon the baby had nuzzled into the folds of his mother's leg, comforted by warm milk and a reassuring trunk.

Watching the birth of an animal in a harsh and dangerous environment makes us all too aware, by comparison, of our own vulnerability and physical weakness. A wildebeest will be on his feet and running with his mother moments after birth. A baby springbok is virtually odorless and so almost undetectable to the hypersensitive nostrils of its enemies. Species perpetually strive to outwit their predators.

Compared with other animals, we are flagrantly conspicuous in the landscape, particularly as we rumble along in our vehicles, audible and obtrusive from miles away. Most animals become aware of our presence long before the skilled trackers can spot them. A leopard has the power to become almost invisible at will. One of the hardest things about wildlife photography is actually finding animals that are relaxed in the presence of humans. We are continually reminded that we are guests in their territories.

There is never enough time to give each subject the photographic attention it deserves. The large number of geographical areas covered by this book necessitated careful selection of locations and species. Also by necessity, some geographical classifications are inexact. The chapter on Antarctica, for example, includes nearby sub-antarctic islands that support wildlife linked to that on the continent. The work of a wildlife photographer is always something of a balance, and there is the ever-present wish to stay longer in each location. My photographic thirst will never be fully quenched. The pictures in this book represent a personal view of a tiny microcosm of the world, like a few grains of sand on an endless beach; grains that change with time as the cycle of life continues.

The mystery of spirit emerges in all life, and is not confined to the single self. An intuitive awareness of others is the very foundation of love. In its purest form it is the sense of being at one with the whole universe, where the self loses its perceived role as the center of everything.

I am humbled by the opportunities I have had to witness the diversity of life in so many places, and through this book I hope to share such experiences. Photography is the means by which I strive to engender in others a feeling of unity with the natural world. There remains the ongoing challenge to portray life in all its manifestations, and create images that reveal the very essence of what it is to be a living being.

—Steve Bloom

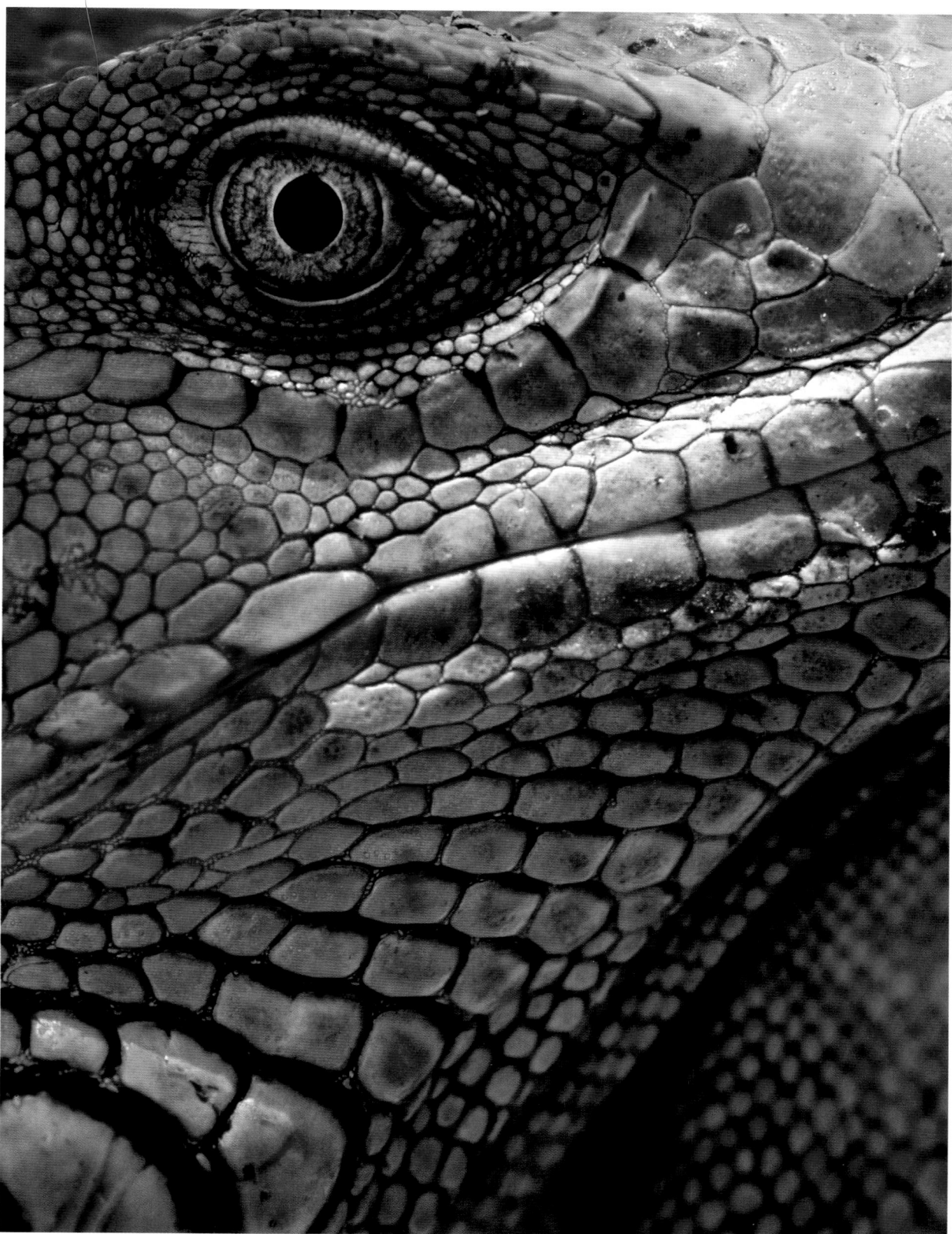

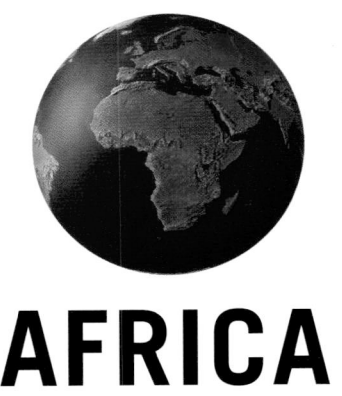

AFRICA

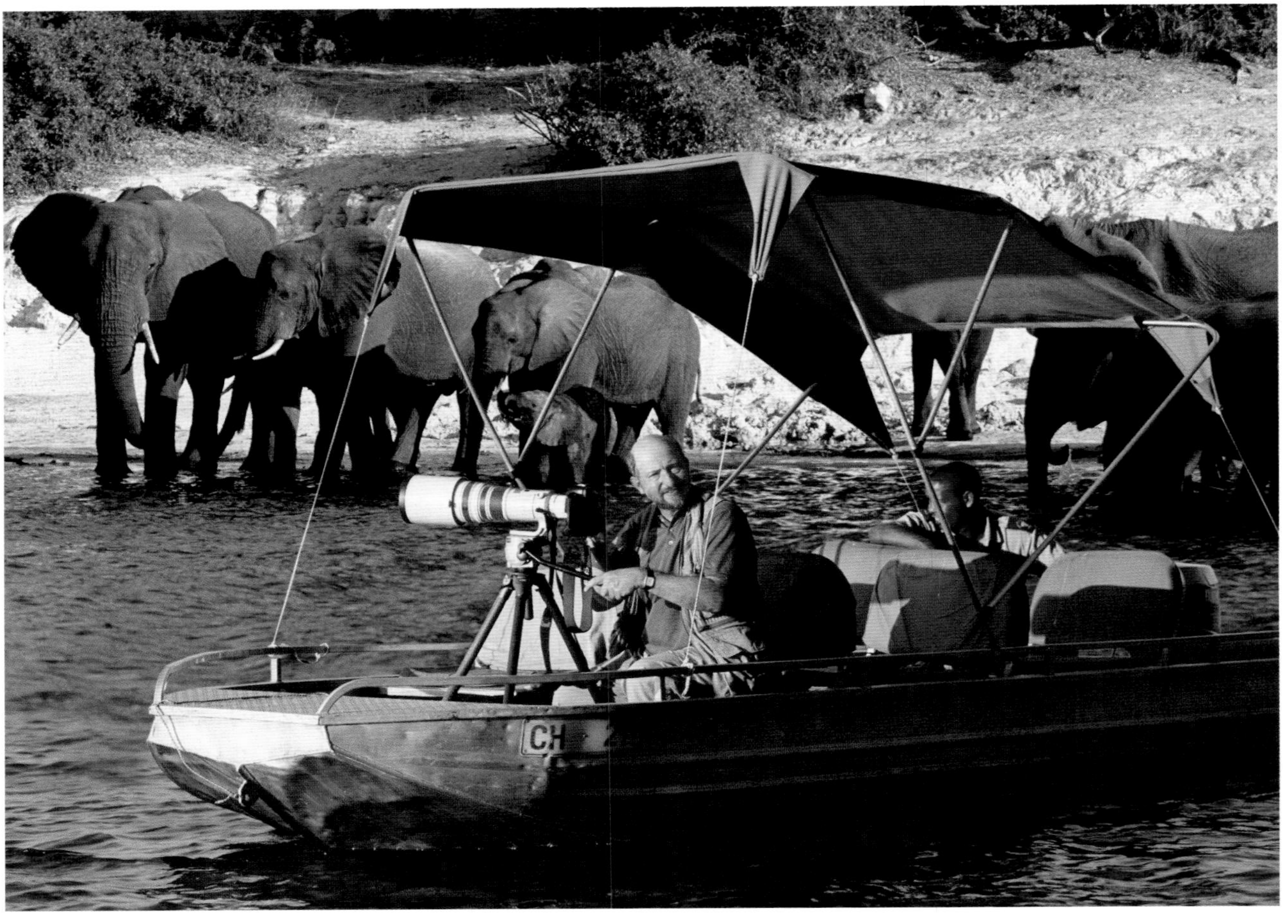

"THE RAW SMELL OF THE EARTH AND A LINGERING SENSE OF PRIMEVAL ENERGY DRAW ME BACK TO AFRICA."

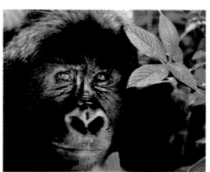

I travel to Central Africa to search for mountain gorillas in an extinct volcanic crater. The journey is grueling. Open fields give way to shrubs and then dense undergrowth. We hack paths with machetes, crawl on our bellies, and struggle with backpacks. Torrential rain batters down in a deafening drumroll. Leaves funnel raindrops from above, amplify them, and bombard us with a relentless onslaught. Later, we find a gorilla, serene in the stillness that follows the storm, soft eyes glistening in the misty light. His gaze penetrates further than the deepest forest.

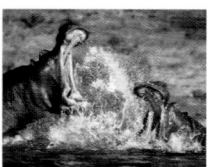

Hippos spend many hours wallowing in water, seemingly without a care in the world. When provoked, tempers explode. Locked in furious territorial combat, they tear at each other. Water crashes to the sound of primeval screams, deafening and terrifying. Then, as quickly as conflict begins the battle subsides, the water settles, and an uneasy peace returns to the pool.

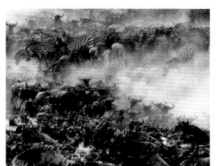

Determined to photograph zebras and wildebeests migrating across Kenya's Mara River, I wait nine long days on the riverbank. The intense boredom and frustration ends abruptly with a burst of wild energy as the herd stampedes across the river. While waiting, the time seems totally unproductive, yet ultimately it yields lasting images.

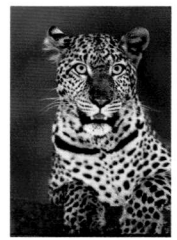

The leopard is a creature of the night. I spend long hours searching for this lonely hunter, this maestro of stealth, so well concealed. We see her on her own terms, and when she wants us no more, she elegantly withdraws into the thorny shrubs. In the night we use our spotlights to search the darkness for her eyes and find them when they return some of our light—two glowing jewels in the blackness. Suddenly the lights go out and she is gone, moving alone through the night with countless stars for company.

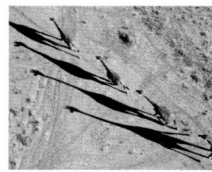

Meticulous timing and a hearty dose of good luck are essential for aerial photography in Kenya's Amboseli National Park. Each day we take off at sunrise in an ultralight aircraft, searching for wildlife as we beat a path through the thick air of the morning. When we finally spot their long shadows formed by the quickly rising sun, we have time for just one pass. I lean out as far as I possibly can, look straight down, and squeeze the shutter.

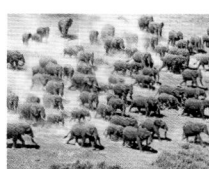

Elephants march silently. Sometimes we fail to hear them approach; their musty smell permeates the air before the sounds of their footsteps reach our ears. Their soft soles spread like shock absorbers, taking their weight as they move across the plain. I have seen fifty elephants marching purposefully, the stillness of the morning air broken only by the occasional soft sound of a cracking twig.

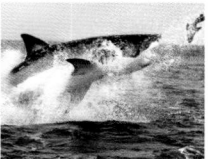

For sixteen days I huddled in a small boat off the African coast in an attempt to get a picture of a great white shark breaching in its hunt for seals. Fast reflexes and a responsive camera were imperative as the boat rolled in the swell. I crouched low for a more dramatic image, fighting seasickness and never knowing when or if a shark would appear. My head throbbed and my muscles ached from holding the camera steady for hours on end. When the shark finally burst out of the water, it was so fleeting and over so quickly that as the sea settled in its wake, I wondered if I was dreaming. The entire sequence lasted less than a second.

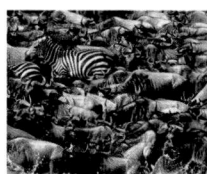

Each year zebras and wildebeests cross the treacherous Mara River in search of fresh grazing pastures. In thousands they gather at the water's edge—a seething mass of bodies. After much hesitation, the surging horde explodes as frantic individuals stampede across the river. Instinct finally conquers fear. Driven by destiny, they follow the rainfall in a desperate bid for survival. Focusing only on the opposite bank of the river, they run the gauntlet of dangerous rocks, treacherous currents, and hungry crocodiles.

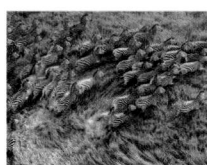

There remain wildernesses on our planet that are especially captivating. A jewel in the desert, Botswana's Okavango Delta is perhaps the finest of them all. Smoke from fires filled the air, so I wait many days to hire a helicopter. Light is delicate and fickle when photographing from the air, and we are further frustrated by overcast weather. We persevere. The clouds momentarily part to let the morning light in and we find the zebras moving through the swamps. Our encounter is brief. The diaphanous light fades quickly; the weather closes in behind us.

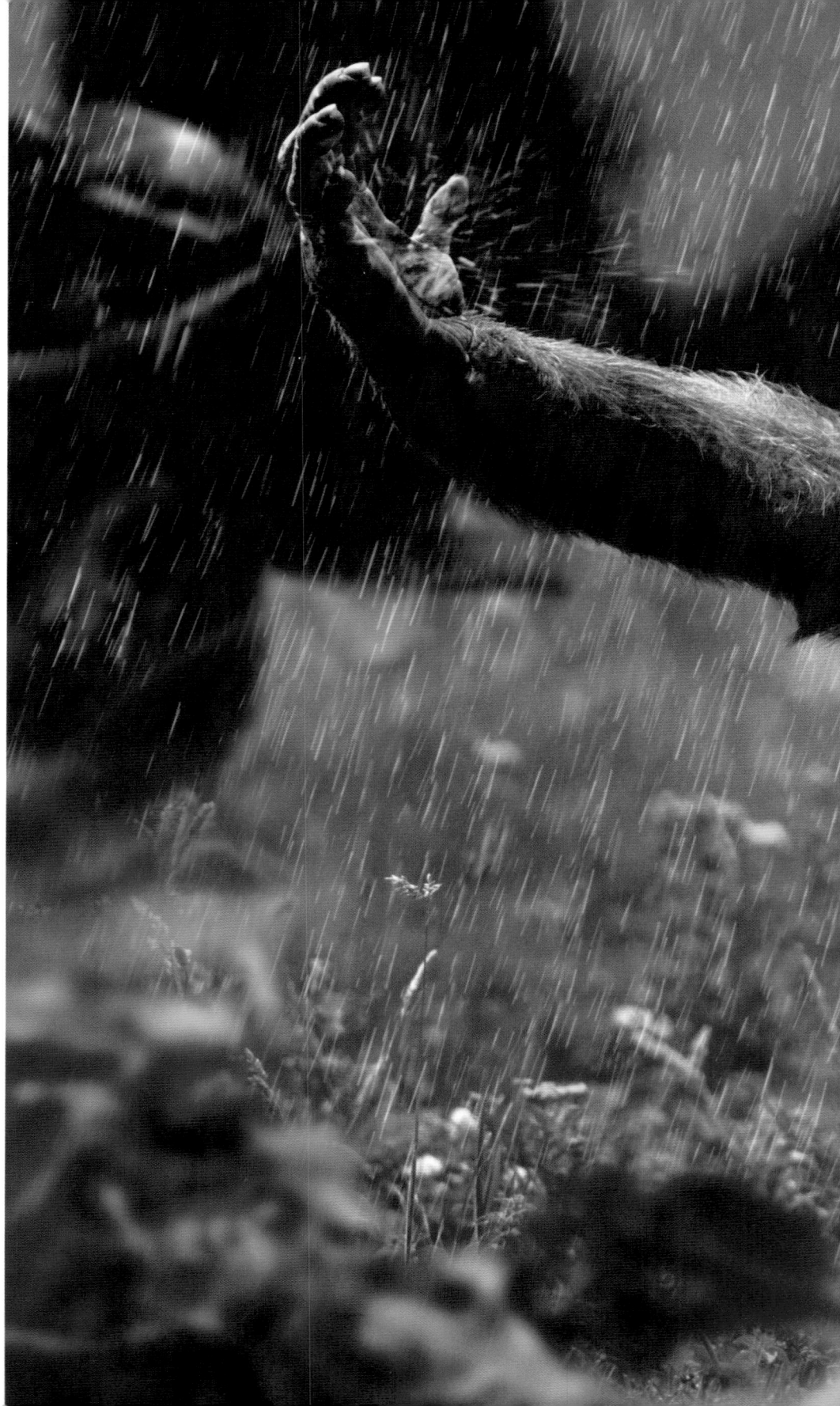

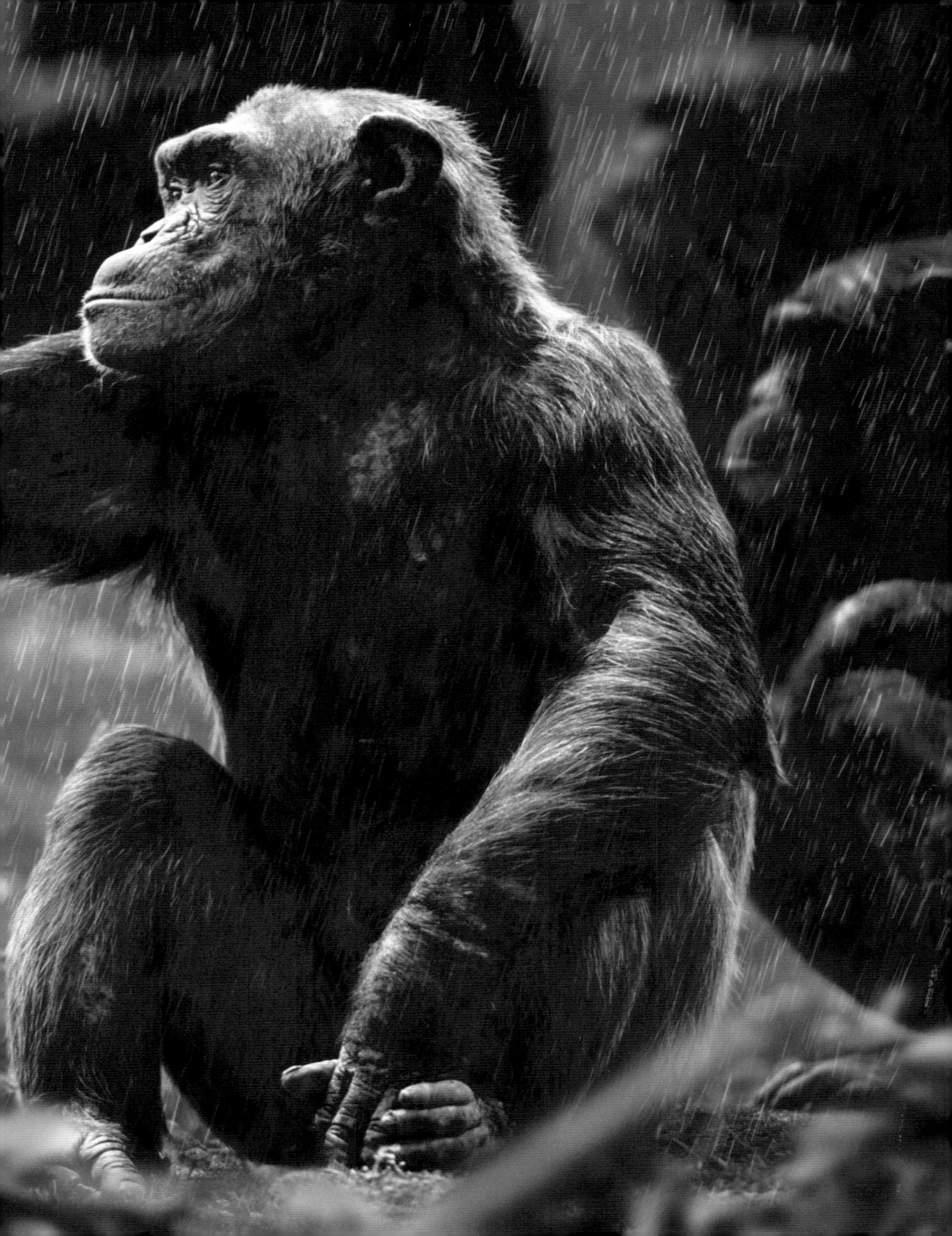

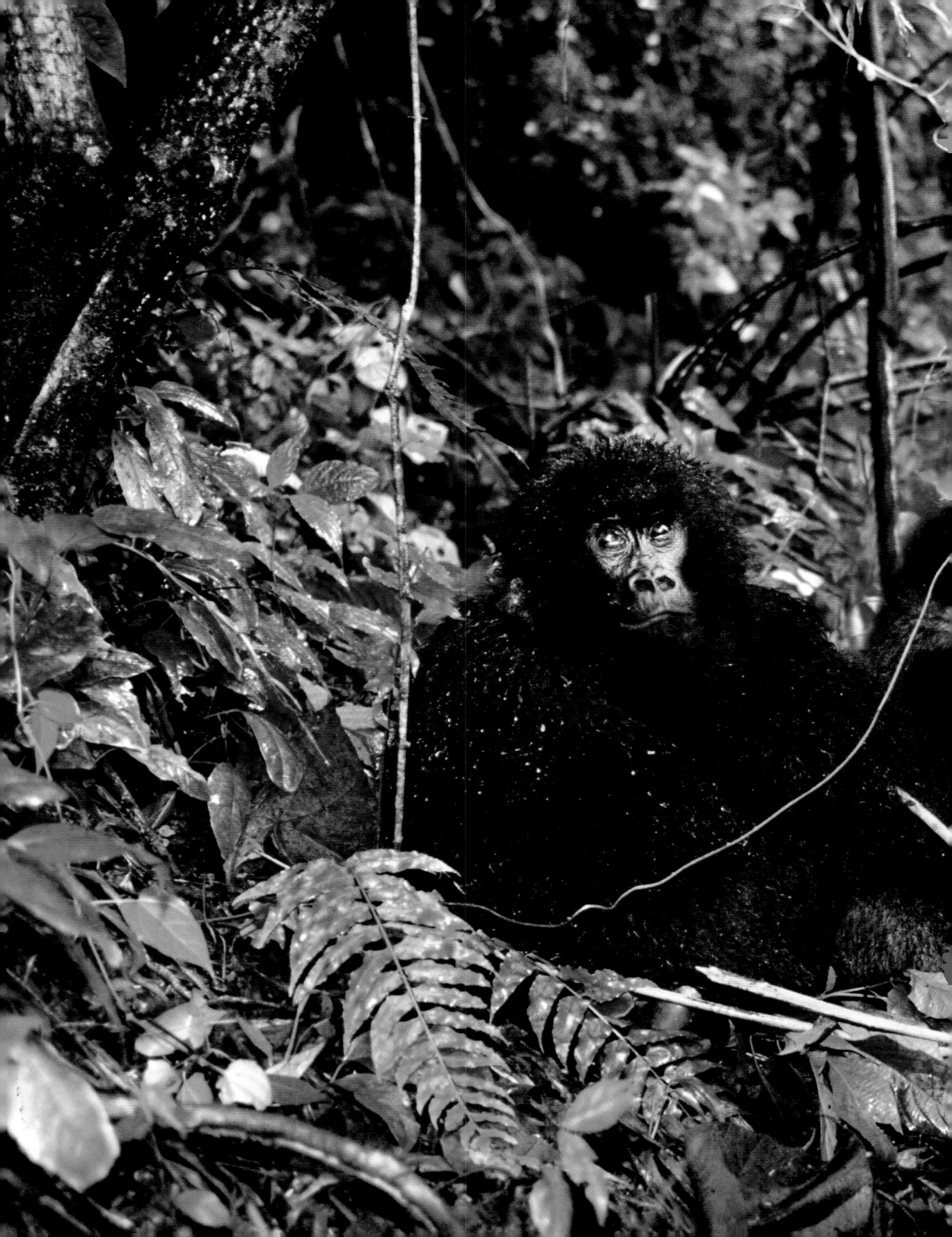

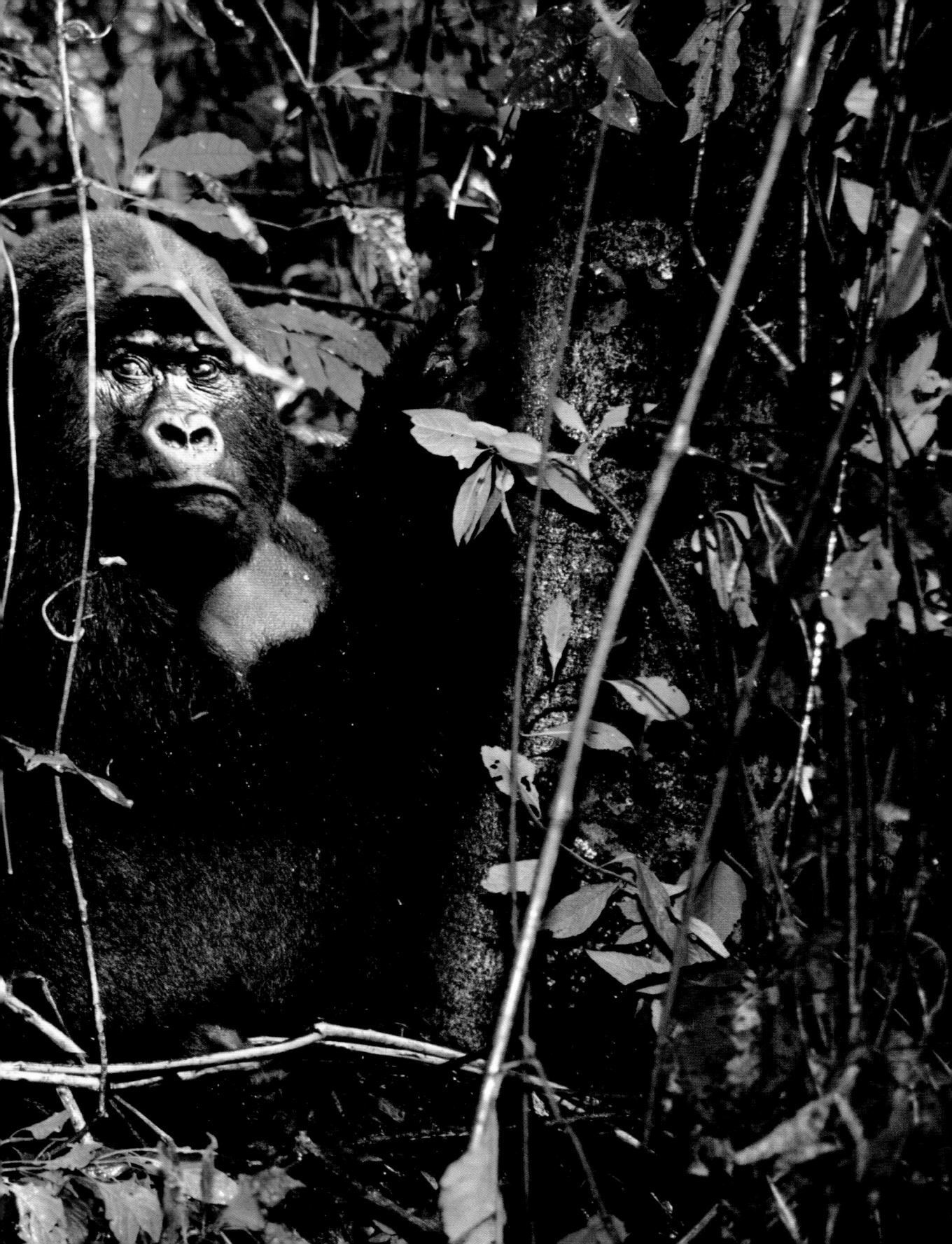

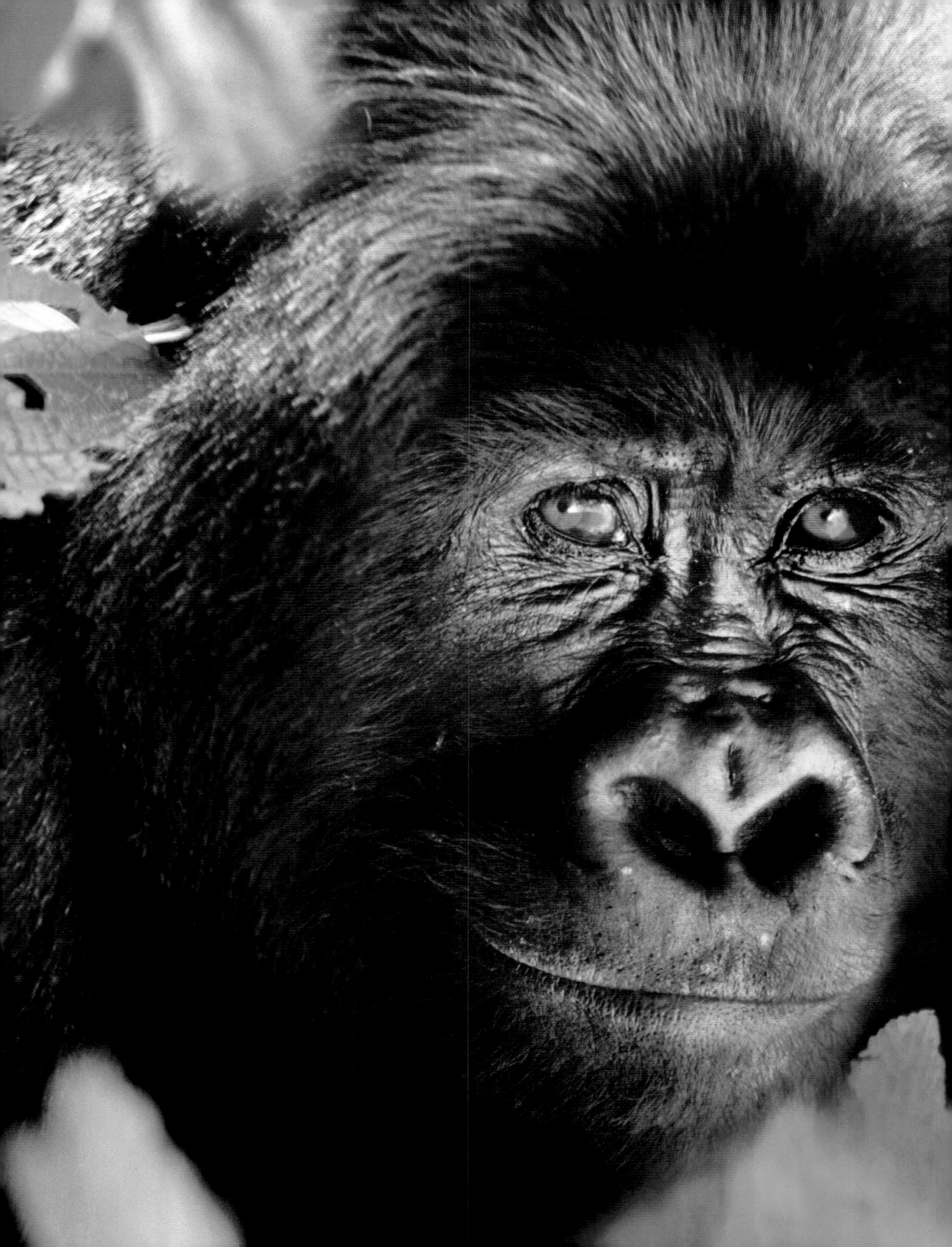

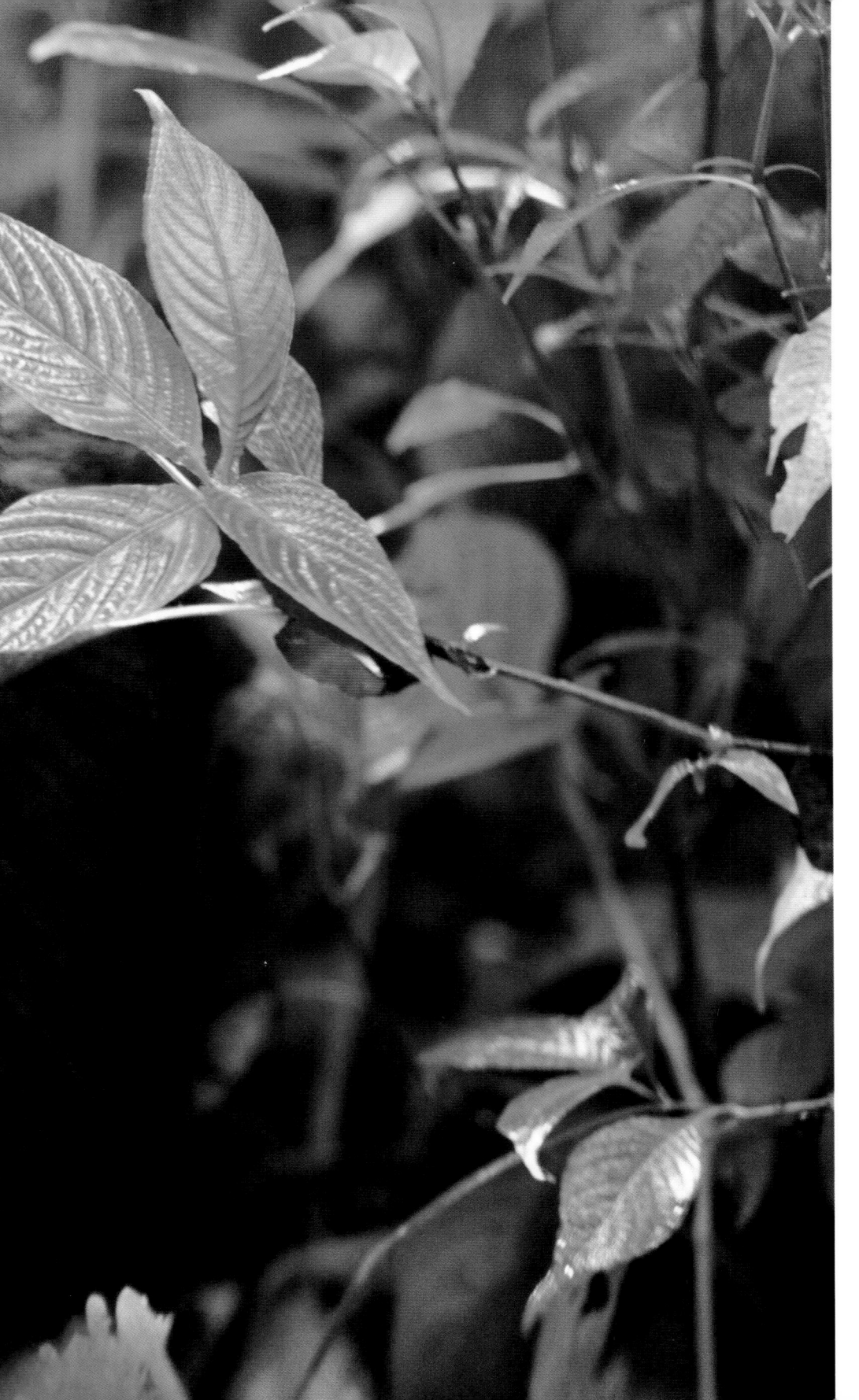

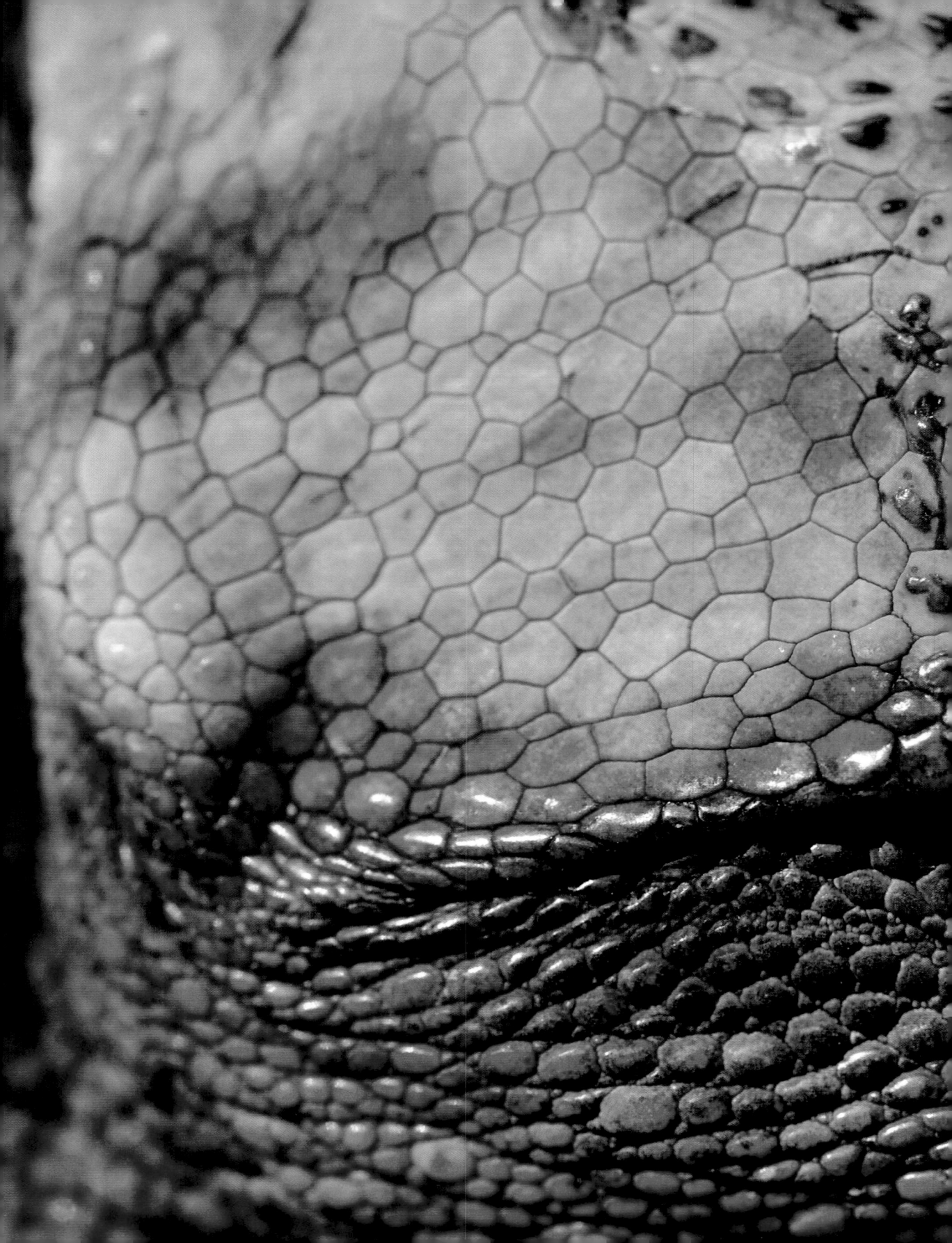

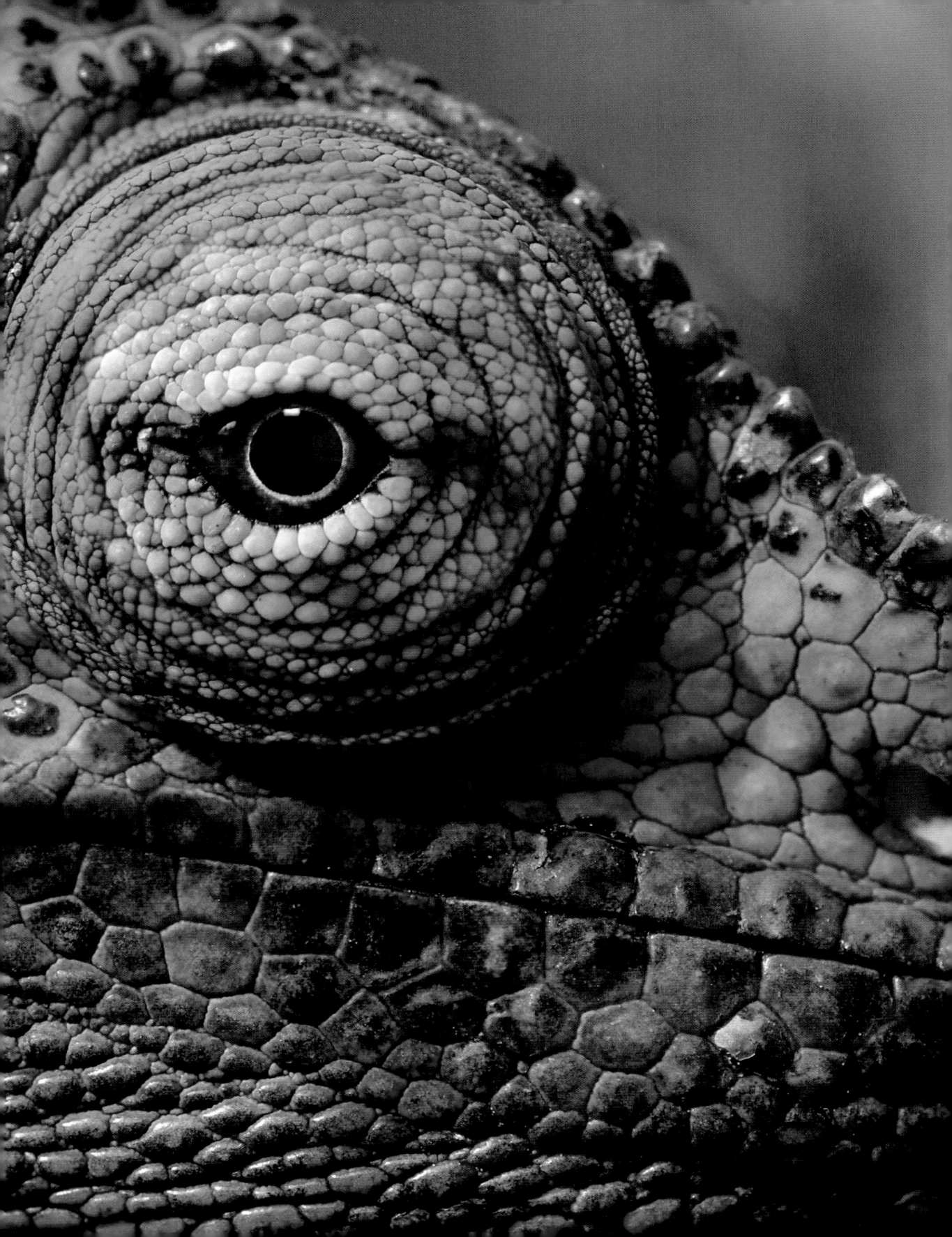

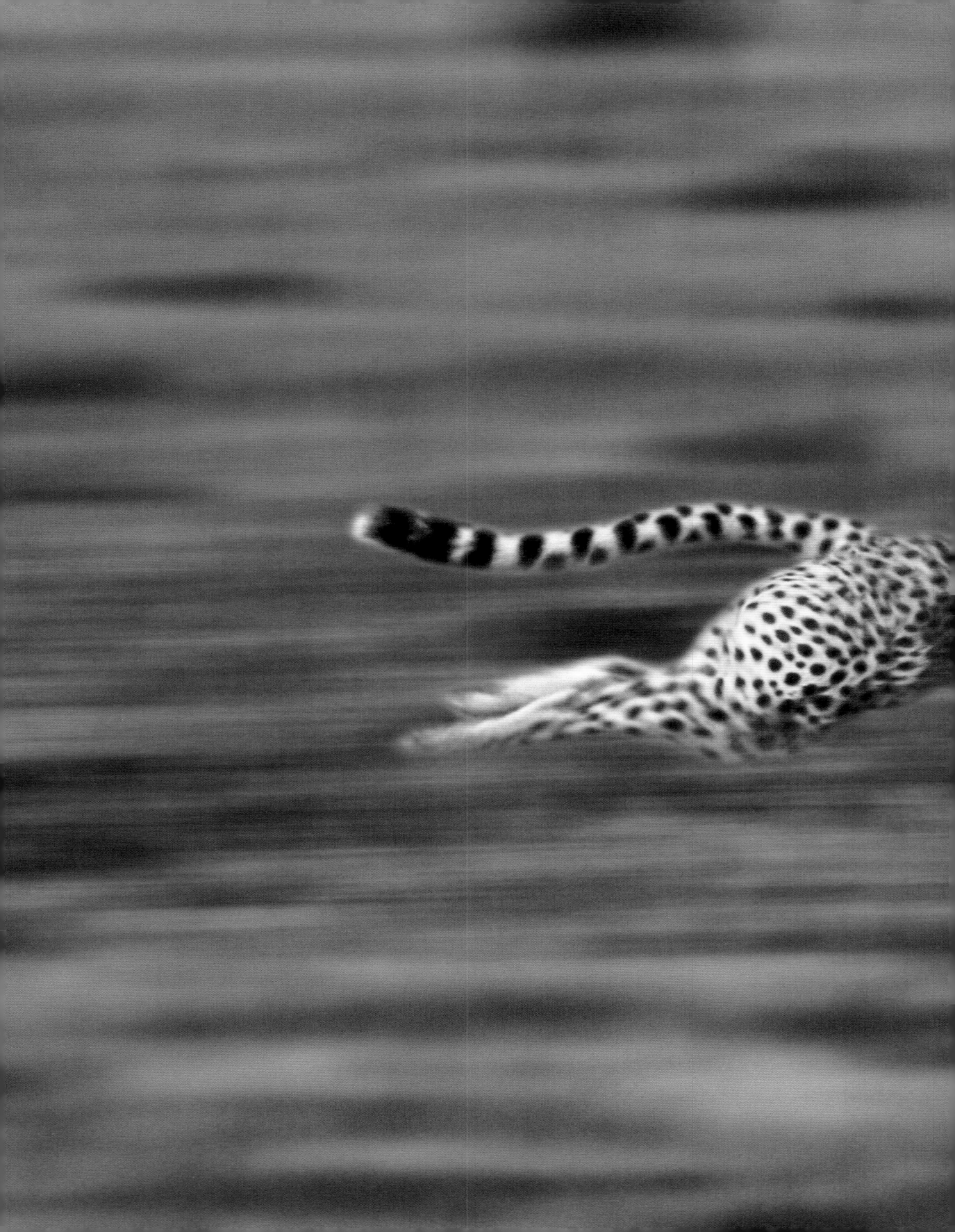

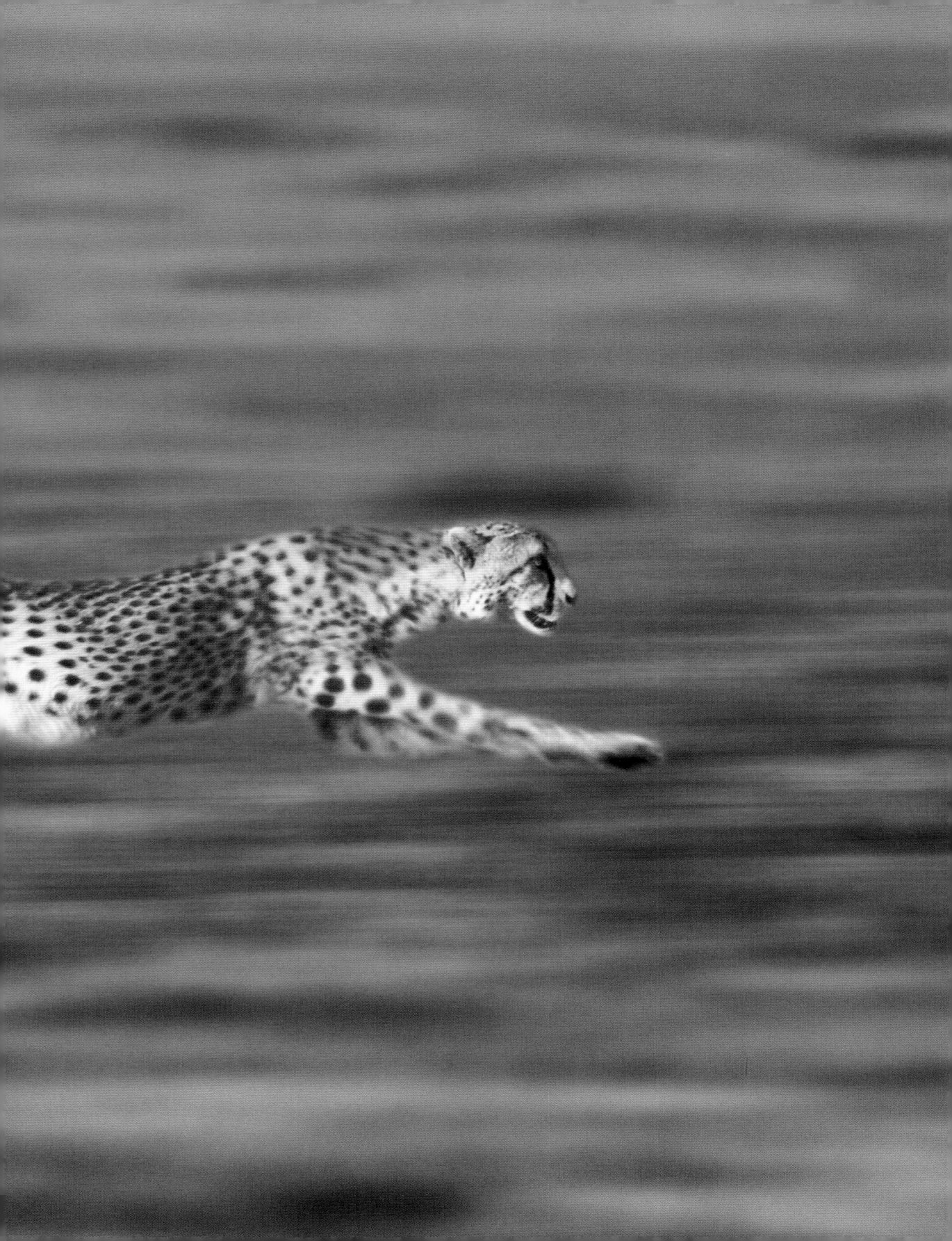

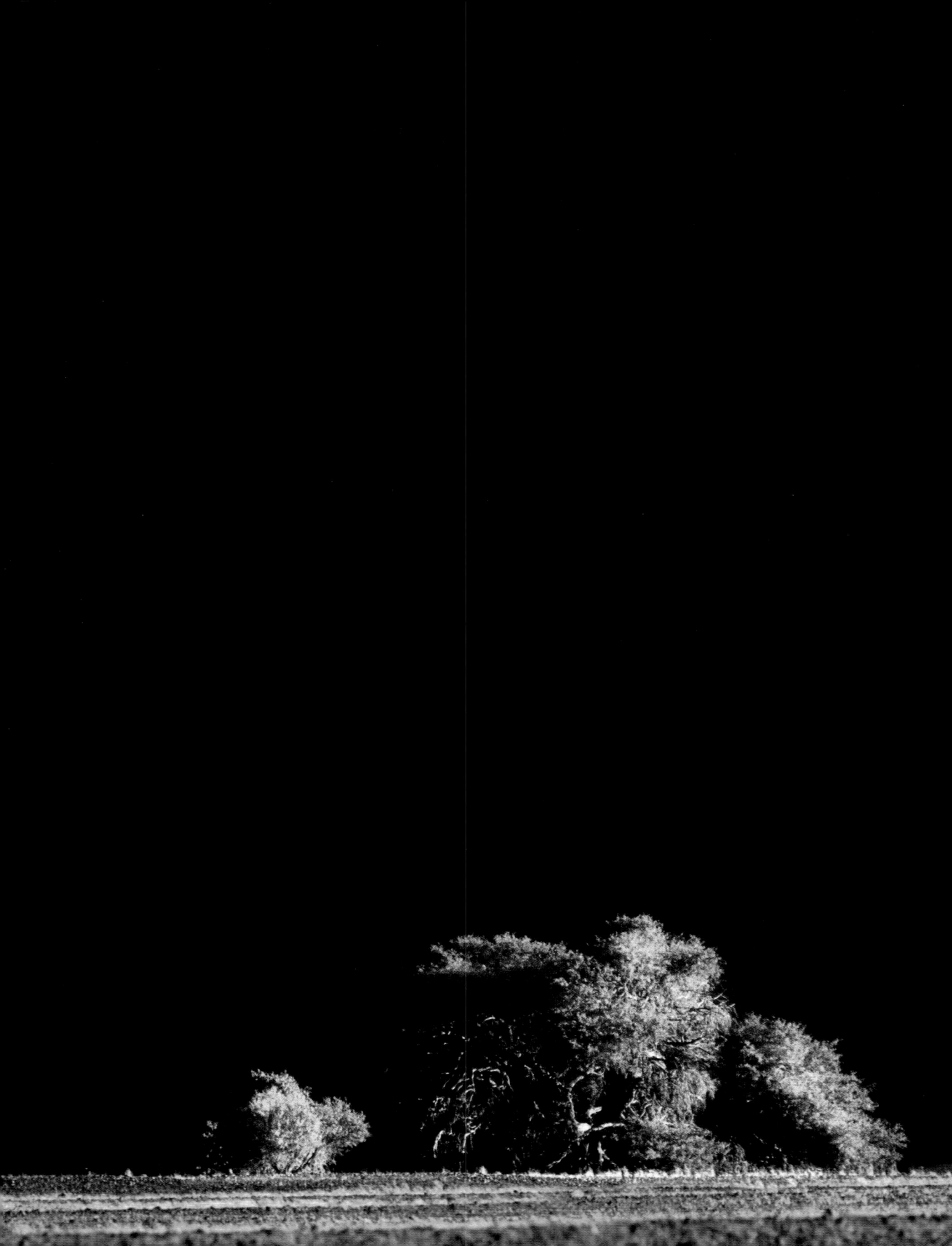

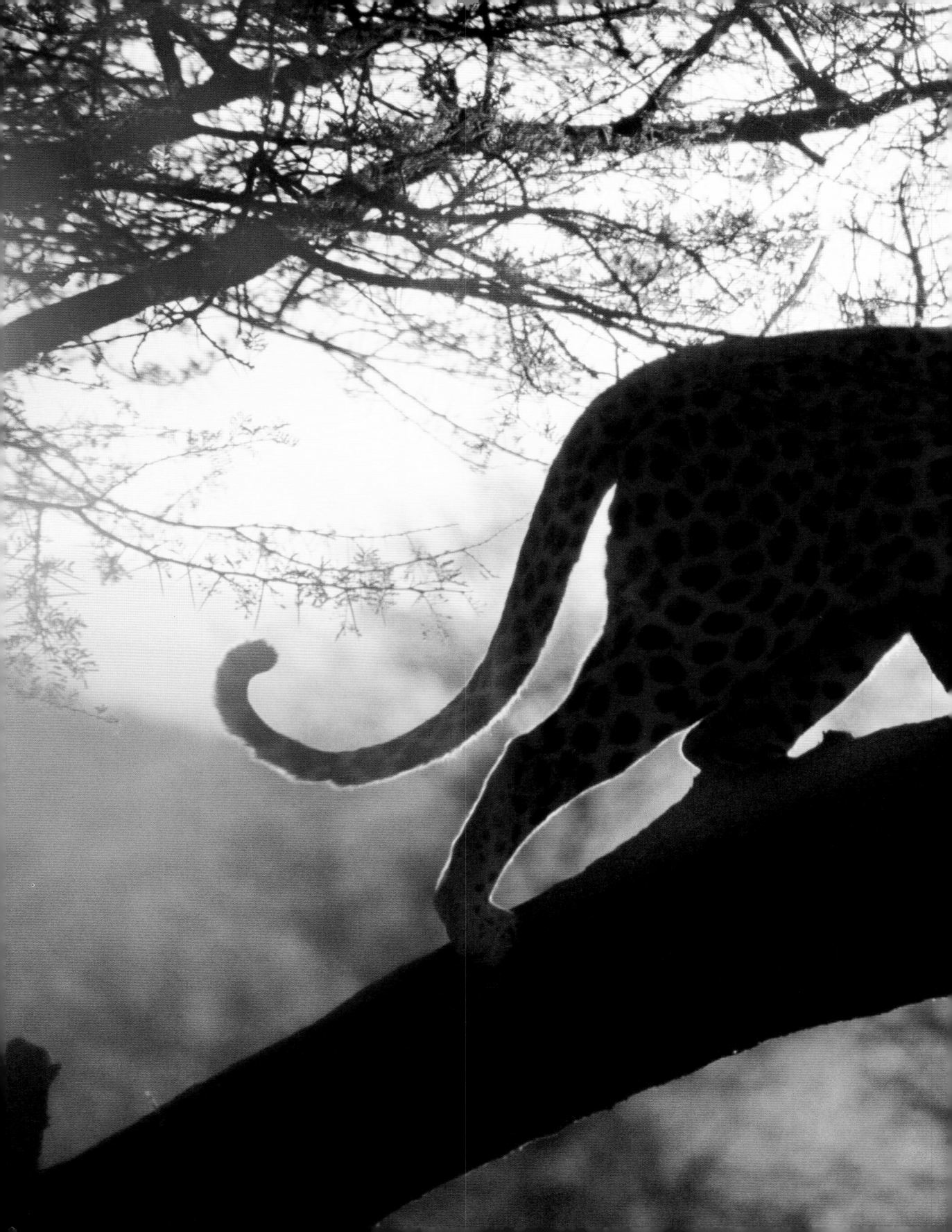

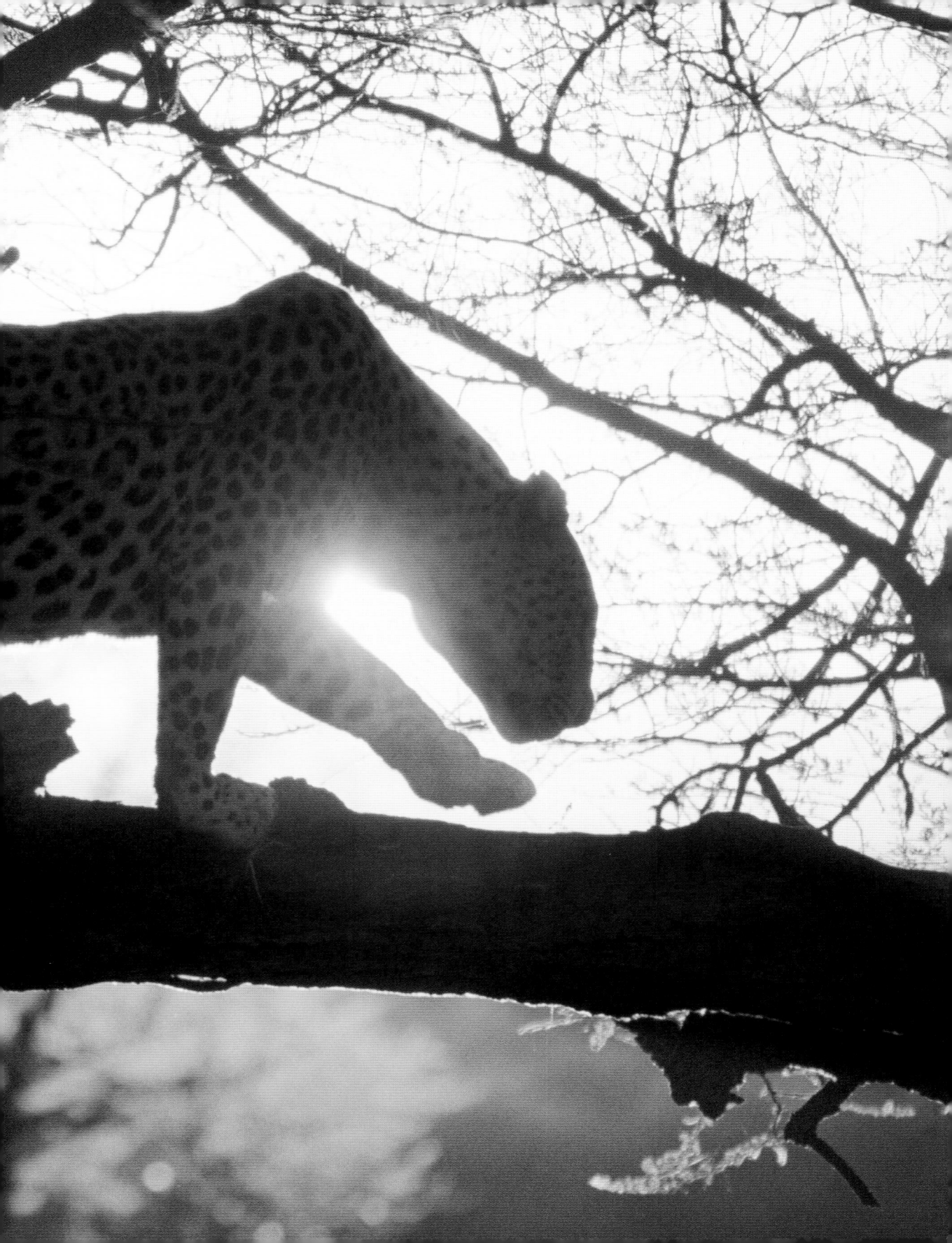

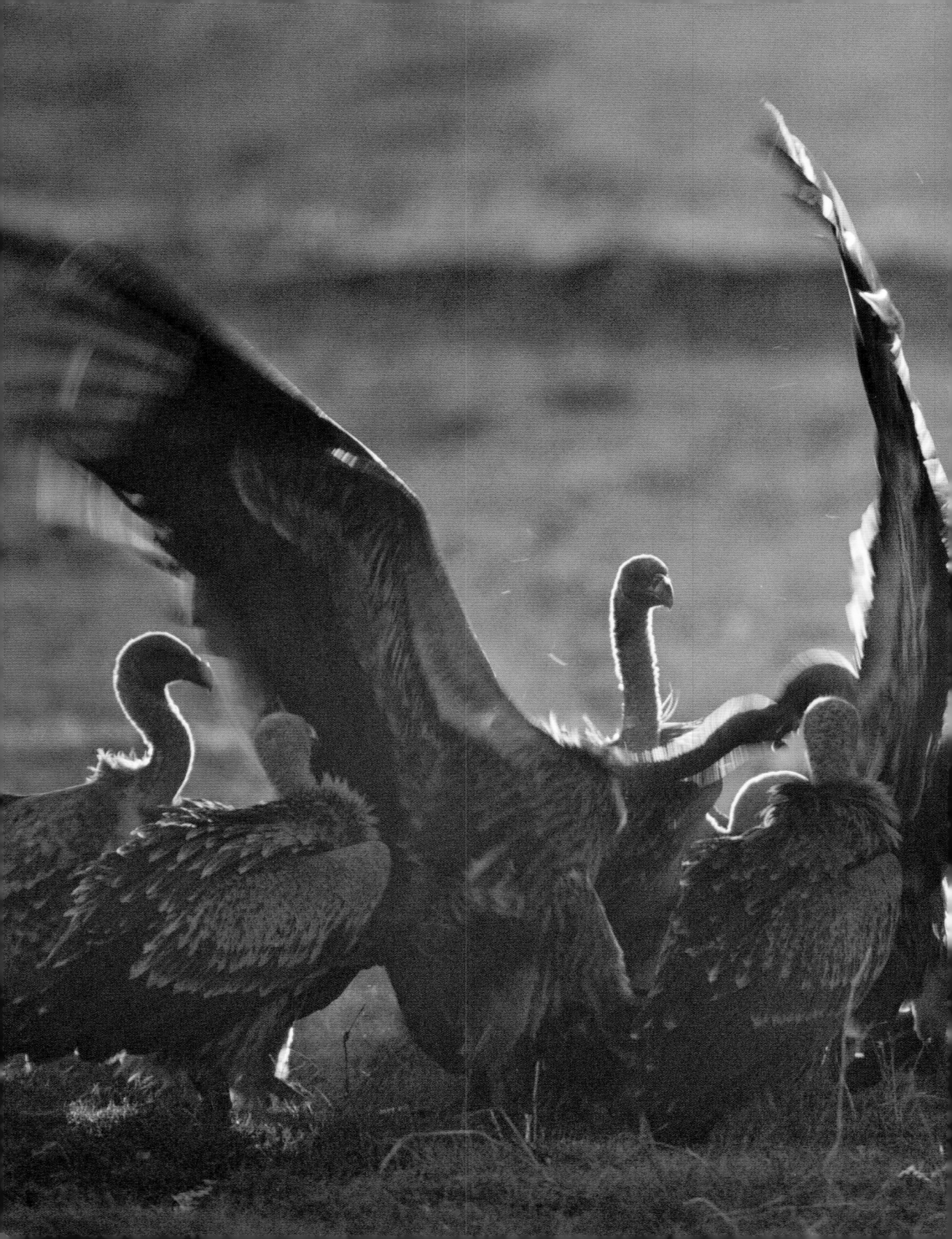

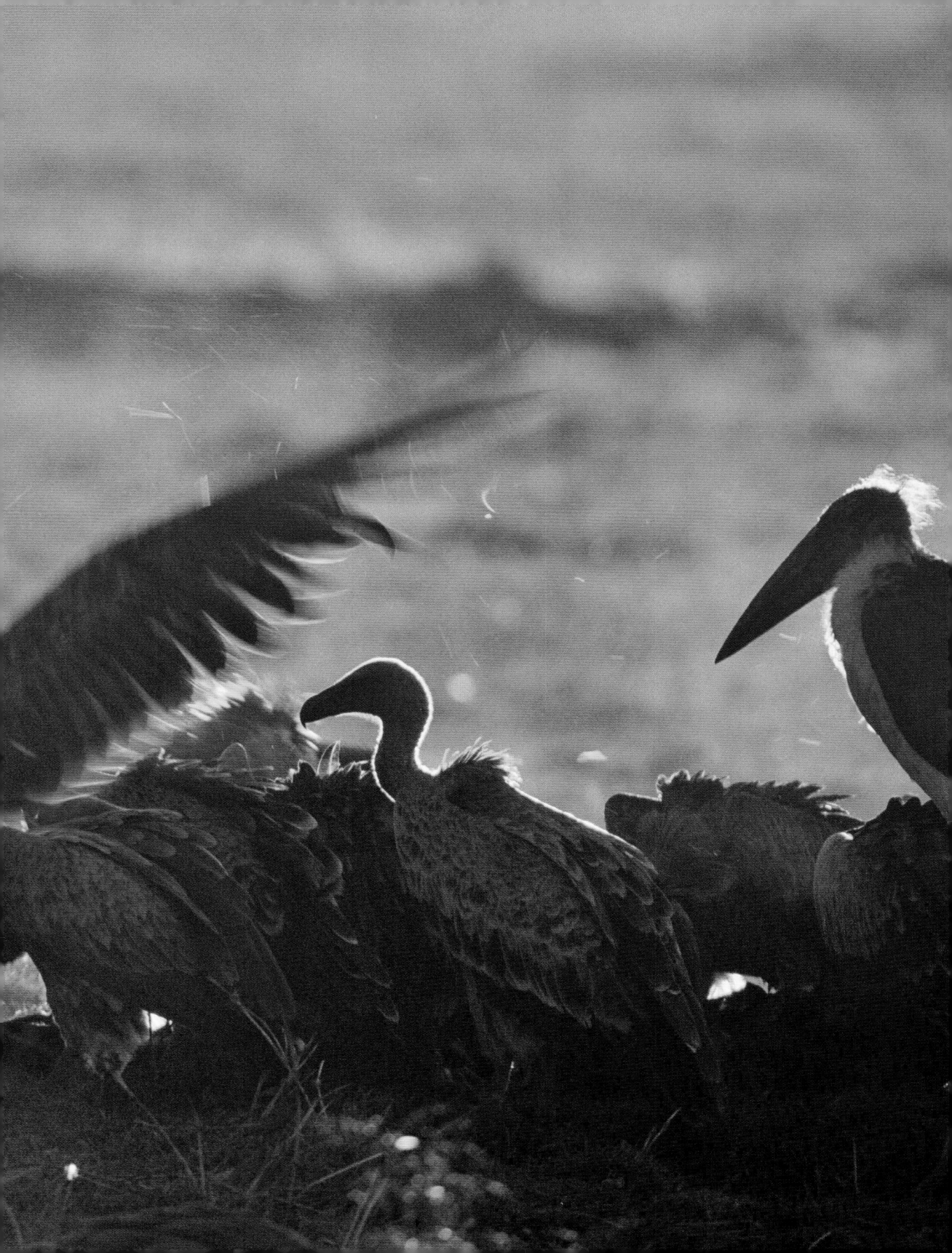

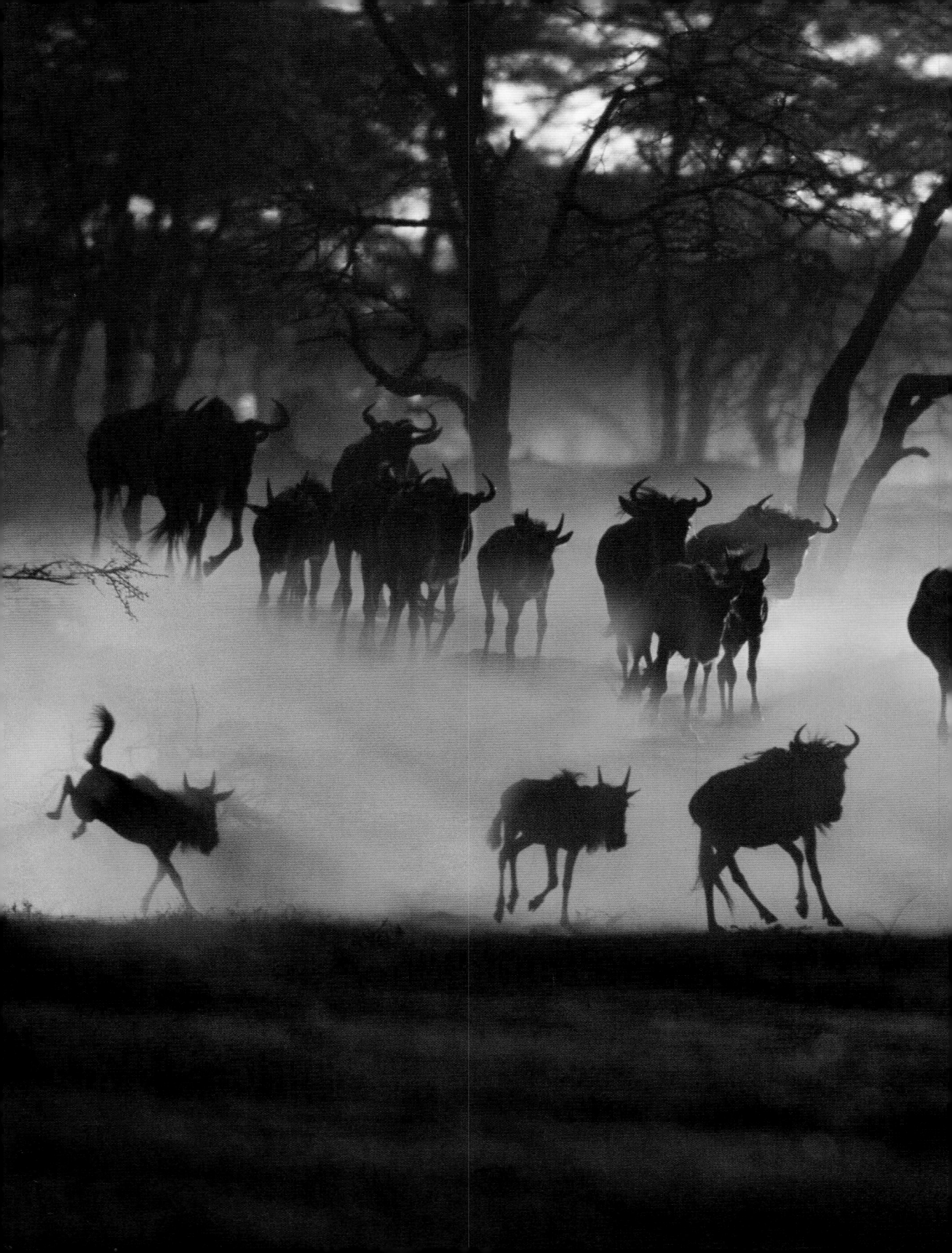

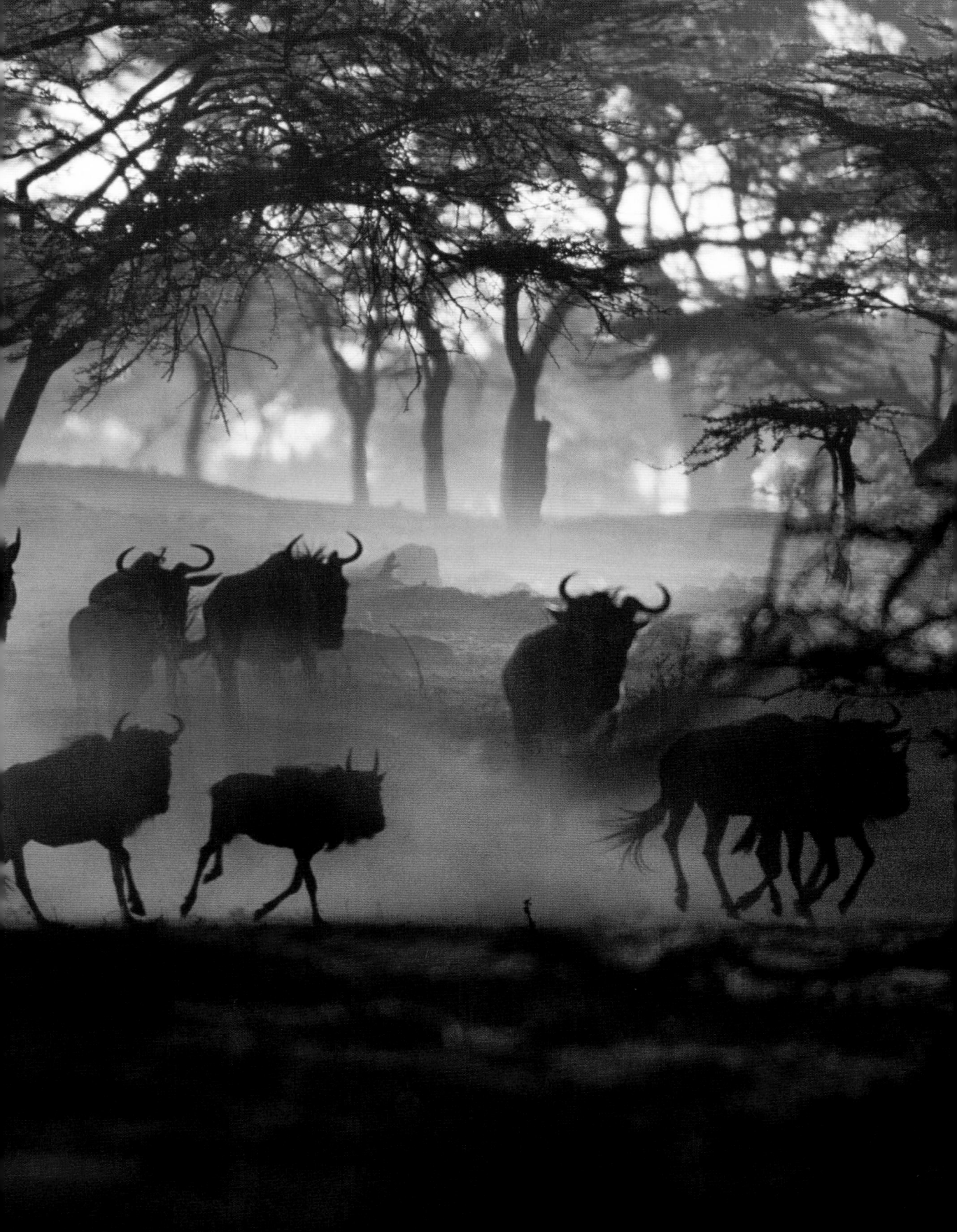

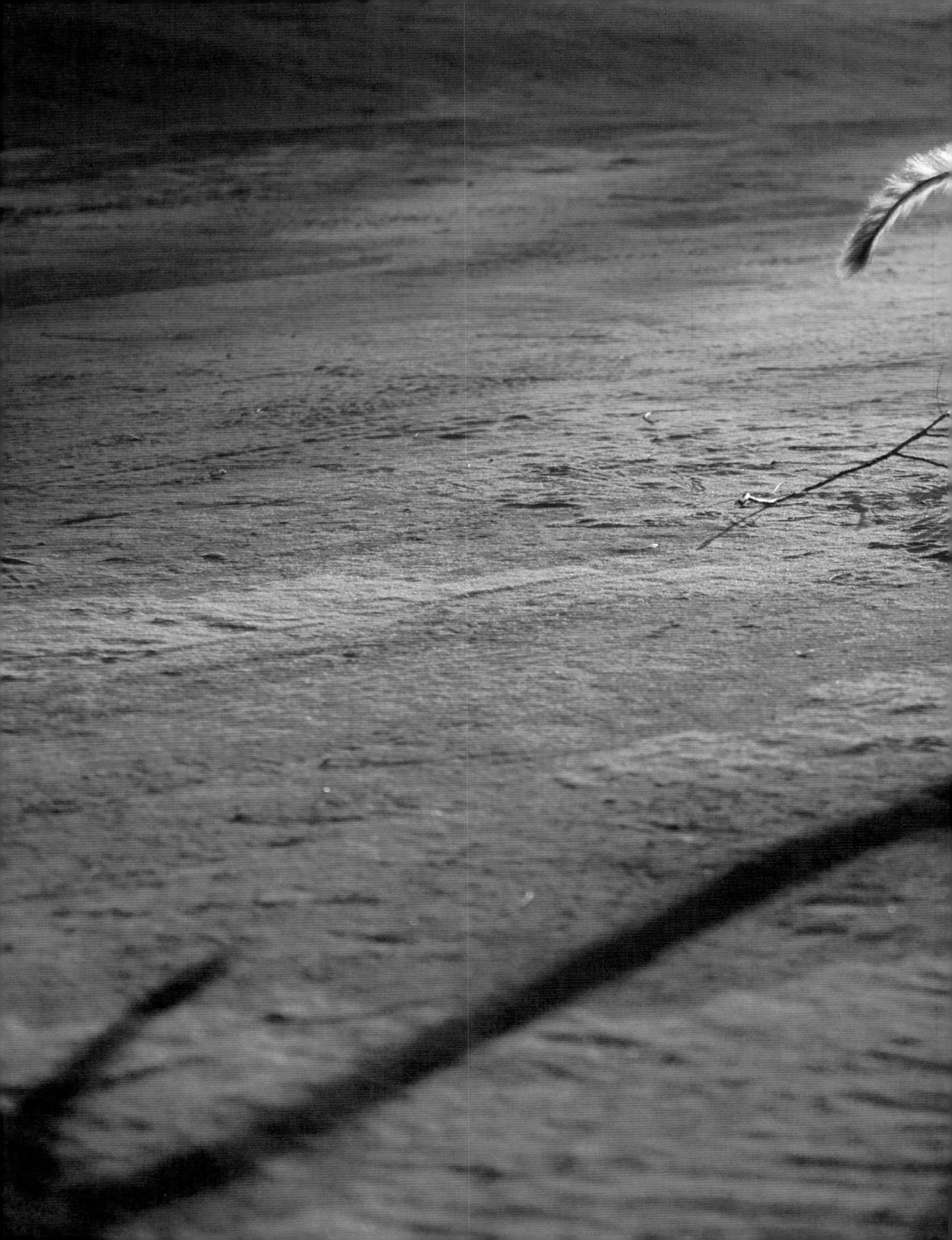

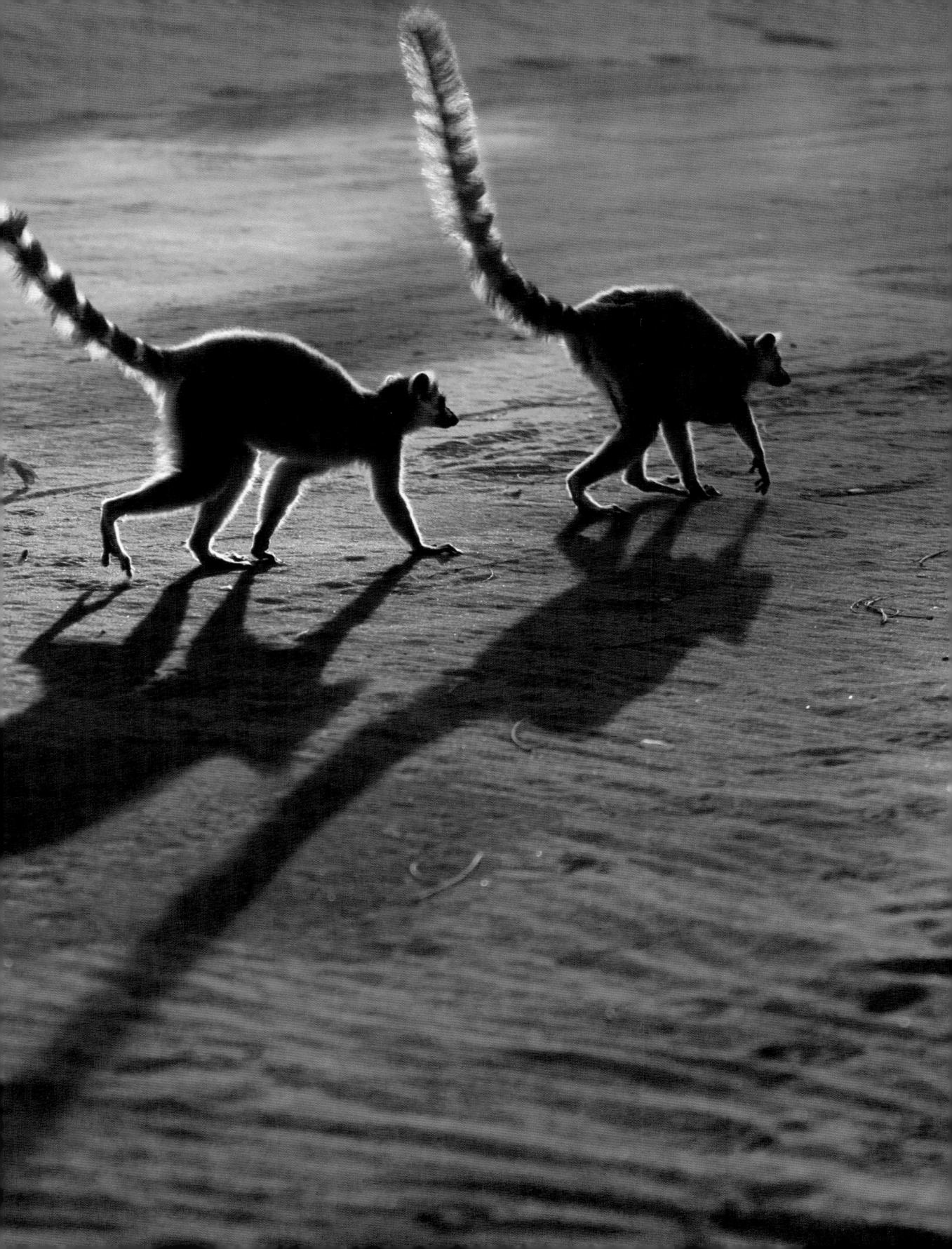

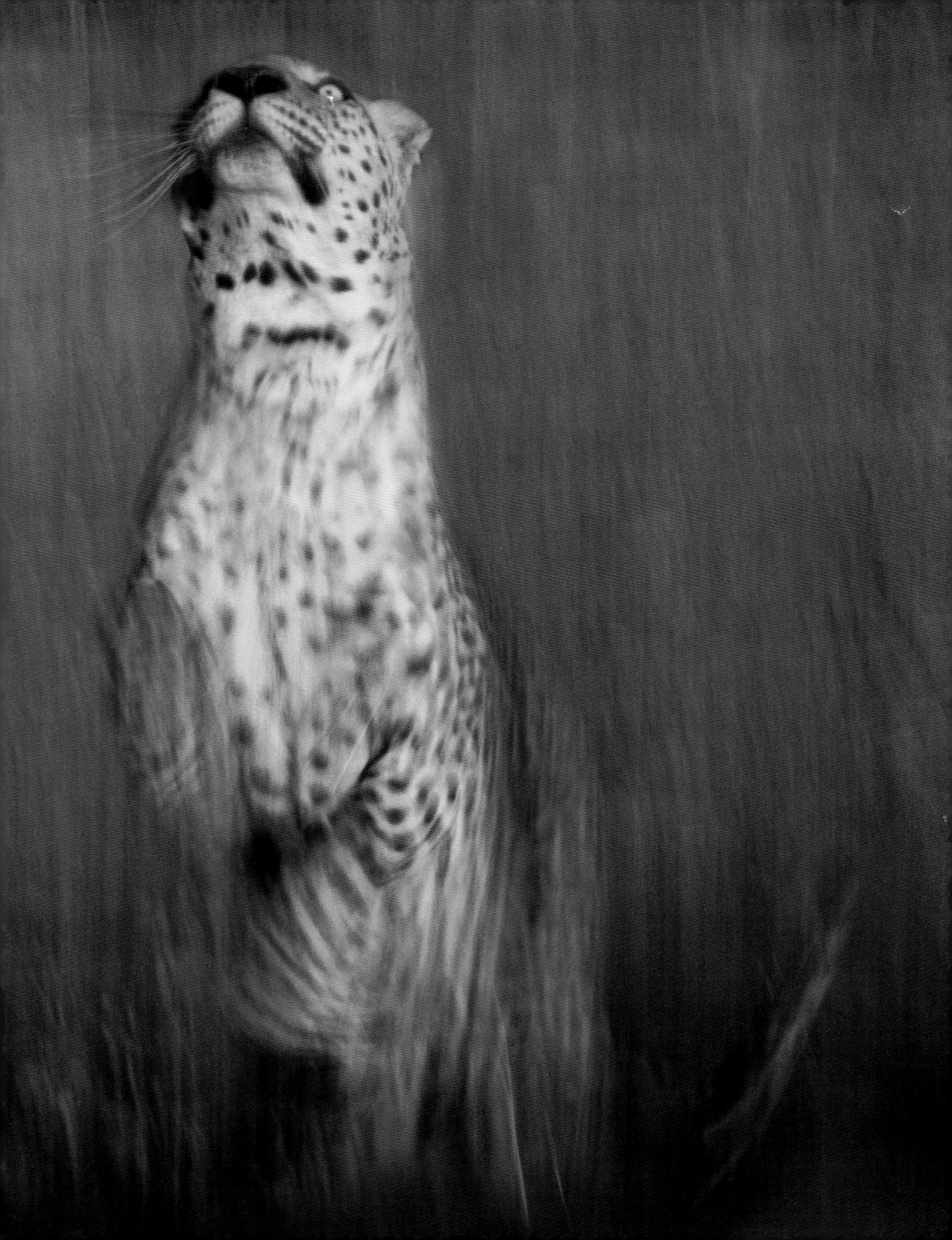

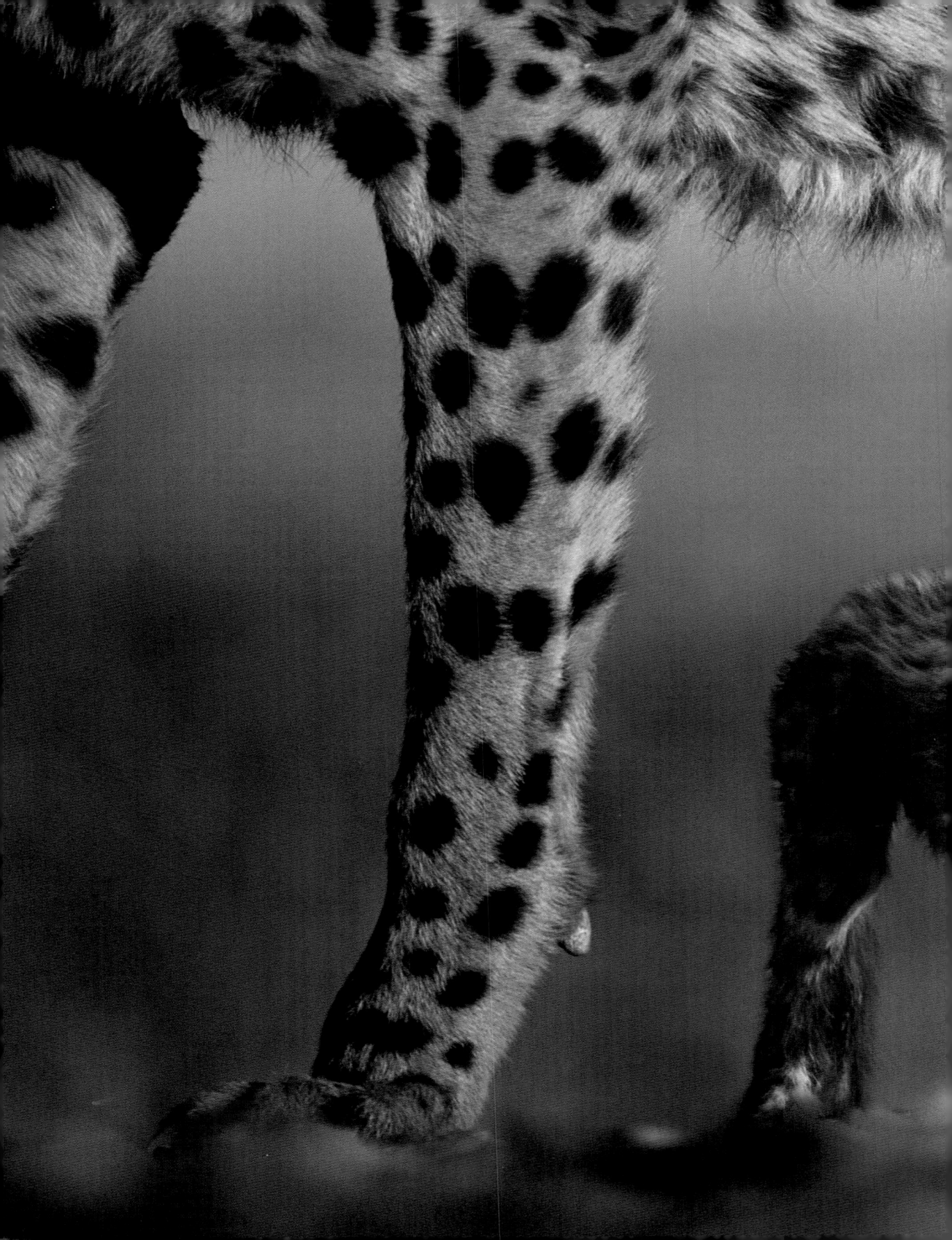

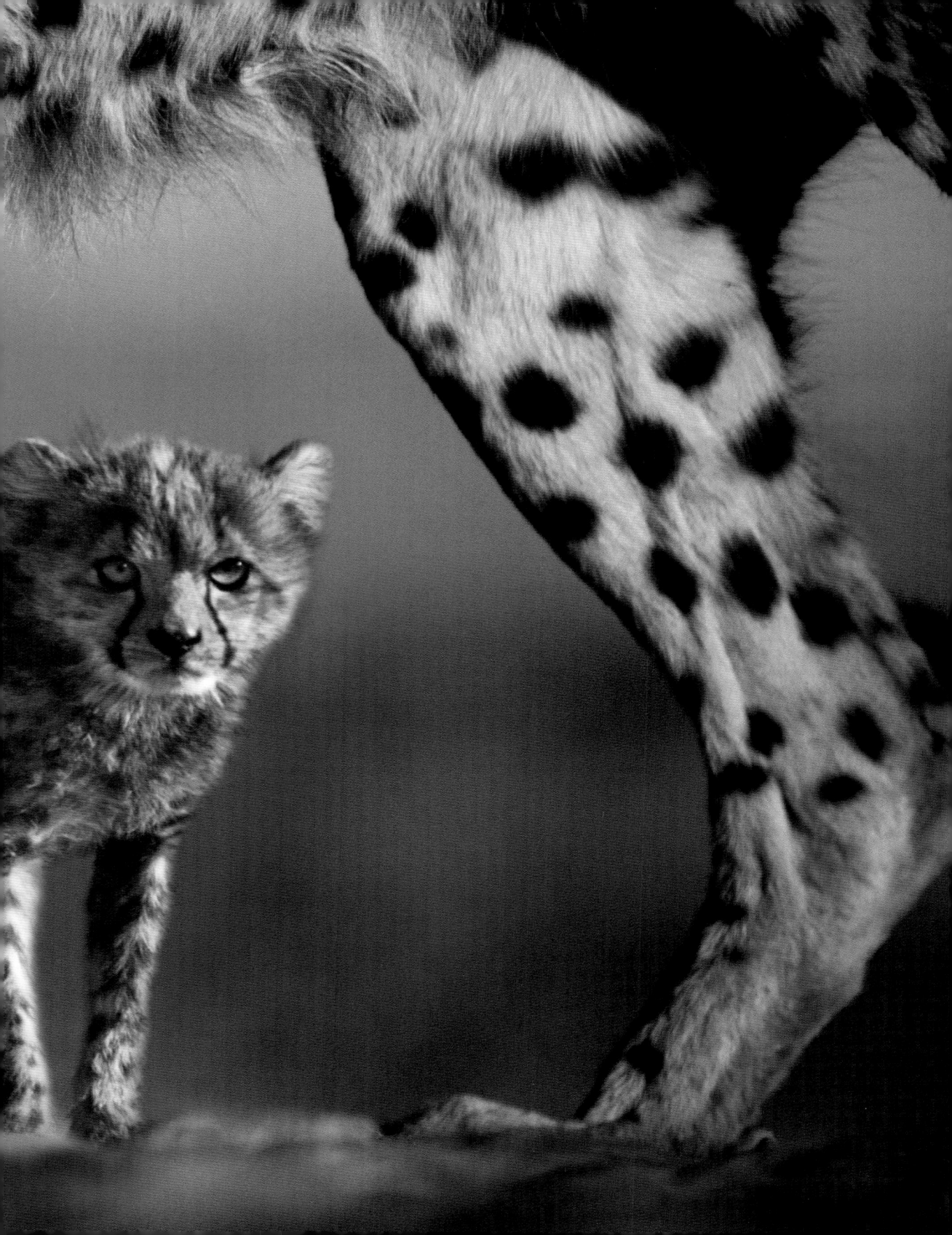

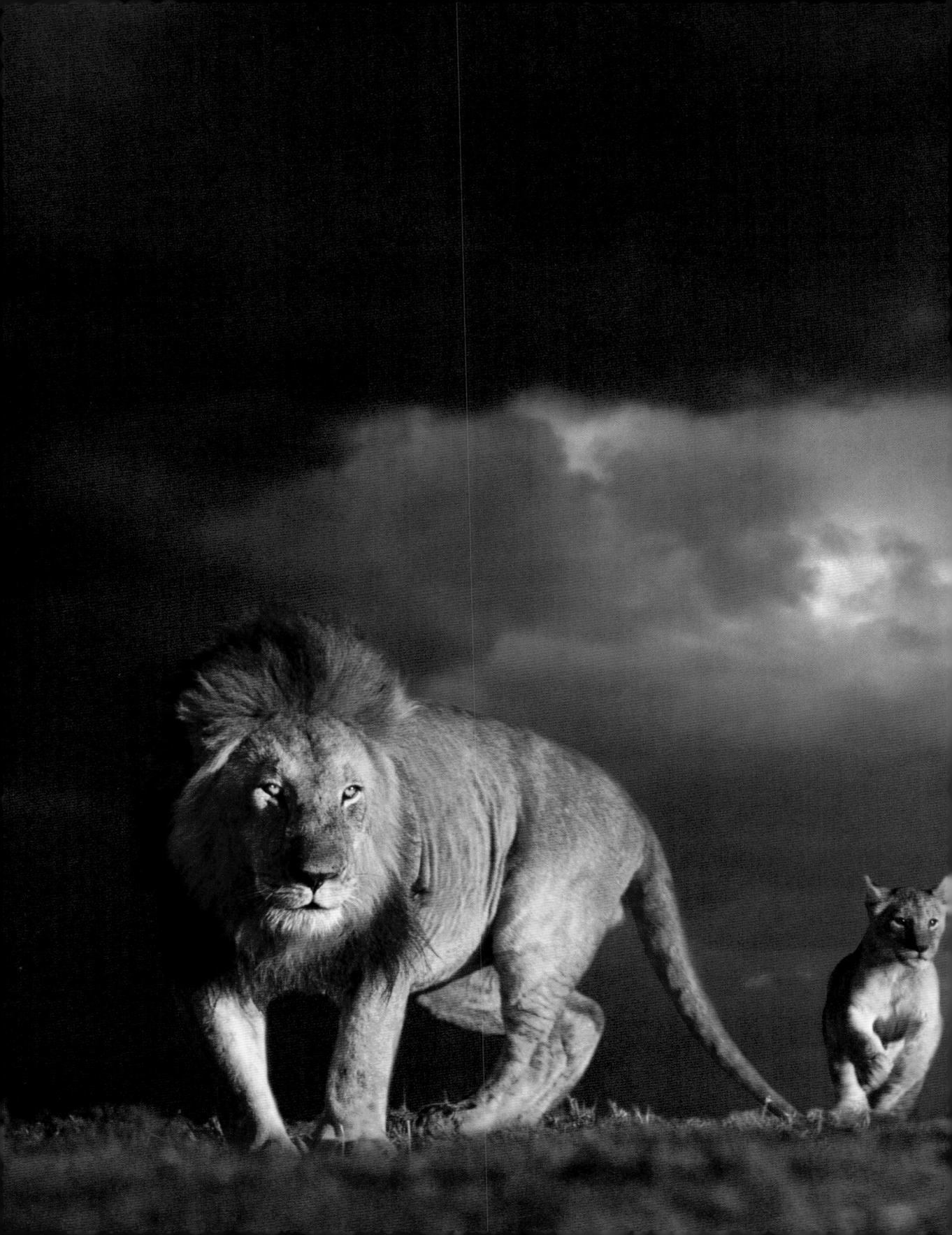

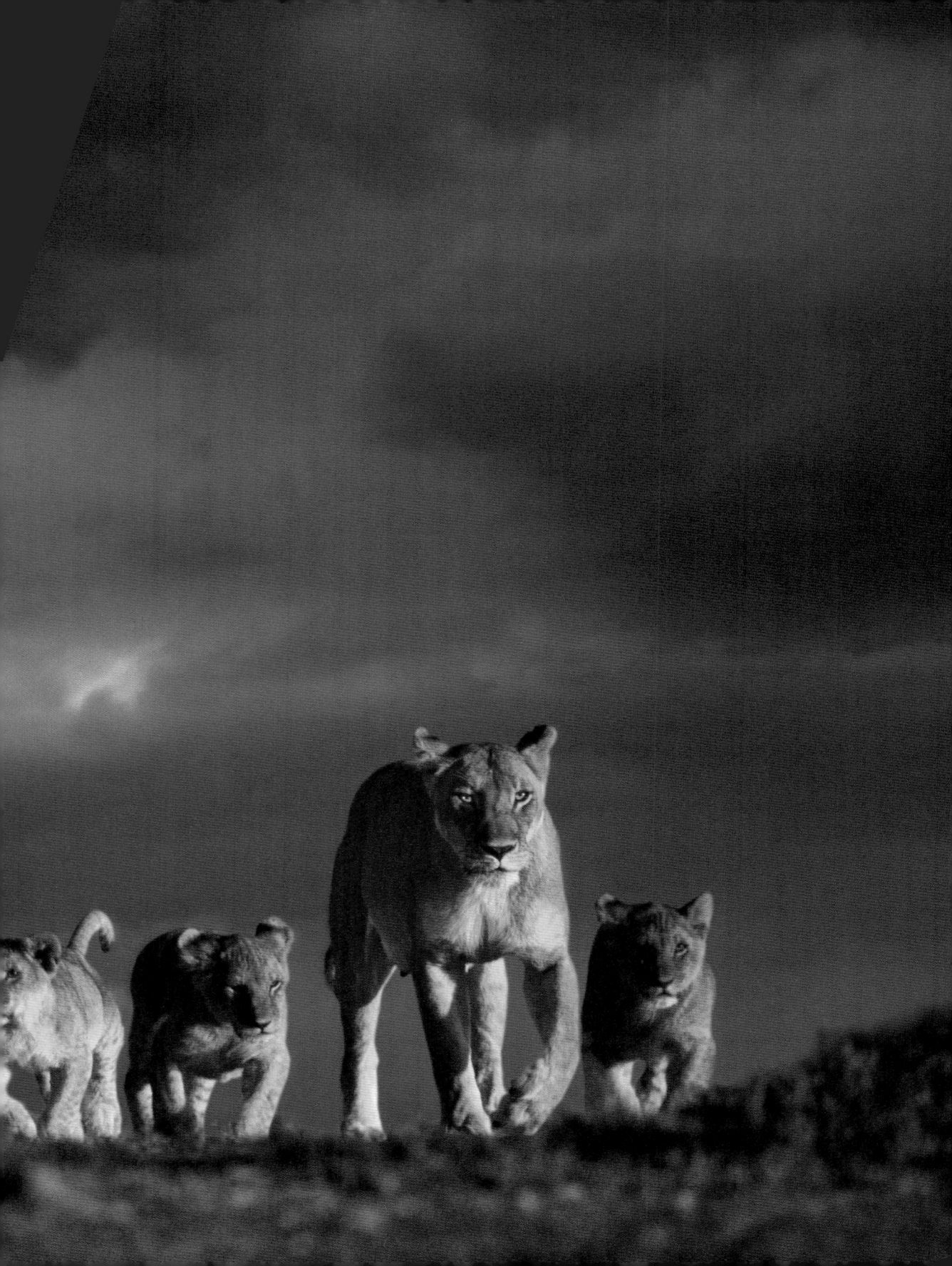

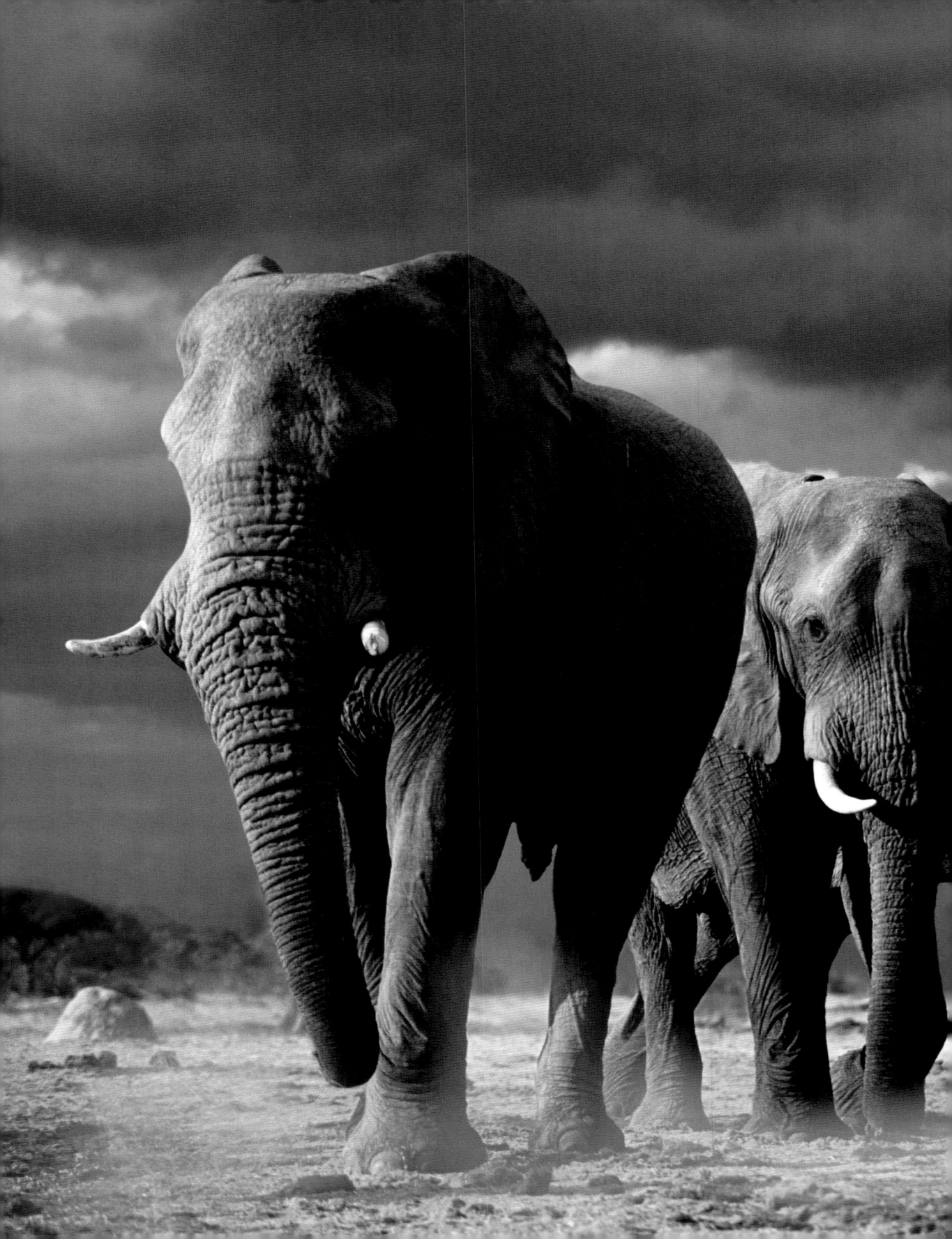

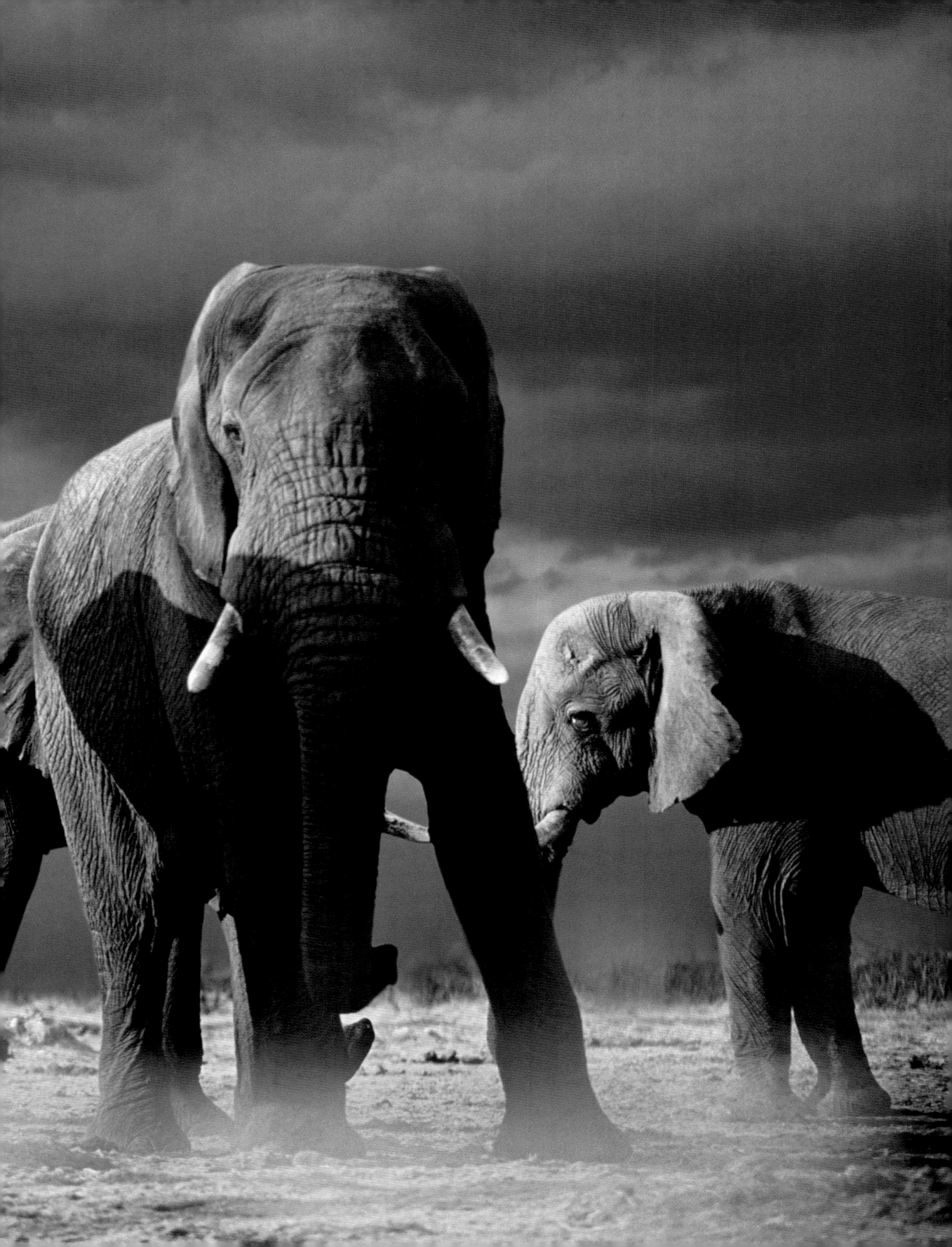

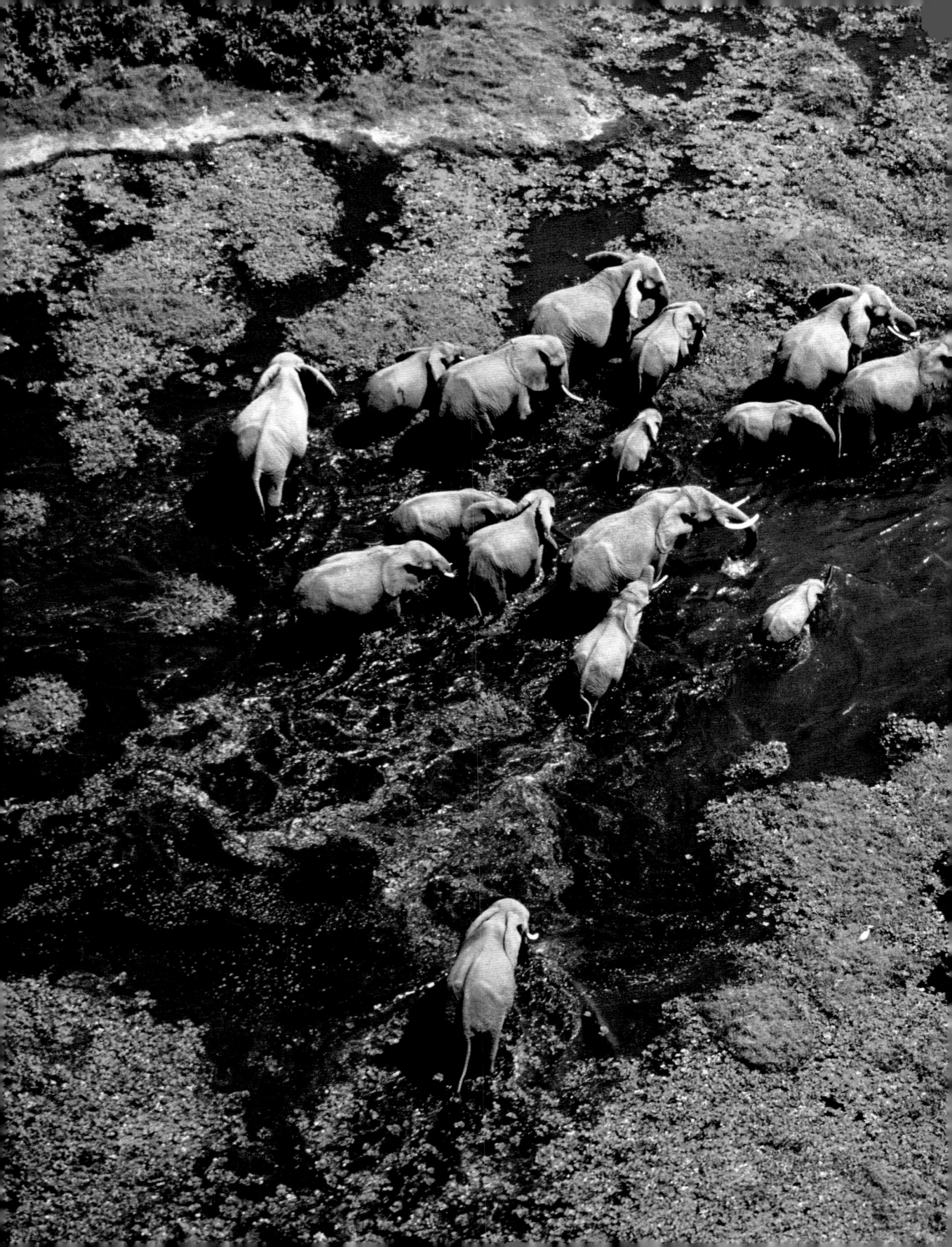

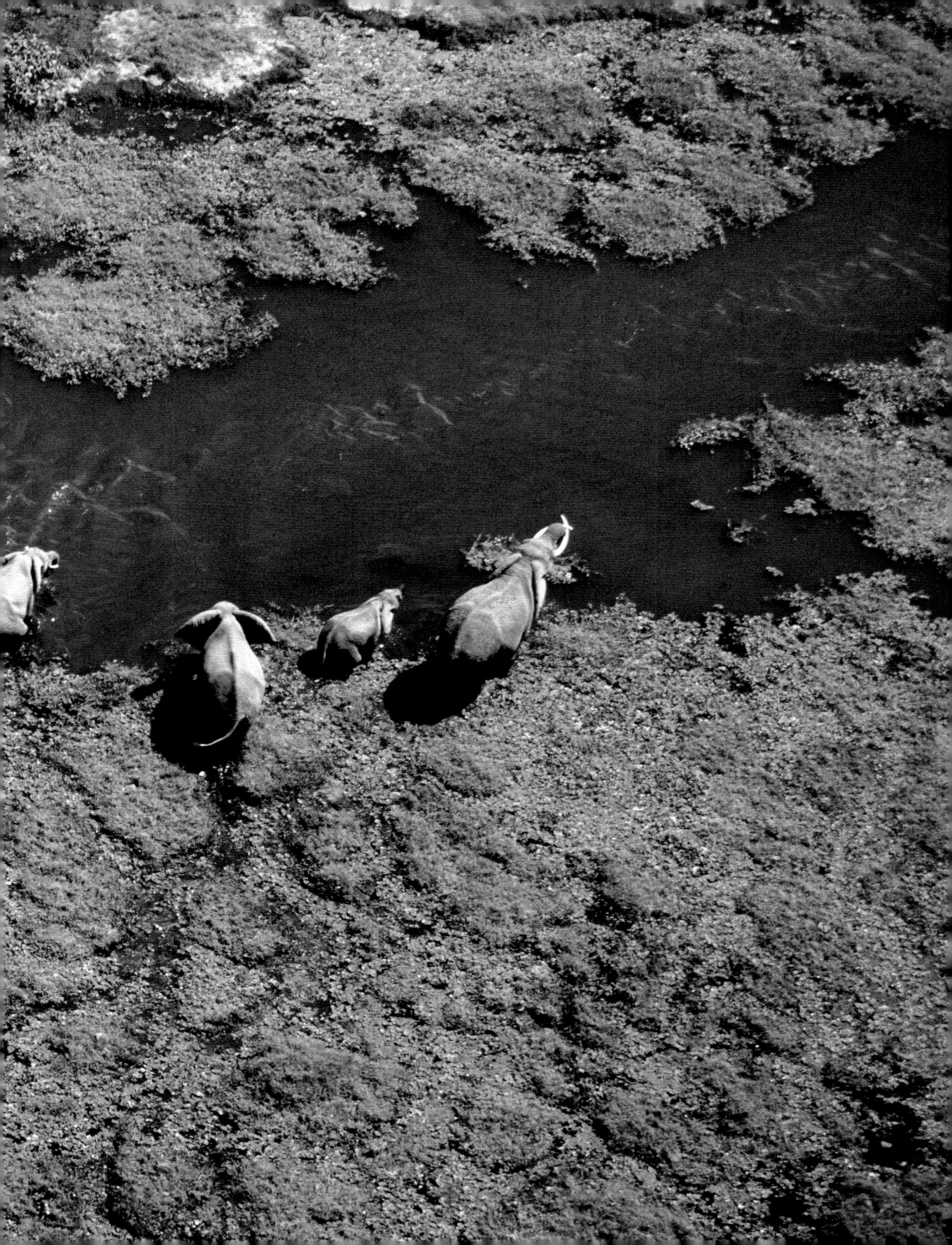

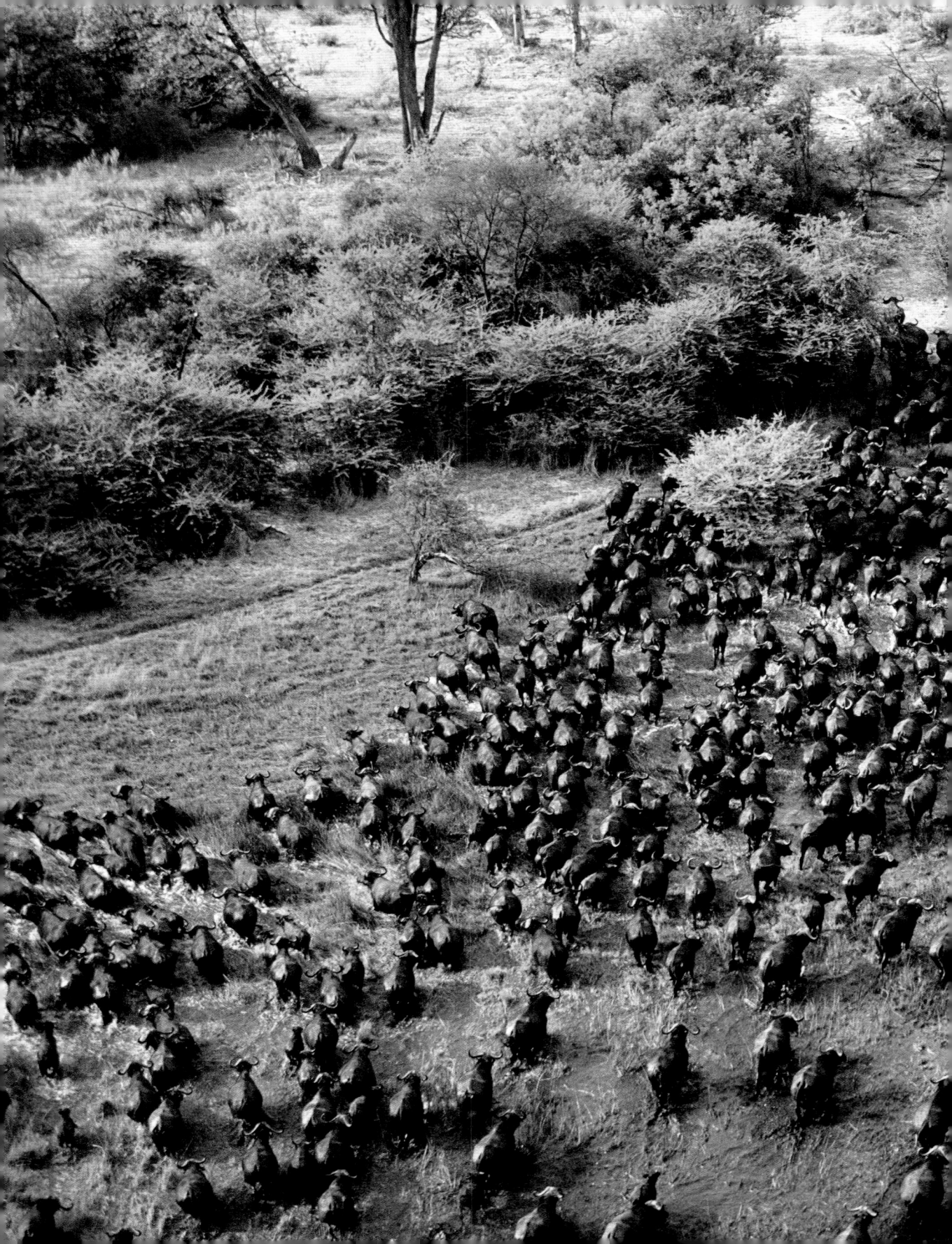

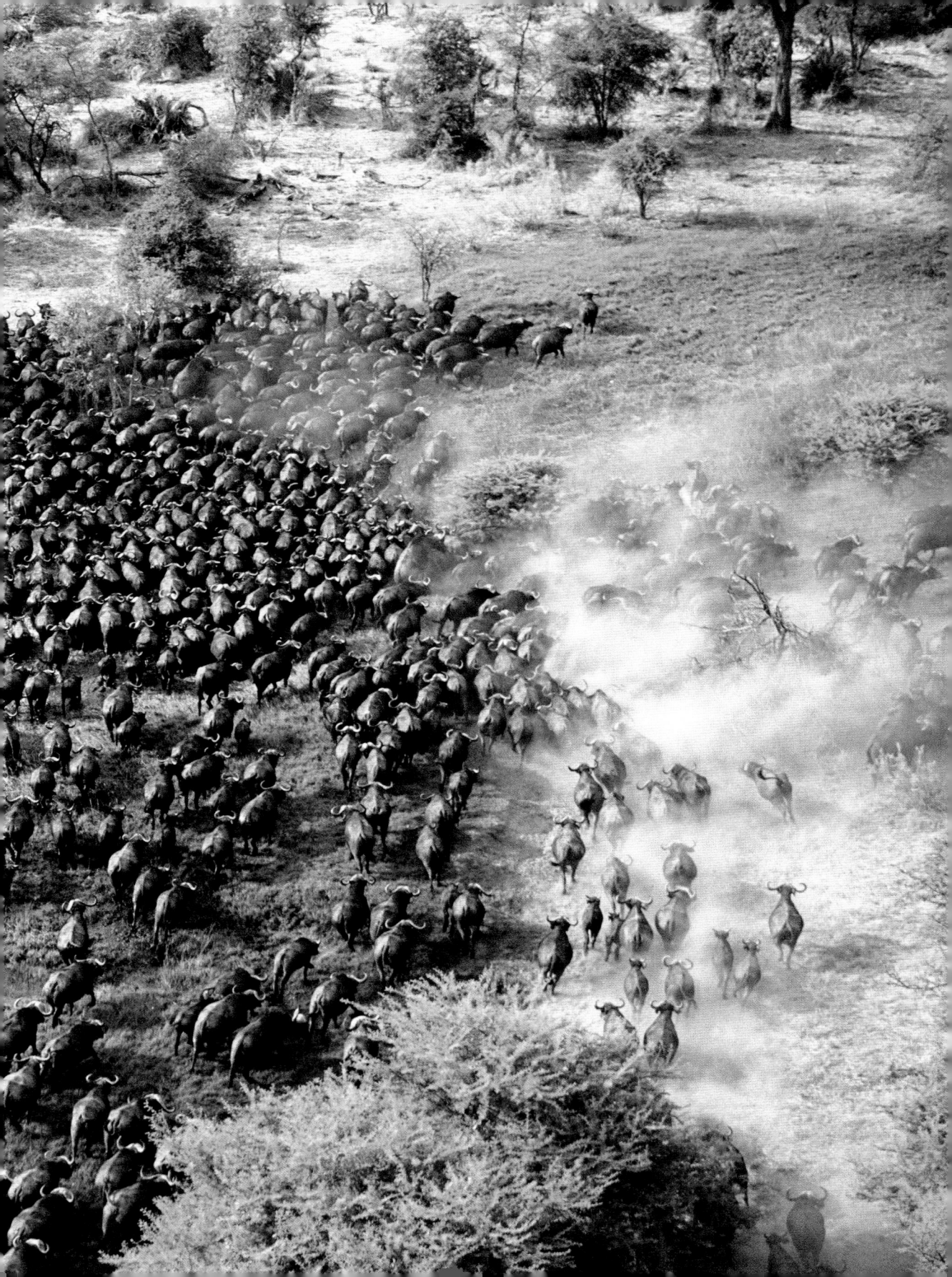

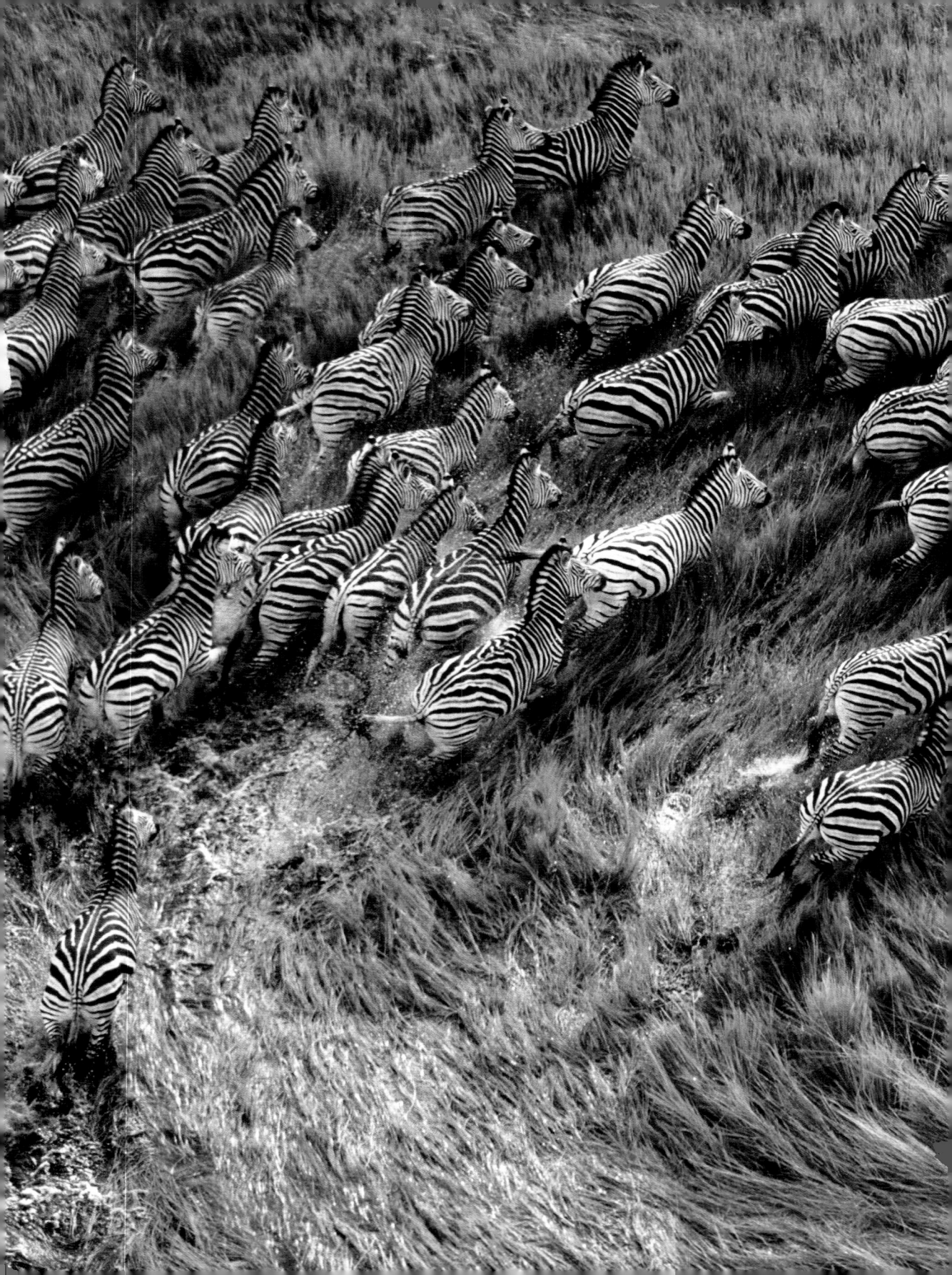

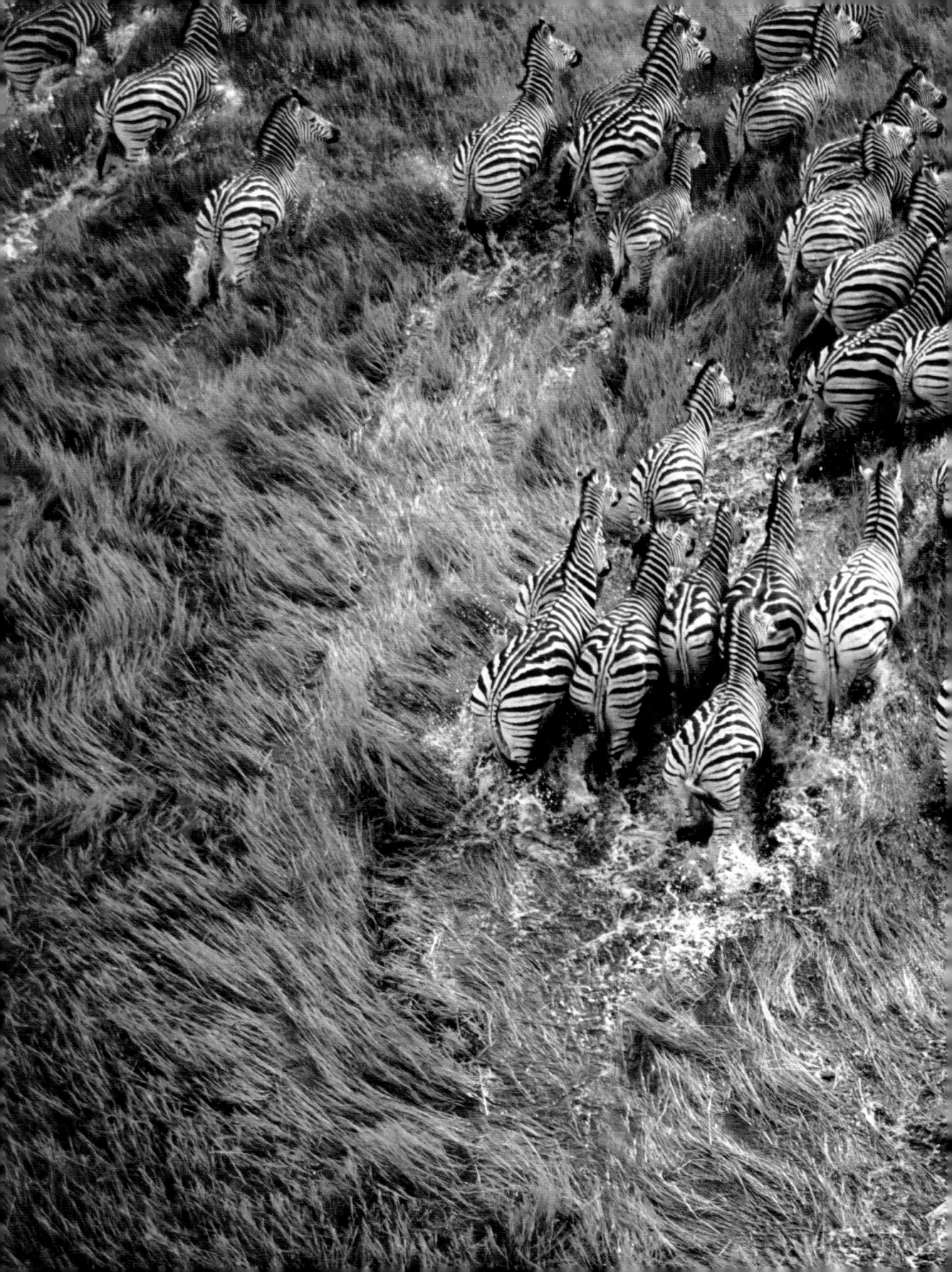

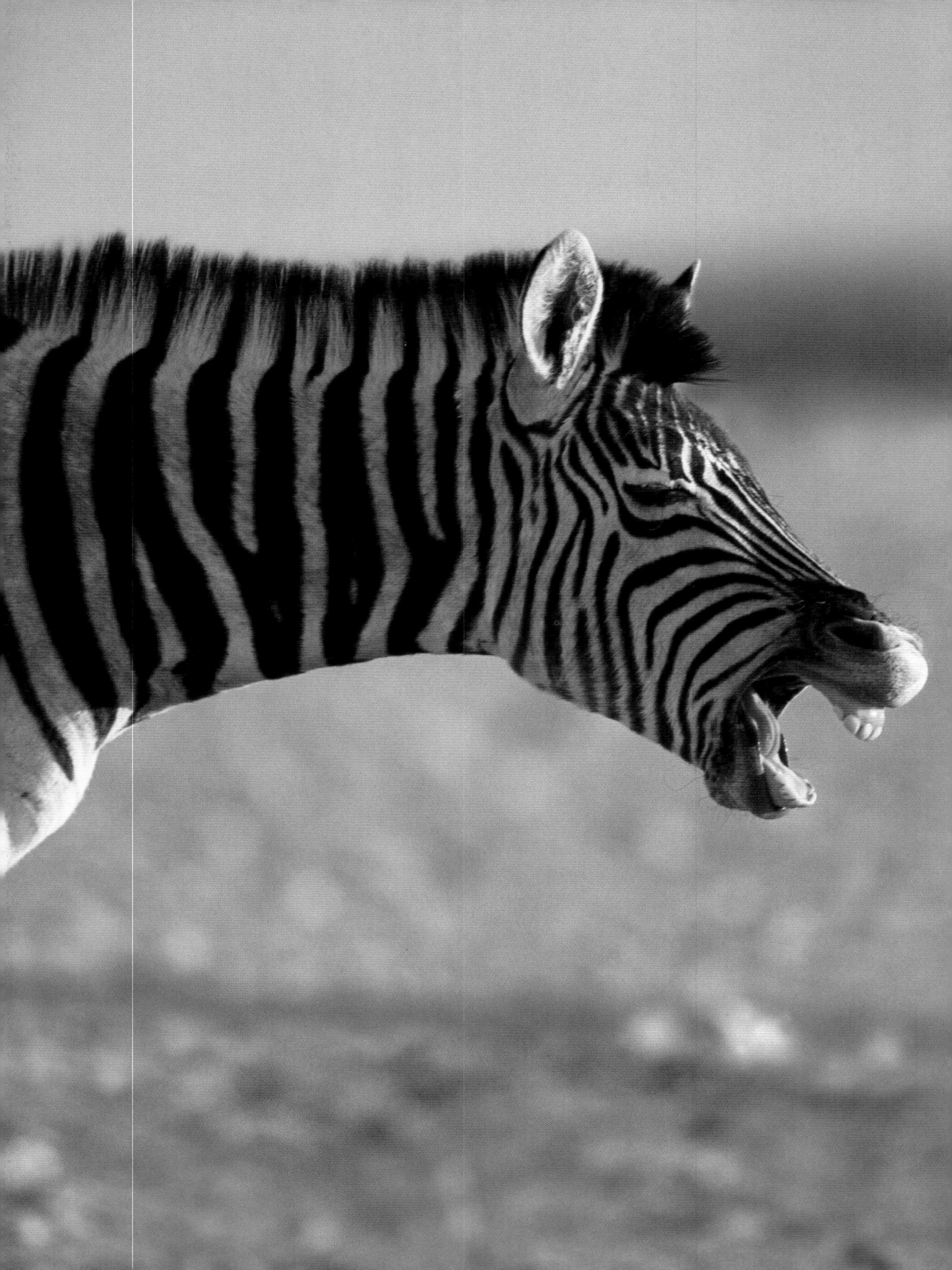

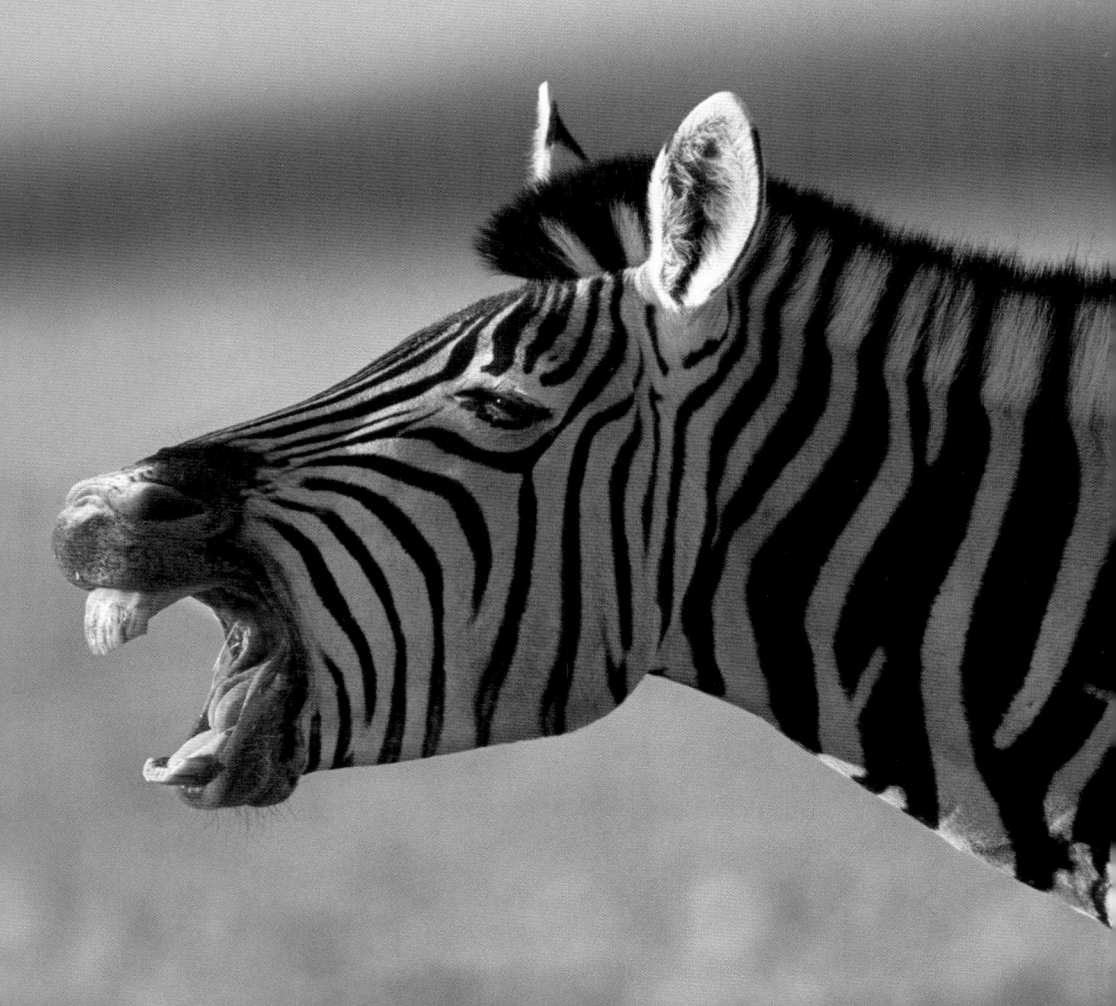

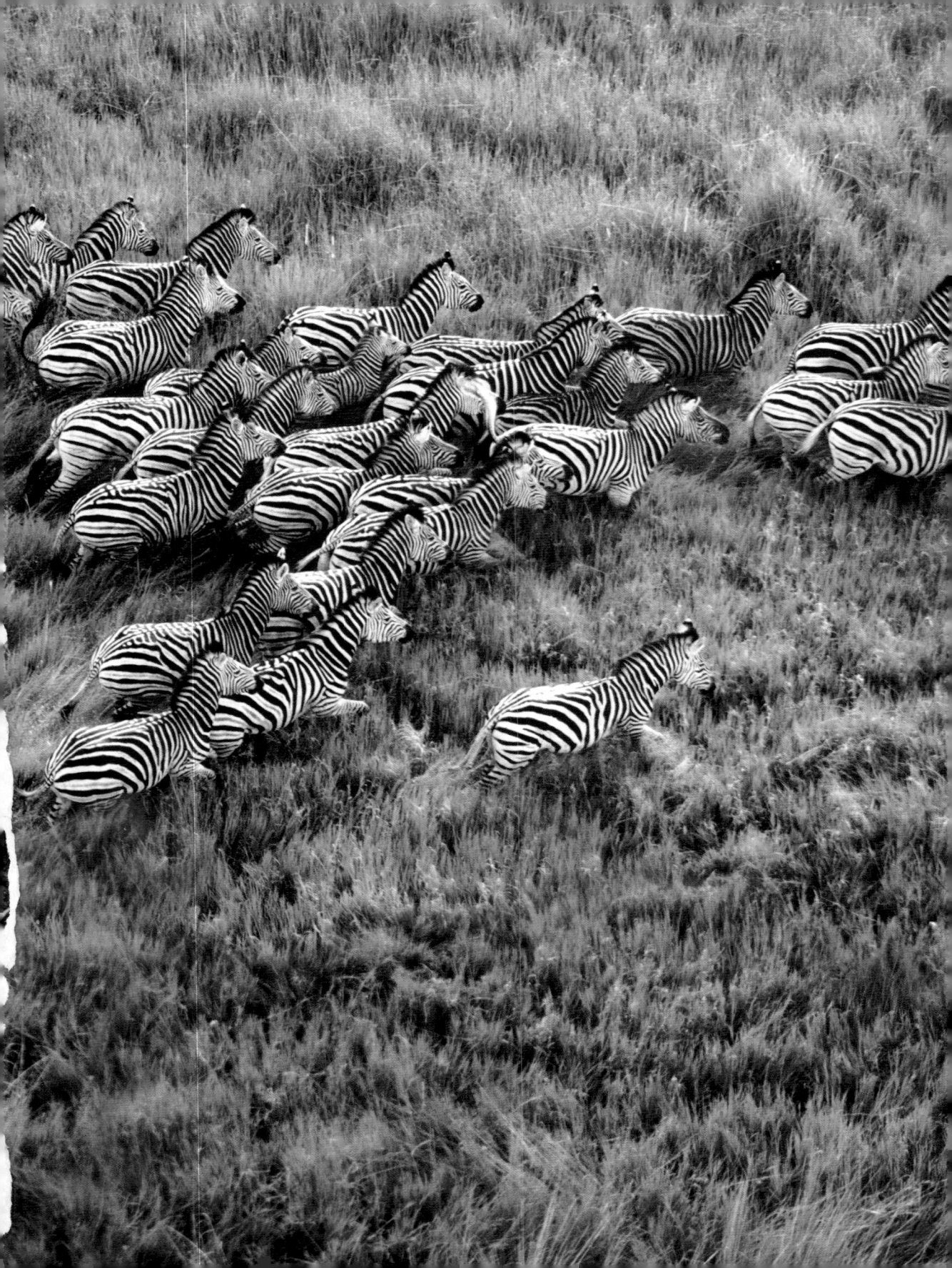

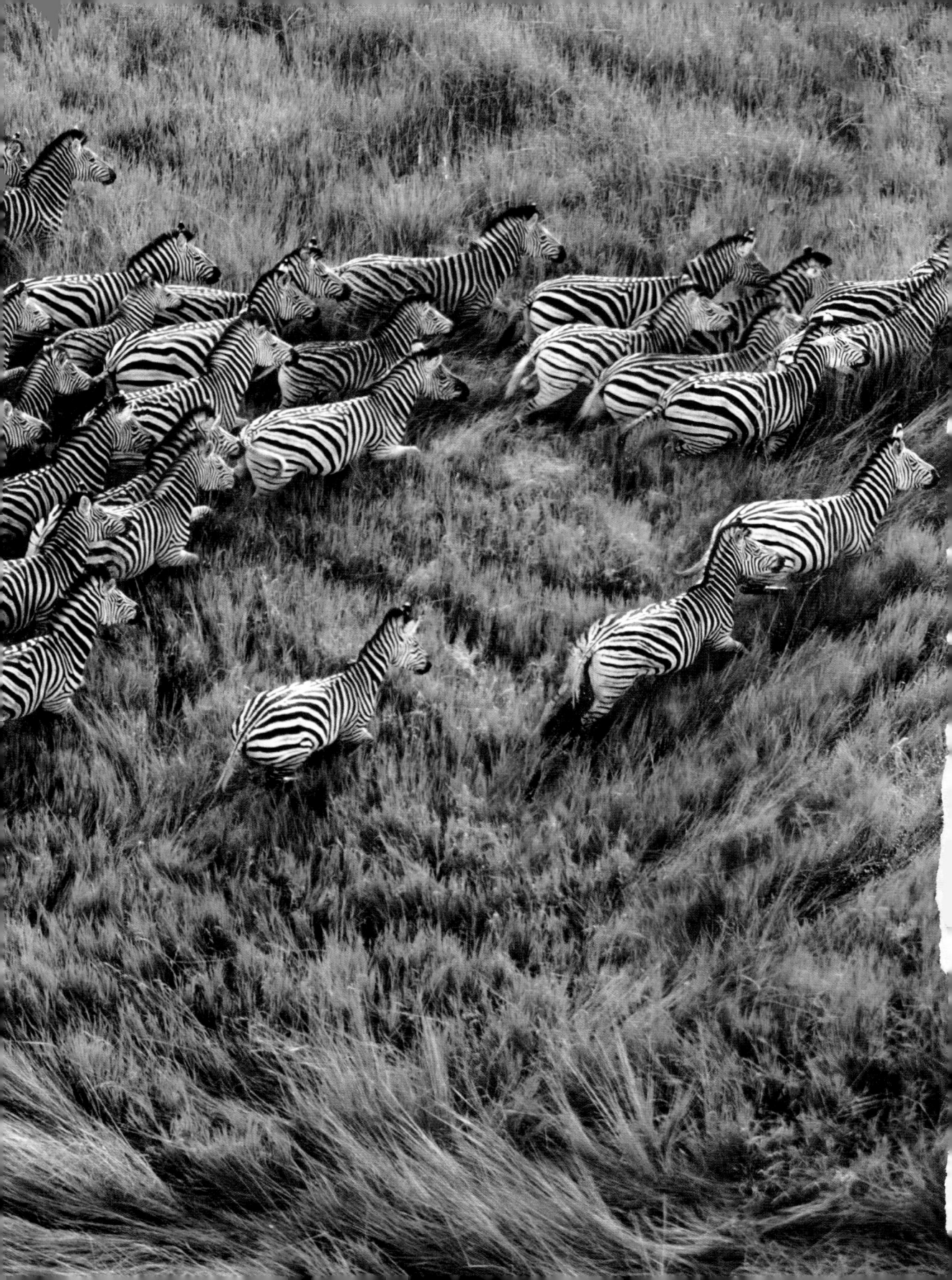

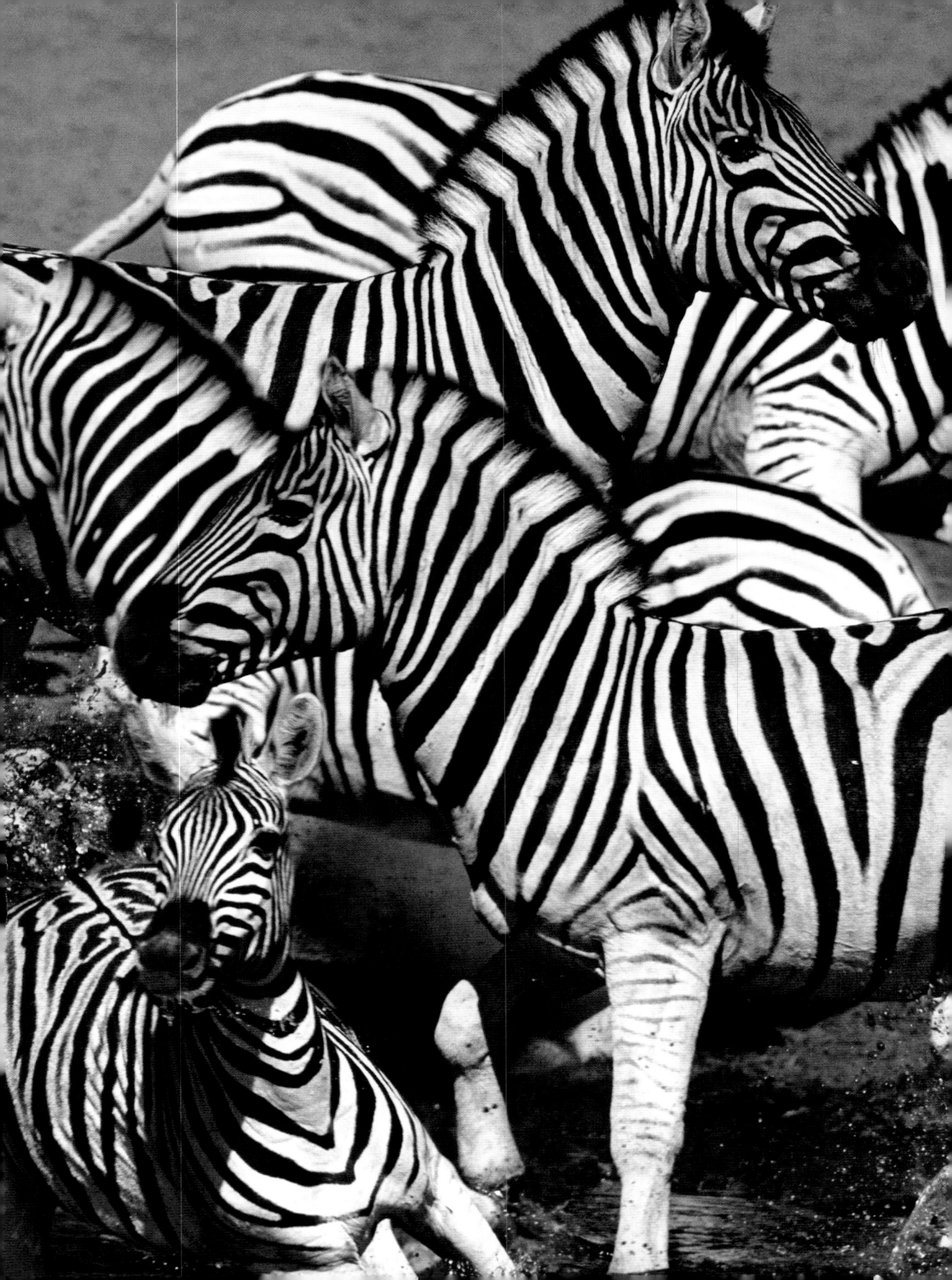

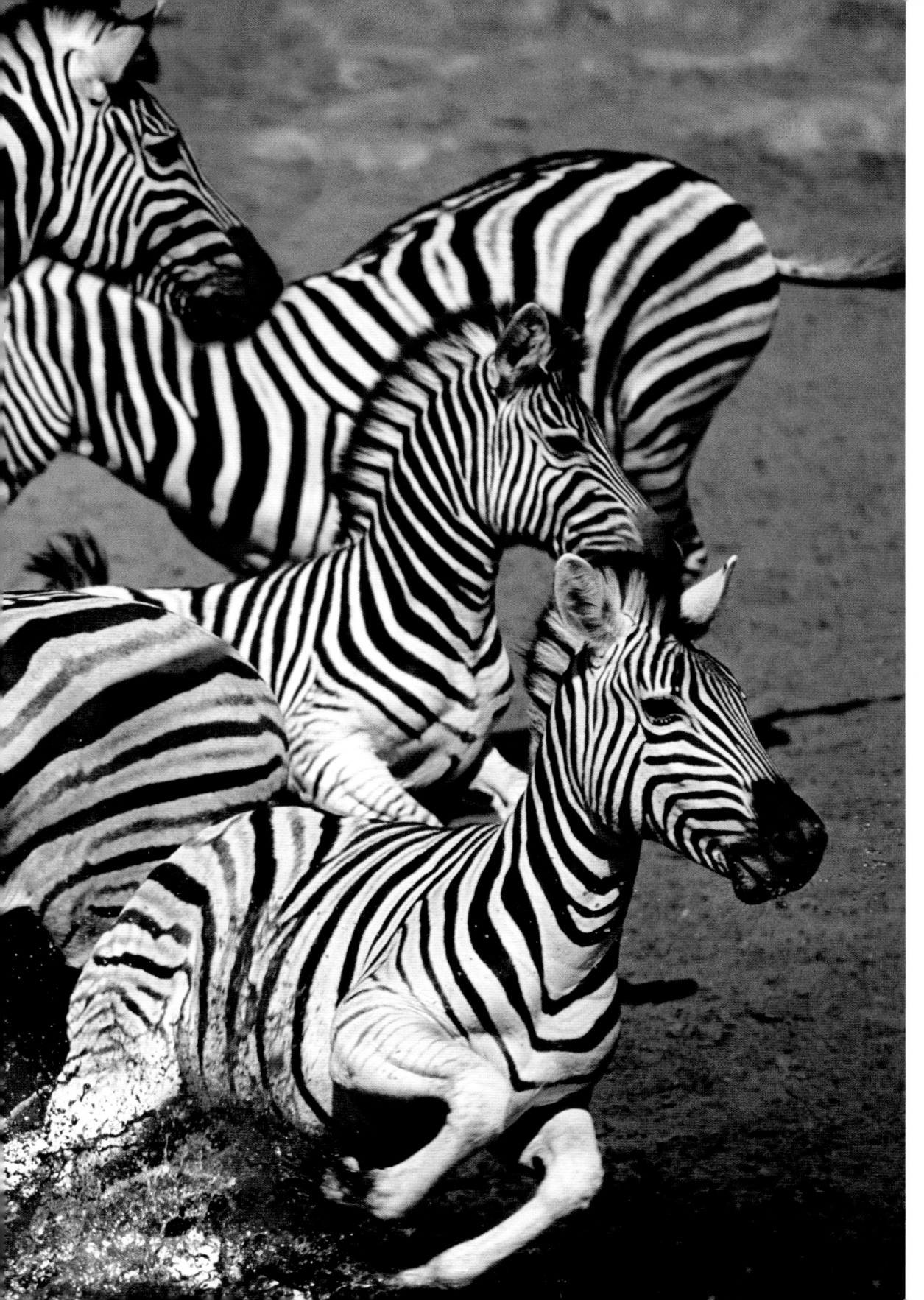

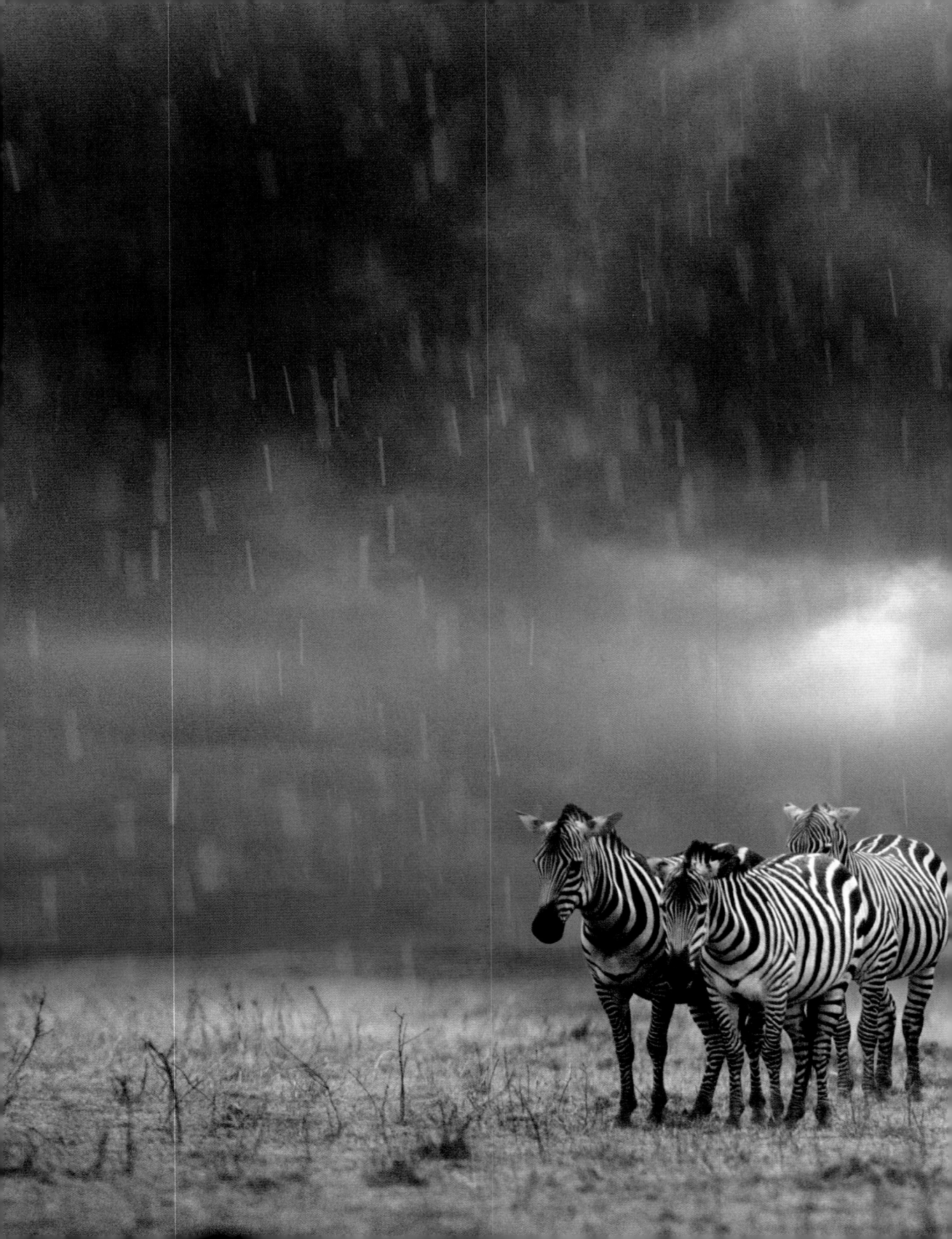

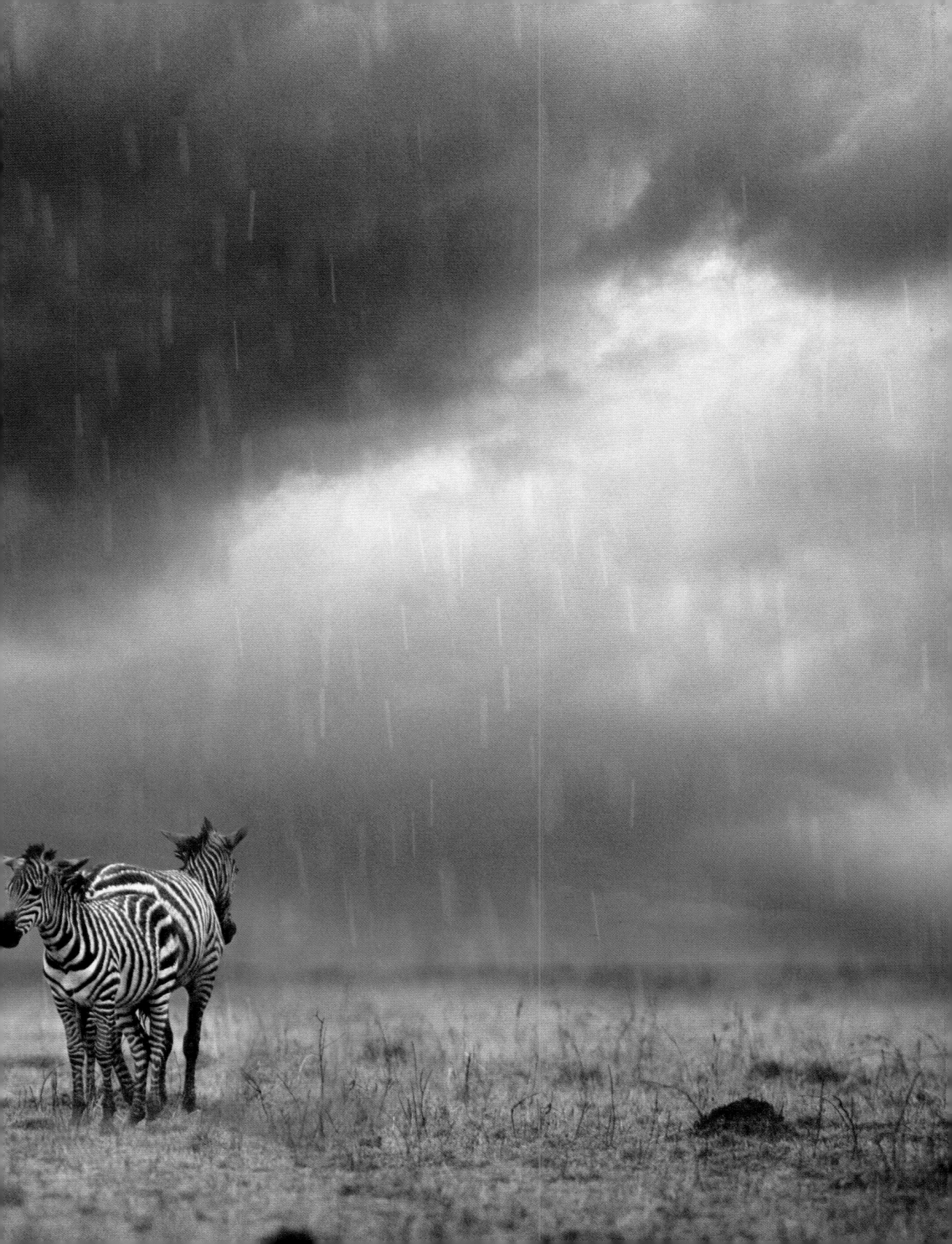

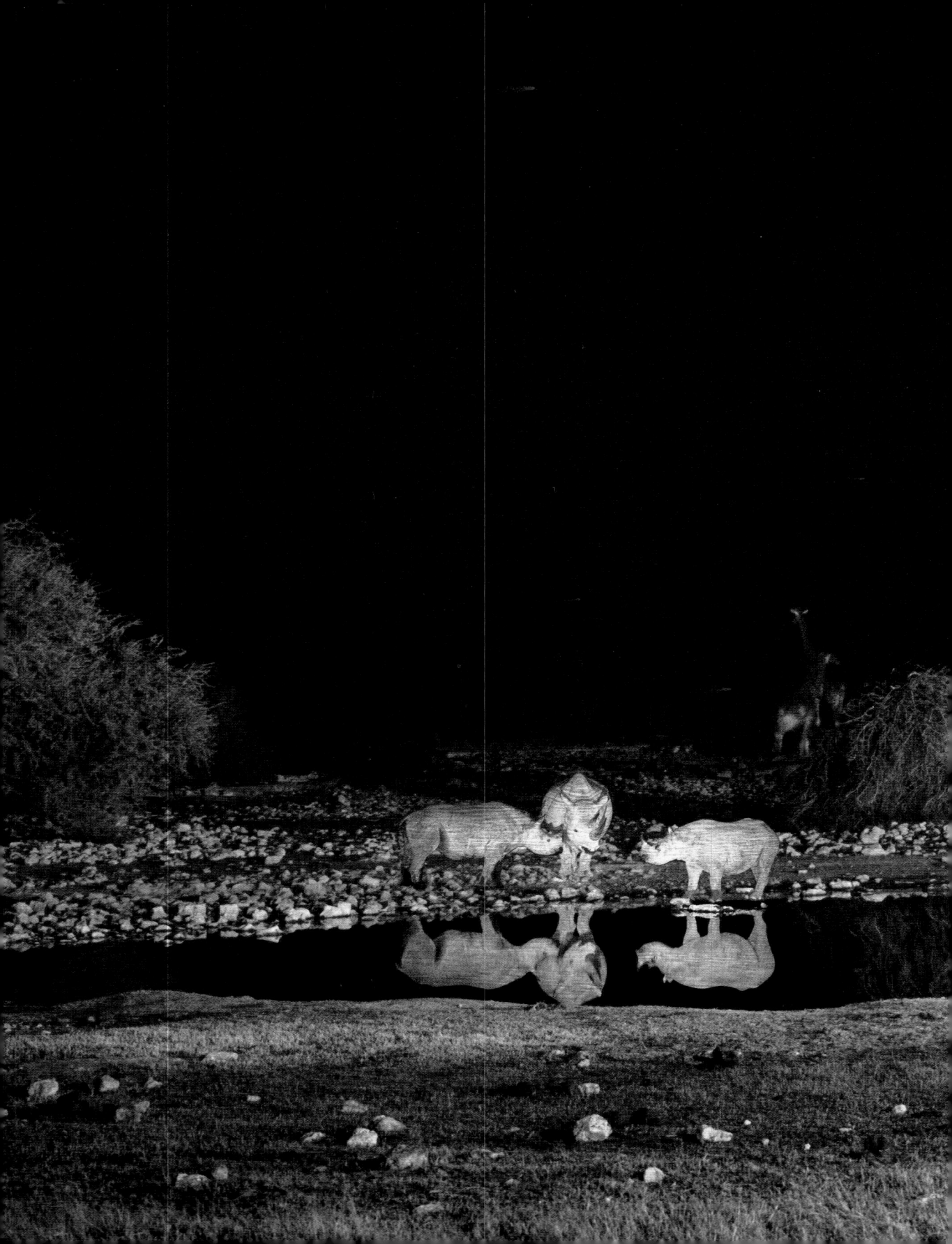

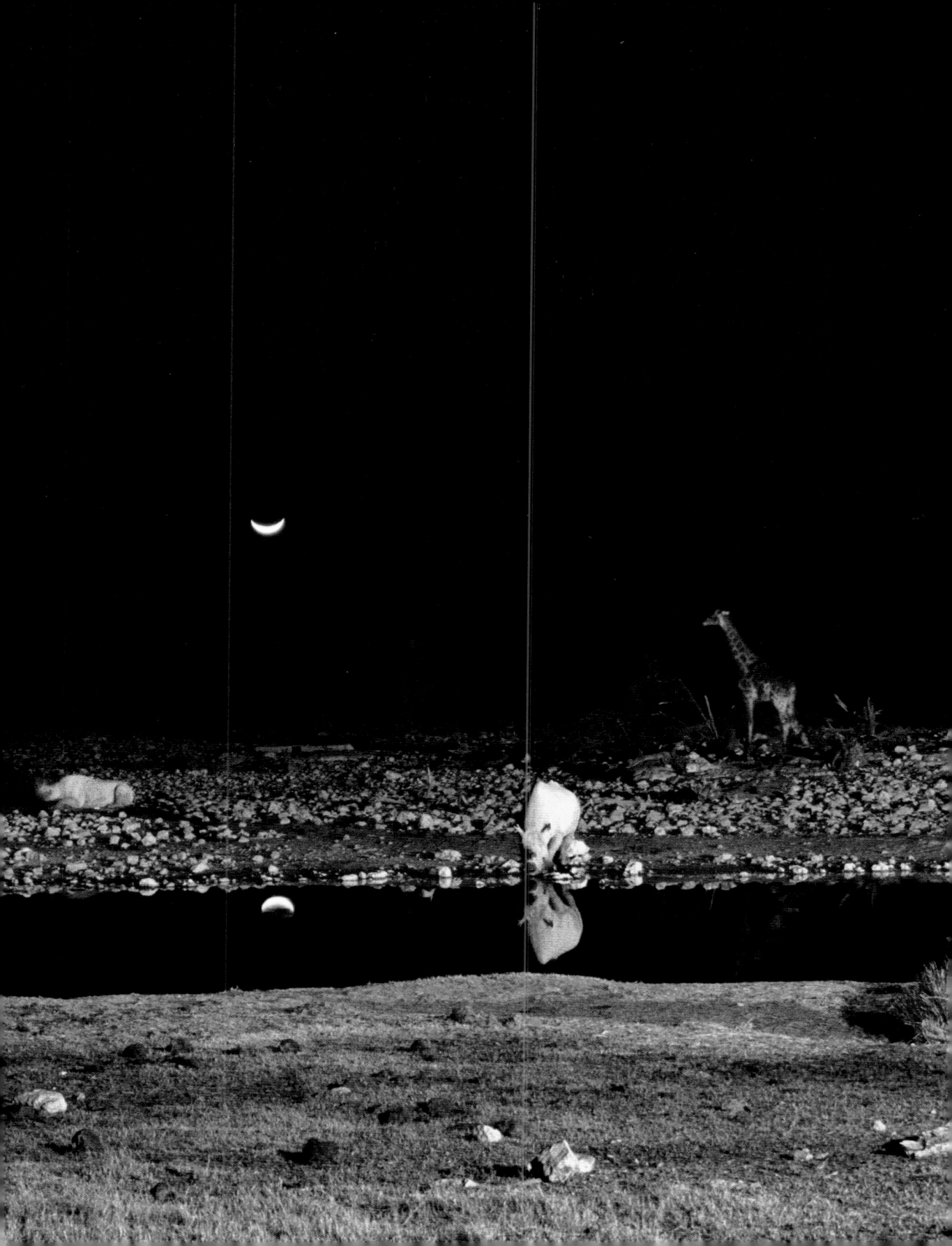

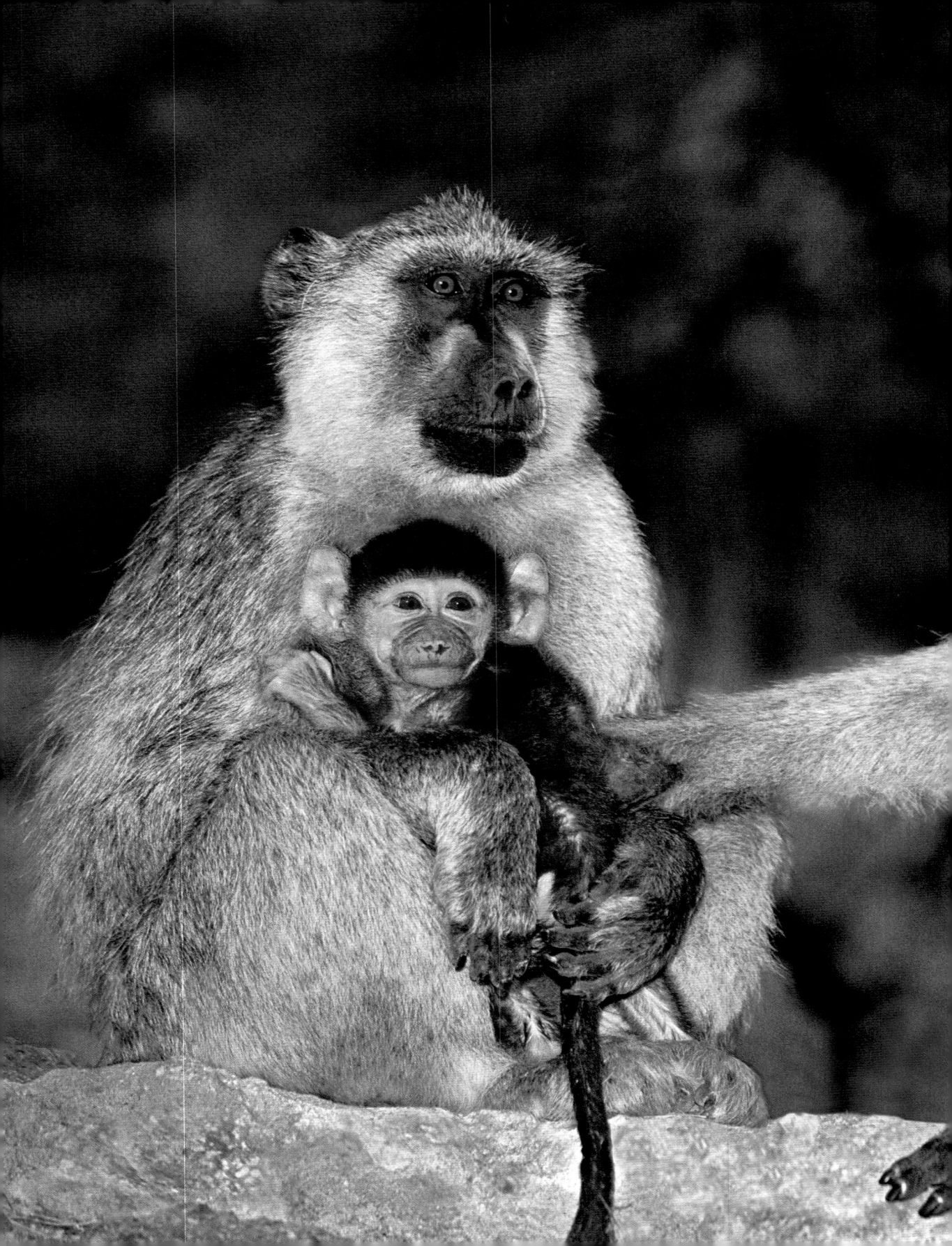

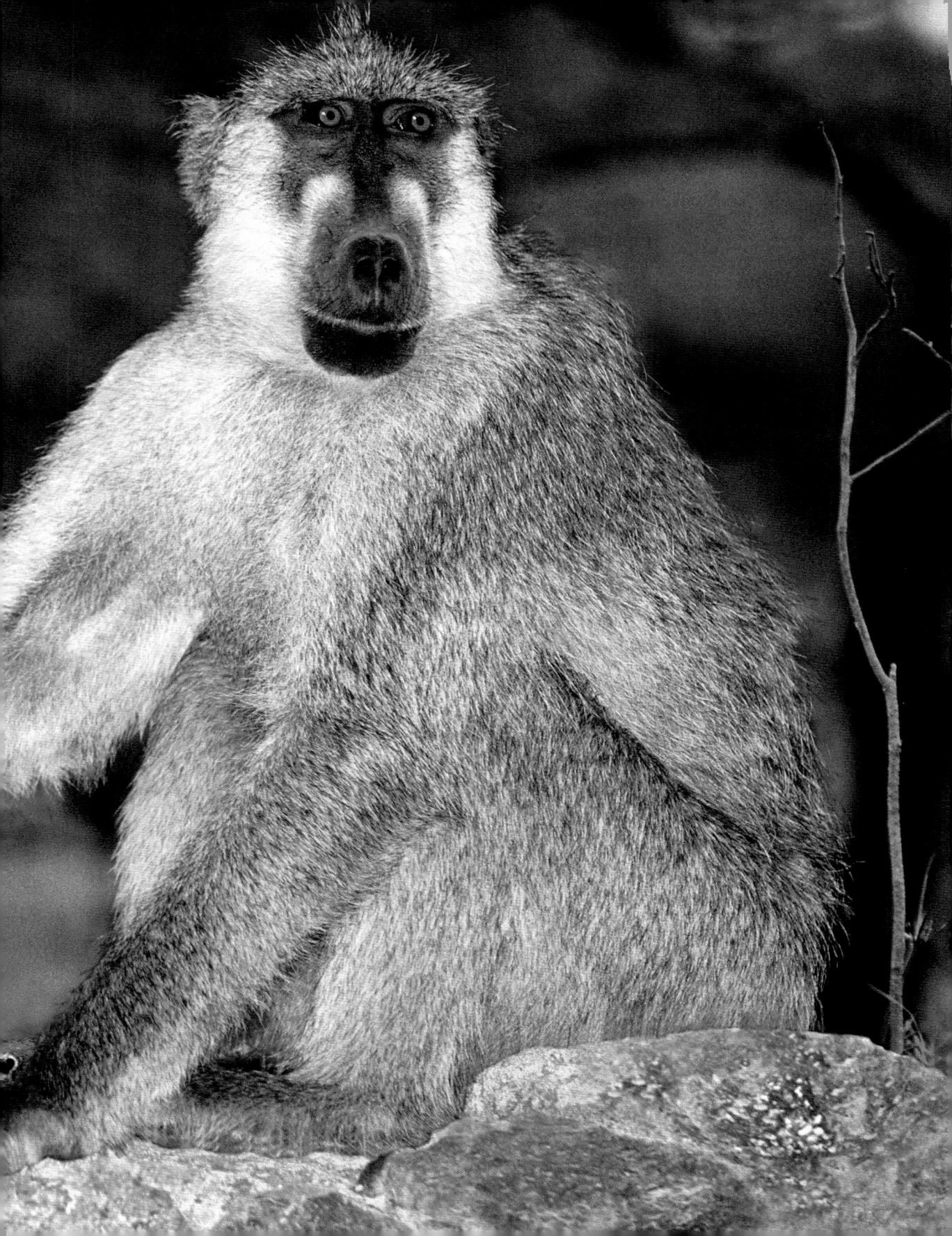

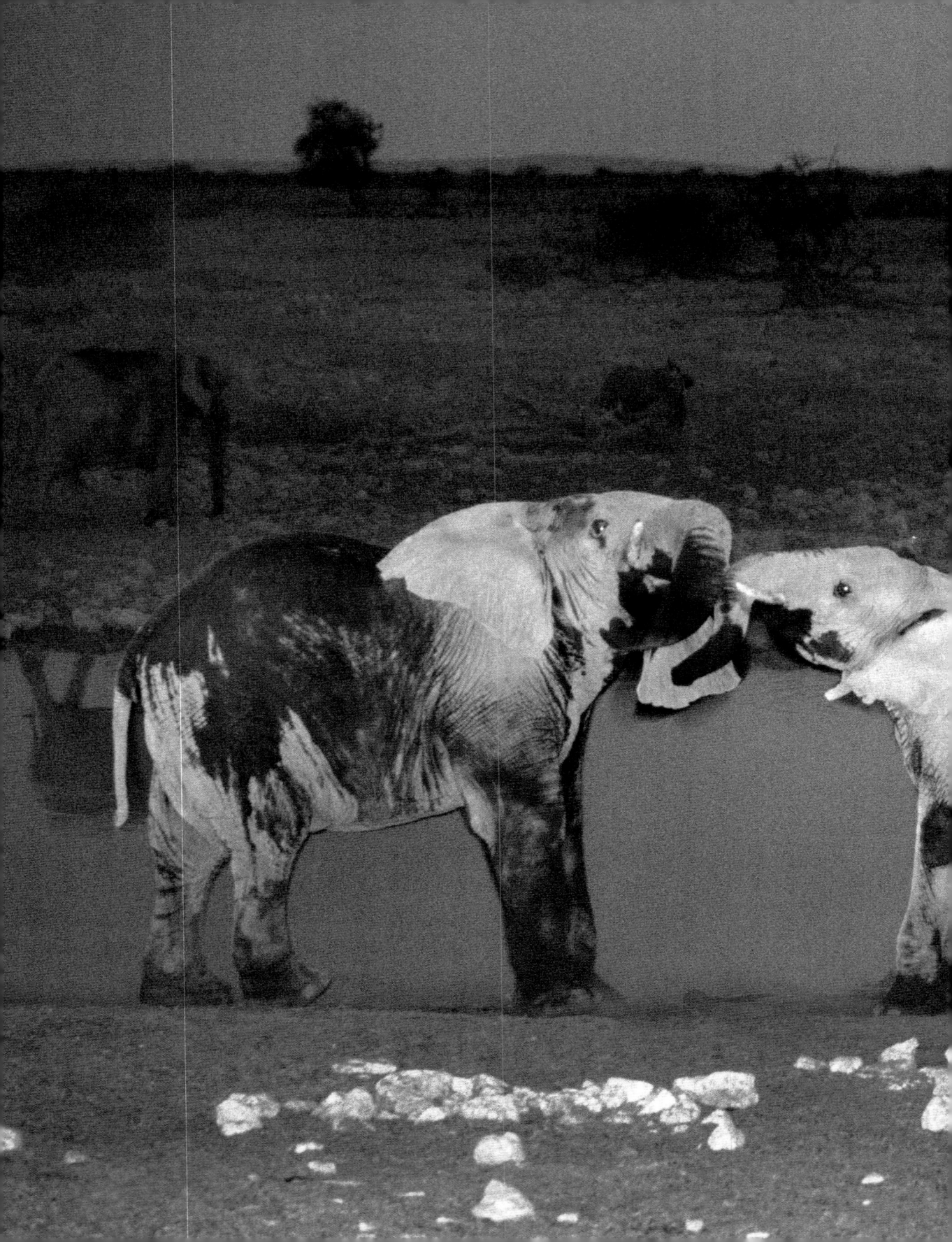

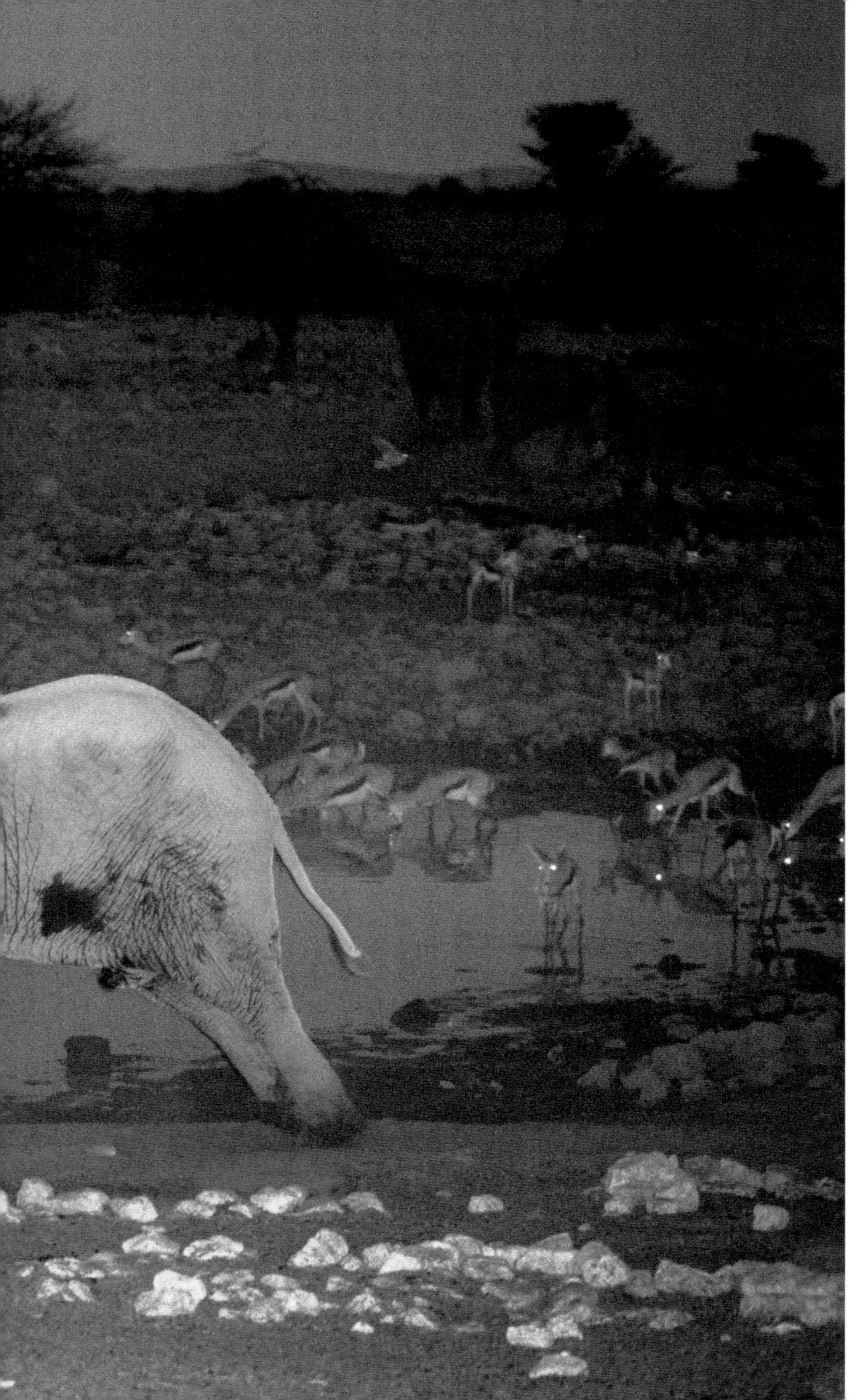

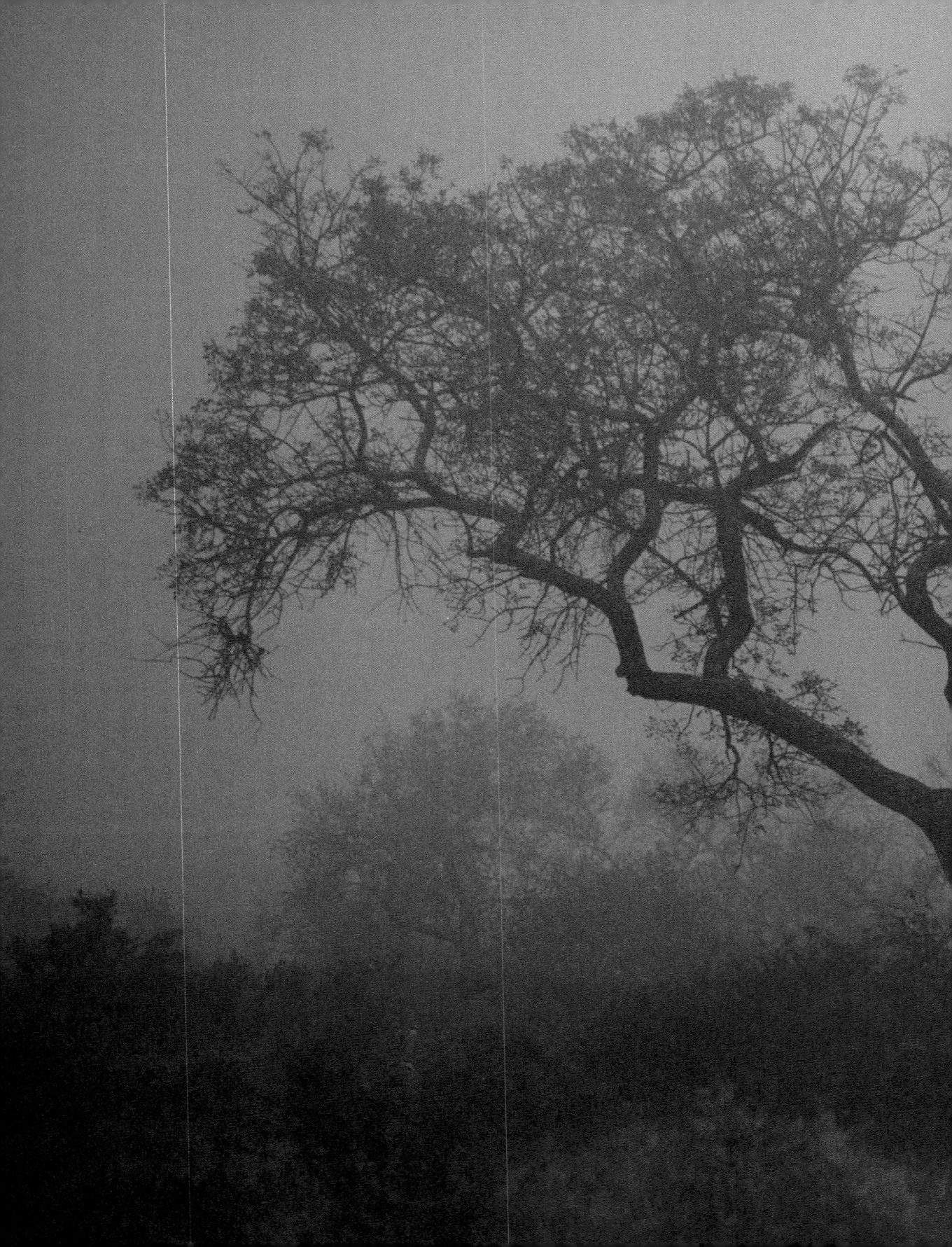

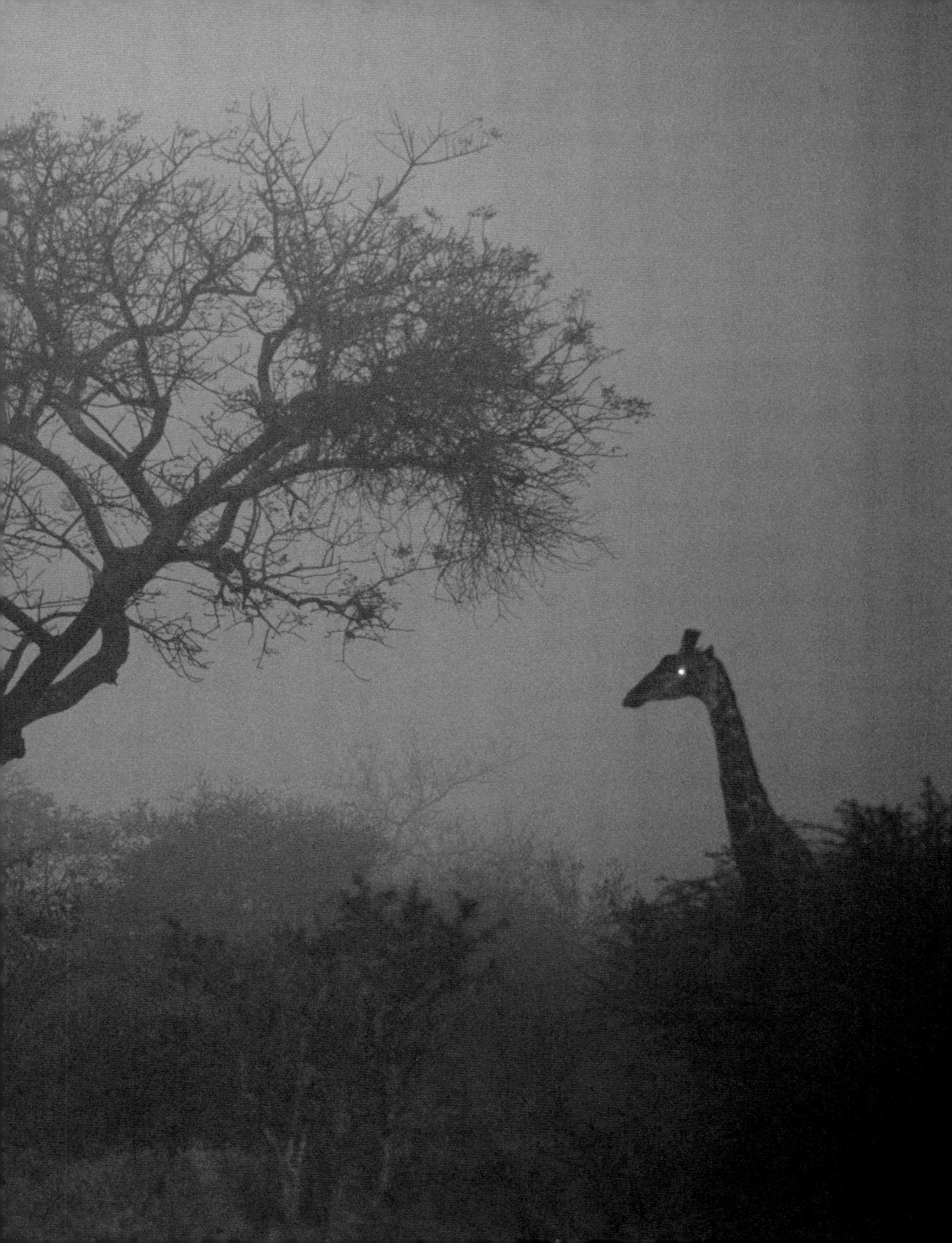

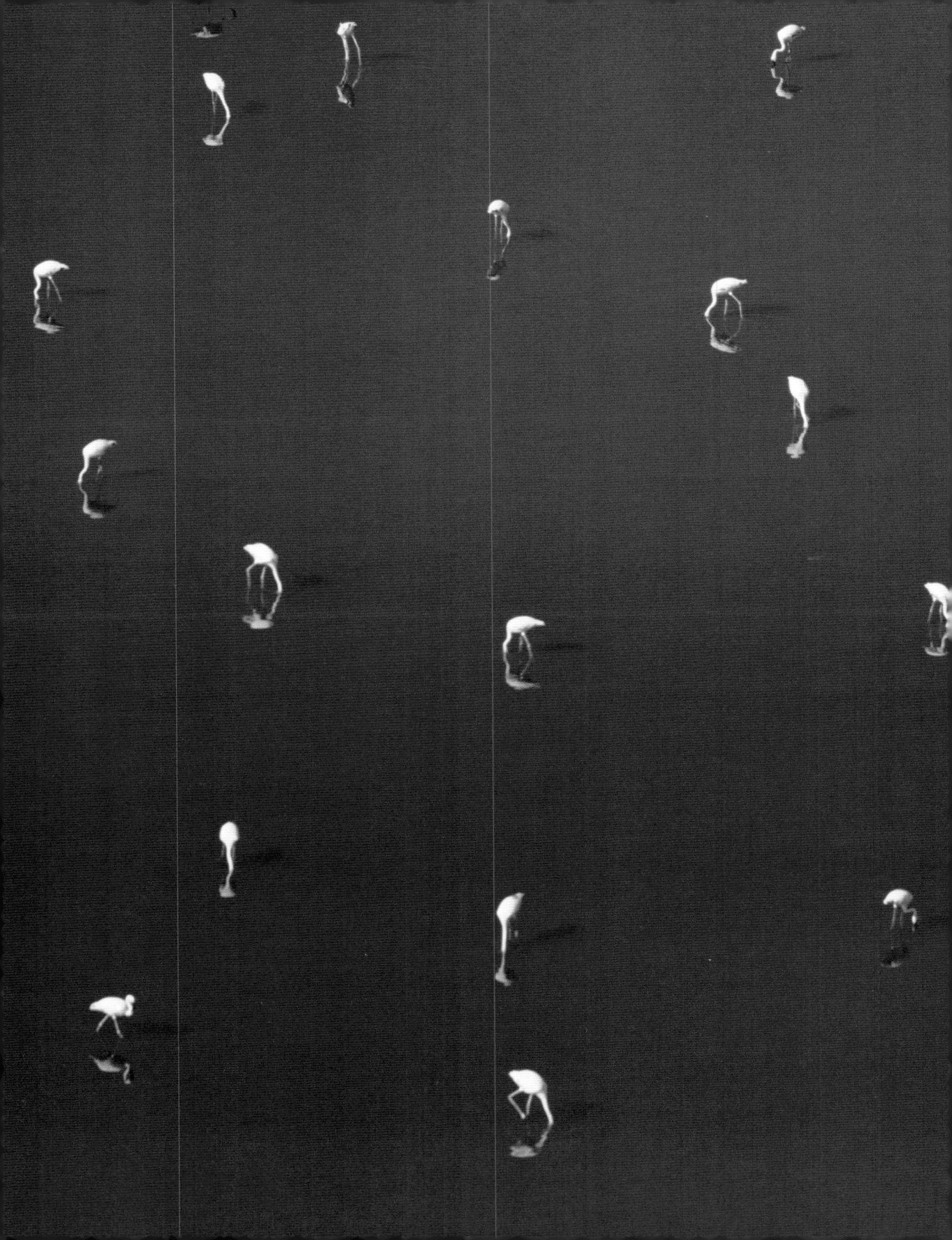

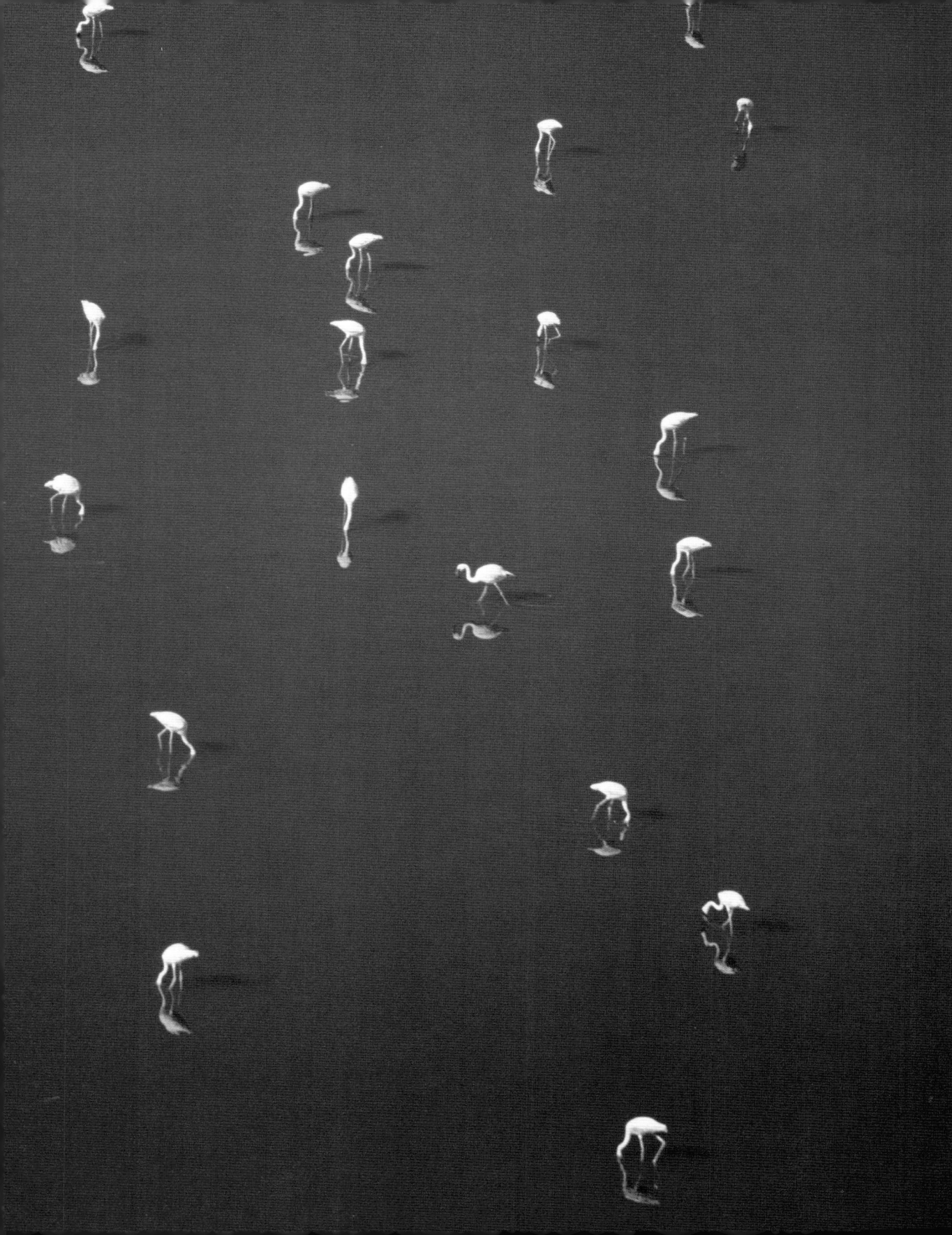

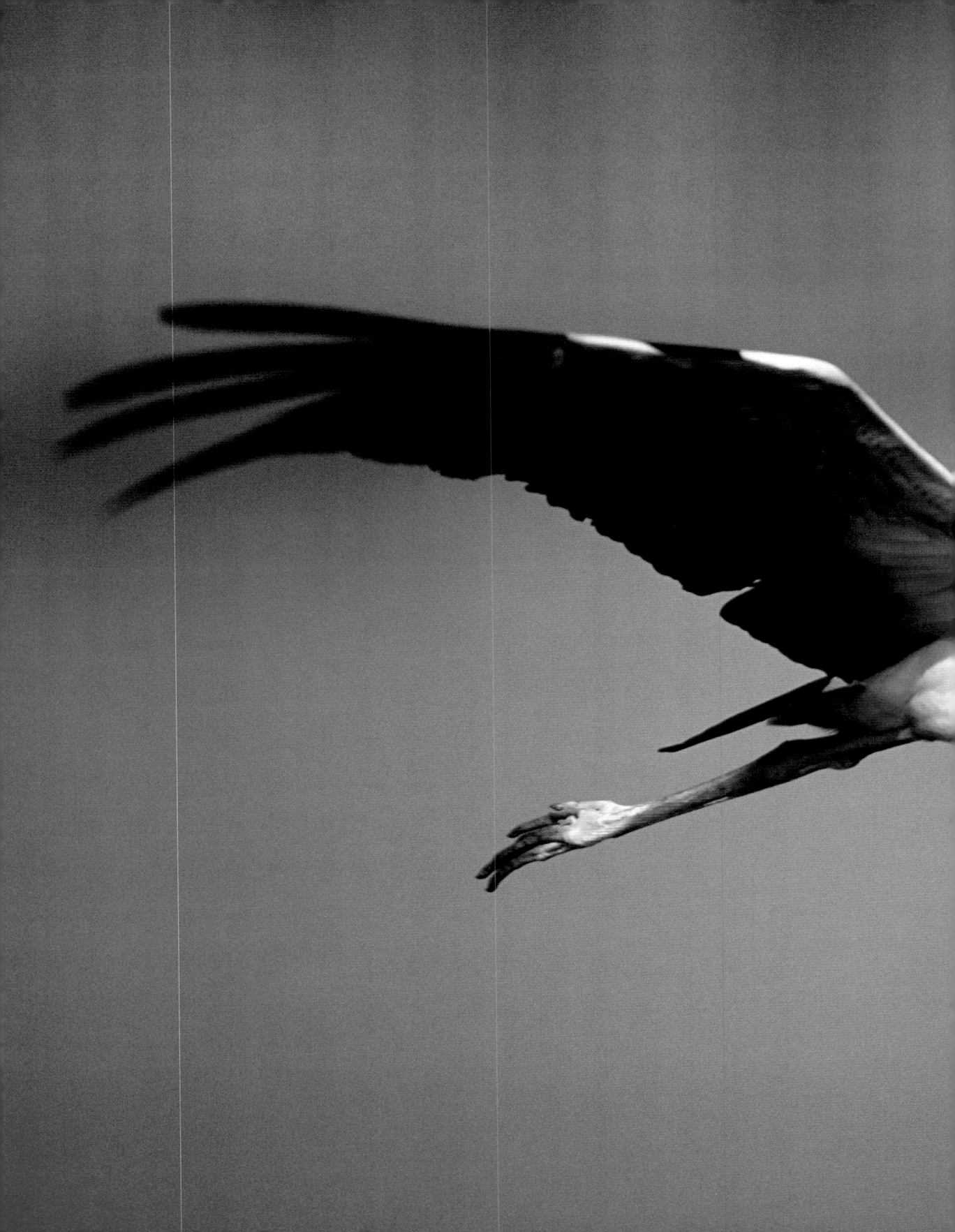

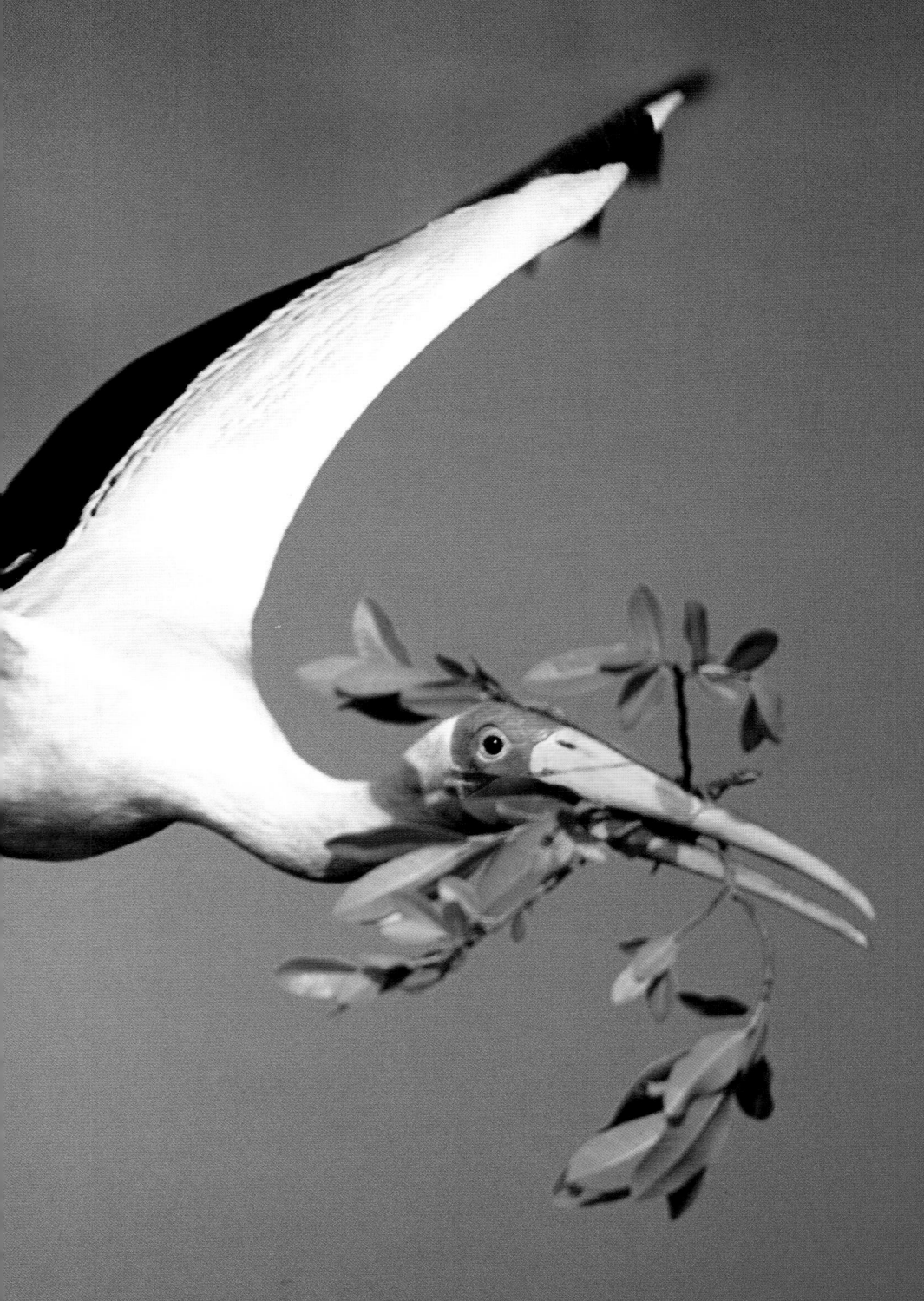

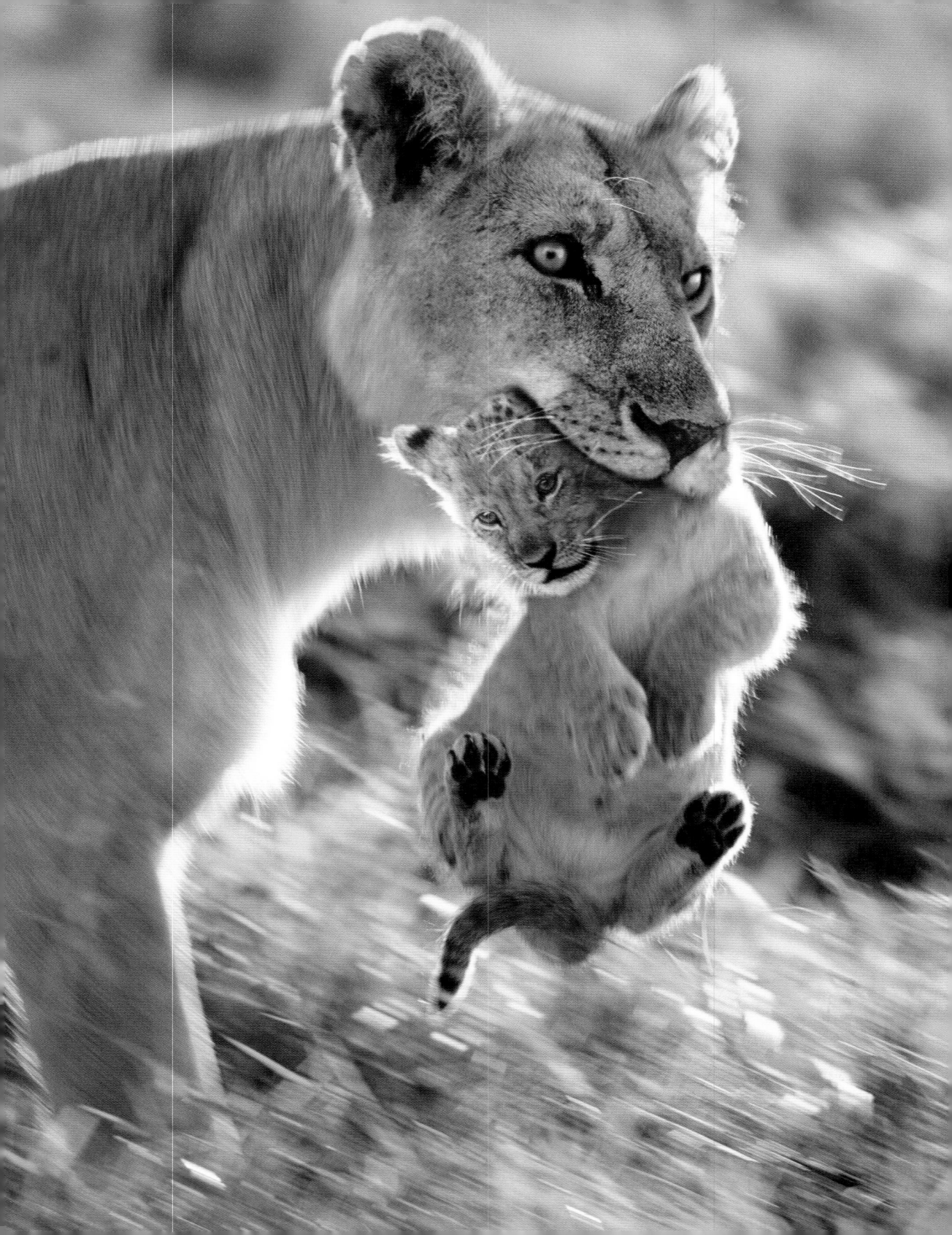

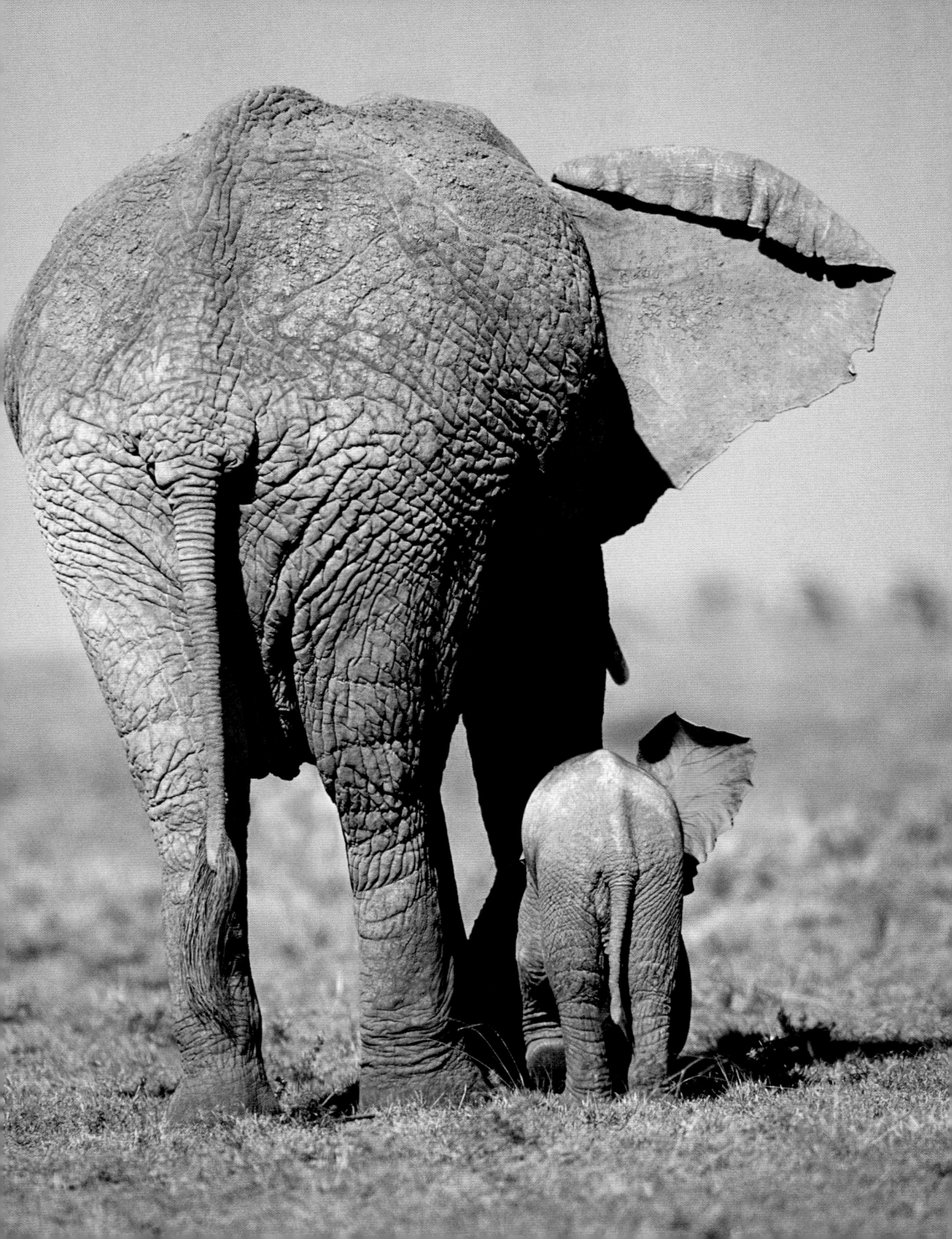

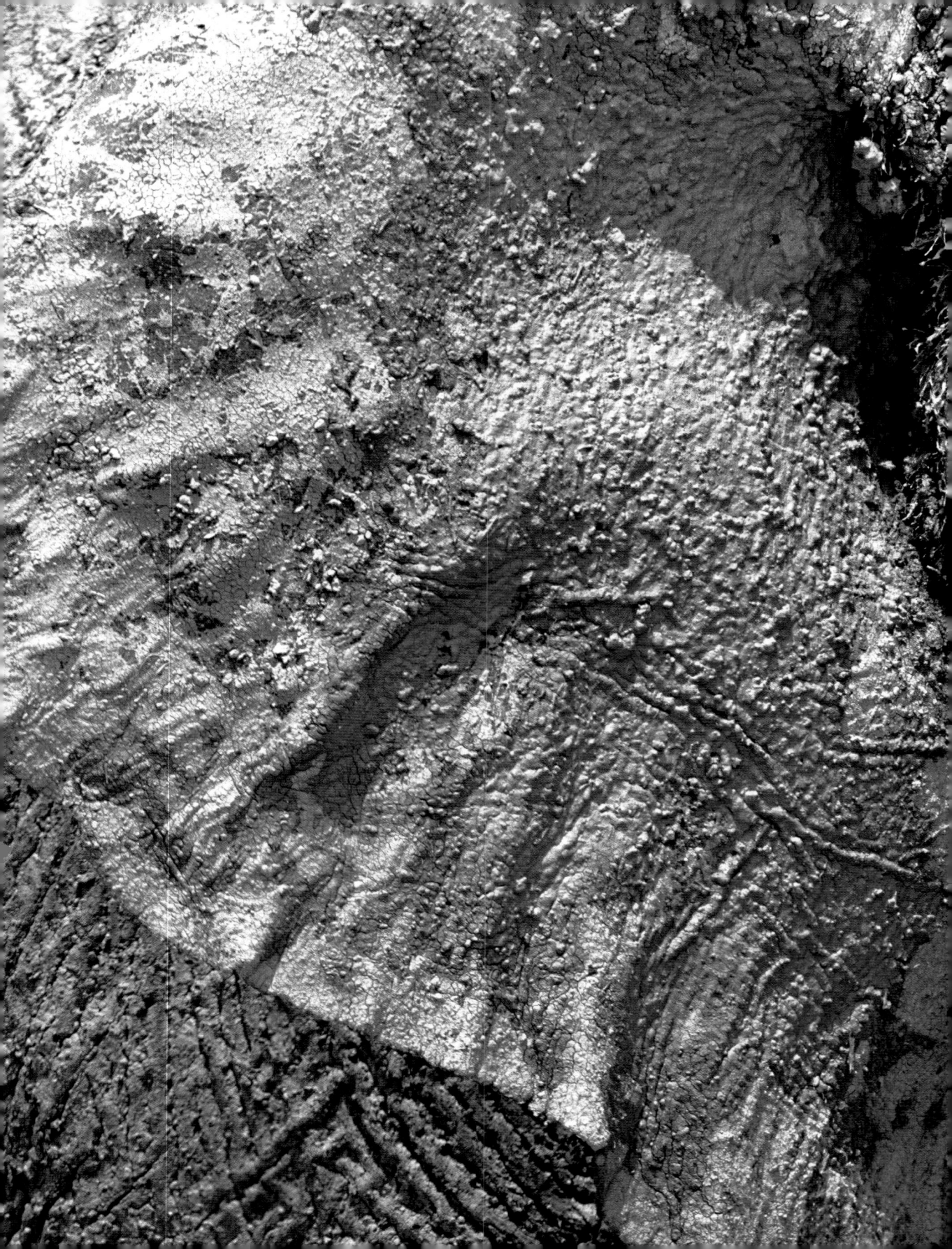

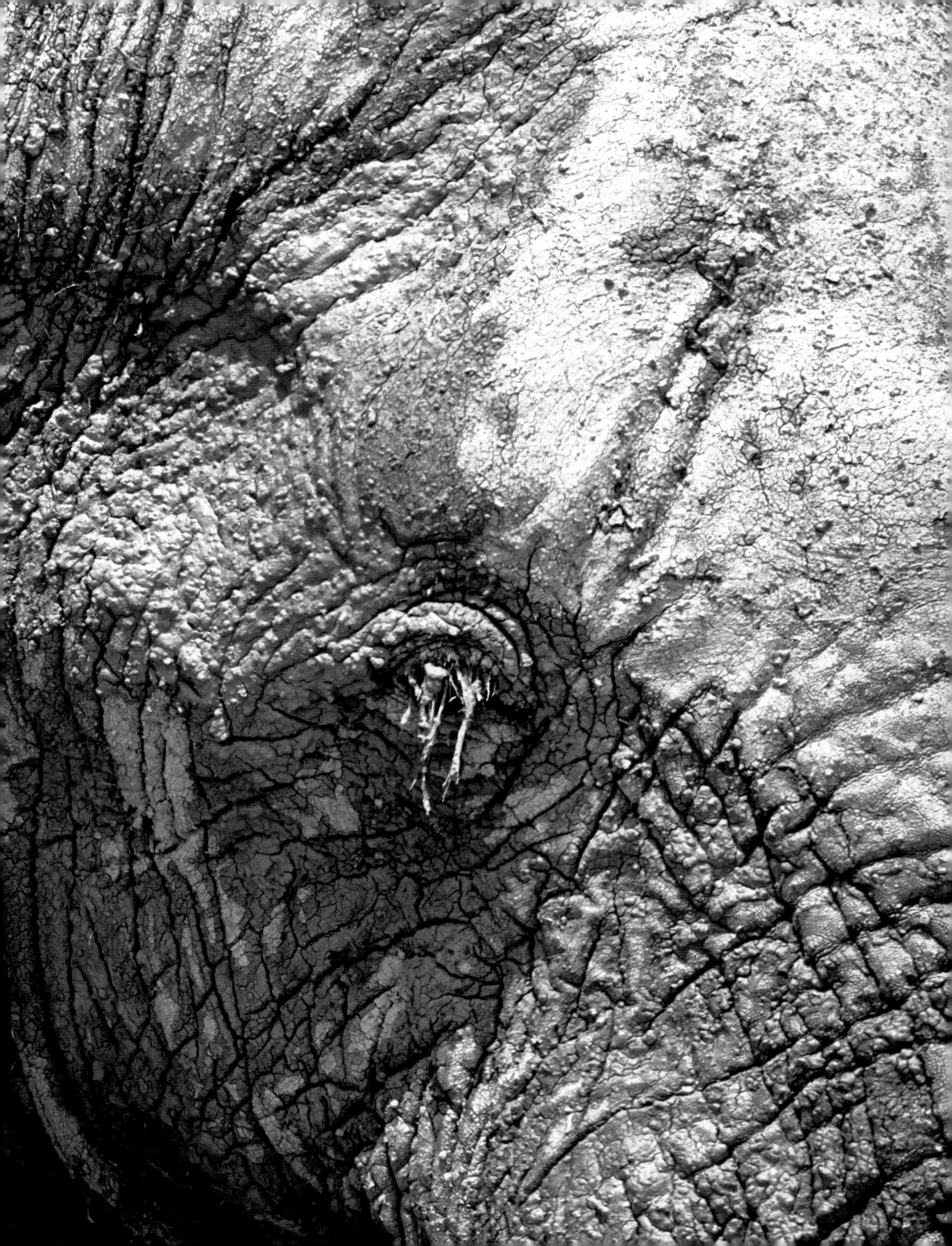

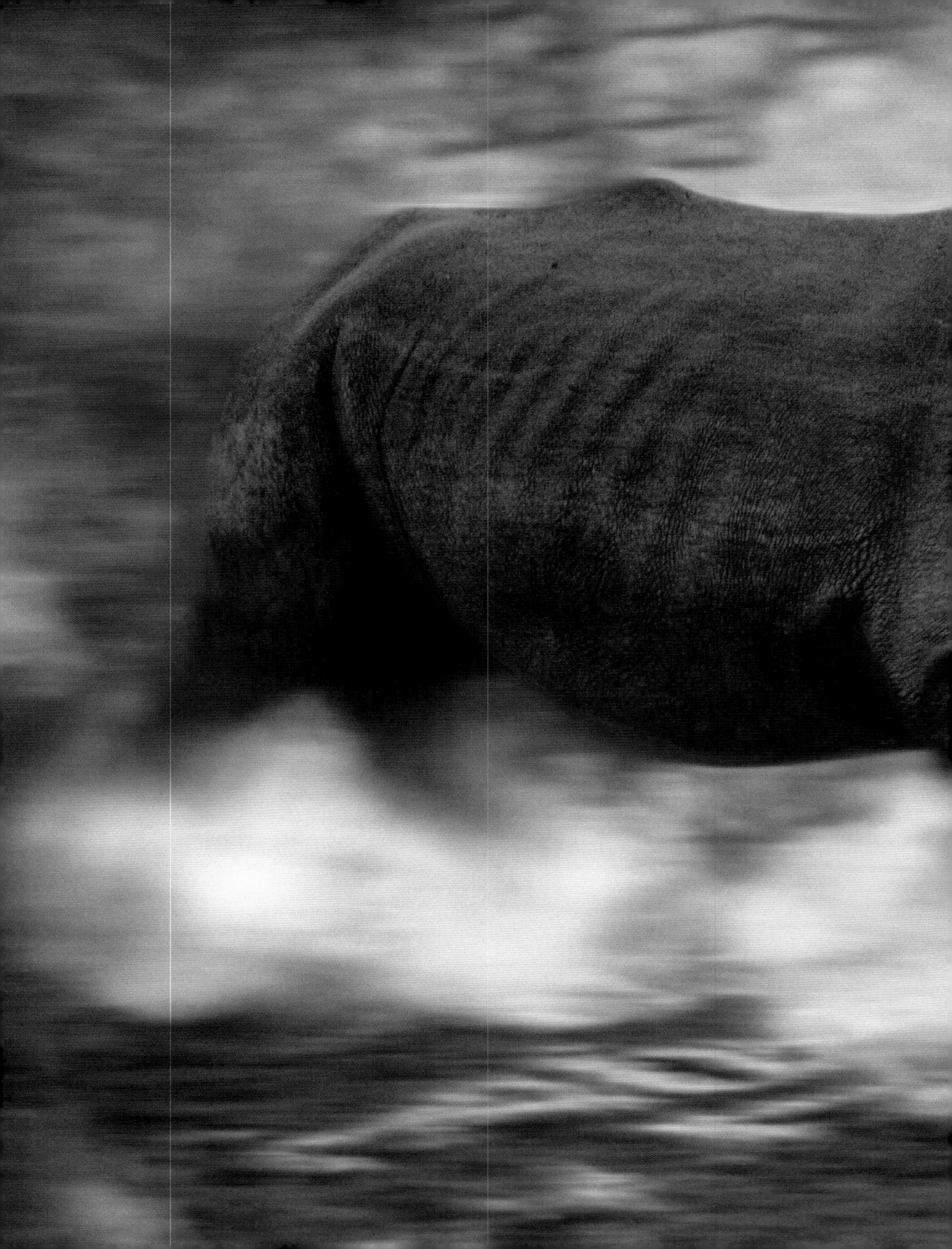

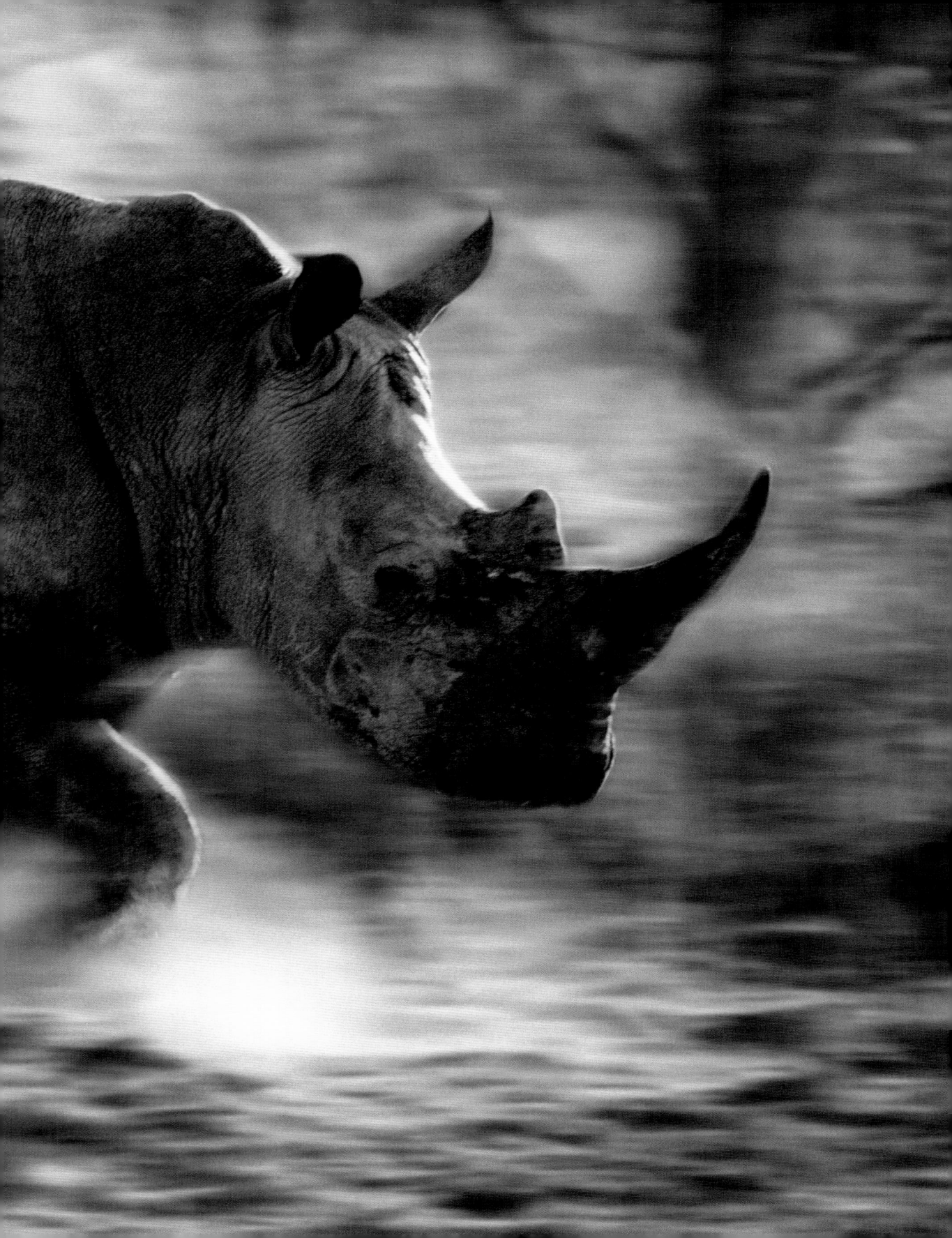

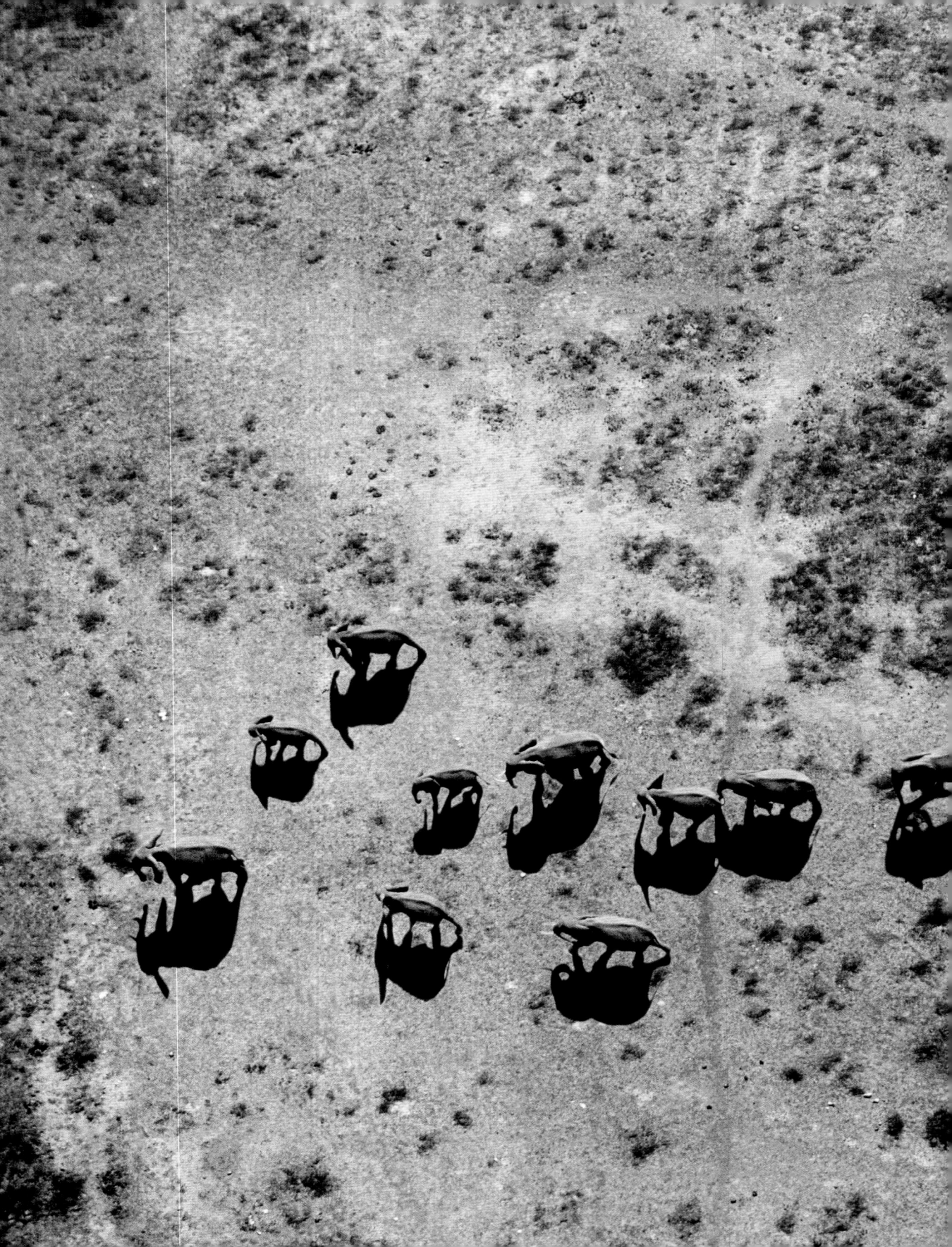

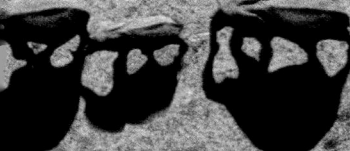

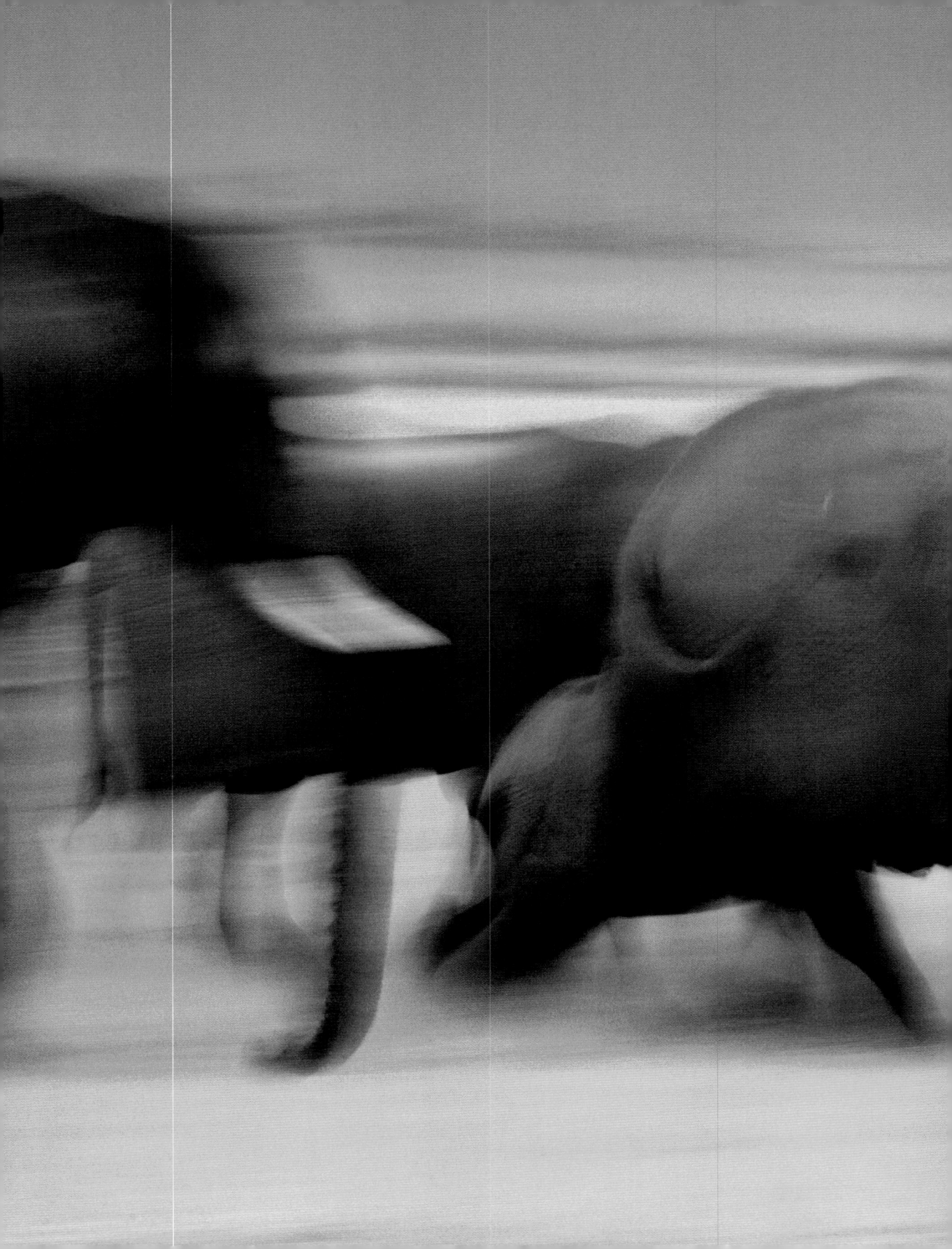

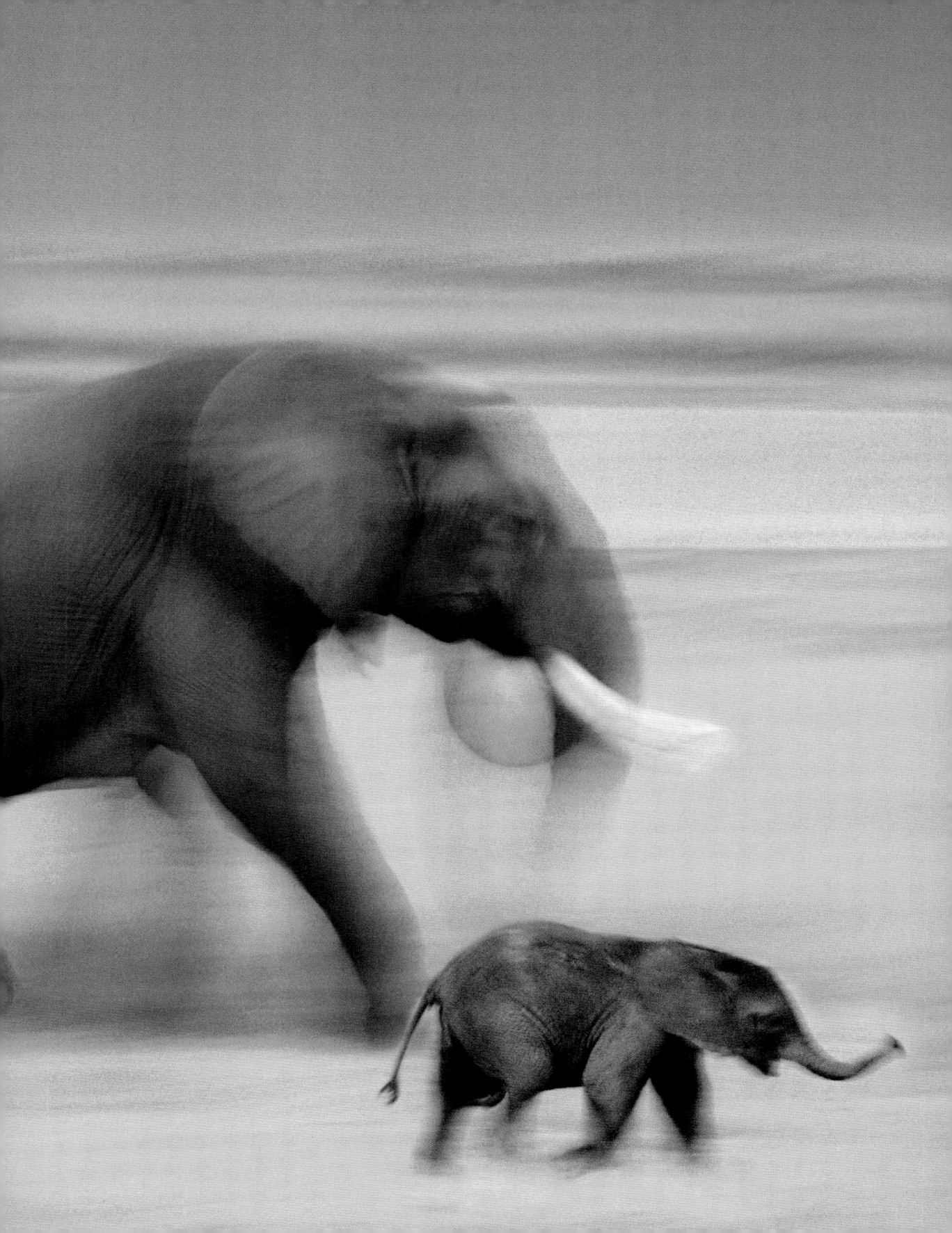

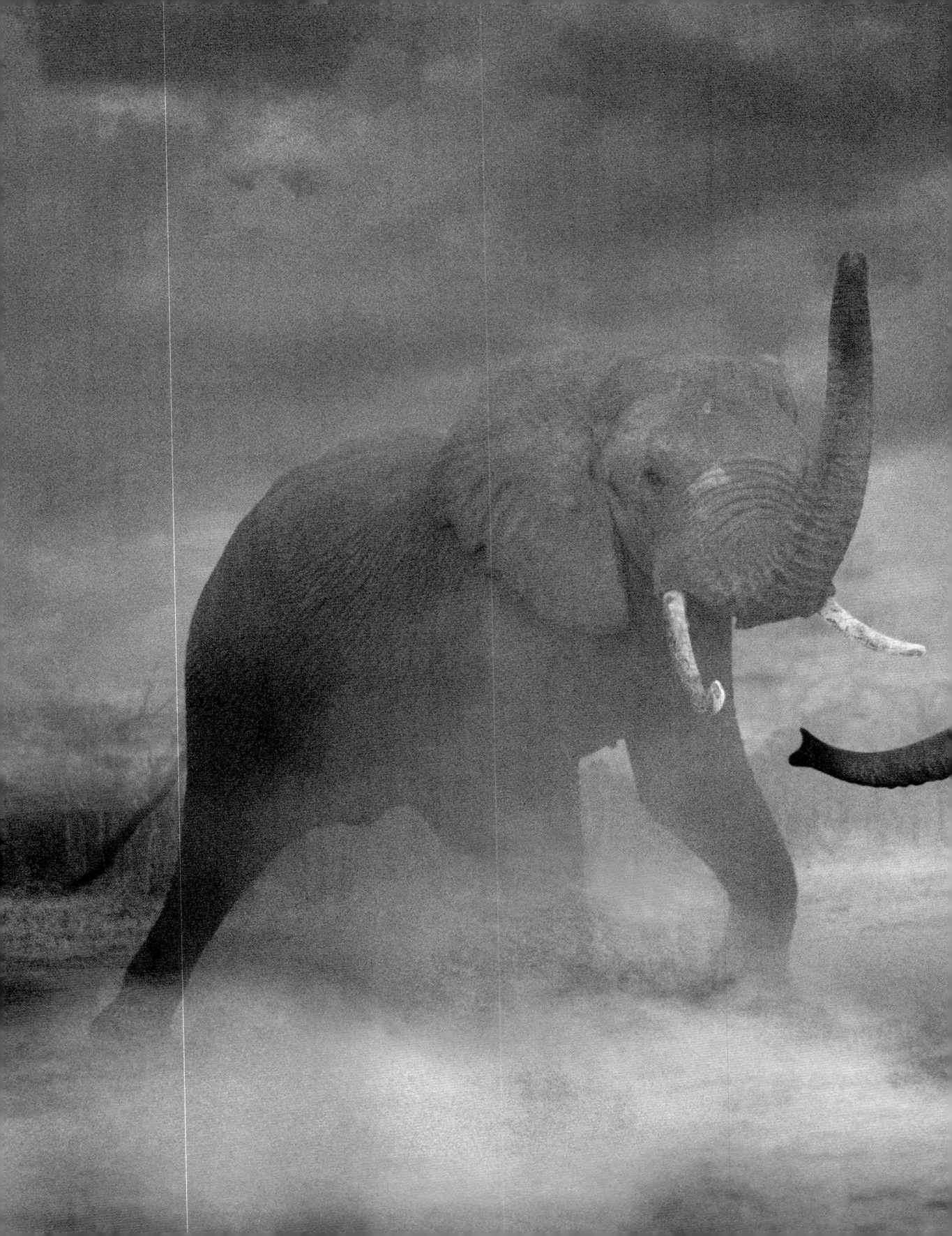

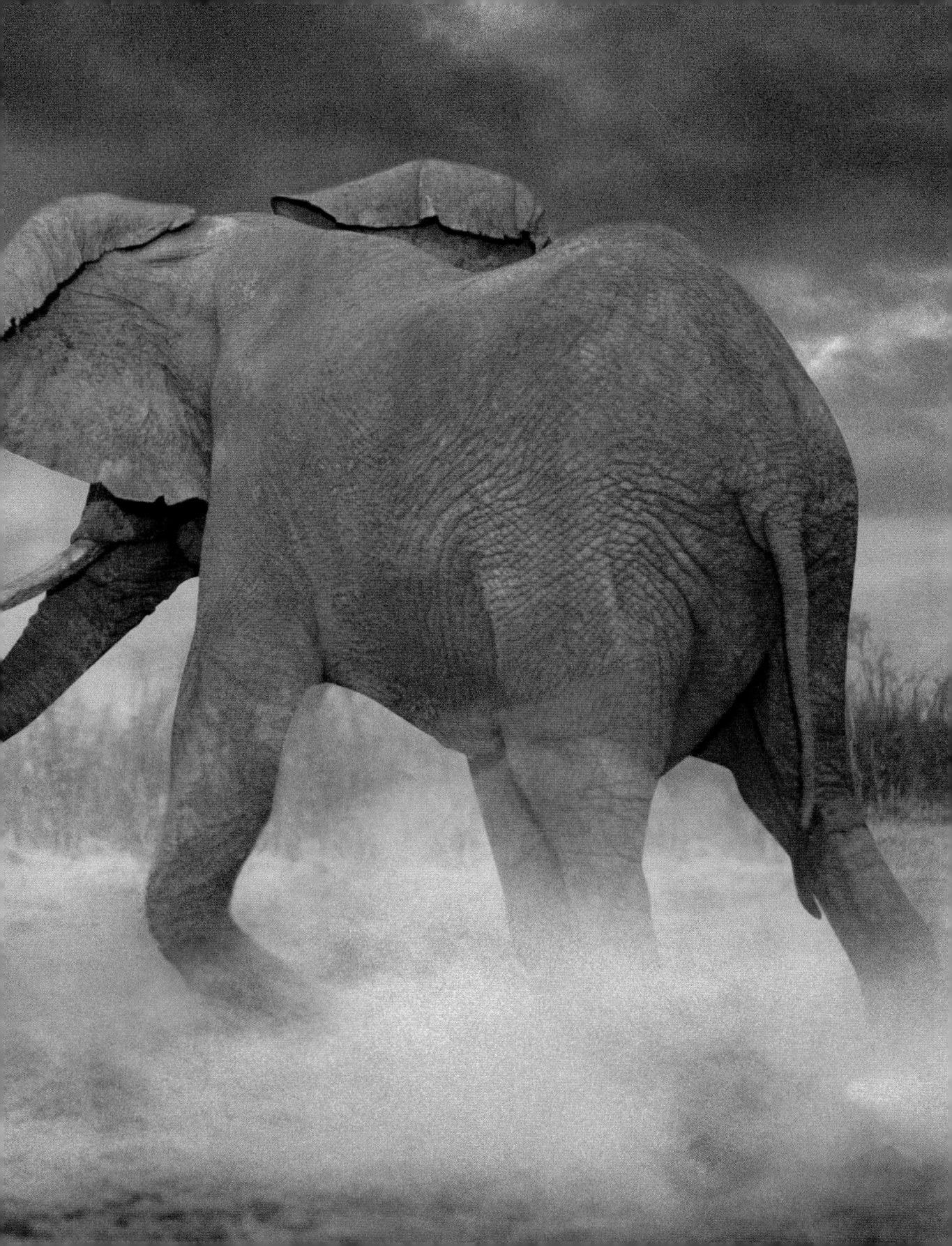

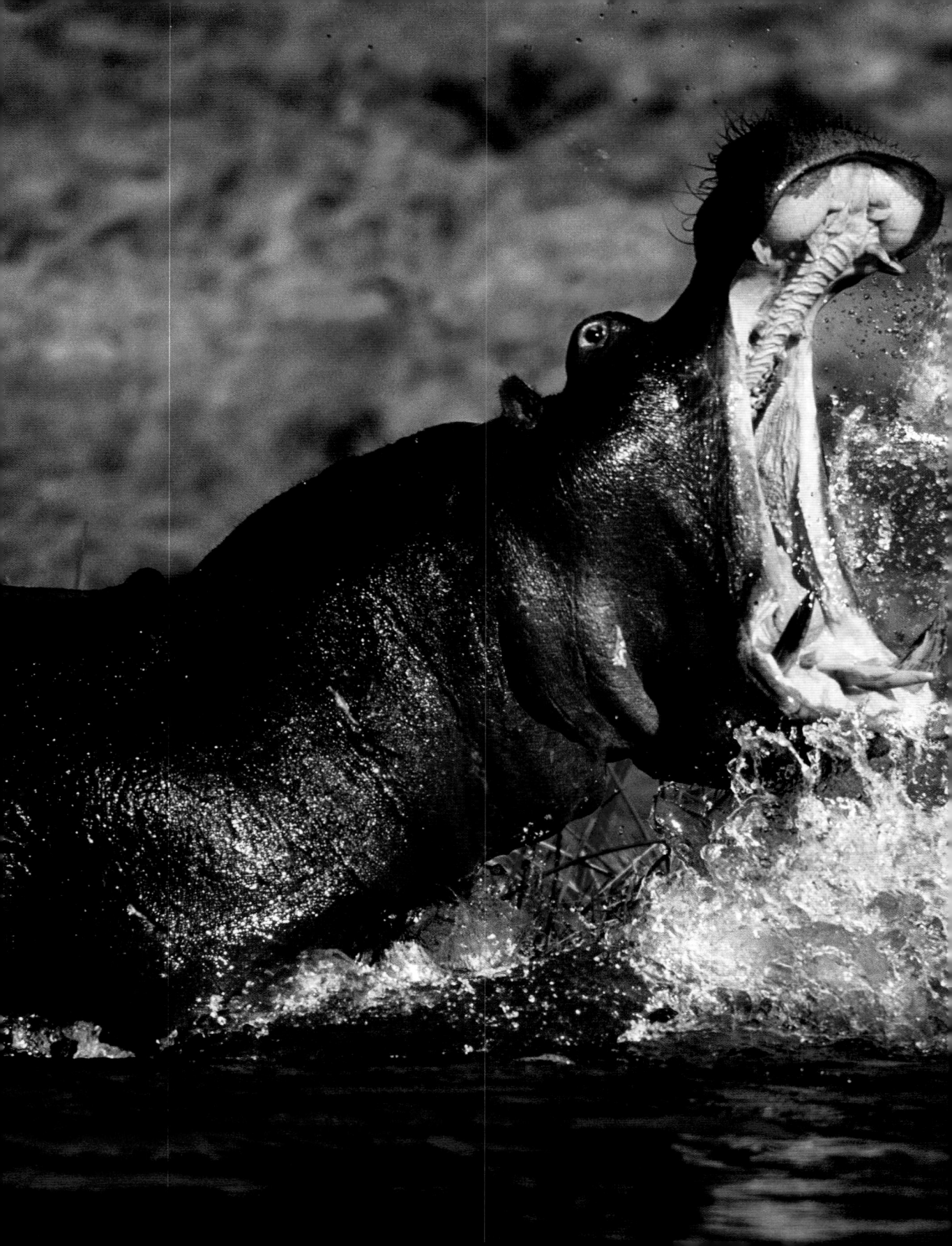

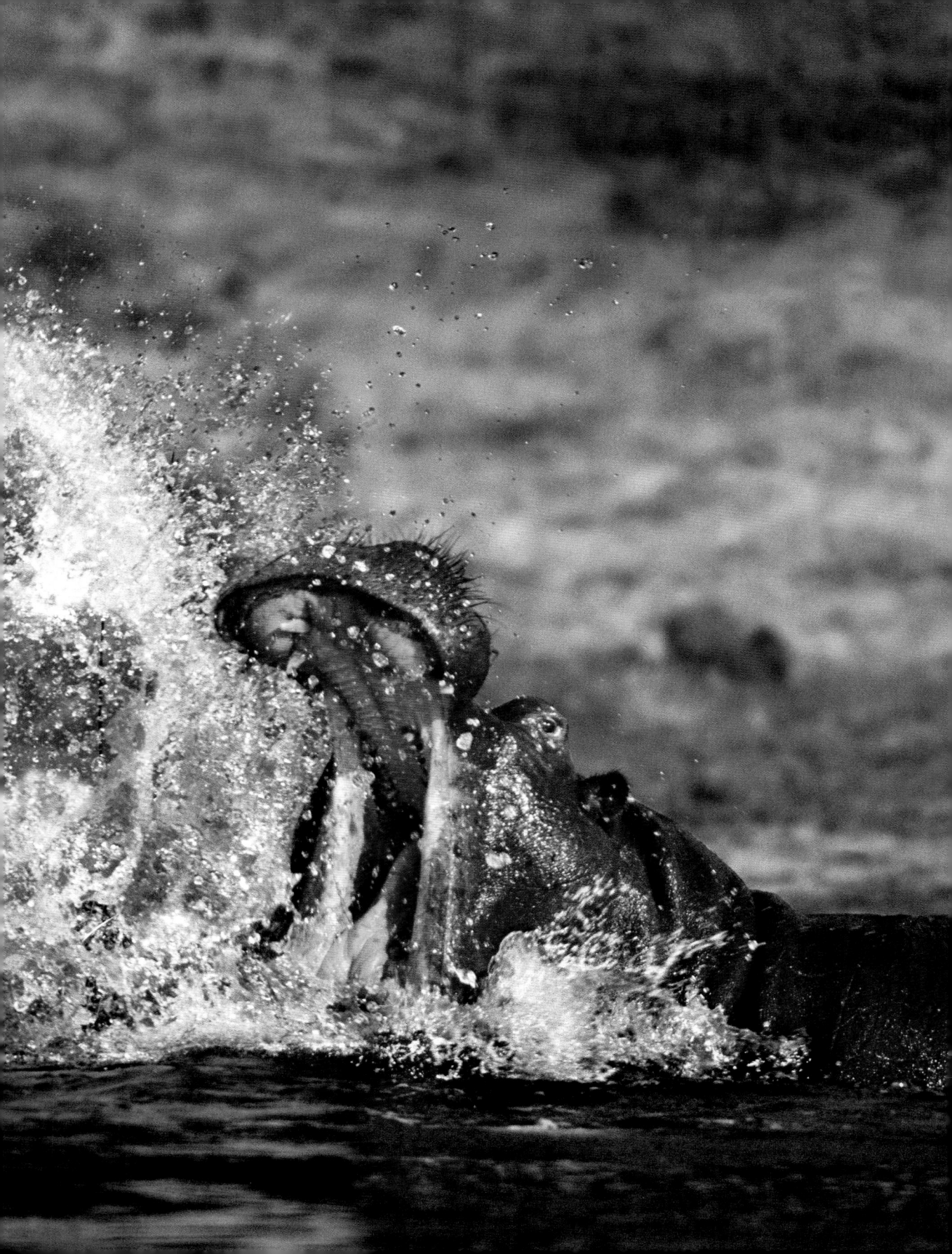

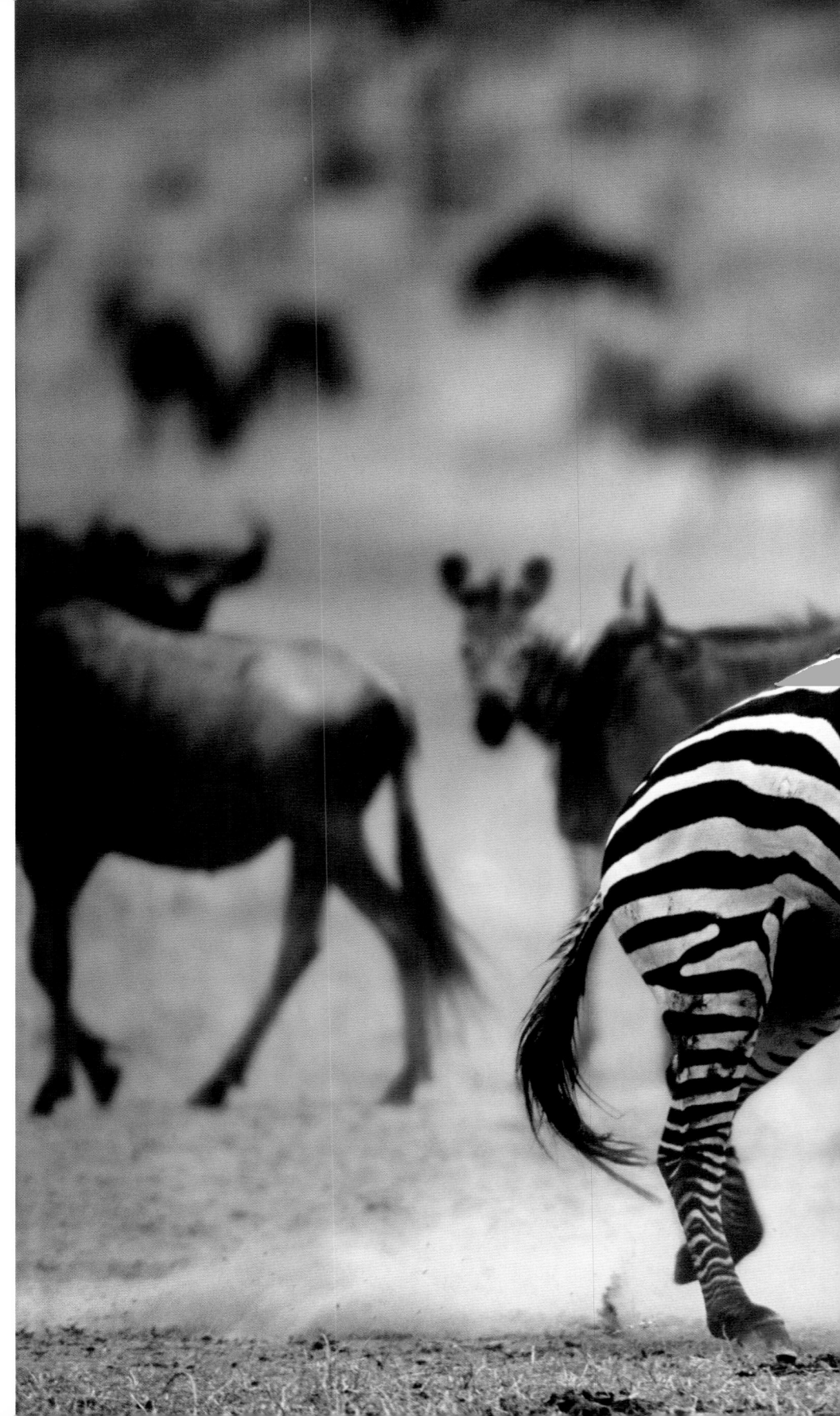

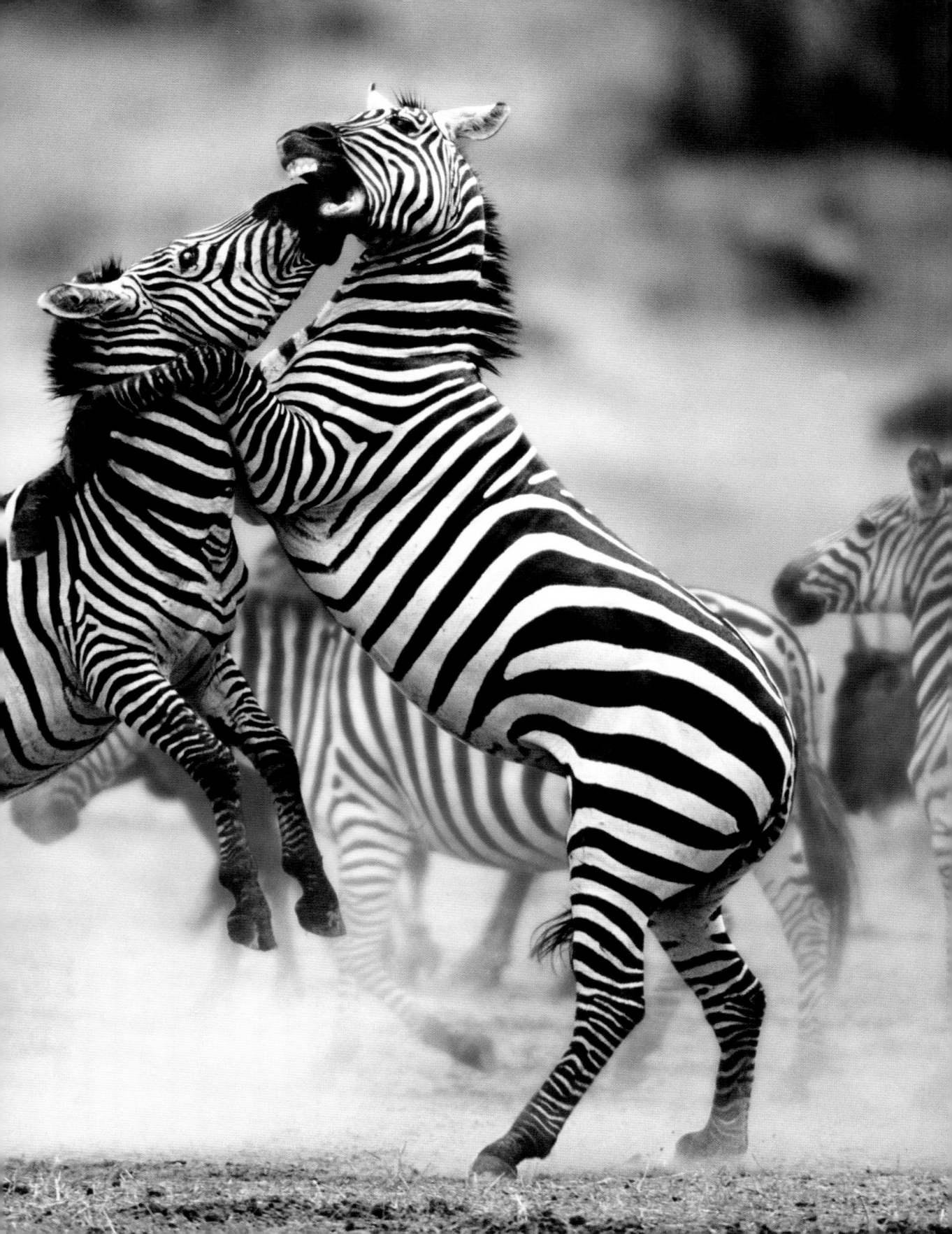

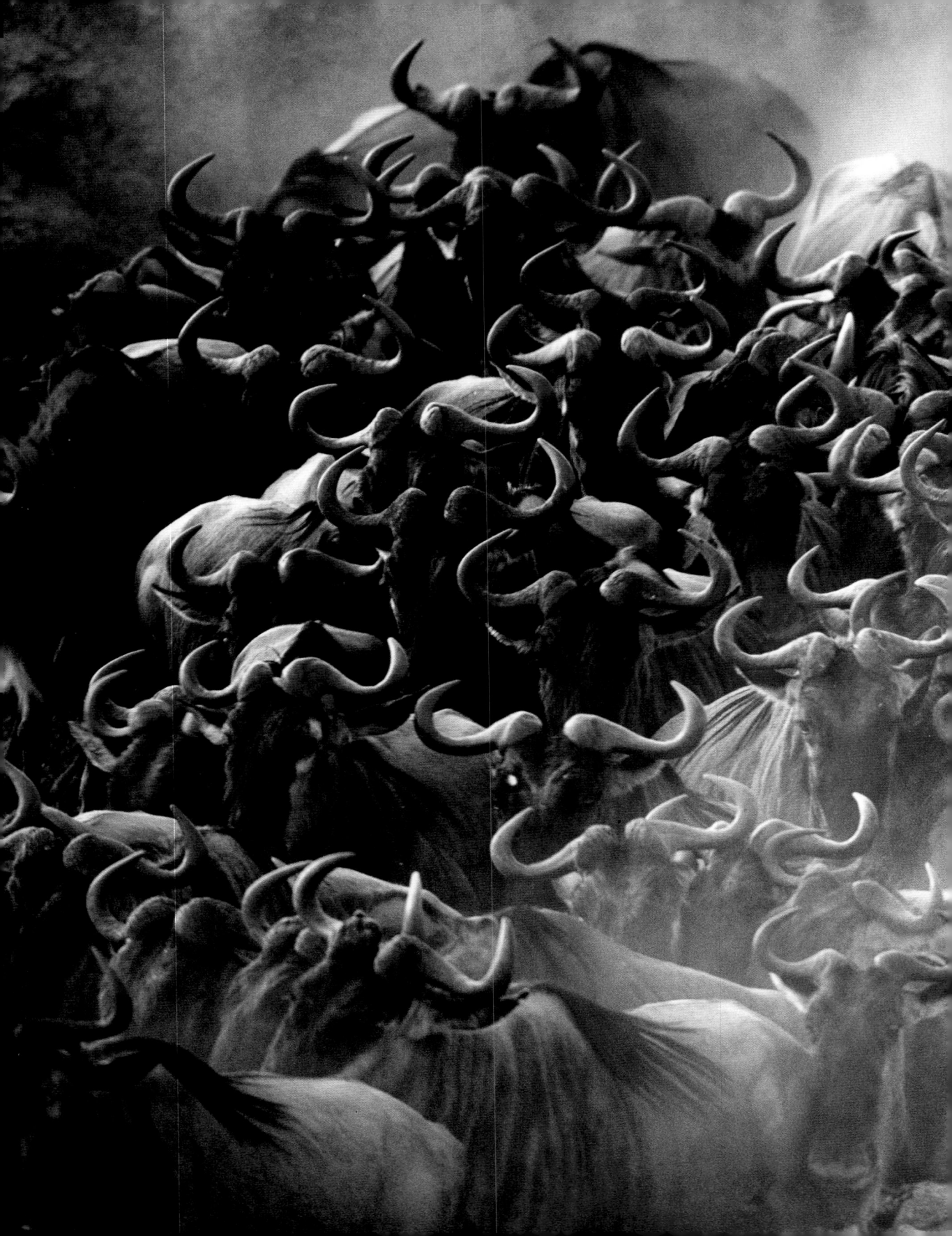

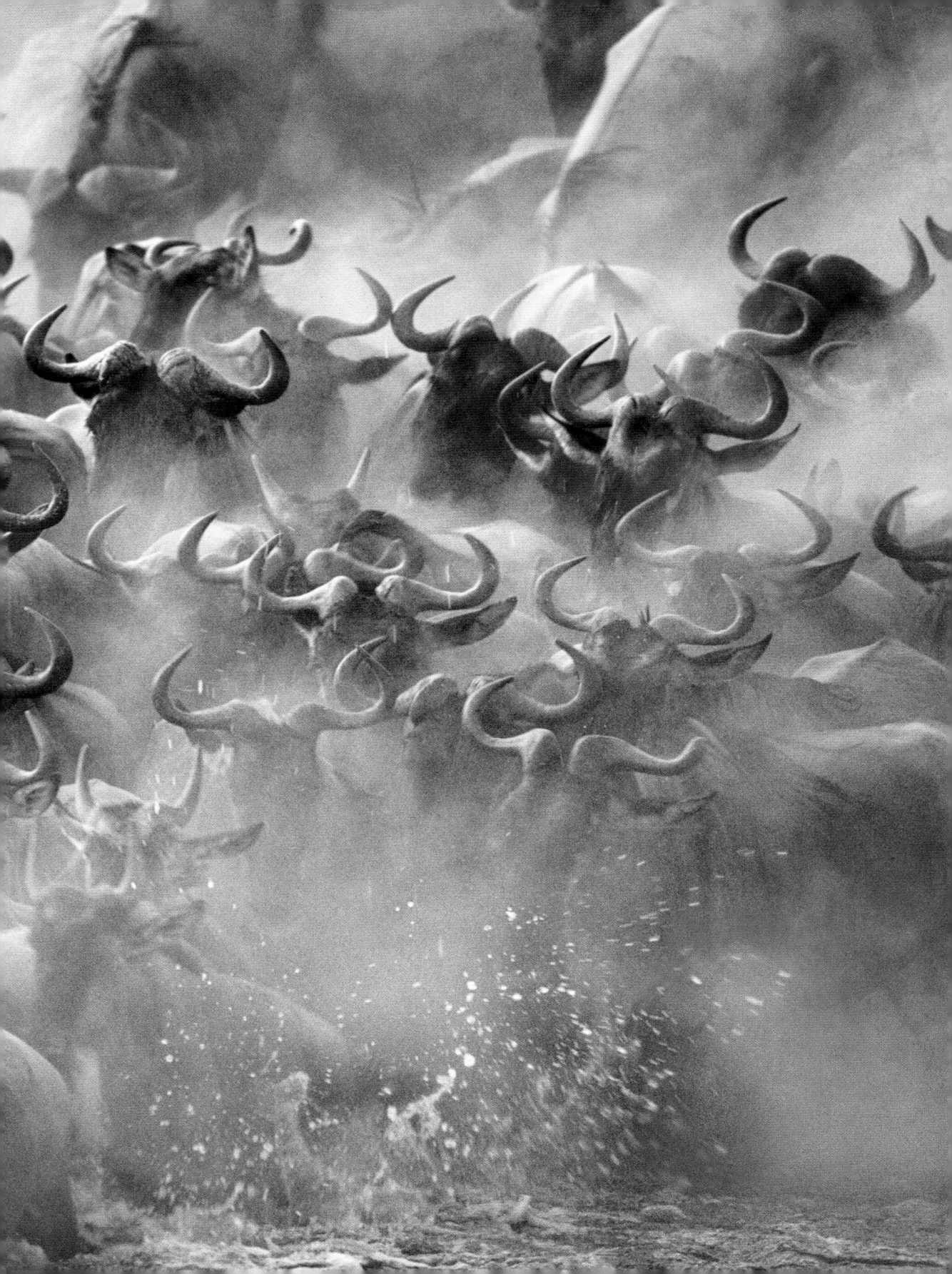

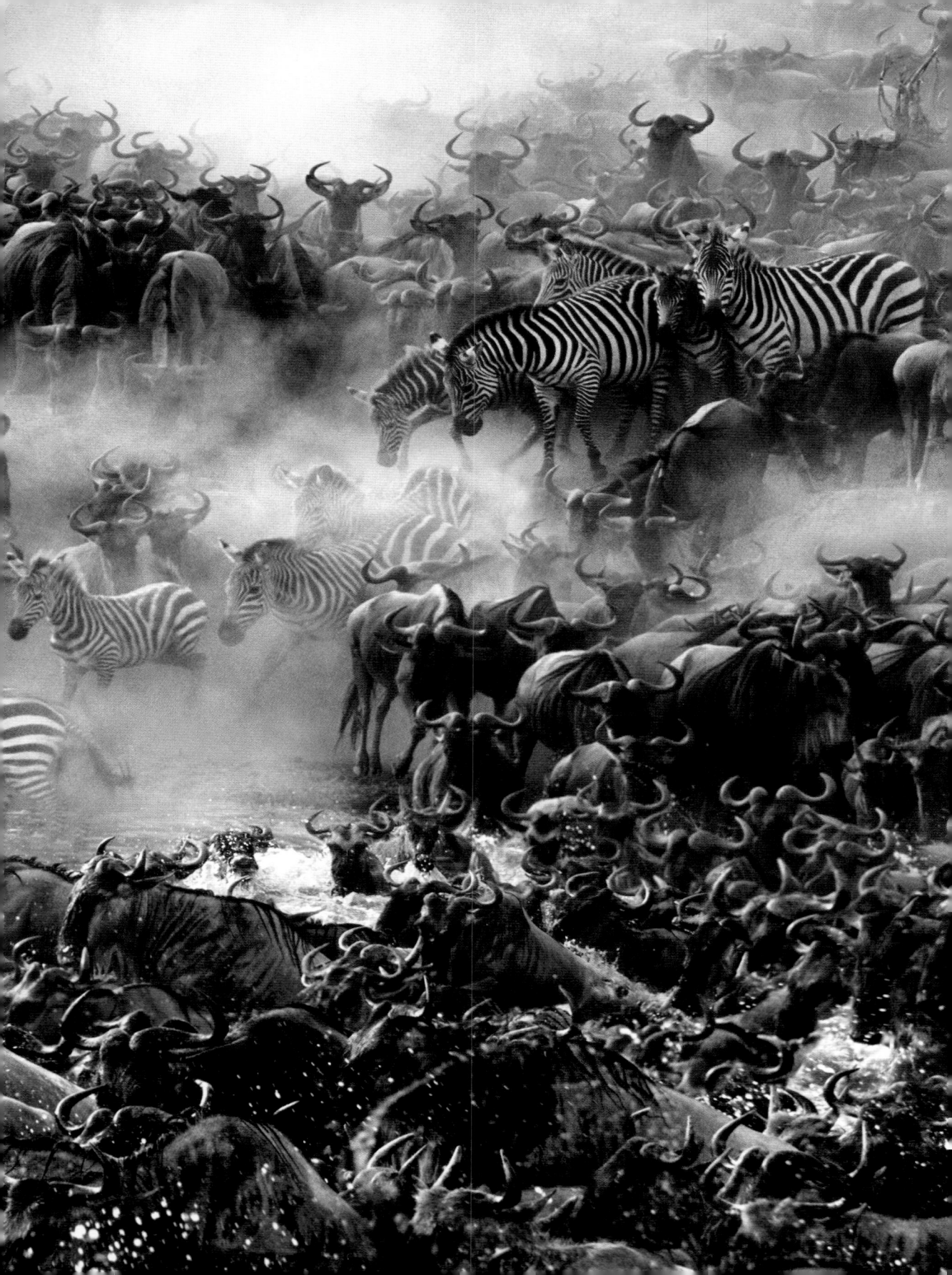

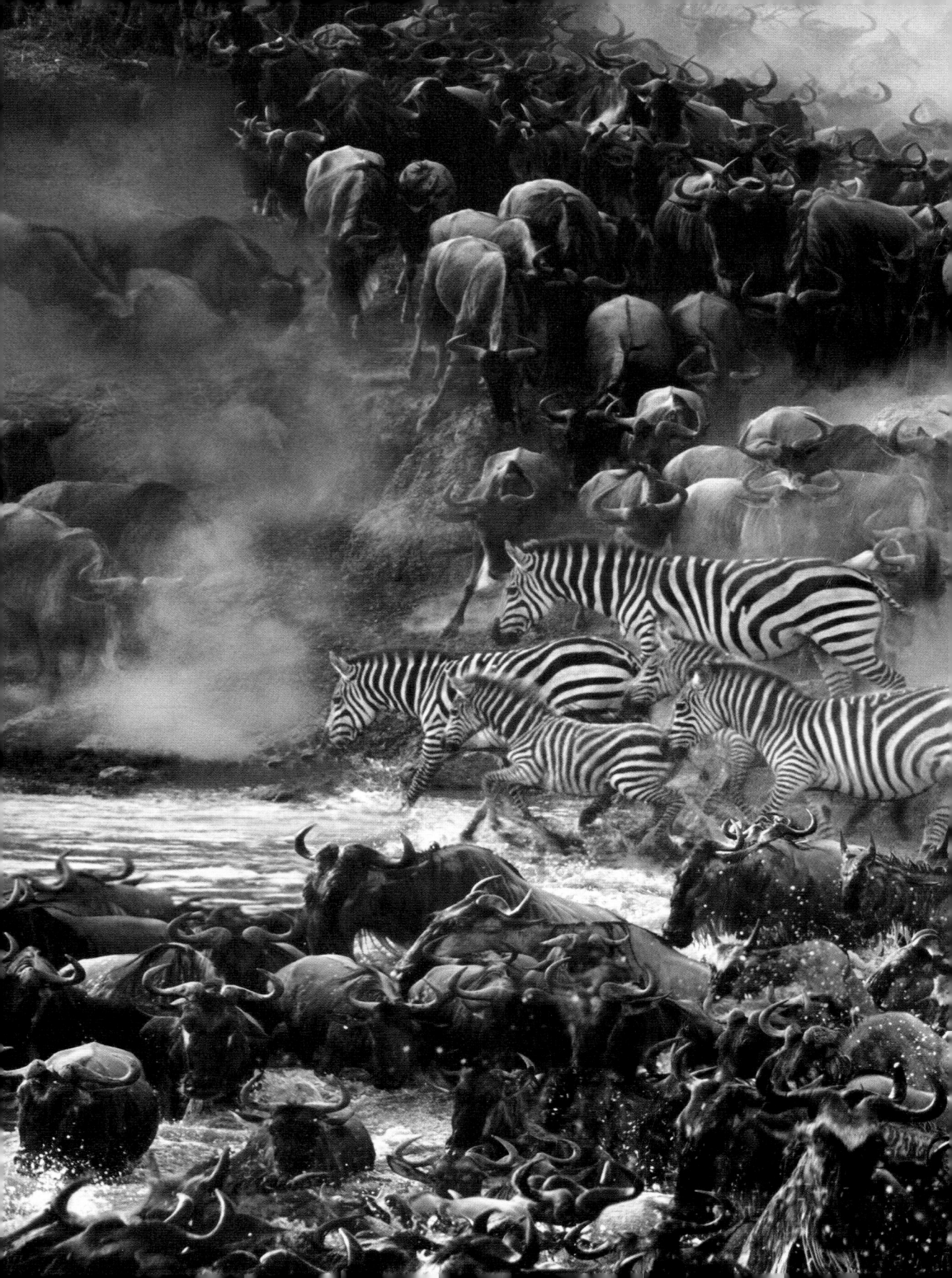

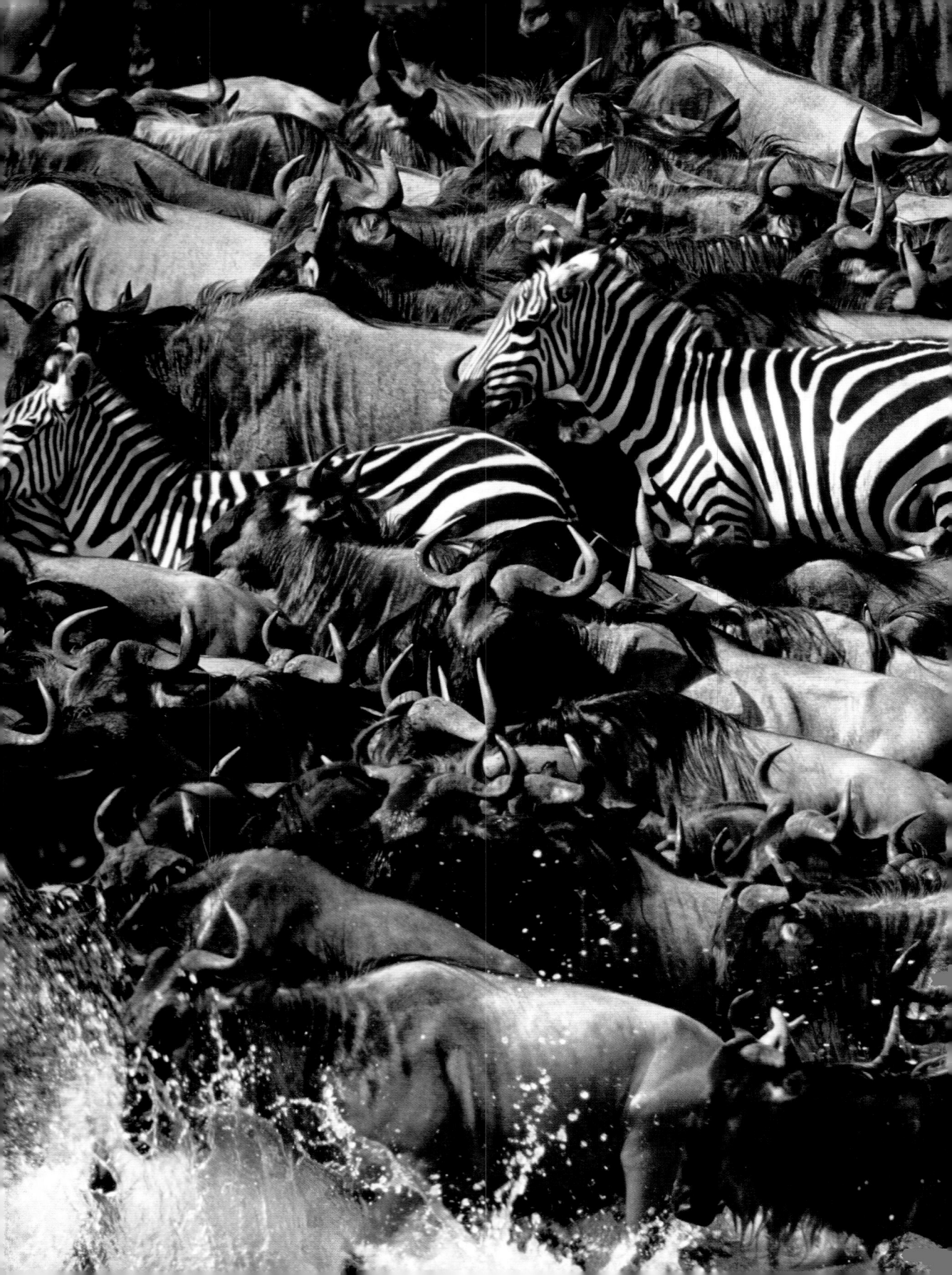

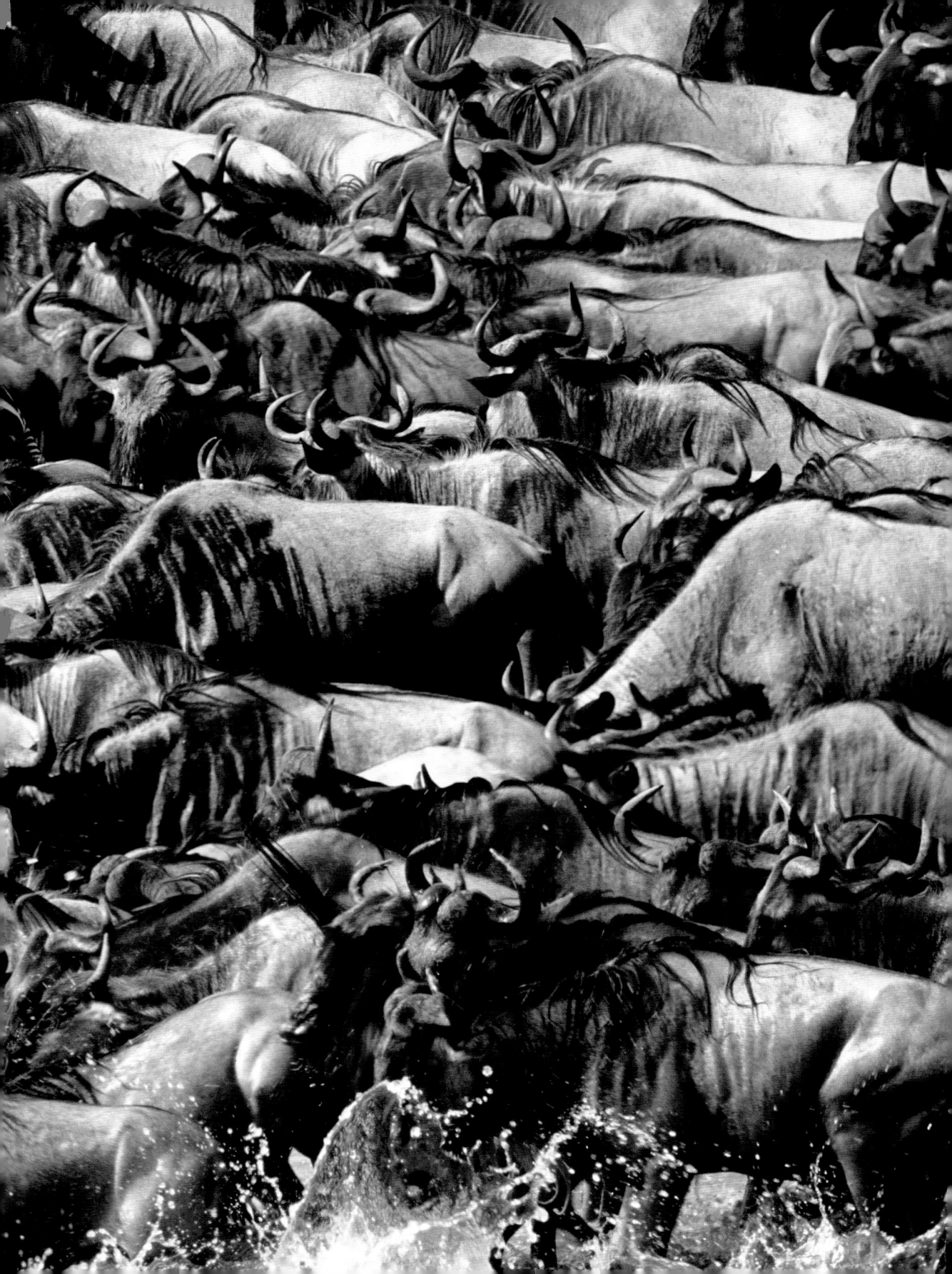

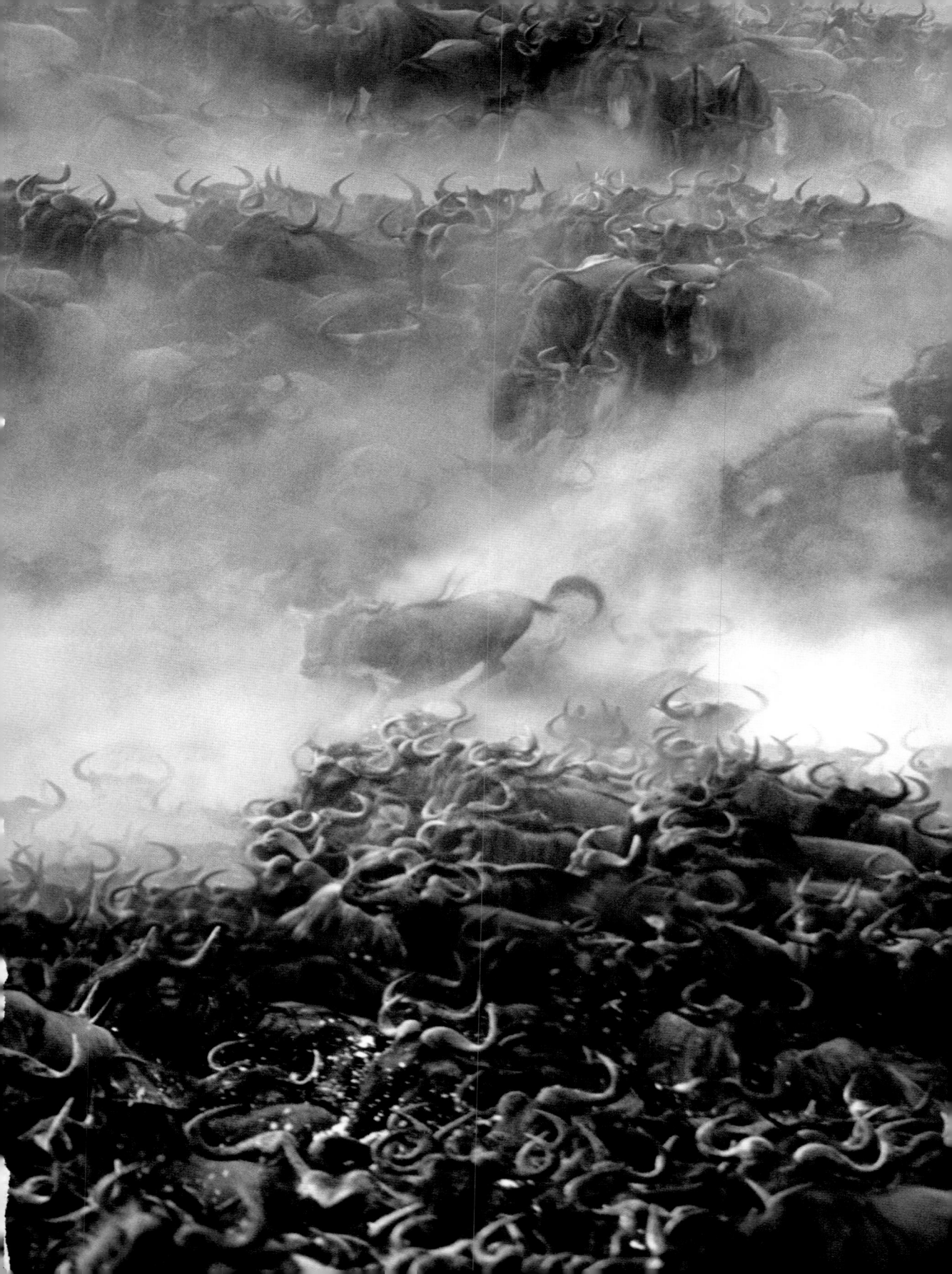

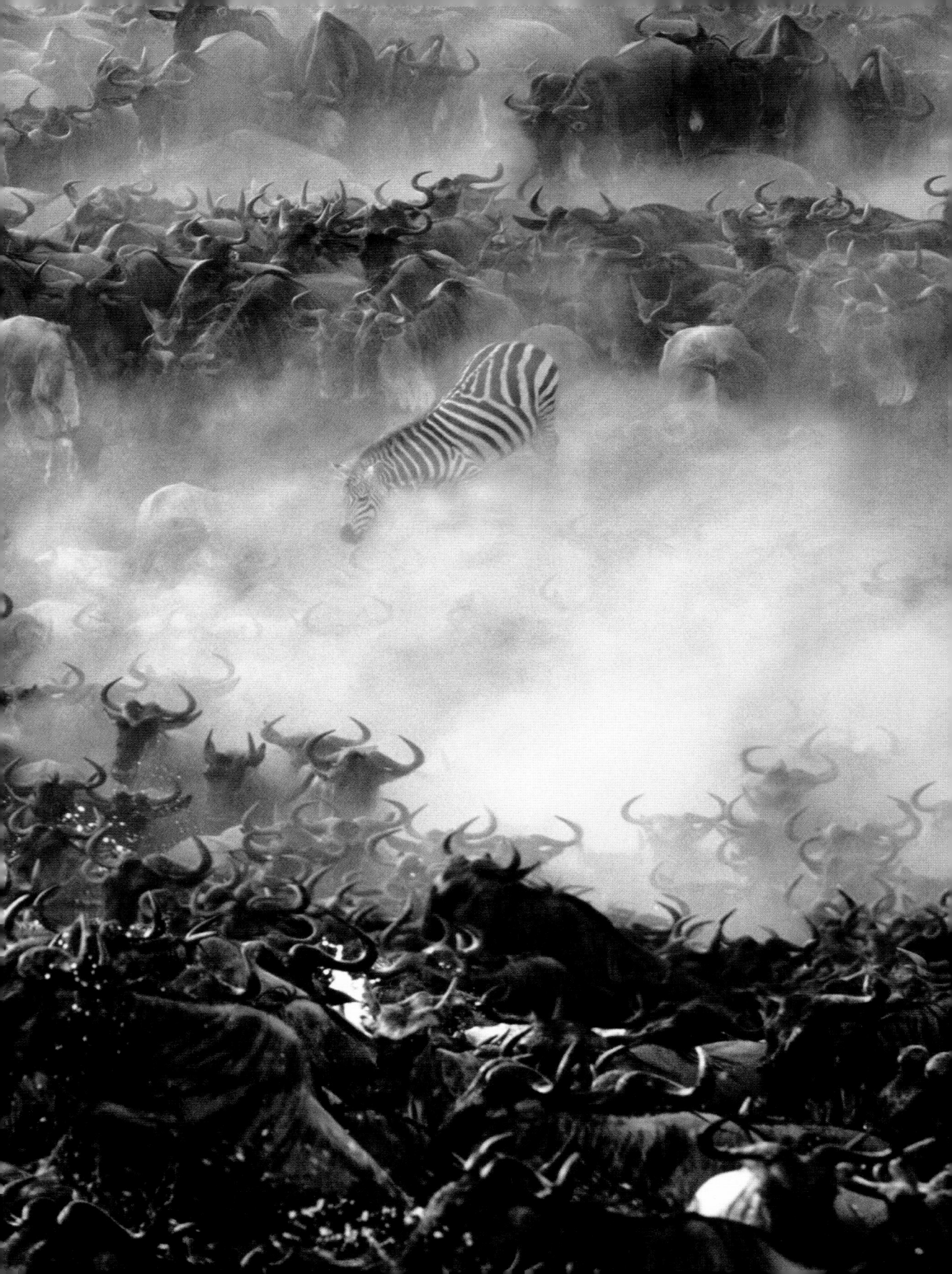

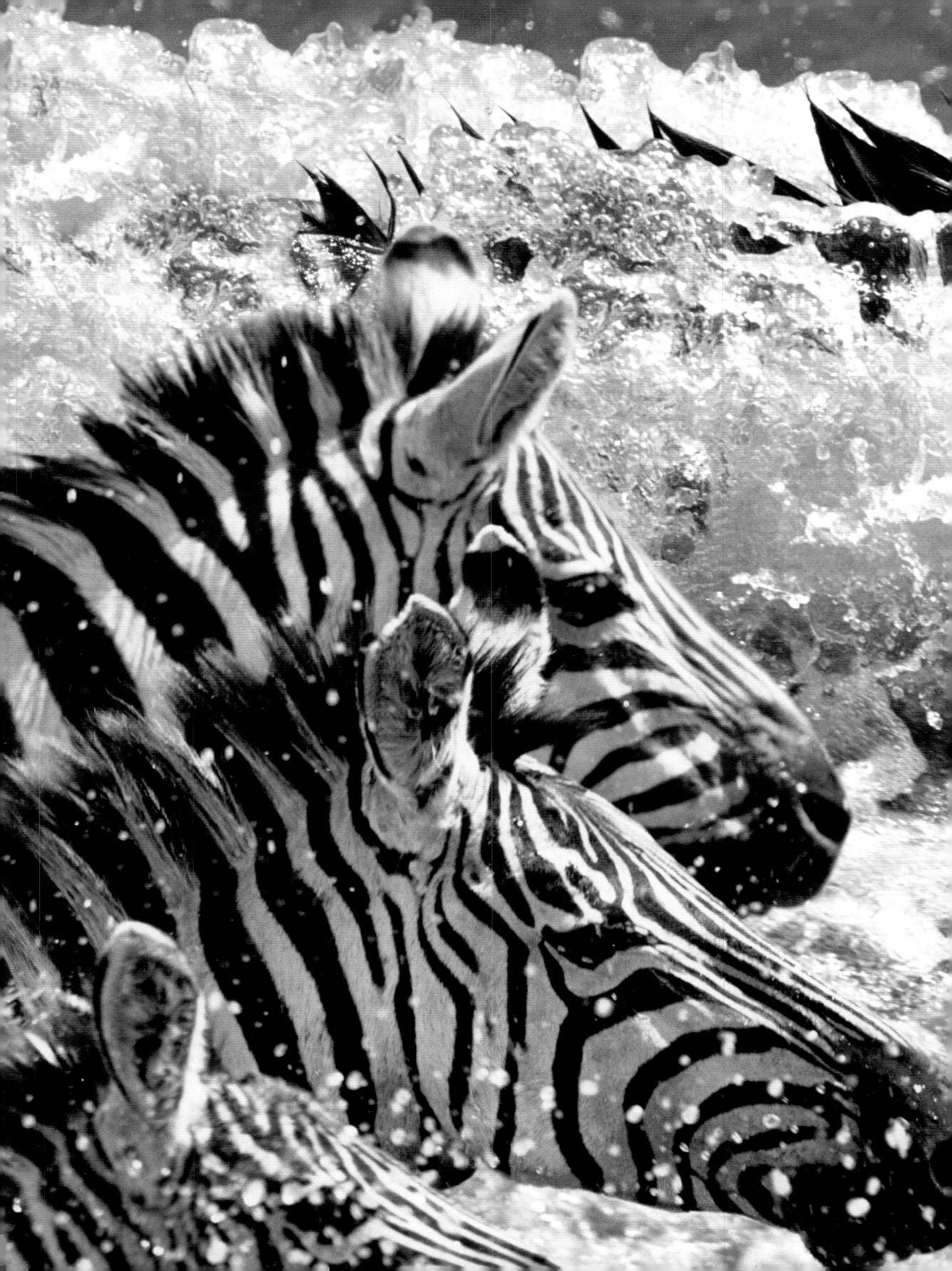

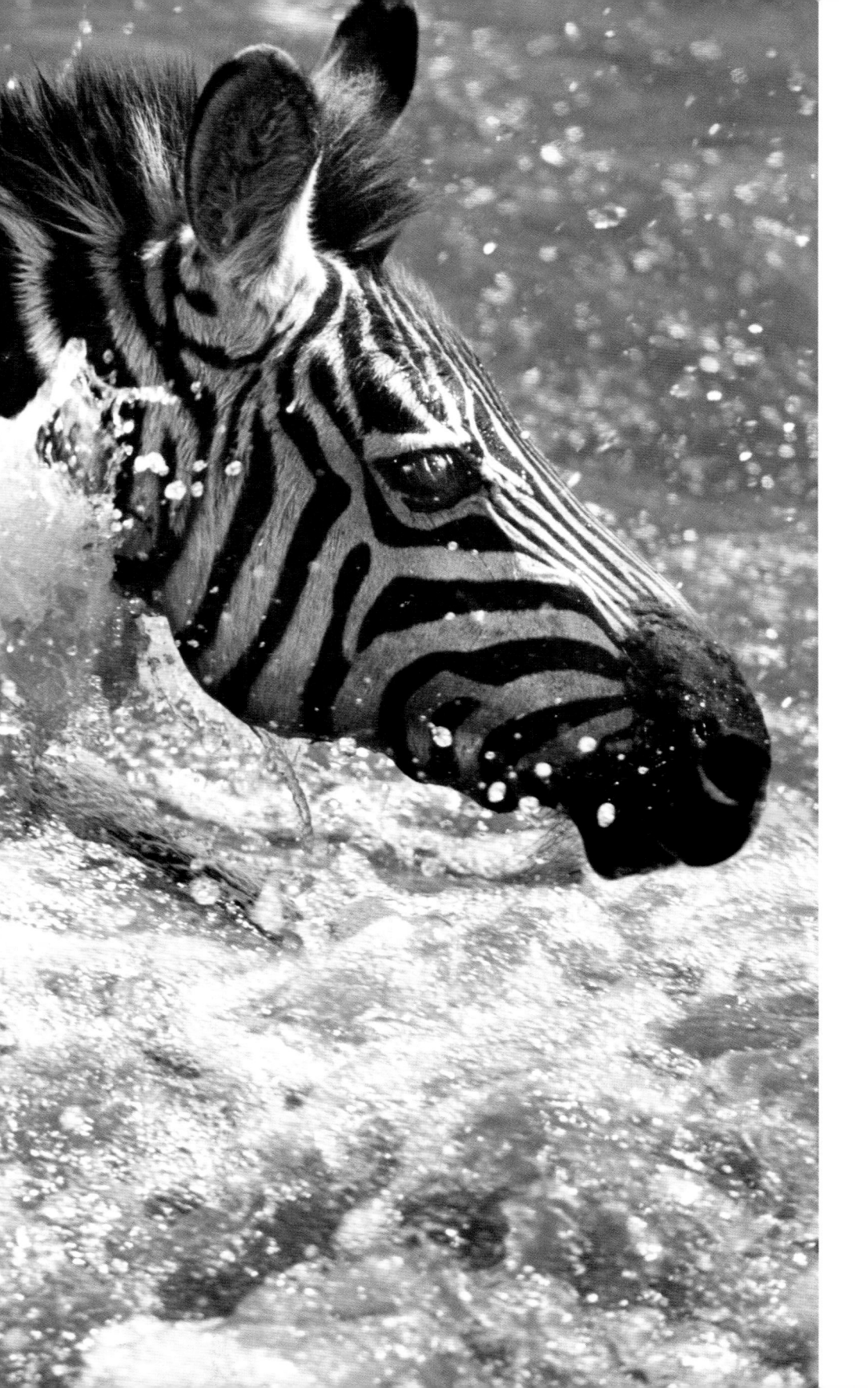

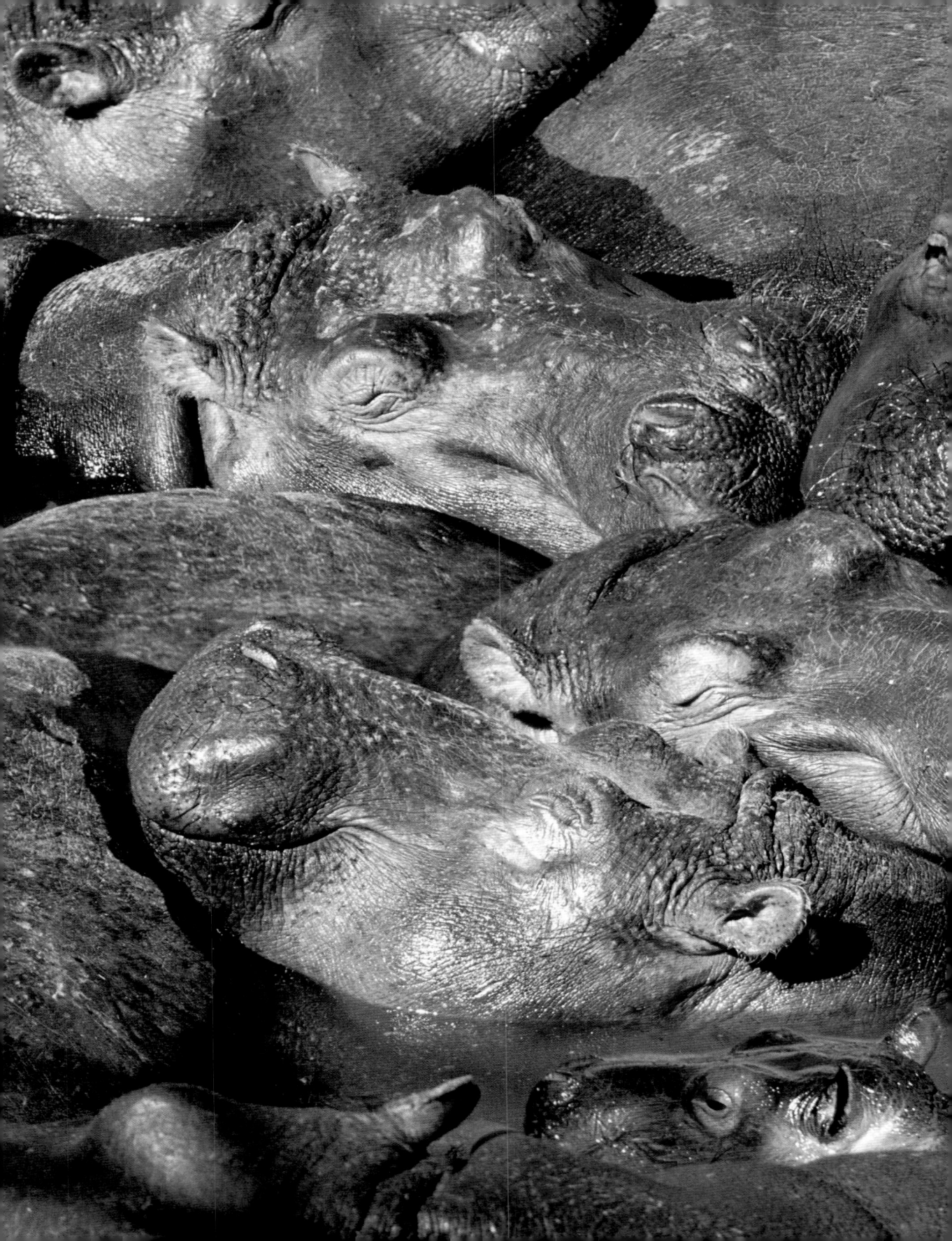

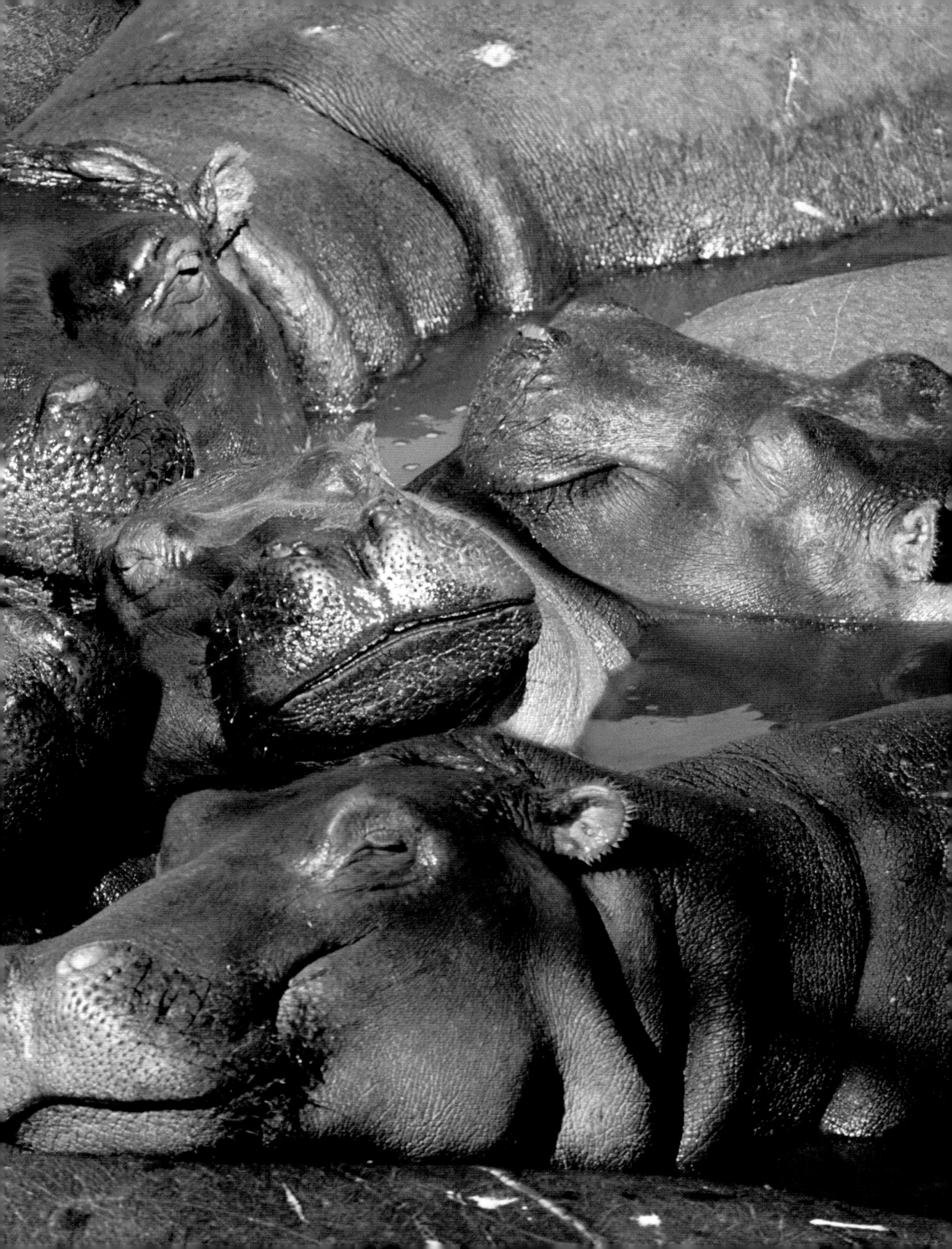

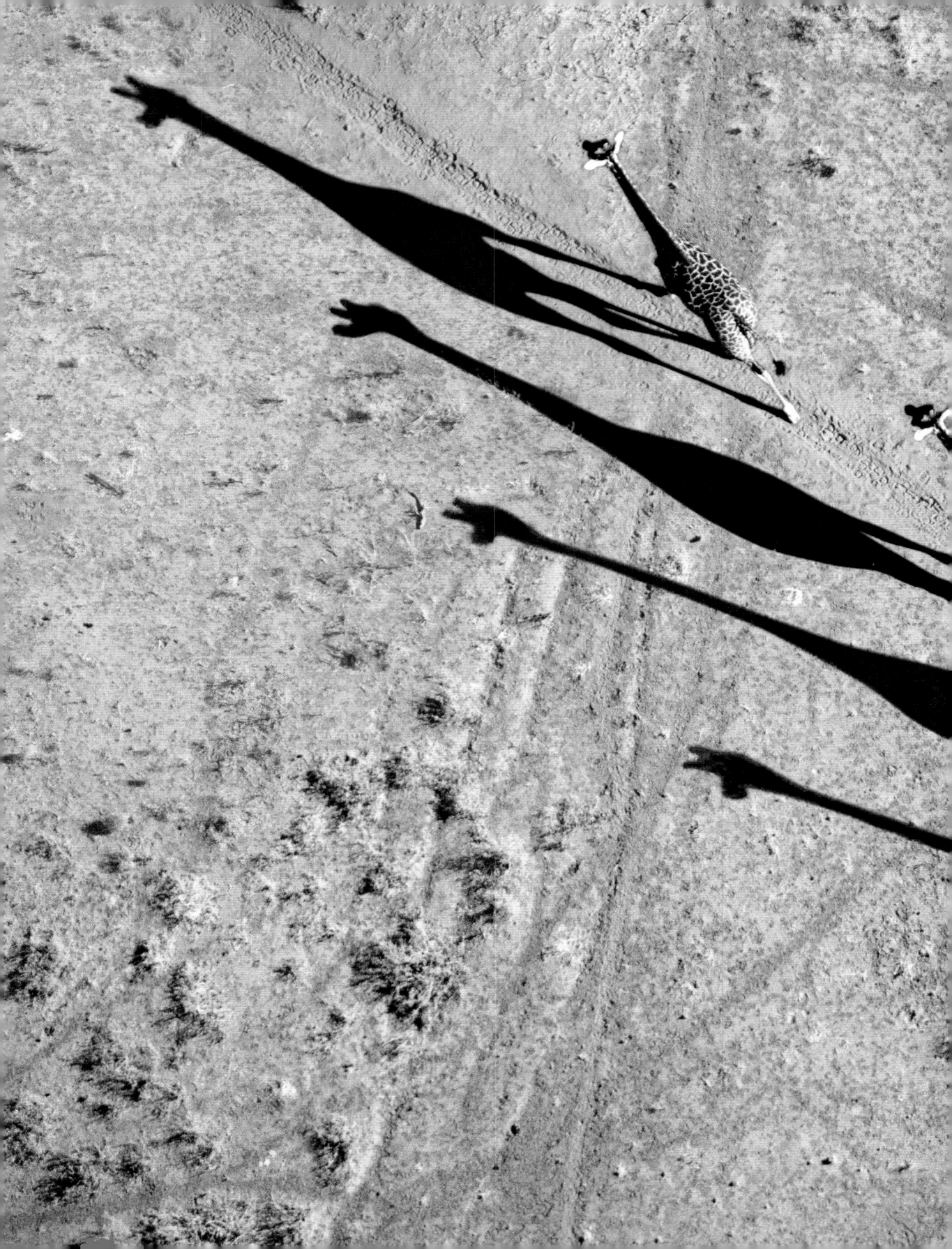

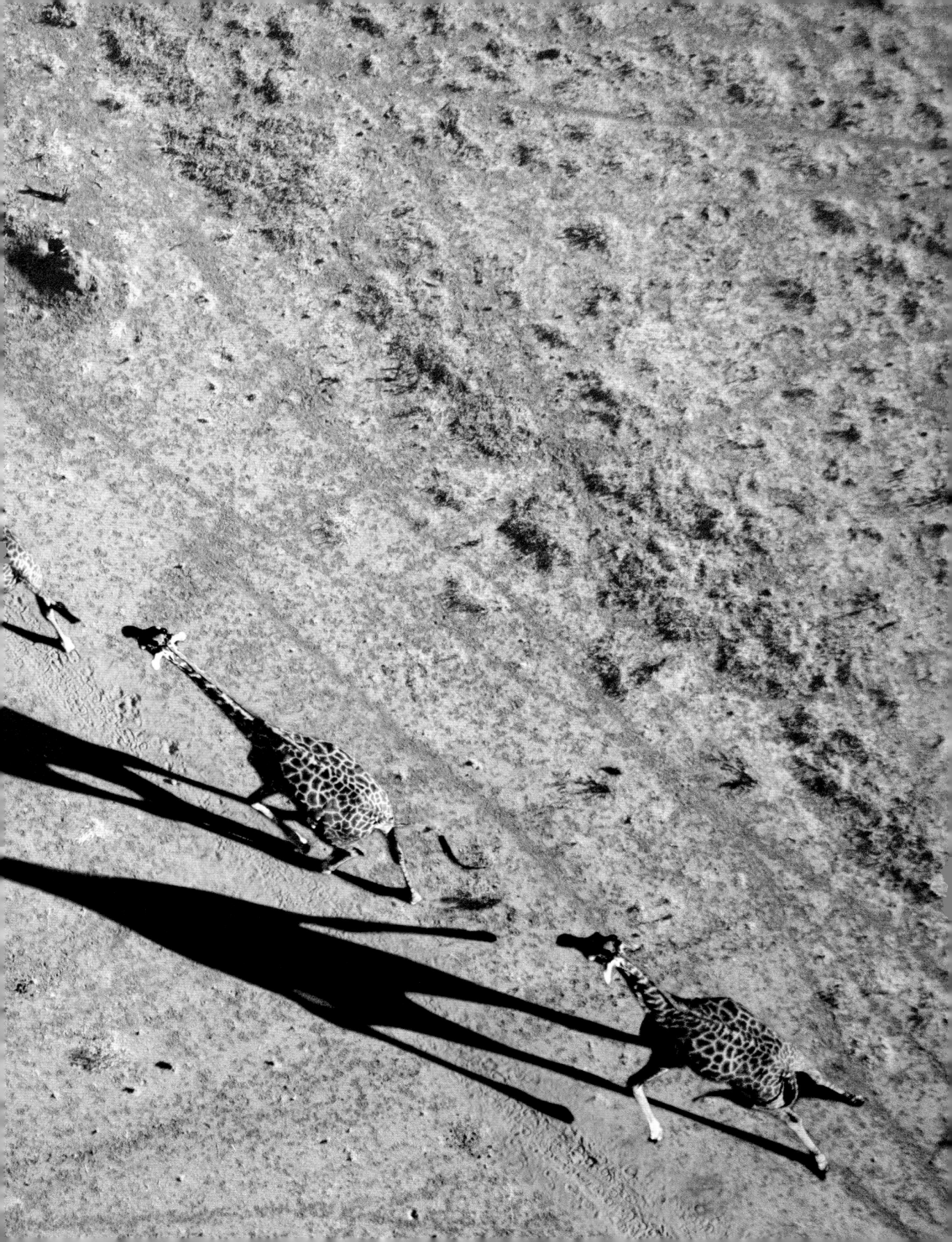

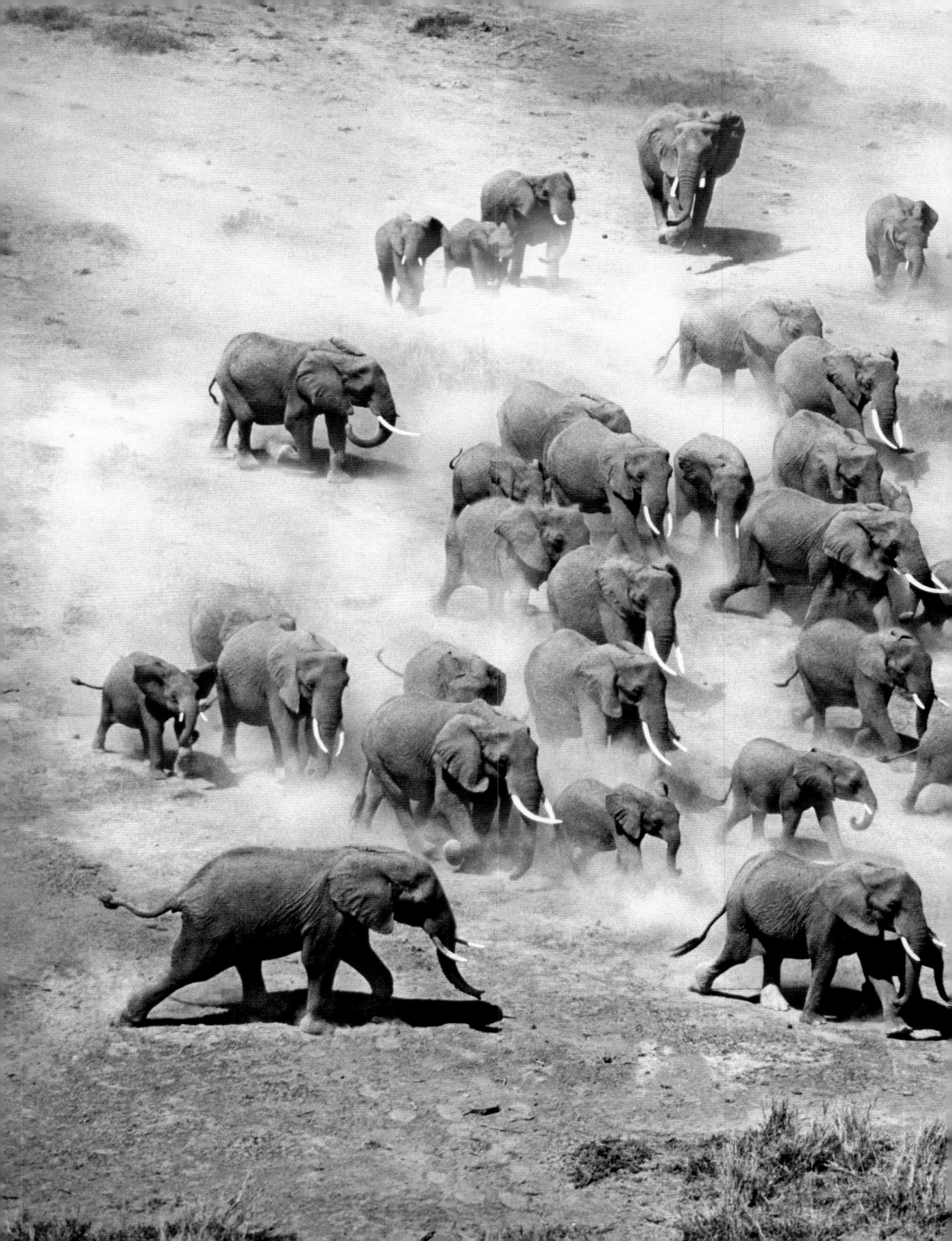

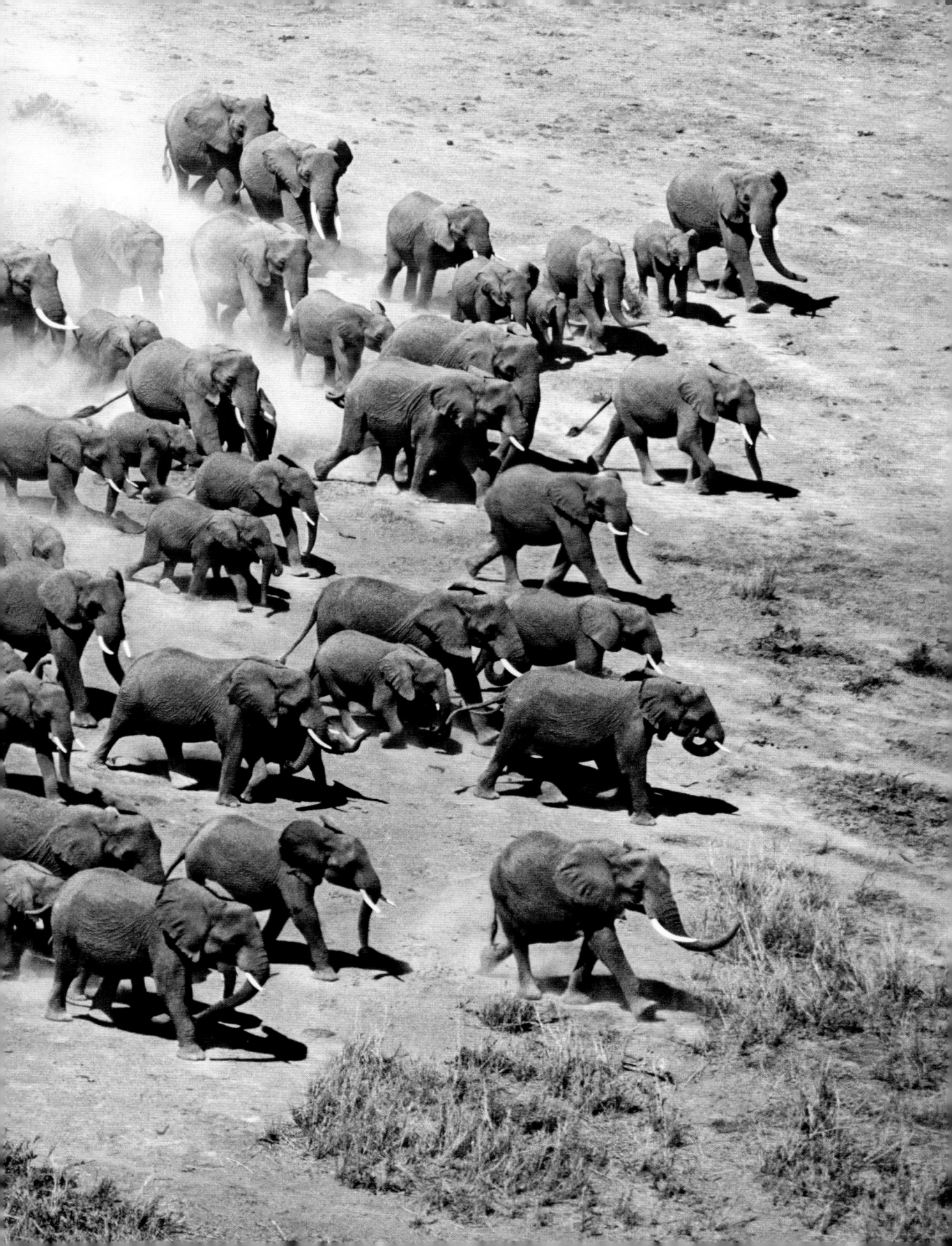

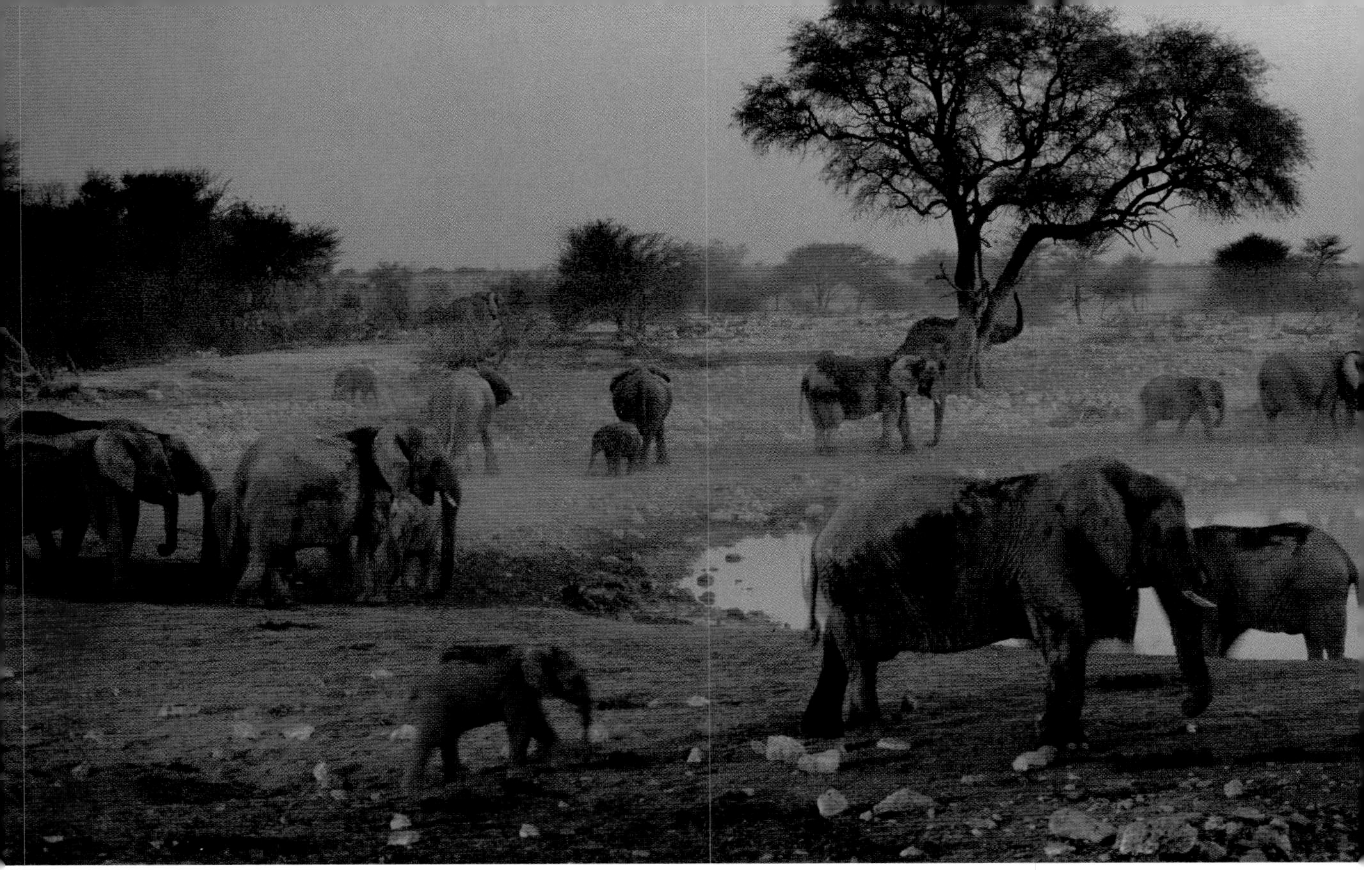

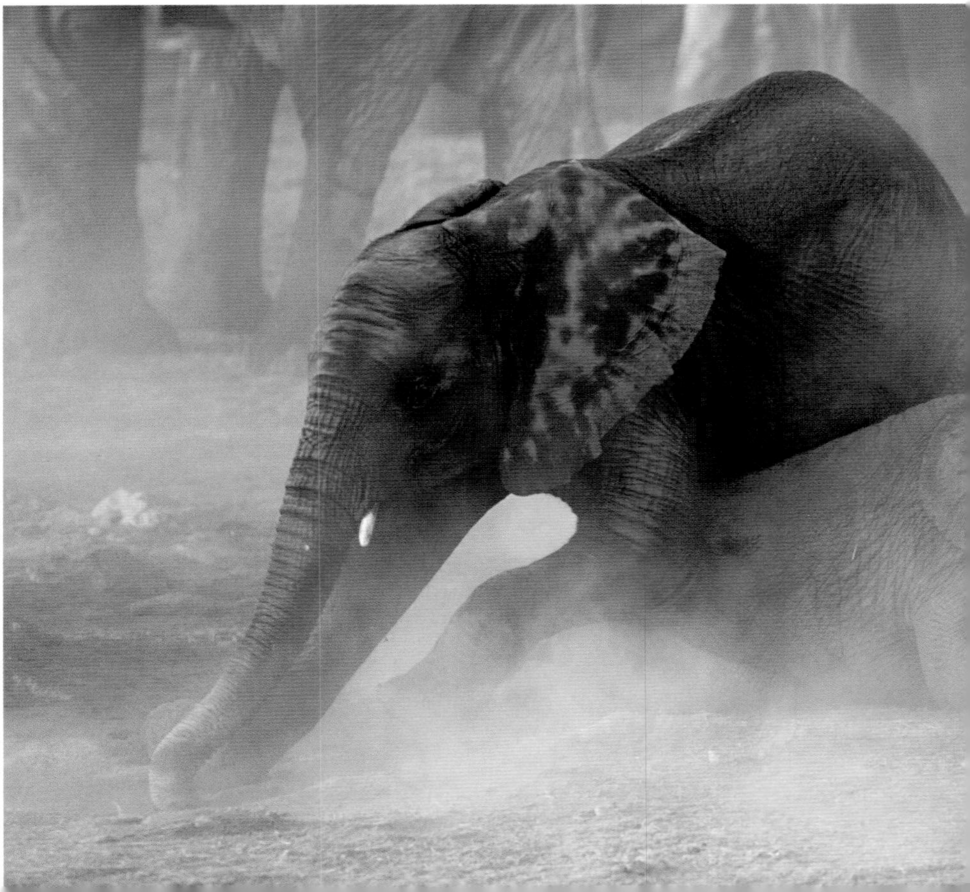

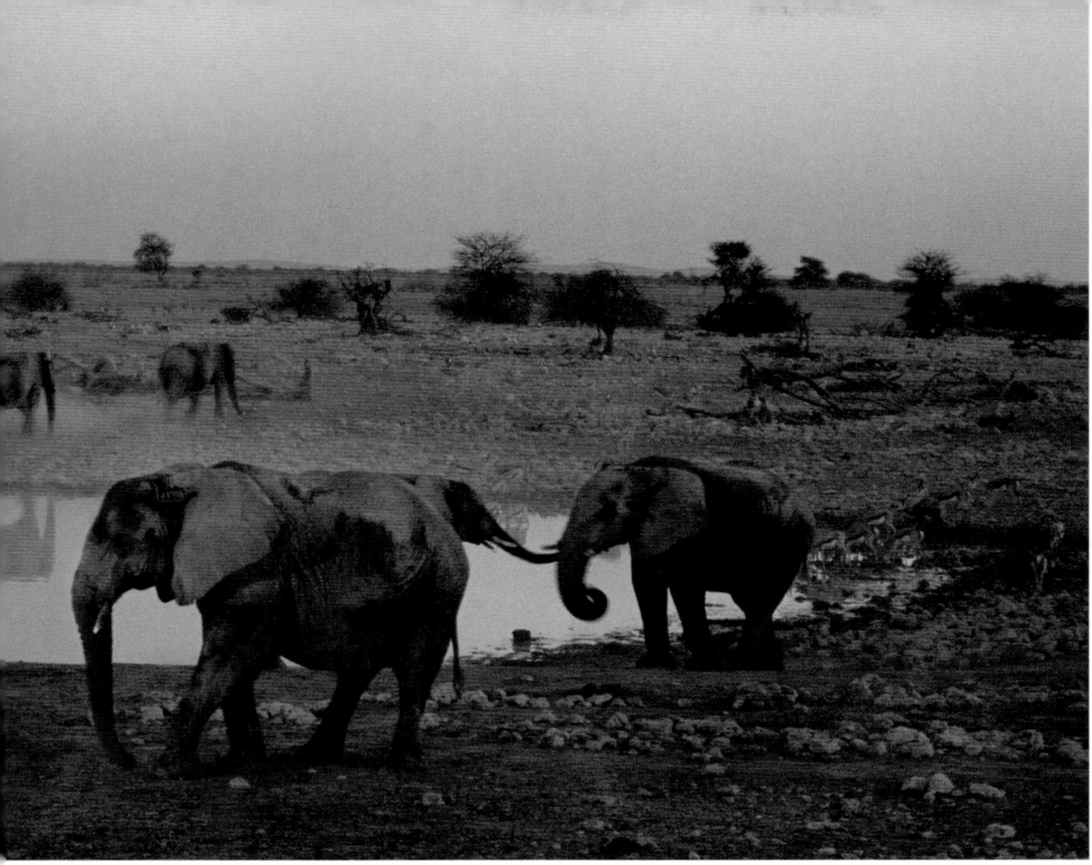

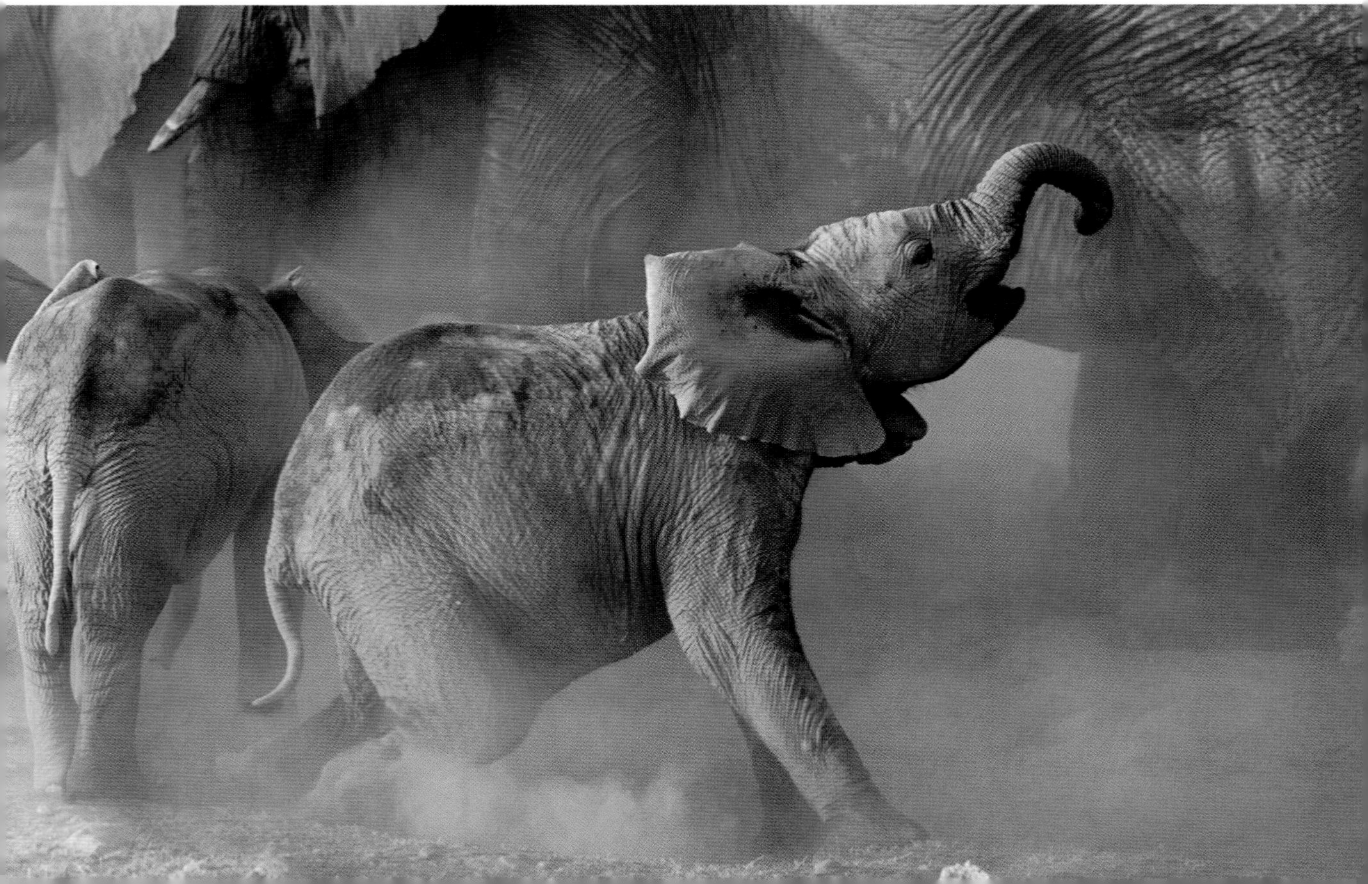

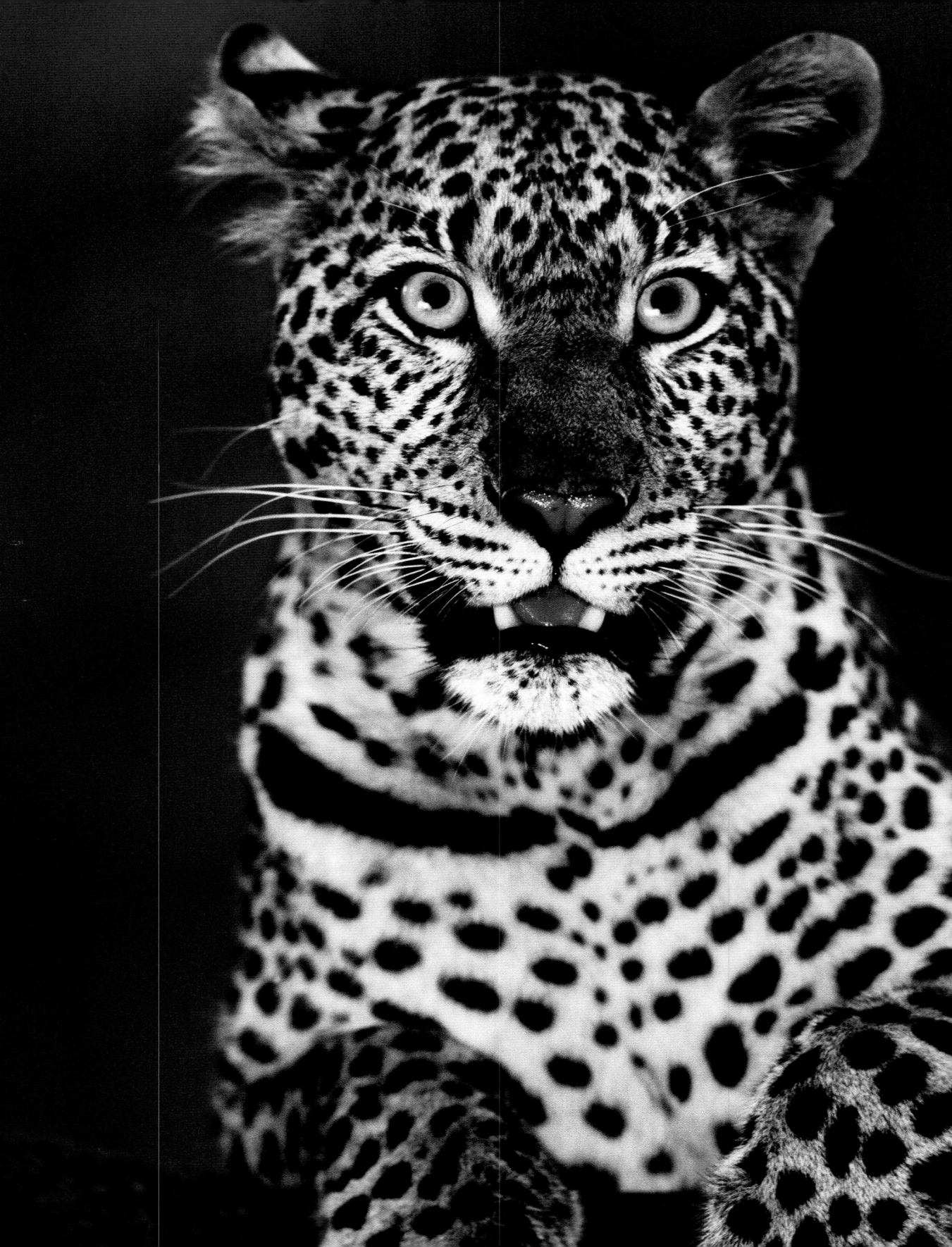

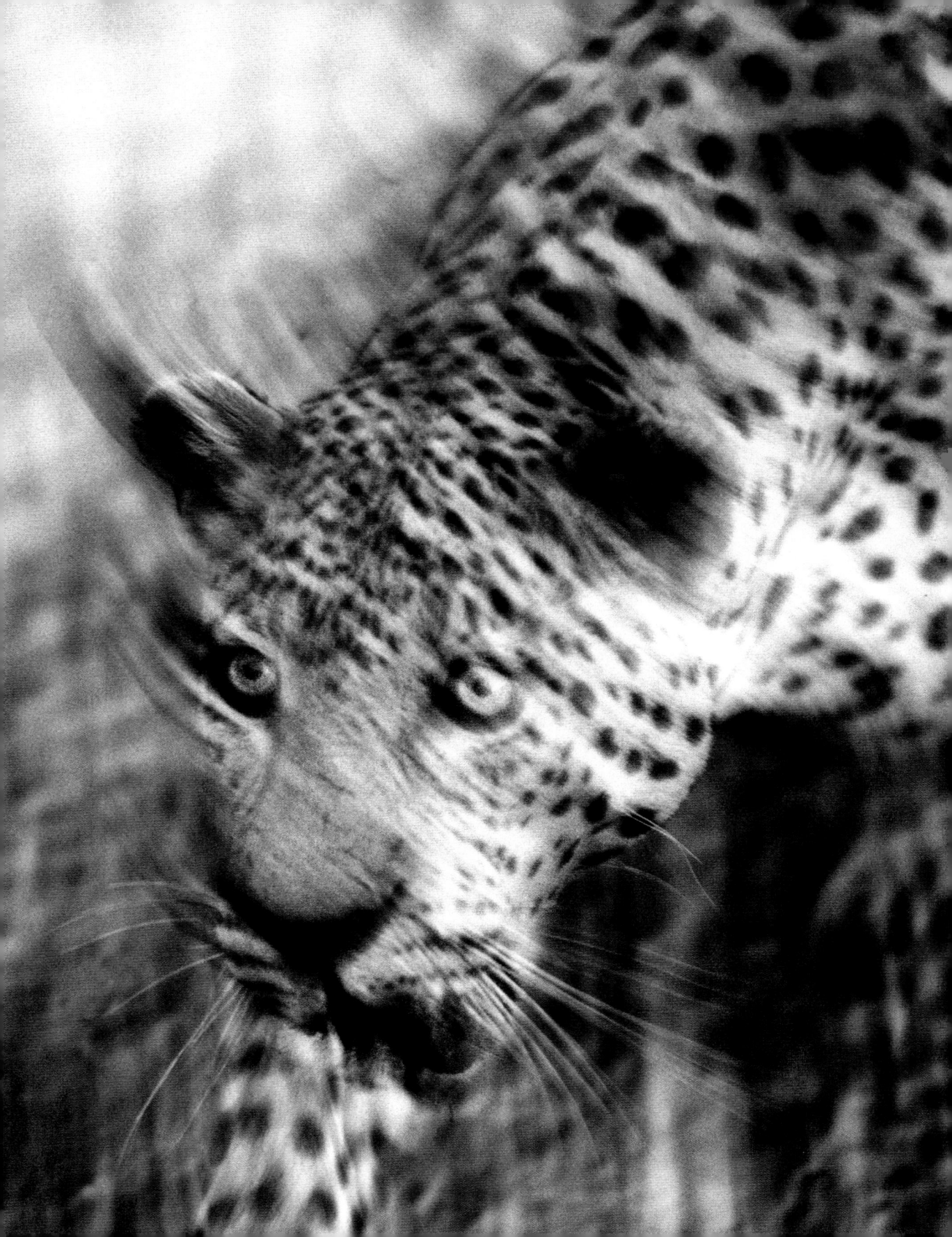

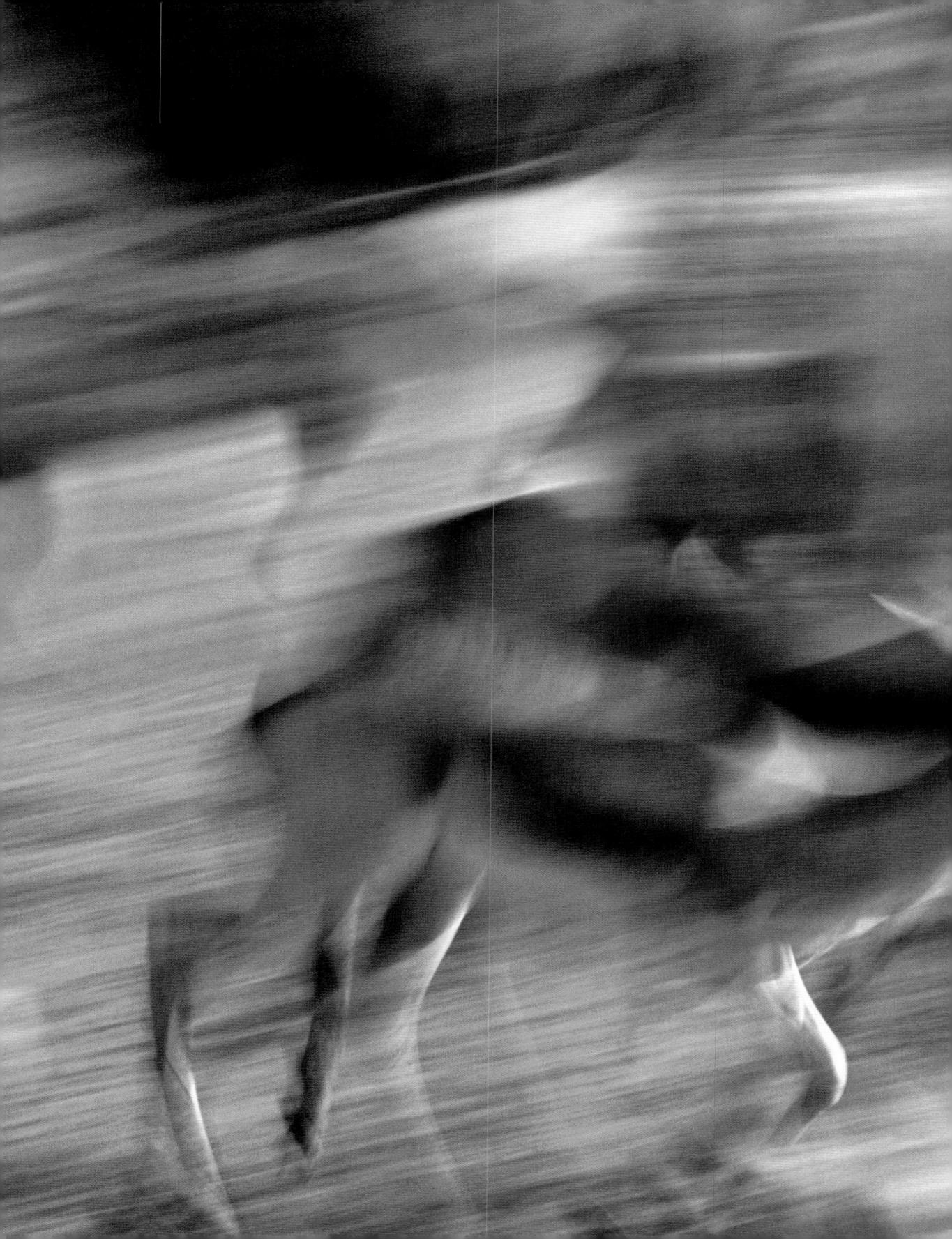

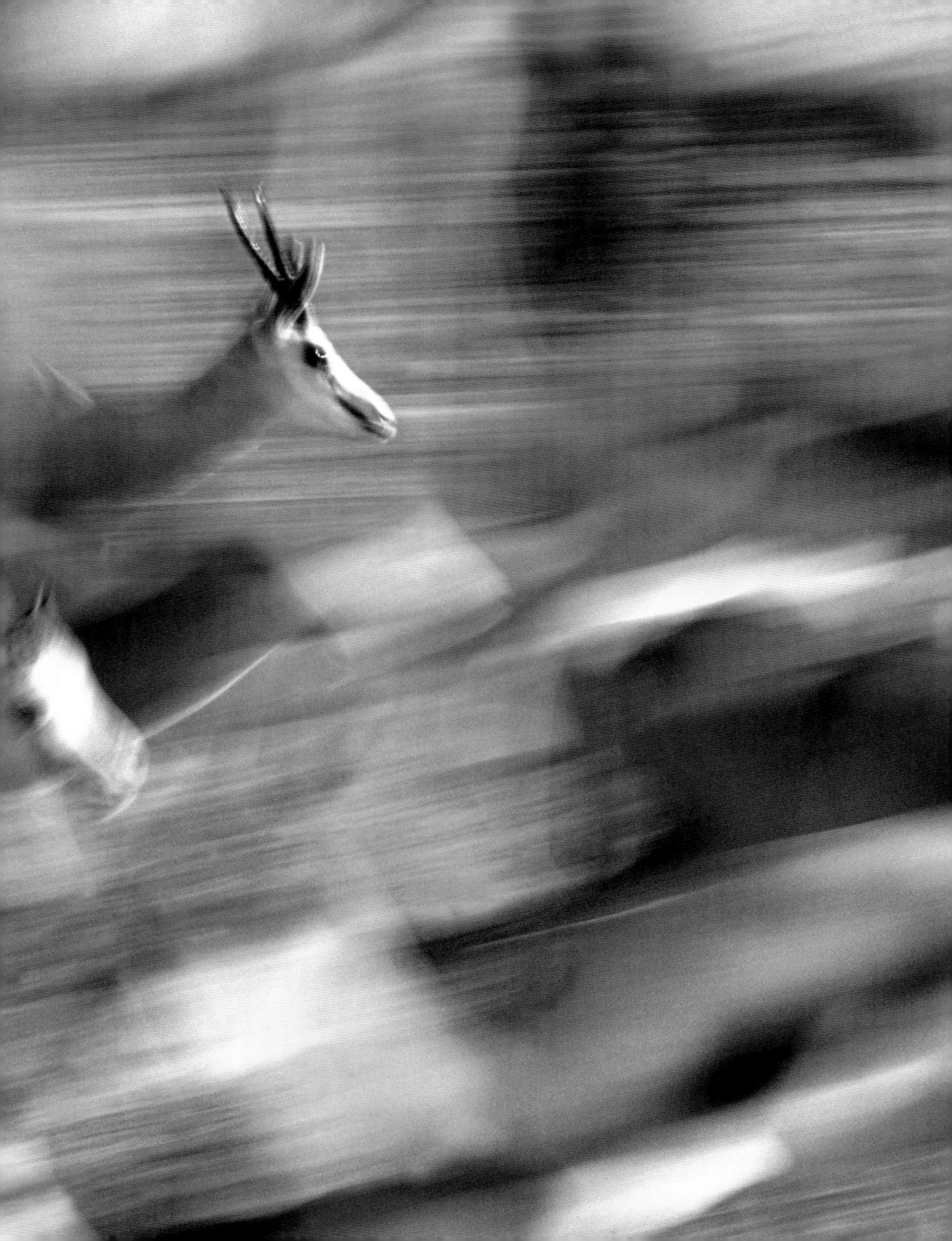

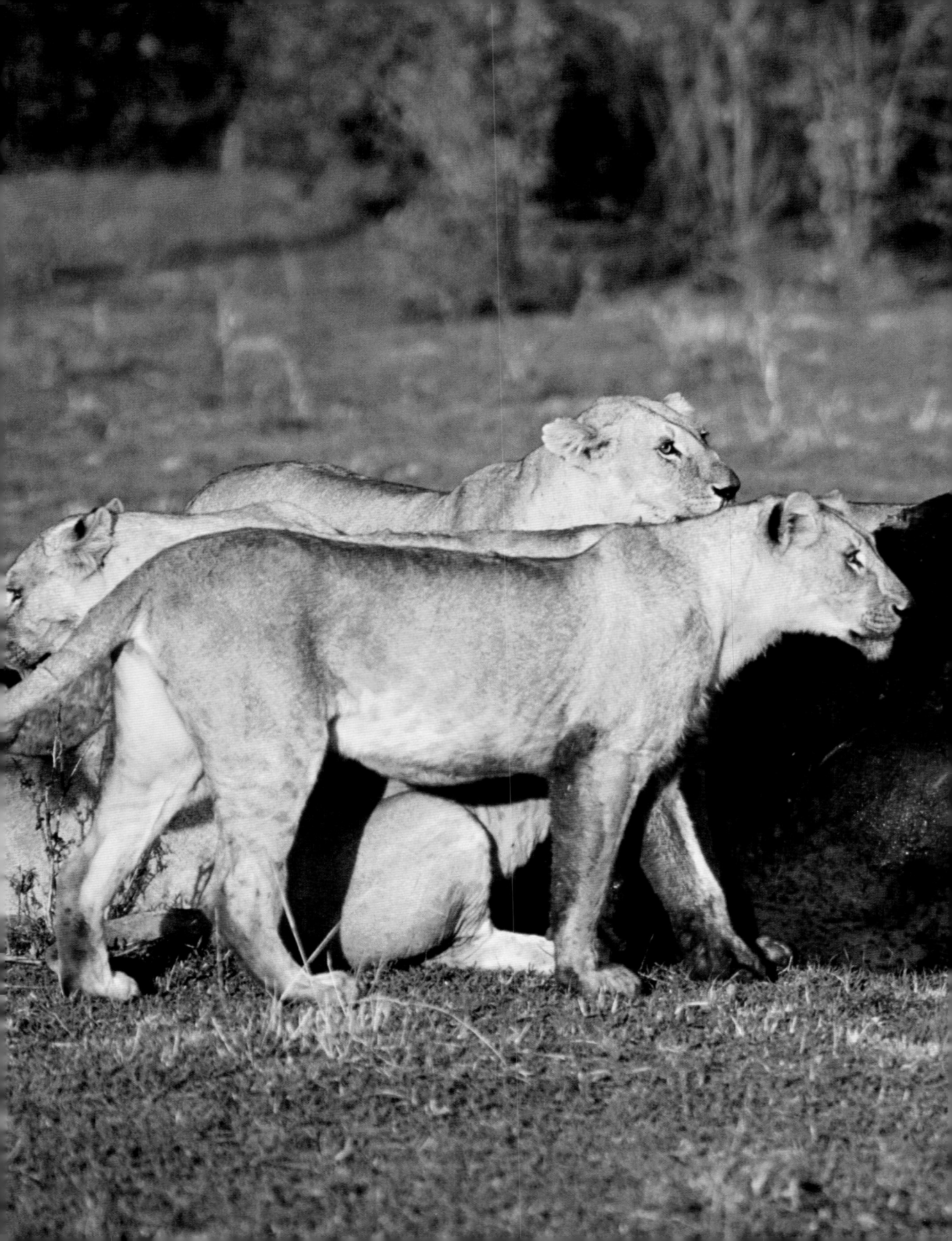

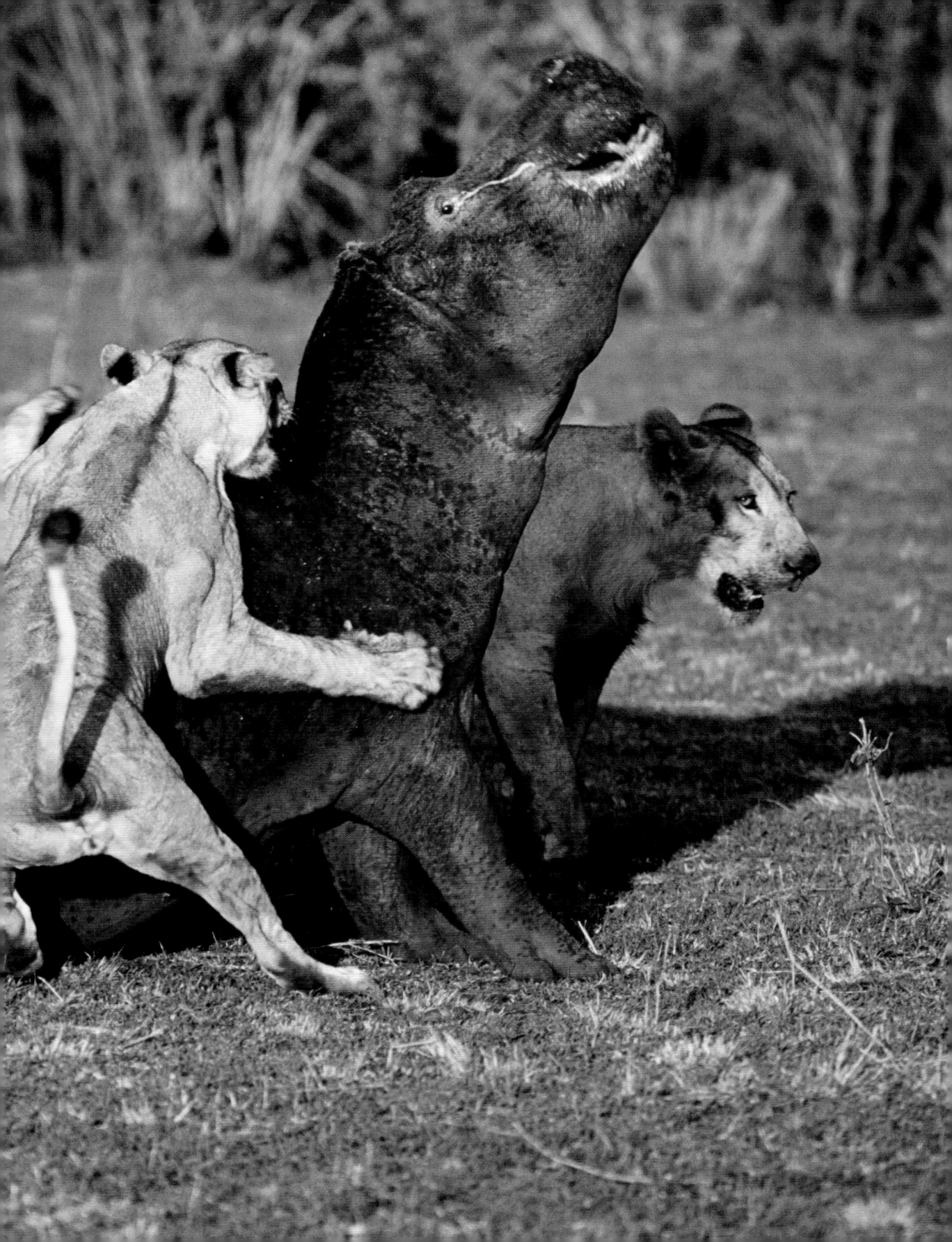

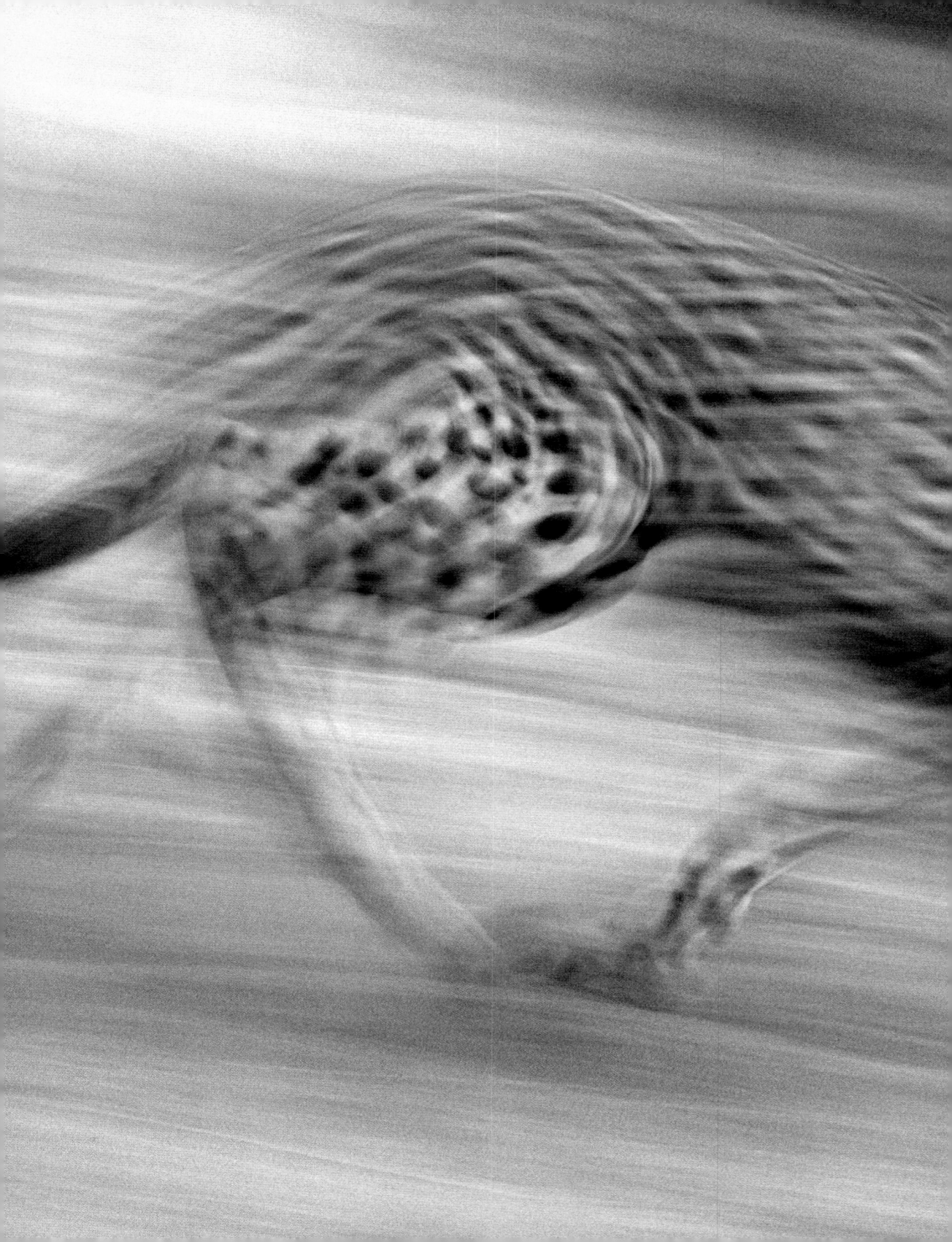

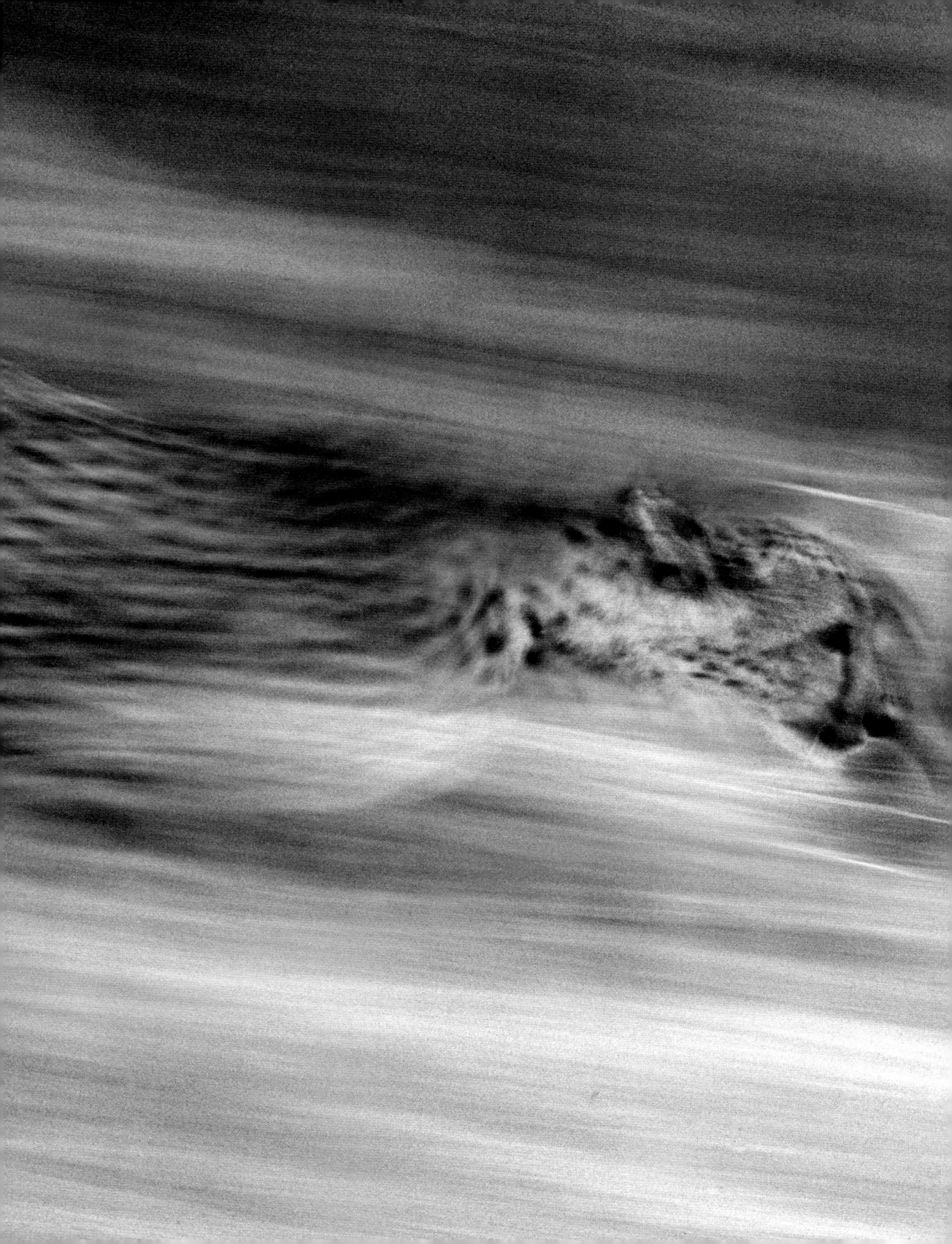

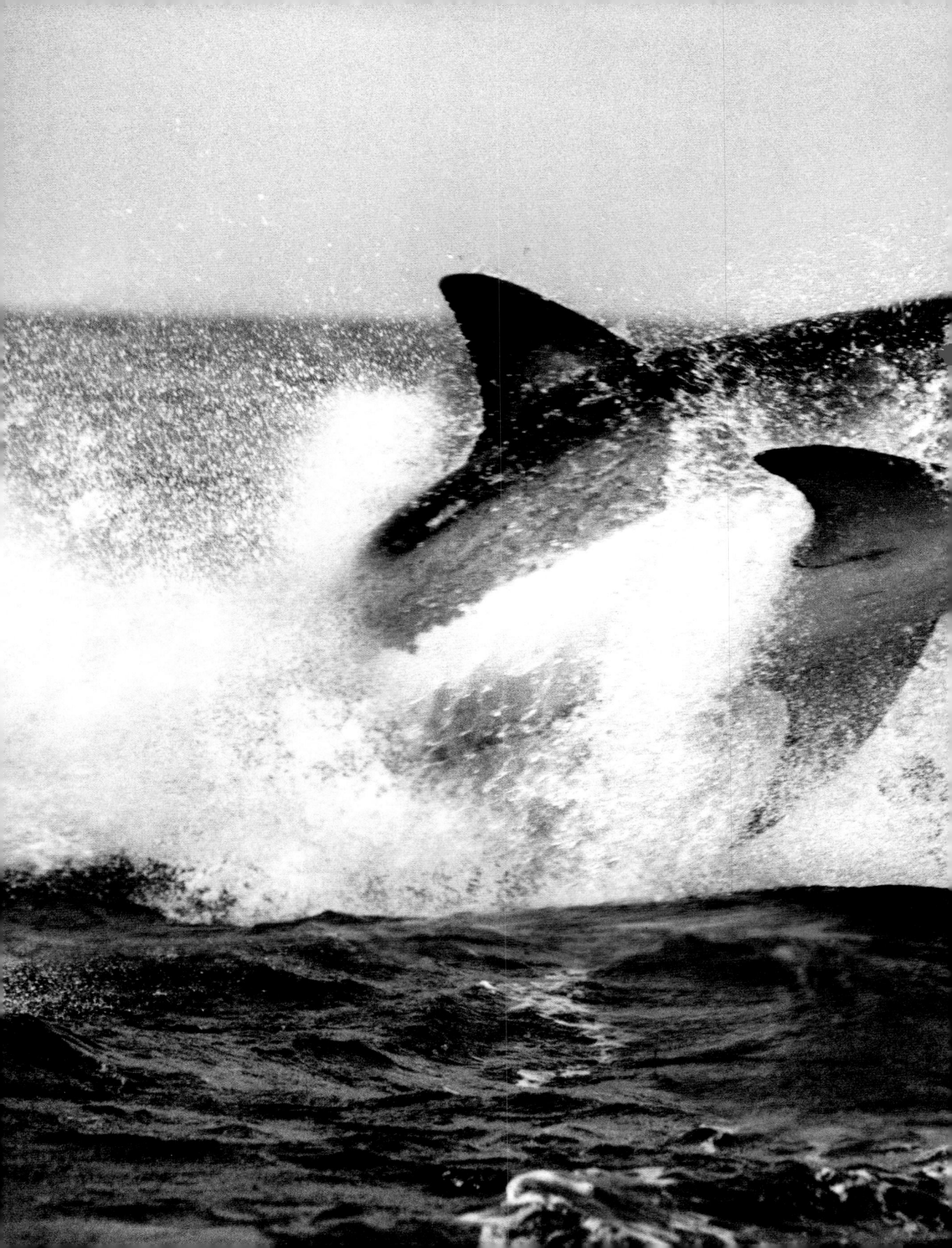

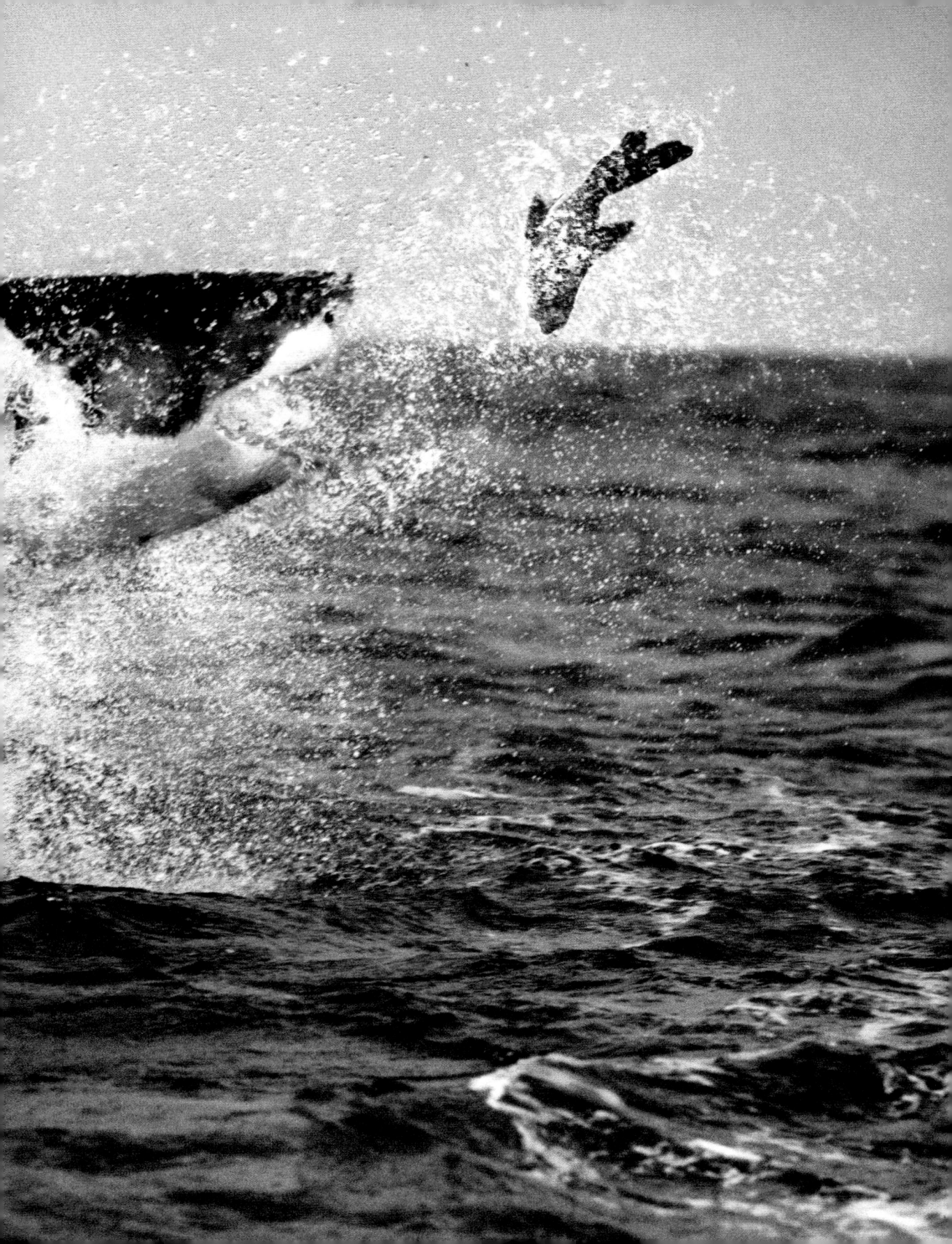

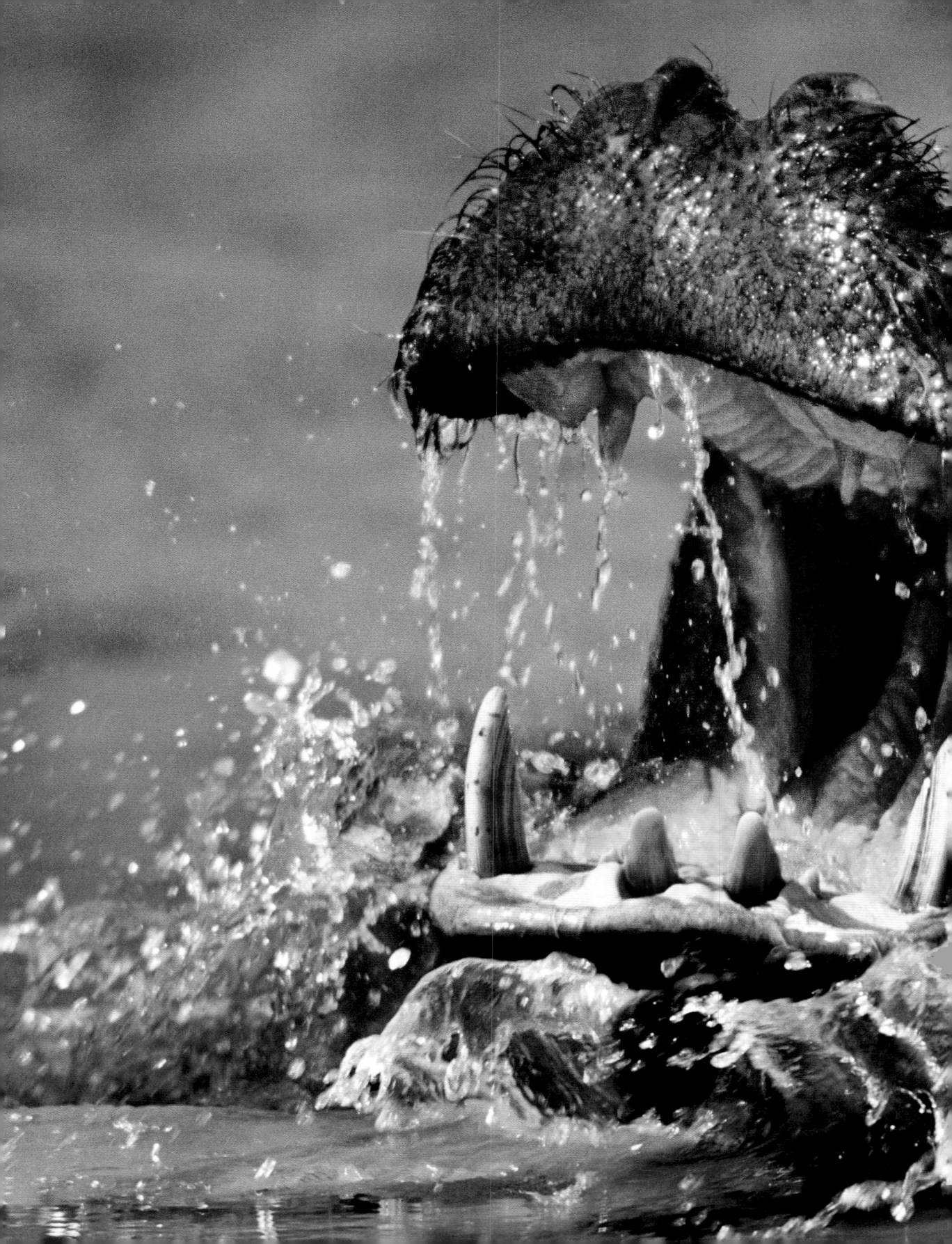

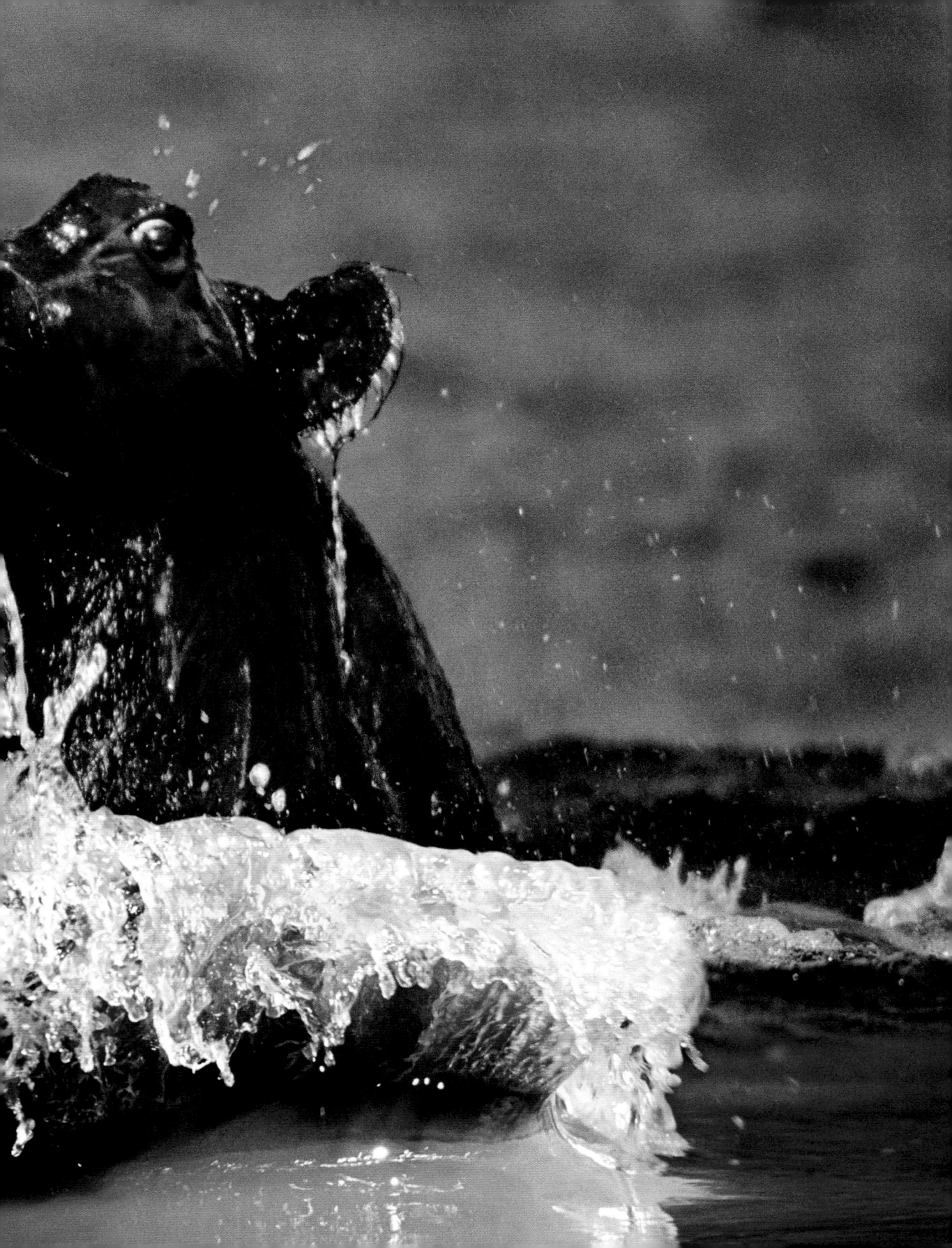

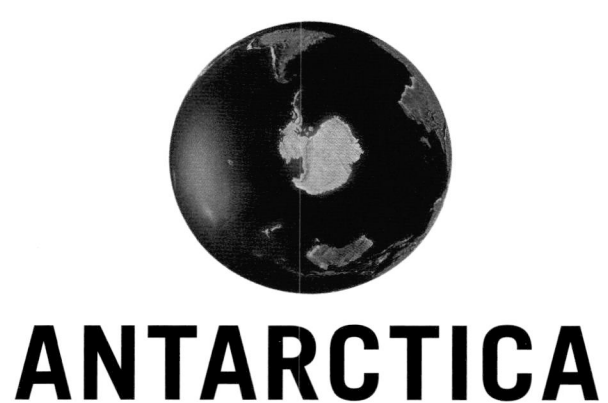

ANTARCTICA

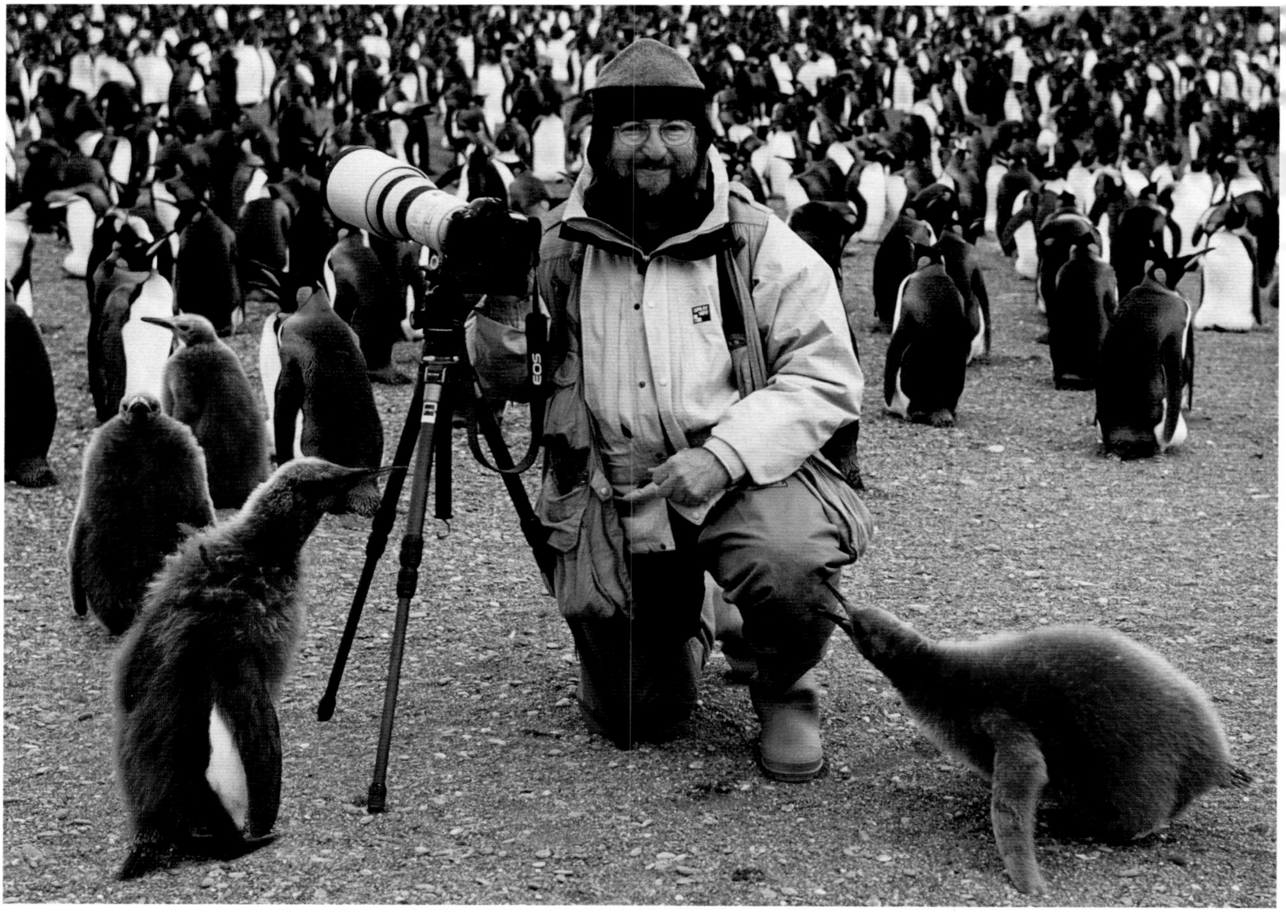

"IN THIS SURREAL WORLD, GIANT ICE SCULPTURES PASS BY, CURIOUS SHAPES FROM DREAMS AND FANTASY."

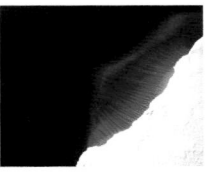

Life can depend on aberrations in nature. Water ignores the usual rules of physics, expanding as it freezes. The difference in densities allows ice to float so that fish swim below, penguins and seals have places to rest, and an ecological balance is maintained. Starfish, crustaceans, and sponges, some centuries old, live beneath the ice. Abundant life, such as diatoms, colors the underside of the floes brown. The most remote places support a rich diversity of life.

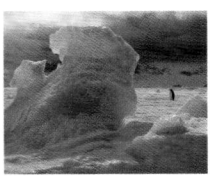

Antarctica is a mystic place, an icy temptress, attracting and enfolding. In this surreal world, giant ice sculptures pass by, curious shapes from dreams and fantasy. Fields of ice tame the ocean, settling the waves that lie flat and obedient below. In such tranquility, stock markets, war, and fashion dissolve into trivia. Here they are mere microcosms in the universe, things that will ultimately pass.

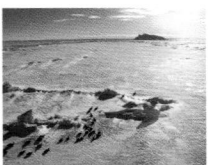

As our icebreaker heaves and churns its way across the pack ice, penguins, when seen from the ship's bridge, become mere dots on the ice floes. Our vessel towers high above the earthbound birds as it ploughs its way in a southerly direction. How much smaller the penguins become when seen from our rising helicopter—specks that soon disappear from view. As the world falls away, the ship also becomes a tiny dot on an ice floe, lonely and insignificant on a colossal ocean of ice.

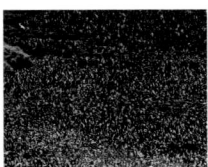

On an island in the Southern Ocean, half a million king penguins stretch as far as the eye can see. As a mass, they are like a giant organism whose incessant racket stays long in memory and whose acrid smell lingers in my nostrils for days. Yet each bird is a distinct and unique individual.

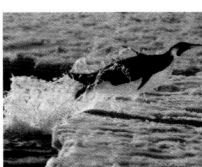

Awkward on land, elegant in water, and impervious to the harshness of weather, penguins epitomize the diversity of life. While others soar in the skies, these birds of the ocean fly beneath the waves. Like torpedoes, they shoot out of icy waters with immense propulsion, defying the notion that they can ever be call "flightless."

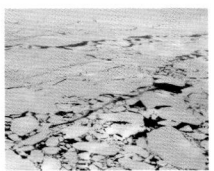

Time is different in Antarctica. The summer day drags on and on and on. Clocks become mere reminders of when to sleep and when to eat. Our ship rides the frozen ocean, forging a path that quickly closes behind us. This is a place of whiteness that is brighter and more intense than anything I have ever seen. It is as if all the light in the universe has gathered together and been scattered upon us. All around, bright white ice merges into hazy sky; our ship a yellow daub on an endless white canvas.

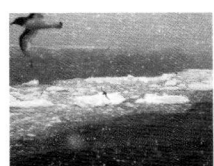

Horizontal shards of searing ice tear through the freezing air. I am a hunched figure in the blizzard, struggling to hold the camera steady in the howling, screaming wind. Through screwed up, stinging eyes, I see Antarctic petrels all around me as they ride the wind with deftness and scour the icy ocean for food.

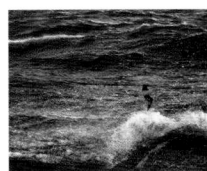

The albatross is at home in the sky. She follows our ship for days, soaring gracefully, enriching the cold, windswept Southern Ocean. I peer out of my warm cabin and watch her ride the wind, content that she is free to wander where she wishes, free to leave the orbit of my metal world that heaves its way across the ocean.

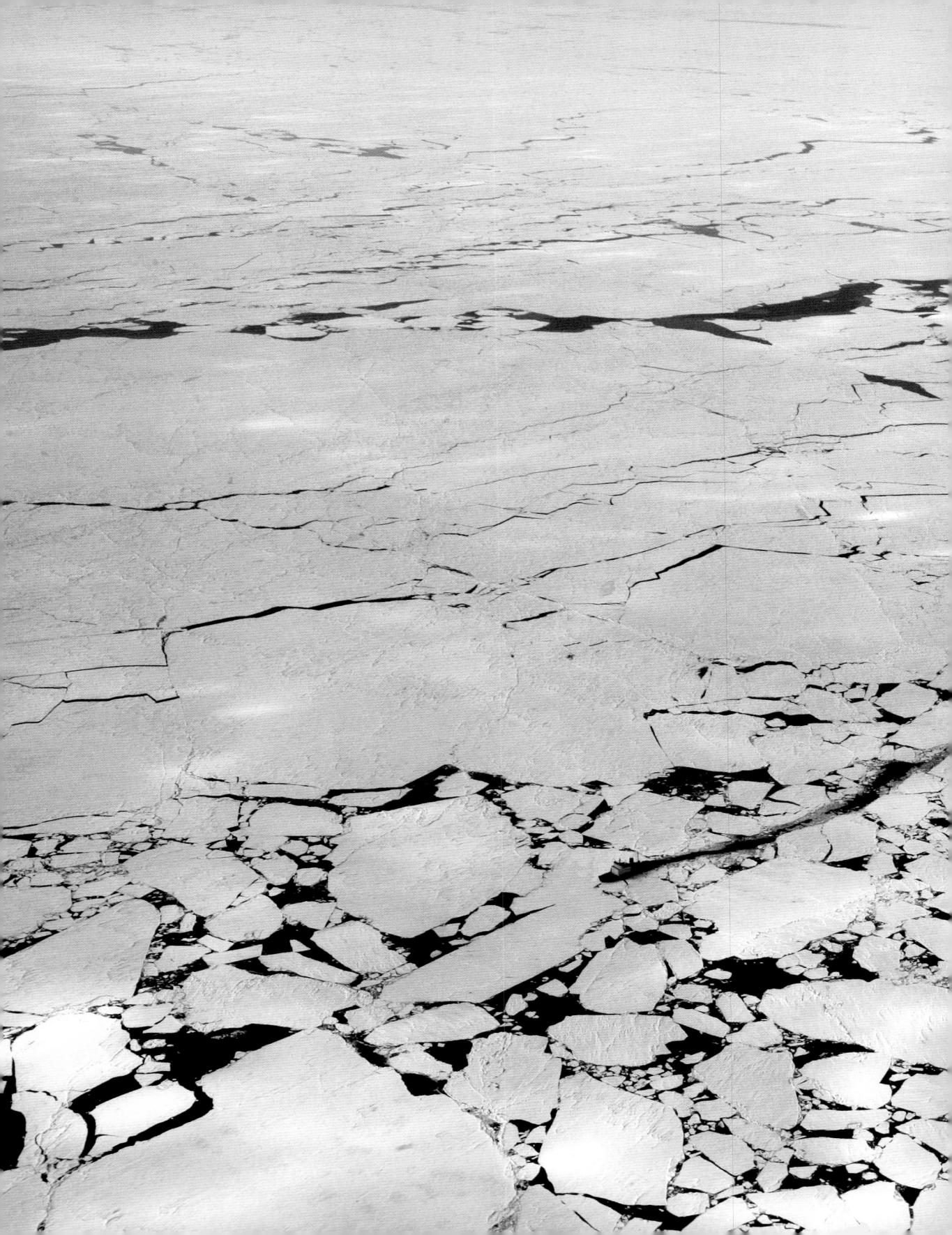

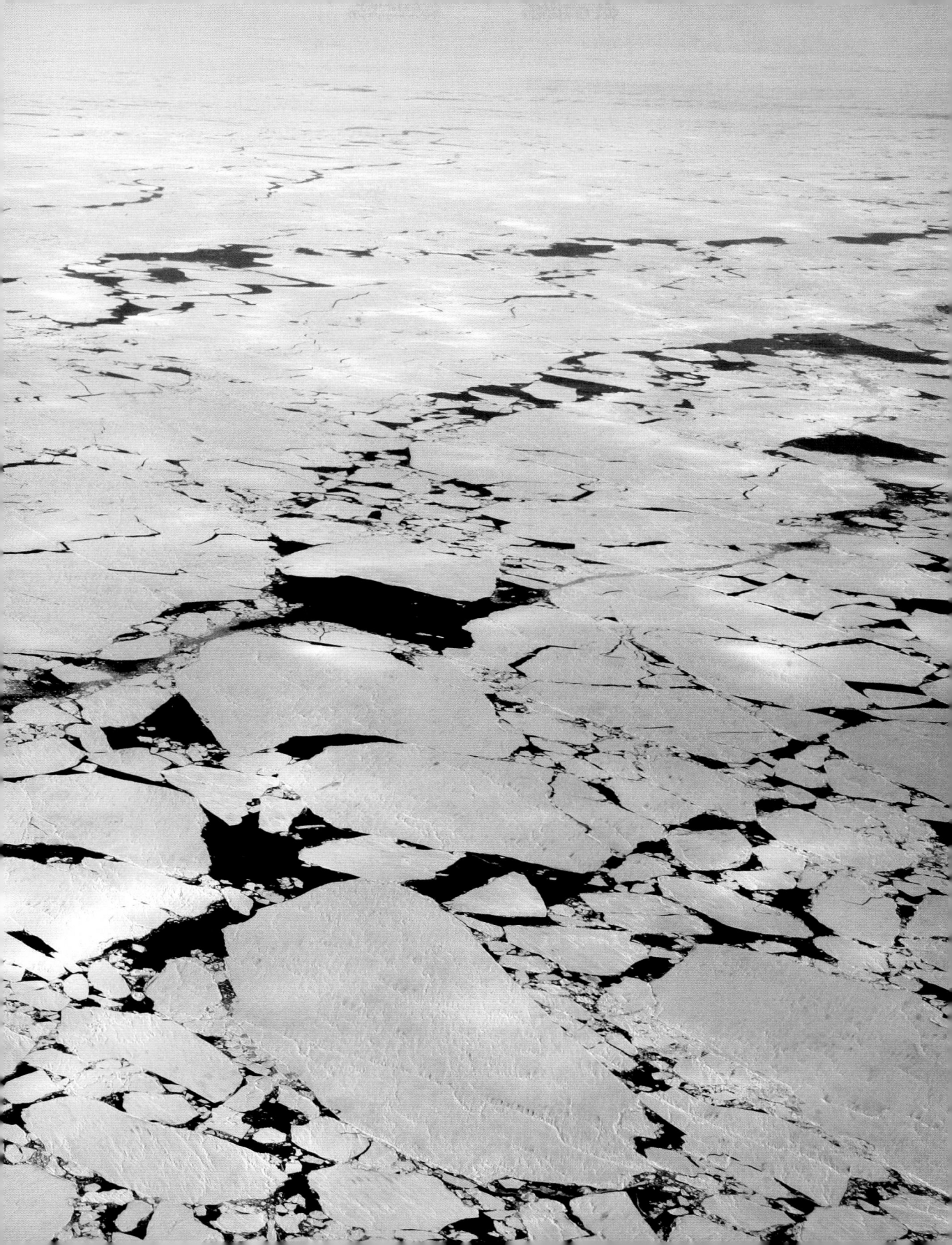

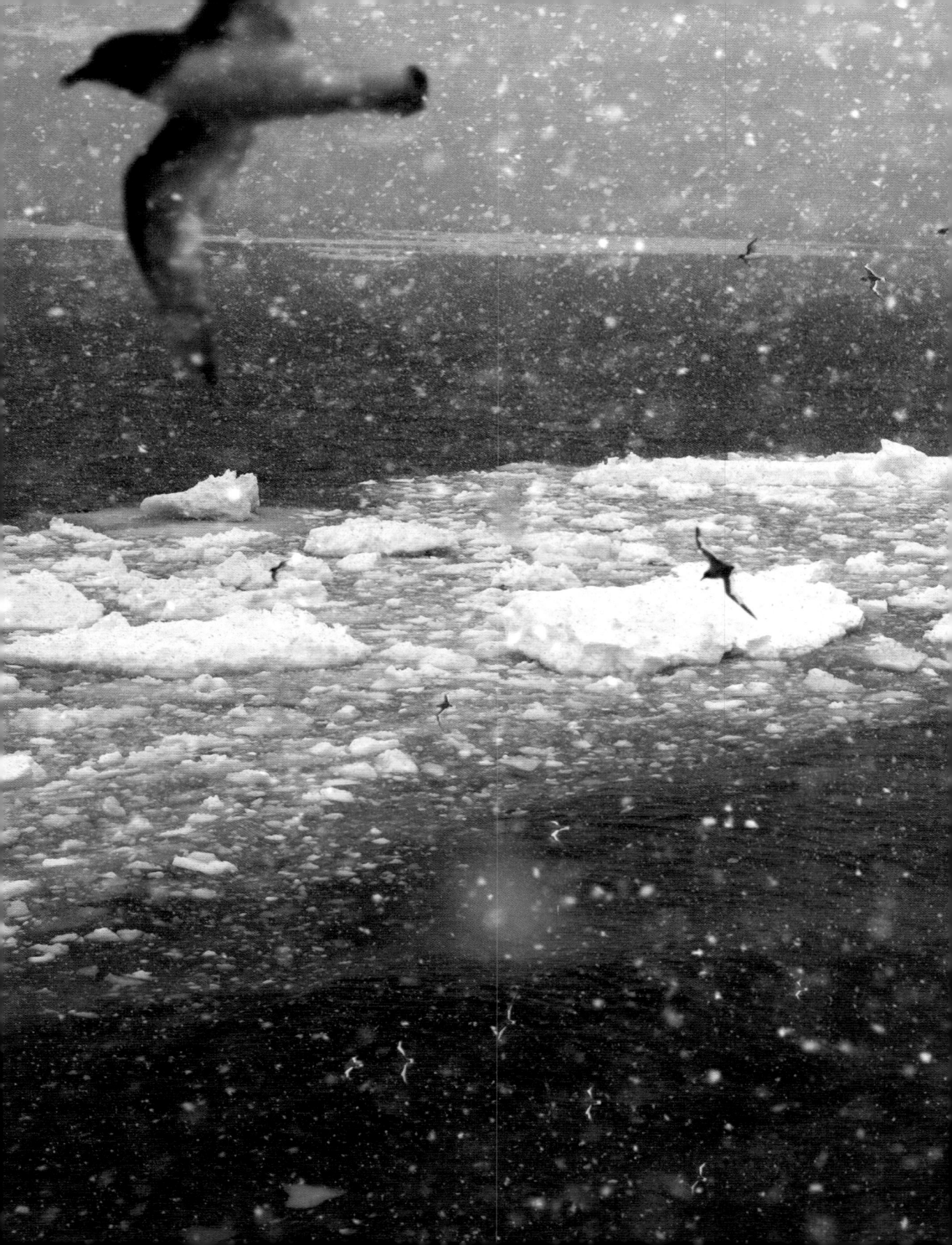

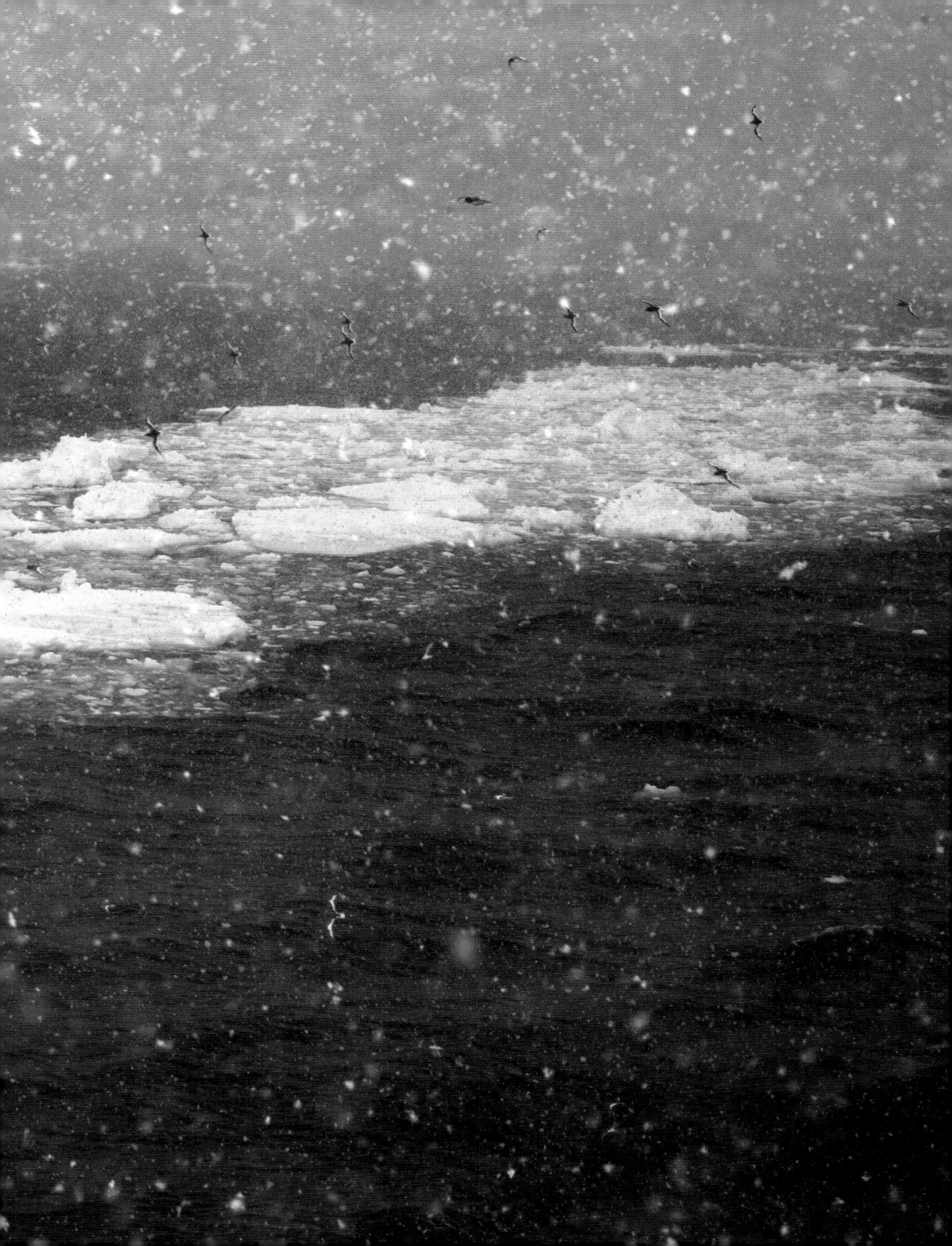

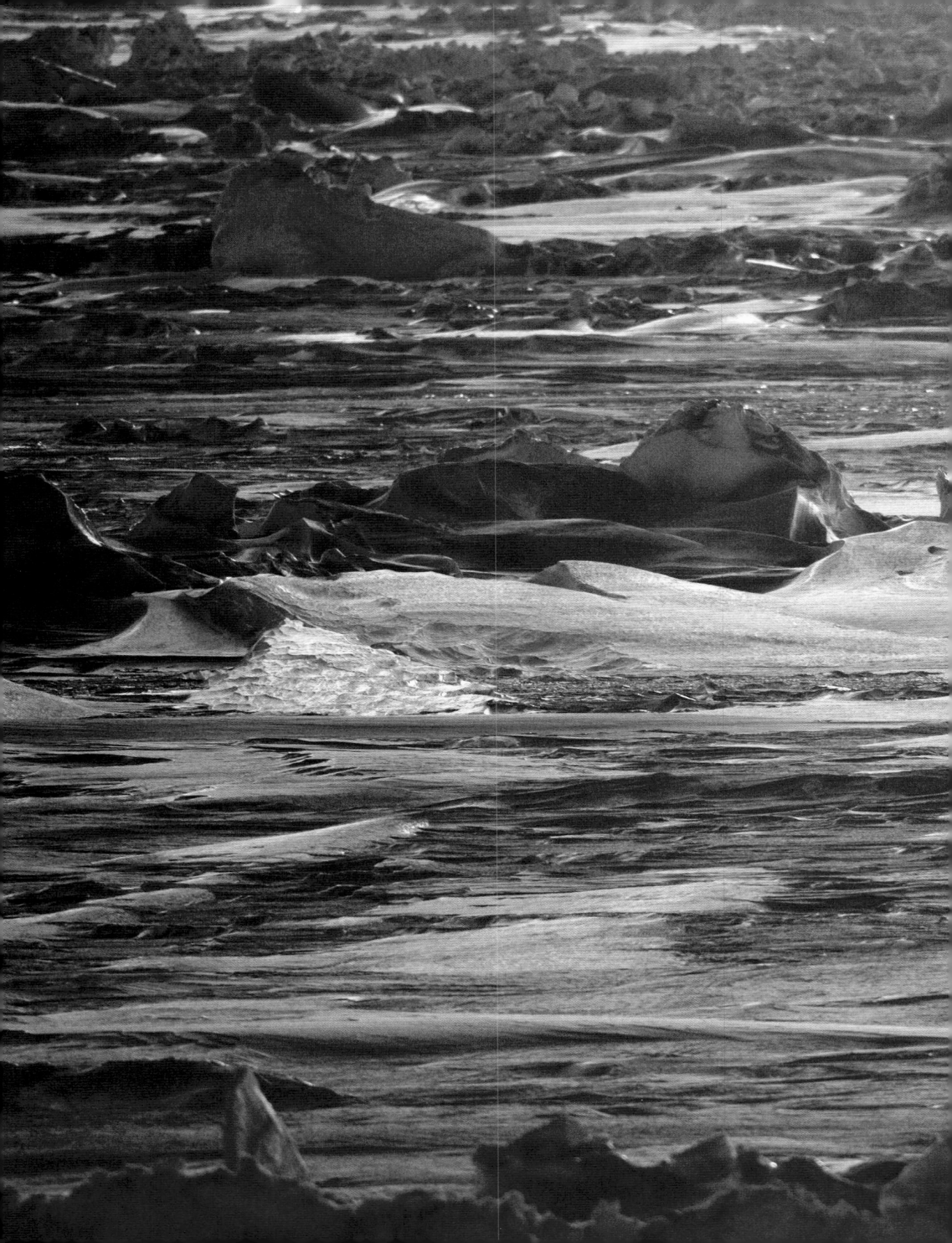

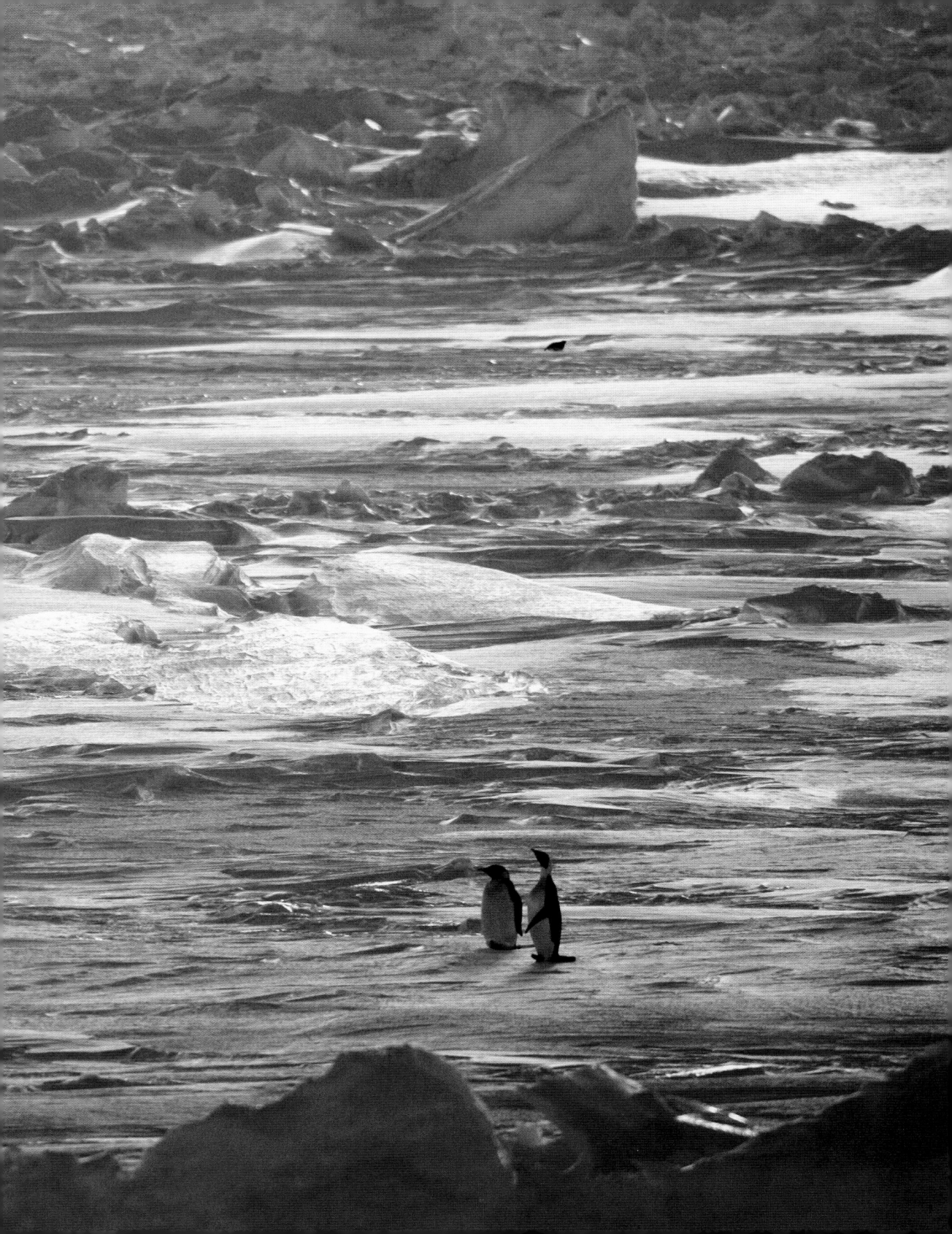

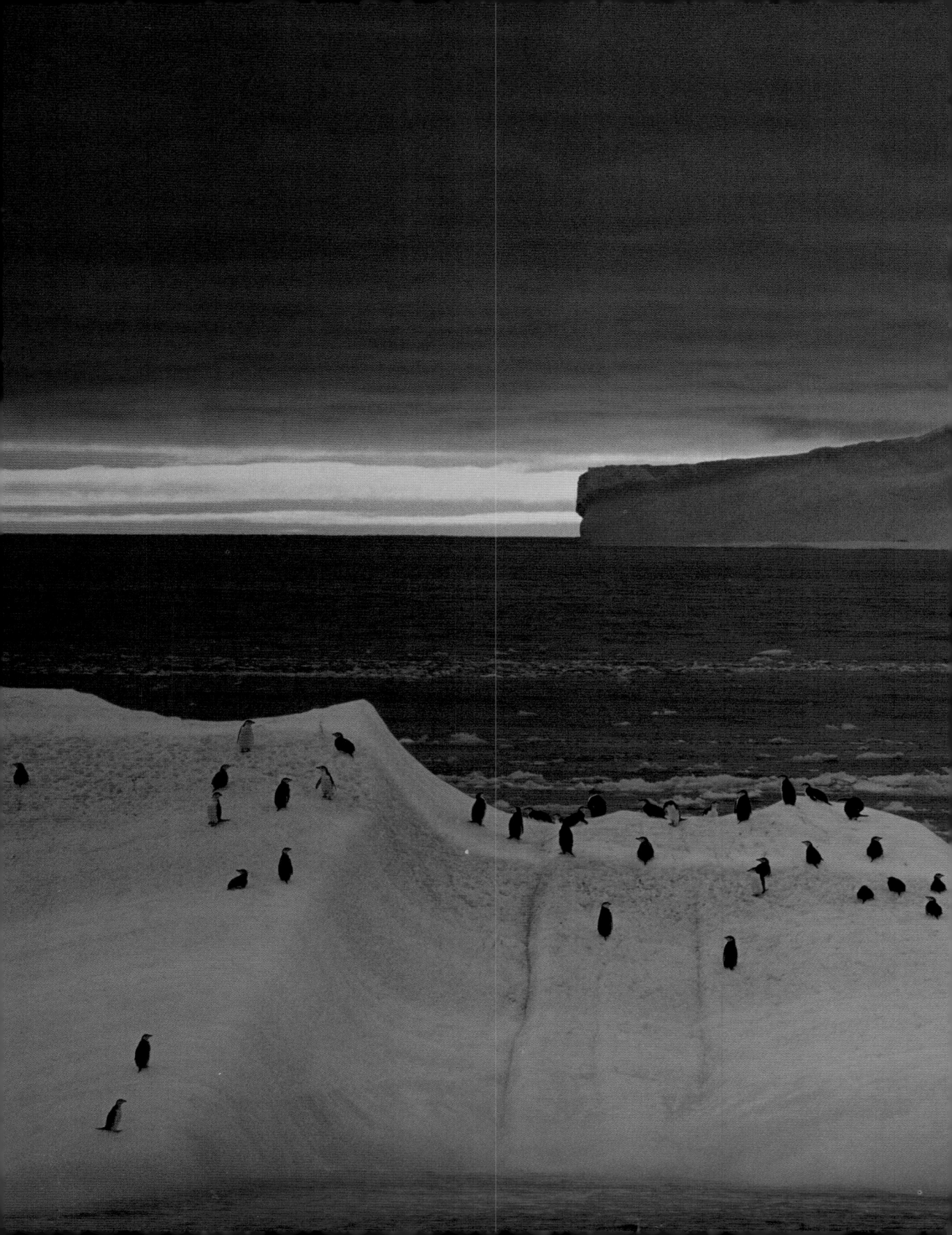

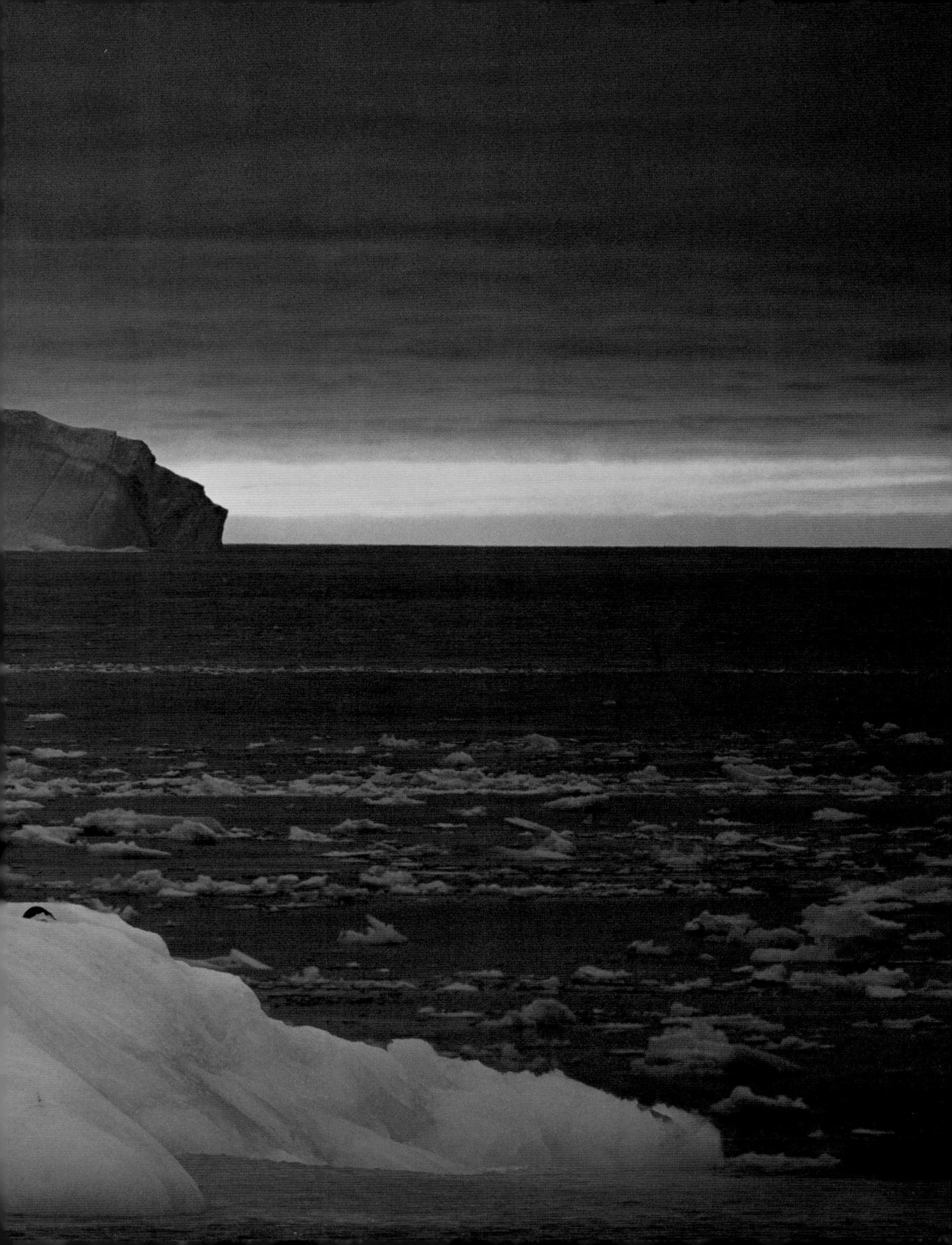

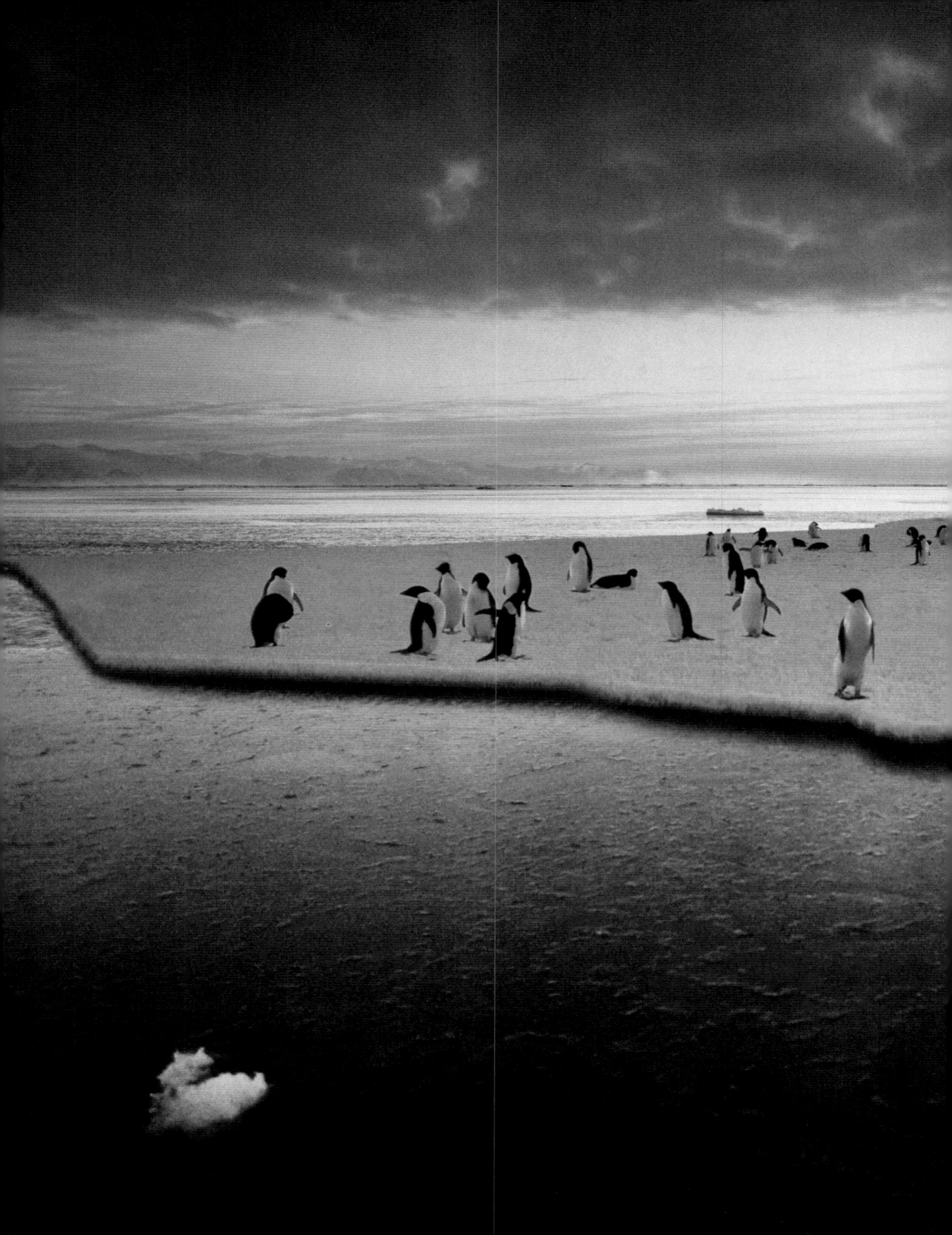

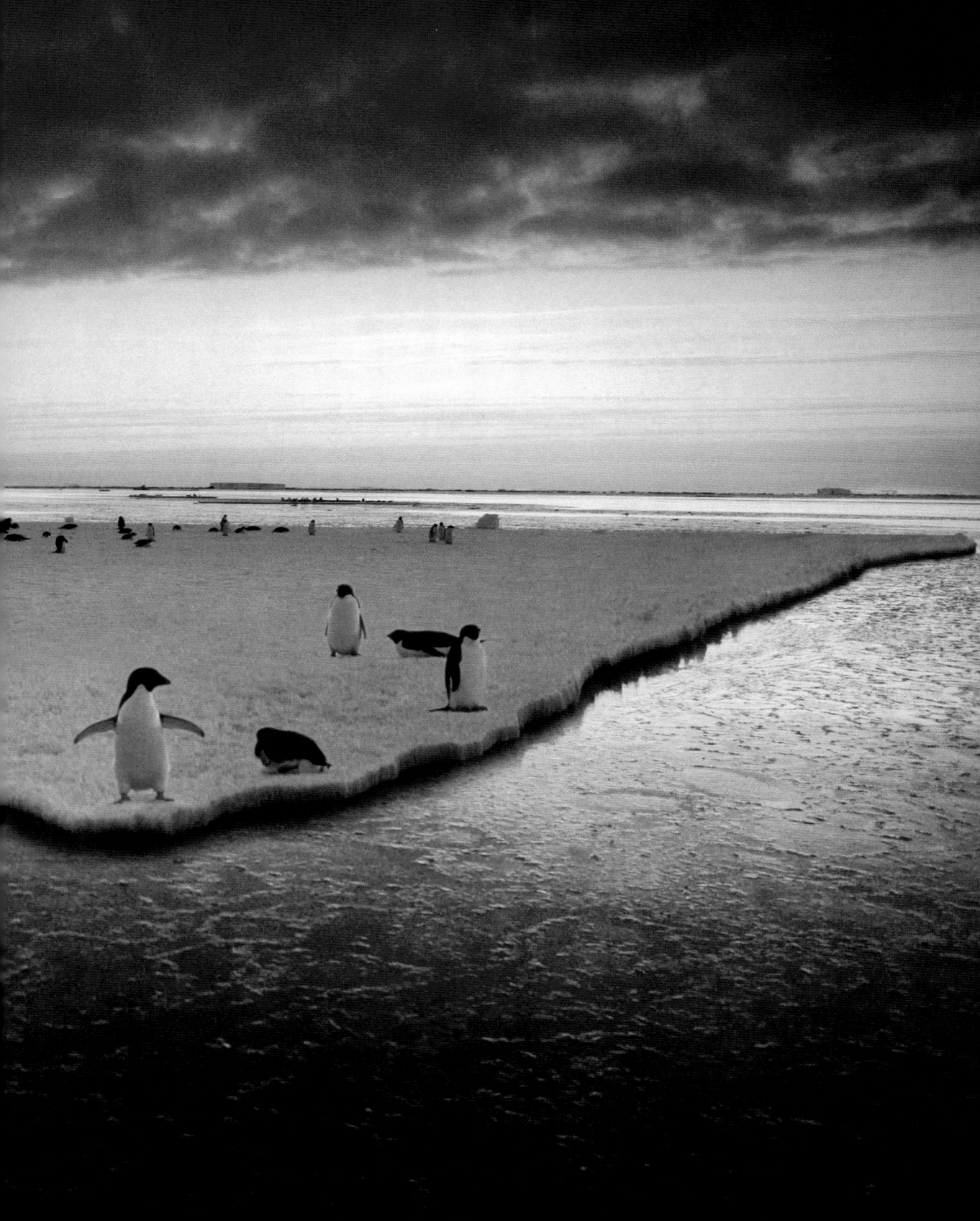

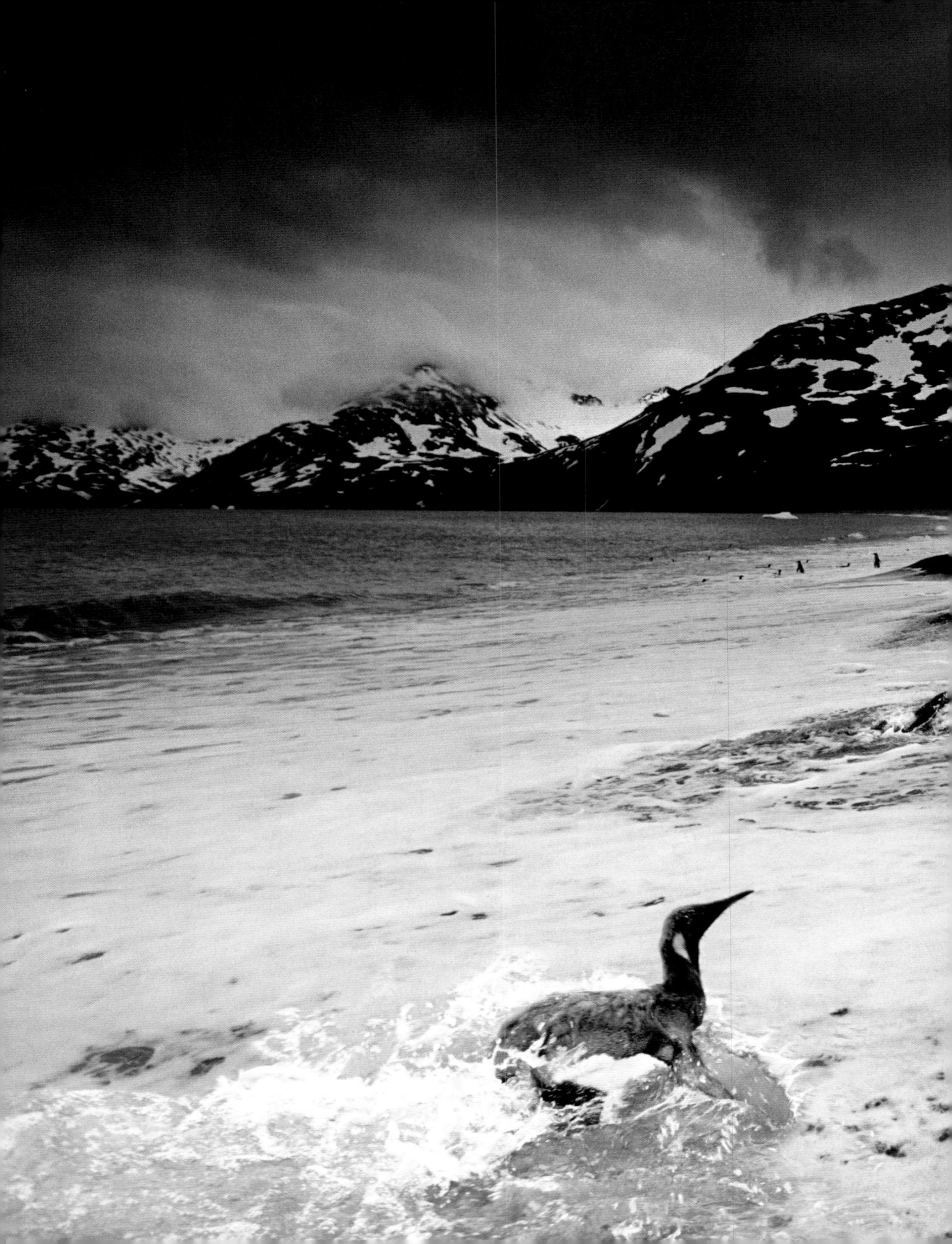

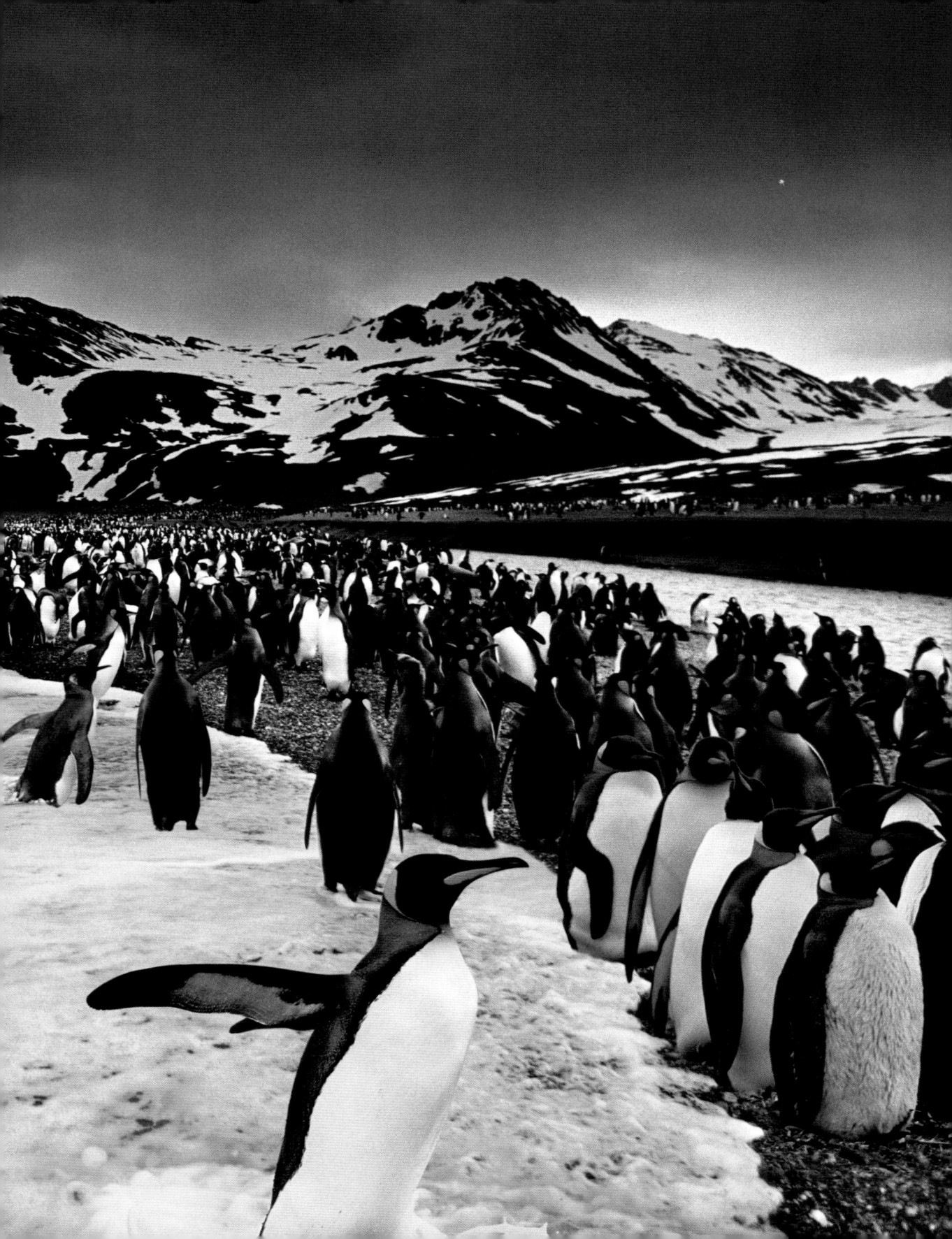

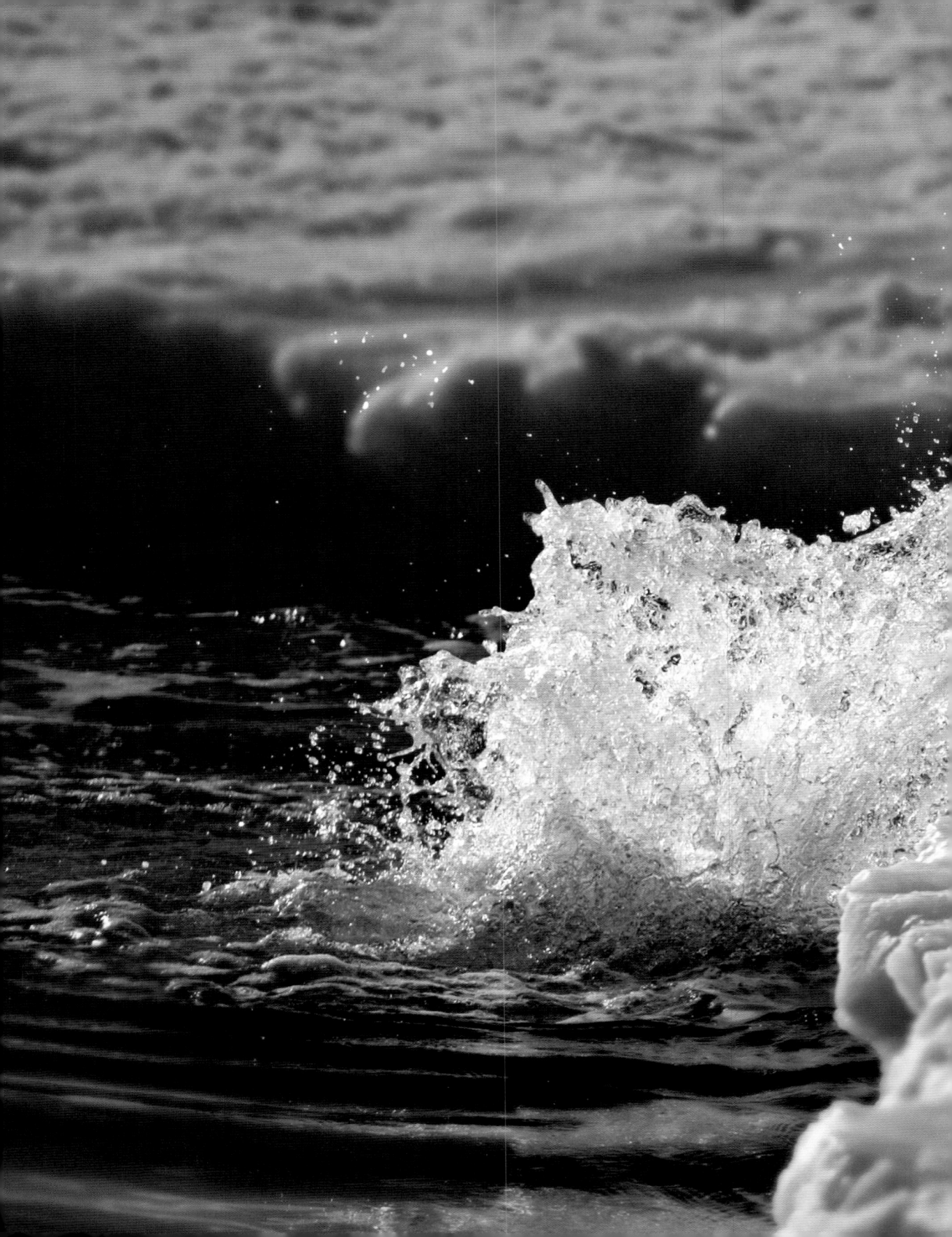

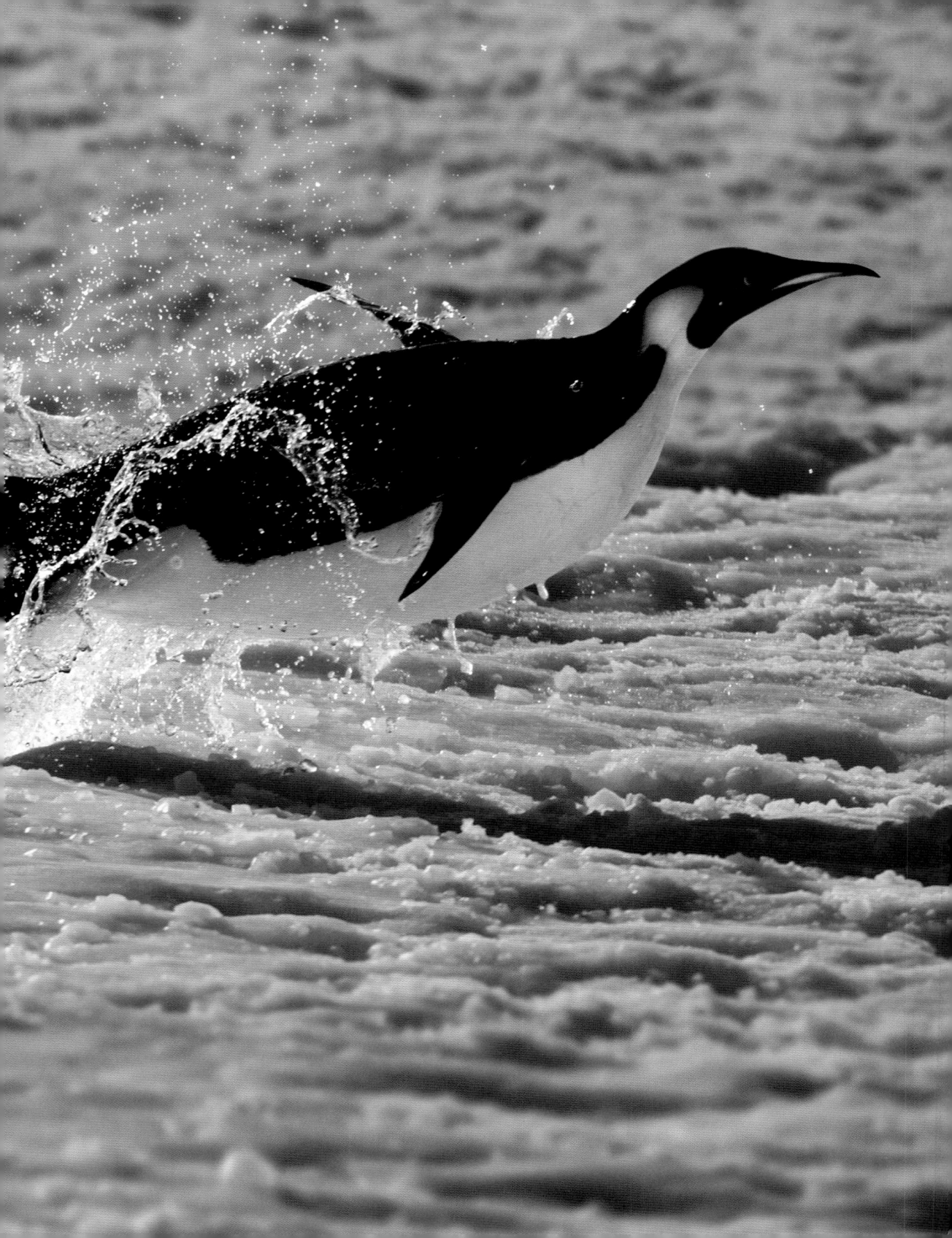

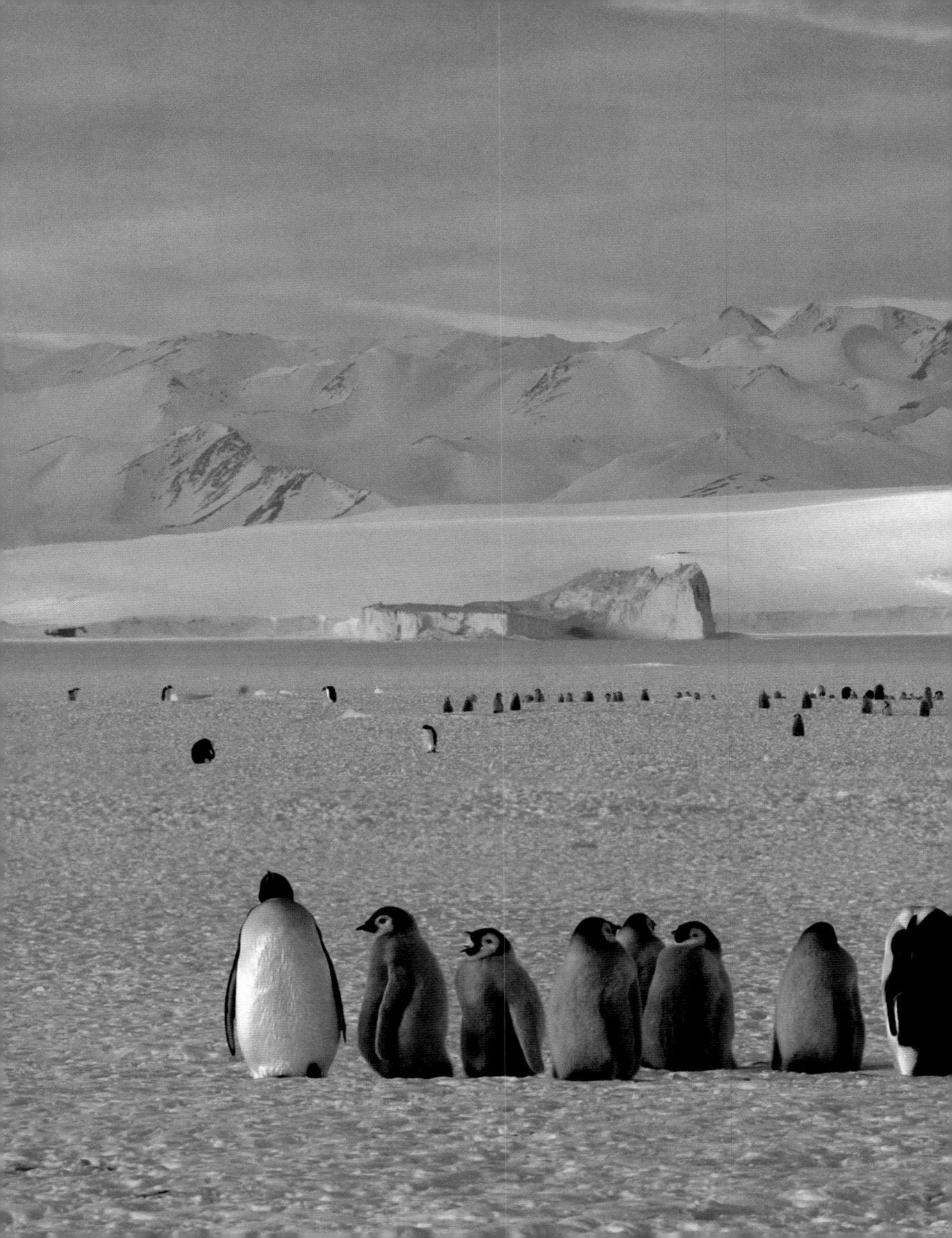

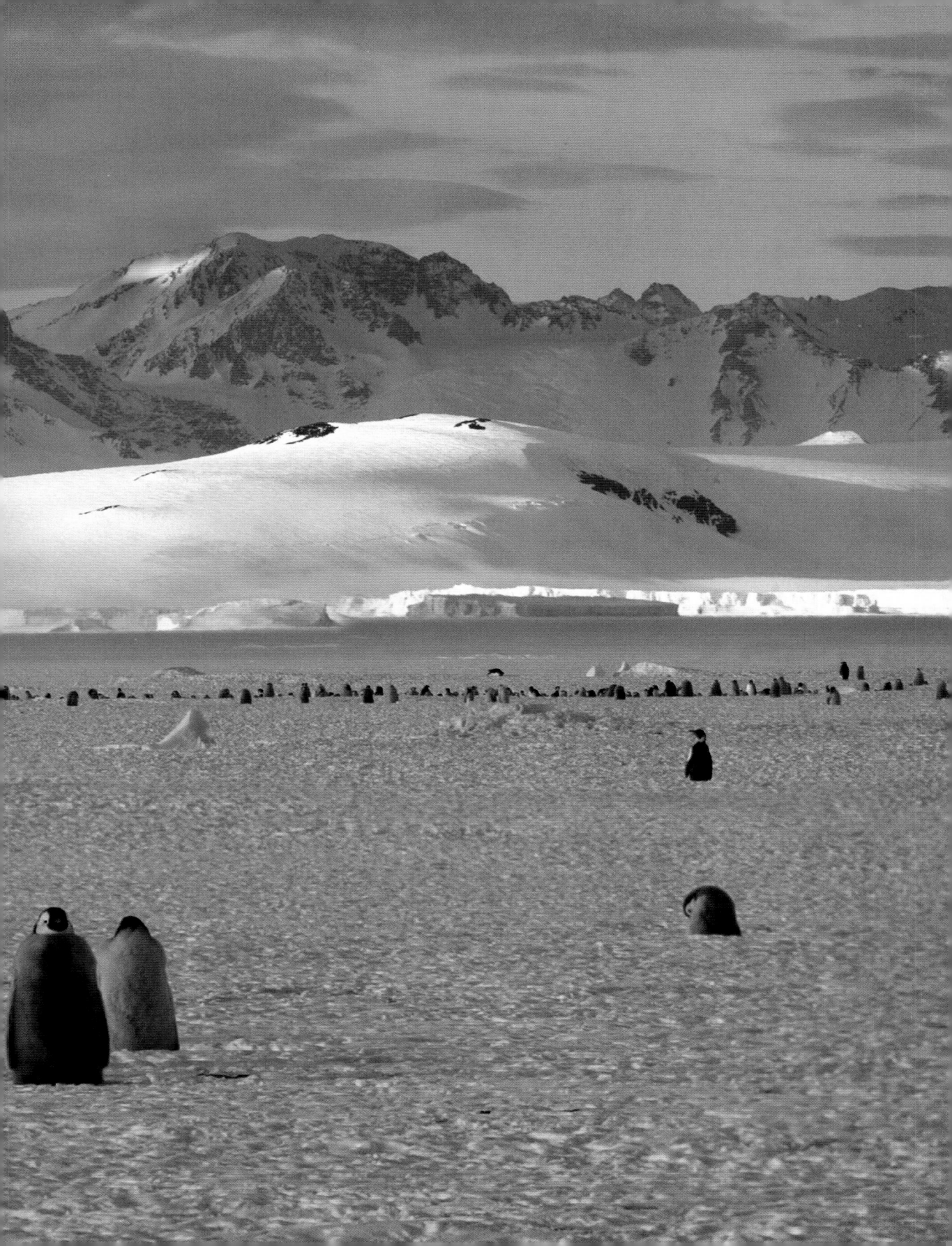

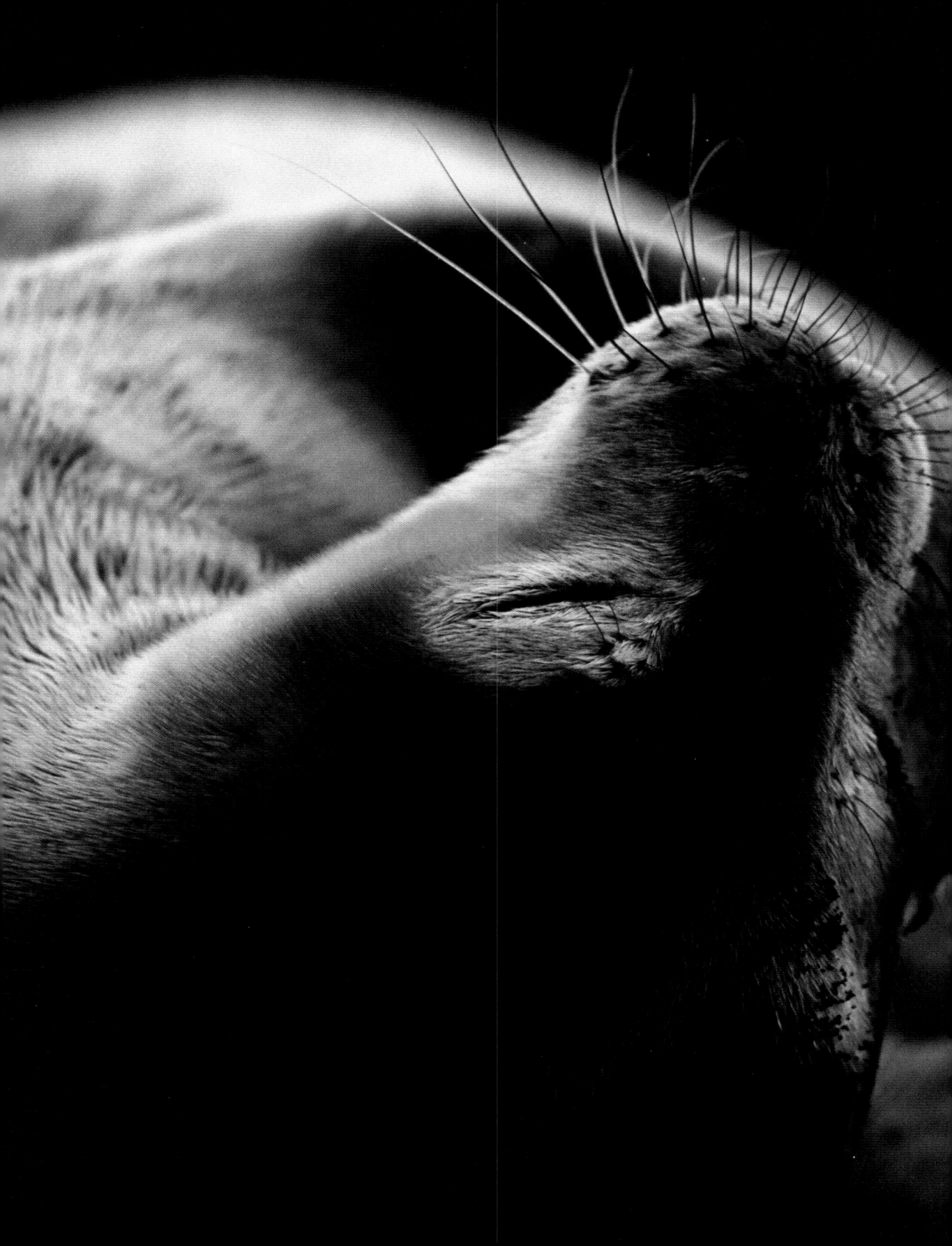

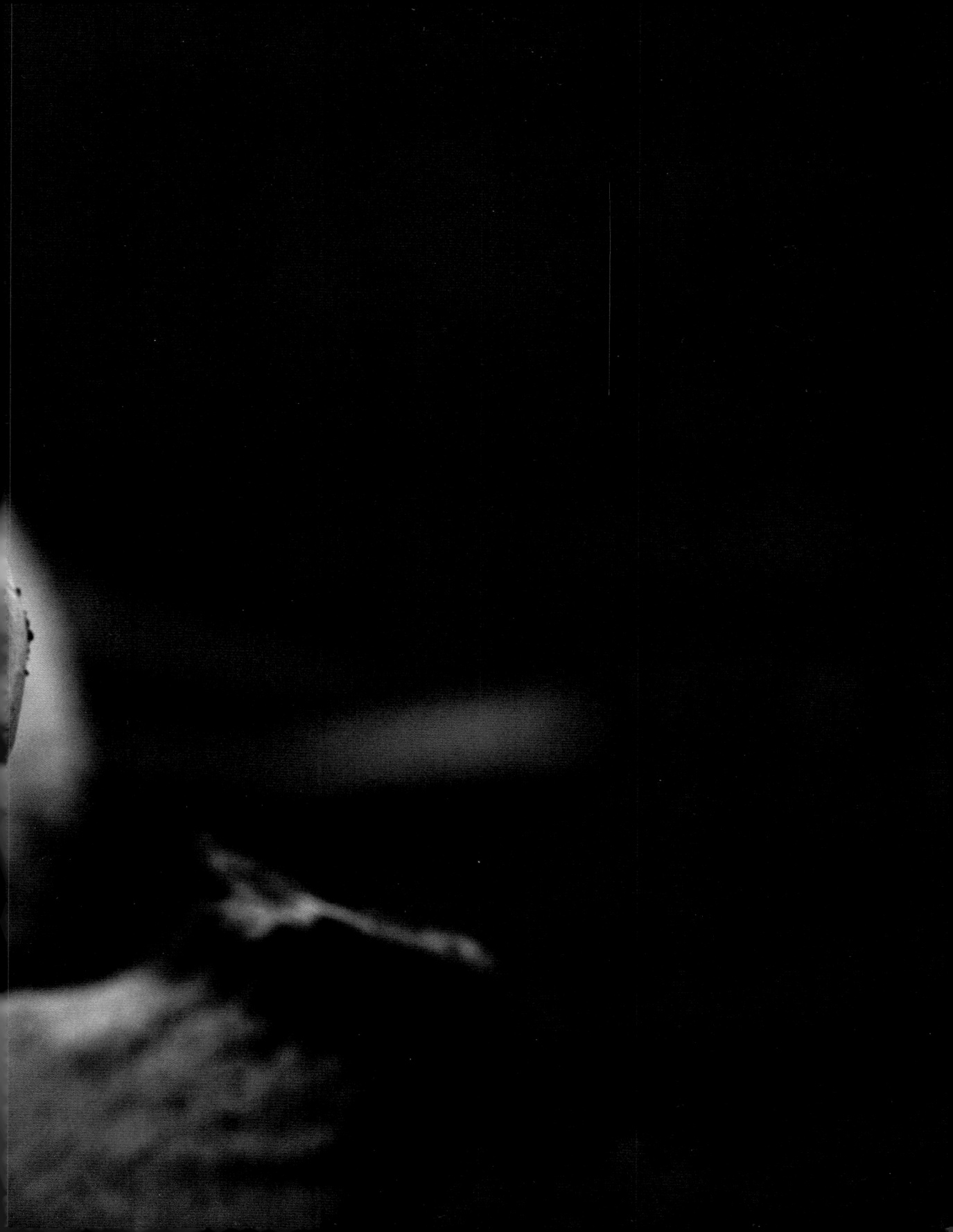

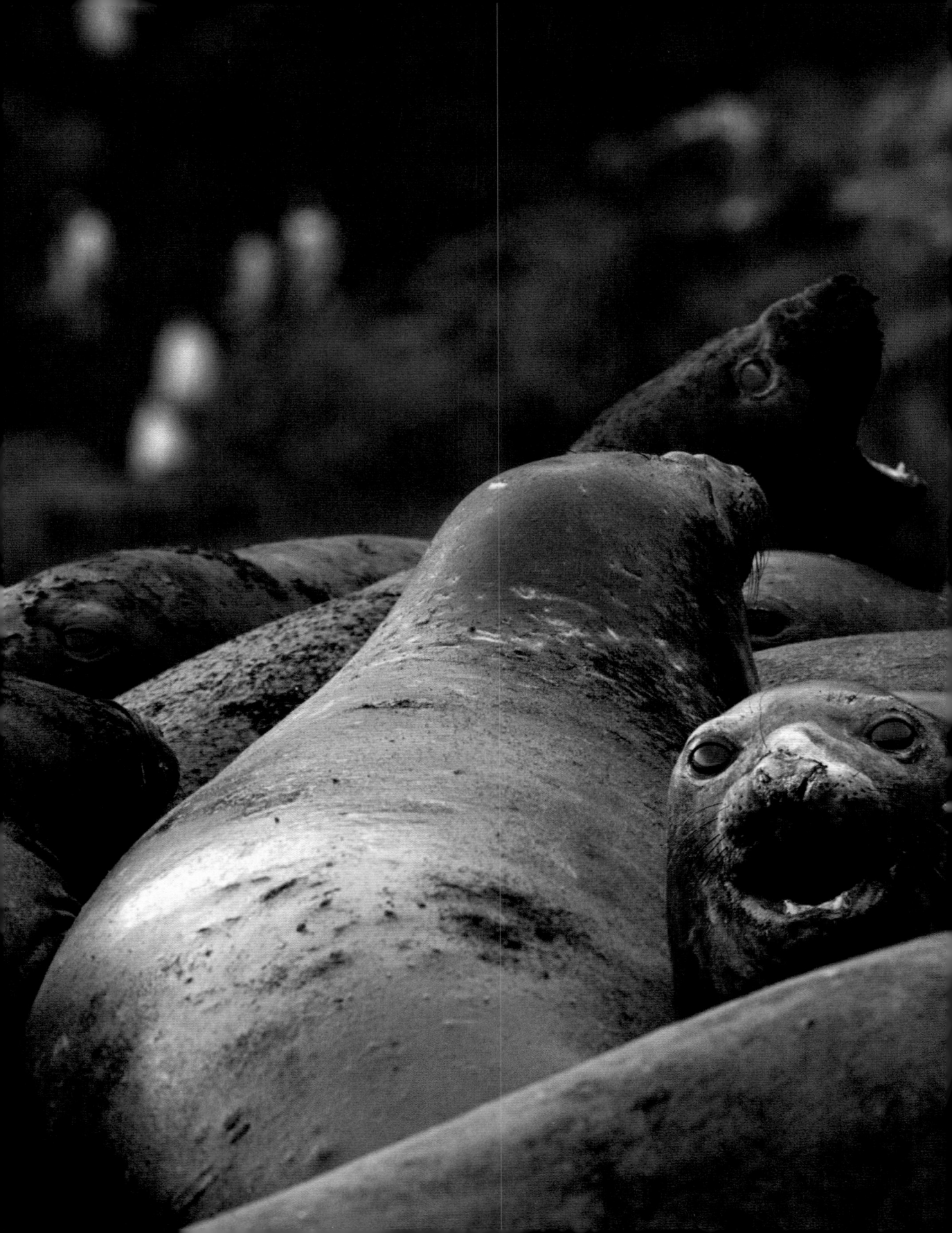

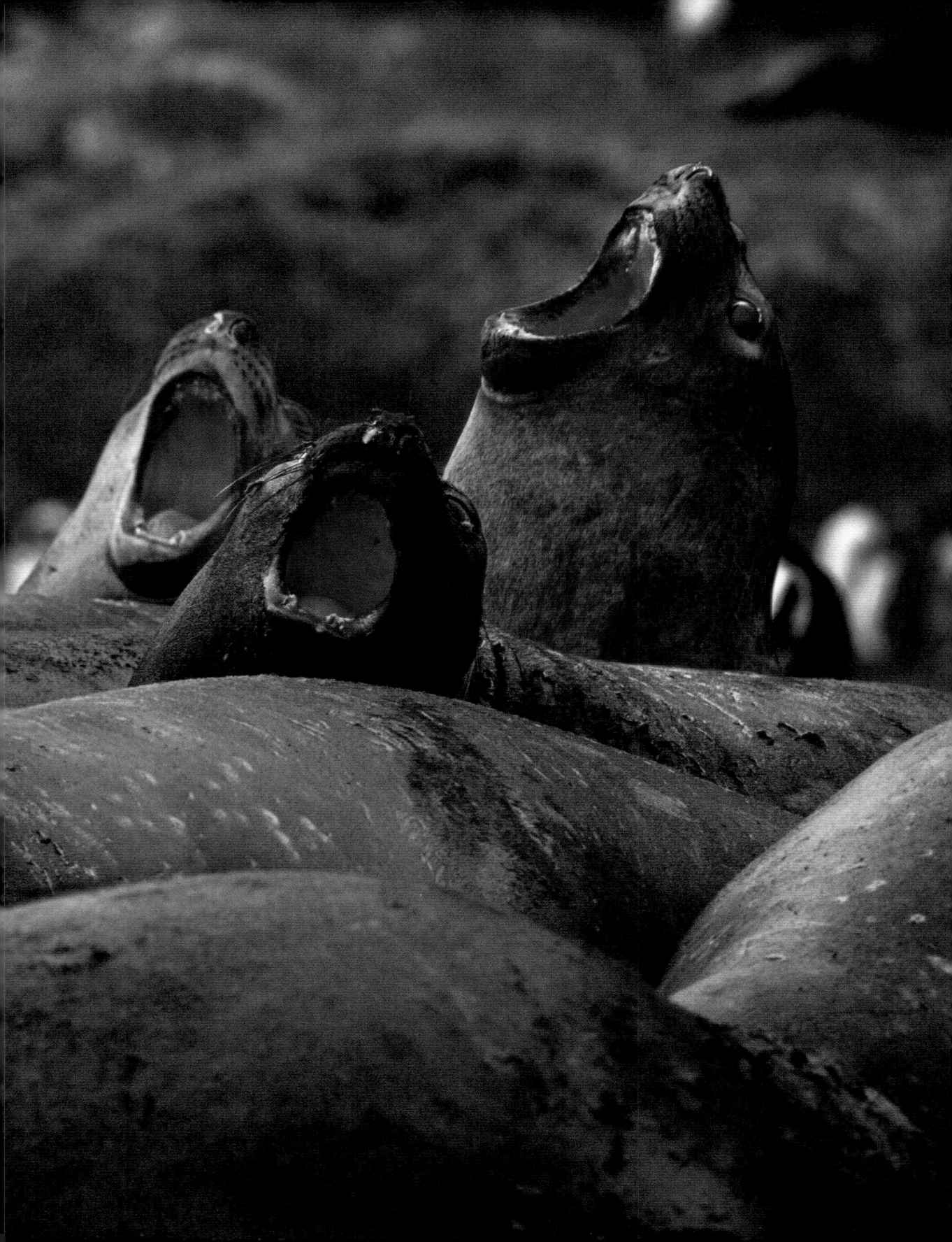

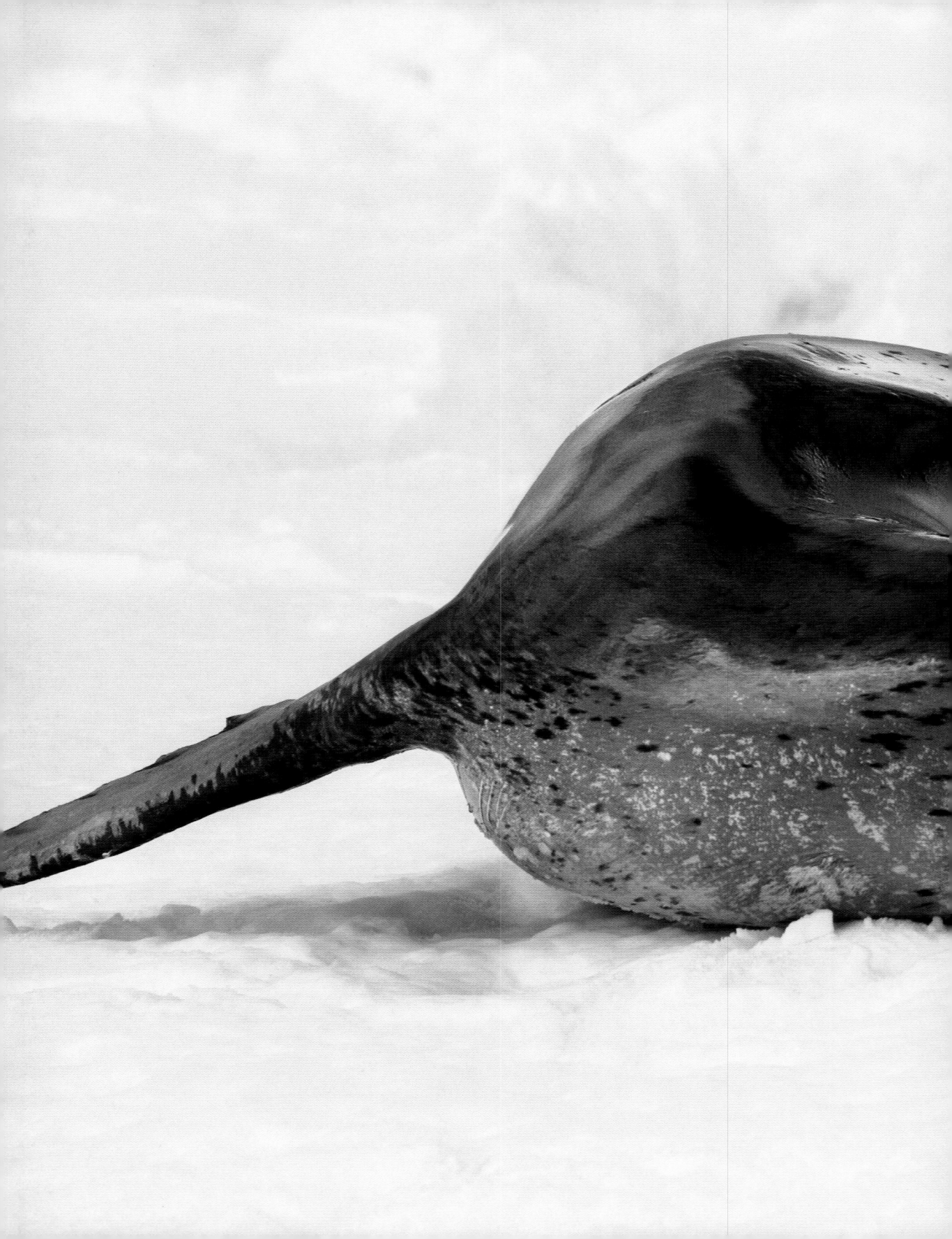

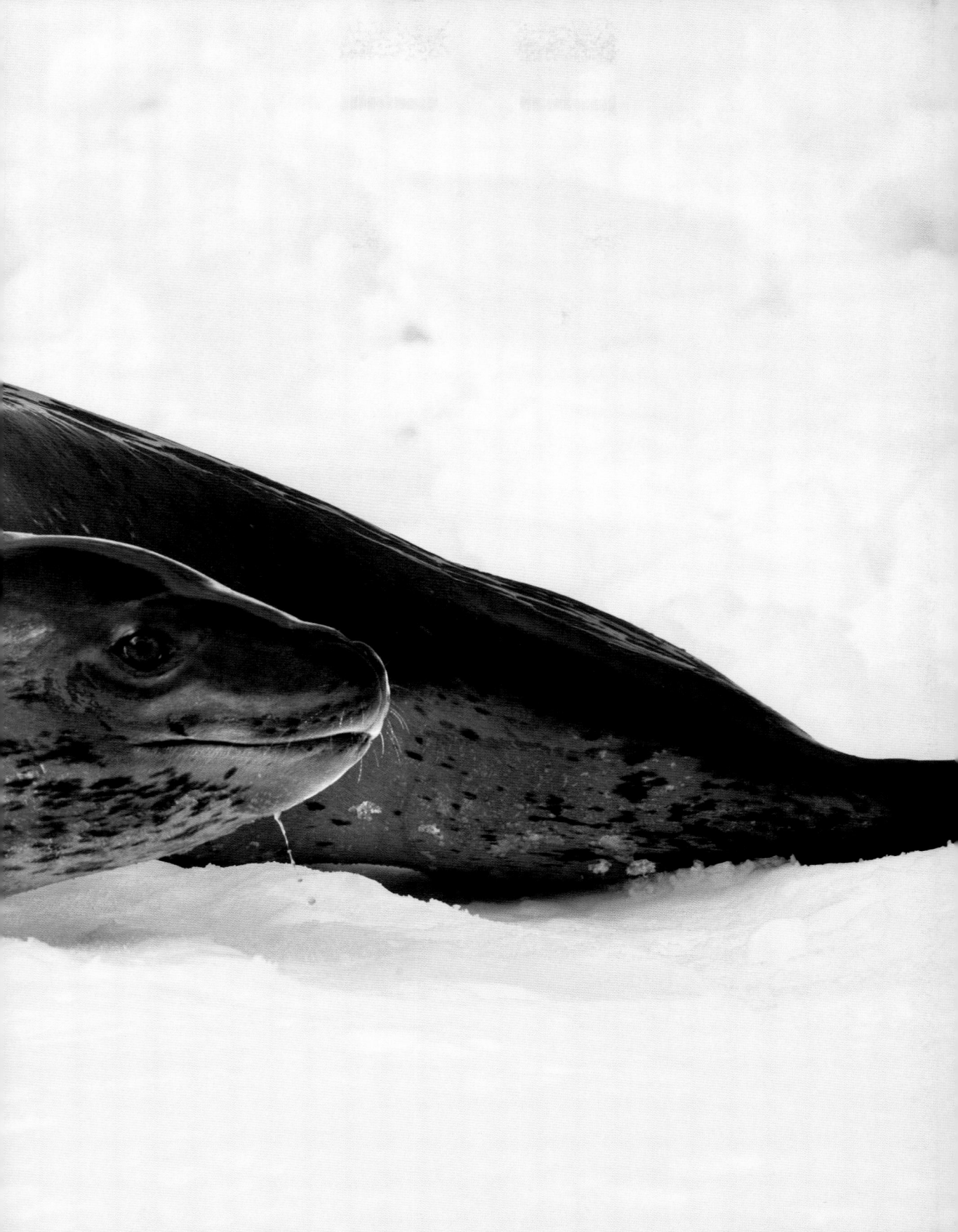

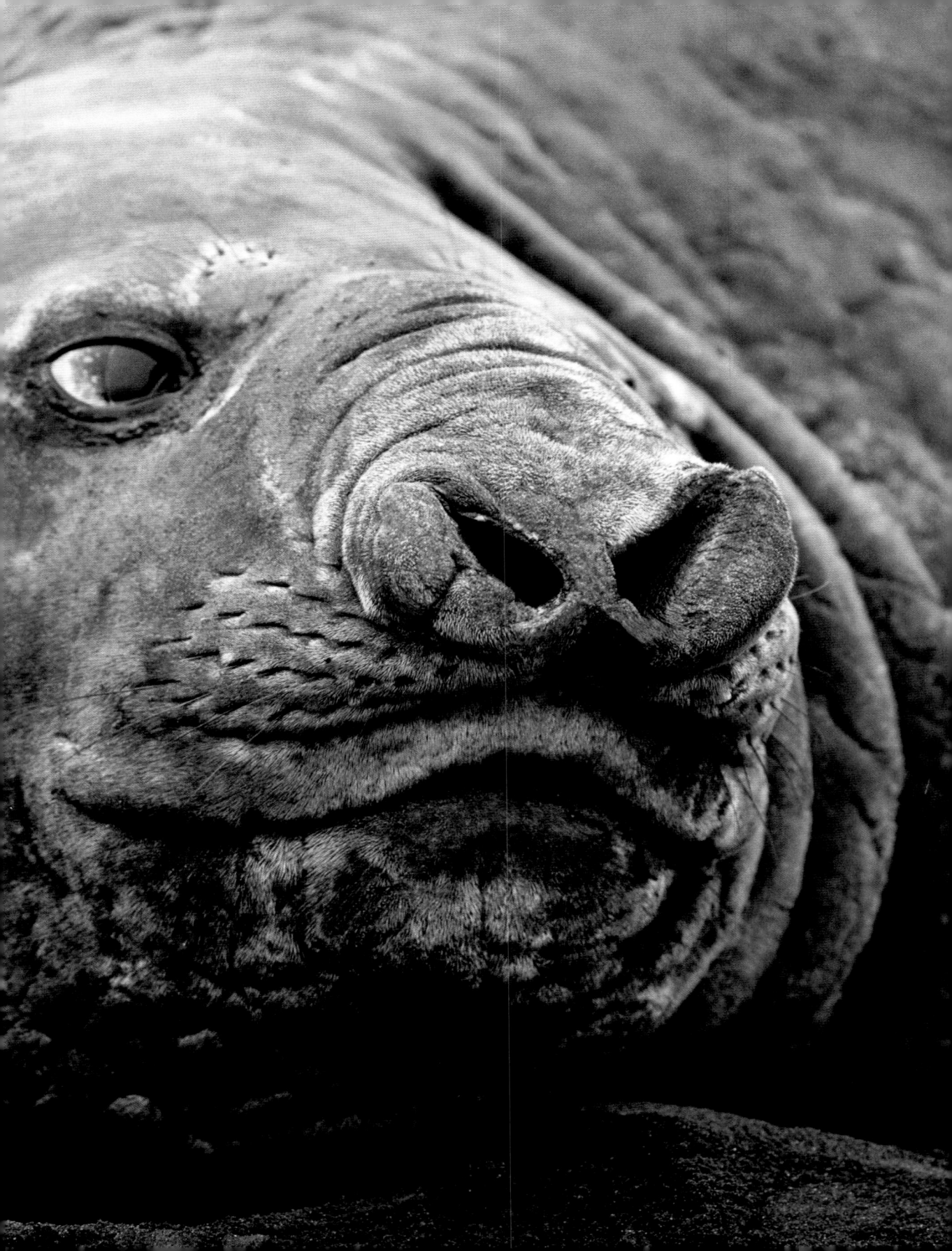

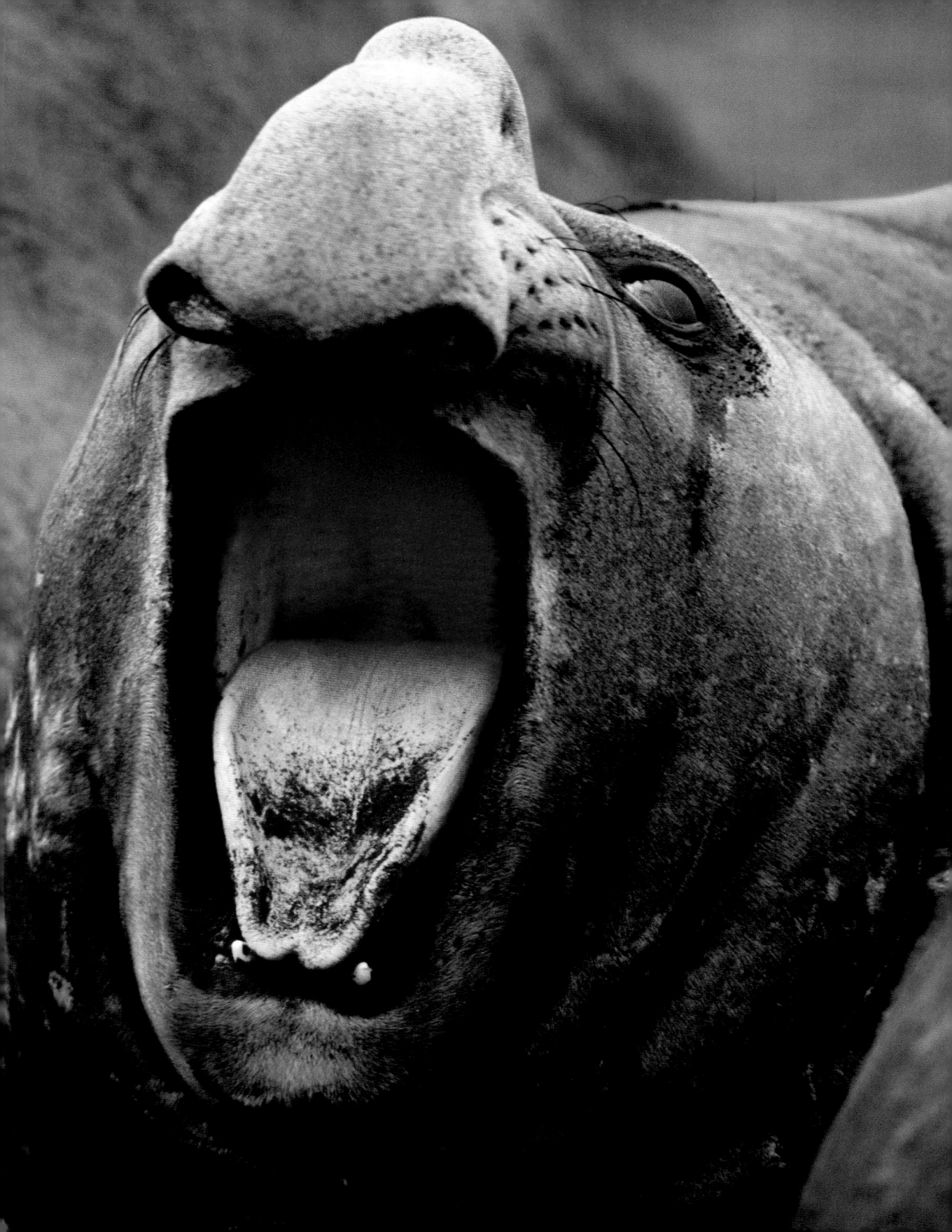

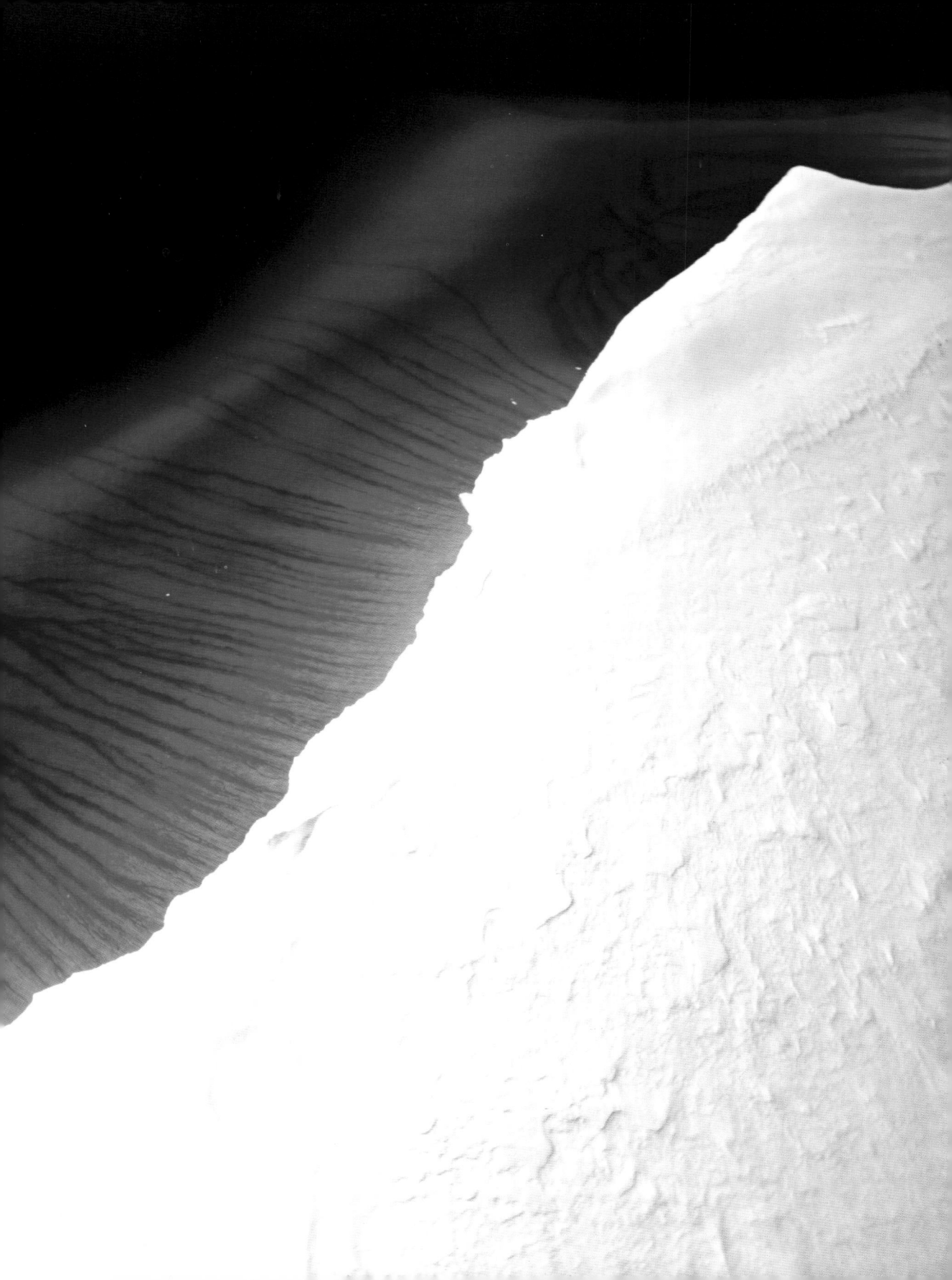

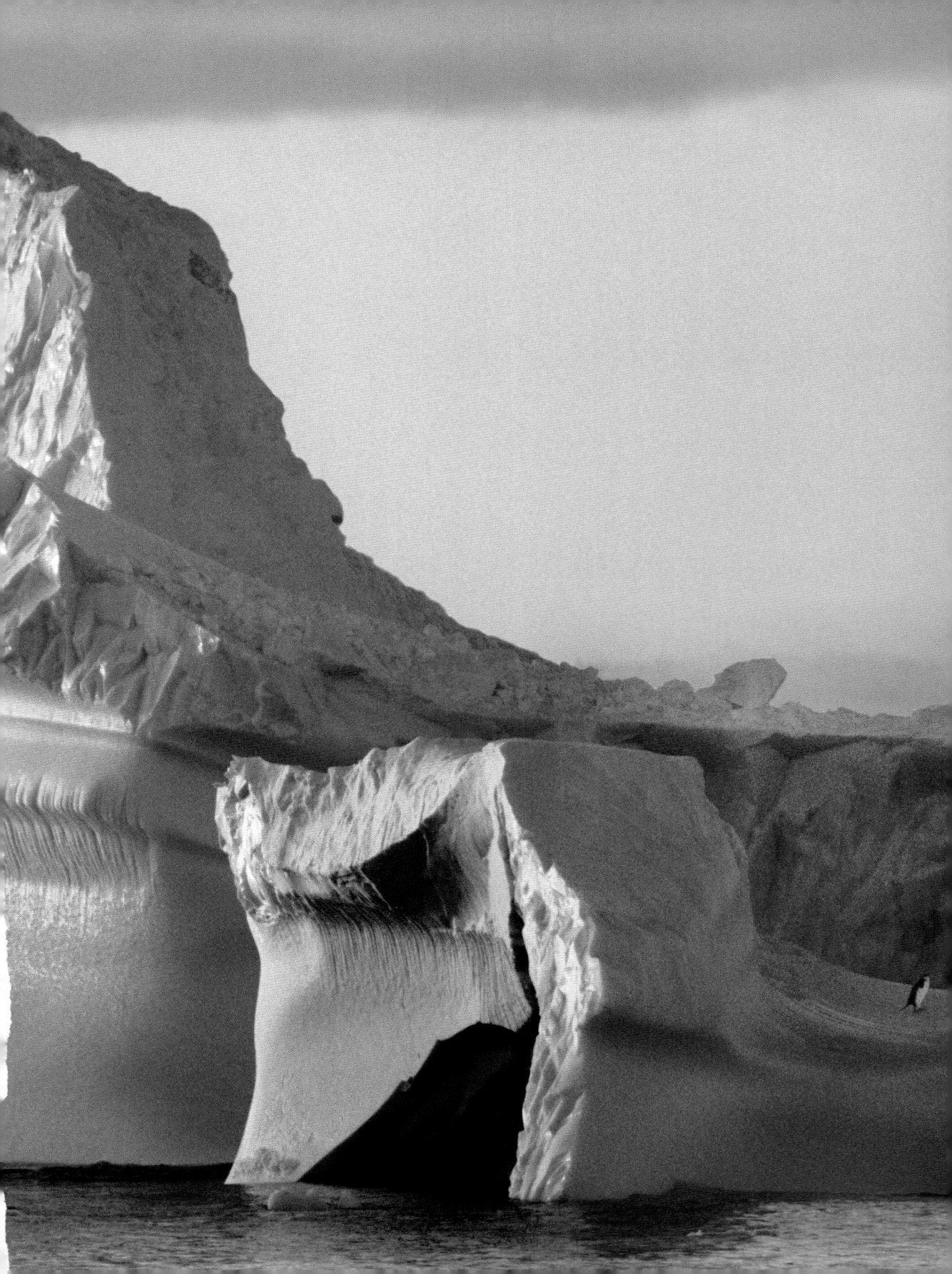

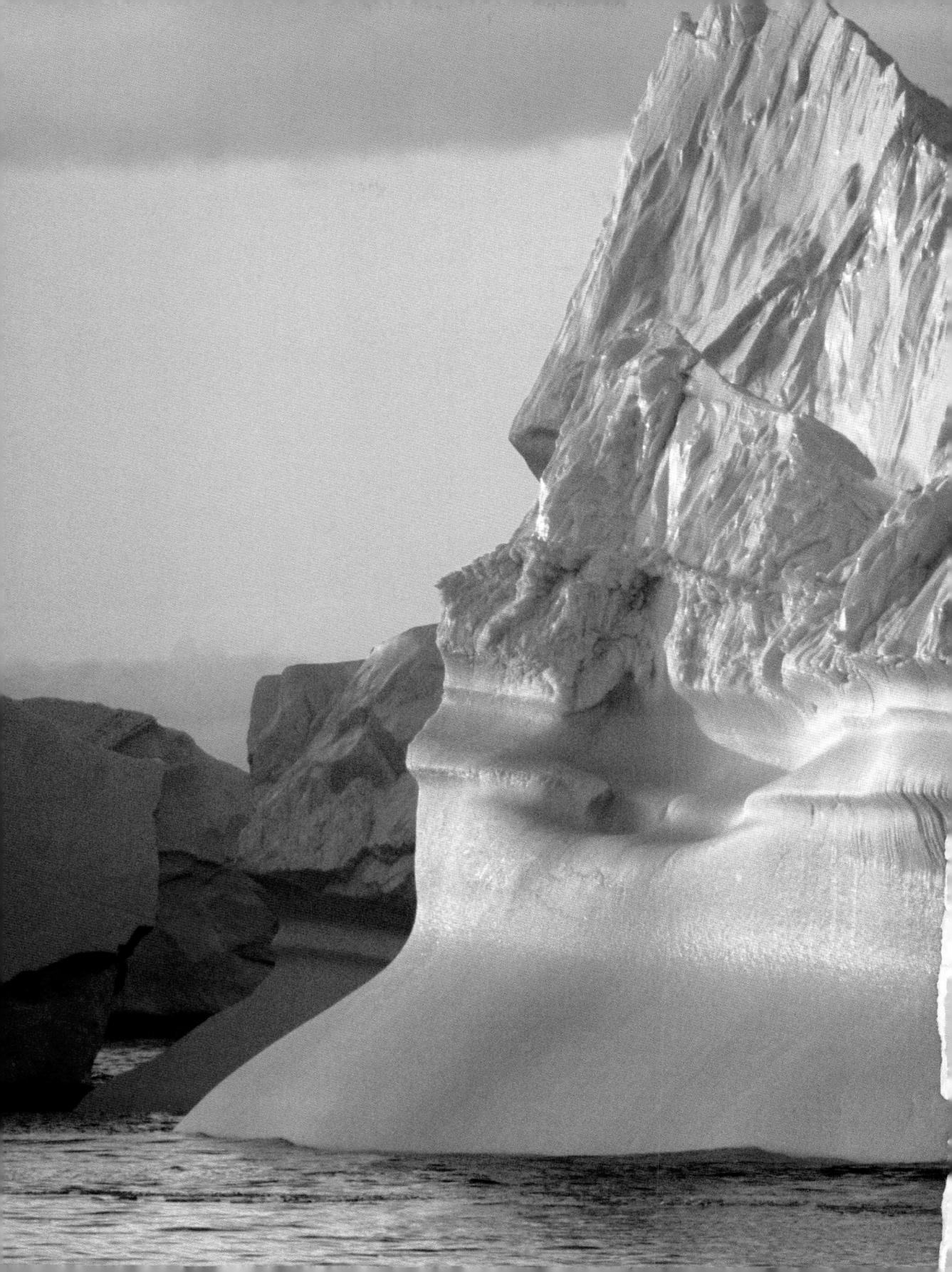

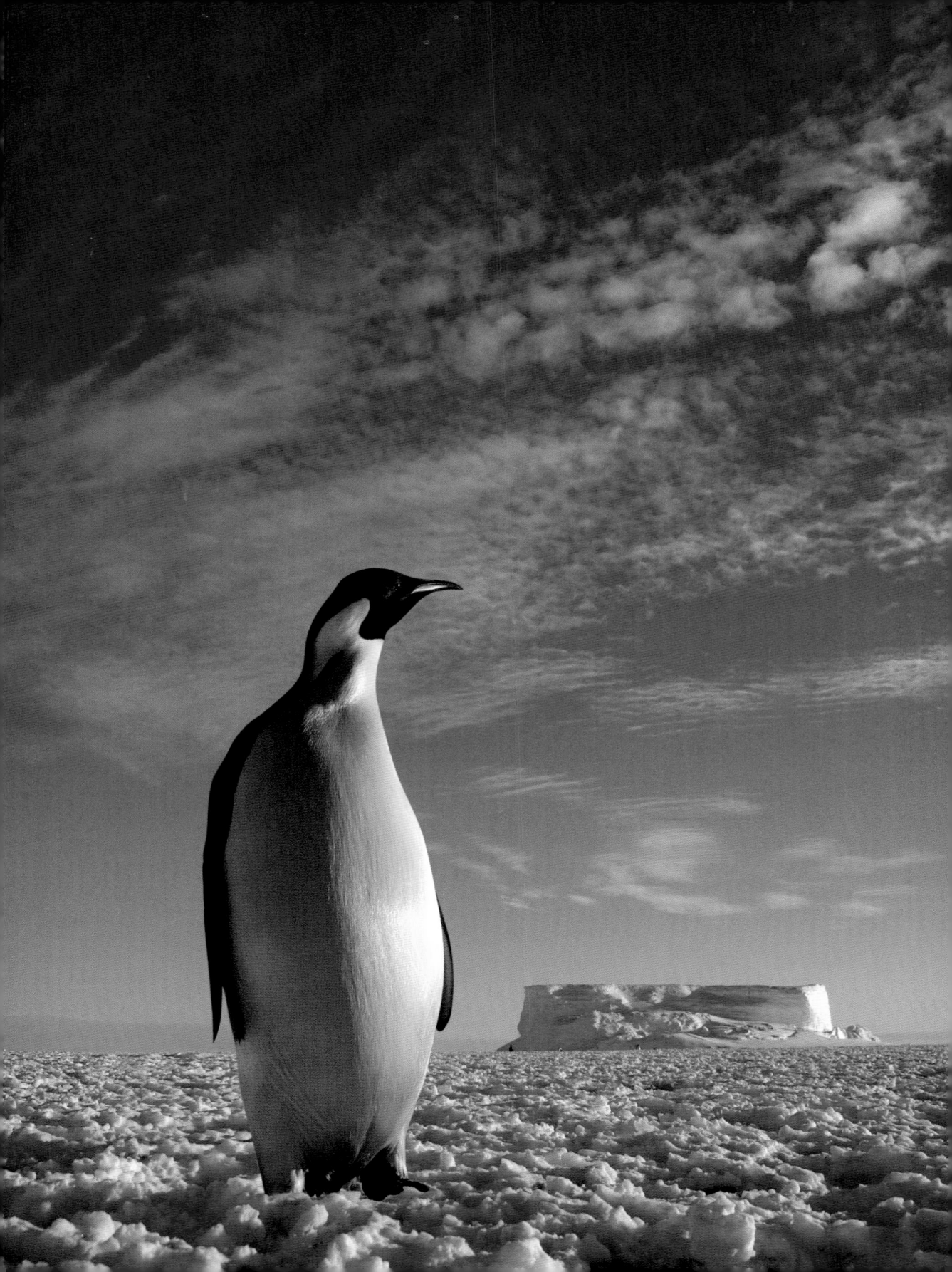

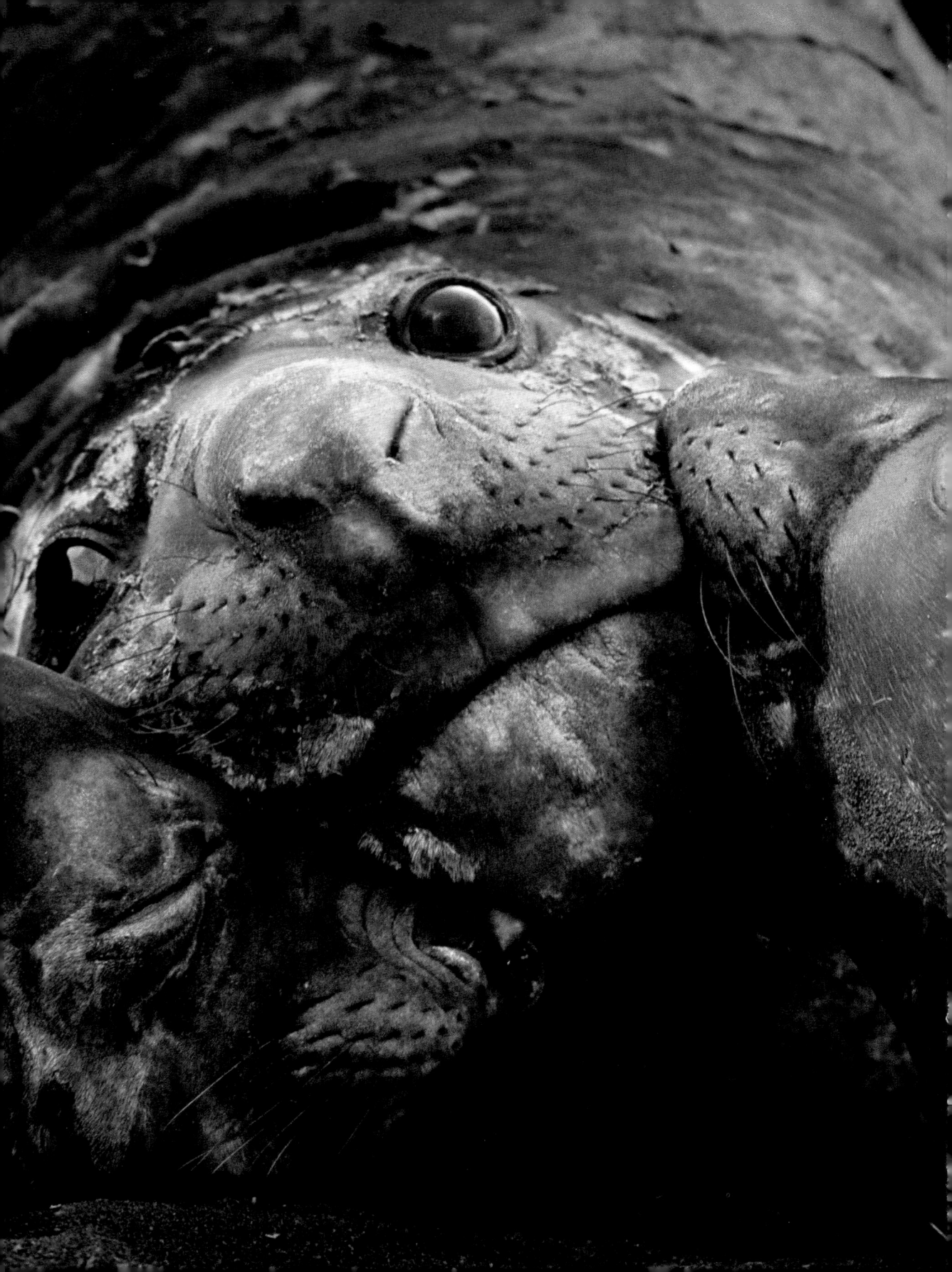

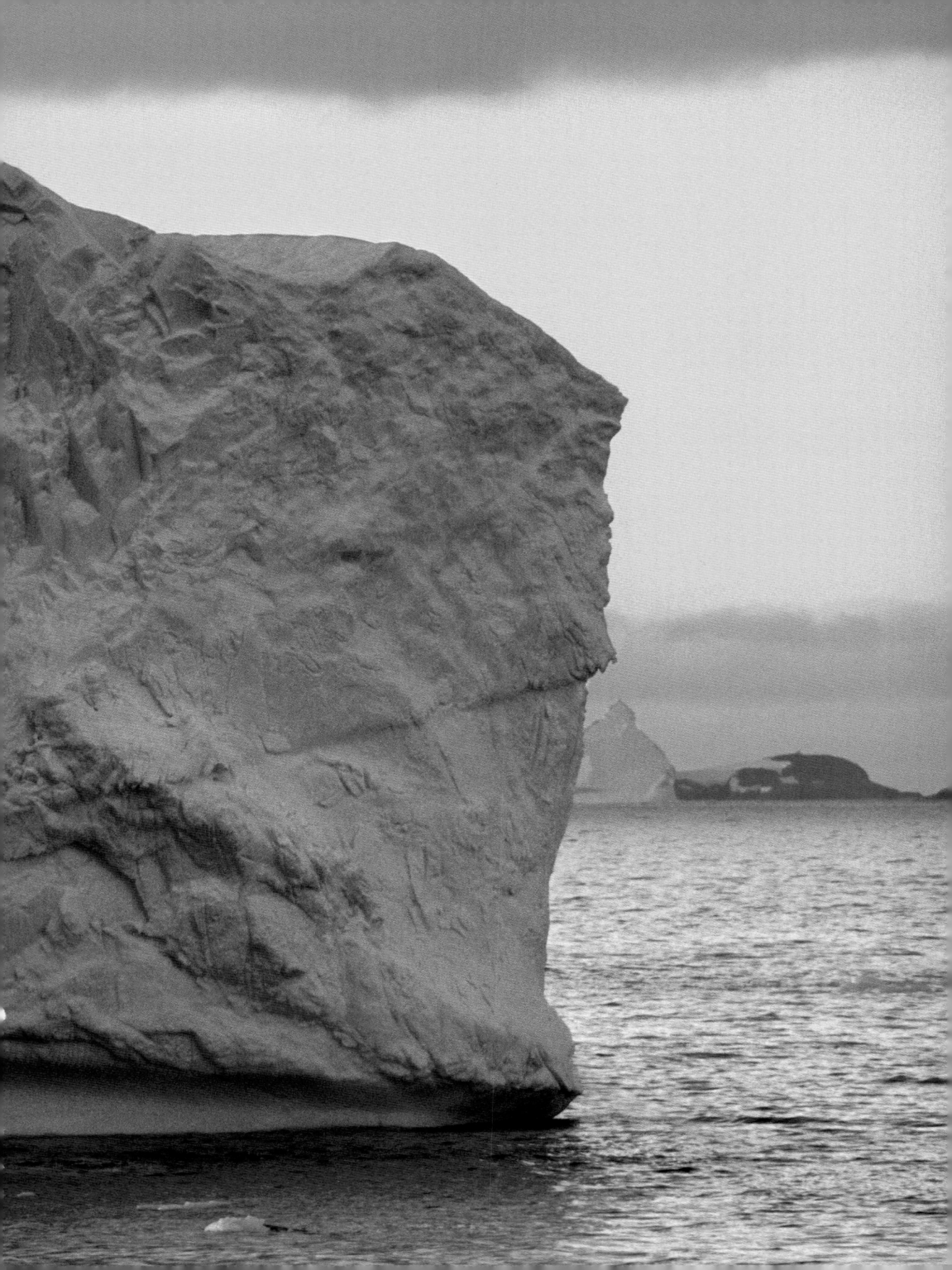

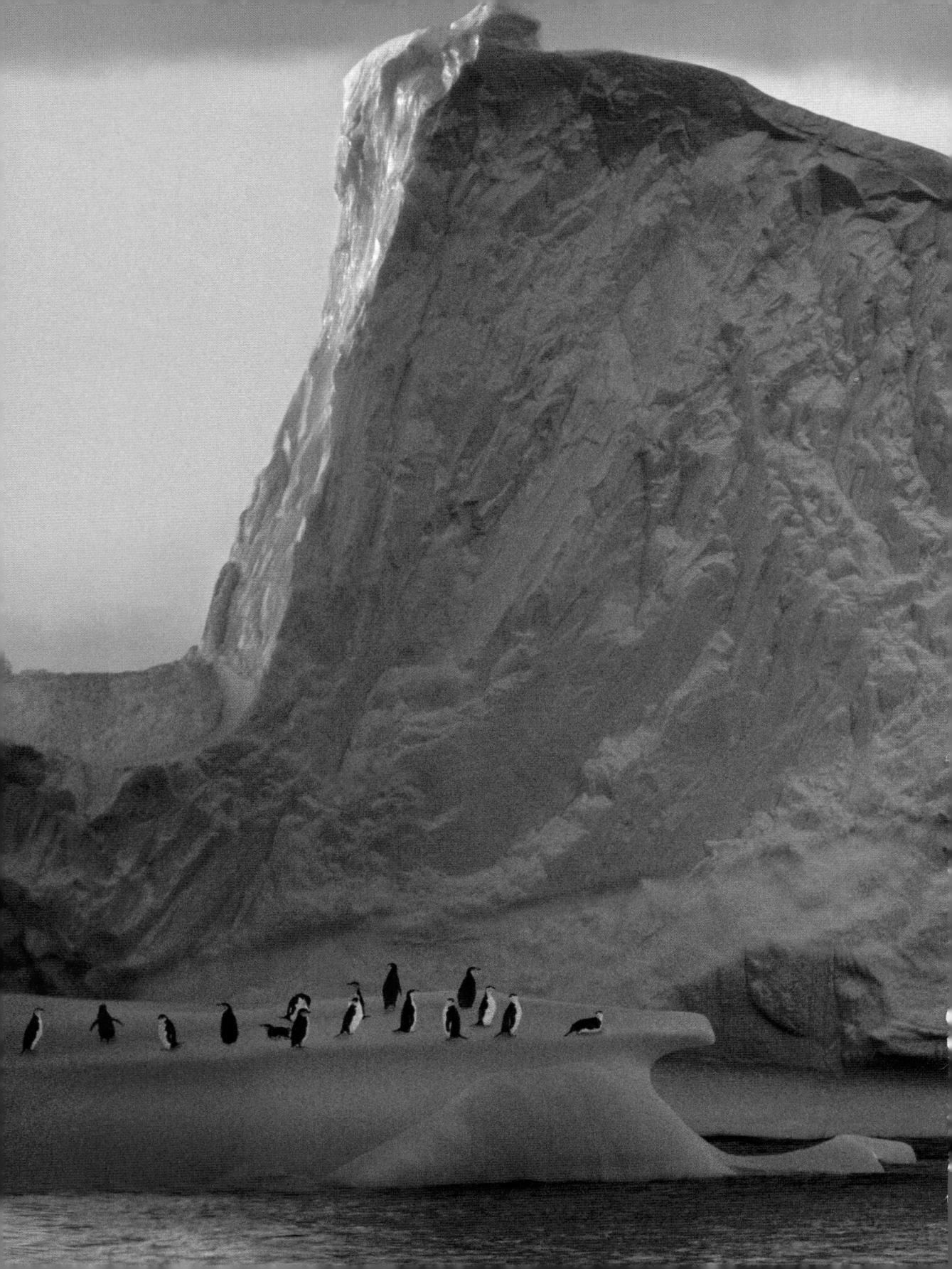

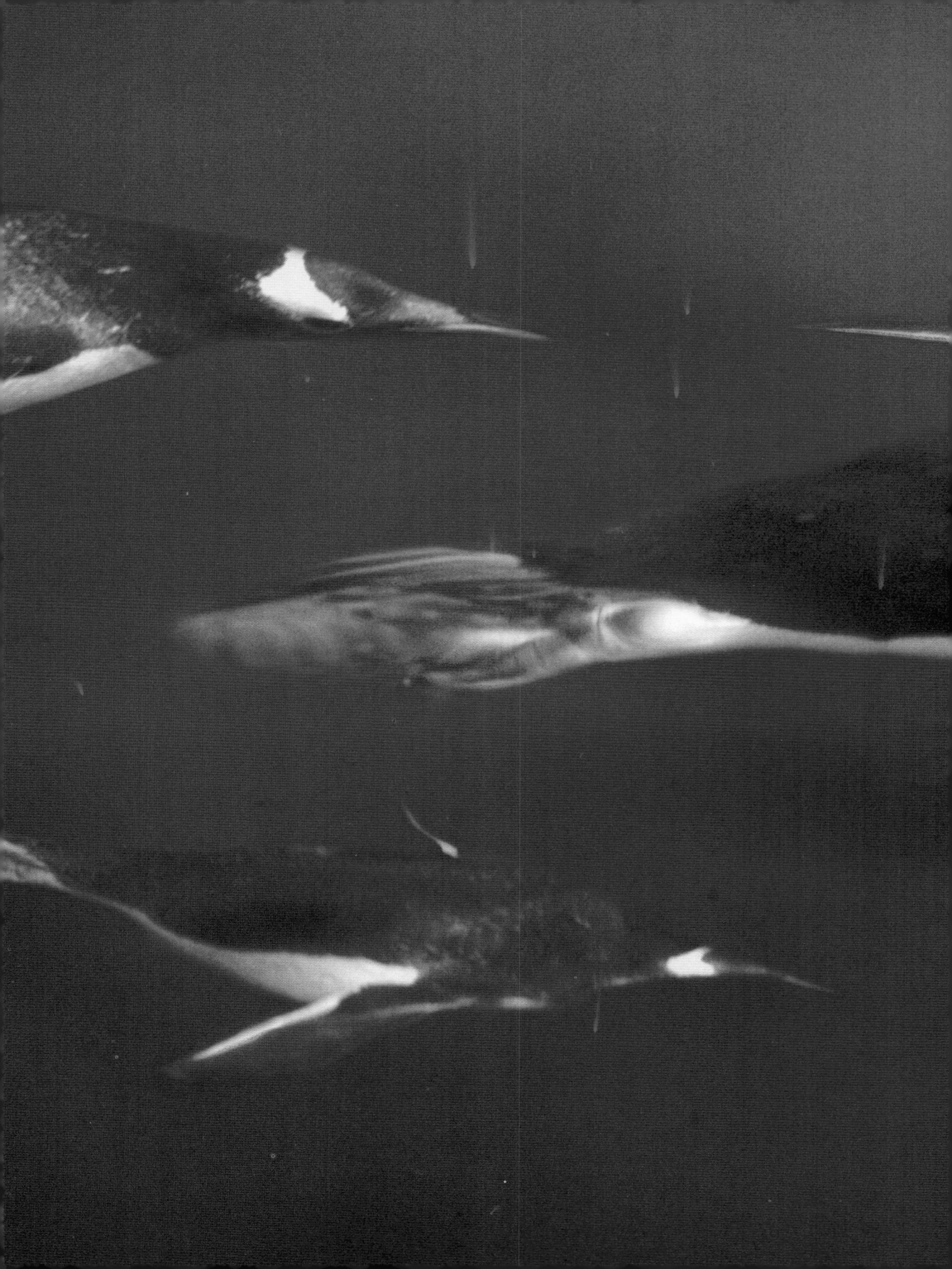

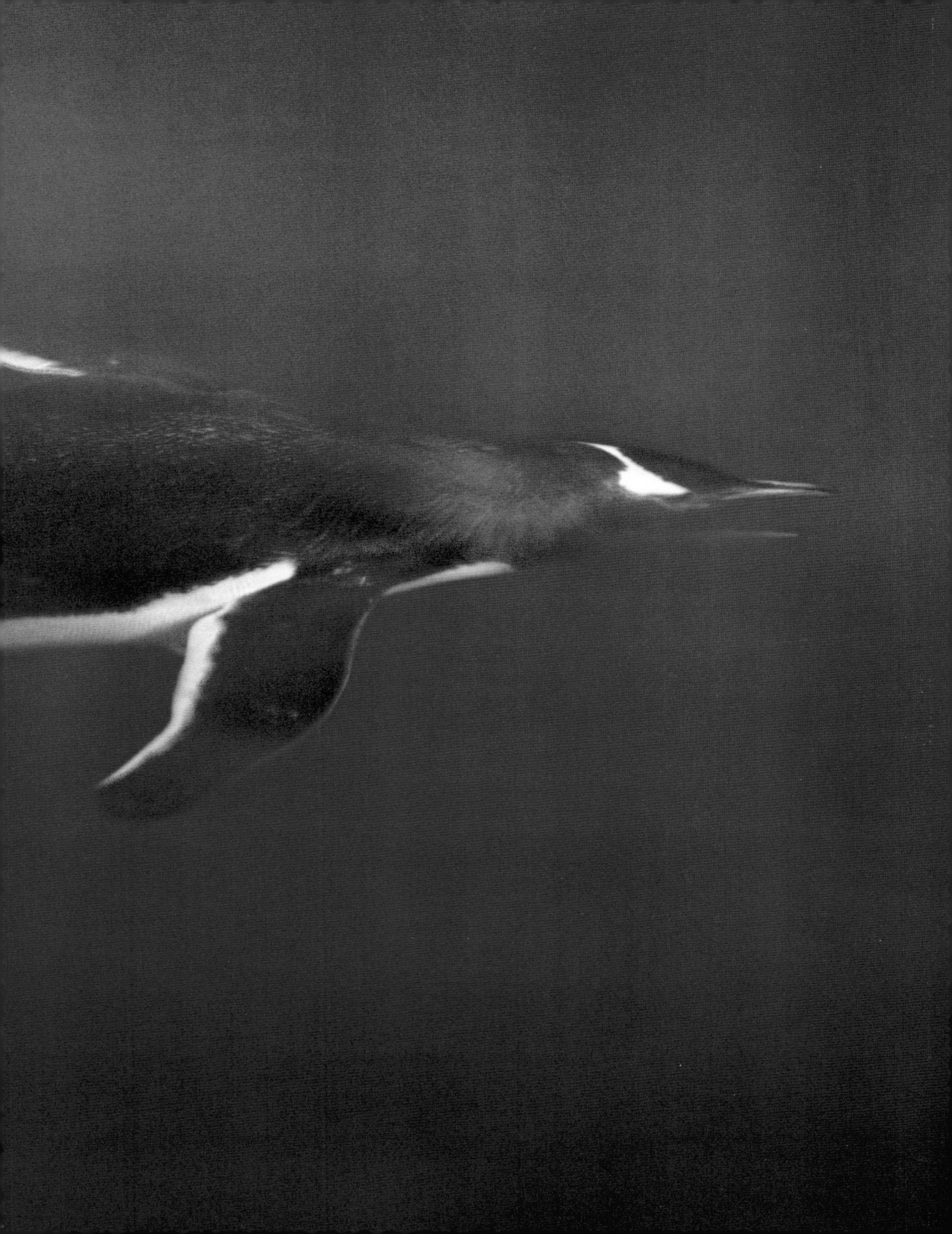

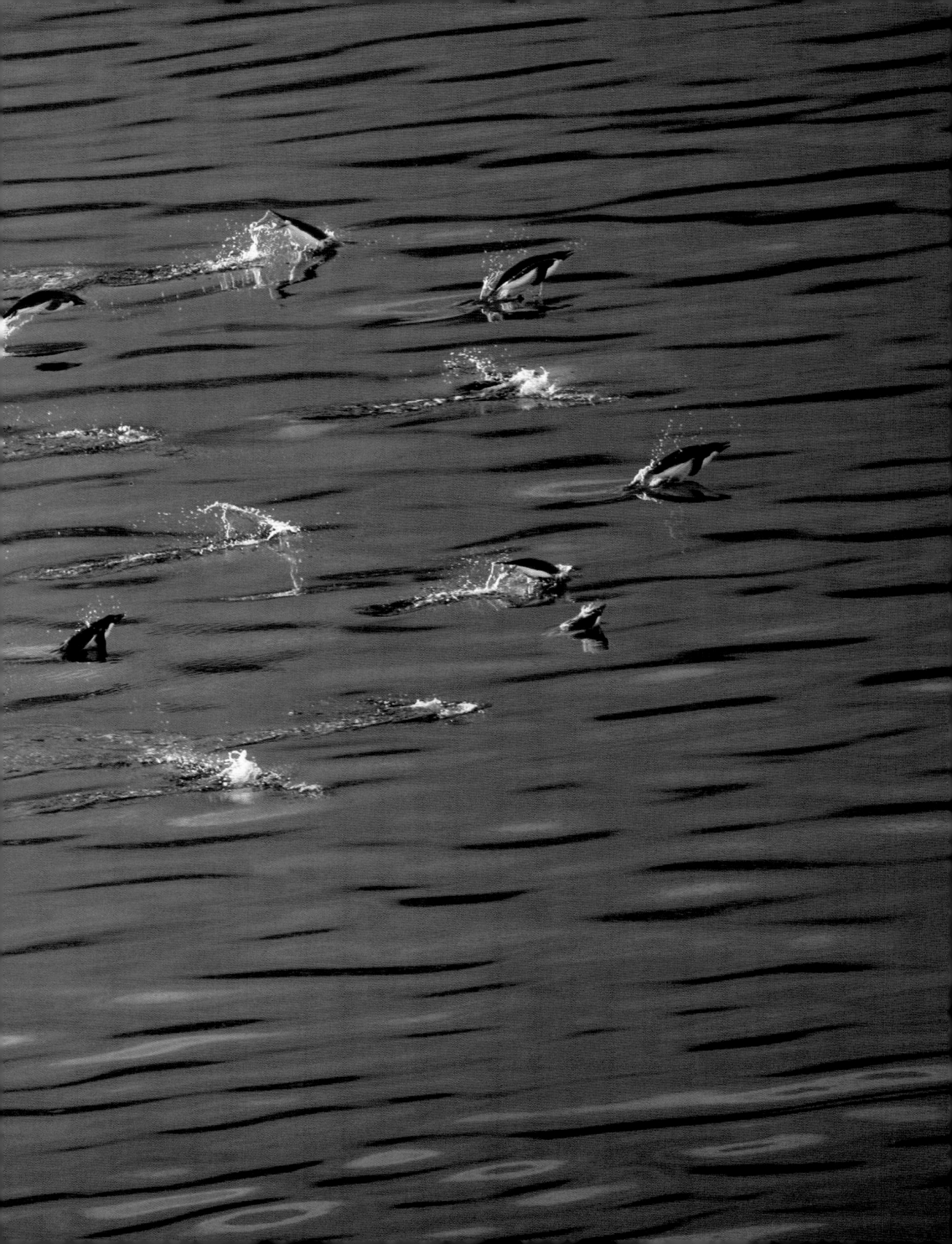

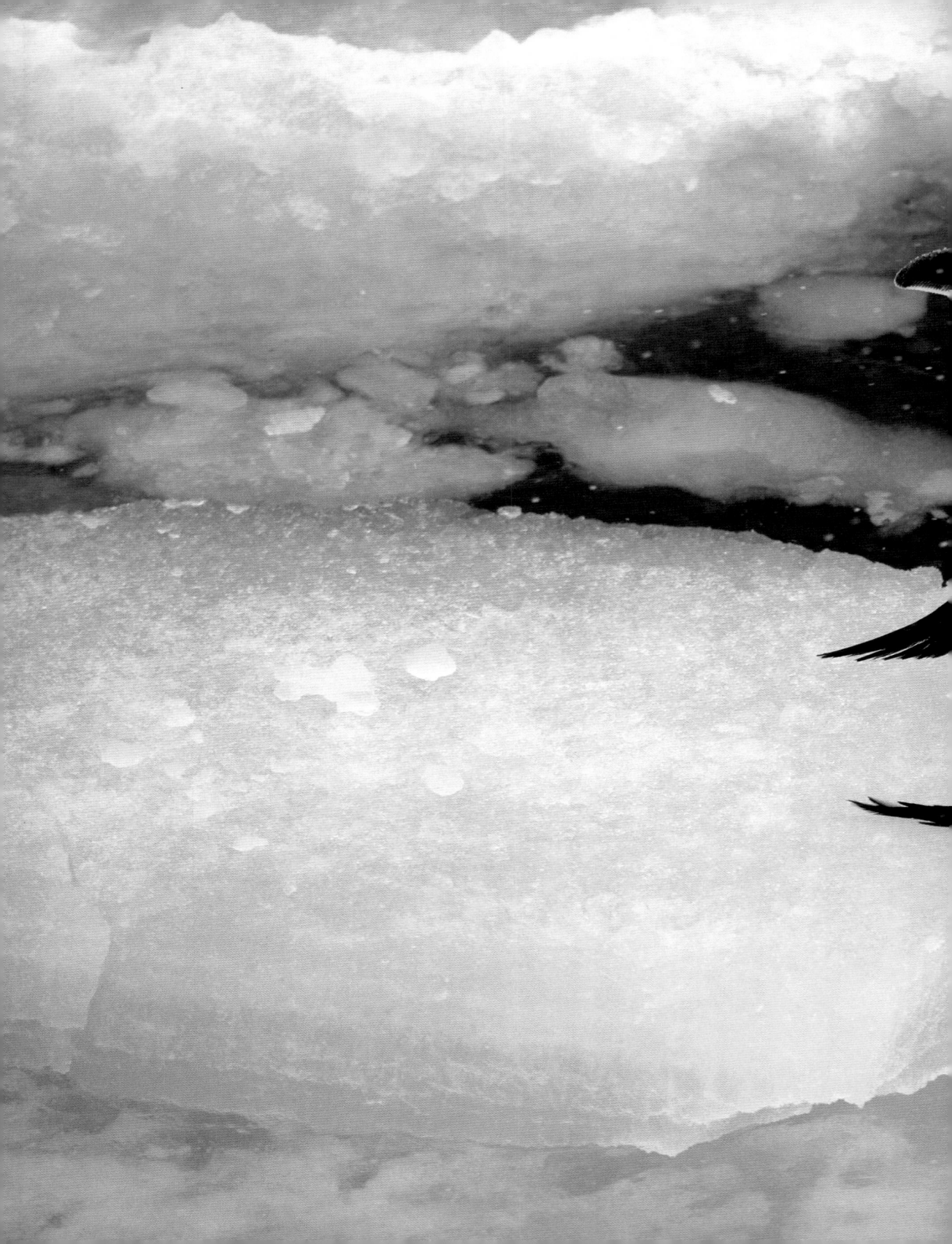

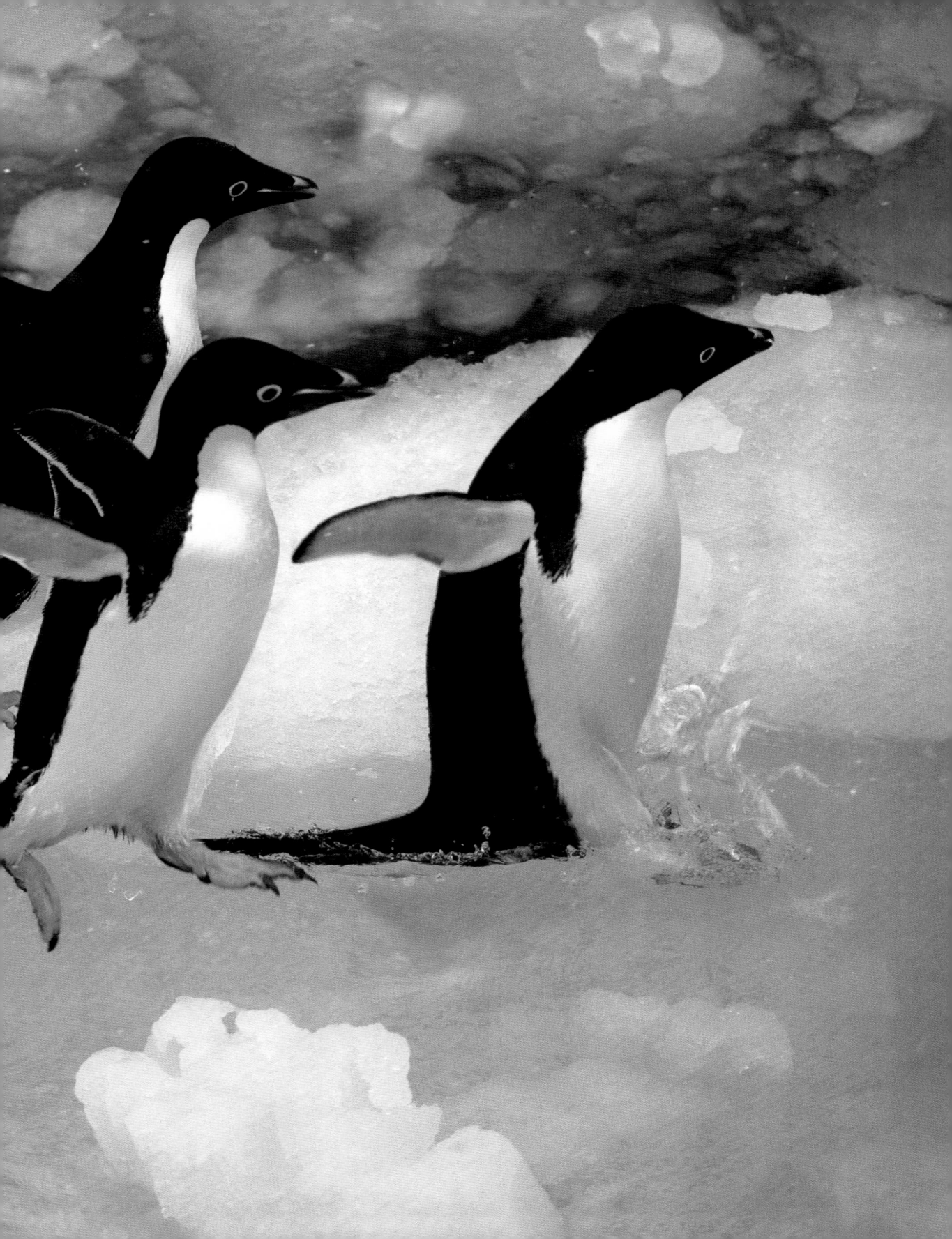

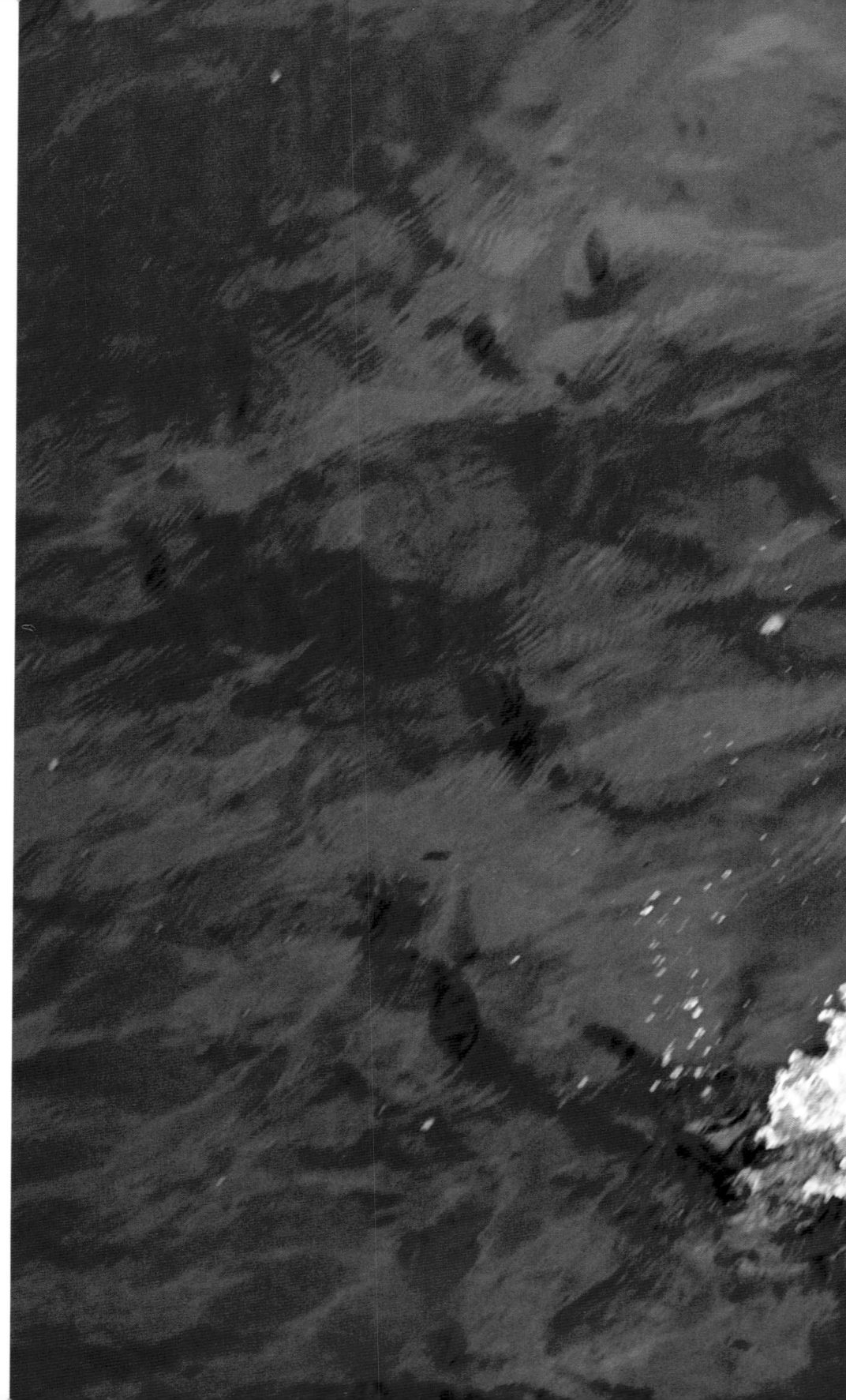

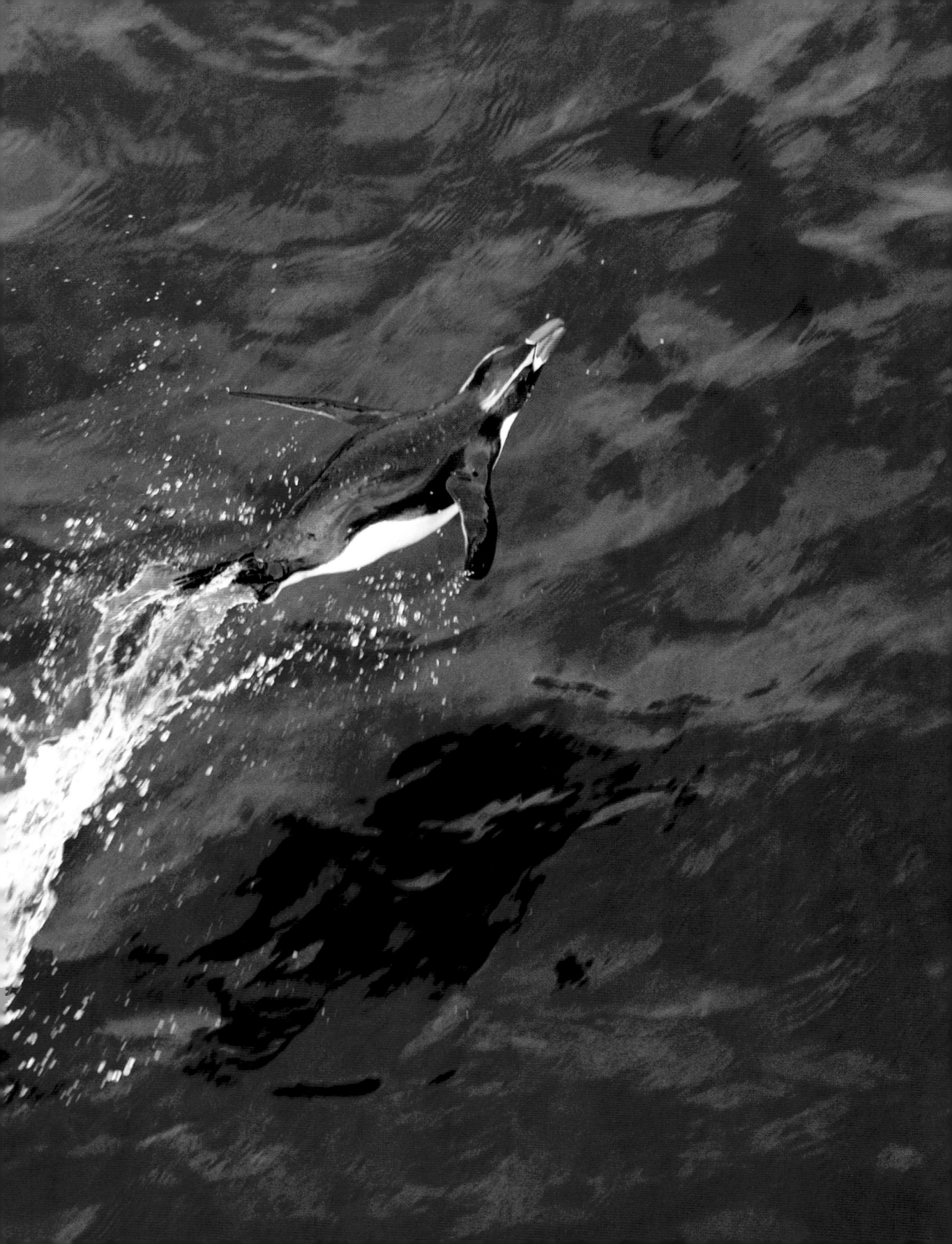

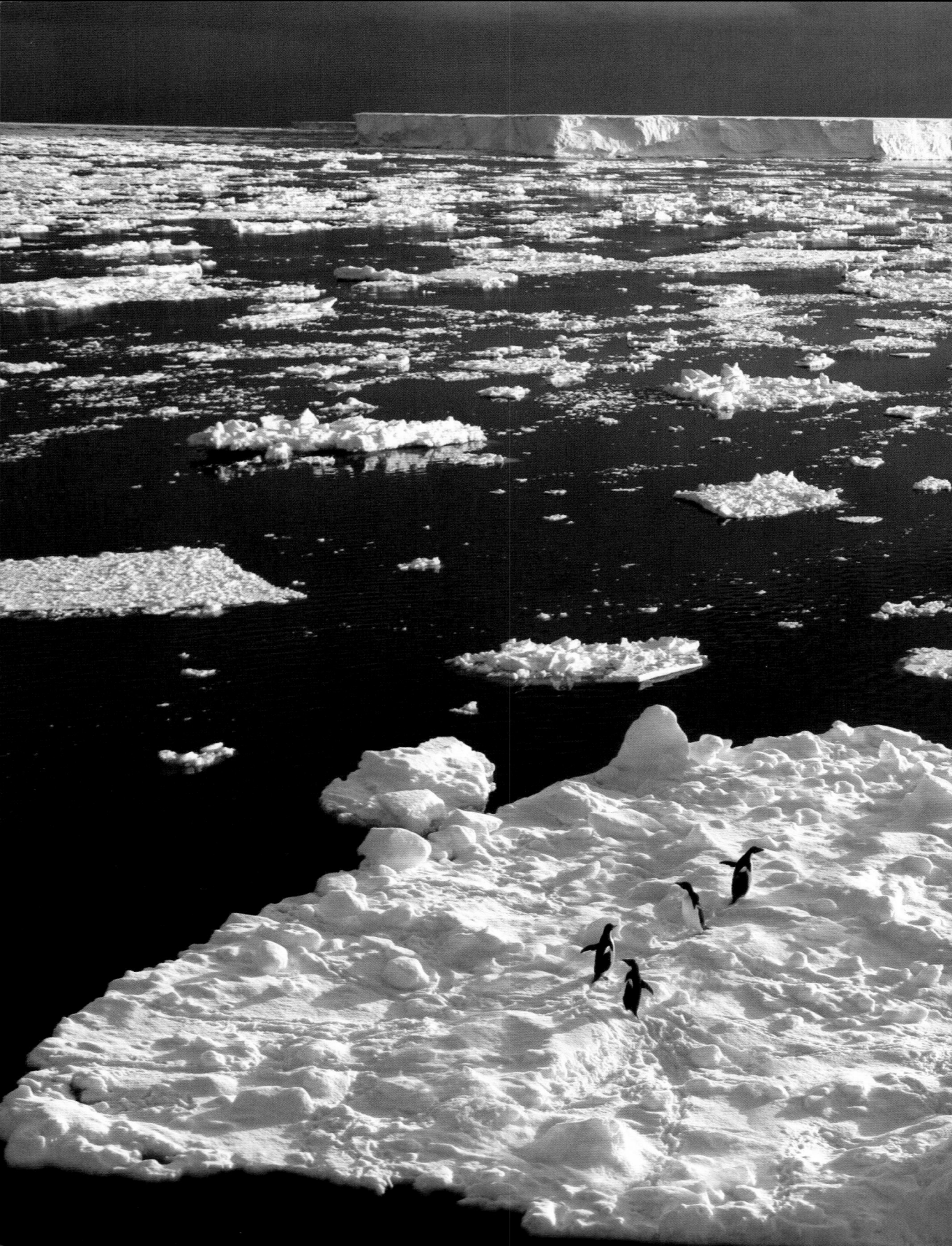

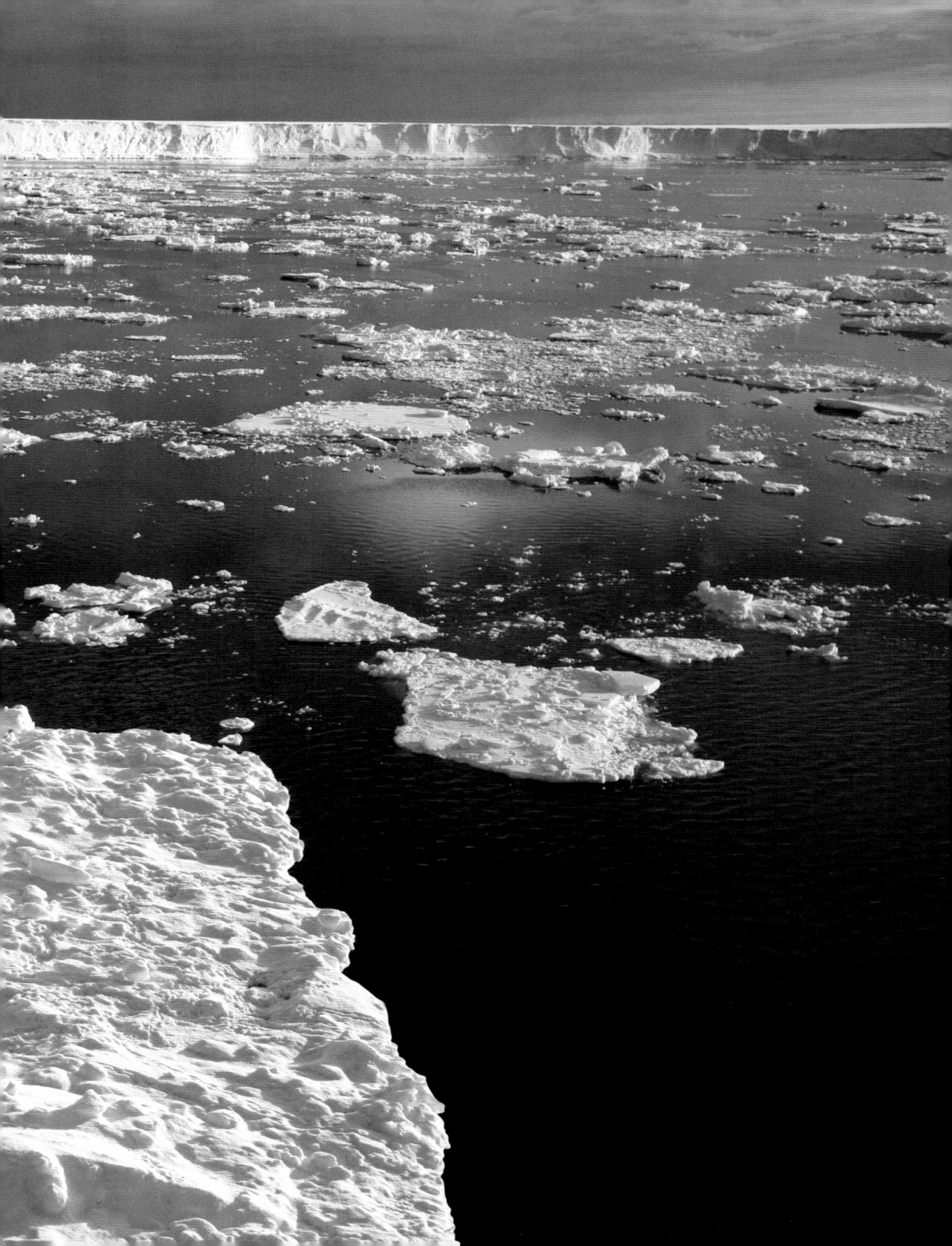

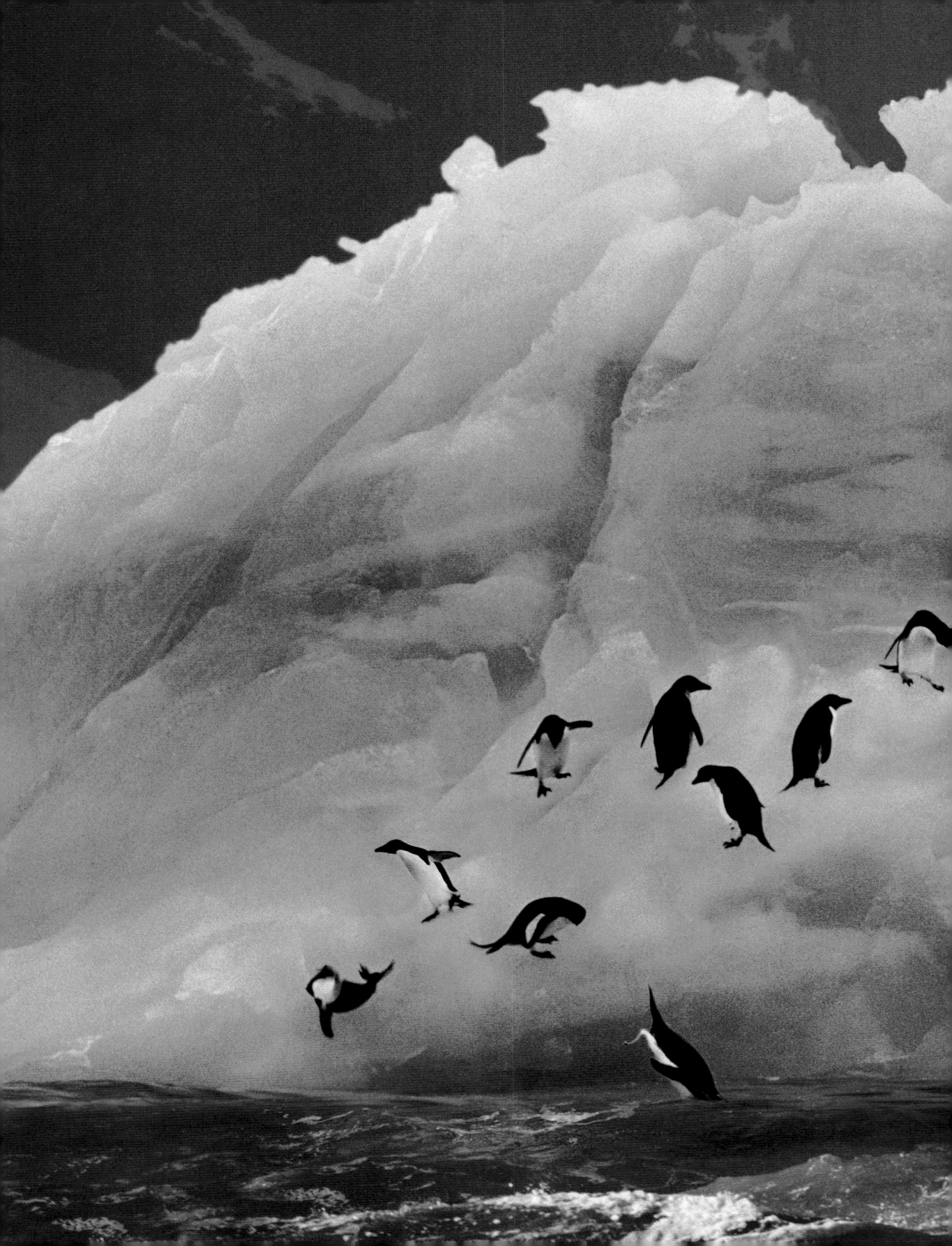

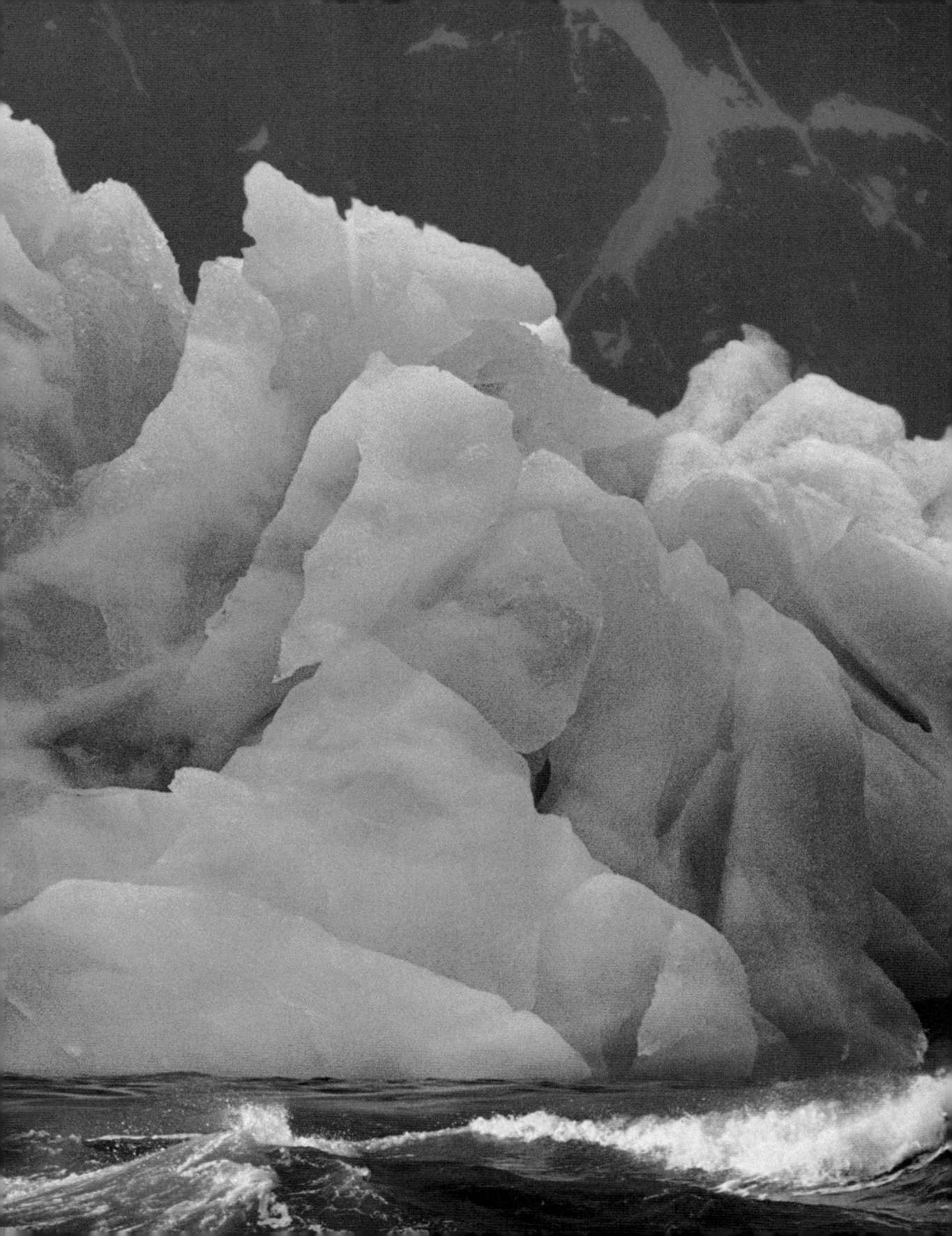

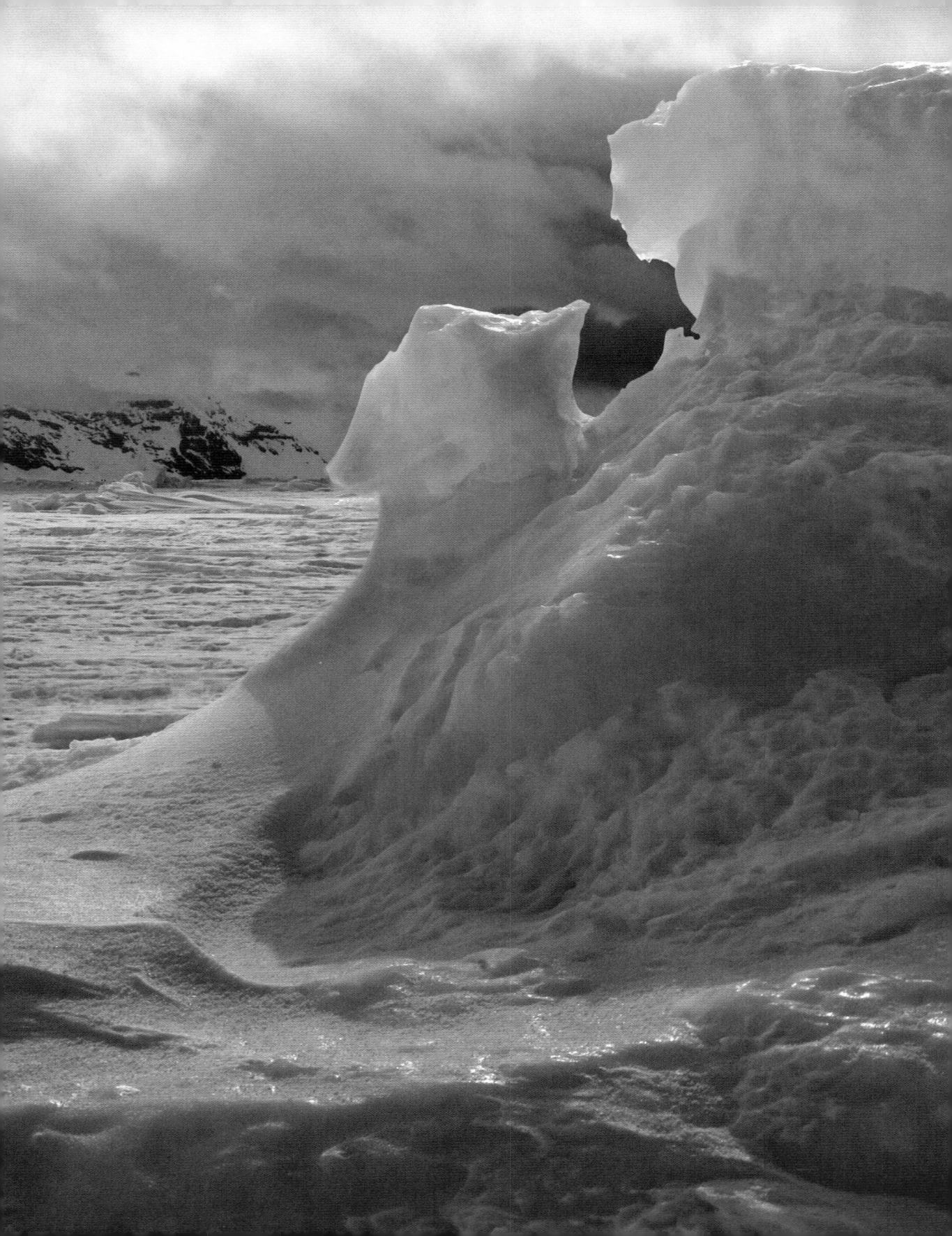

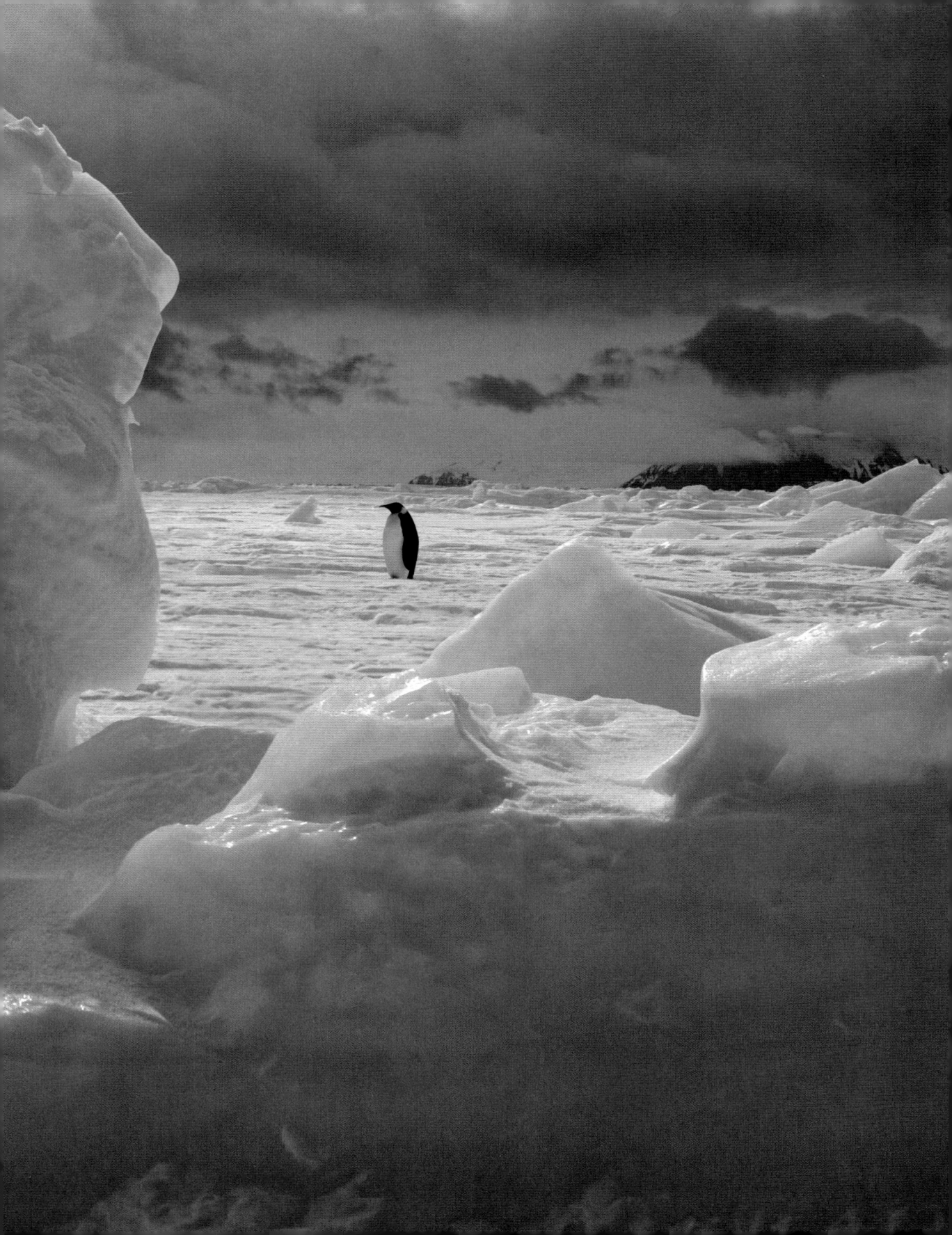

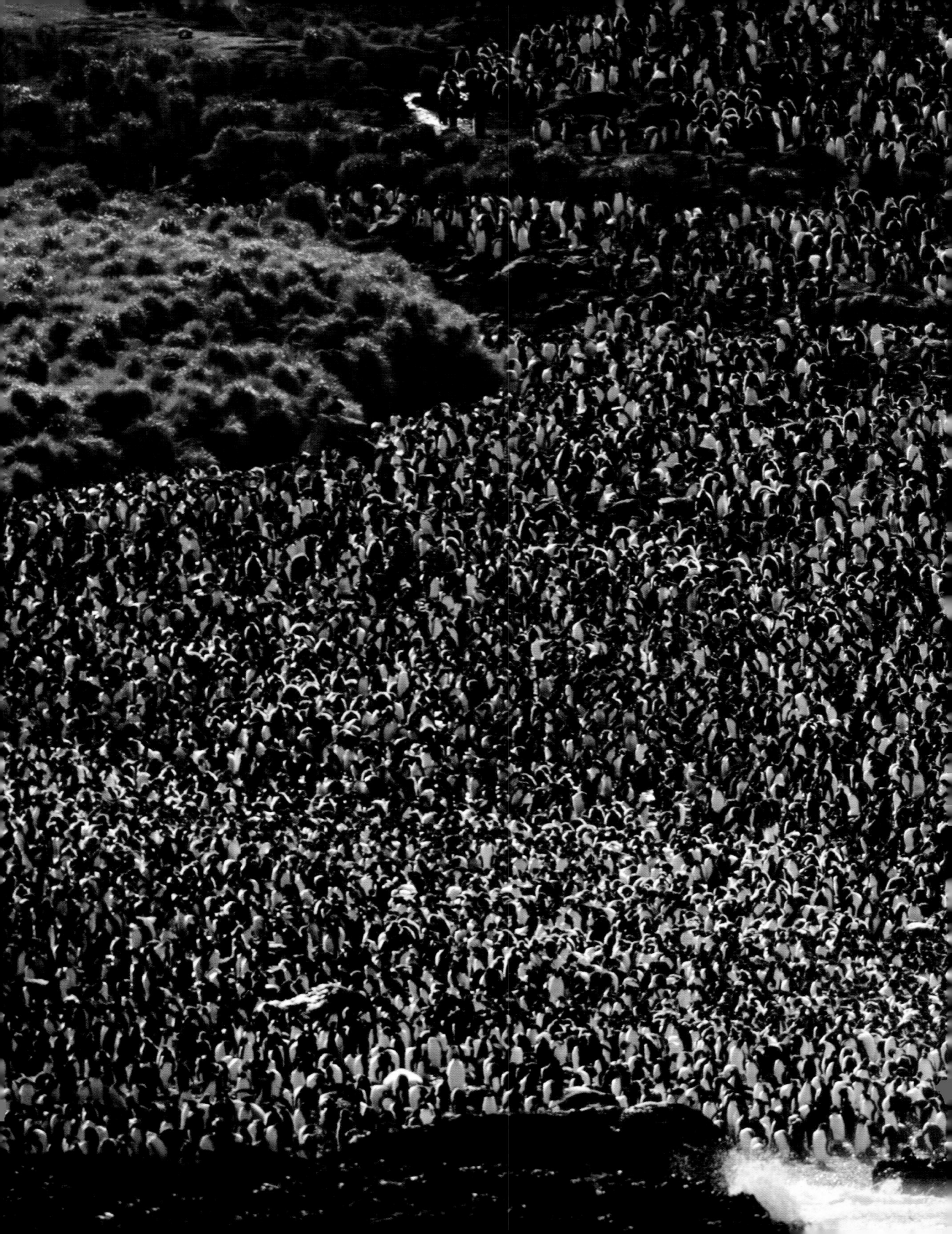

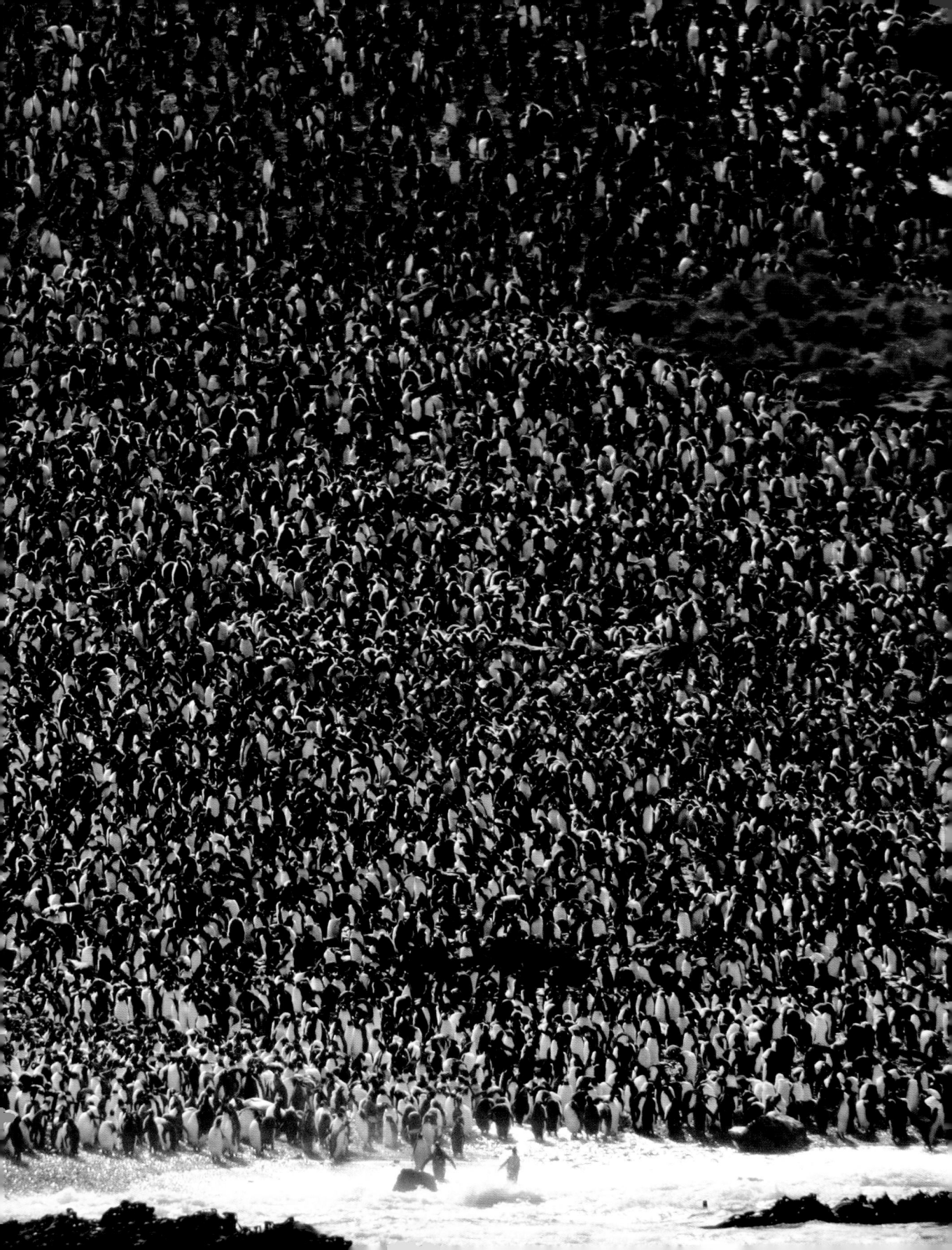

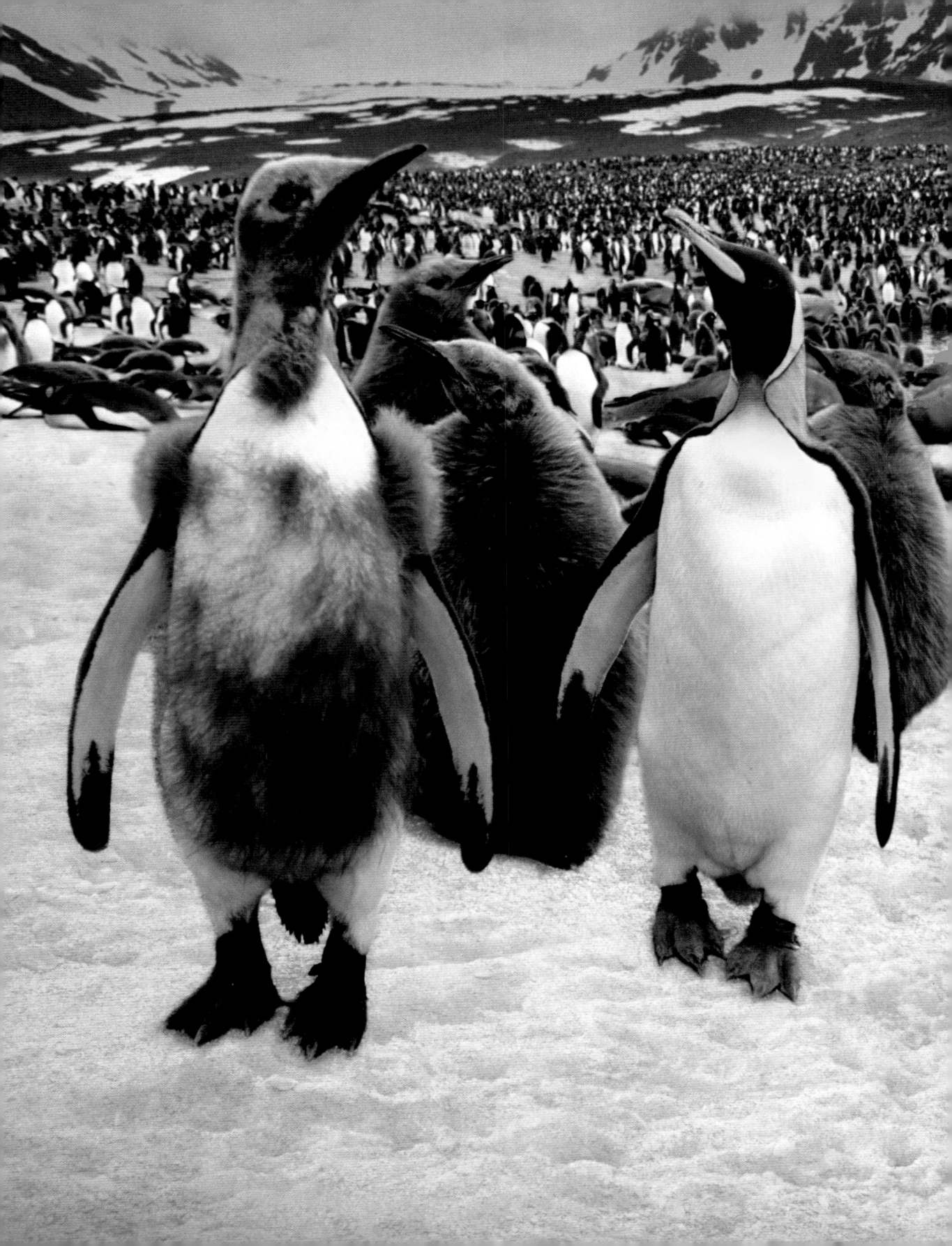

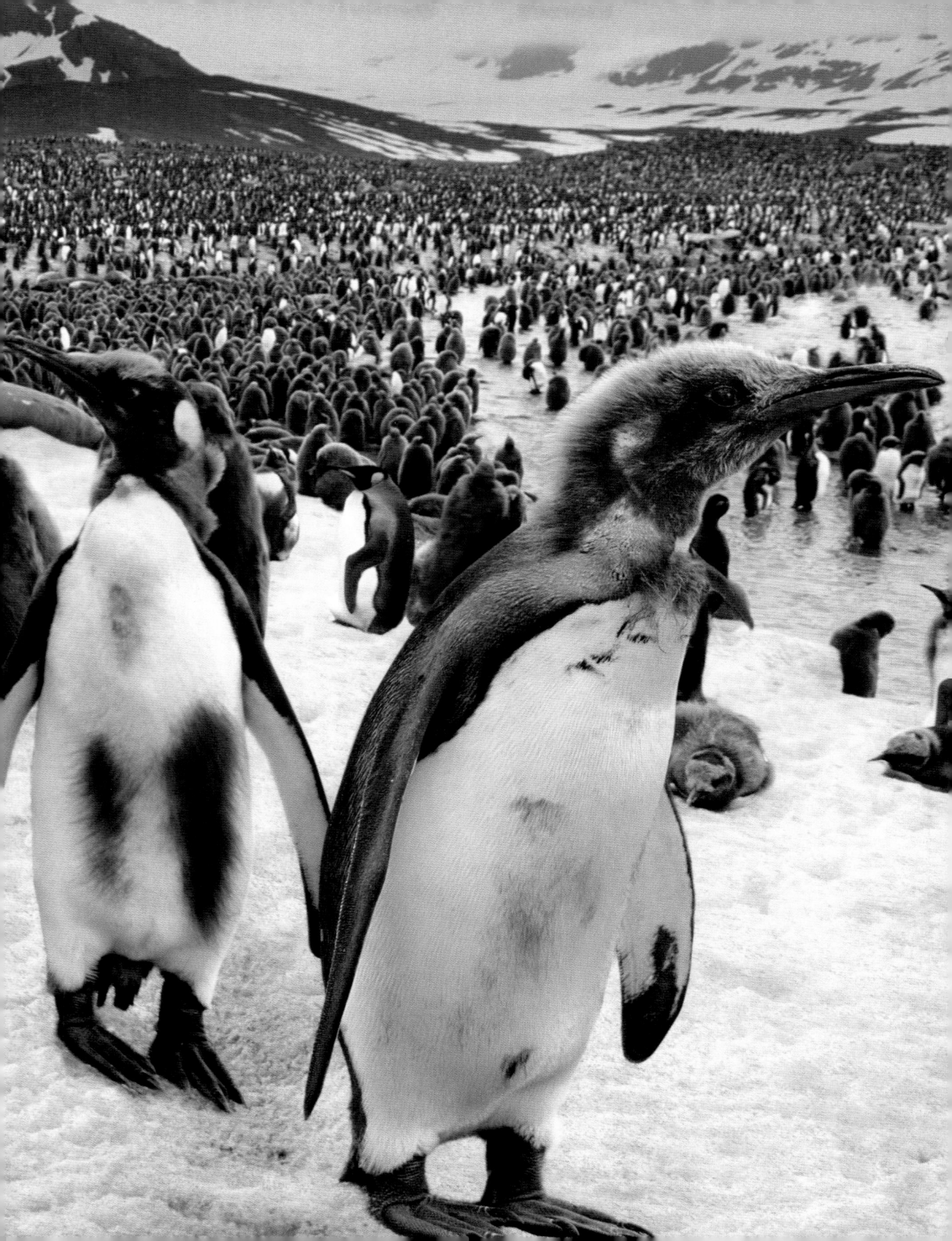

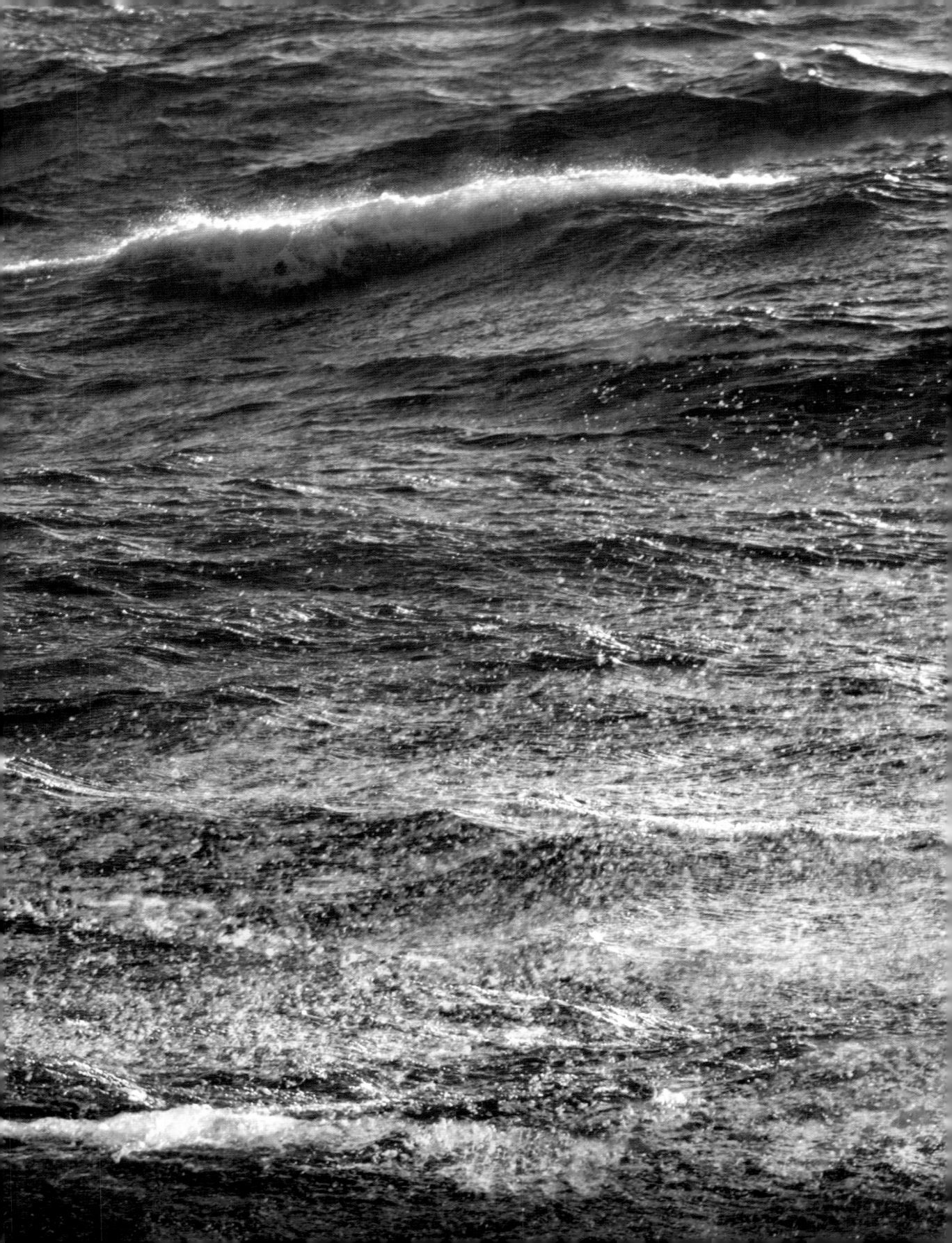

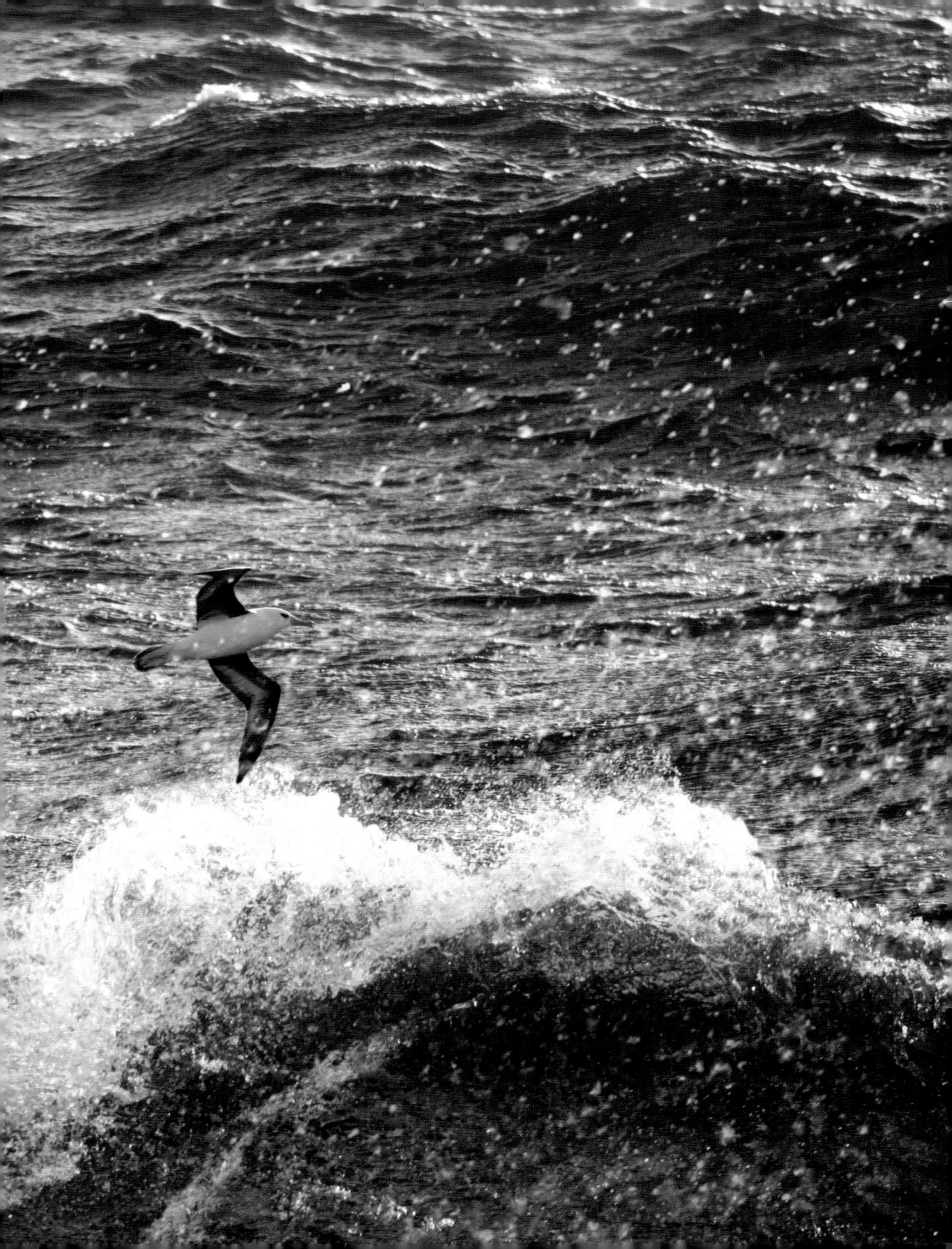

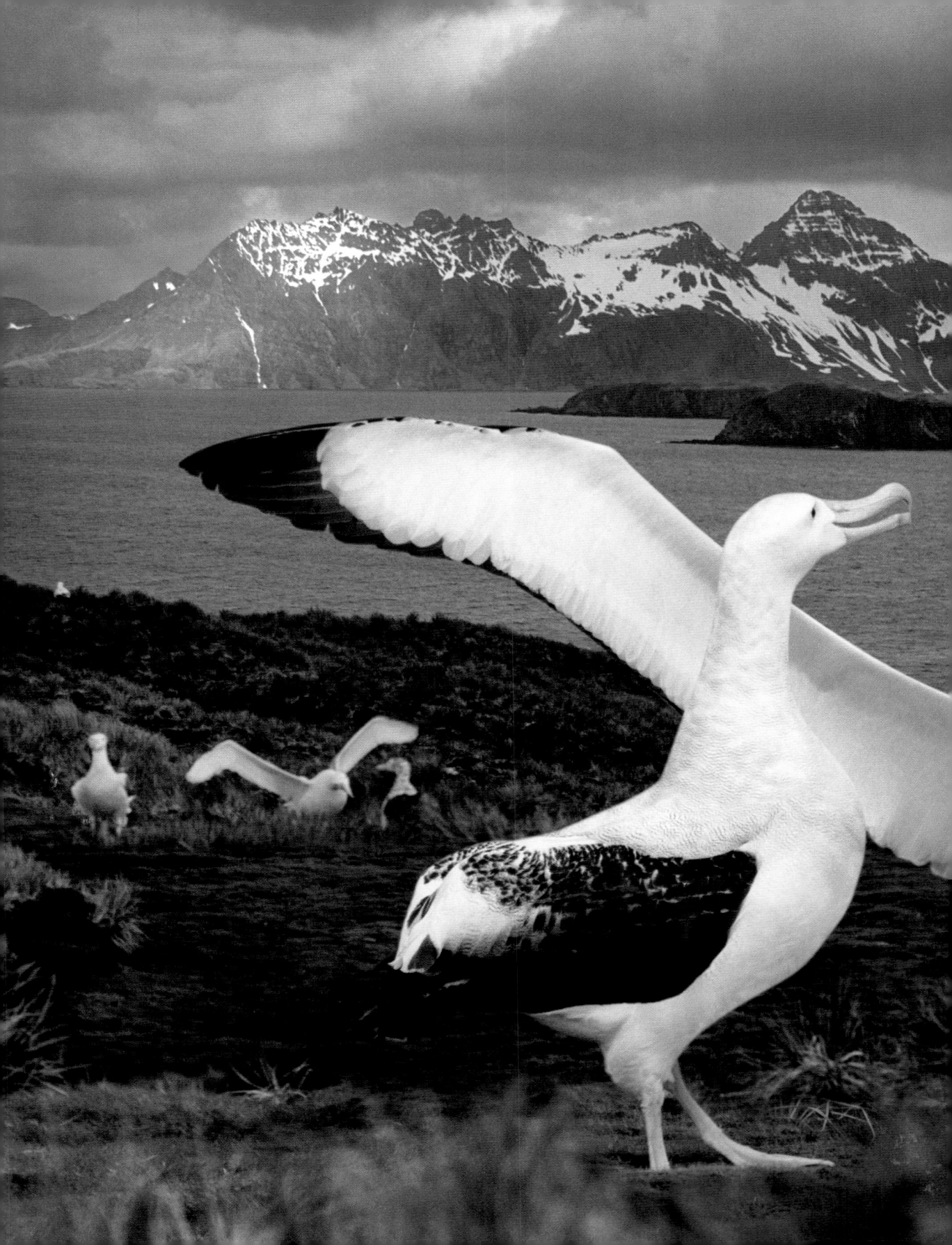

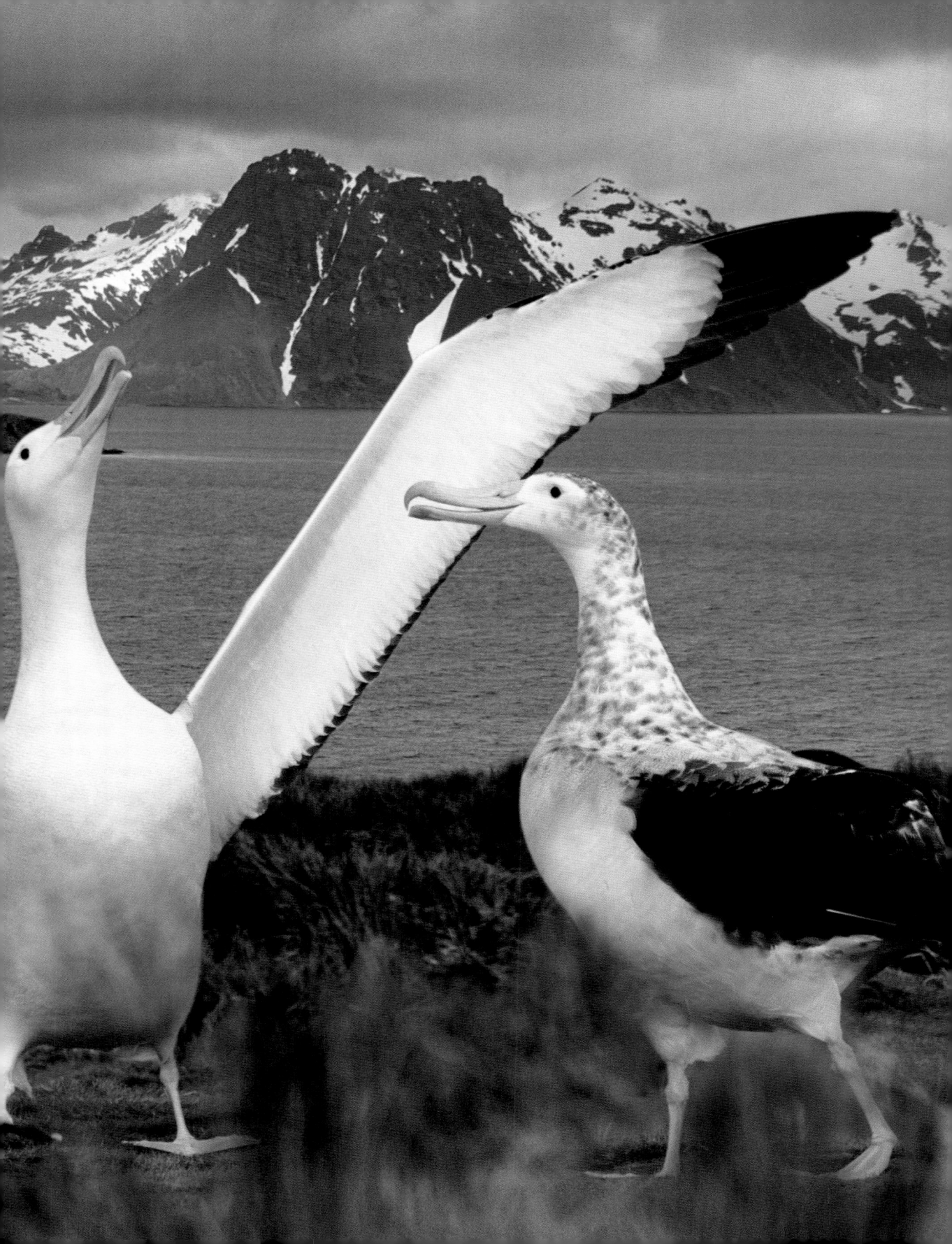

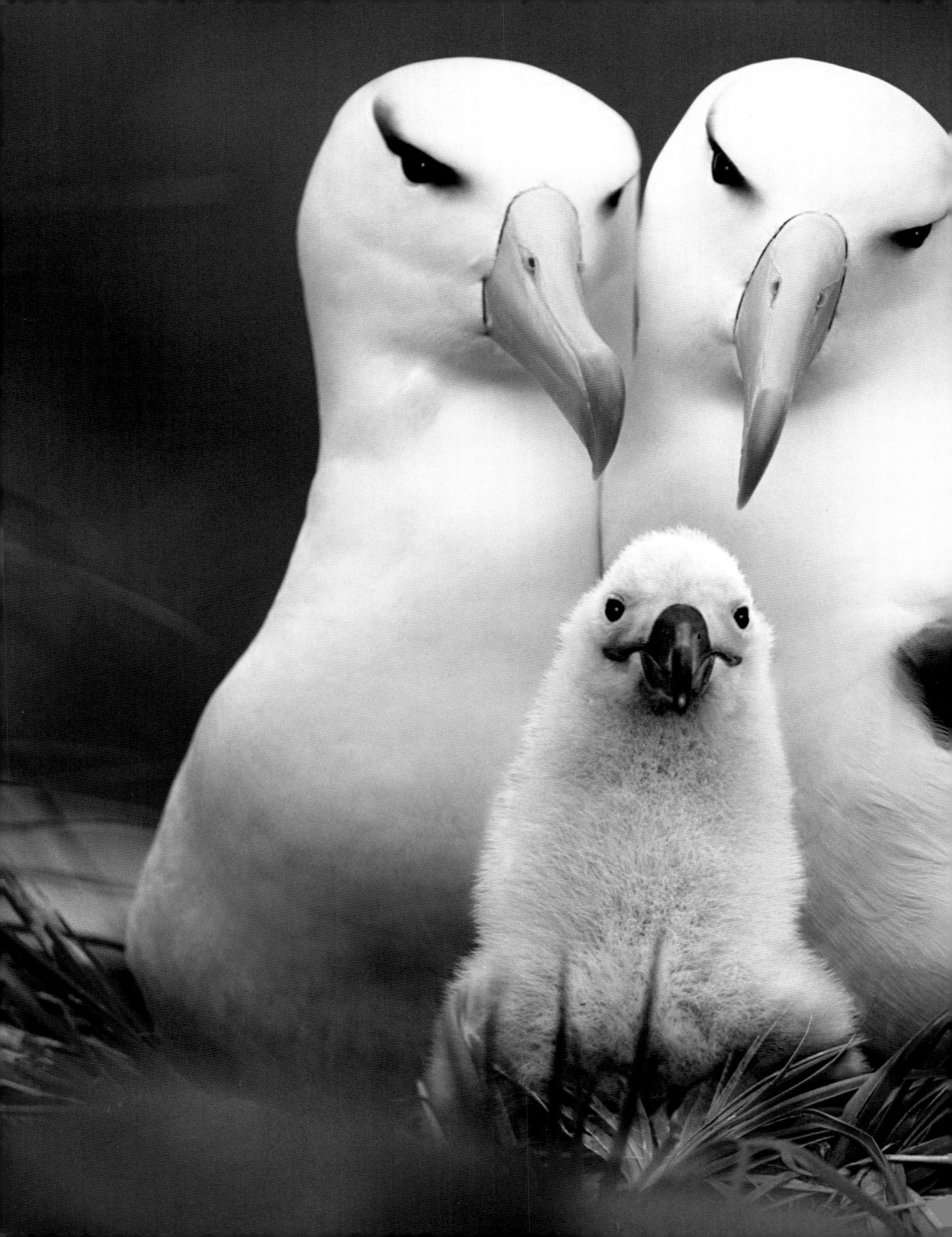

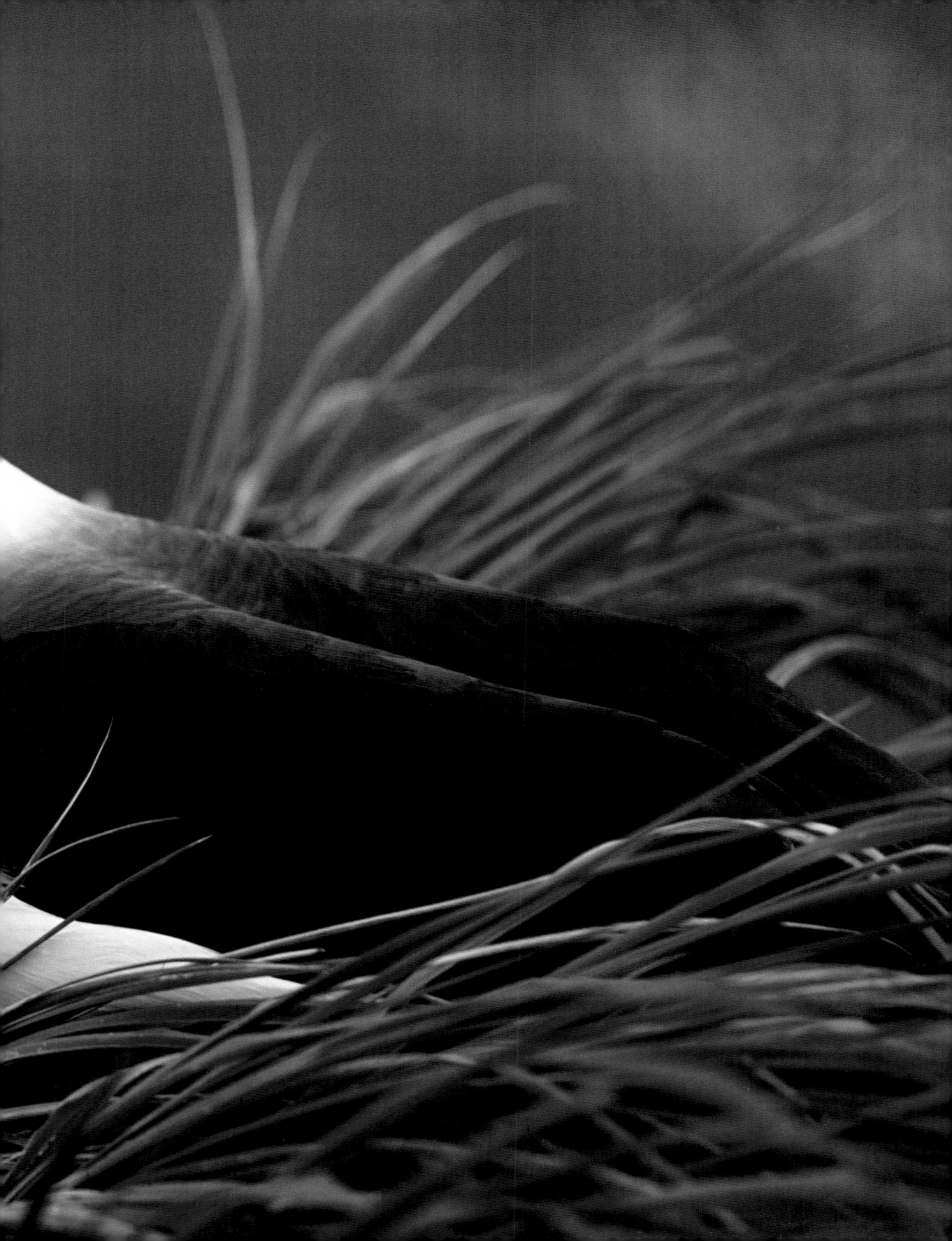

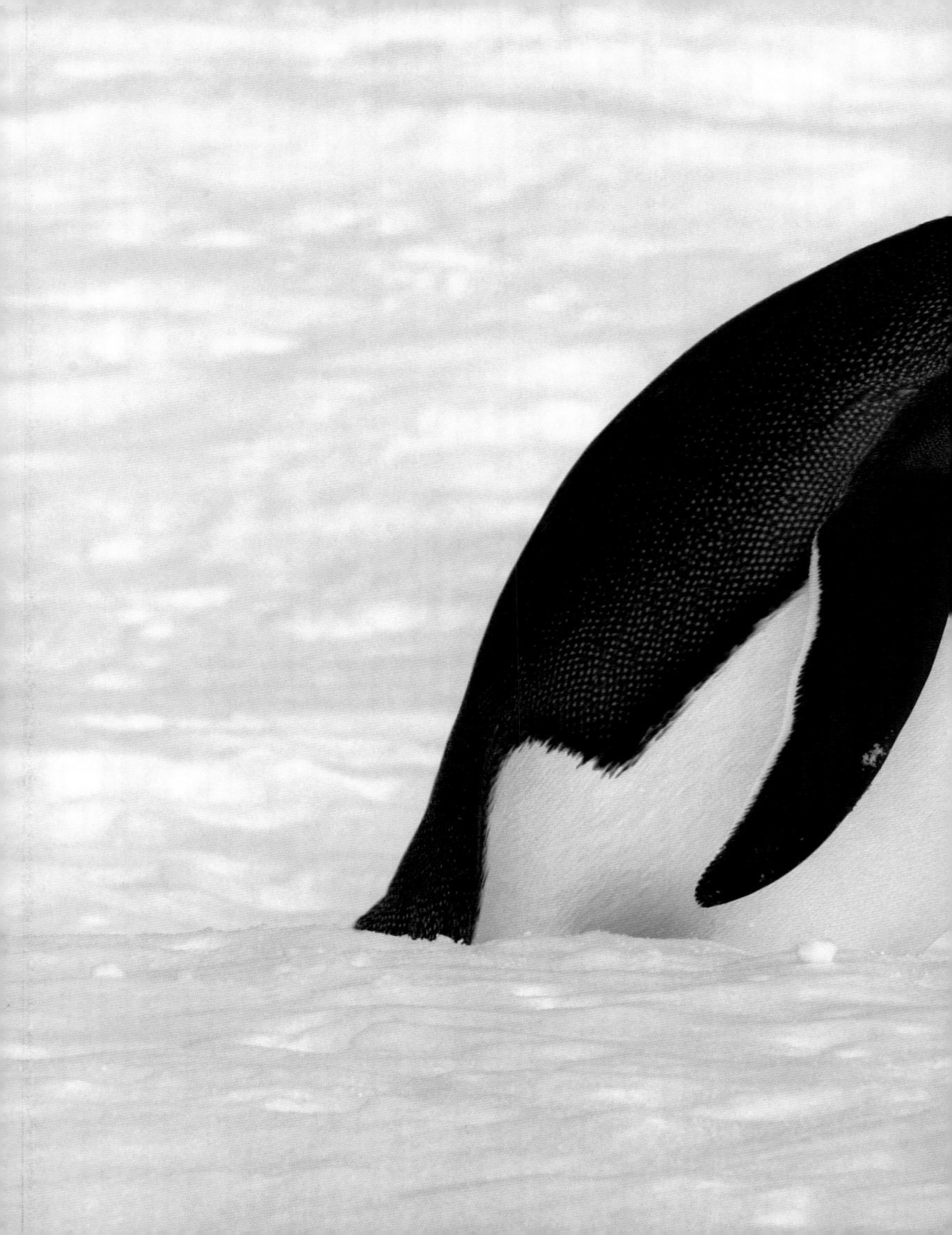

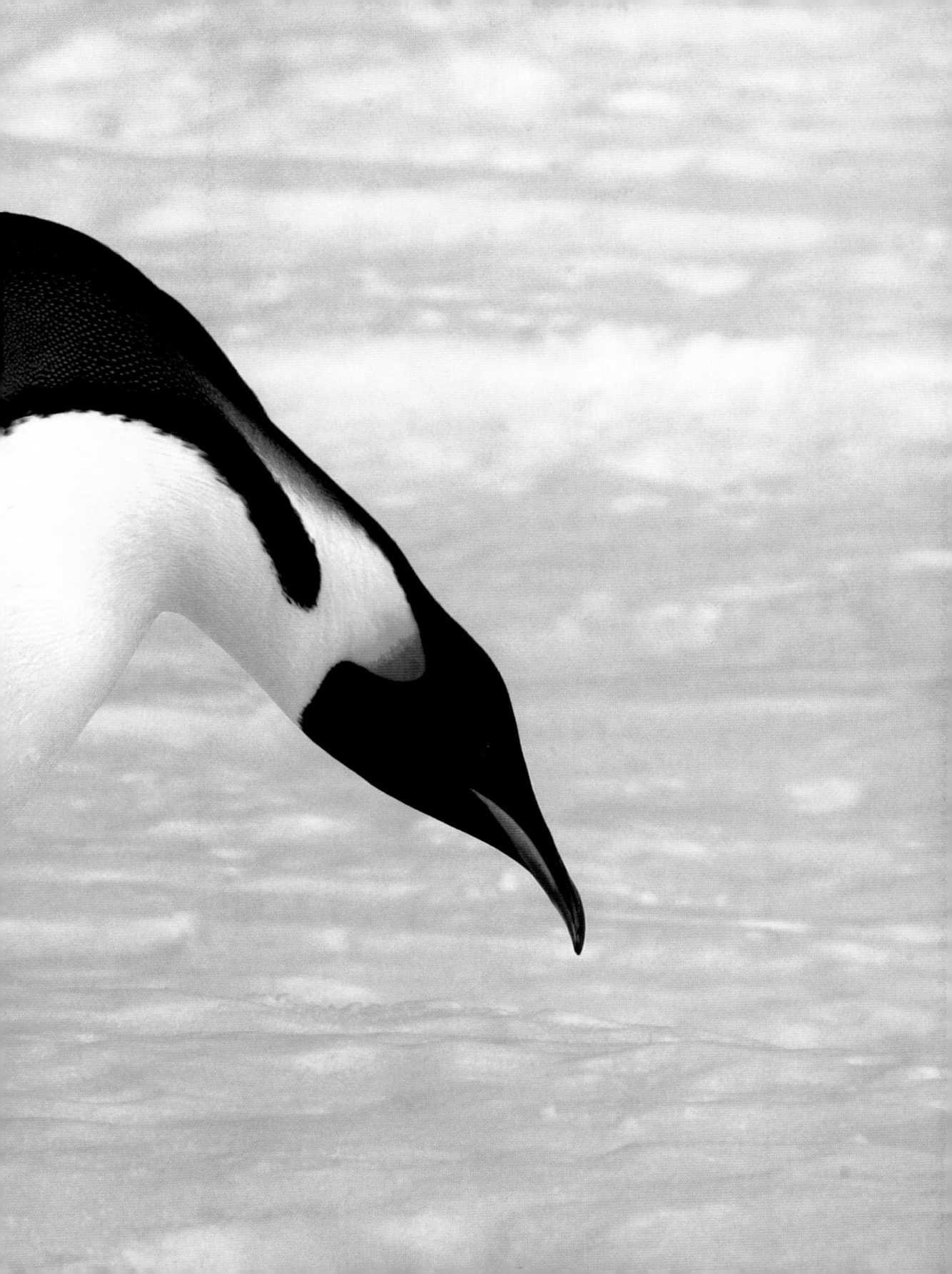

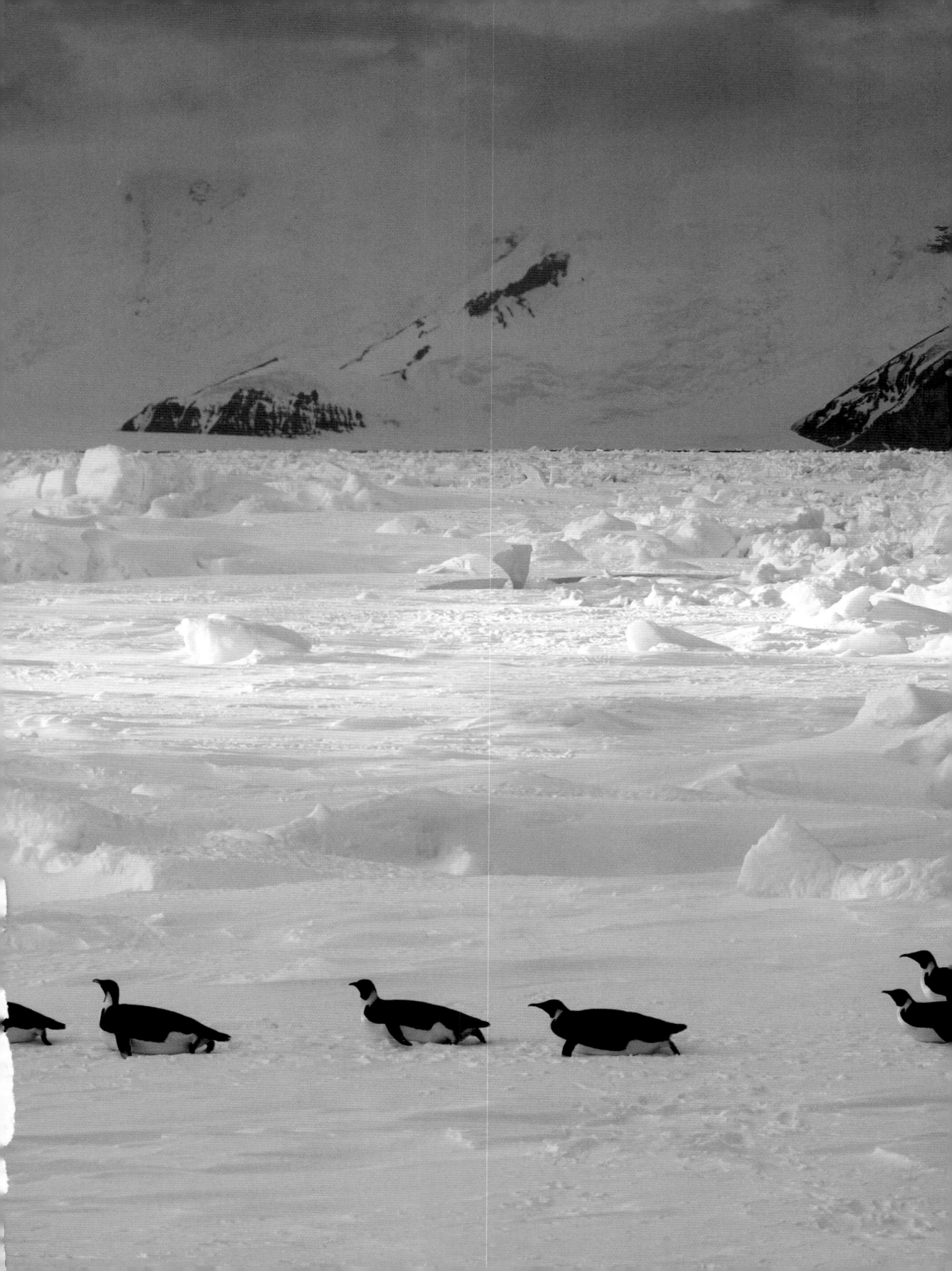

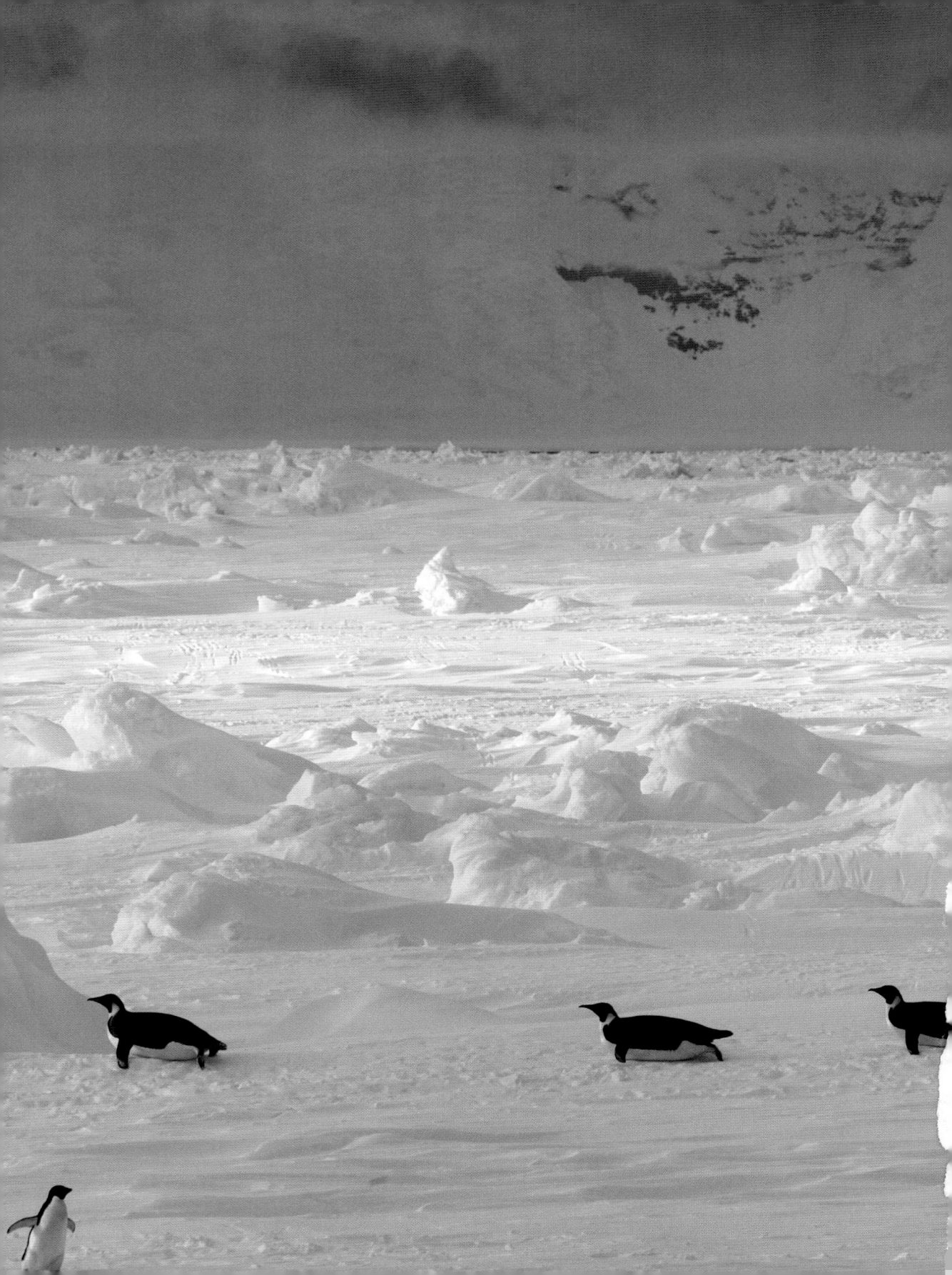

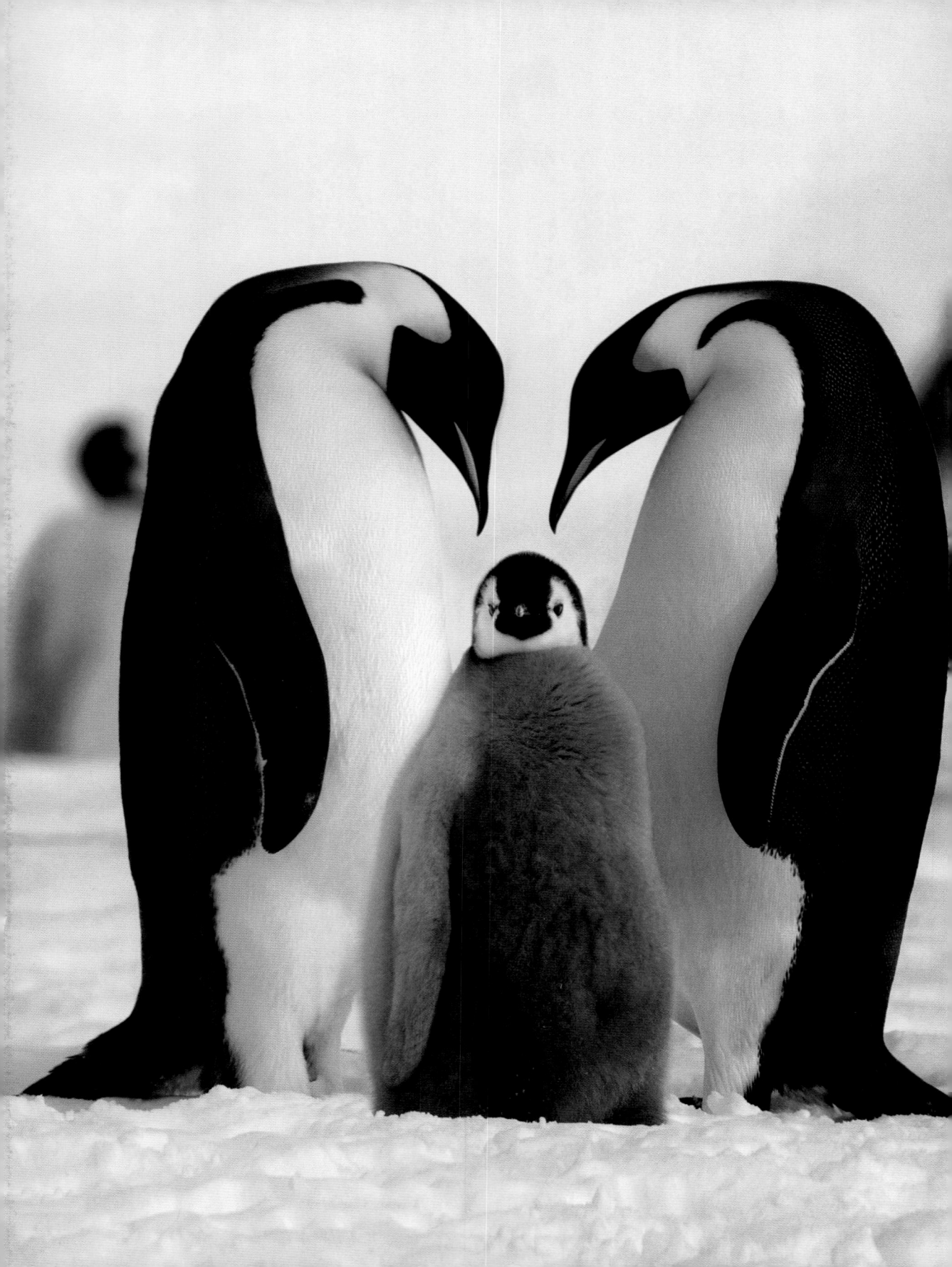

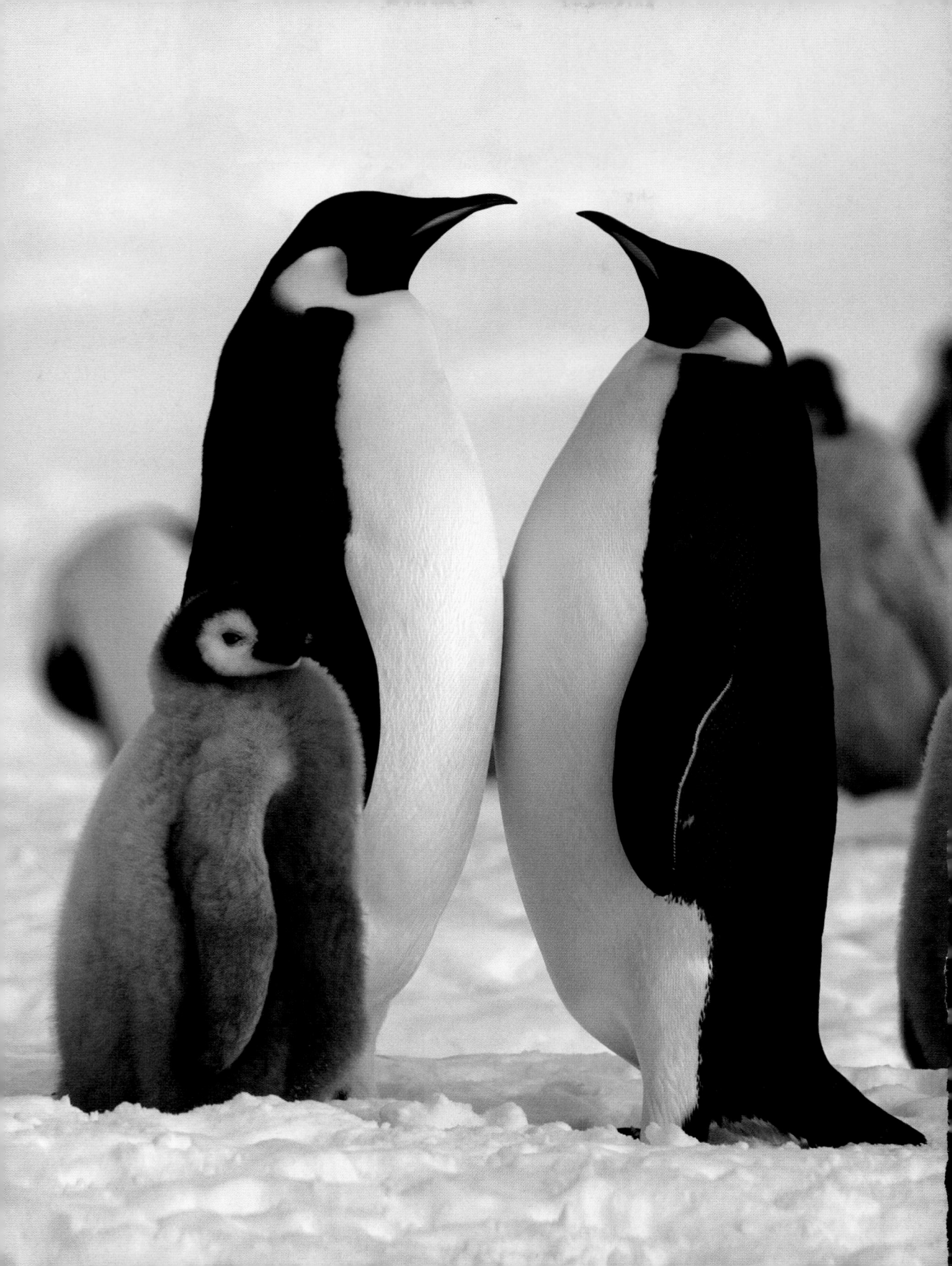

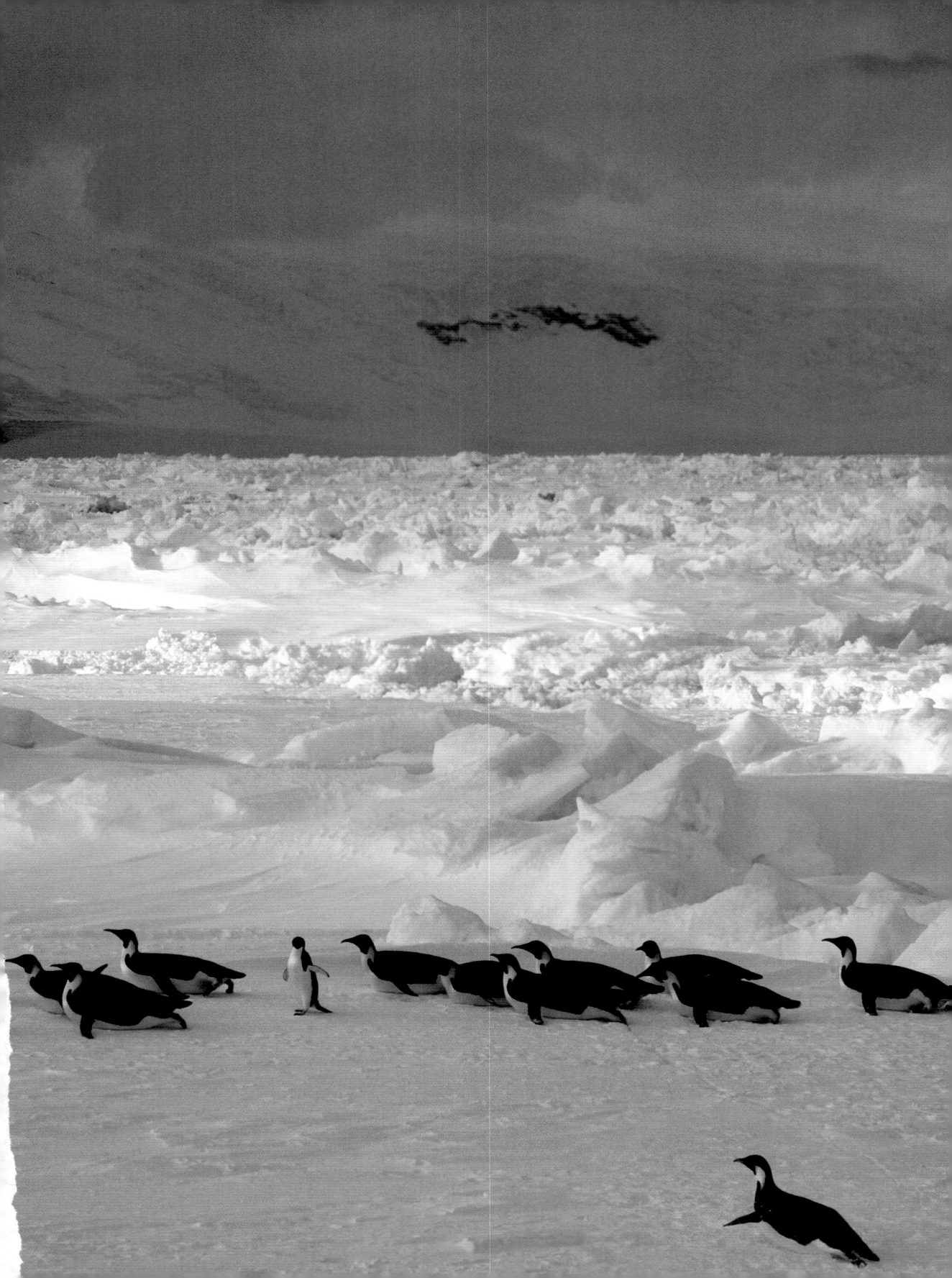

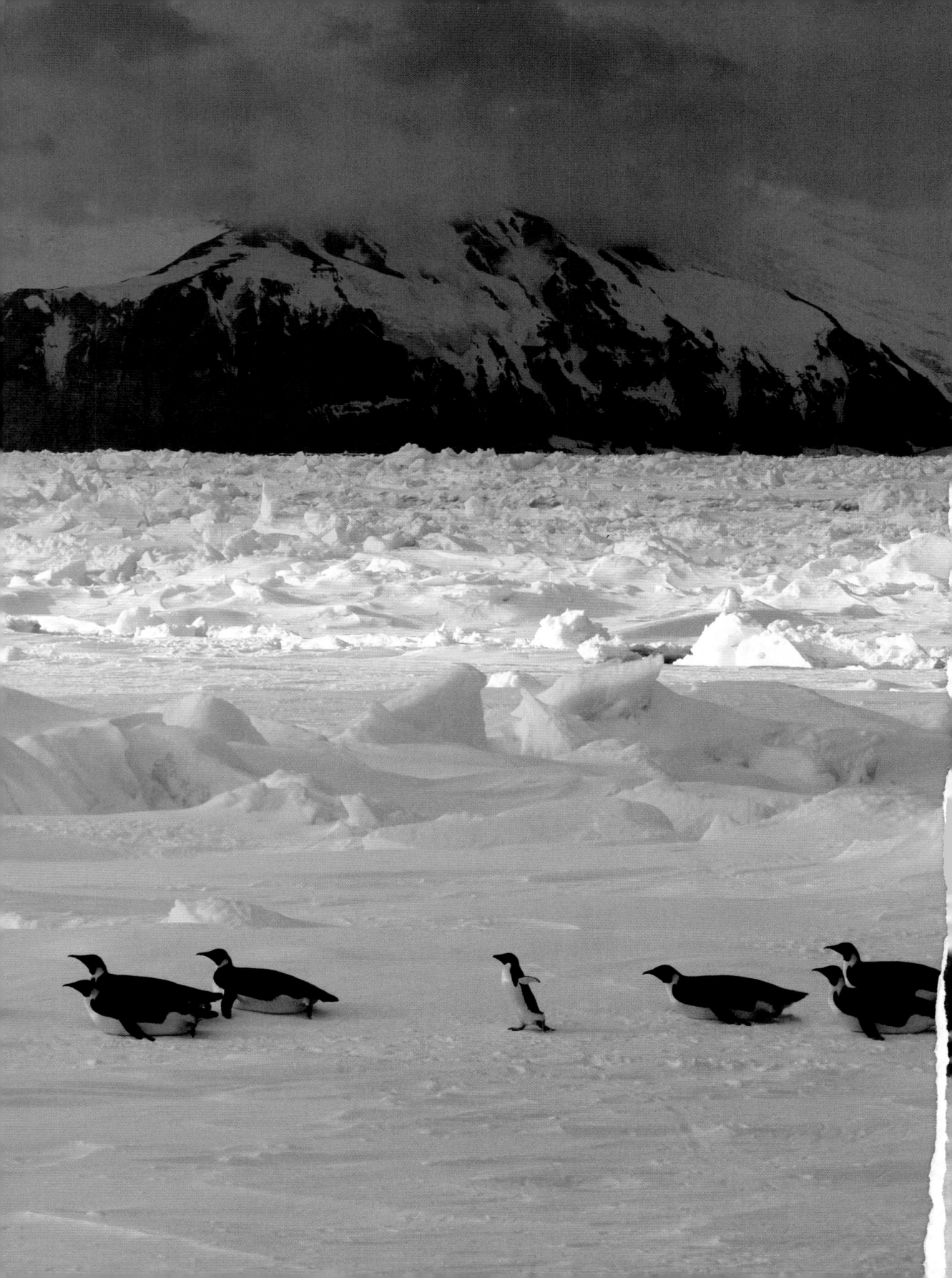

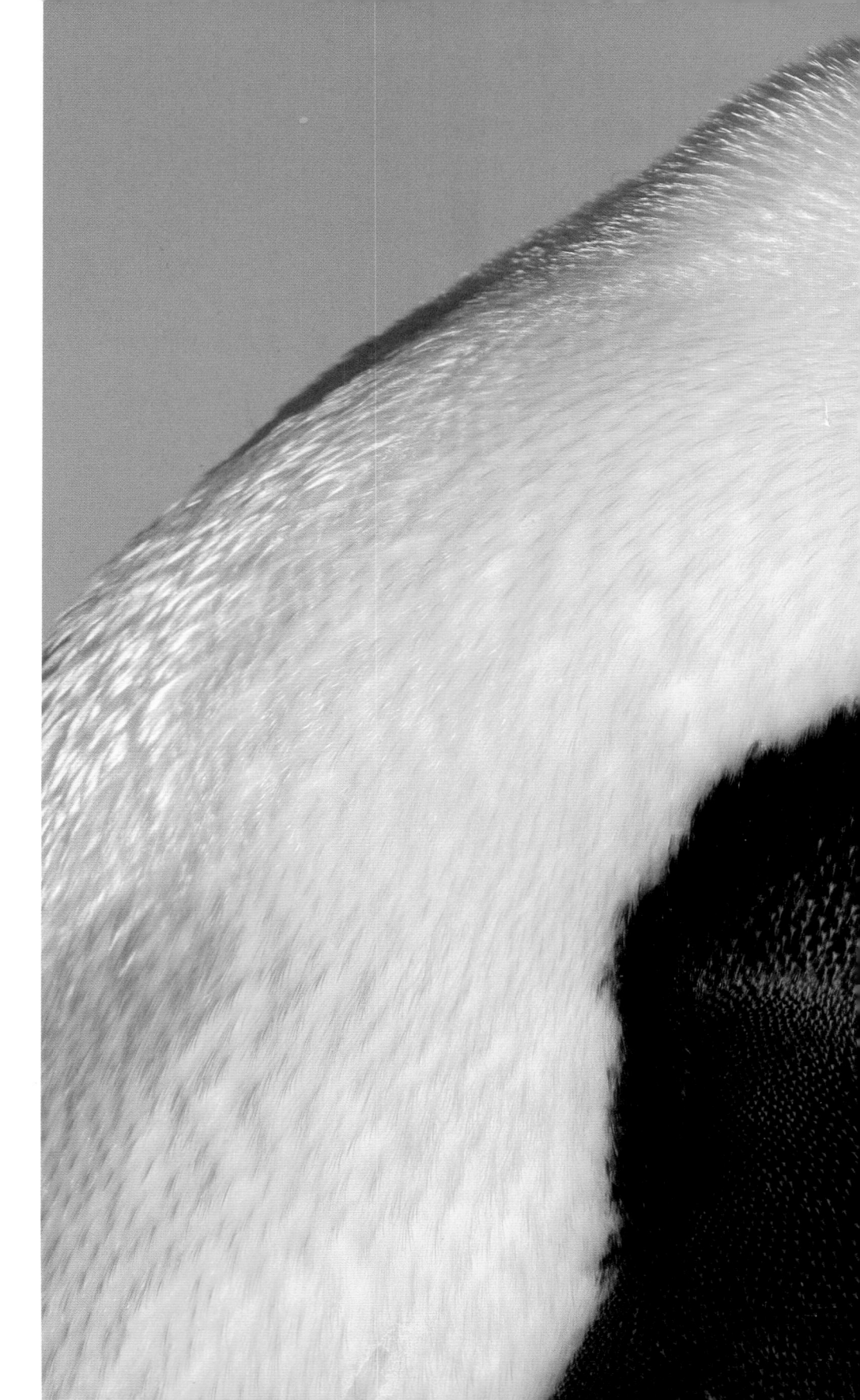

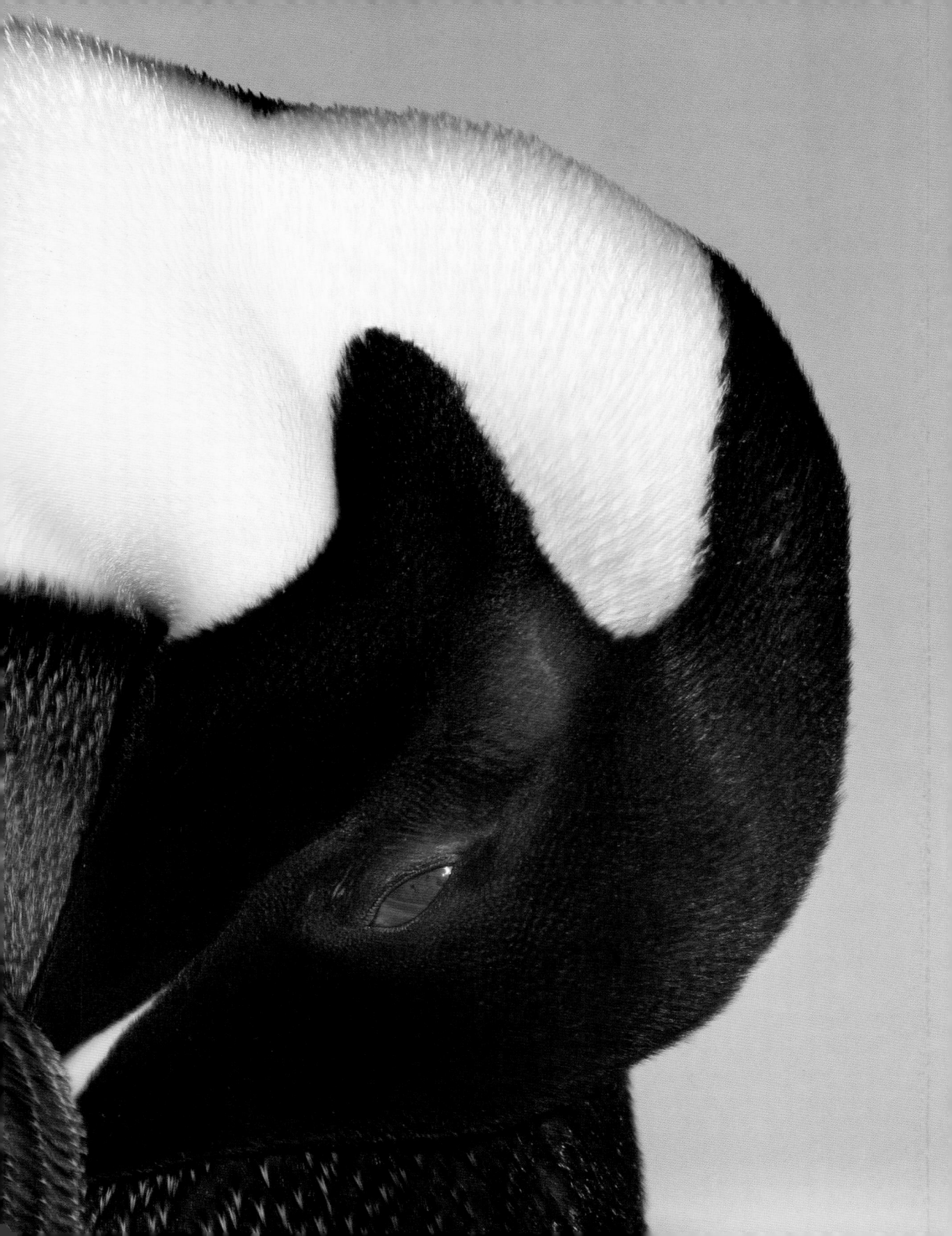

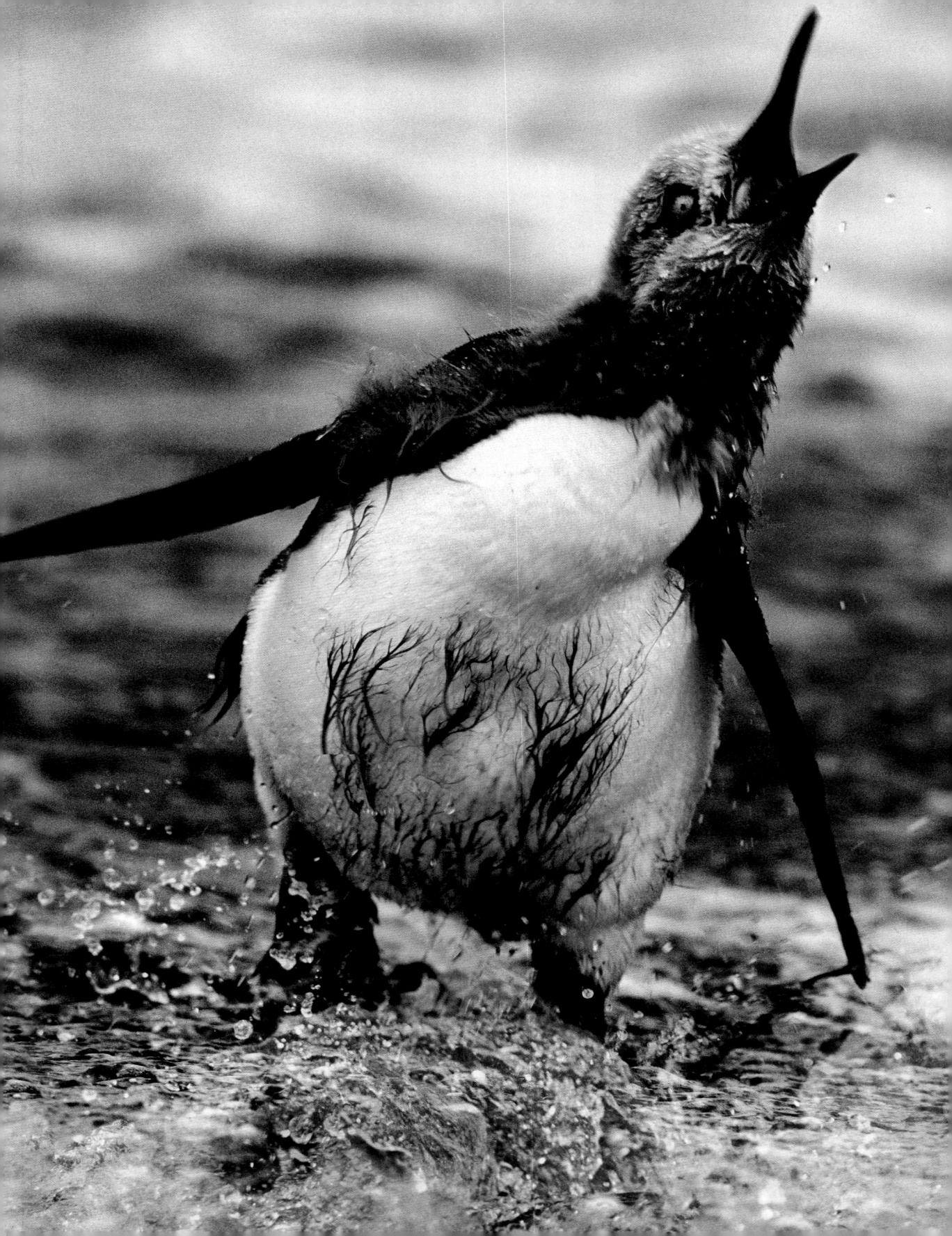

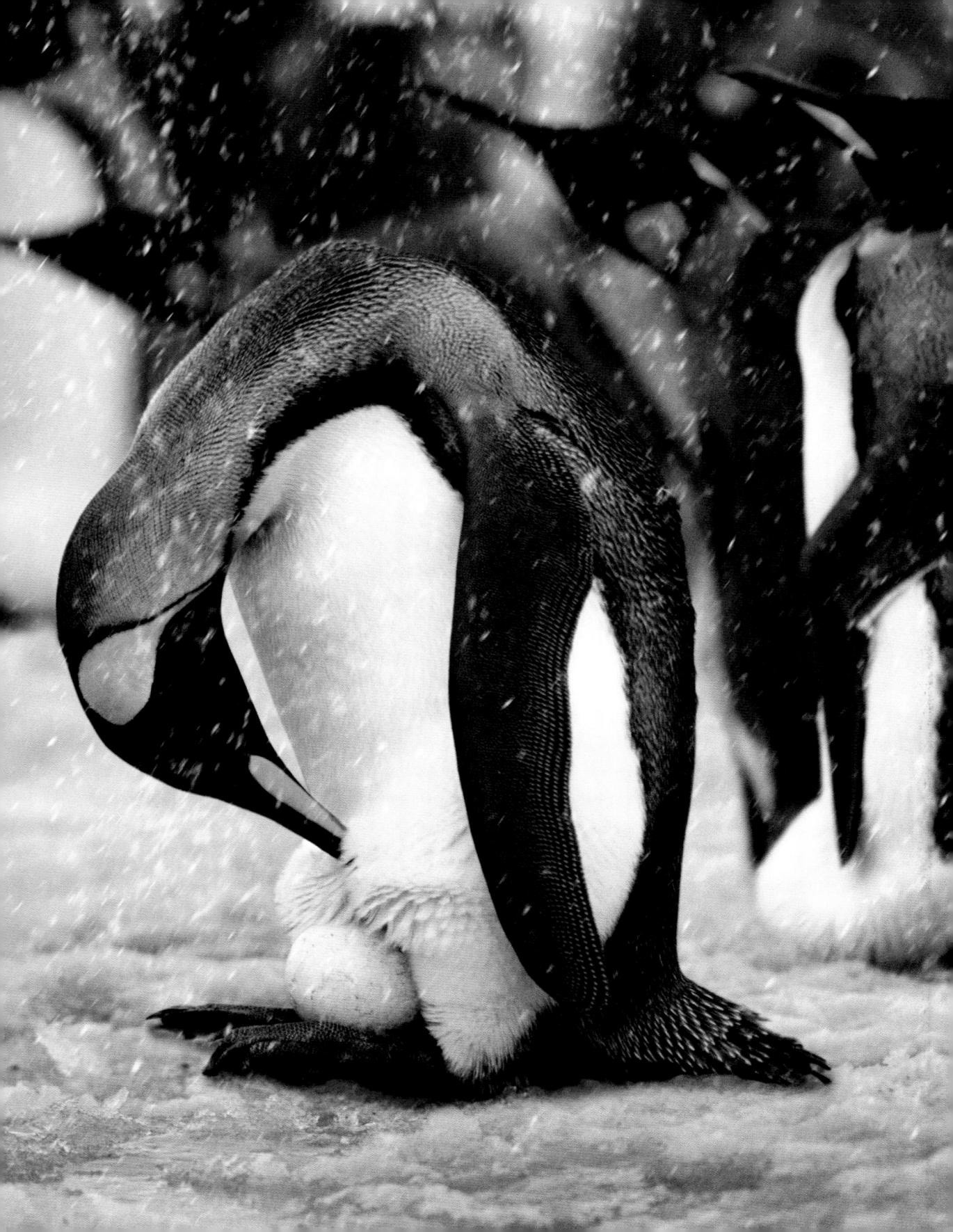

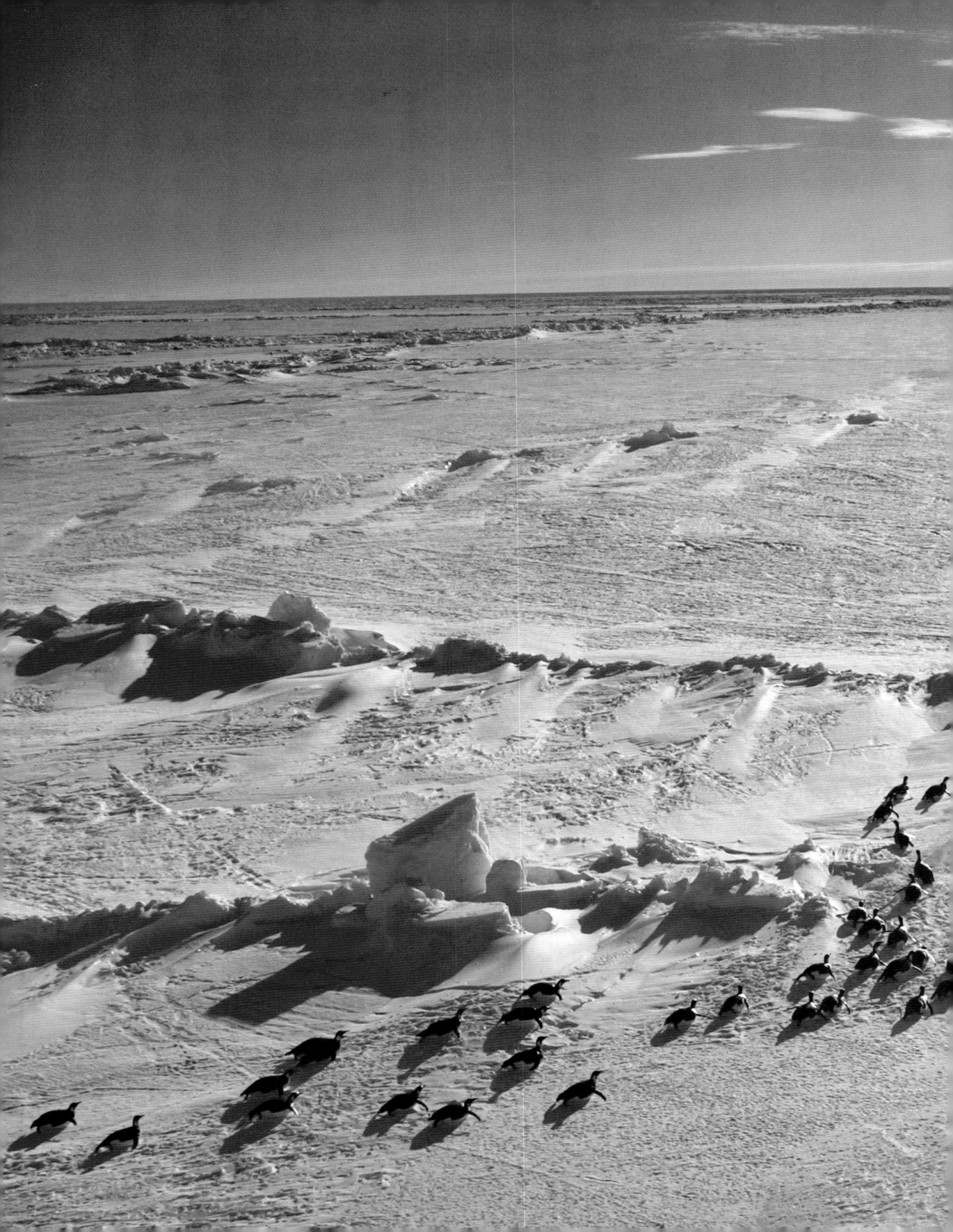

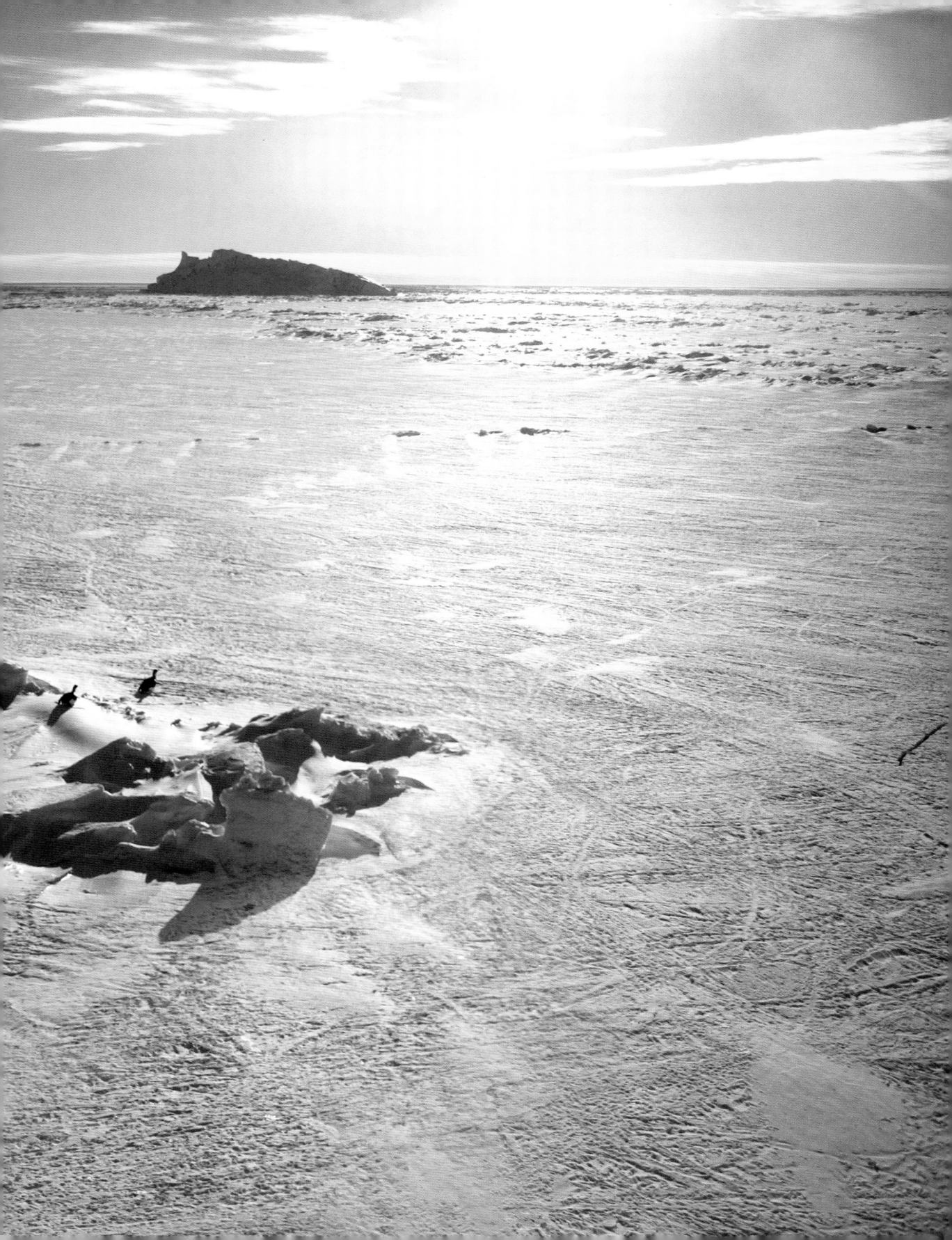

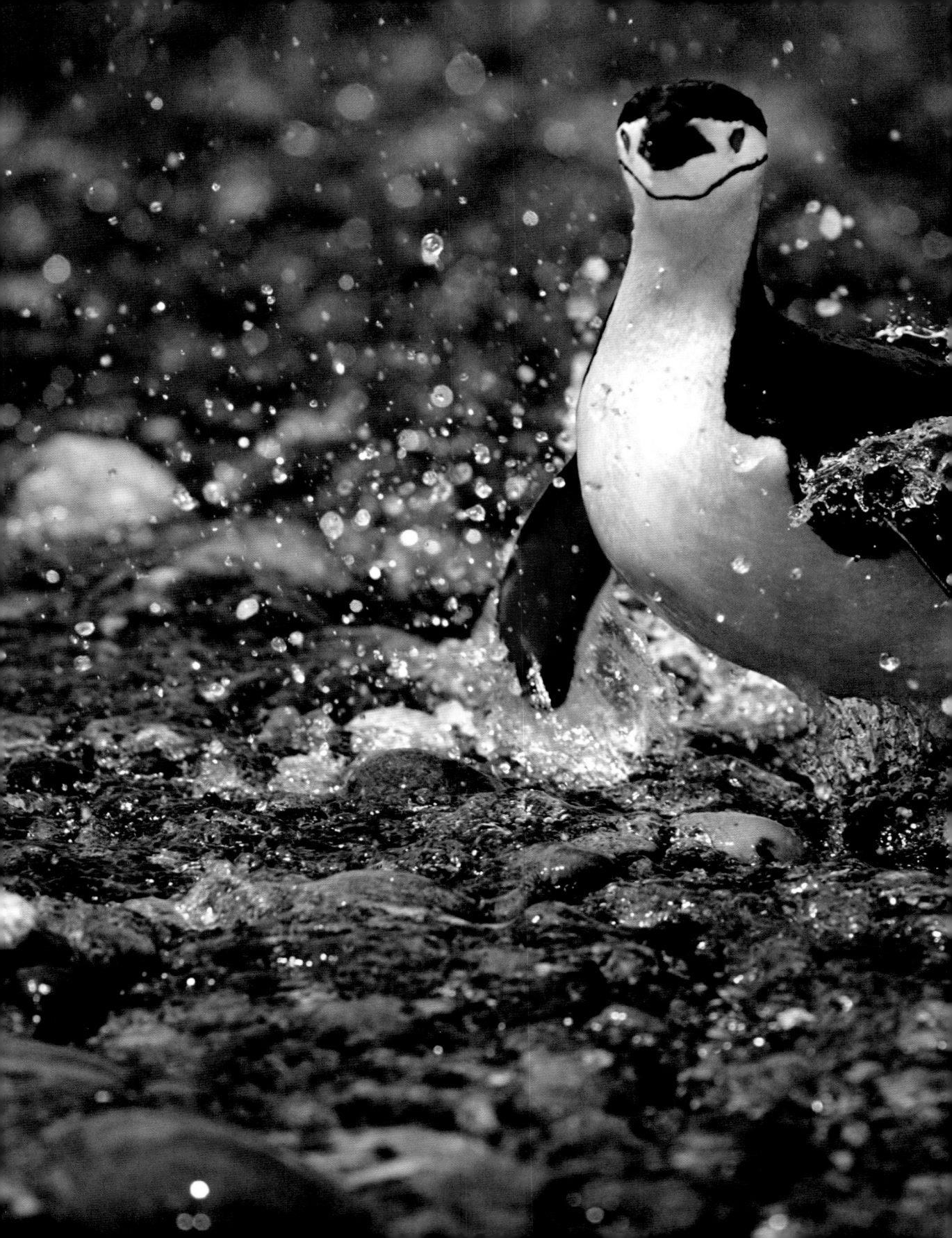

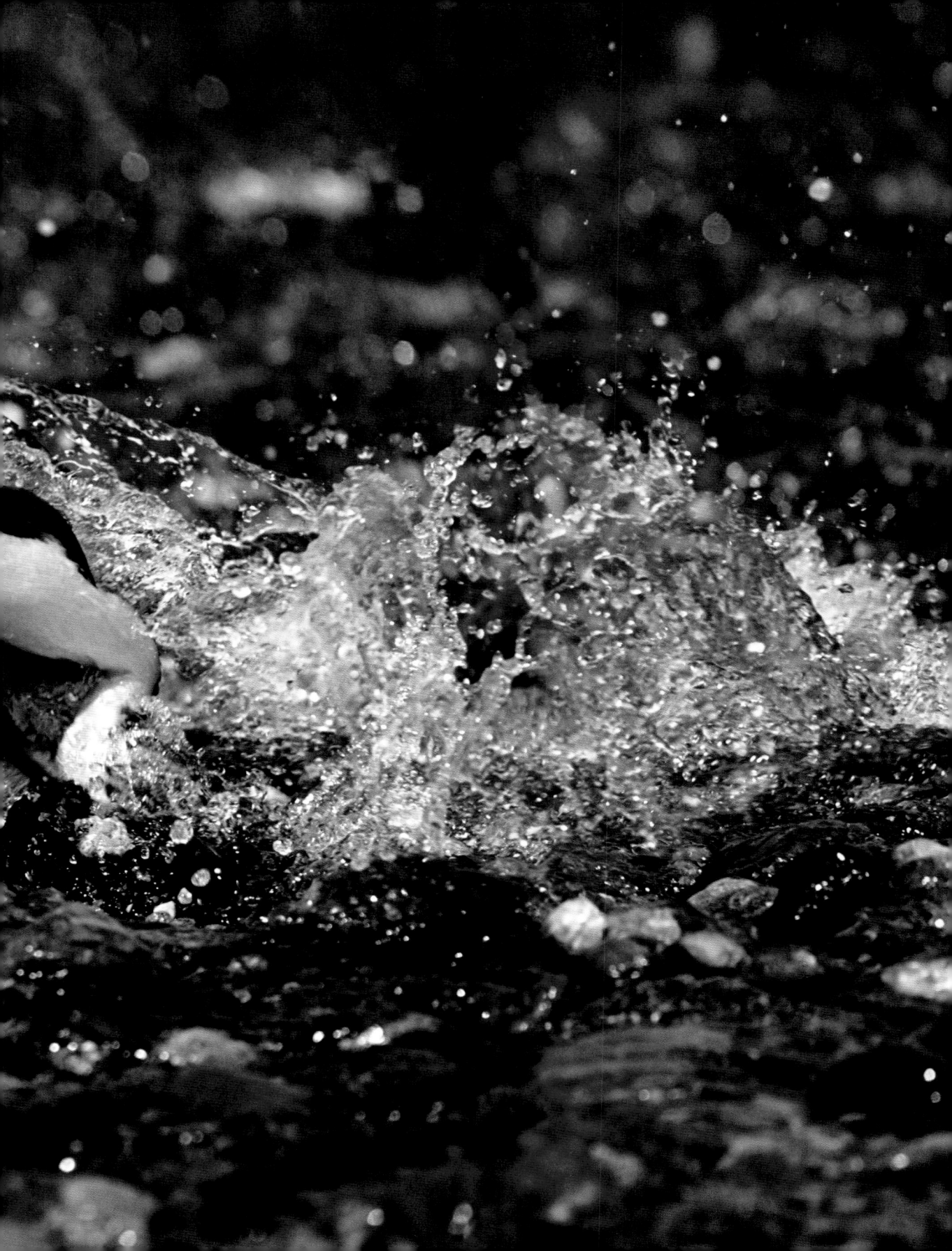

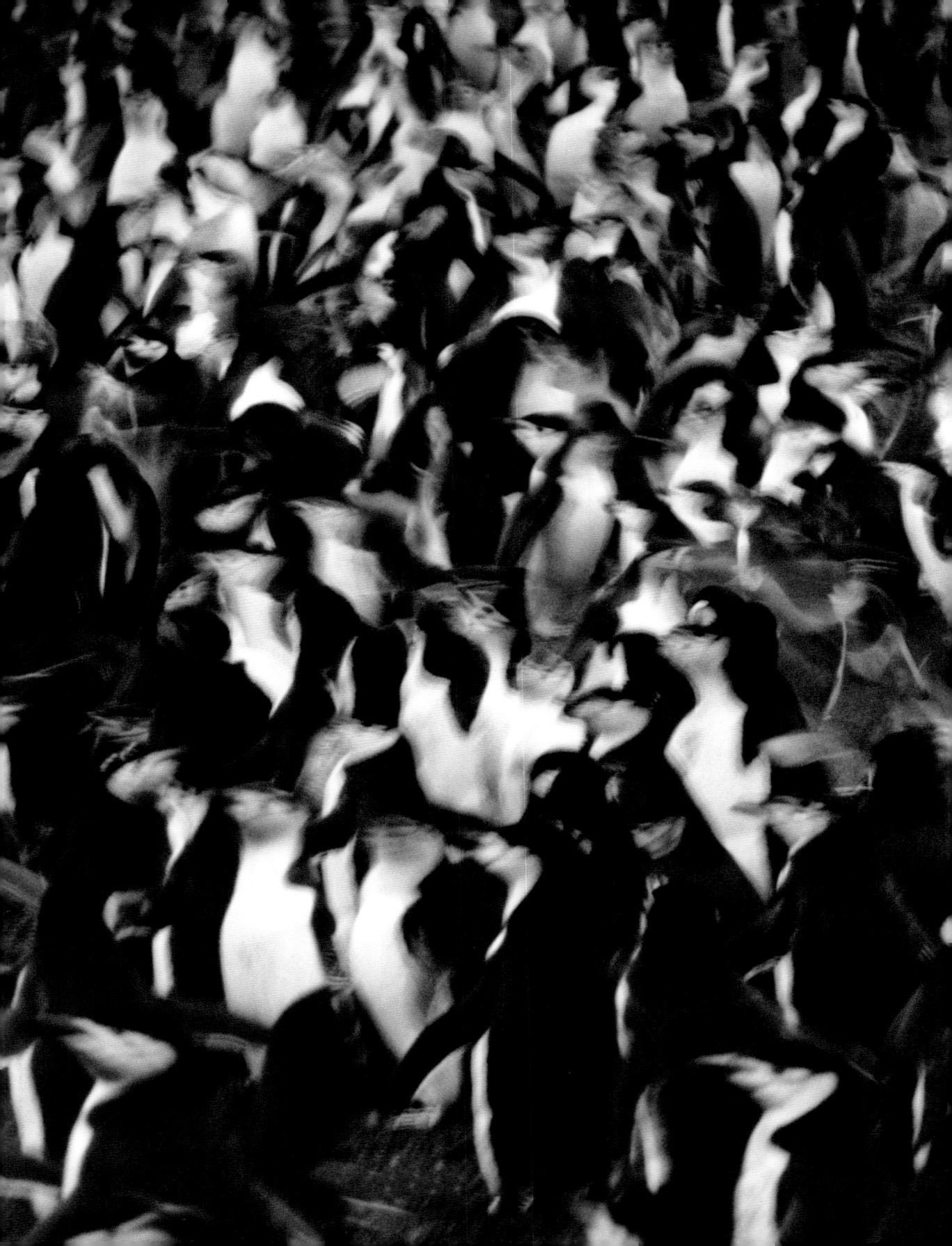

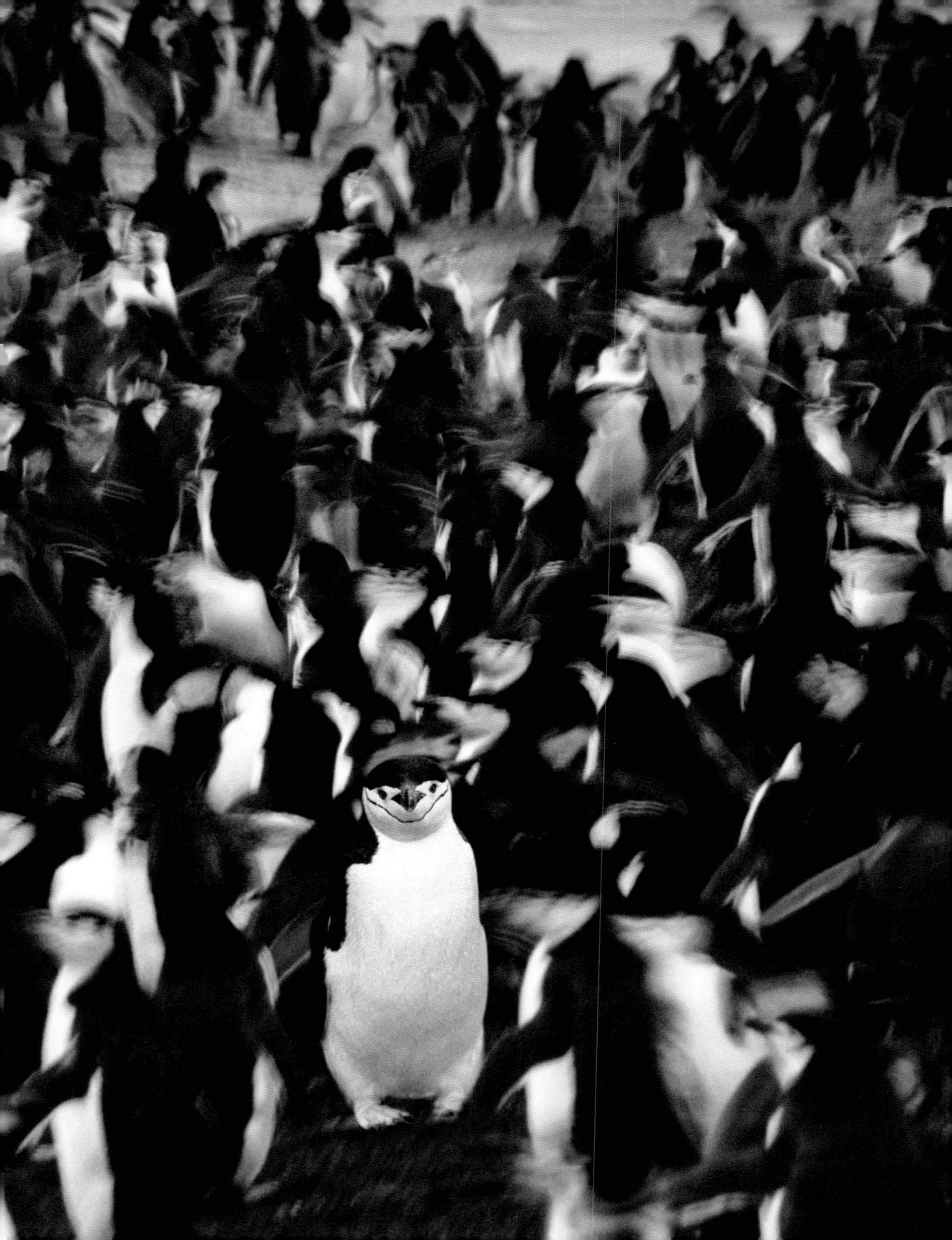

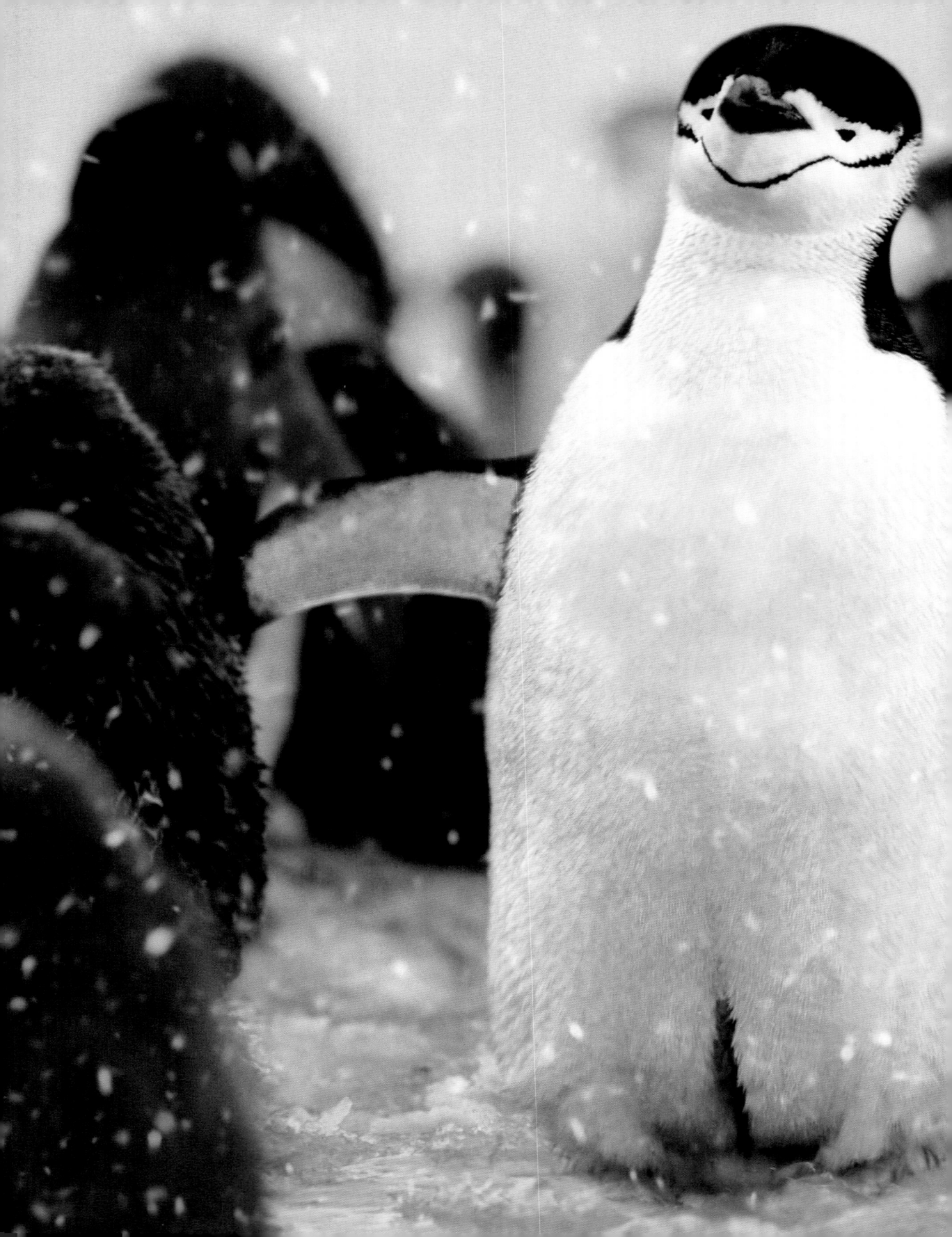

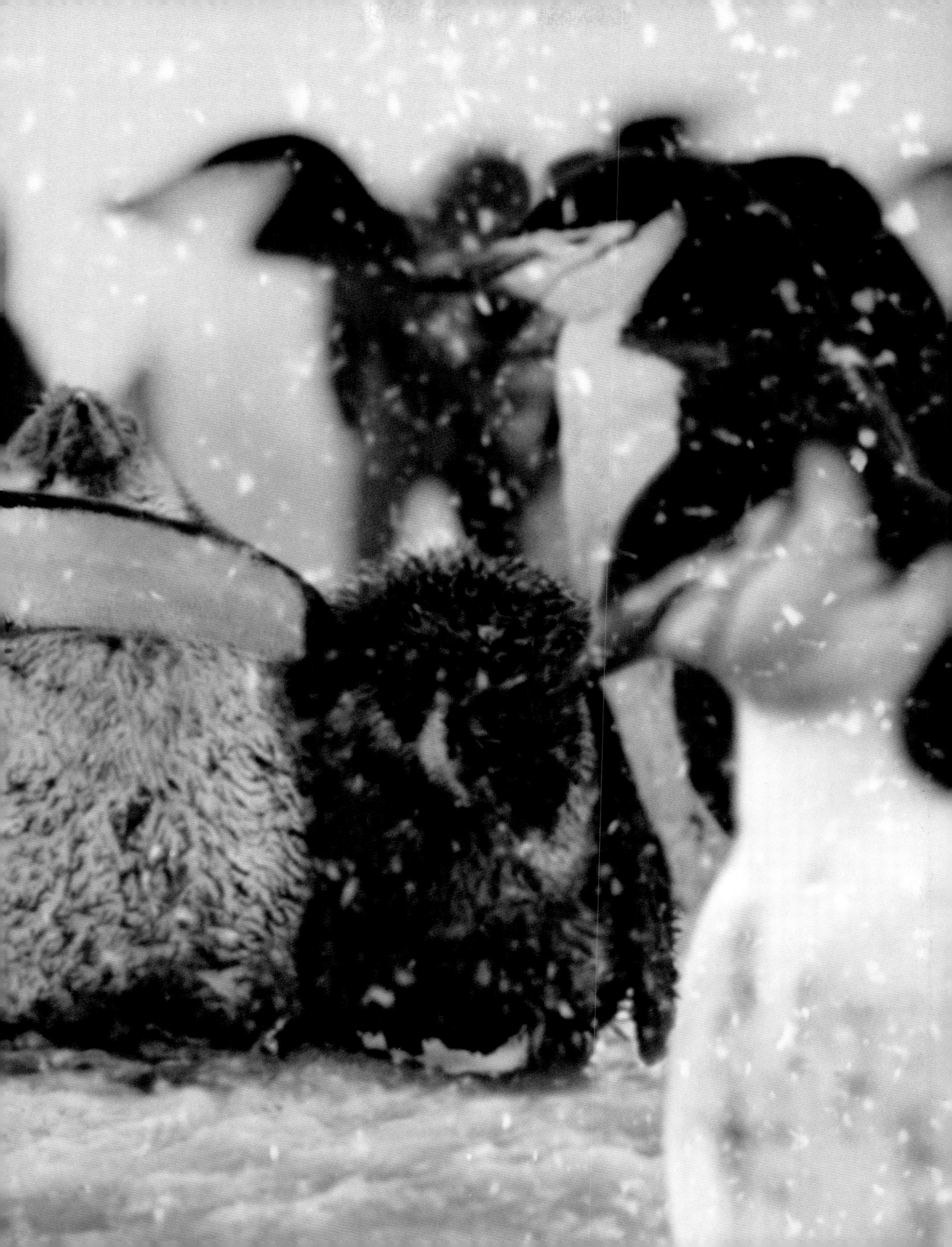

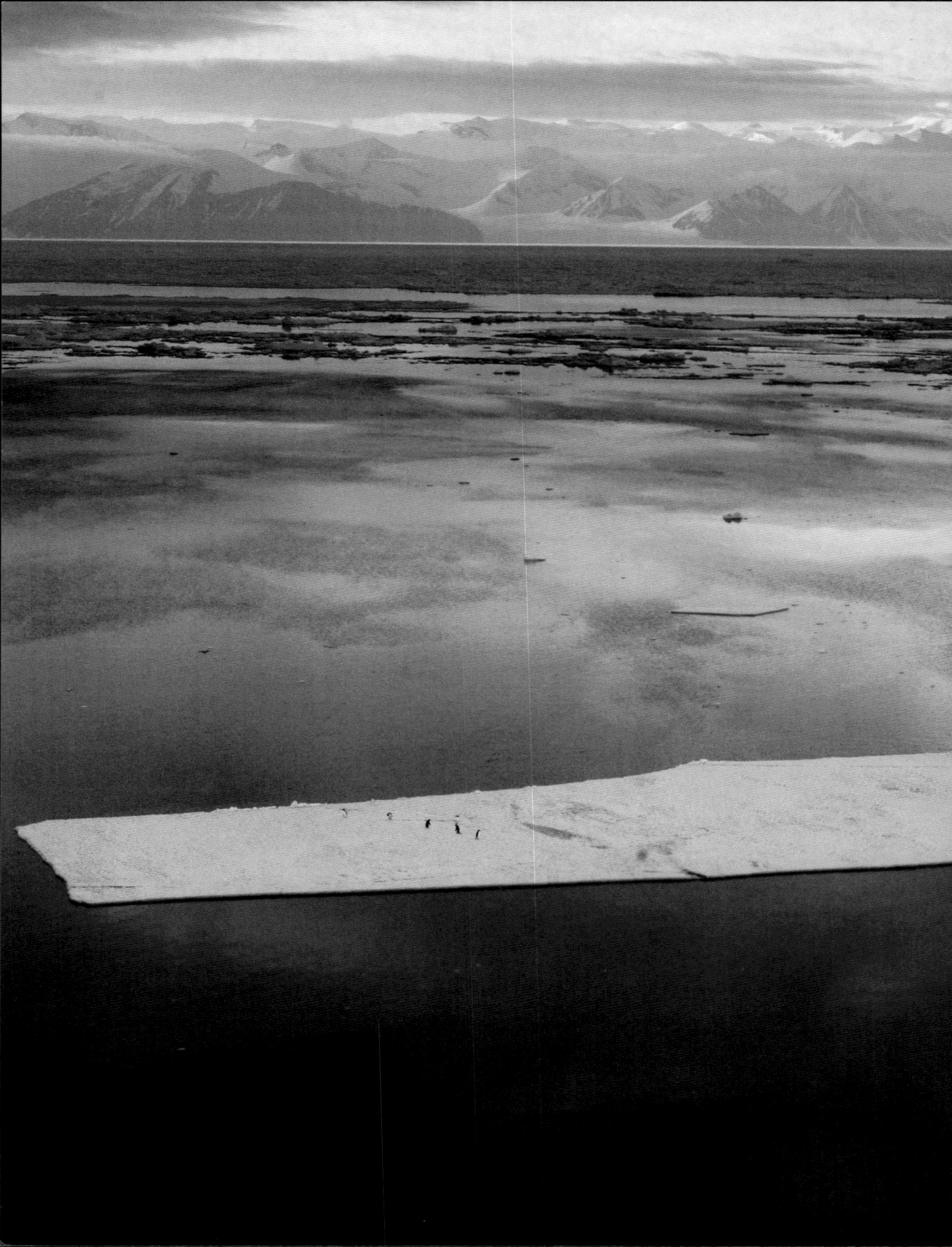

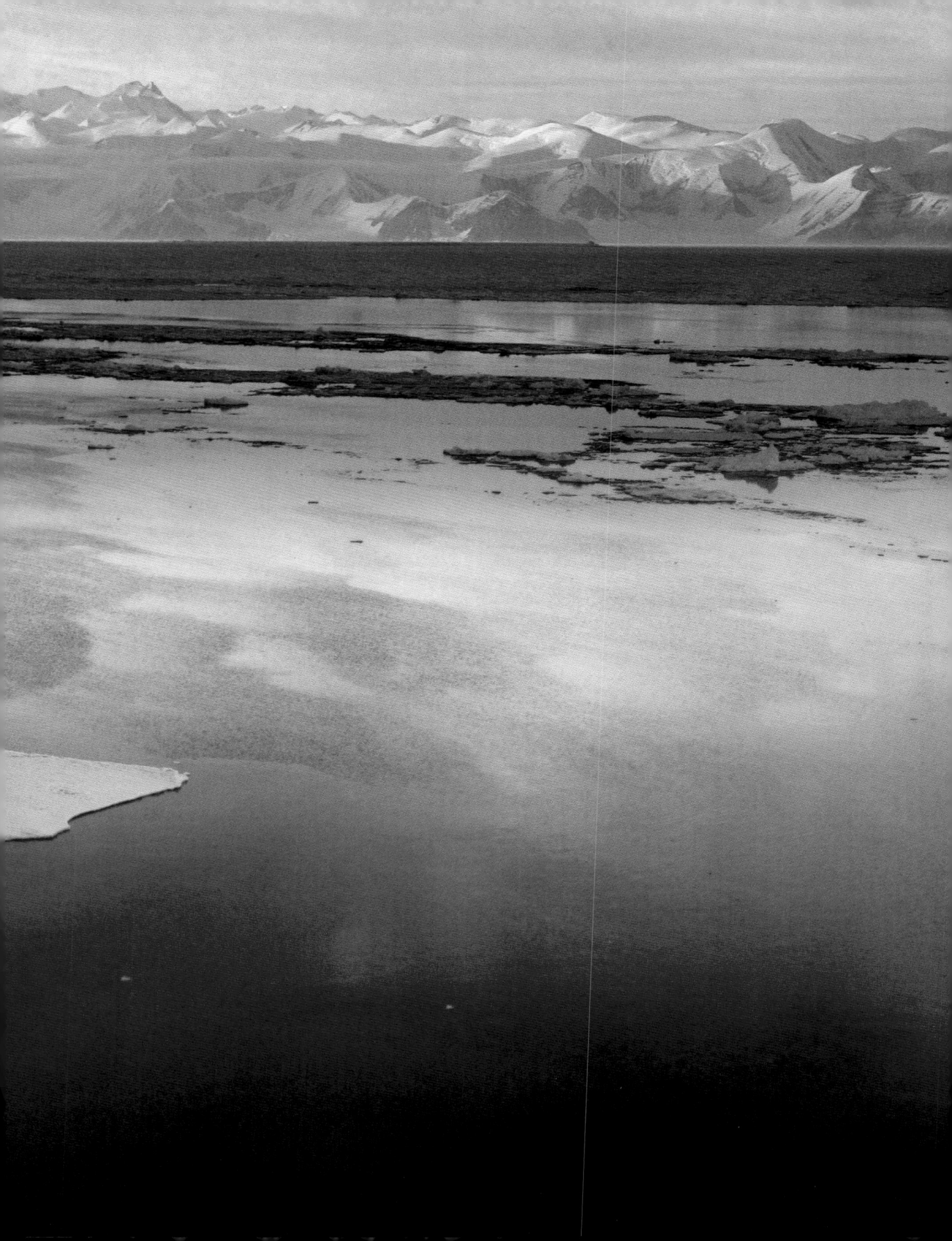

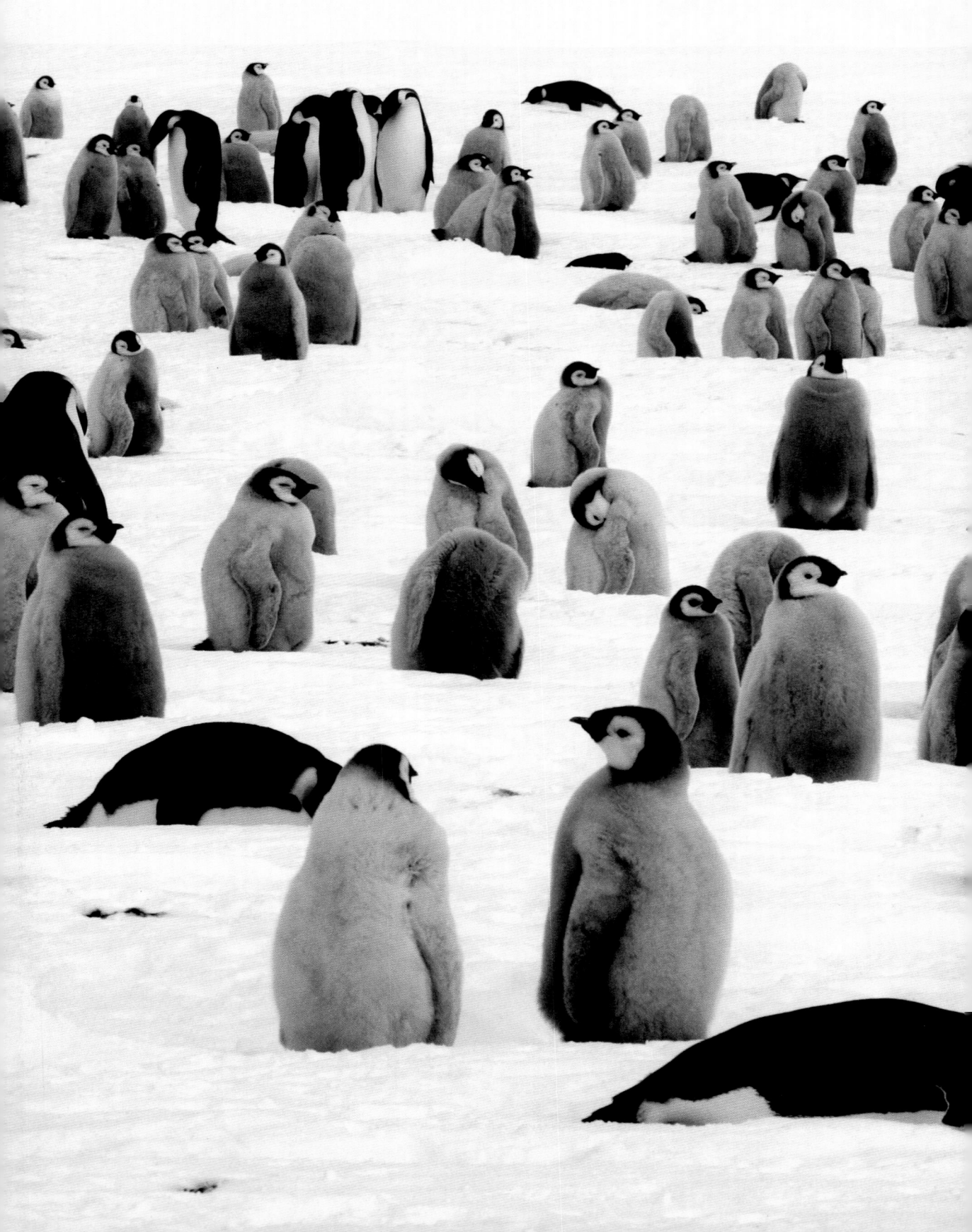

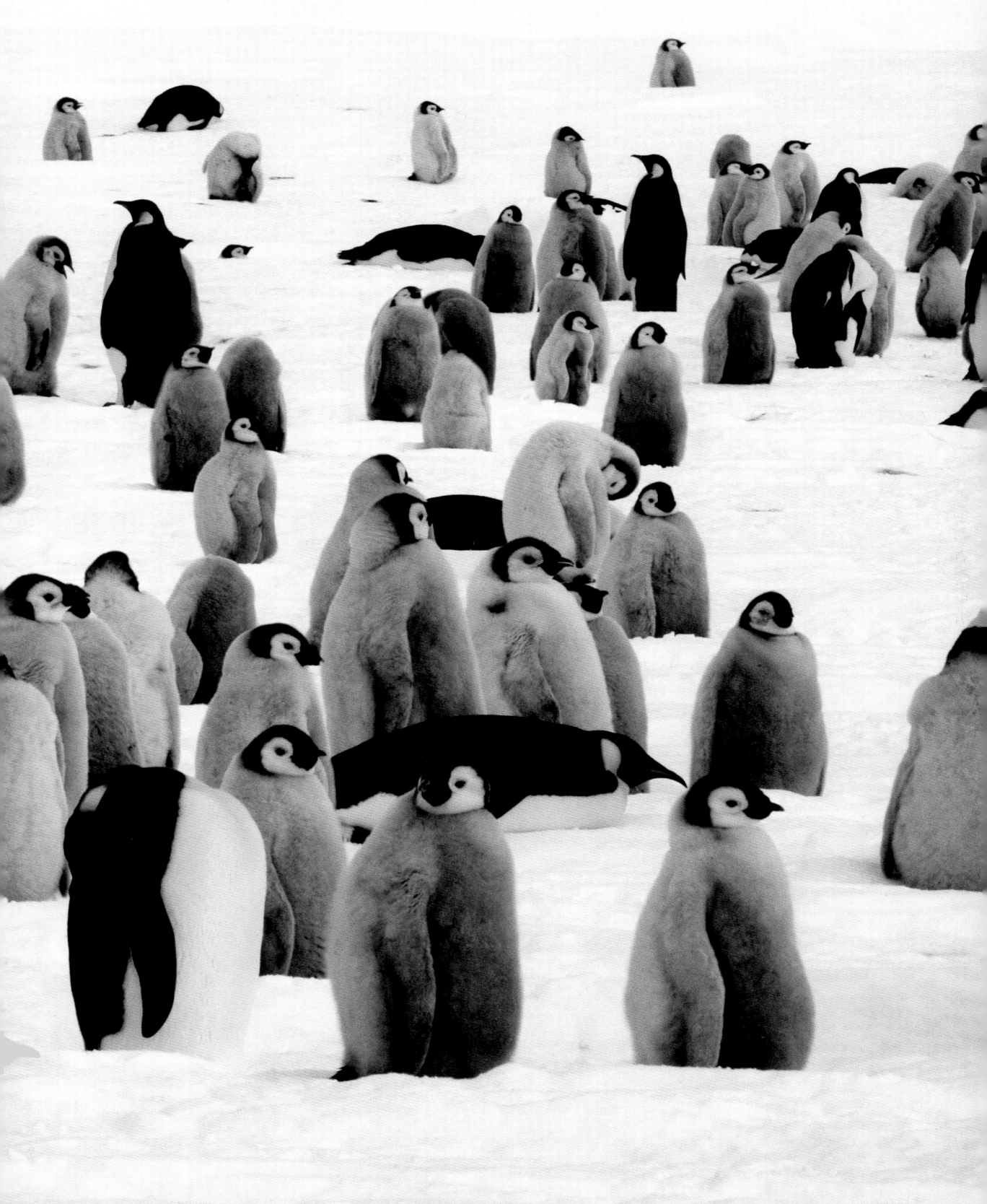

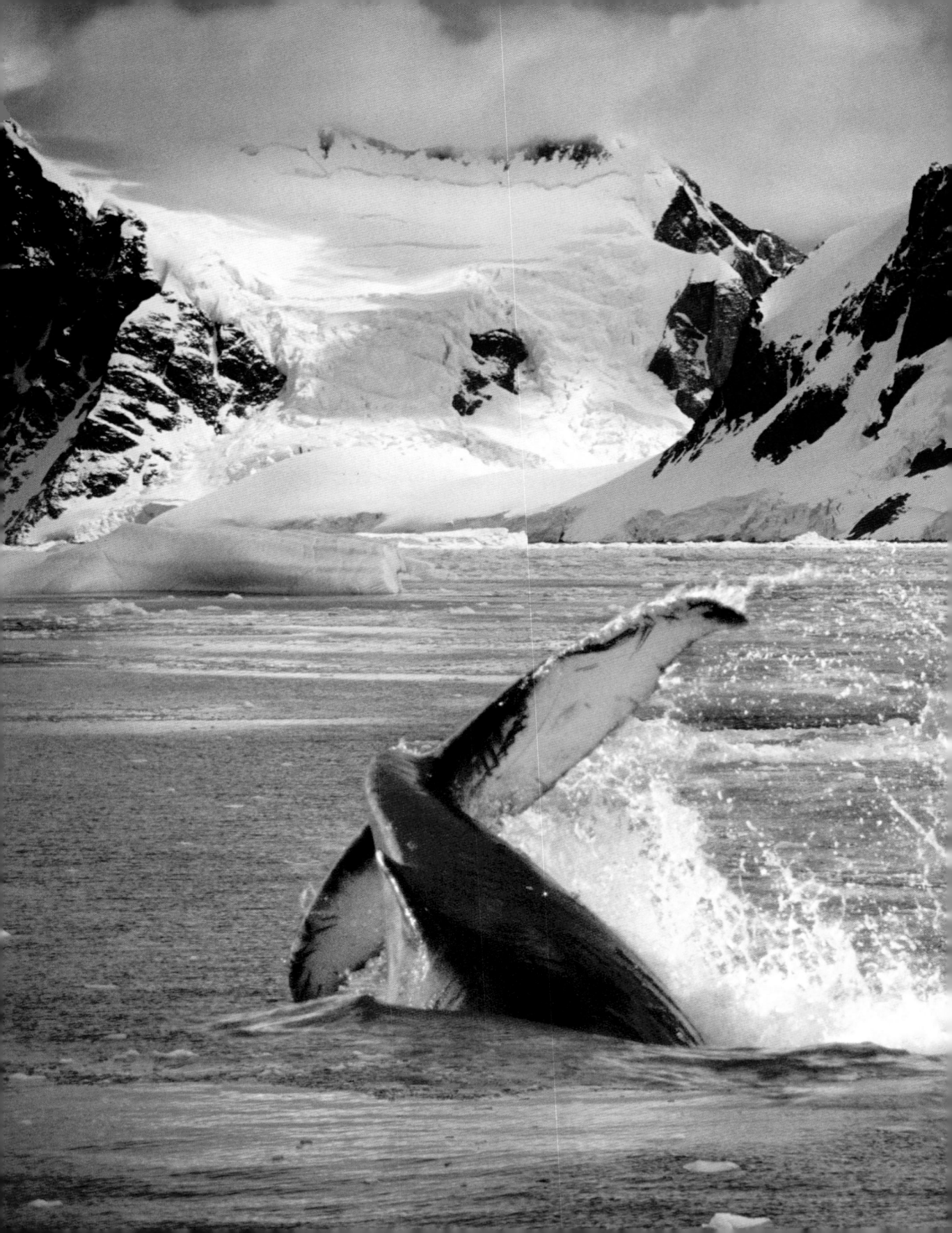

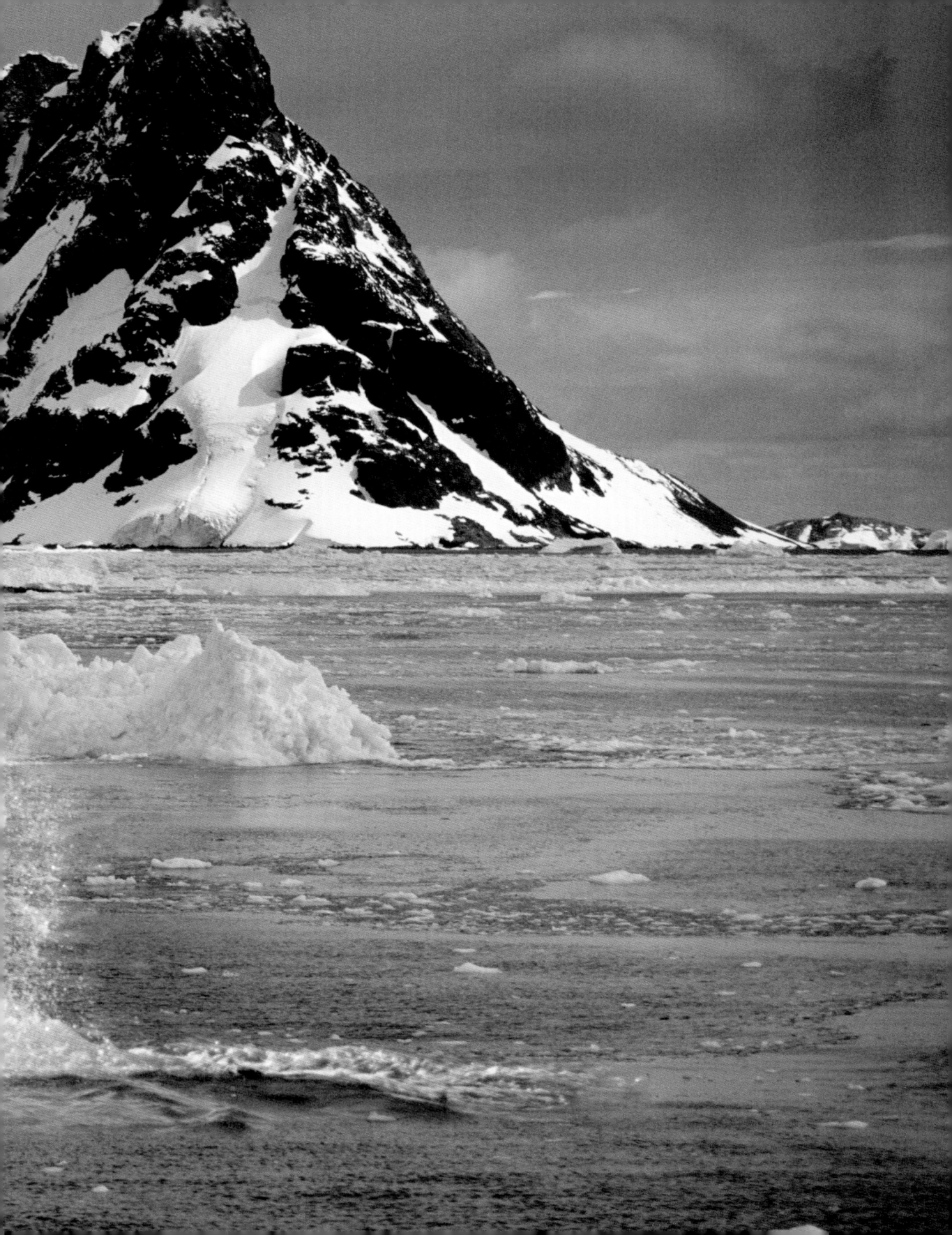

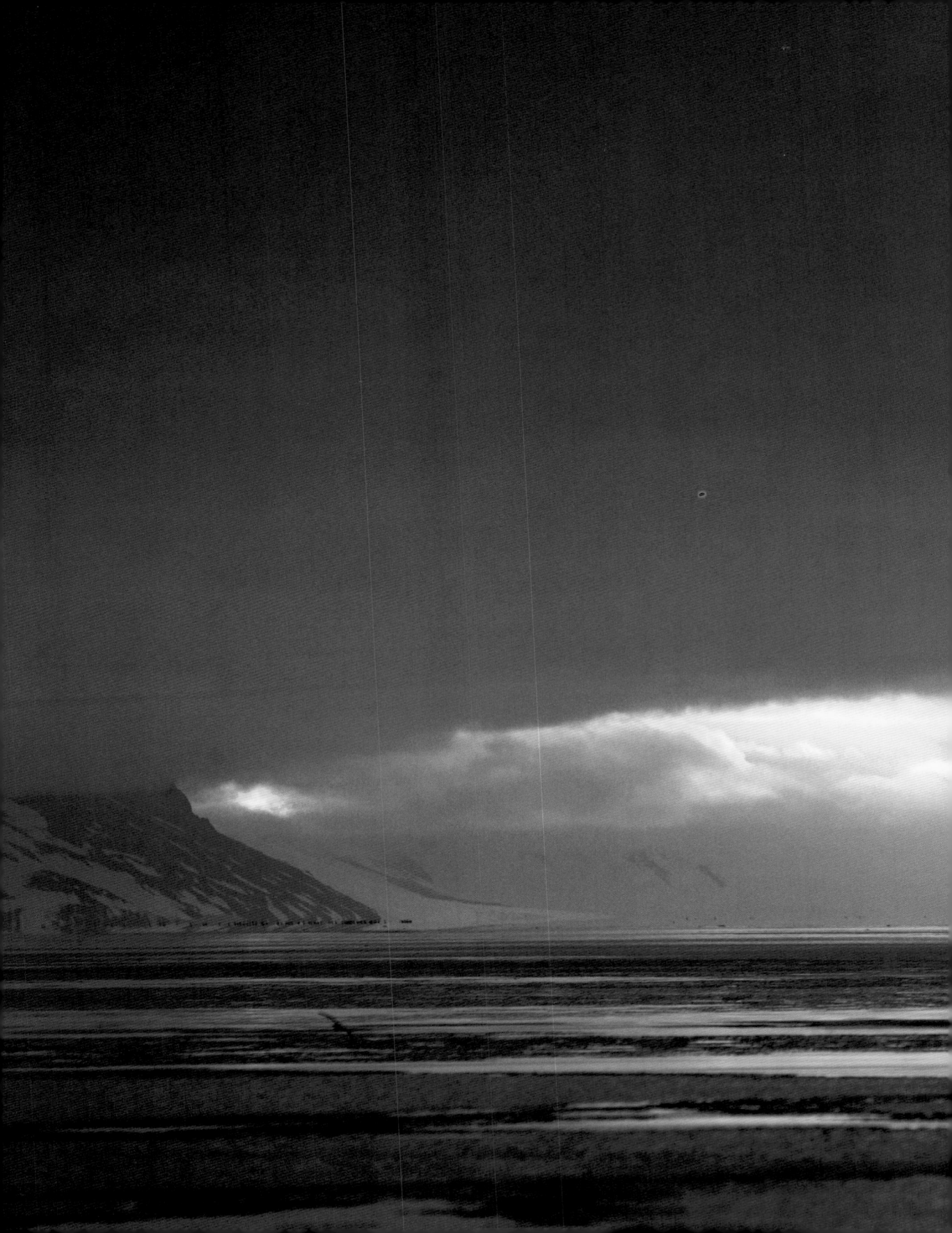

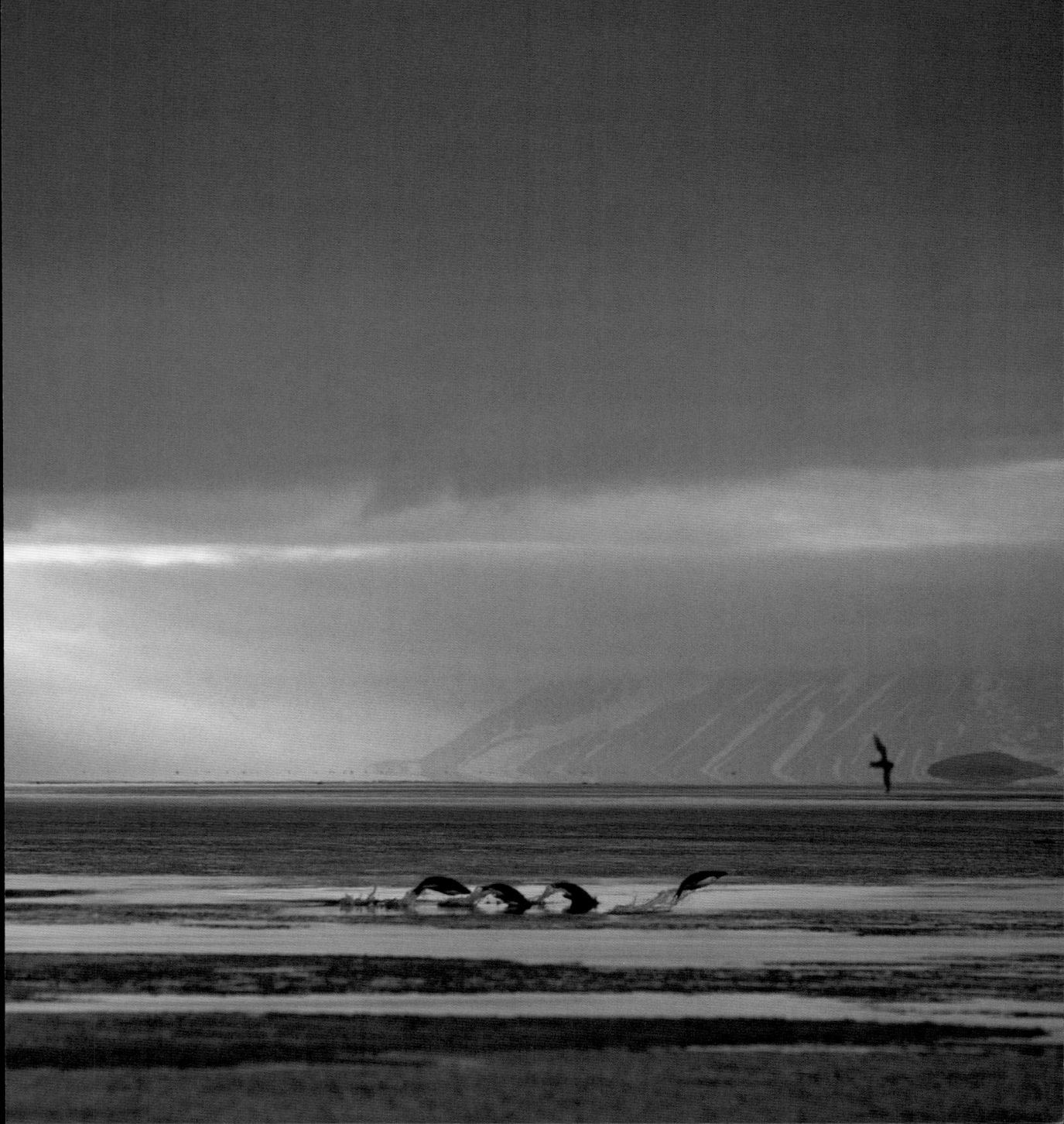

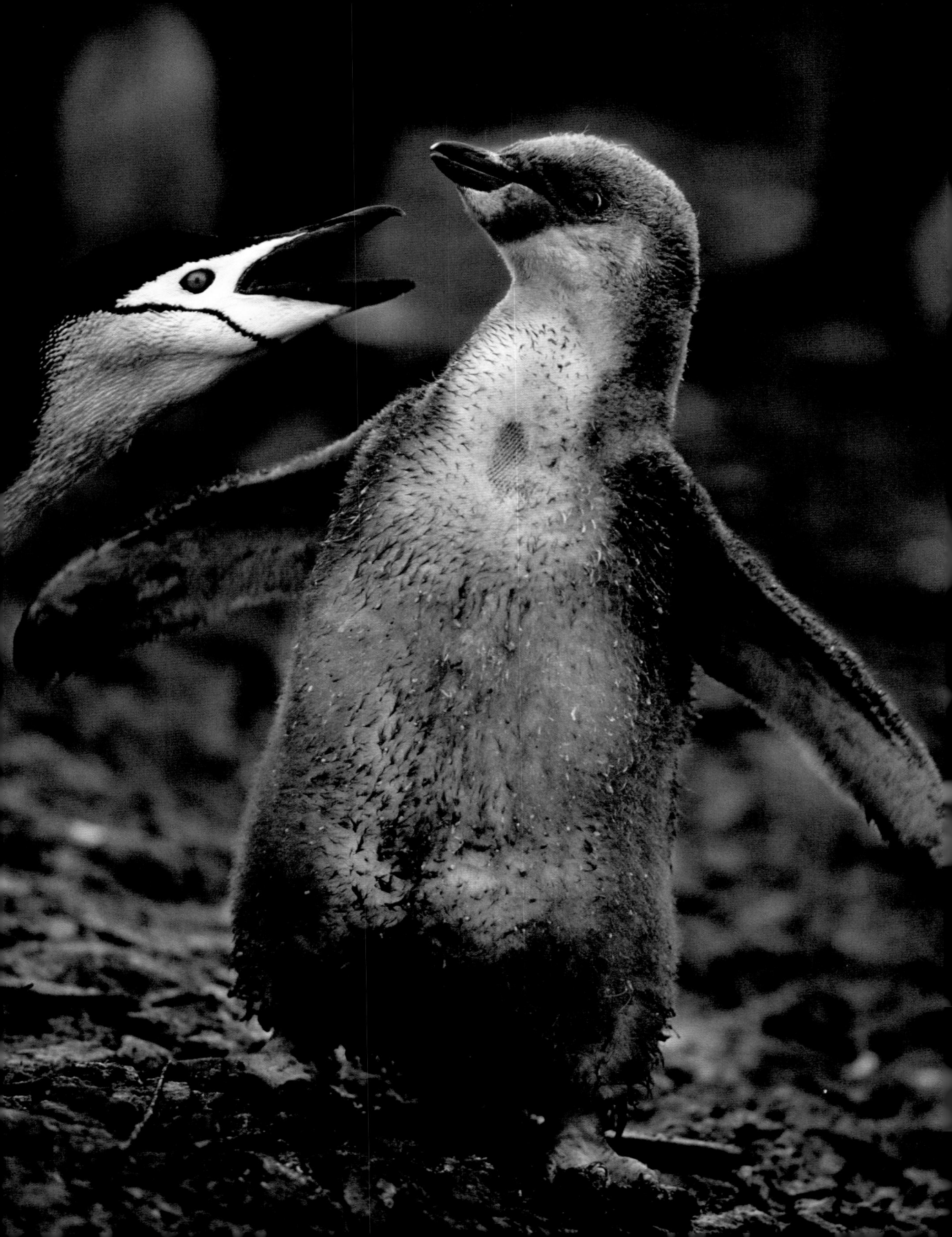

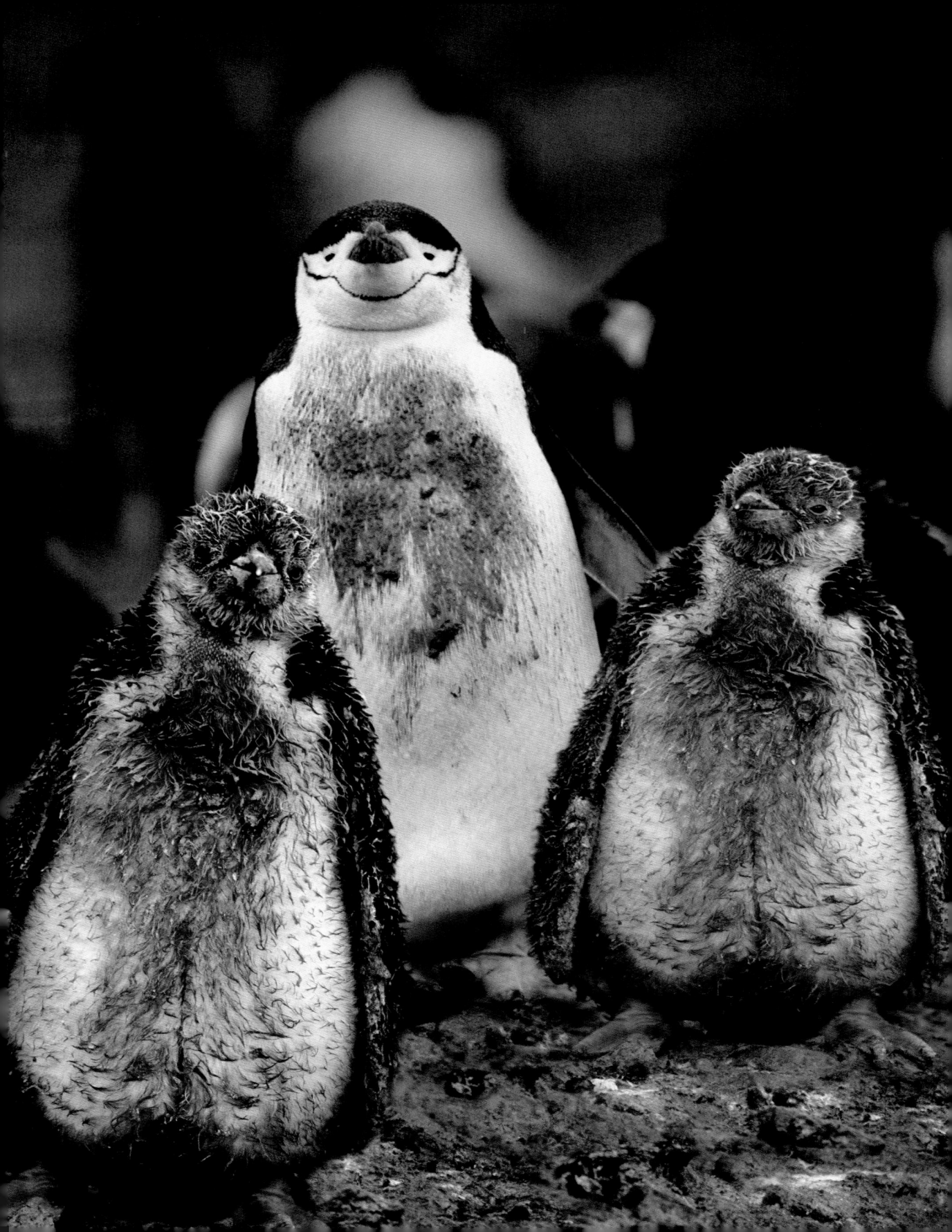

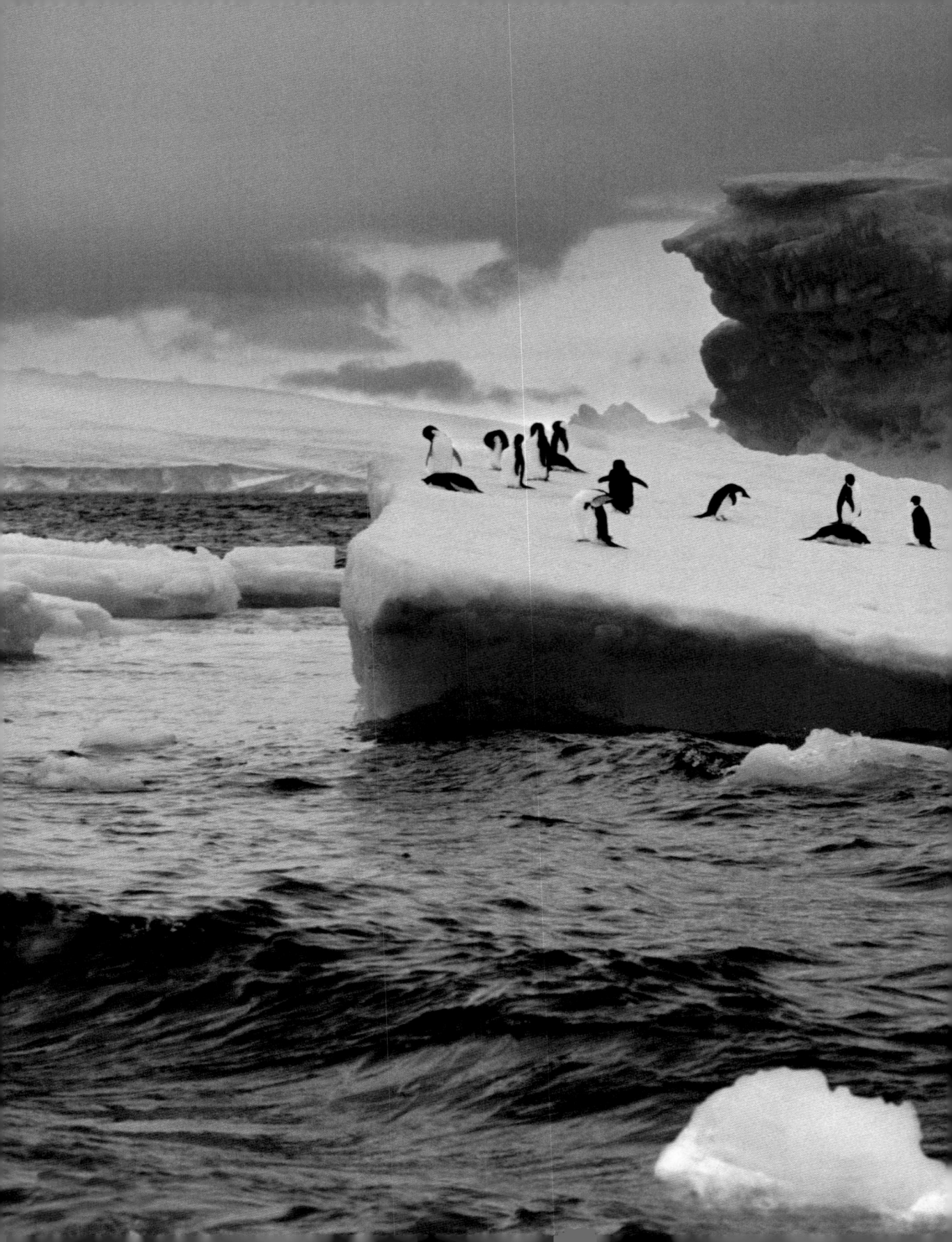

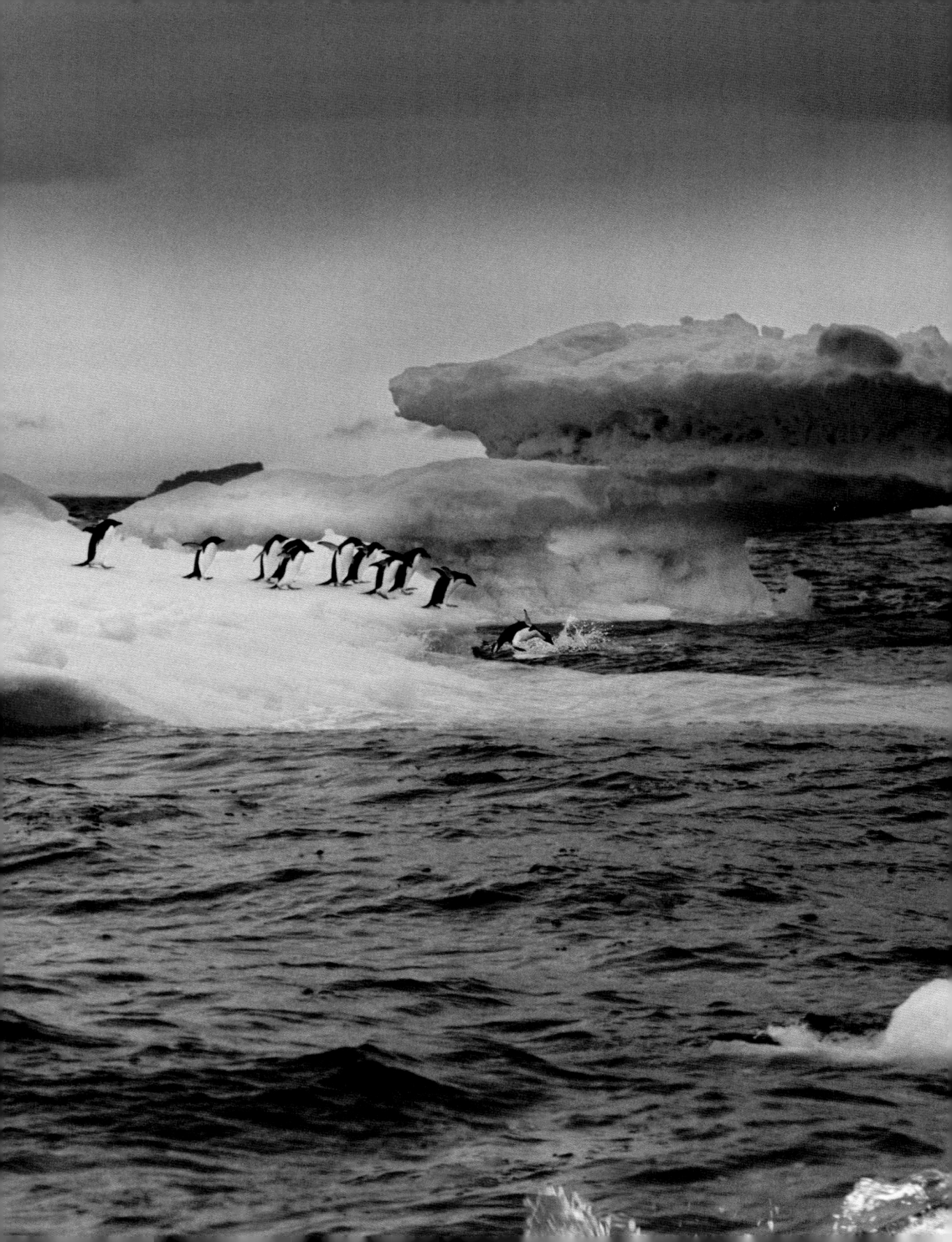

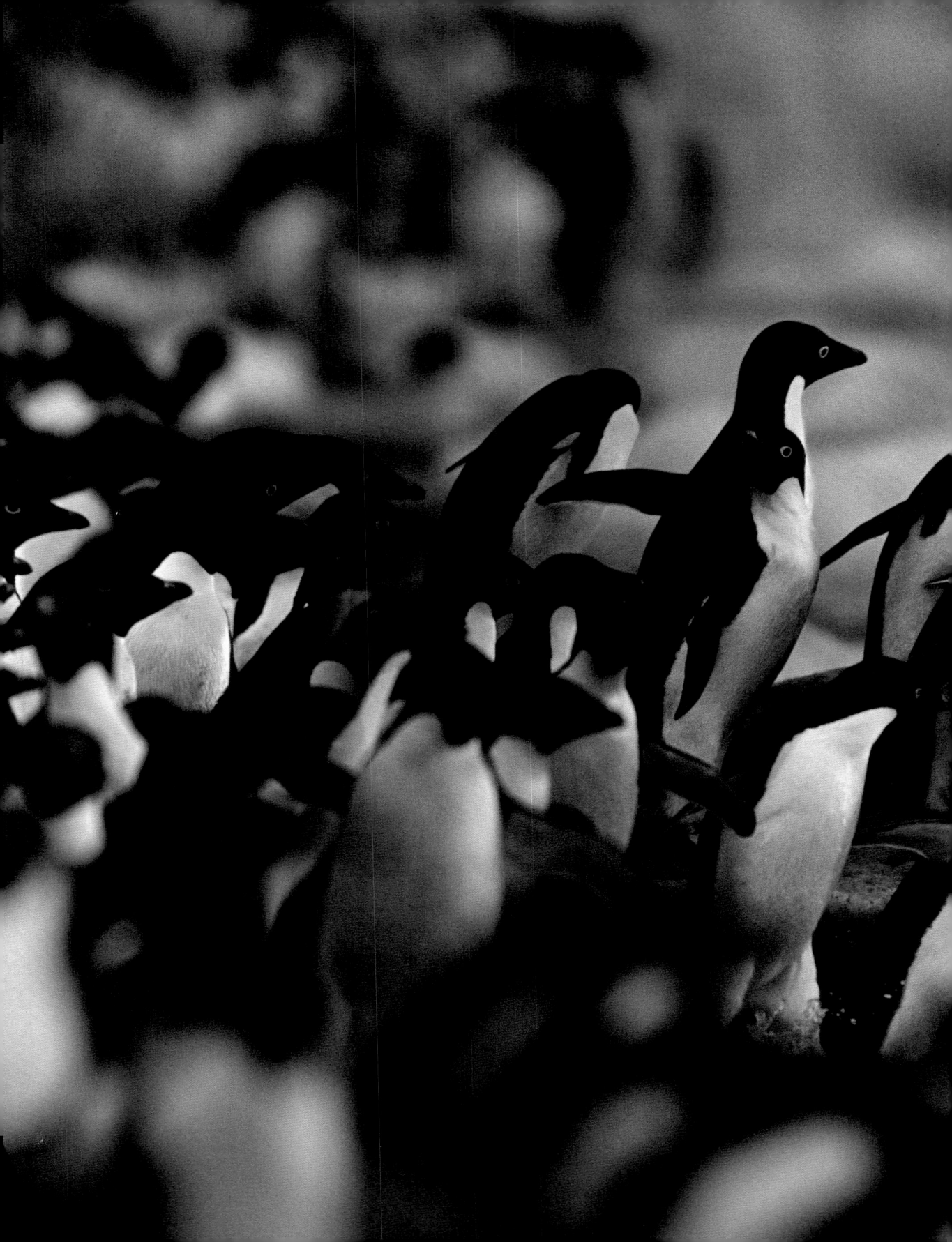

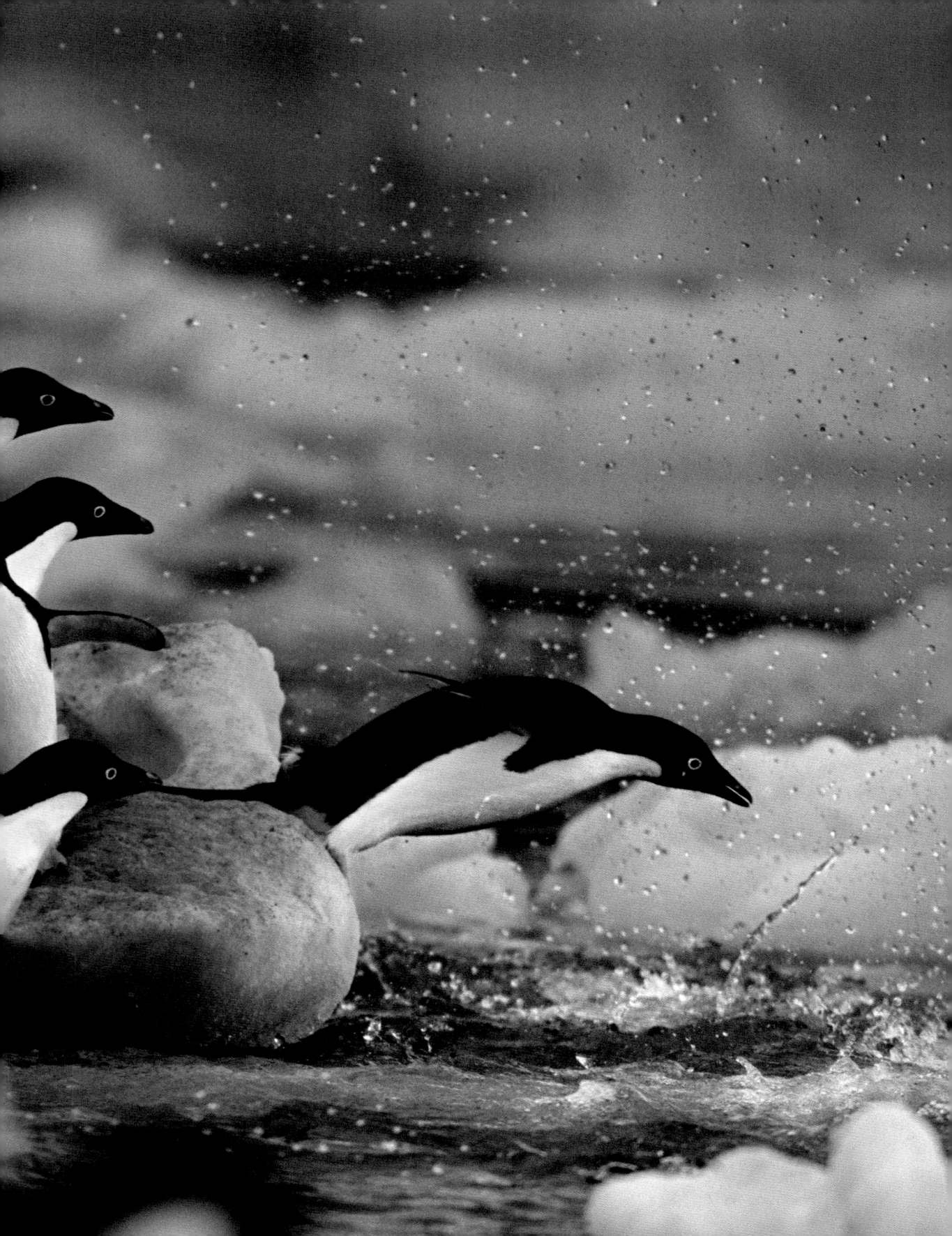

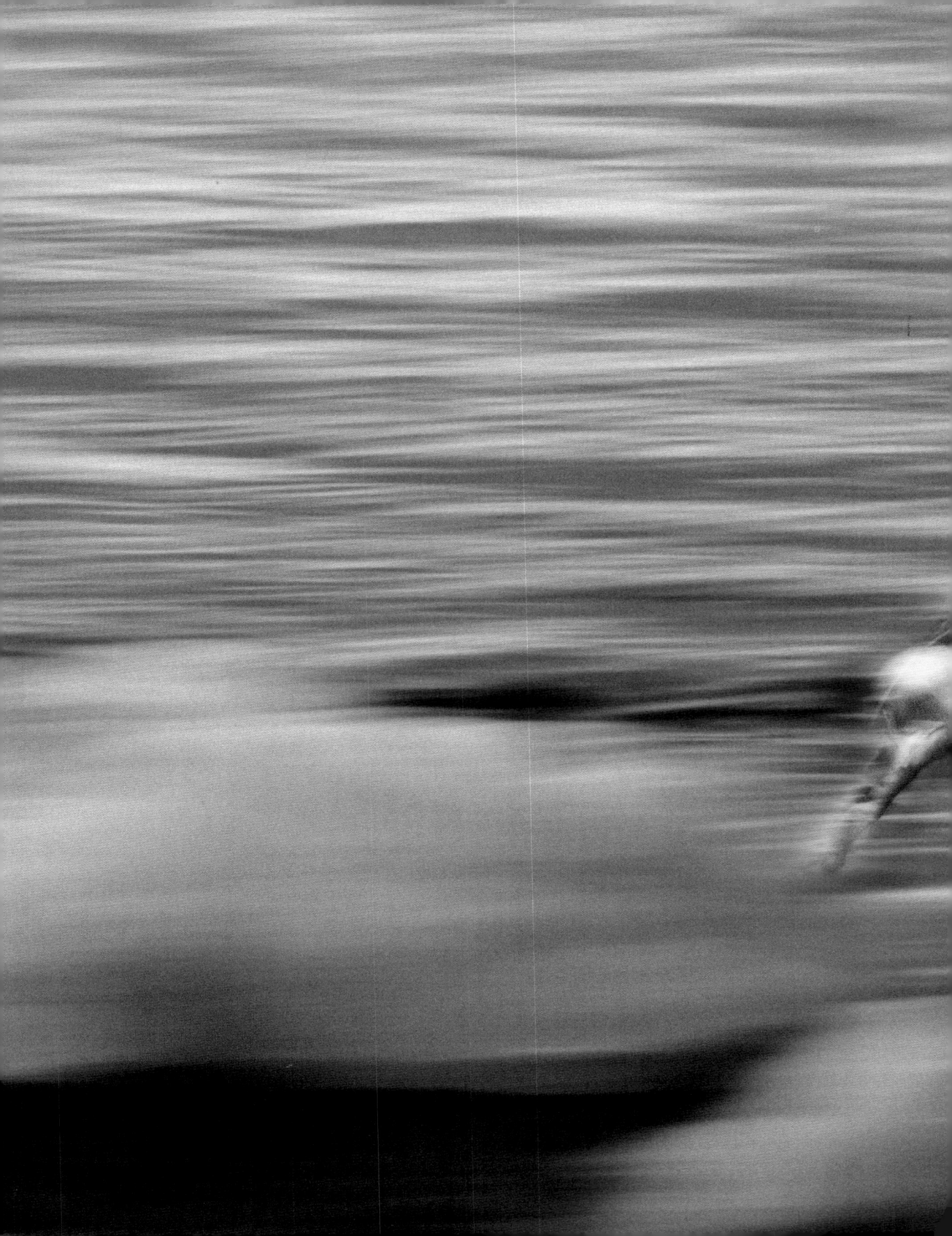

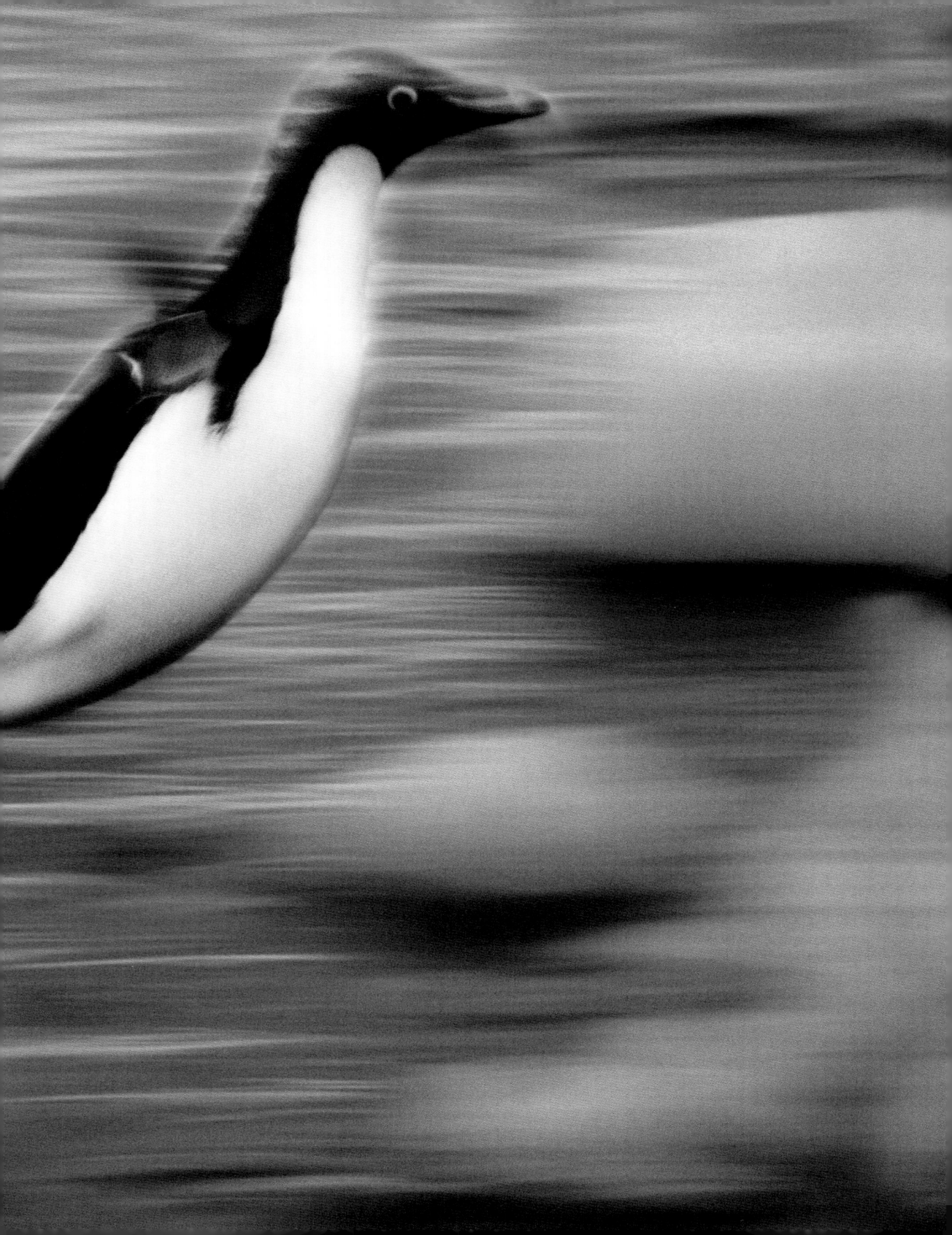

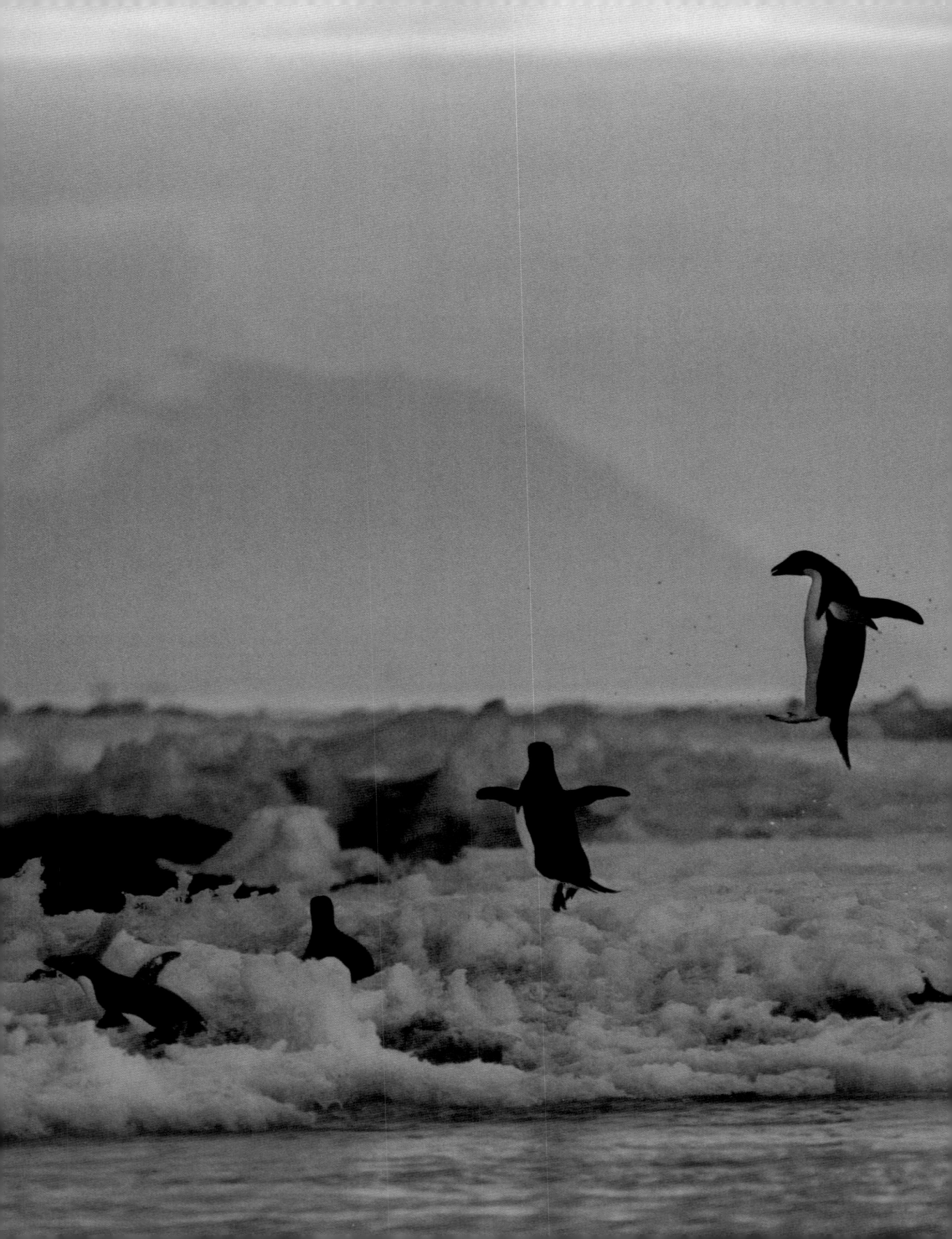

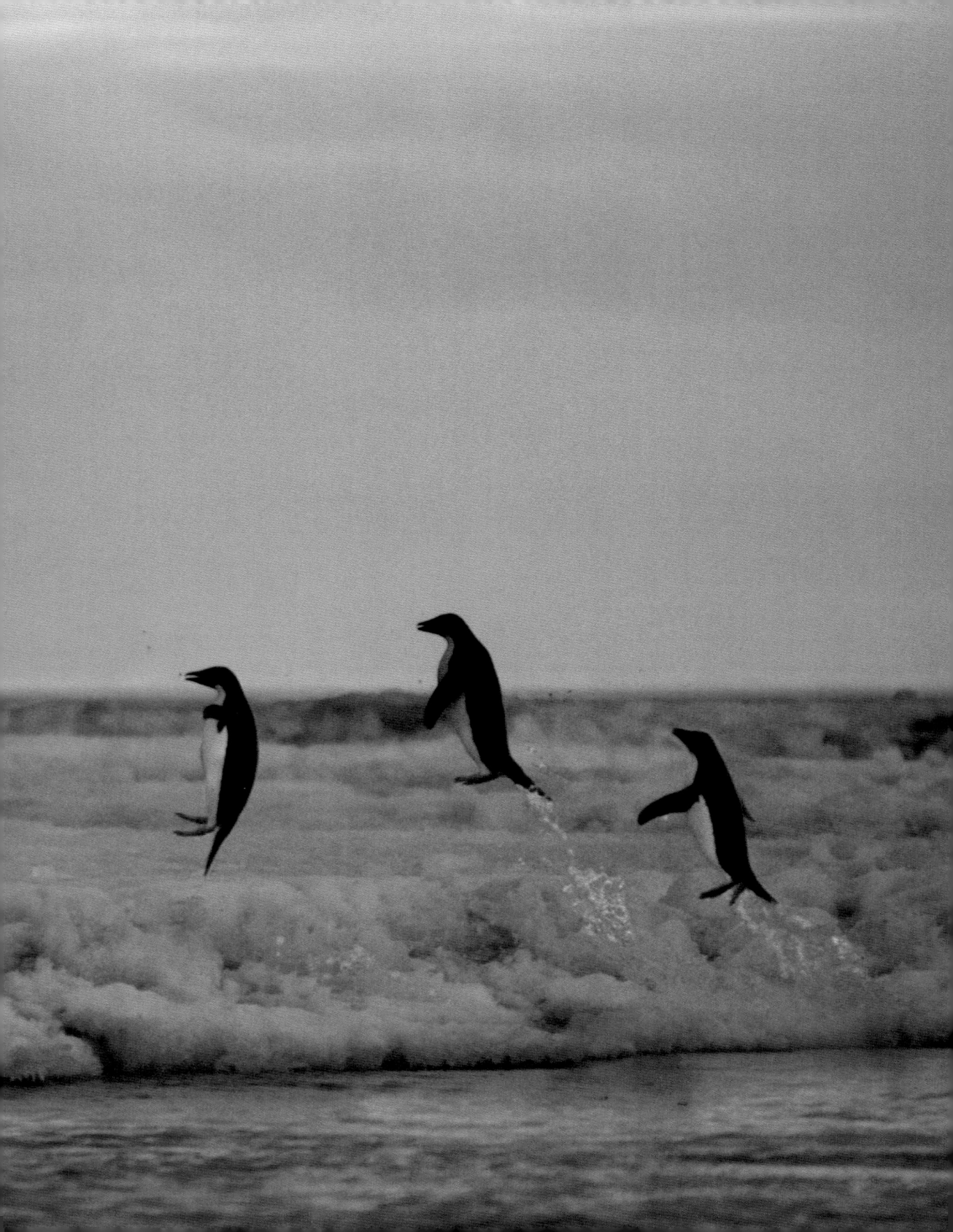

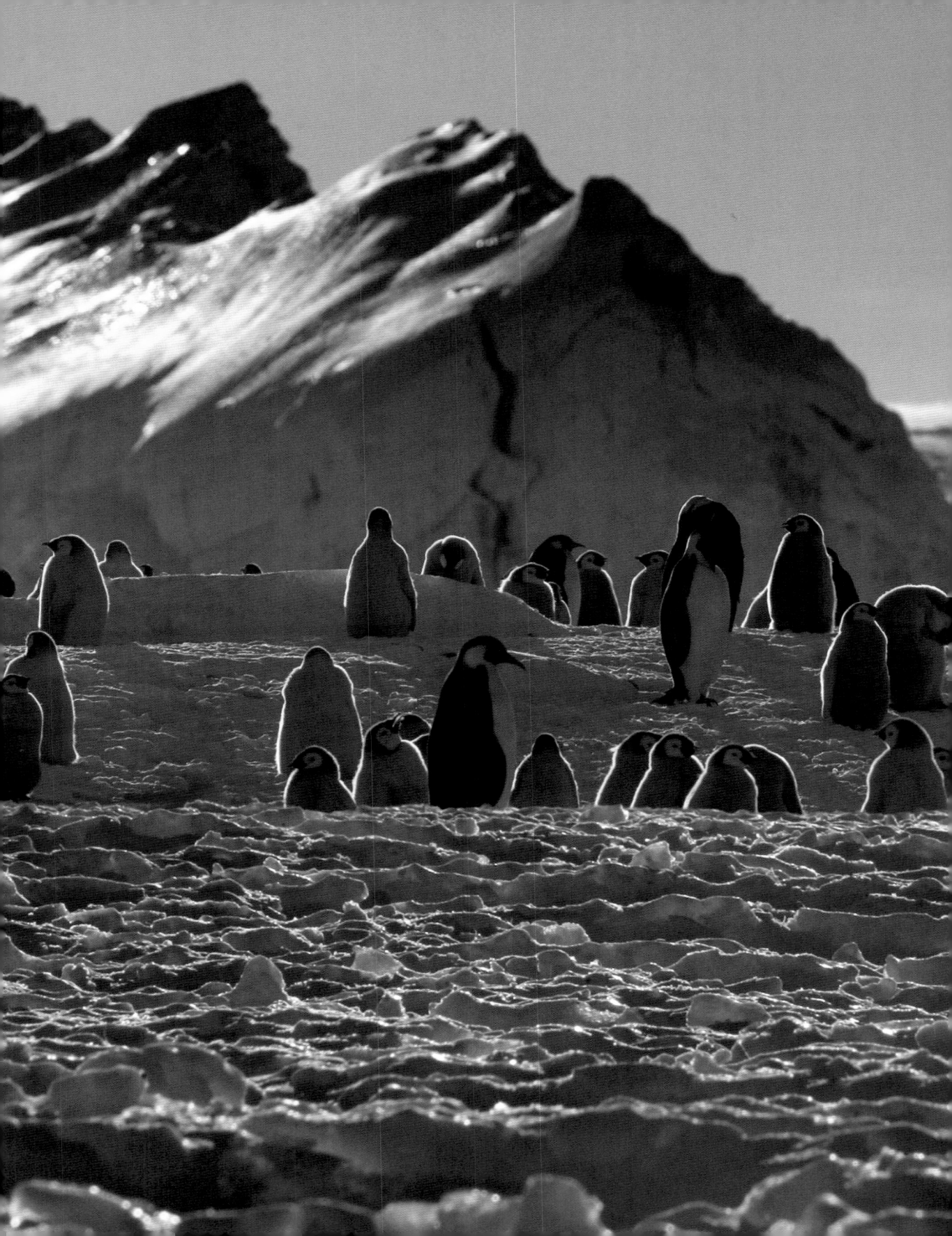

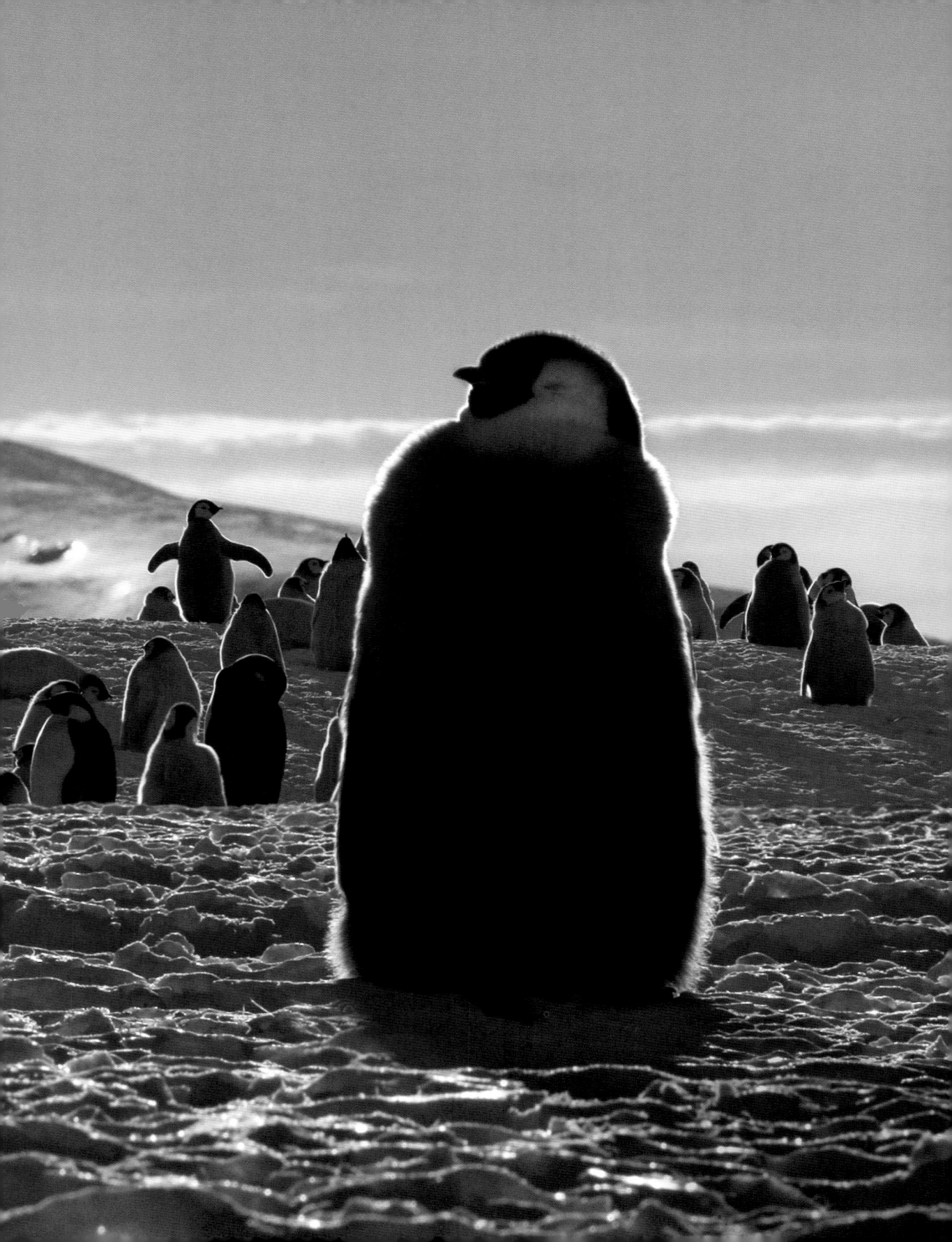

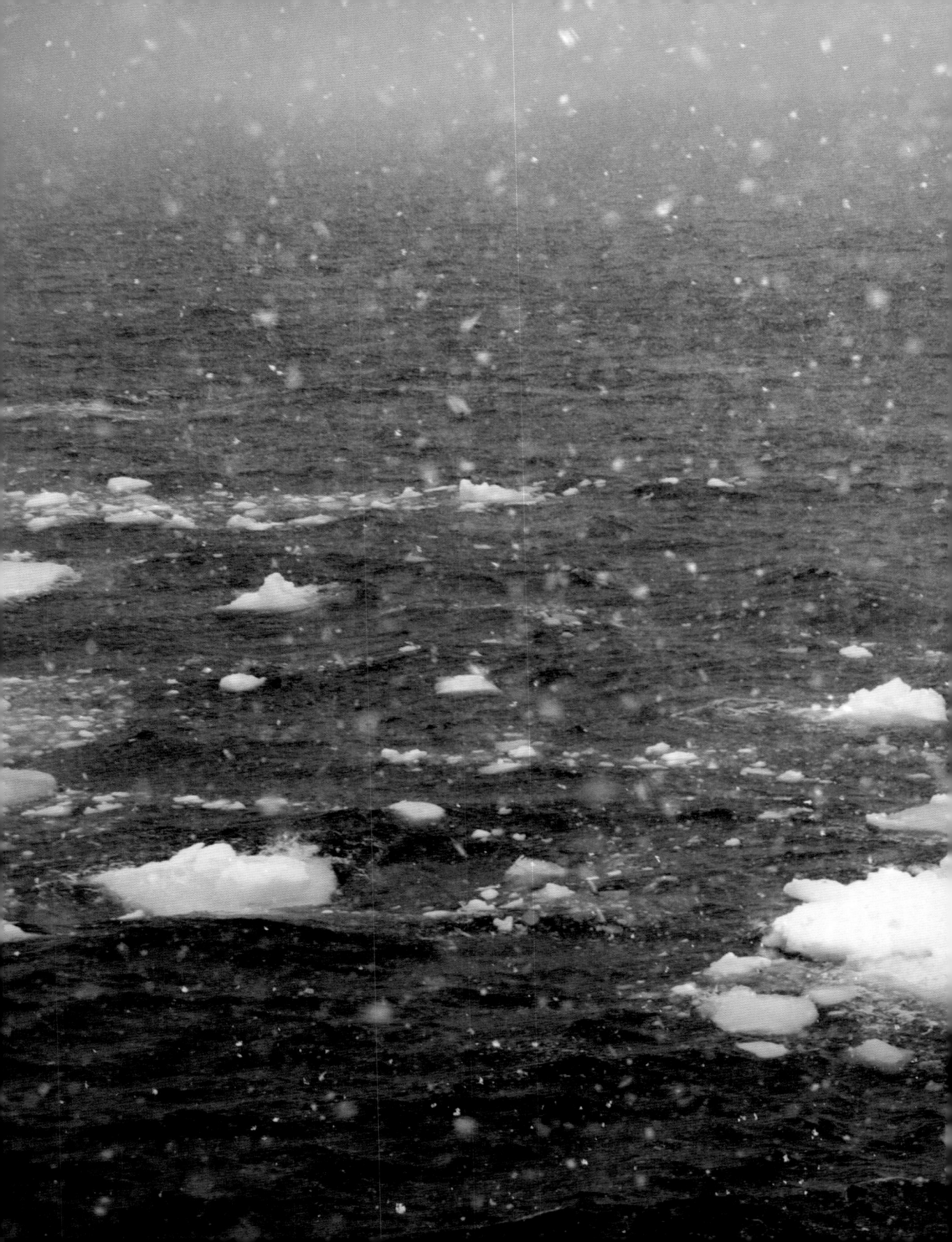

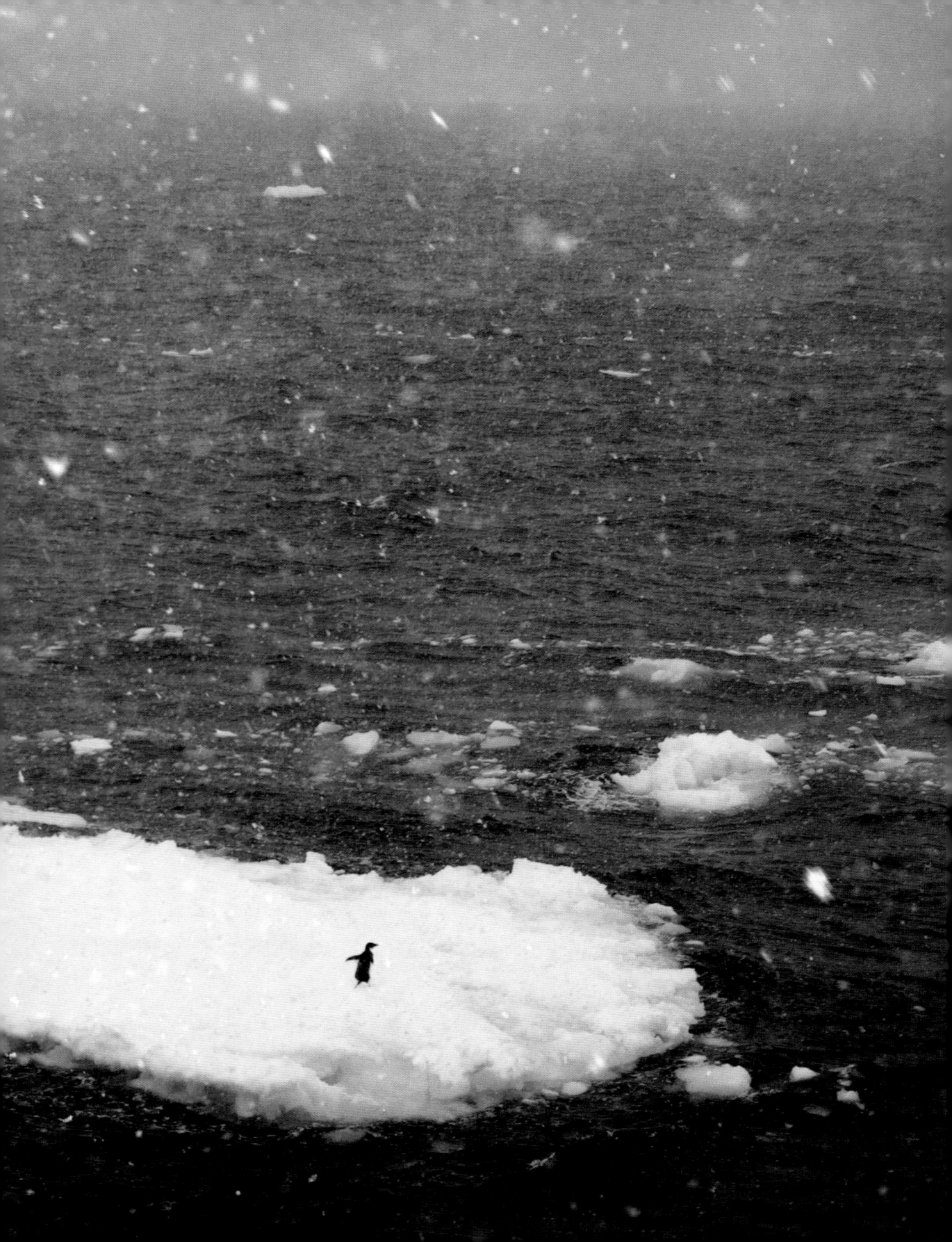

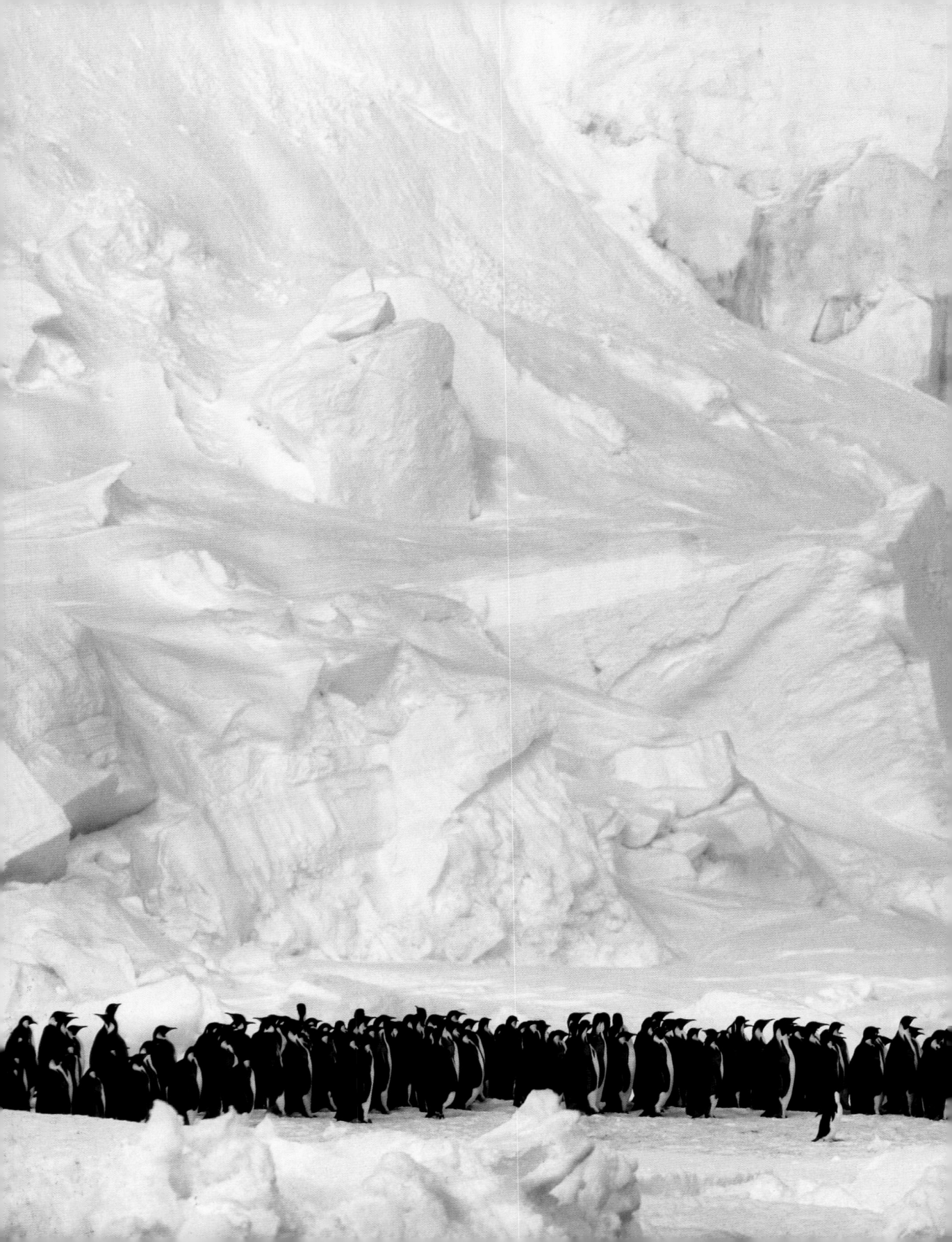

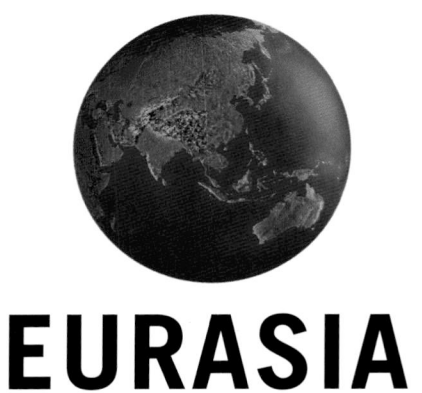

EURASIA

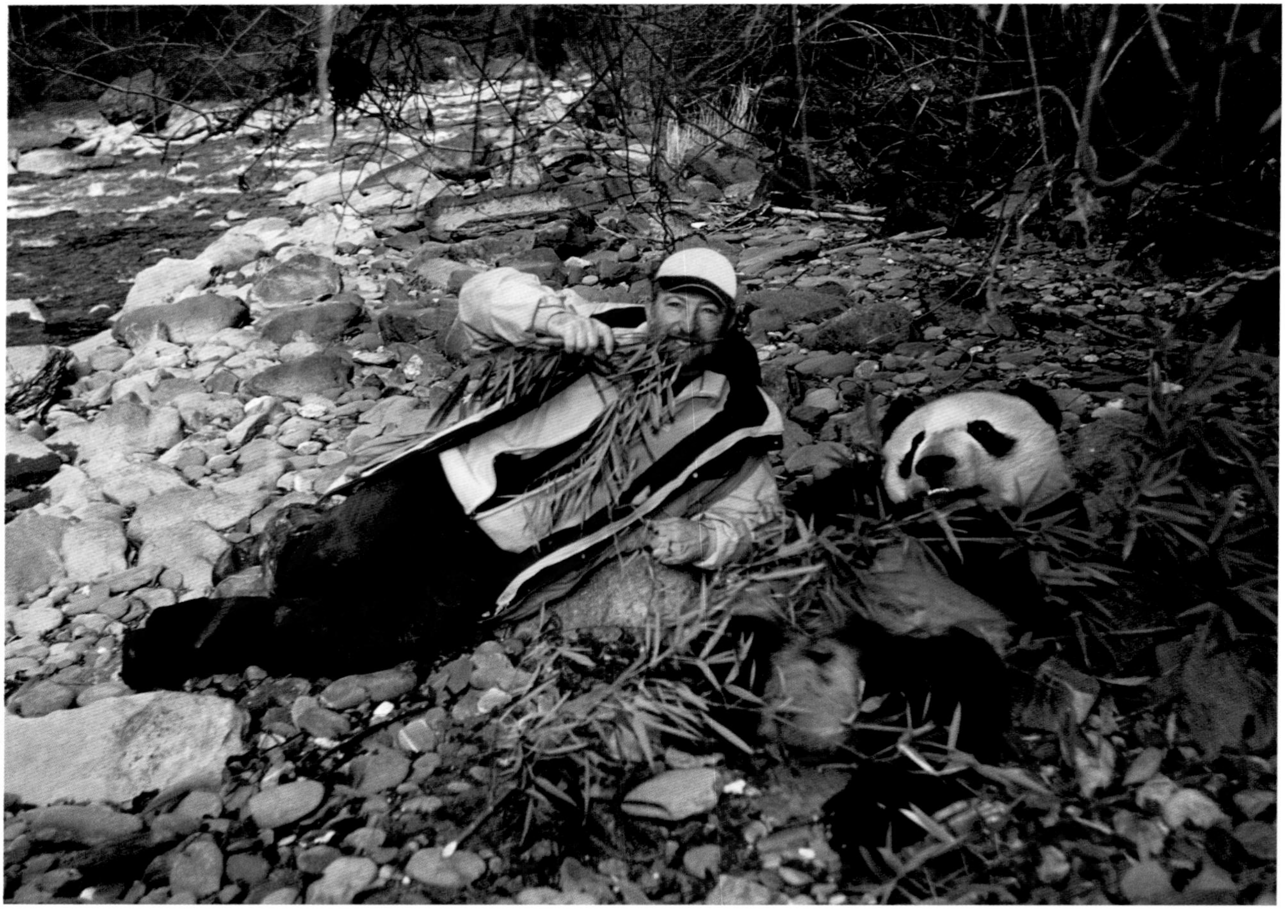

"ALL ALONE AND DESPERATELY ENDANGERED, THE TIGER LOOKS UP, INSTANTLY STRIKING A CHORD OF POIGNANT AWARENESS."

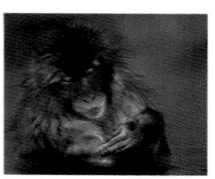

A snow monkey appears through a translucent veil of rising steam. The hot spring is her sanctuary, her small oasis in the vast chill. Immersed in the warmth, she gazes intently at her own arm. I, too, am drawn into her contemplation, discovering her long, elegant fingers, perfectly formed nails, and intricate folds on her knuckles—details so like yours and mine. The separate parts embody the threads that bind us together, a perfect acknowledgment of all that we share.

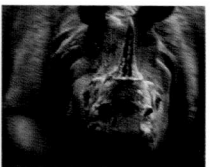

Shortsighted and stubborn, a rhino in full charge is a raw and formidable force. I face the wrath of an angry rhino thundering toward me, his enormous bulk growing rapidly in the camera frame. He is too close; focus is lost, peripheral vision a blur of moving gray. A split second before impact he swerves, narrowly missing my small, open vehicle. The only sound I hear is my heartbeat. Rhinos move me deeply; they remind me of lonely and hunted refugees from a prehistoric age, determined to stand defiant on their own dwindling ground.

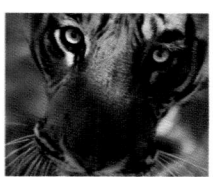

Deep in the jungles of India I strive to find the elusive wild tiger. Our party searches first by vehicle, then on the backs of elephants. We heave and crash through dense undergrowth, clamber down gullies, and grapple with overhanging branches. Just as the frustration of failure challenges our will, the guide finds two glowing jewels peering from beneath a shield of leaves. The tiger's eyes seem brighter than anything else in the jungle. All alone and desperately endangered, she looks up, instantly striking a chord of poignant awareness. The moment is all too brief; she swiftly turns back into the shadows, as if to echo her own extinction.

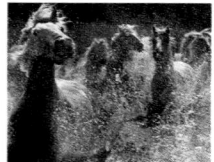

The Camargue in southern France is home to the magnificent Camargue horses; they graze the land adjoining the marshes. It has long been my ambition to photograph them, portraying the raw energy and collective spirit of these hardy animals. It takes several attempts, standing thigh deep in marshes for many hours, enduring biting insects in the hot sun. Filled with vigor, the horses stampede through the water toward me. I love every minute of it.

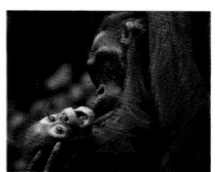

Beyond the banks of Borneo's Sekonya River, the forest abounds with primates. We travel in our small boat; proboscis monkeys, gibbons, and macaques turn their heads to watch us as we pass. I see my first orangutan in the distance, a flash of orange partly obscured by branches. I follow with my eyes until I see her no more. Later, at Camp Leakey, I encounter many more orangutans who reach out to me with their gentle eyes. They are an essential part of the ecological harmony of the rainforests. I carry precious memories of this place.

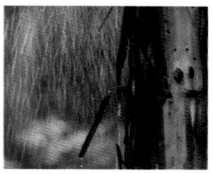

I encounter a juvenile forest in southern Australia. Reclaimed from farmland some thirty years ago, the rainforest is filled with vitality. Abundant life forages in the undergrowth; the young canopy is beginning to close over in its struggle toward self-sustainability. My guide, also thirty, is dwarfed by the towering trees. I contemplate how differently each has grown in three decades.

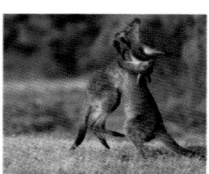

I feel a deep sense of peace after my long walk to a grassy place in Australia. Each morning and evening I photograph kangaroos going about the business of, well, simply being kangaroos. Trudging under the weight of my backpack, I am inspired by the comparative simplicity of their lives, free from complexities and baggage that we find so burdensome.

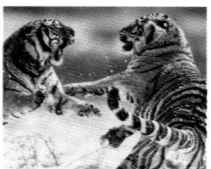

I travel to northern China to photograph Siberian tigers. Despite being undeterred by the ravages of the harshest winters on earth, they have been driven to near extinction. There are now more tigers in captivity than in the wild, a sad reflection on their endangered plight. Captivated by their presence, I feel impervious to the cold.

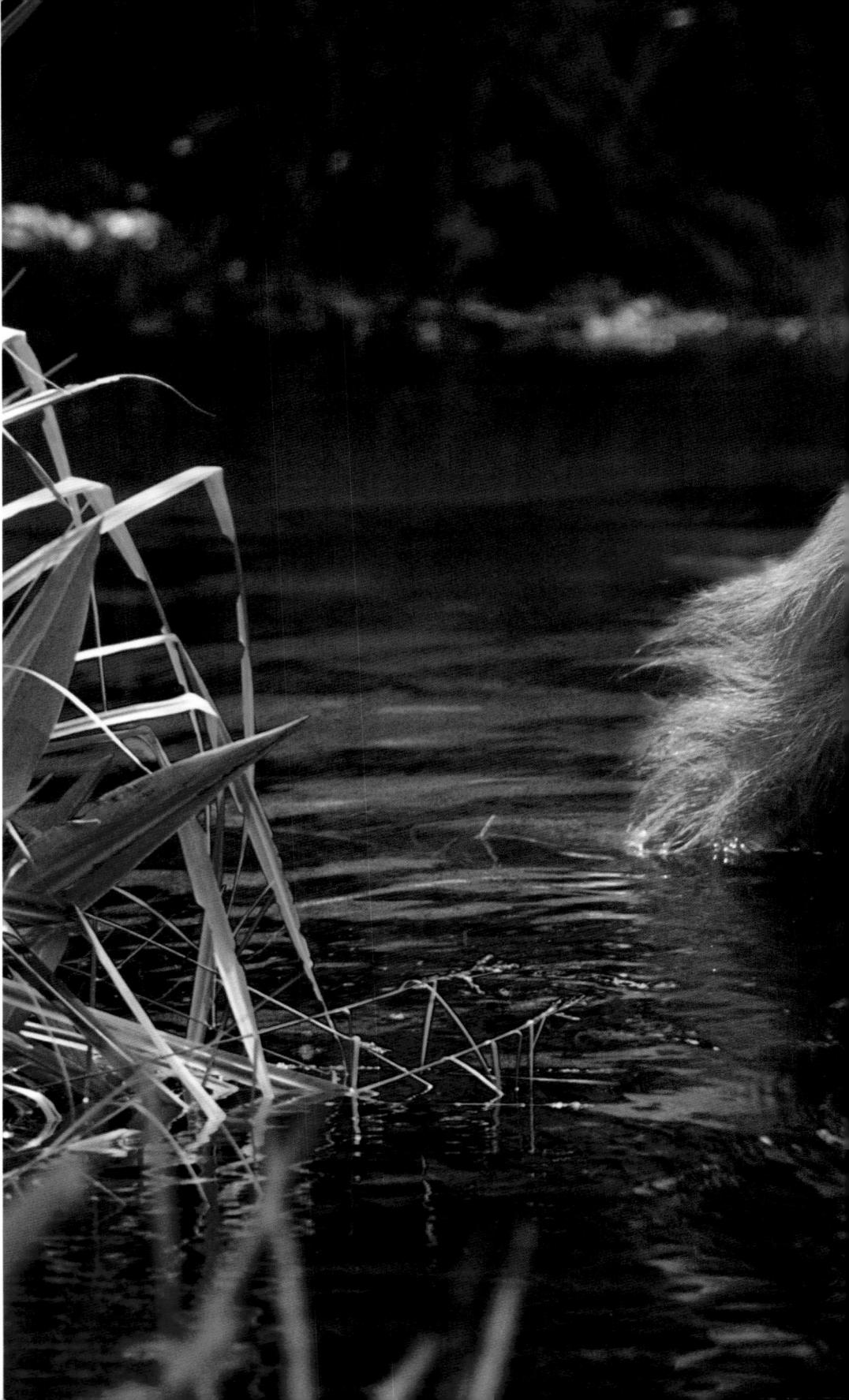

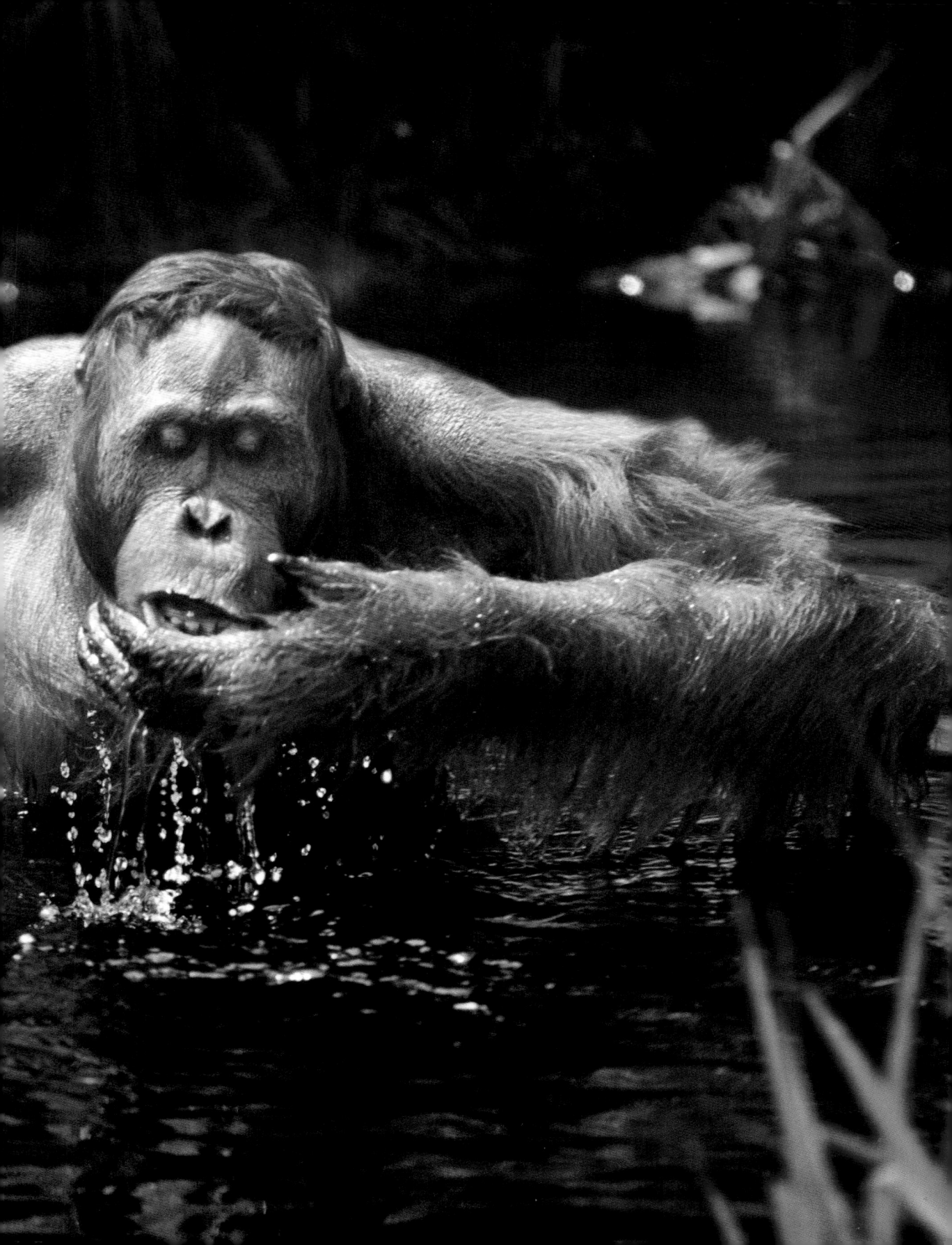

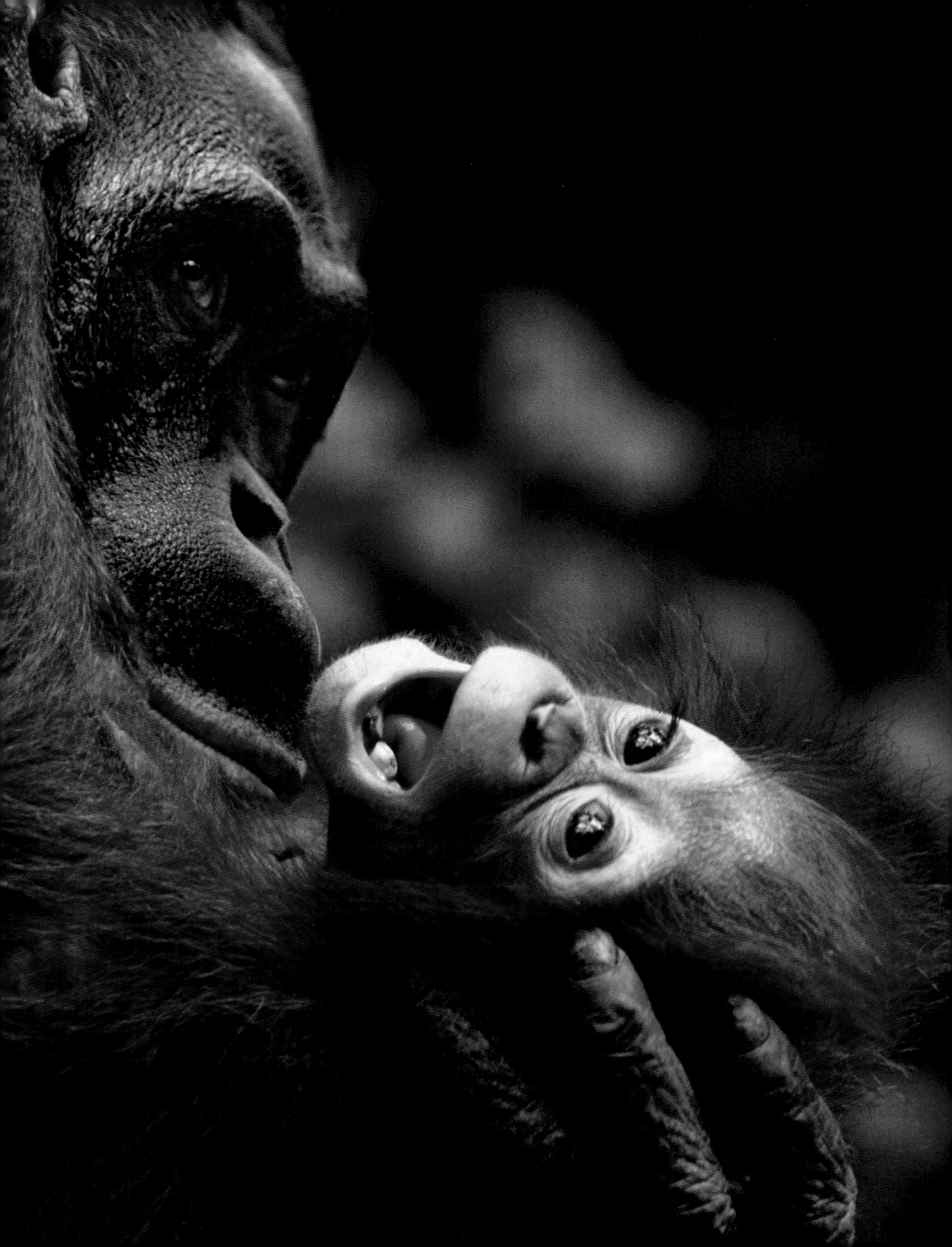

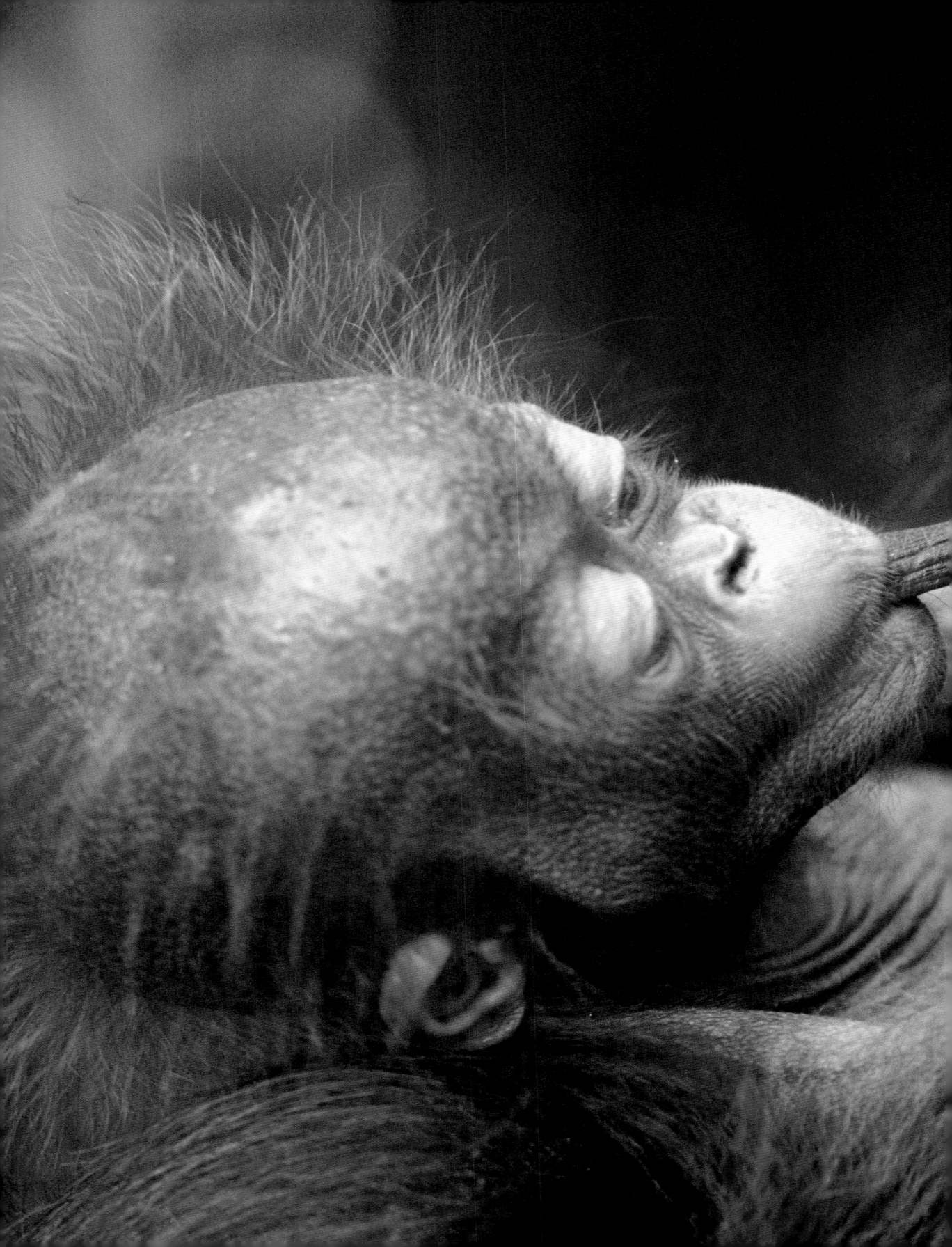

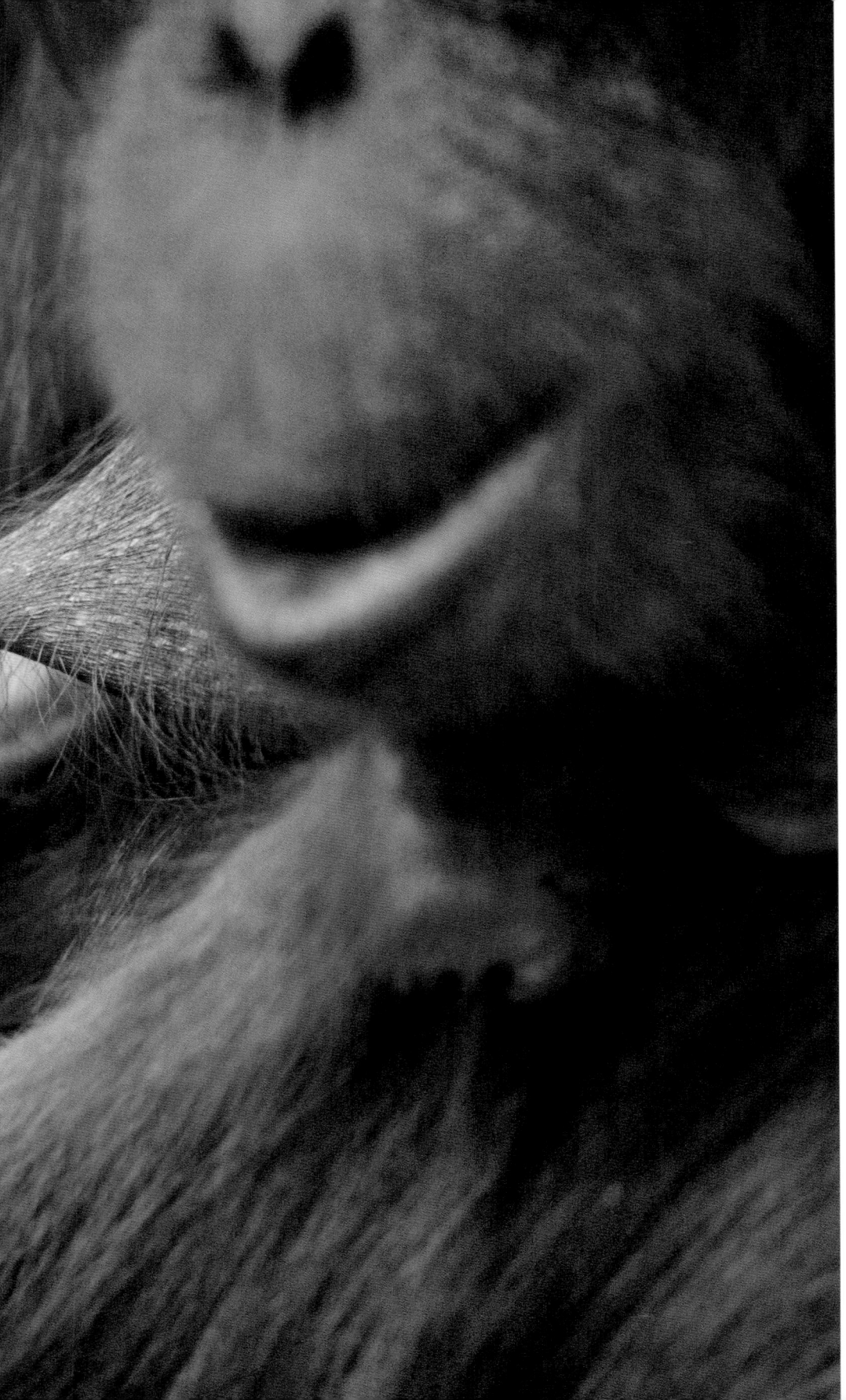

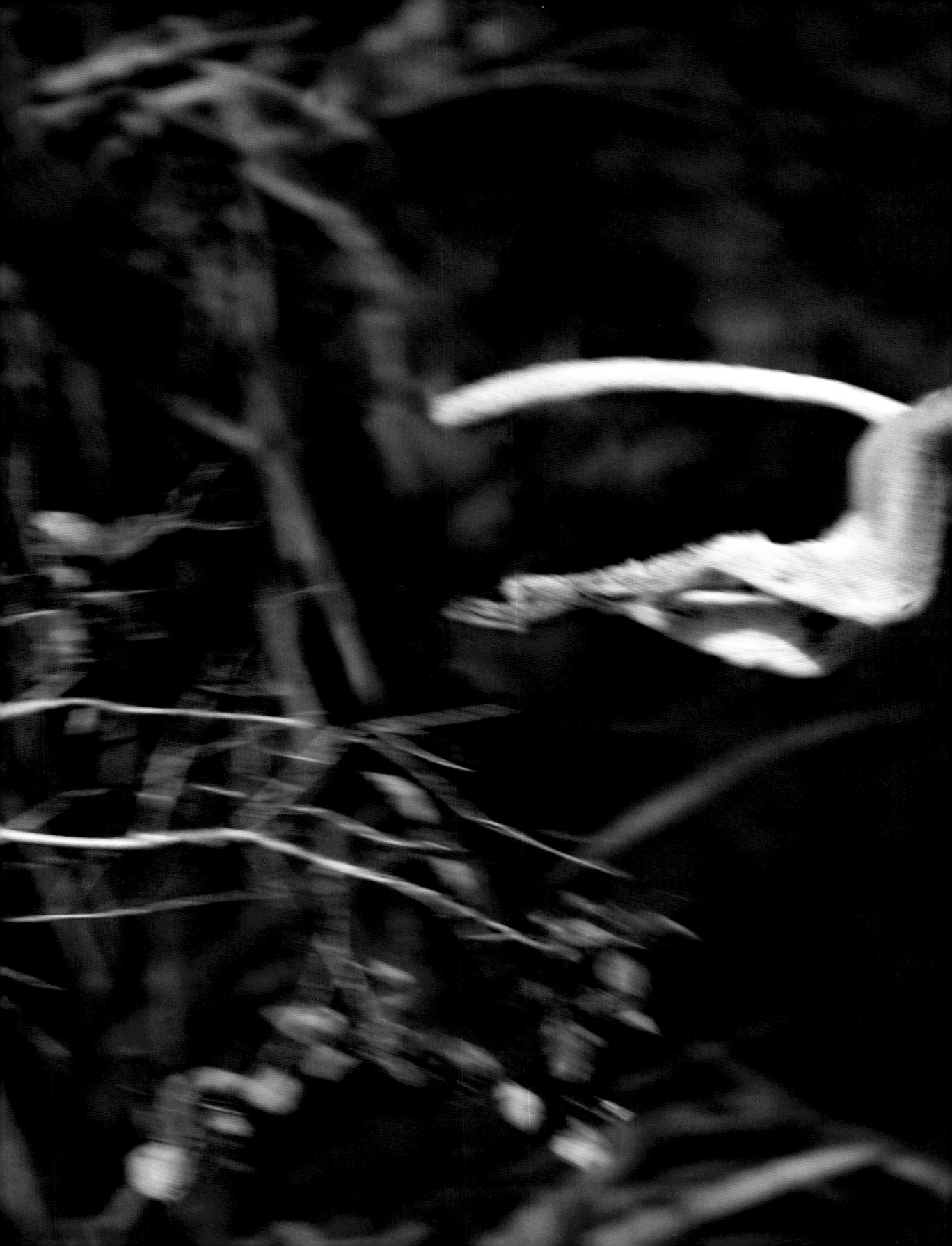

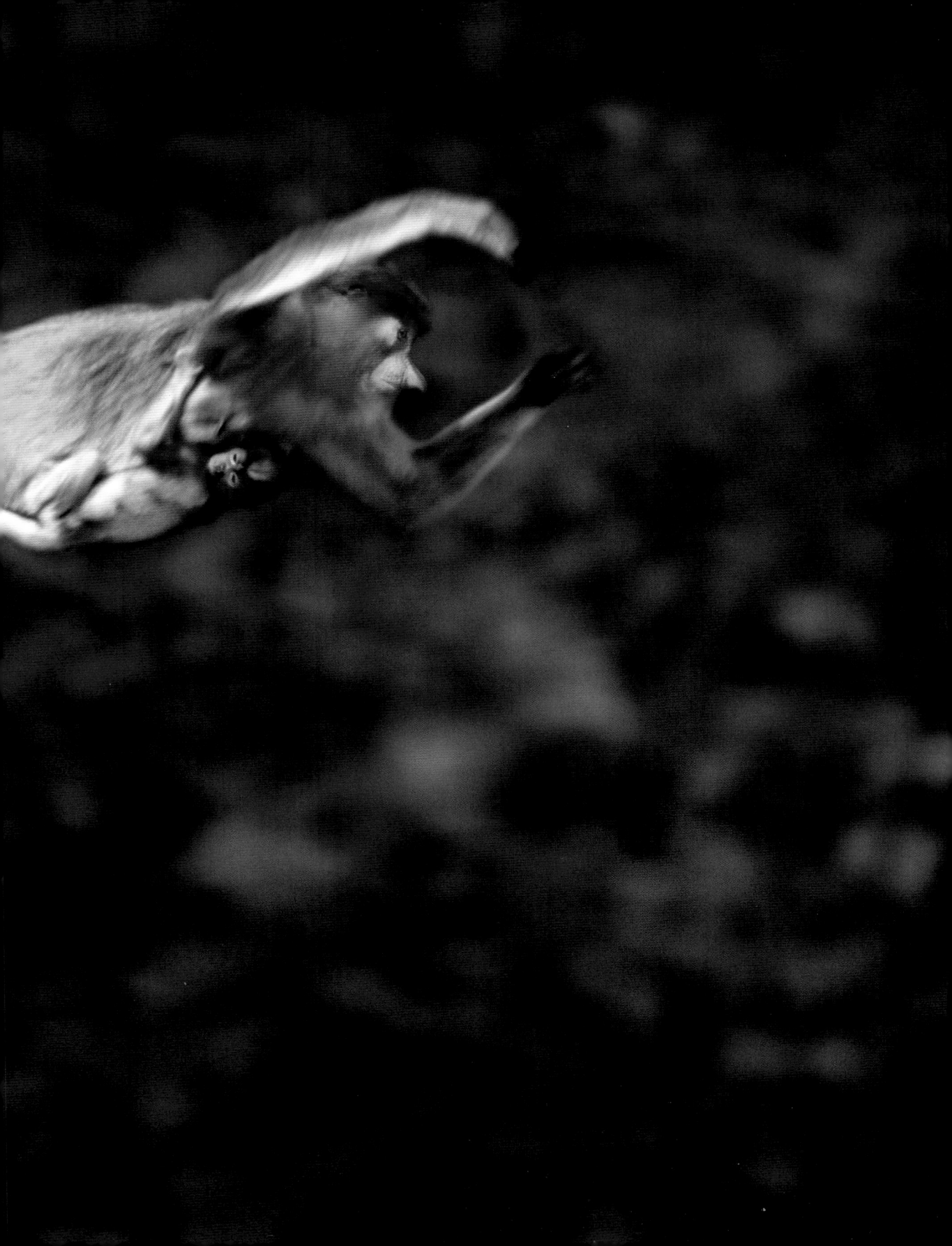

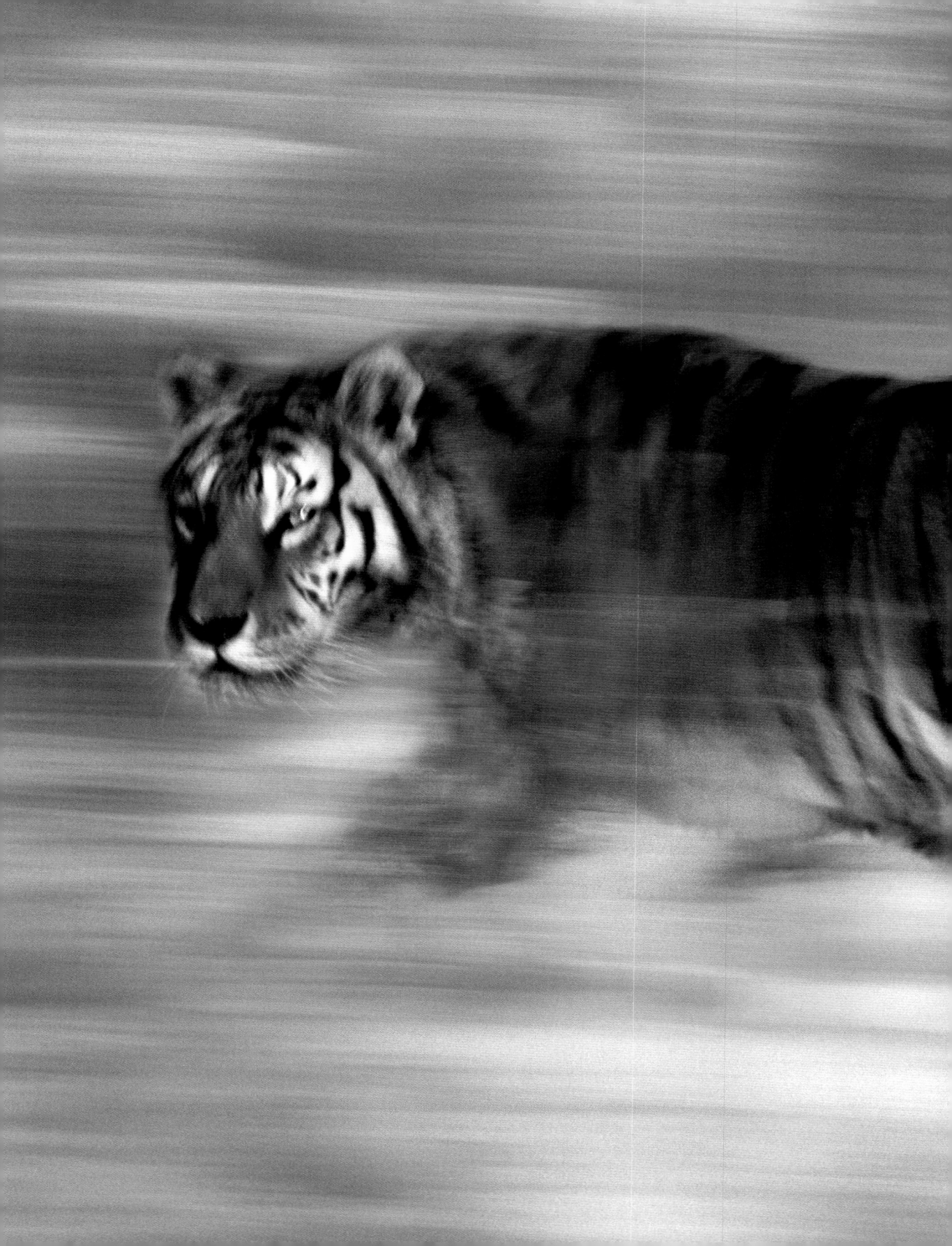

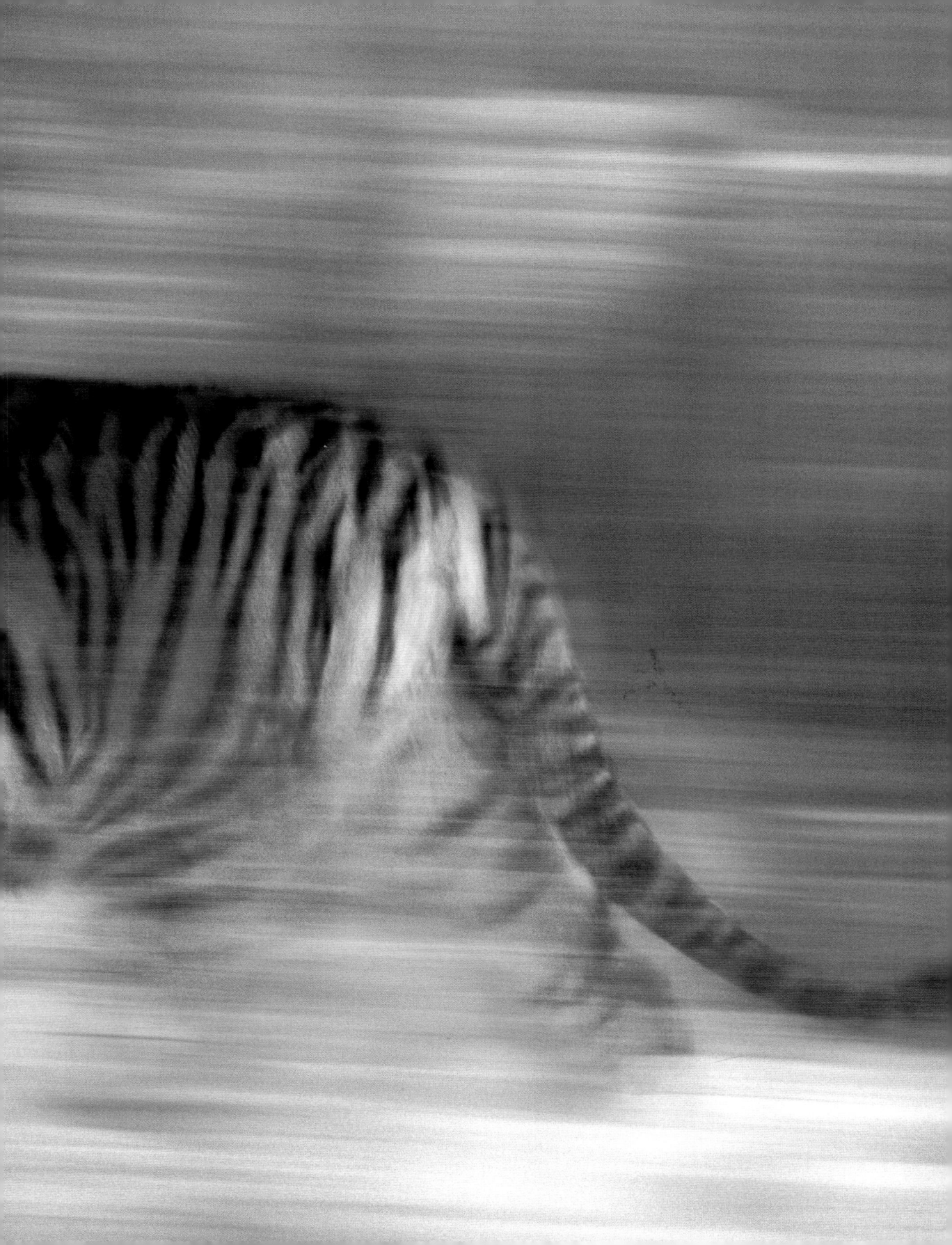

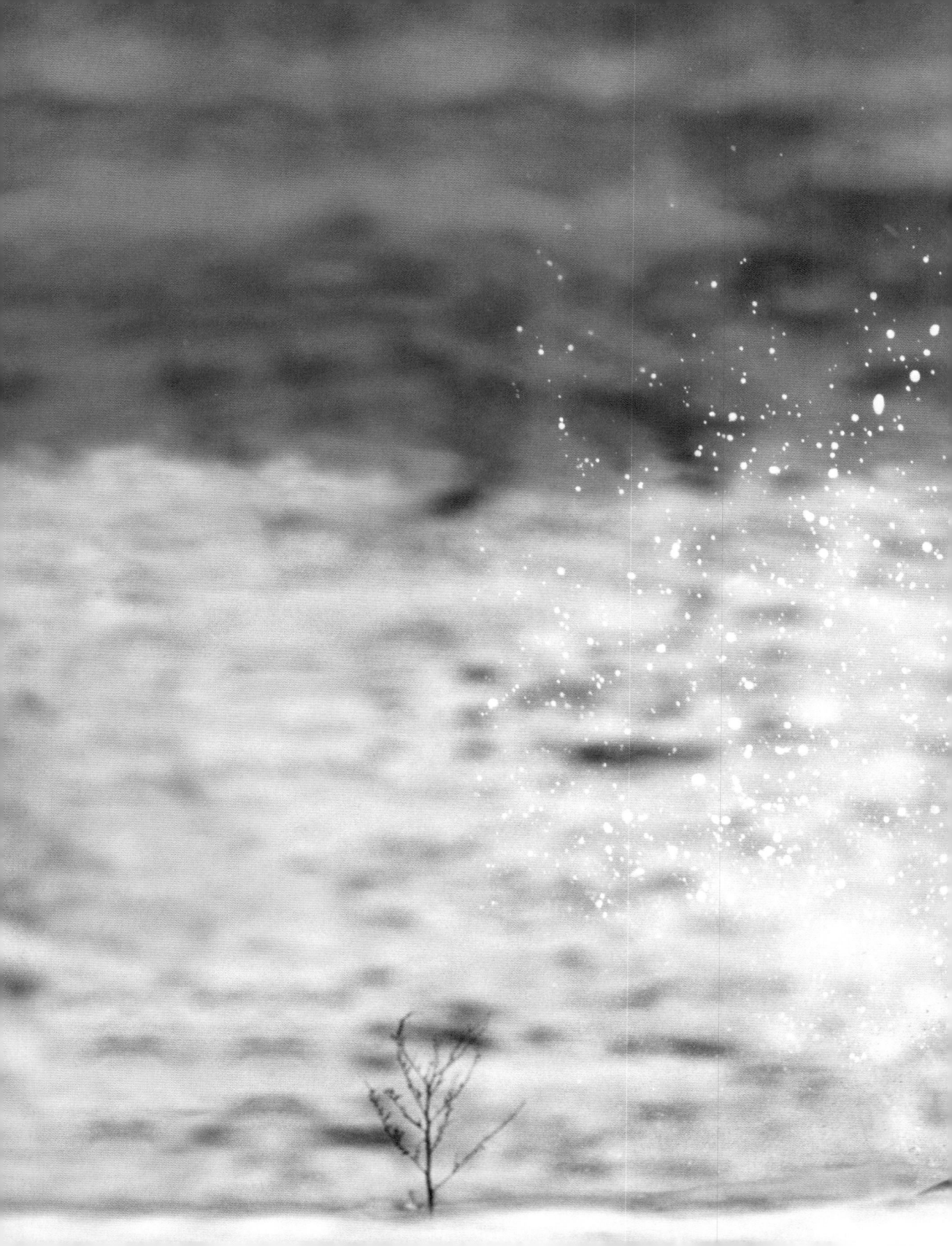

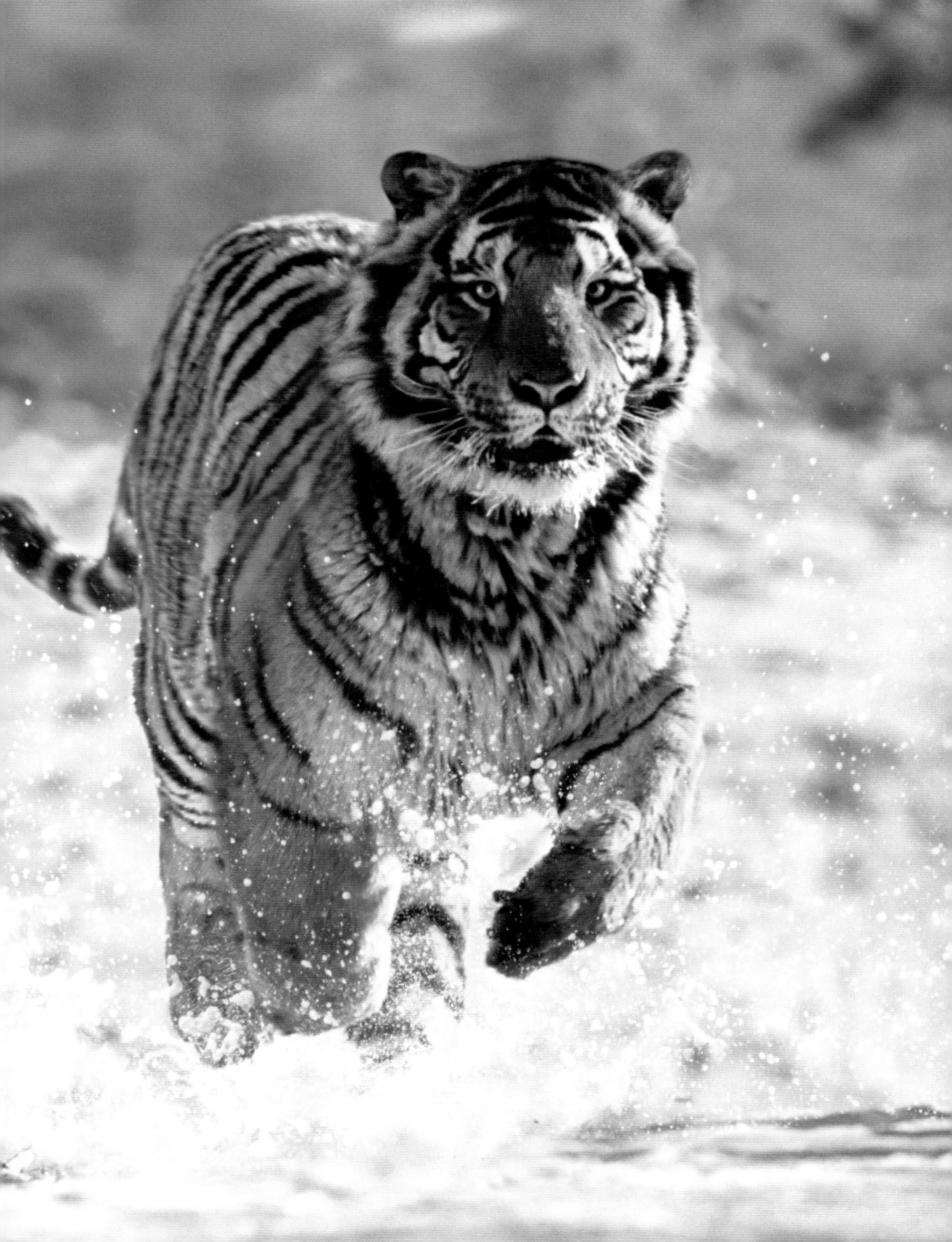

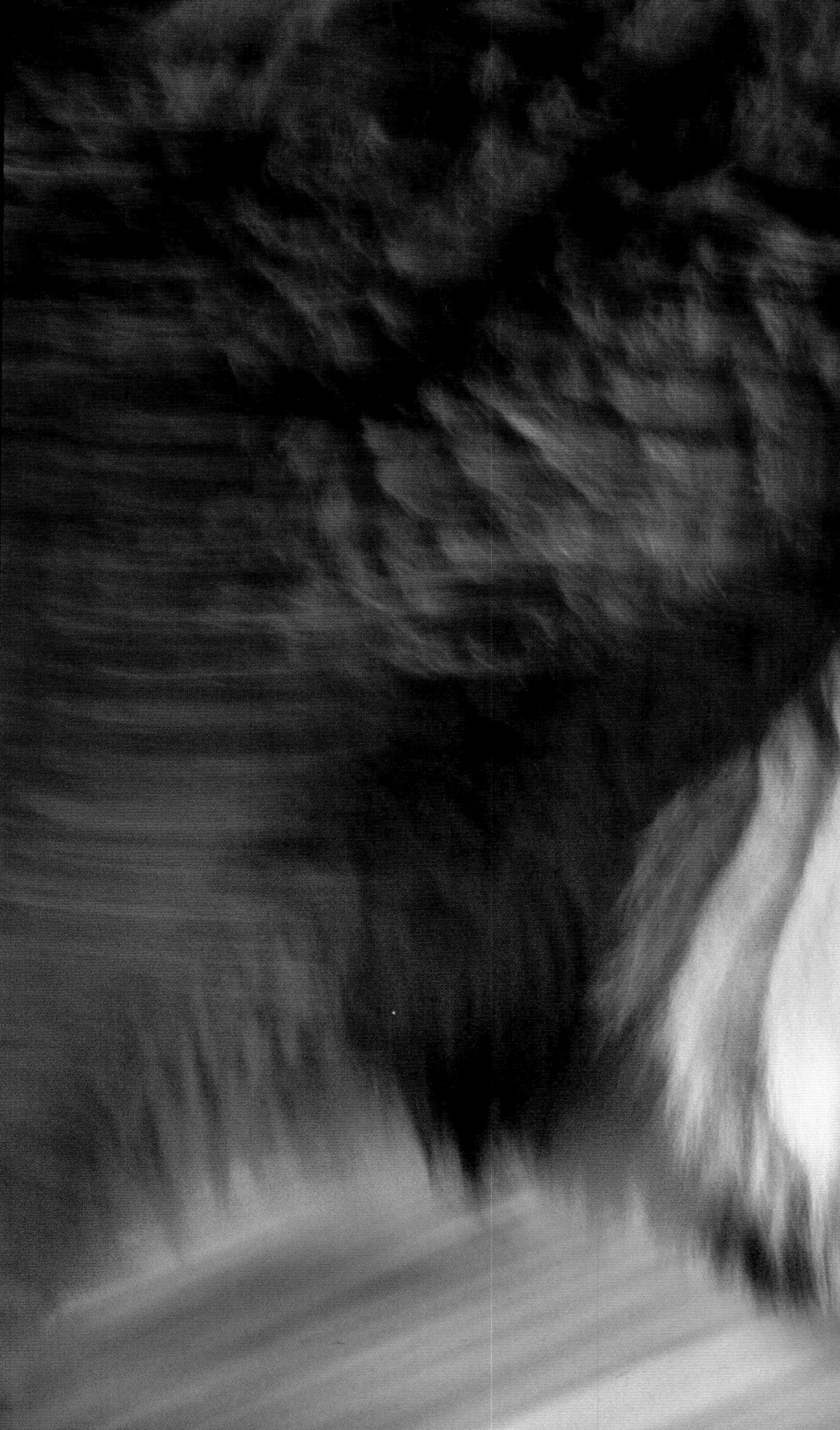

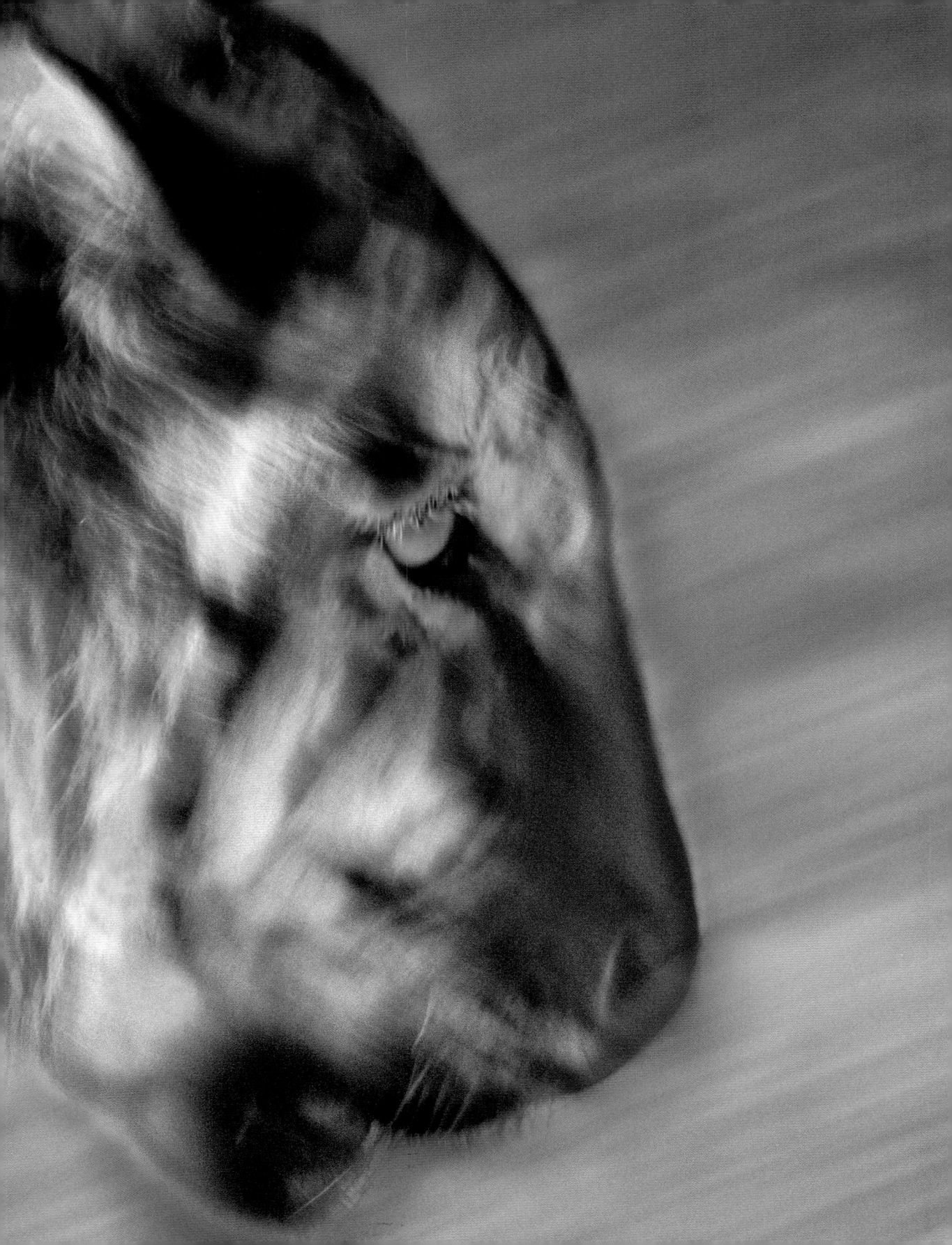

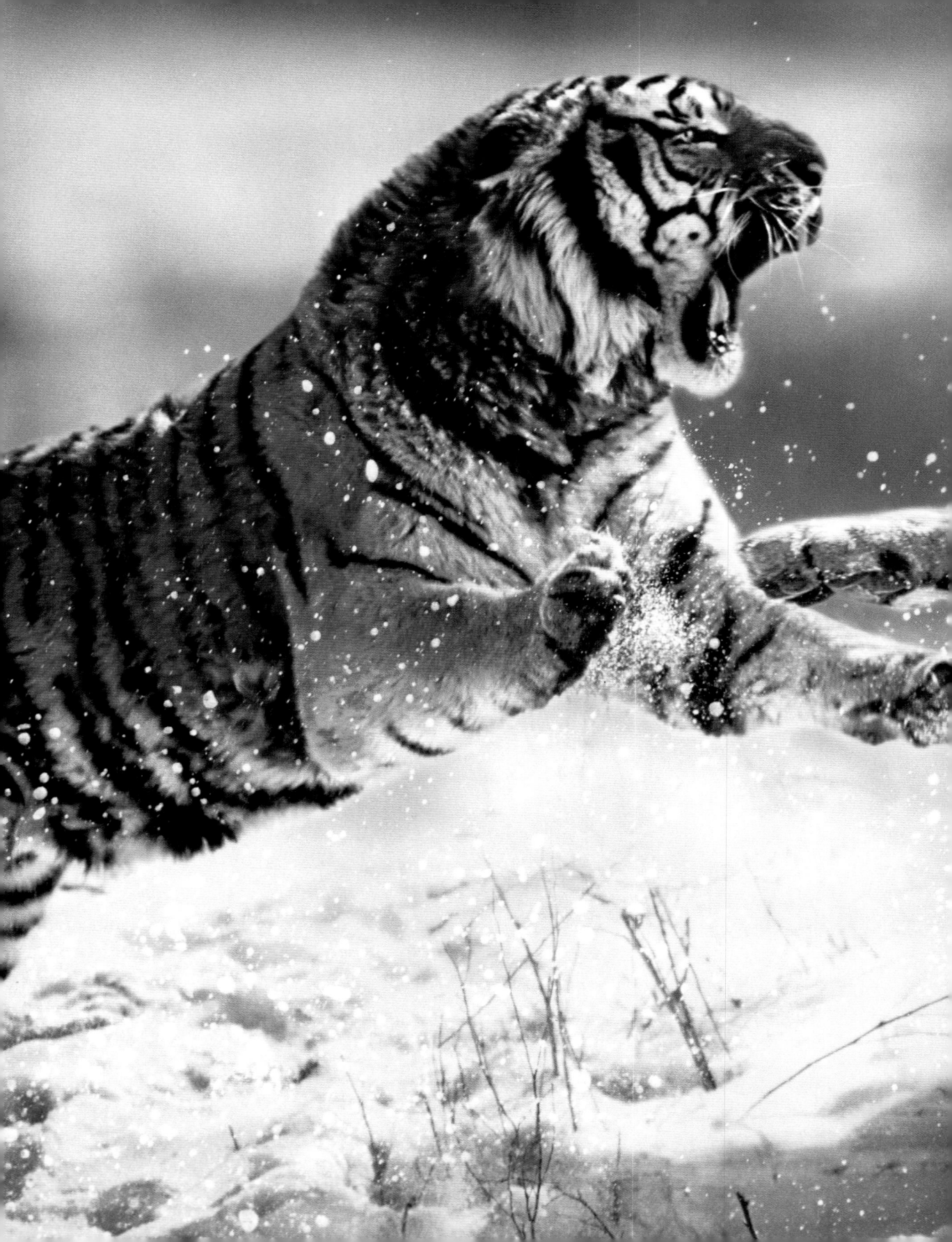

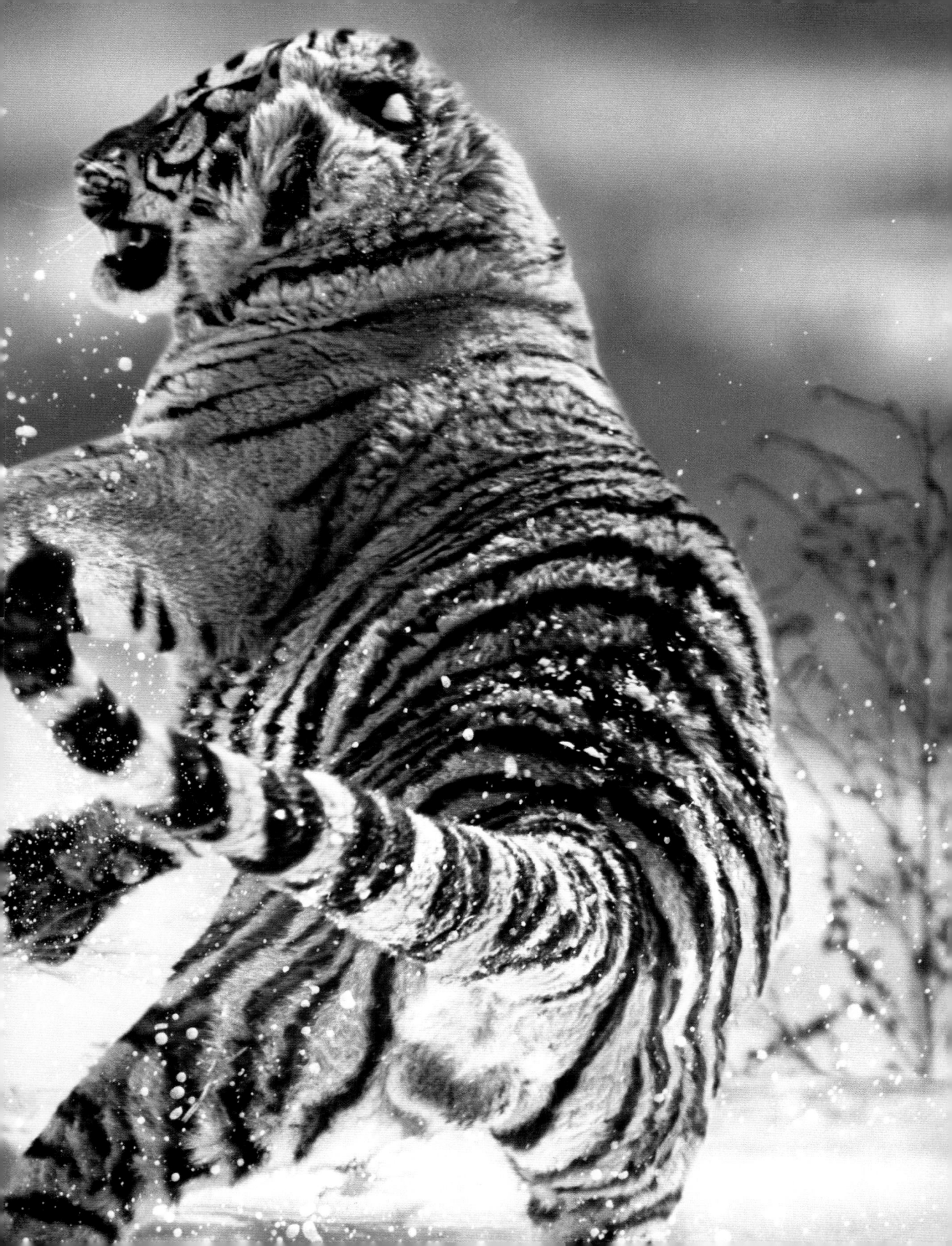

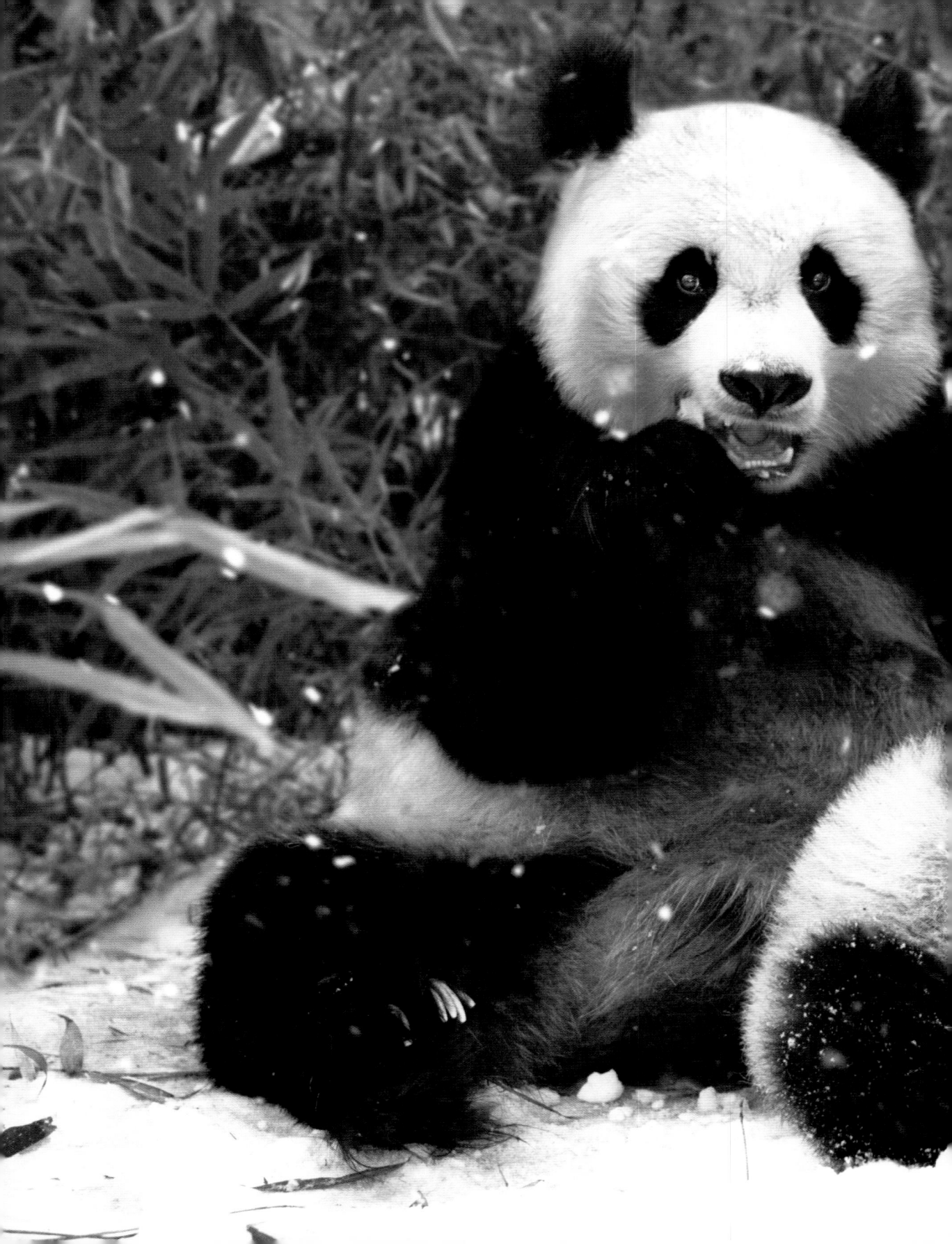

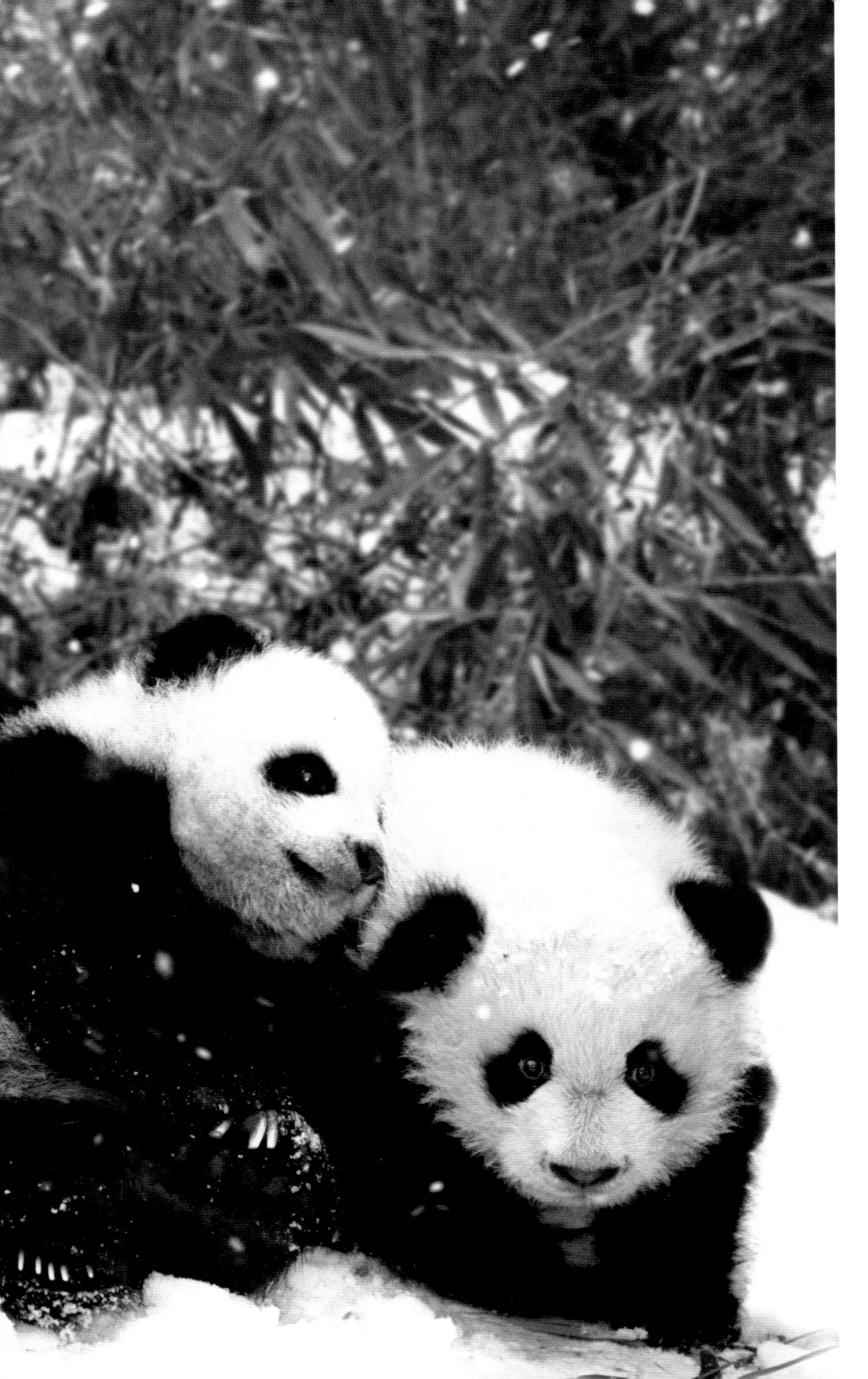

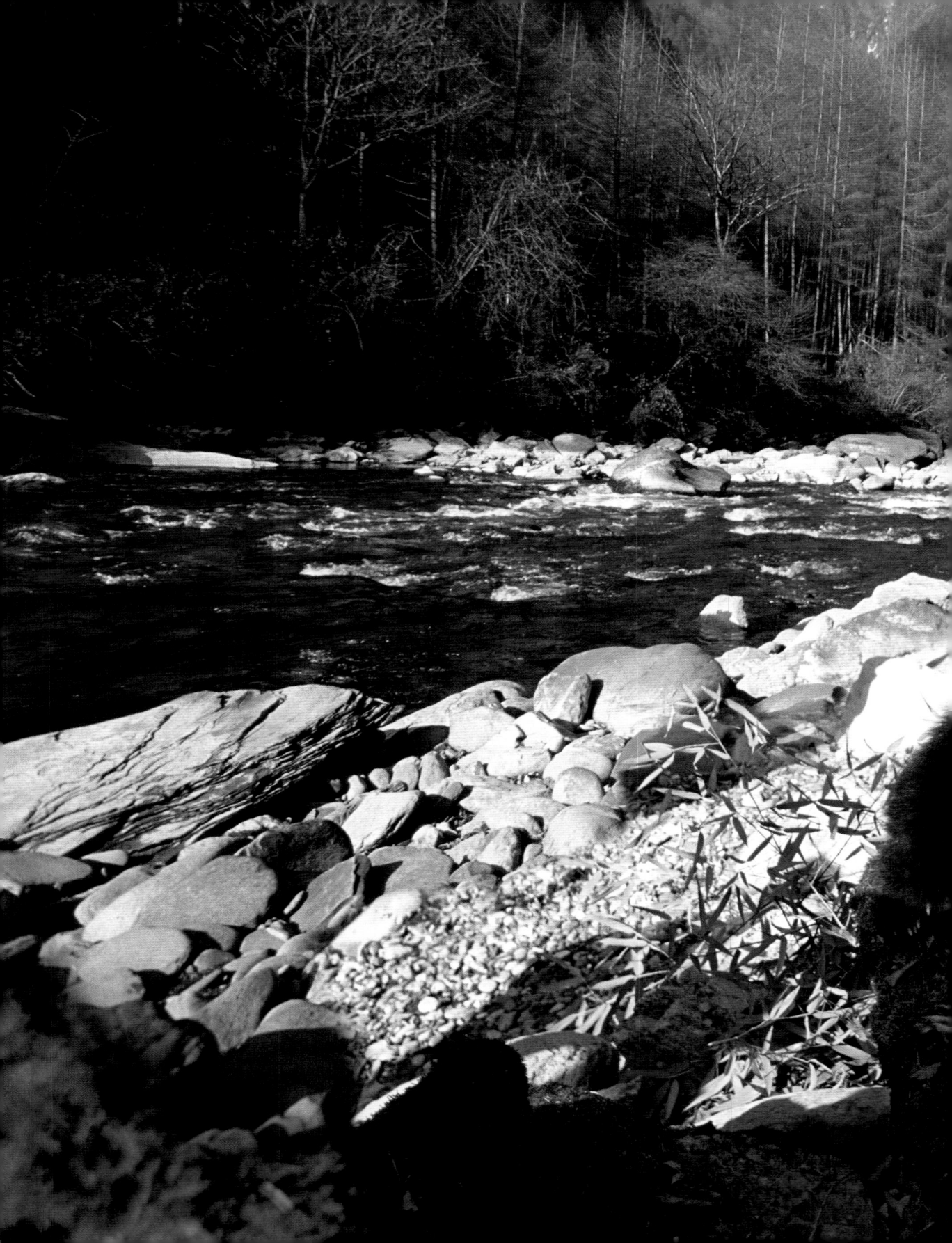

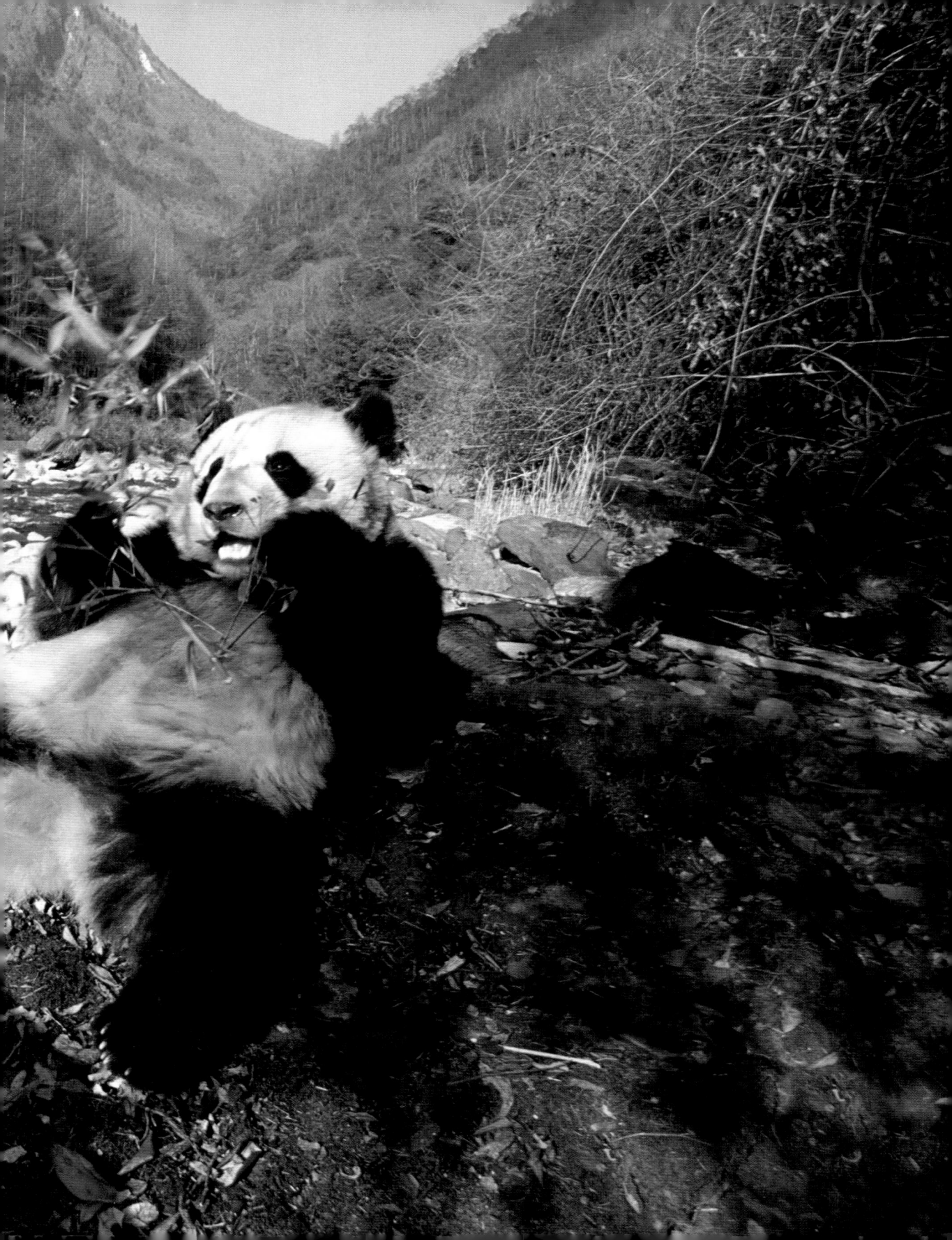

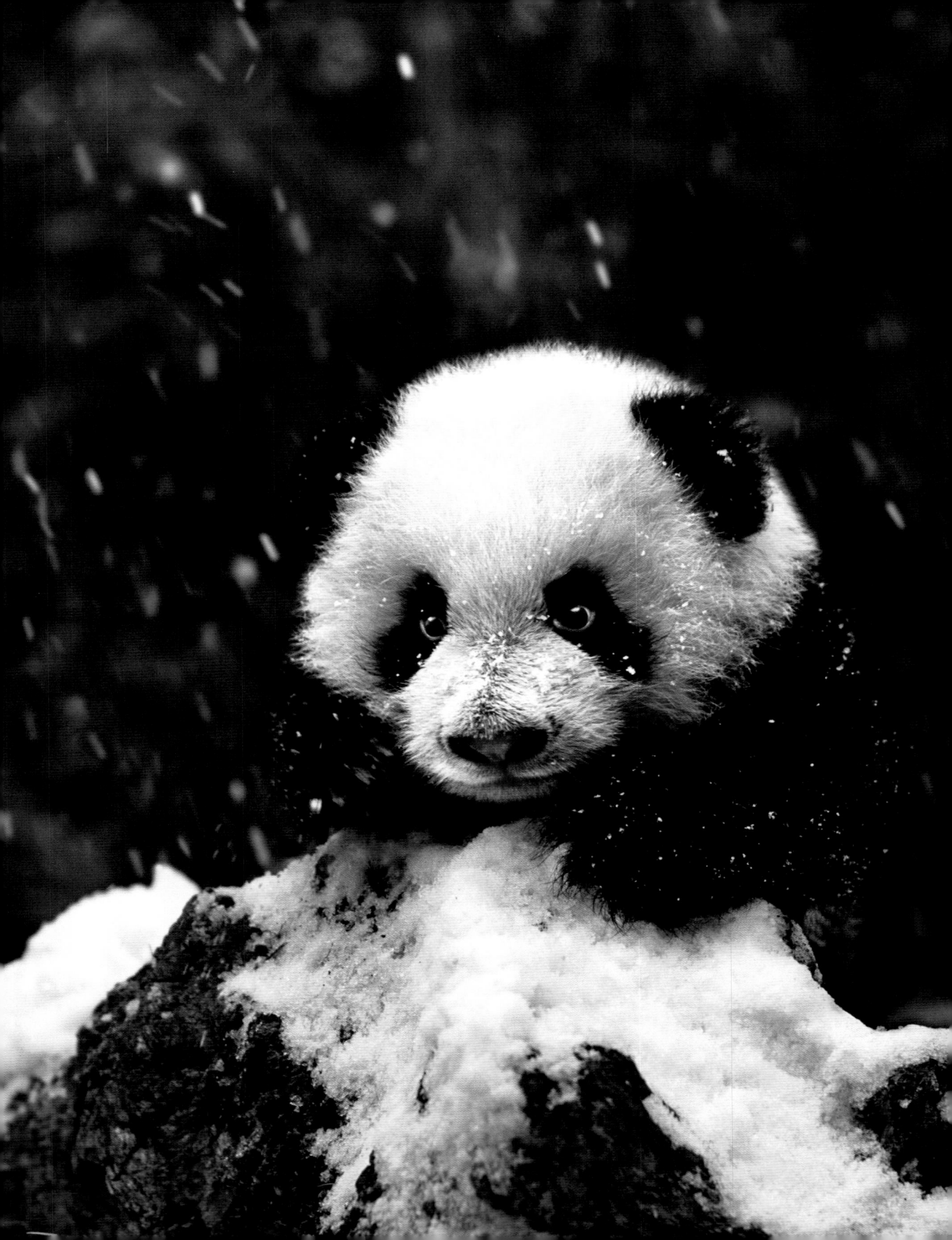

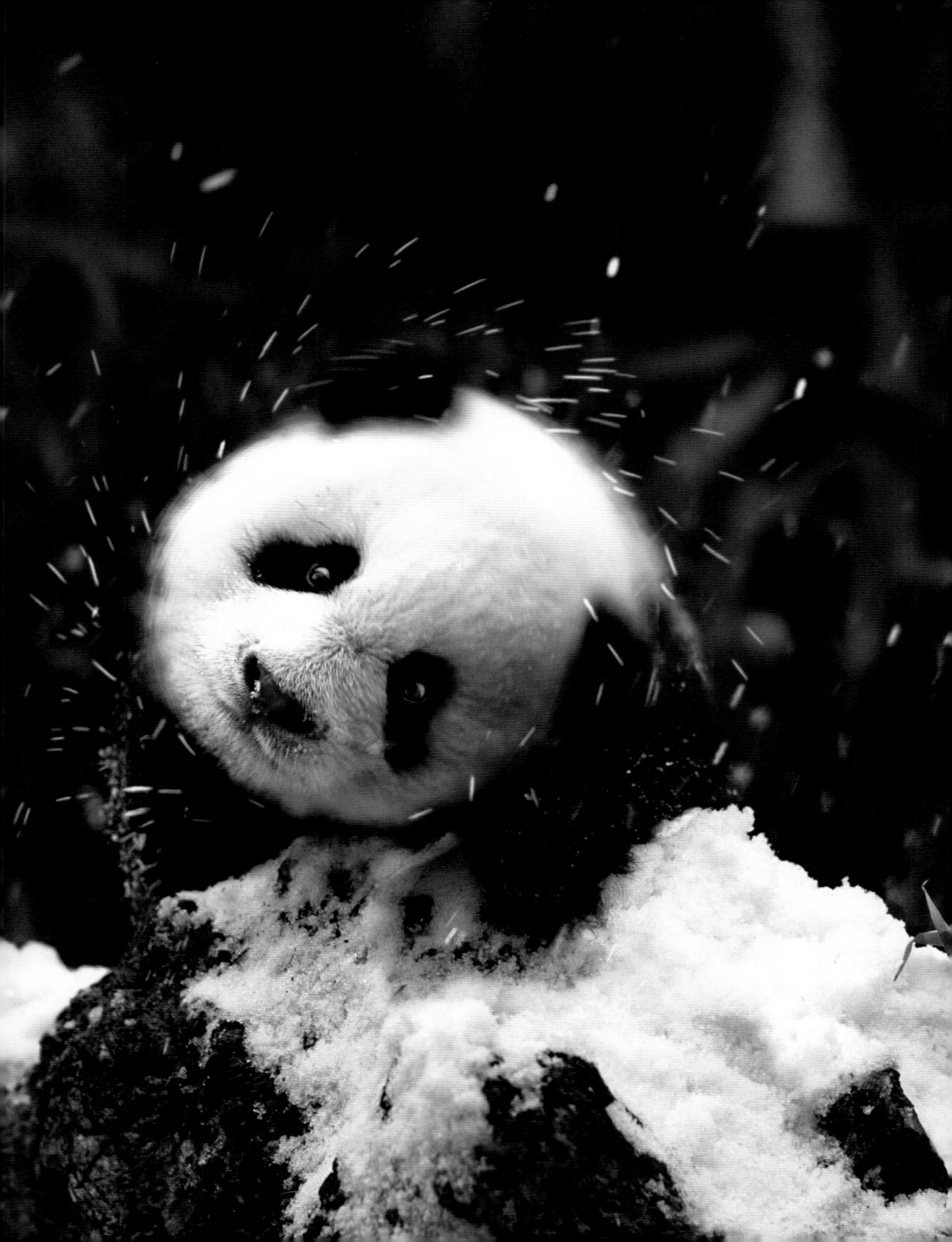

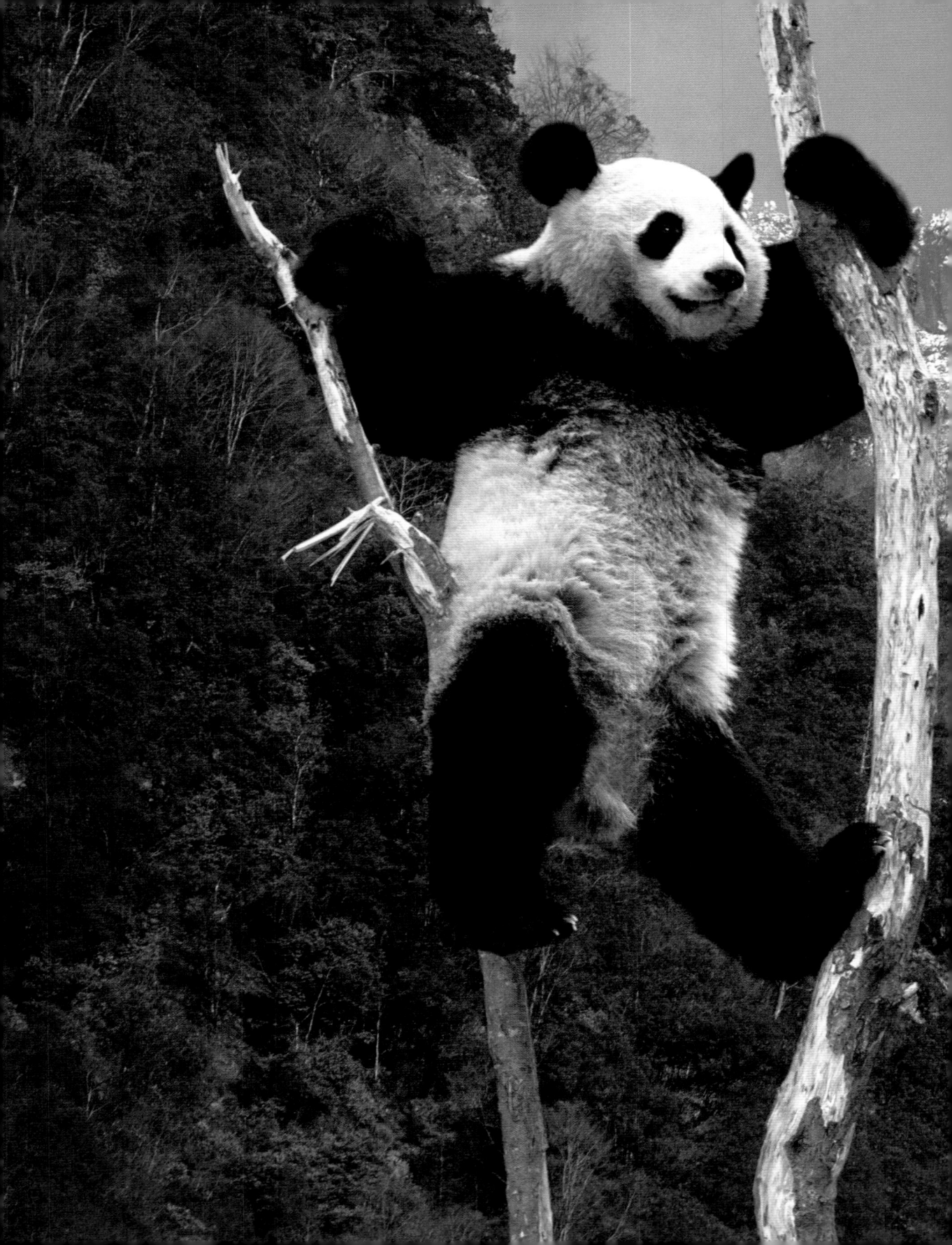

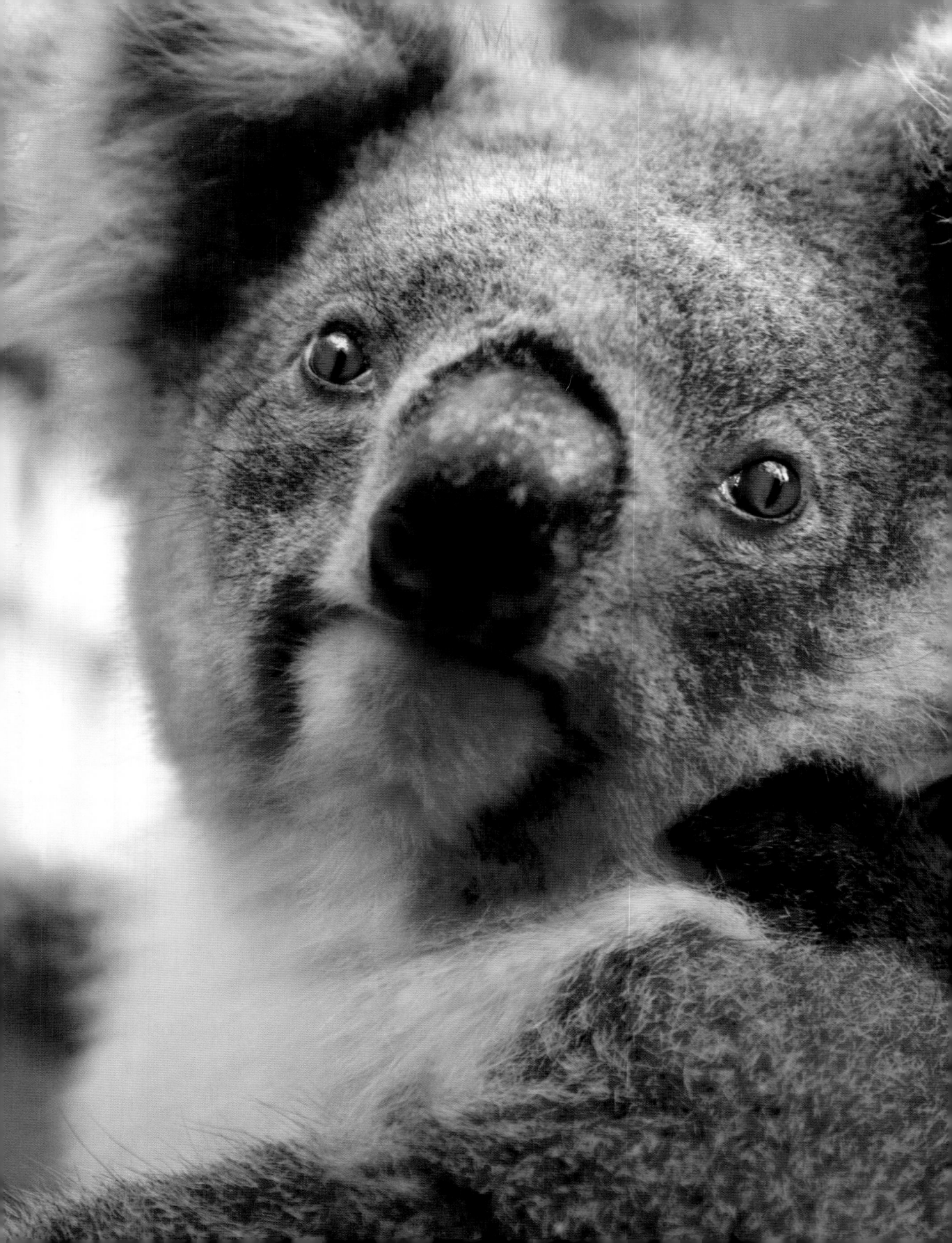

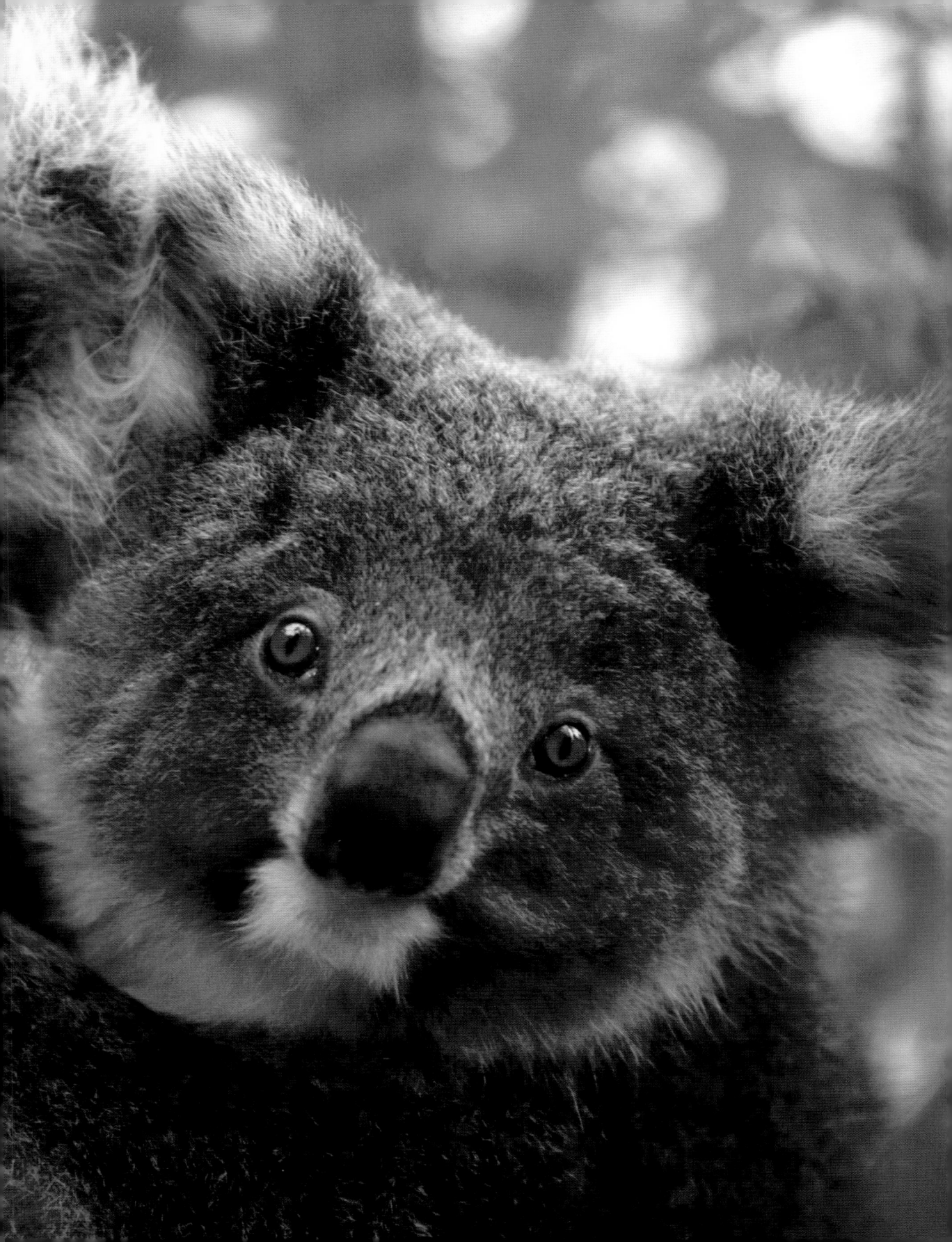

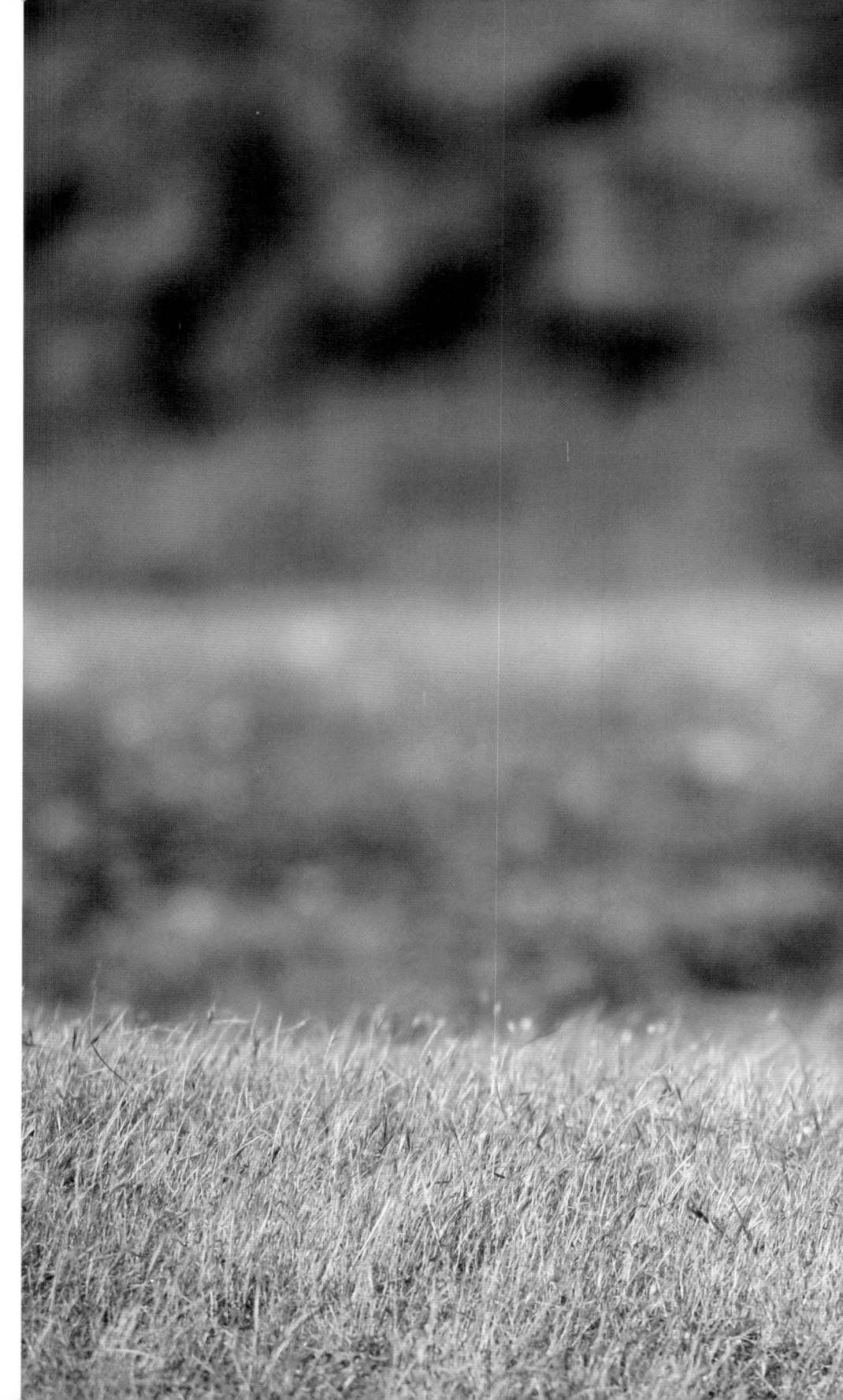

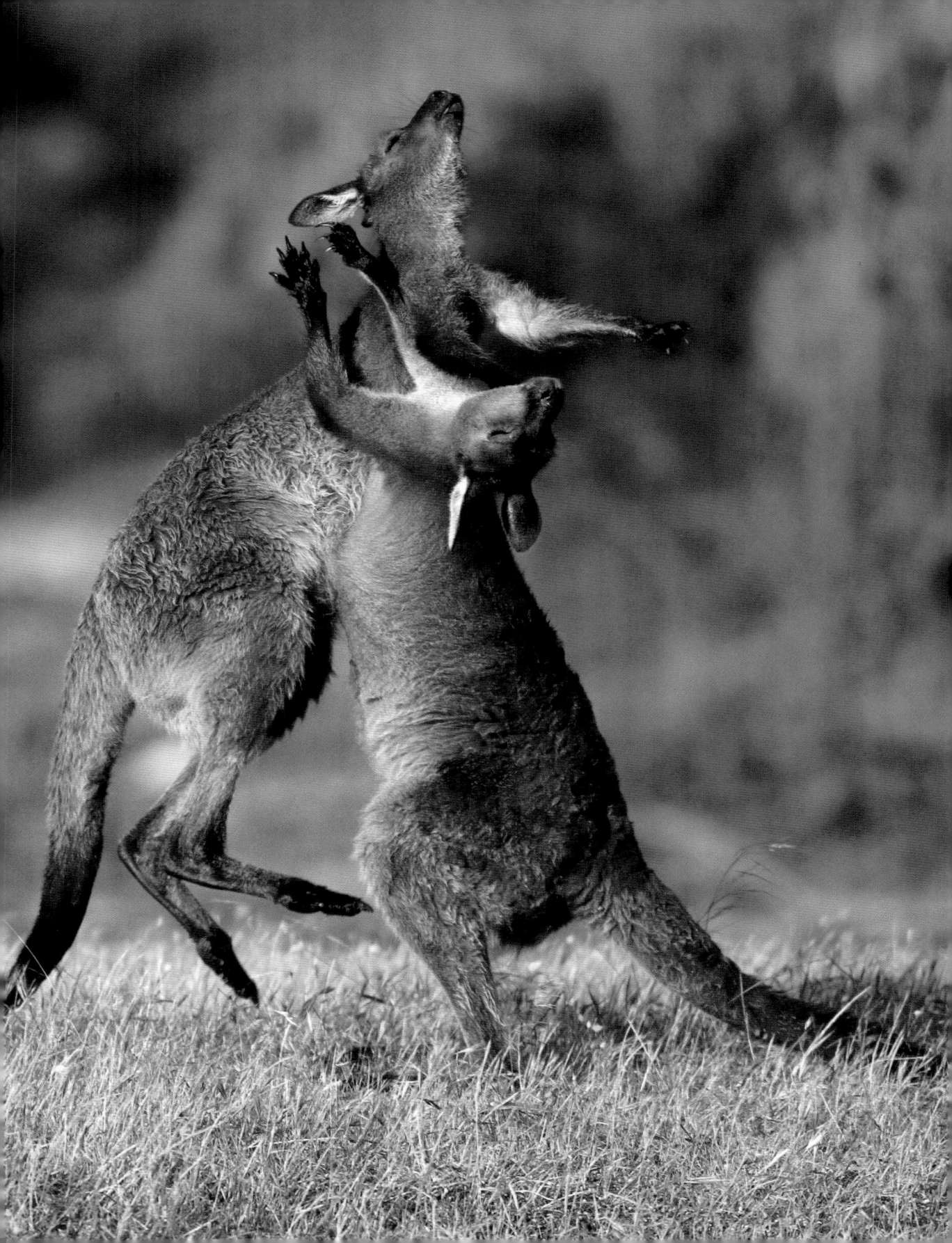

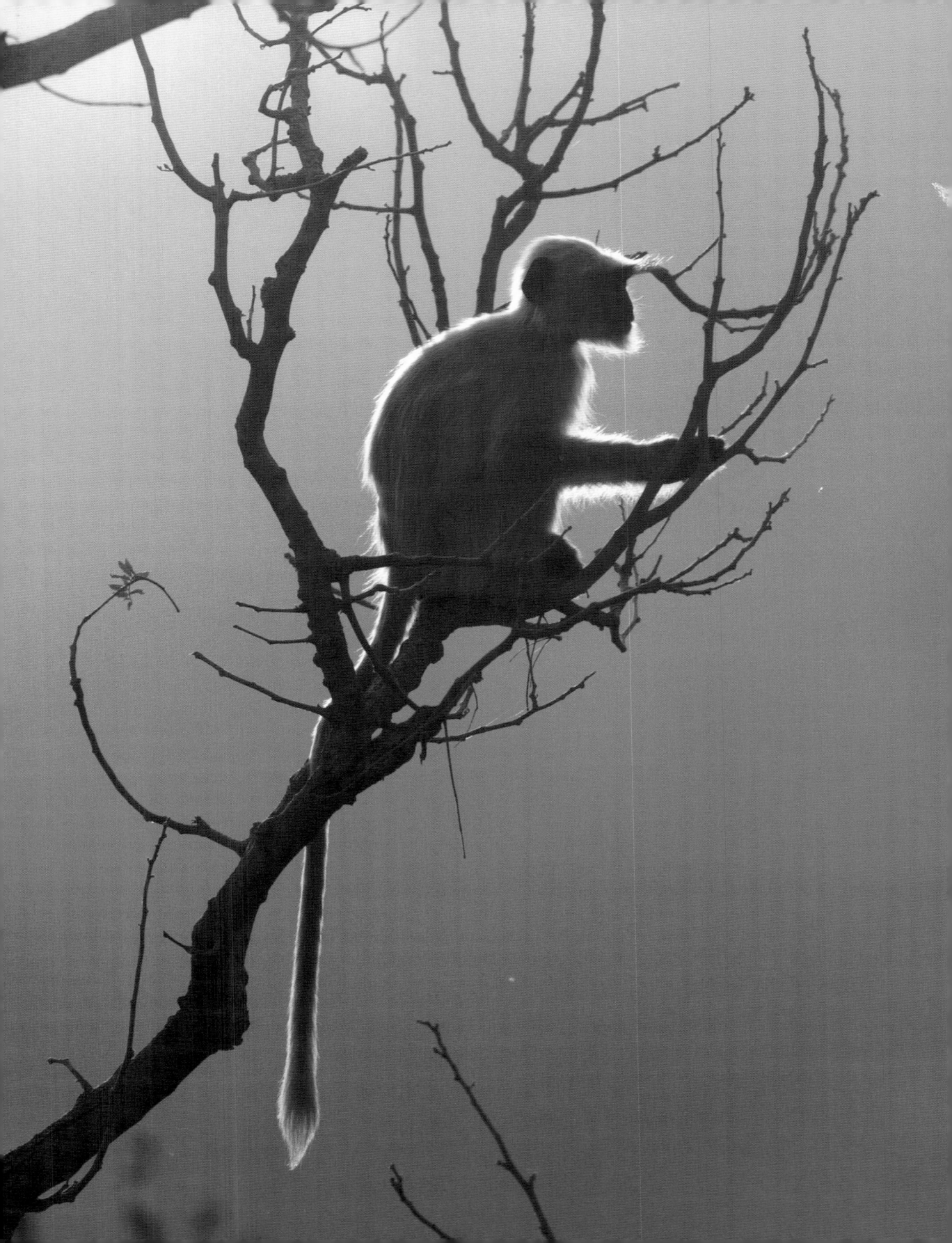

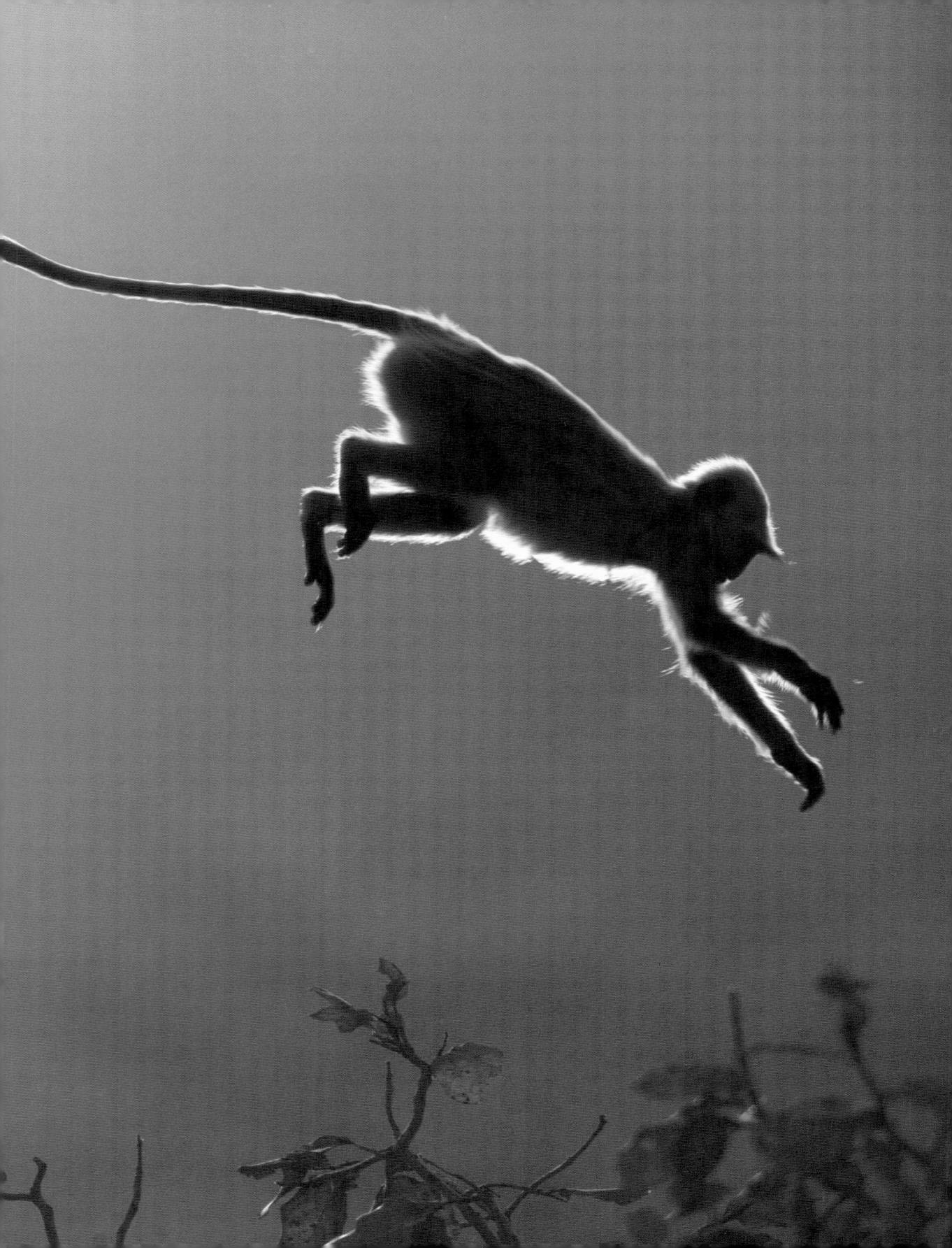

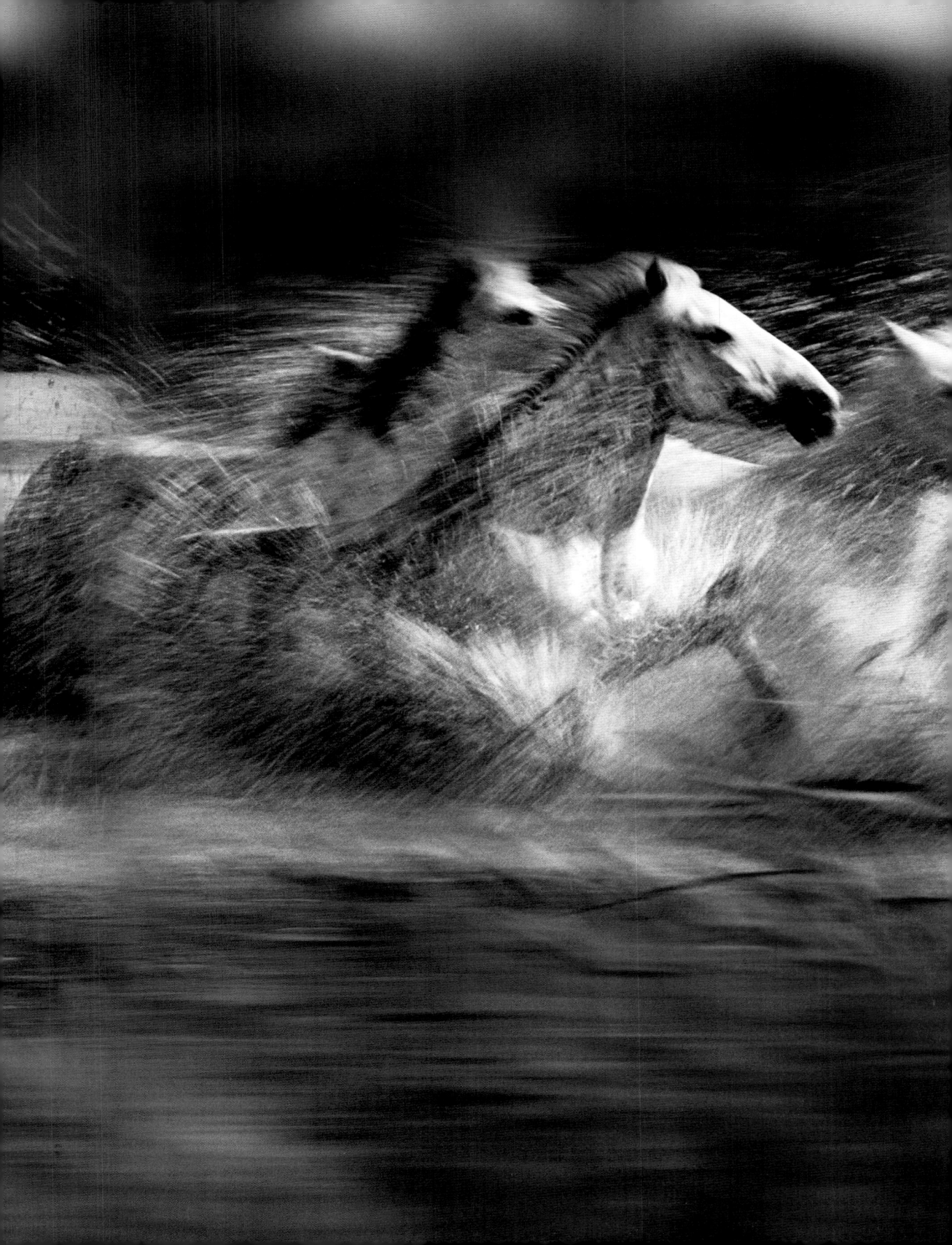

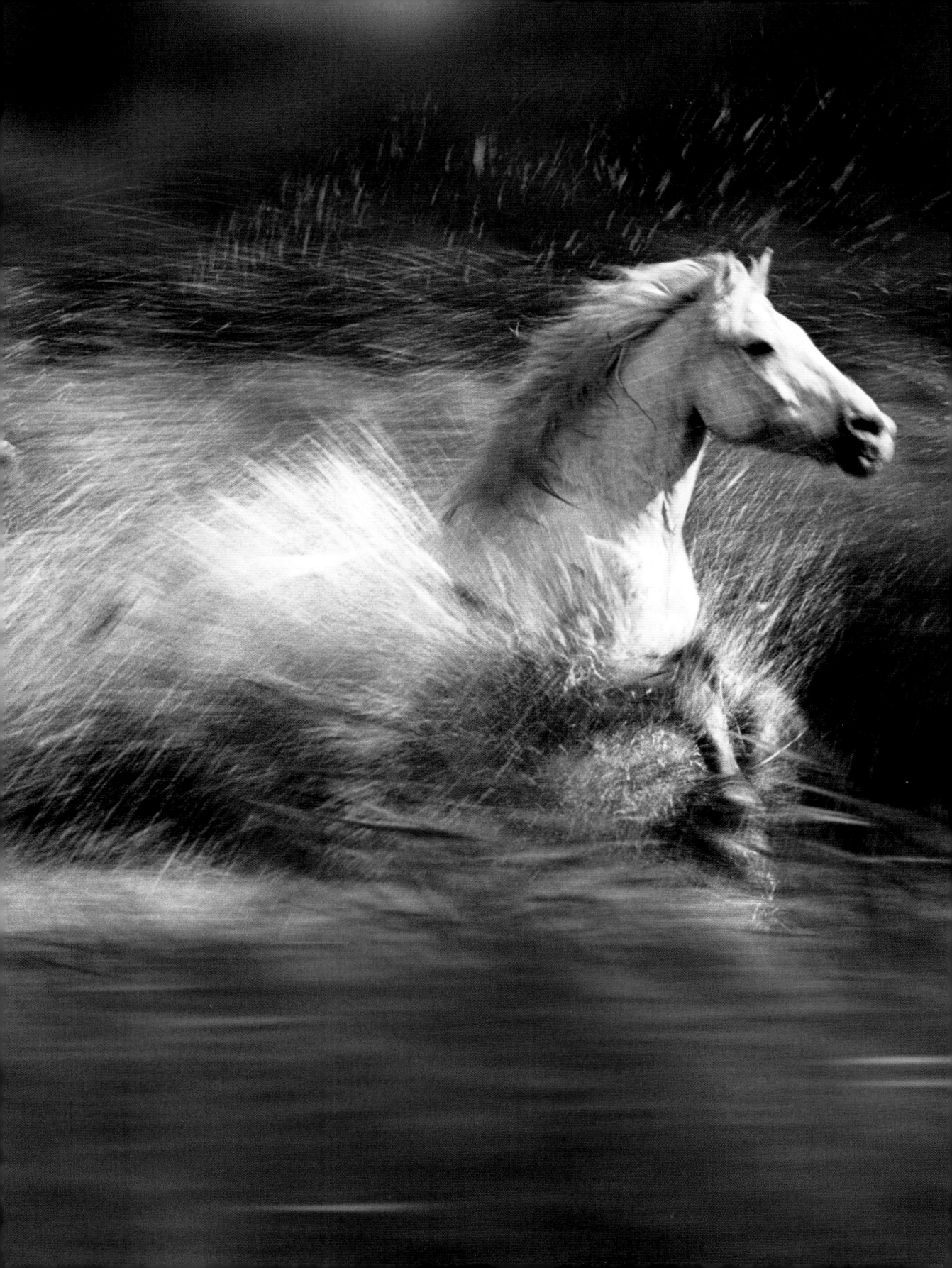

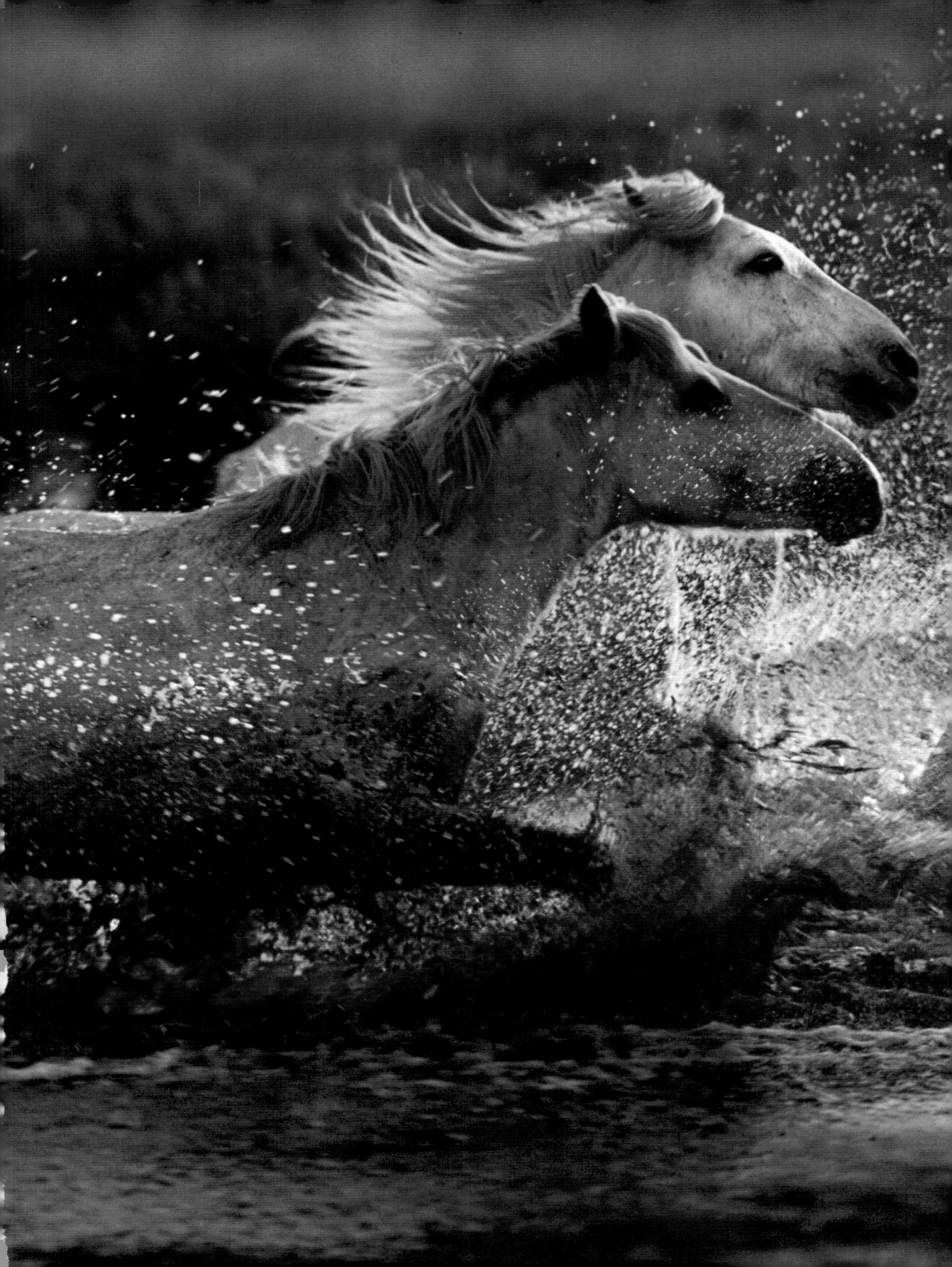

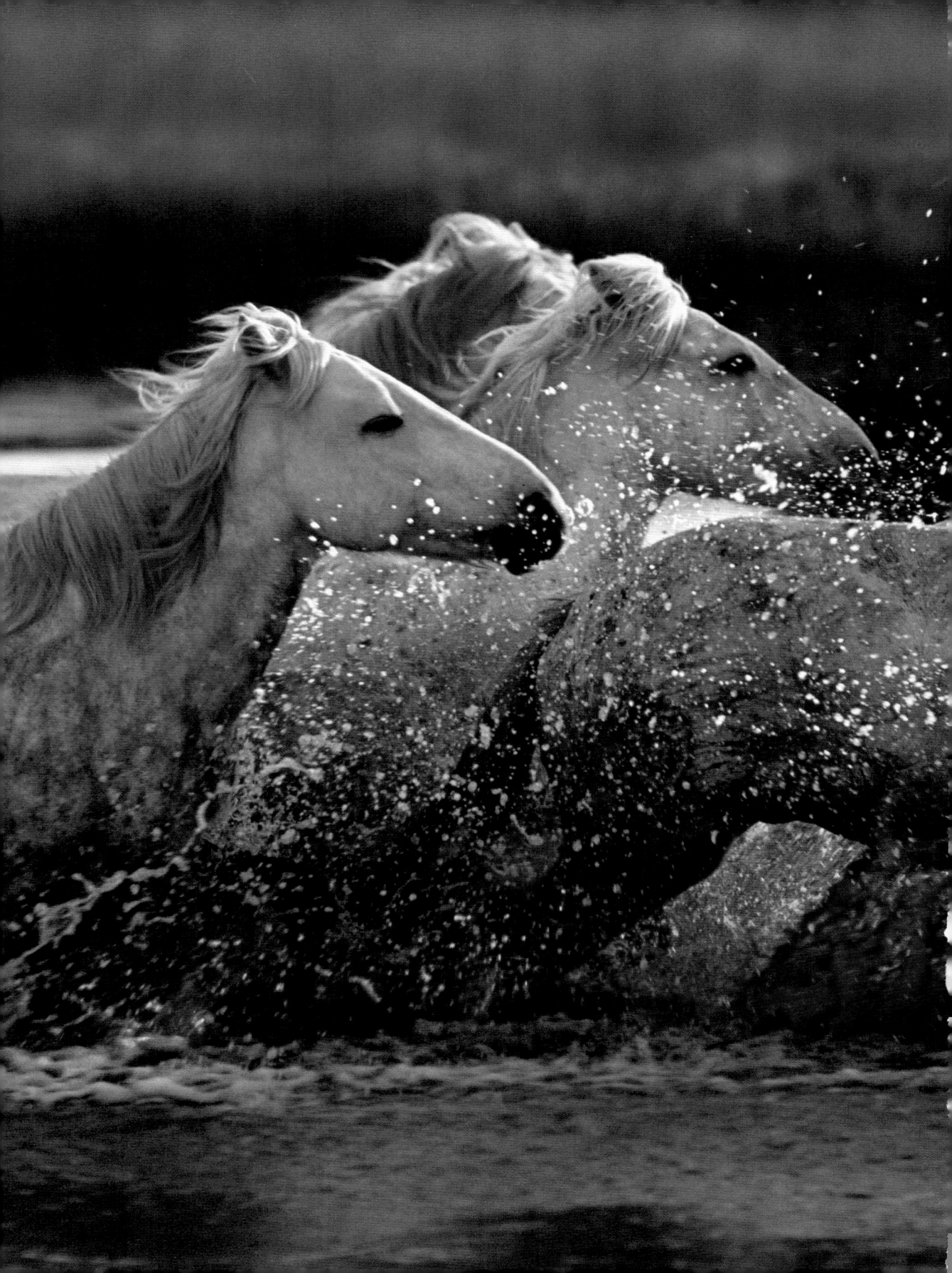

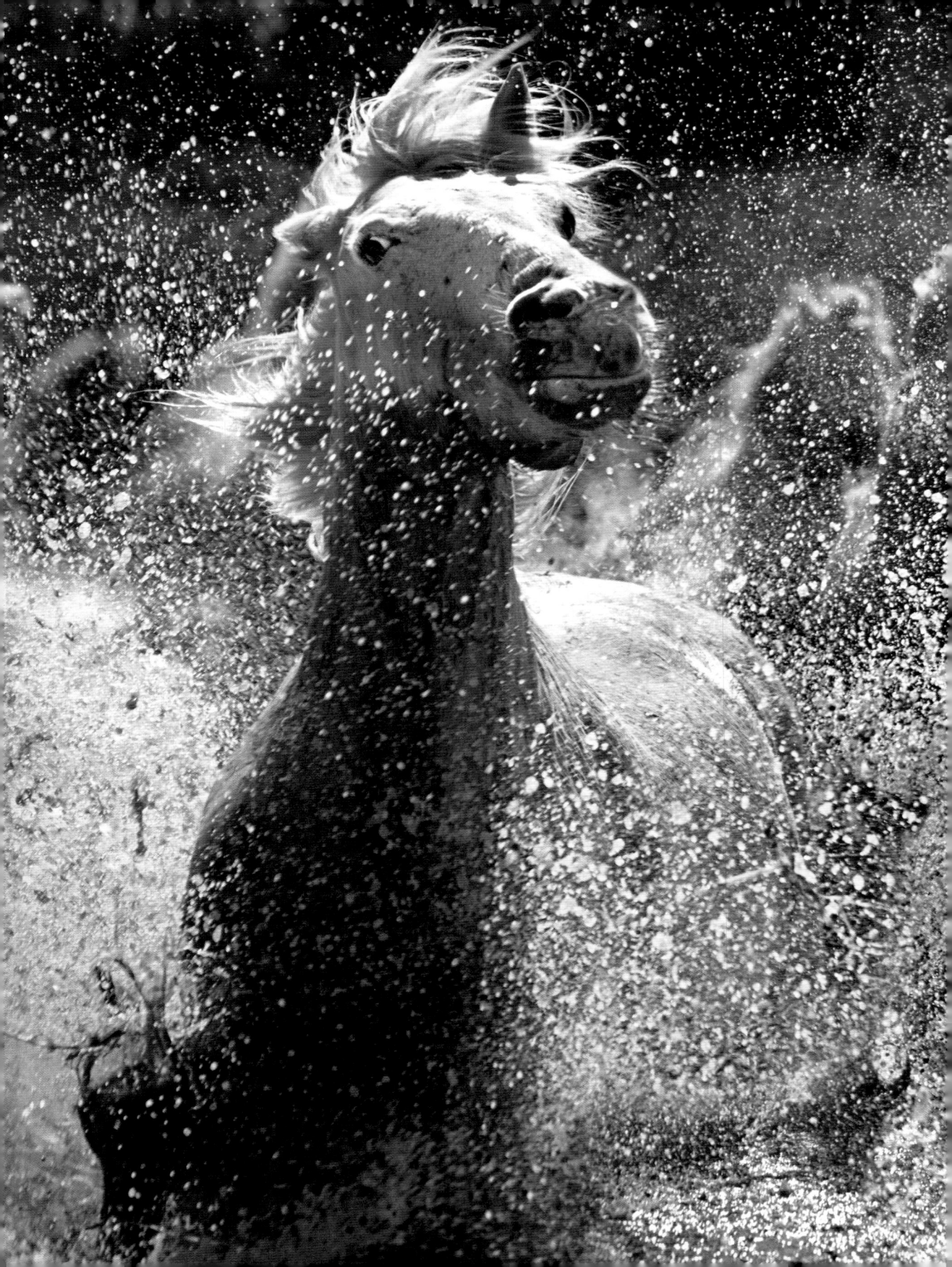

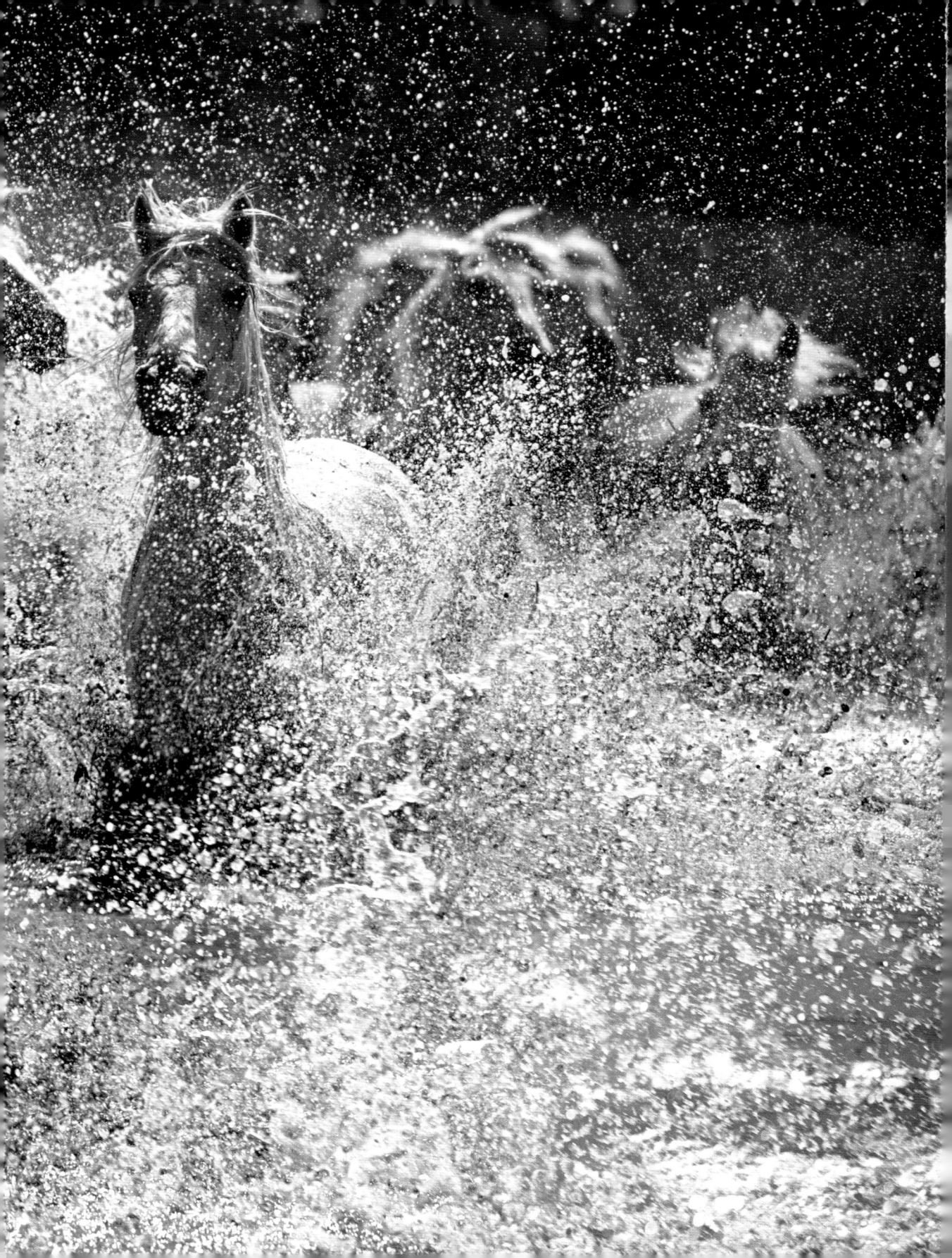

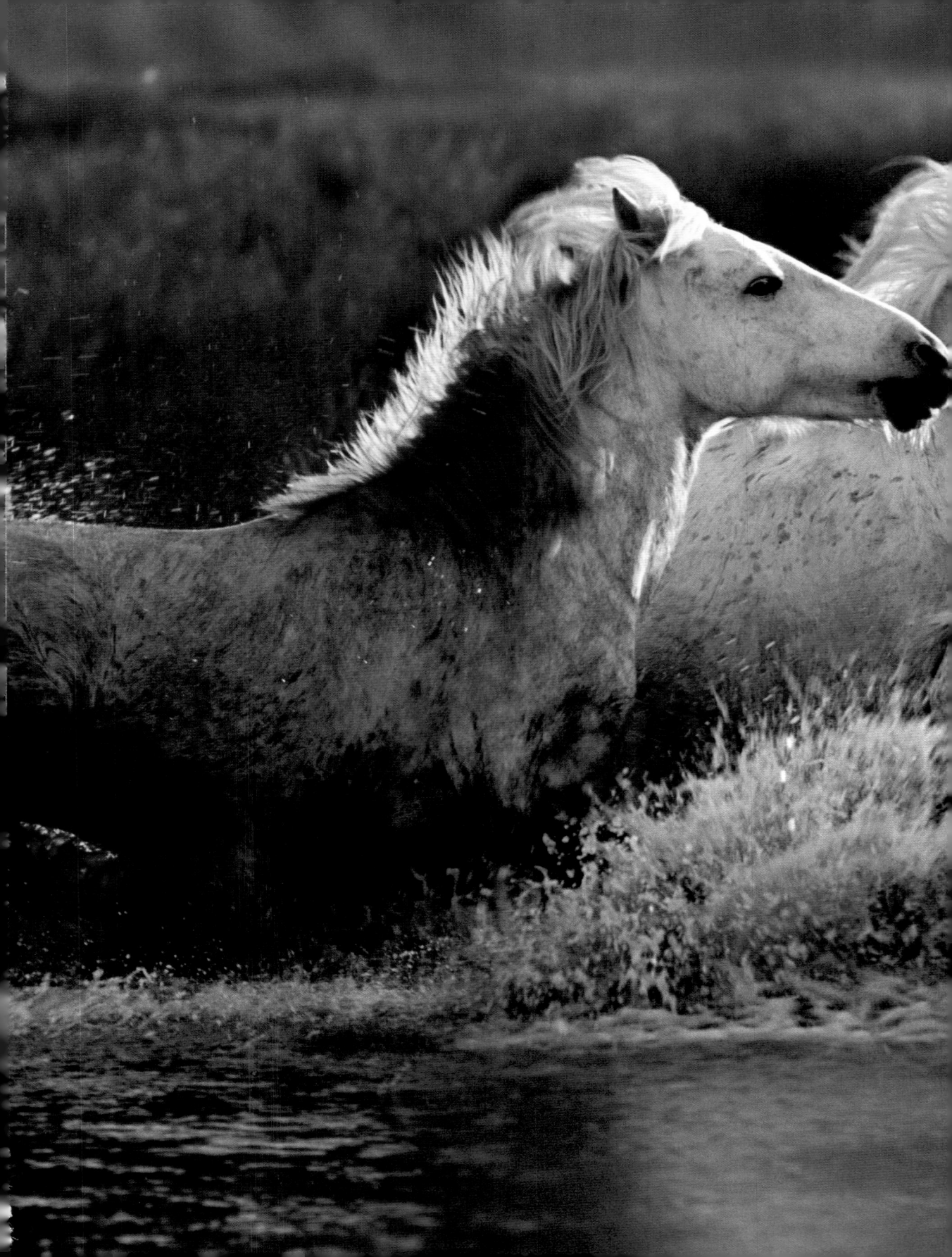

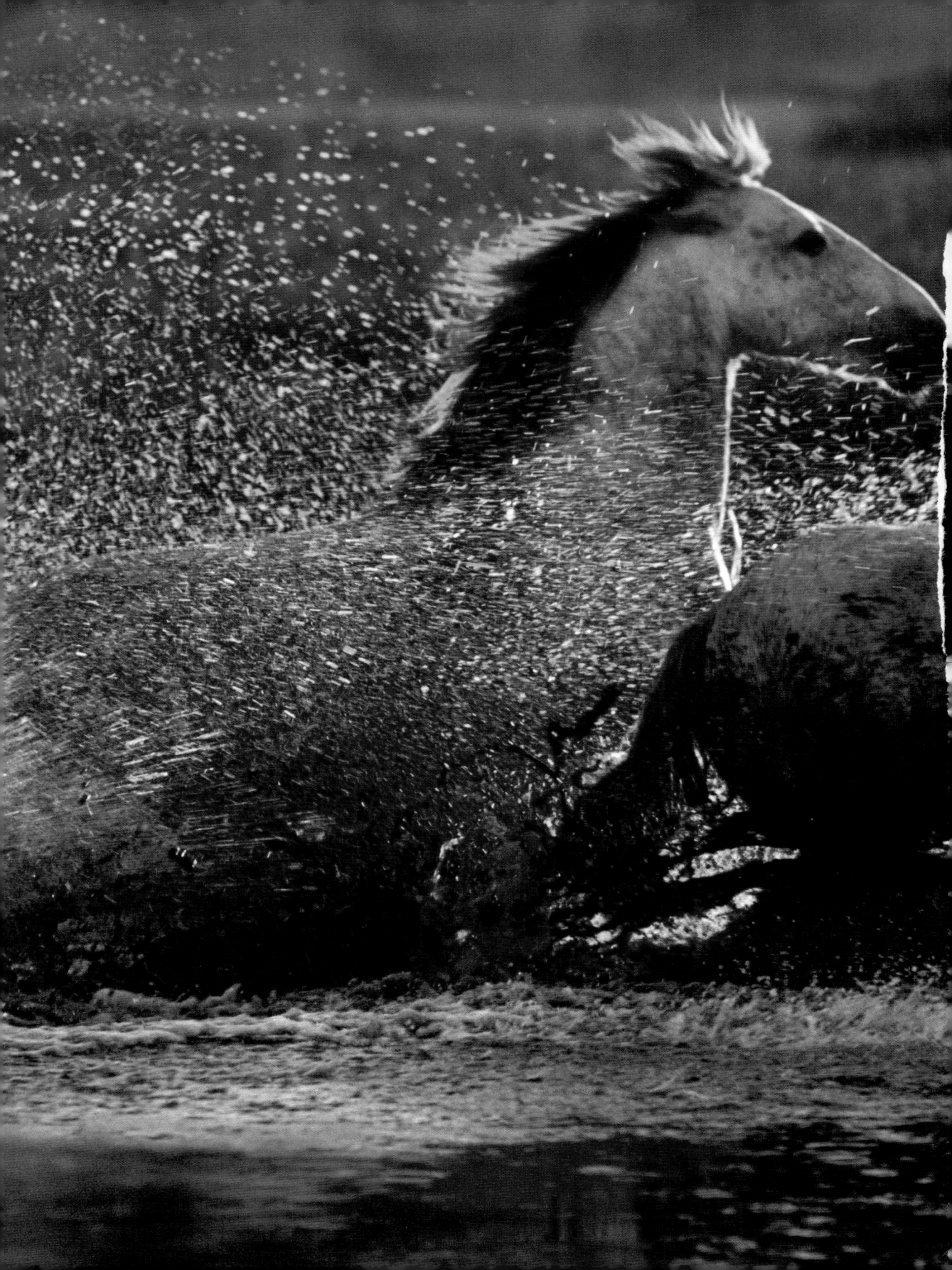

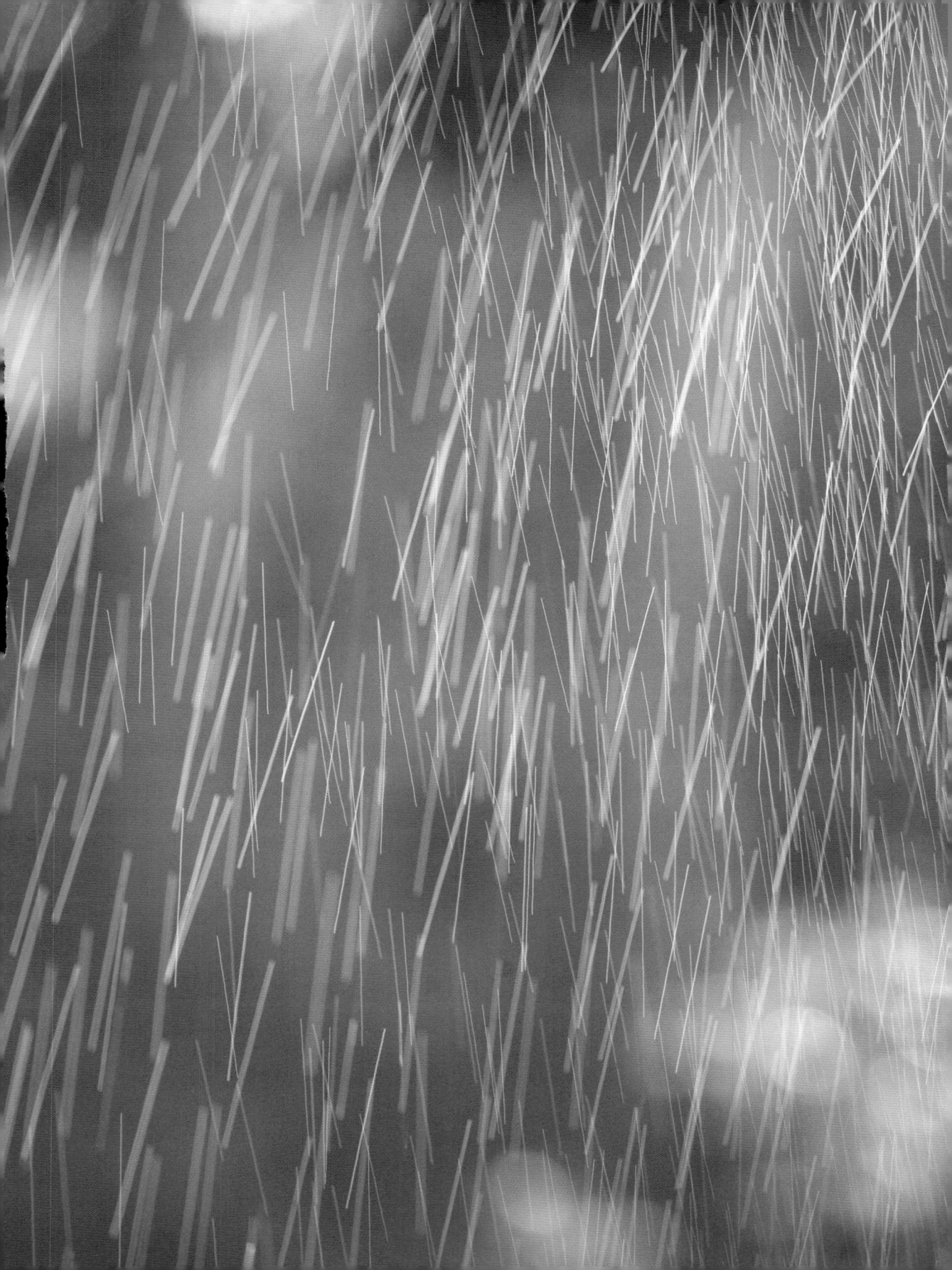

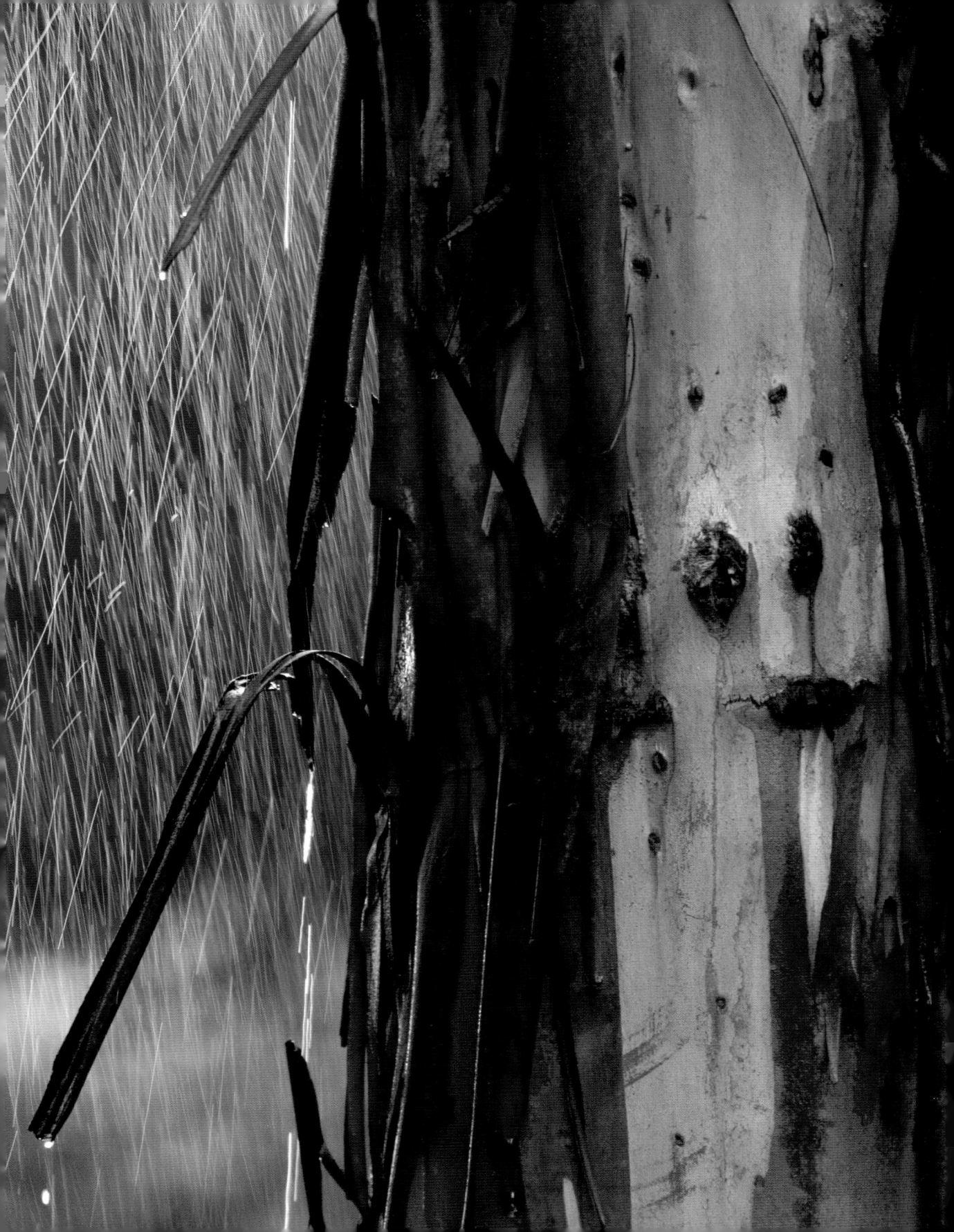

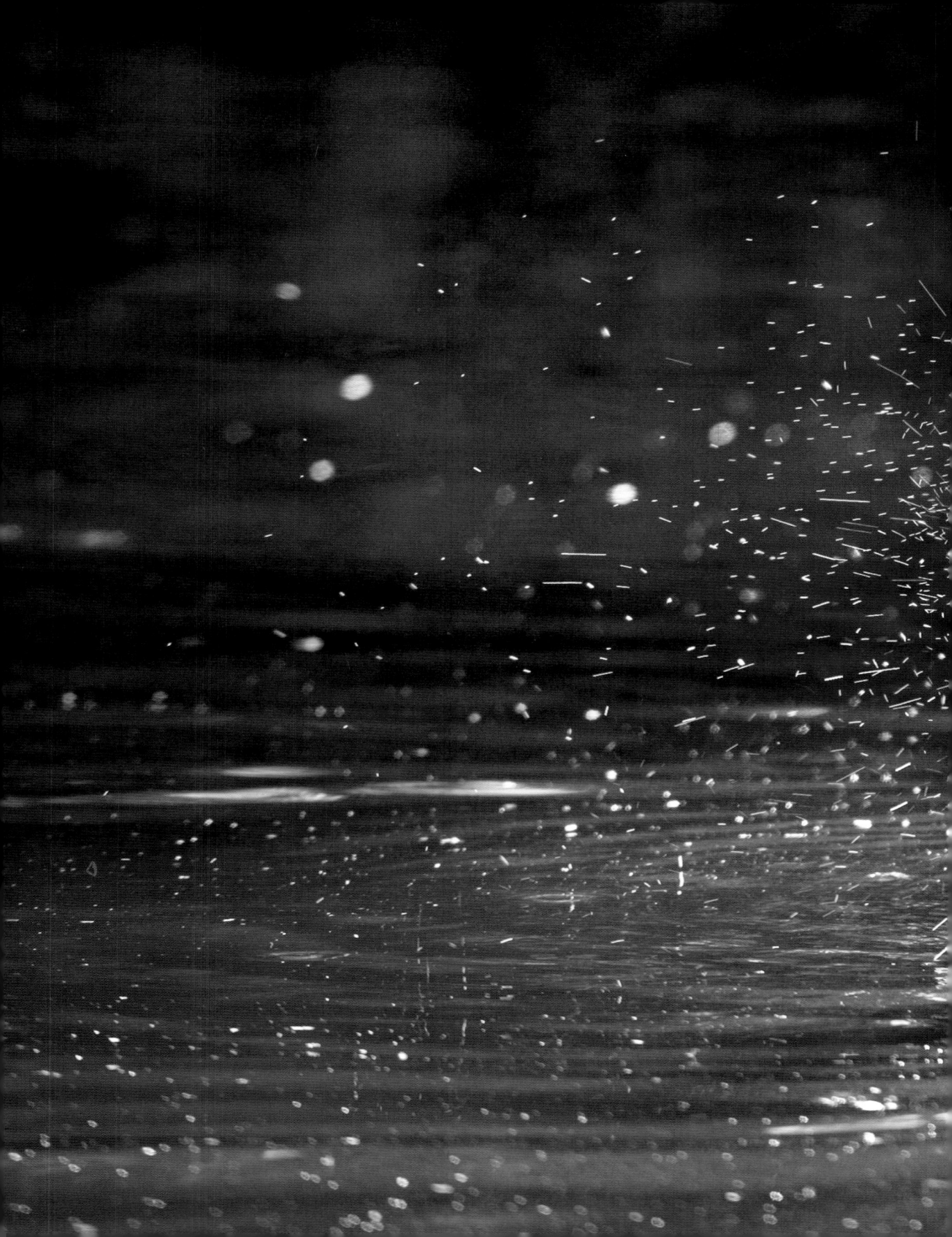

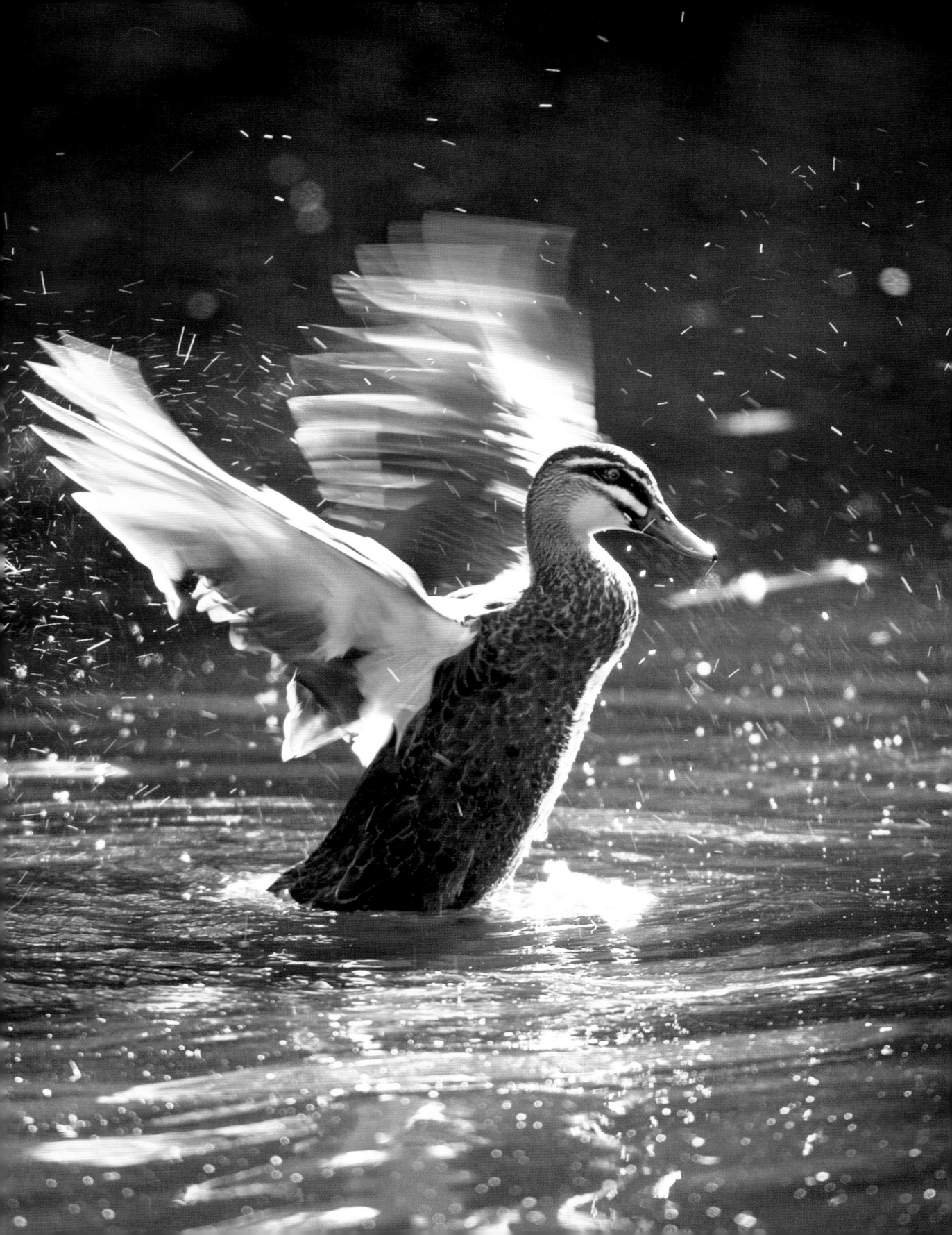

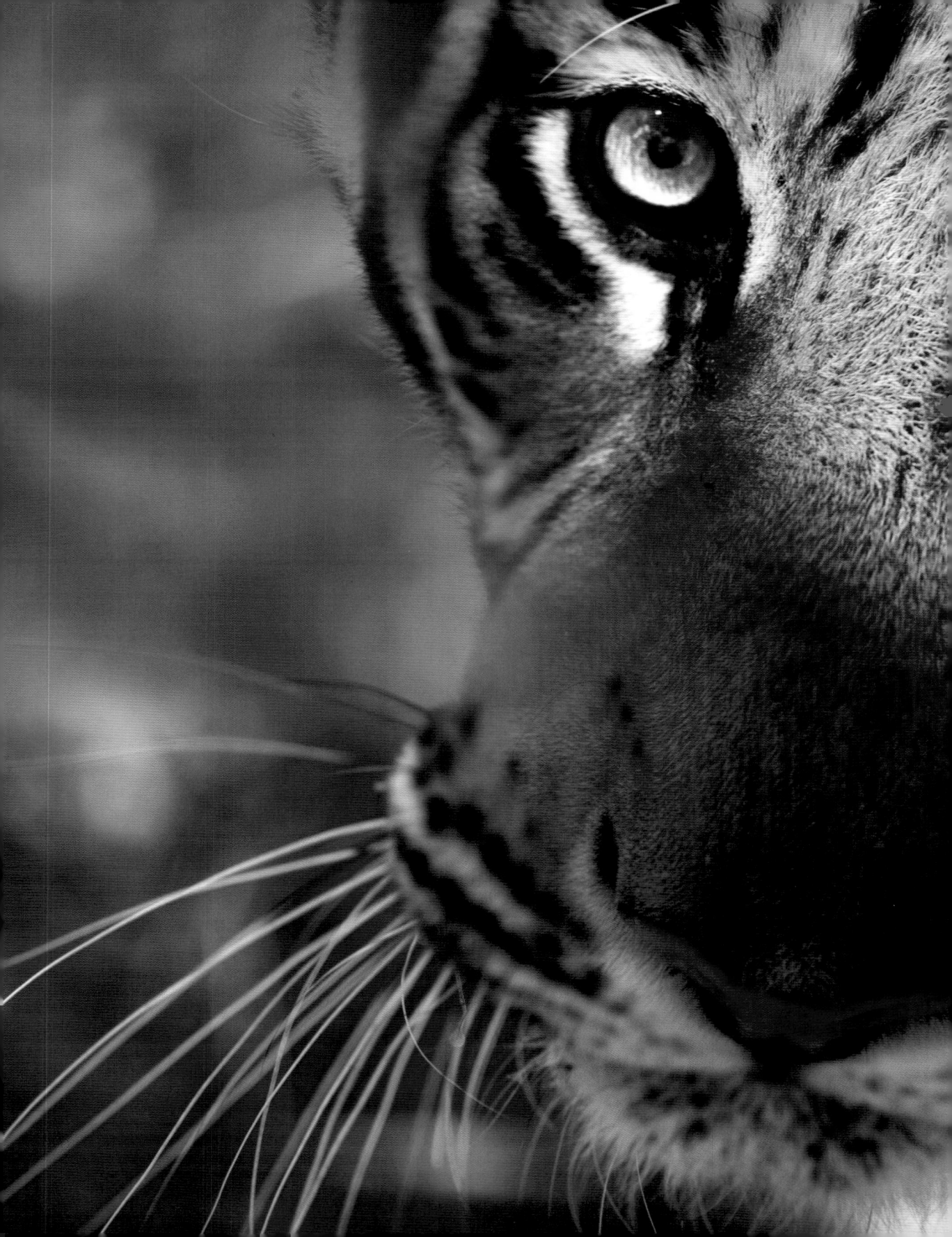

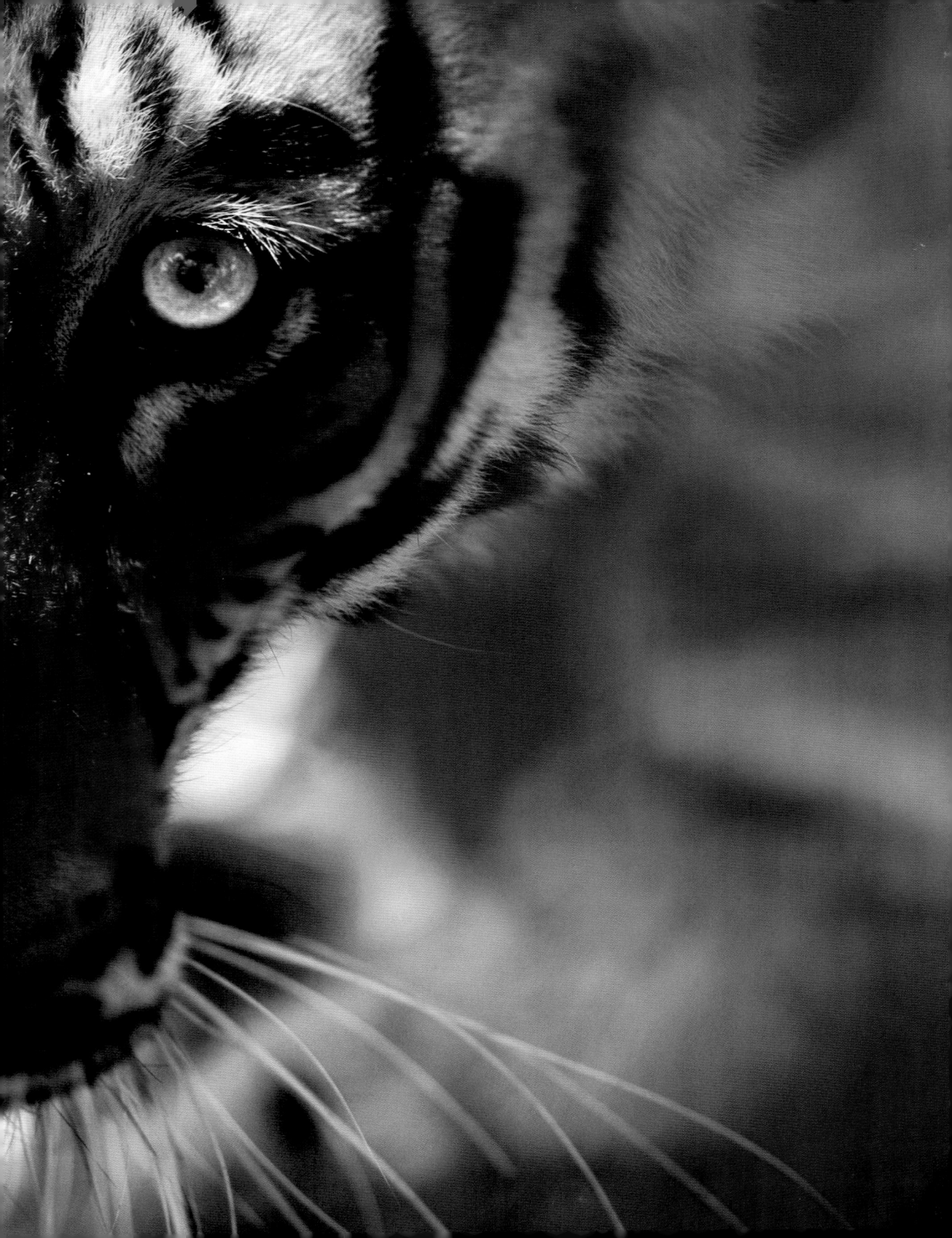

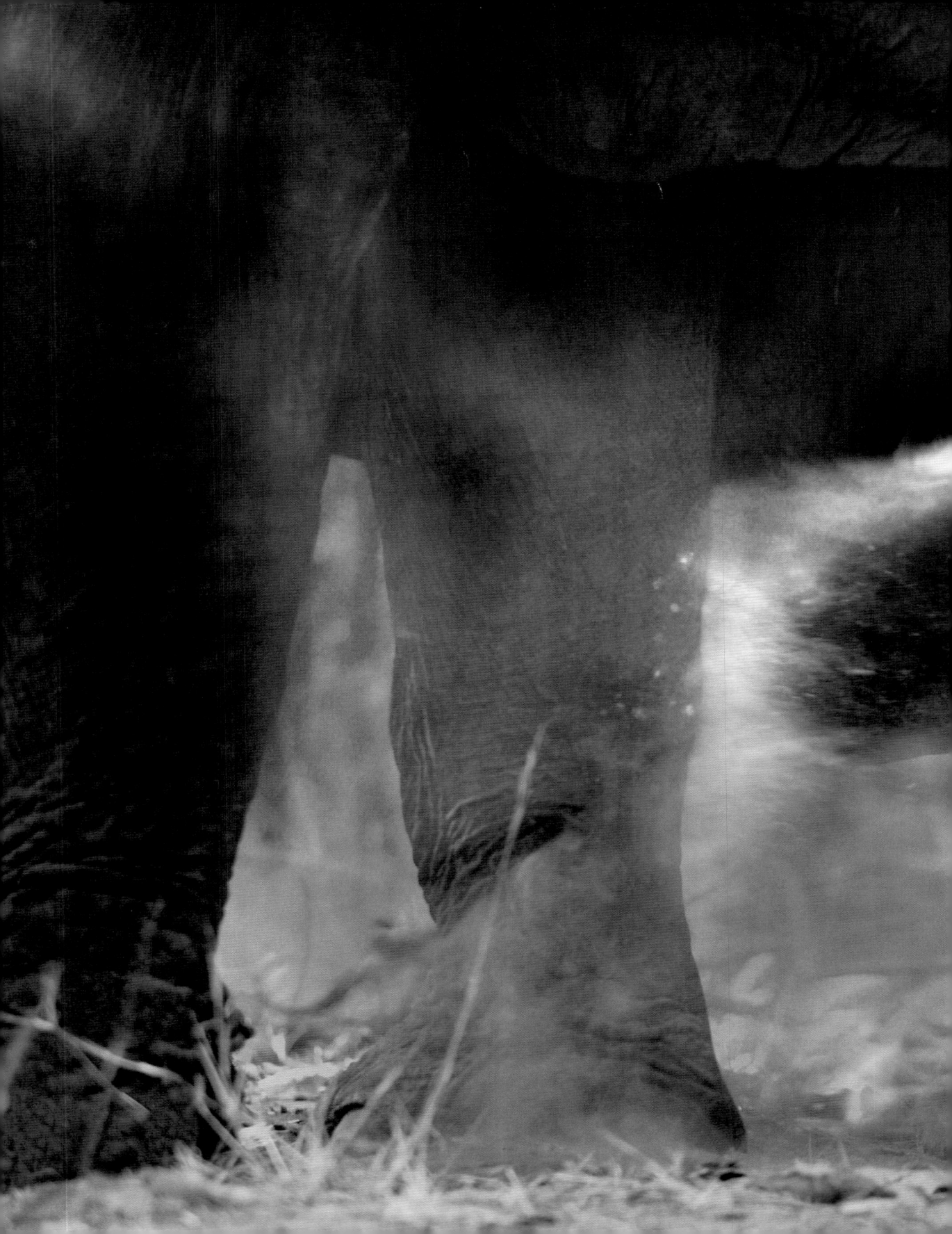

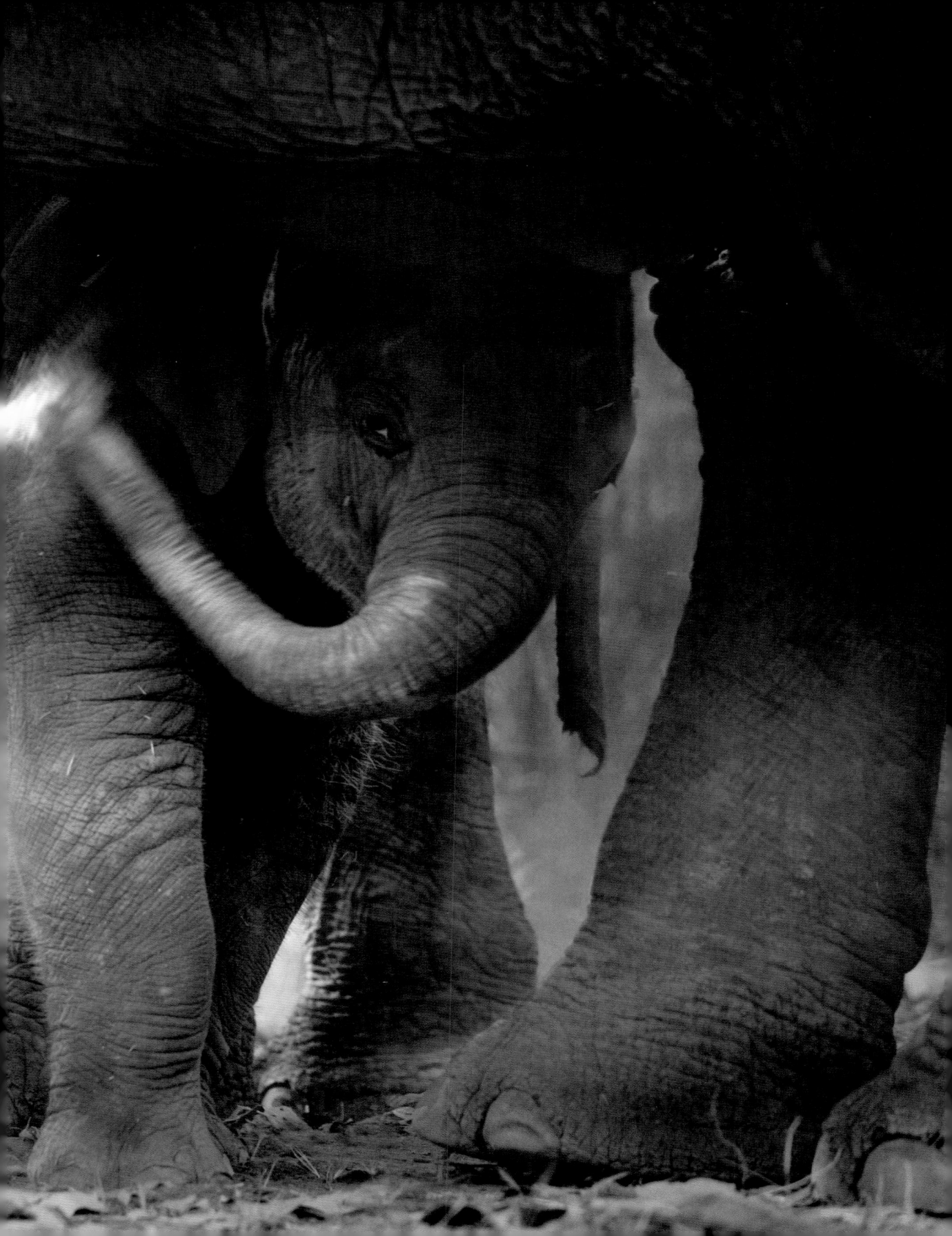

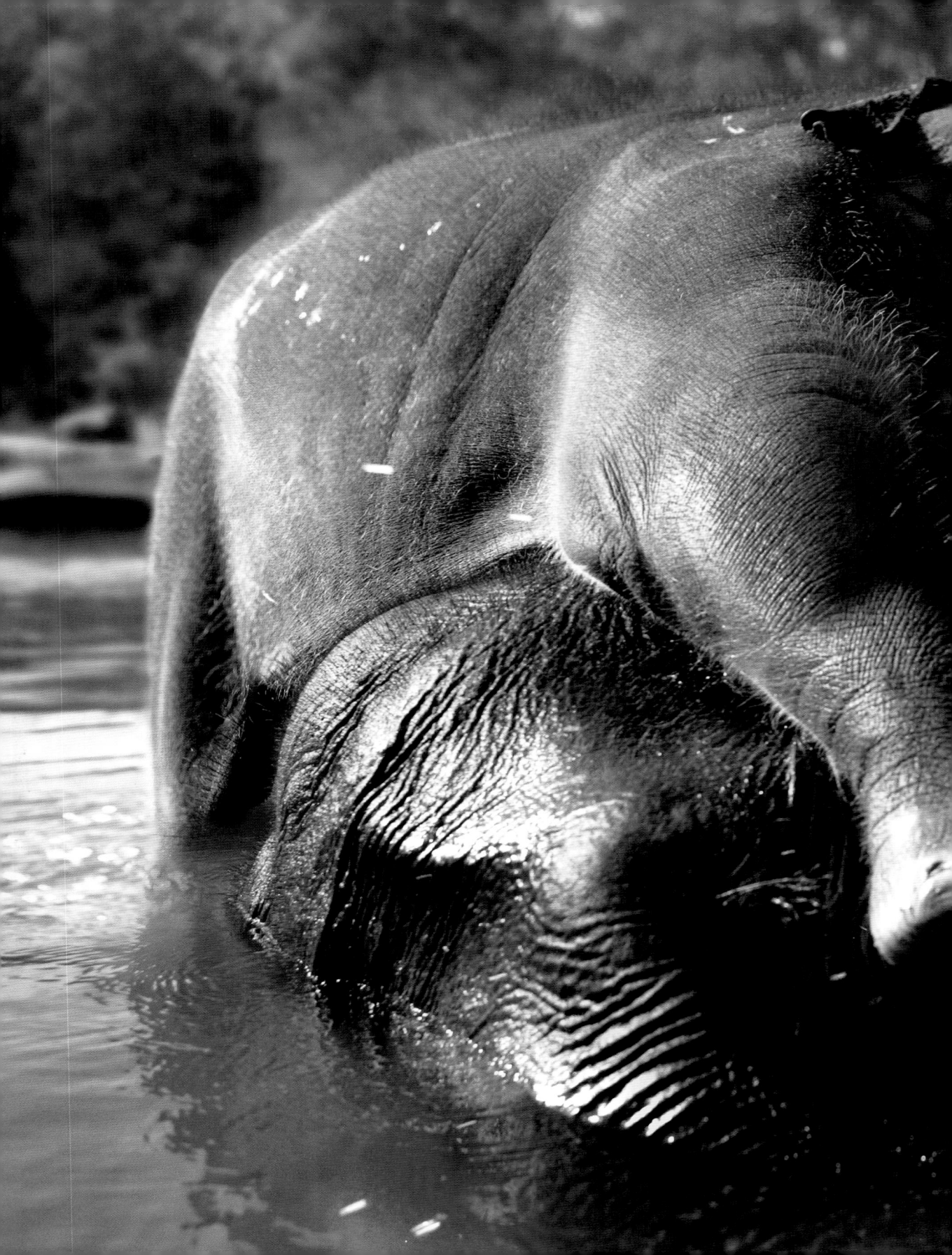

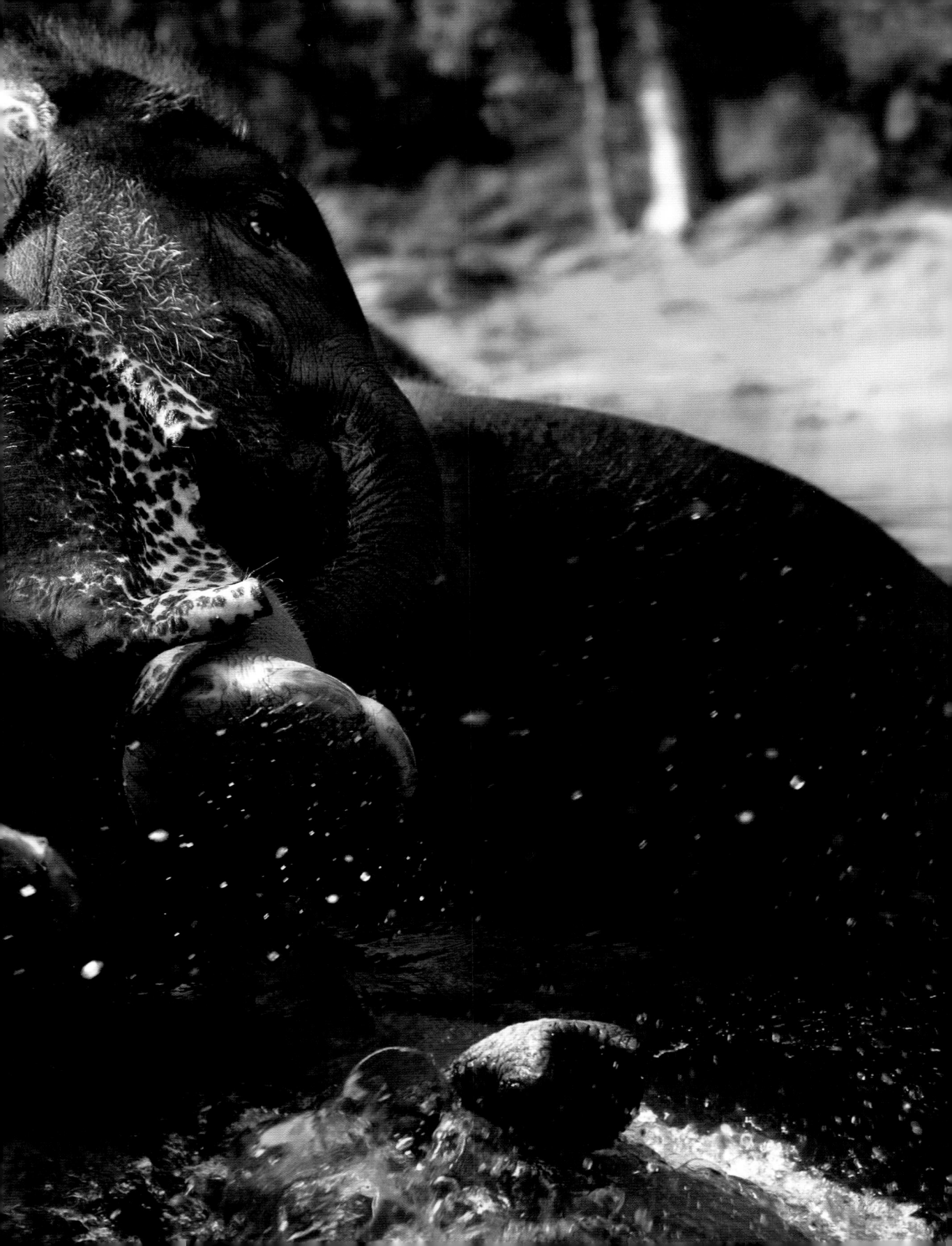

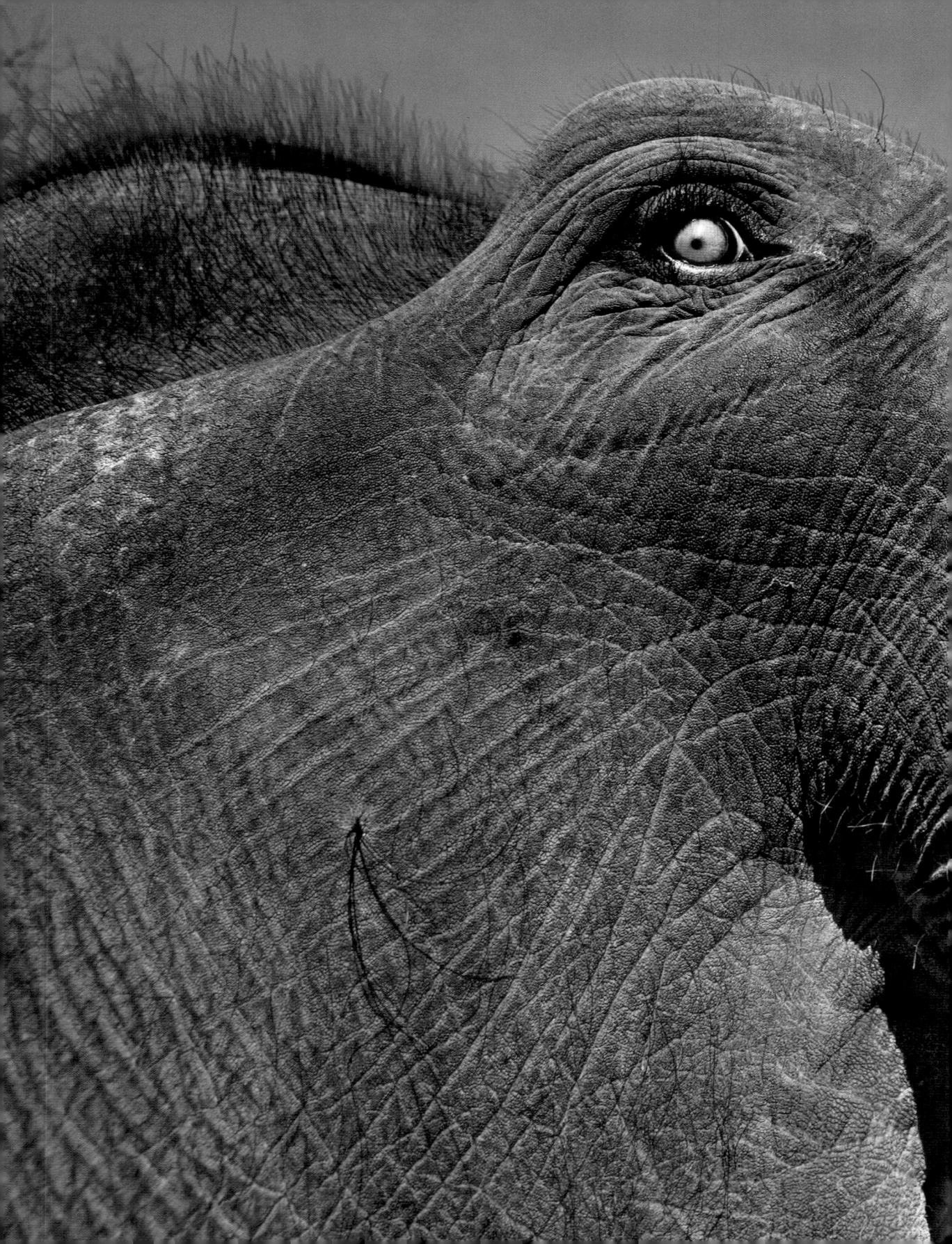

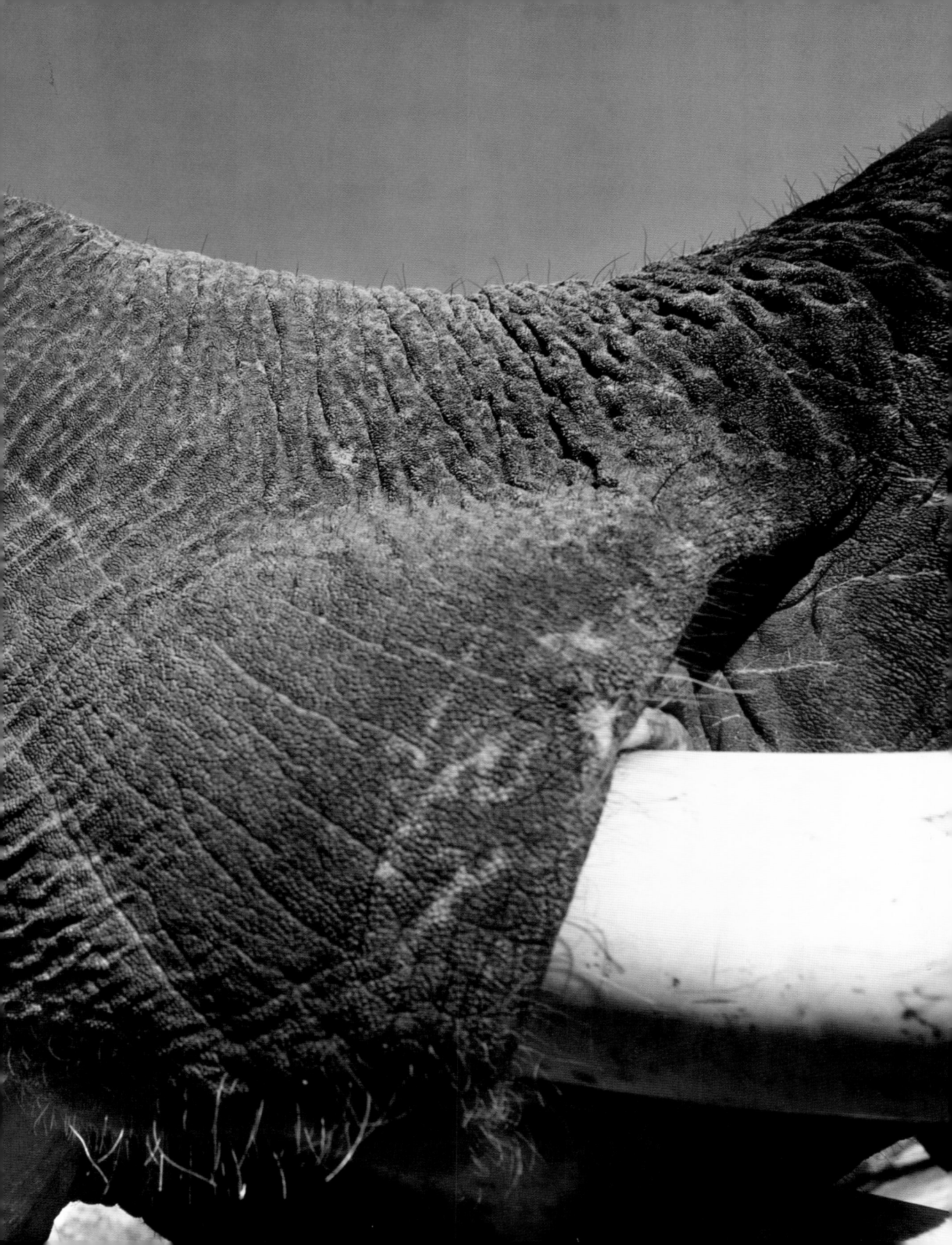

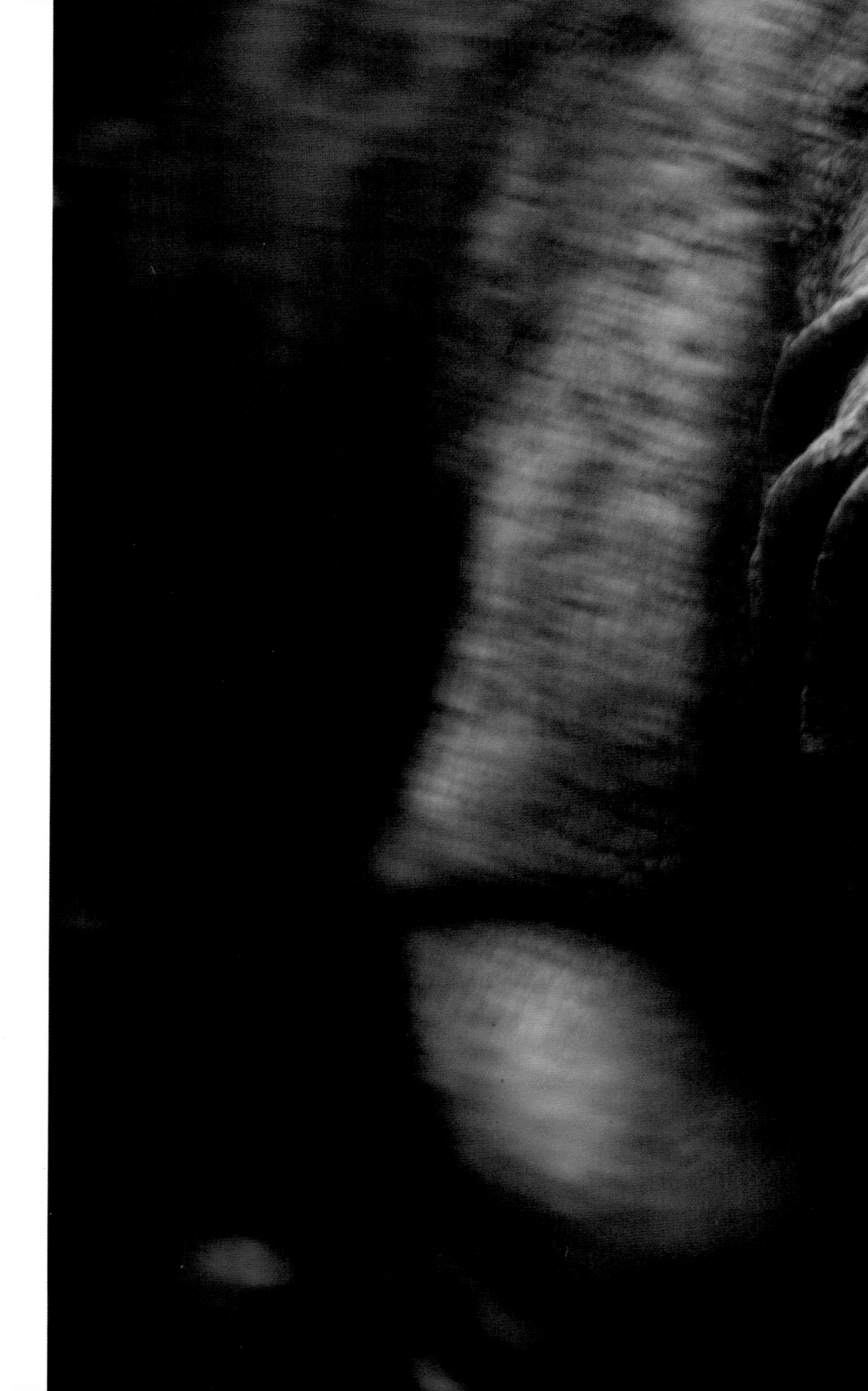

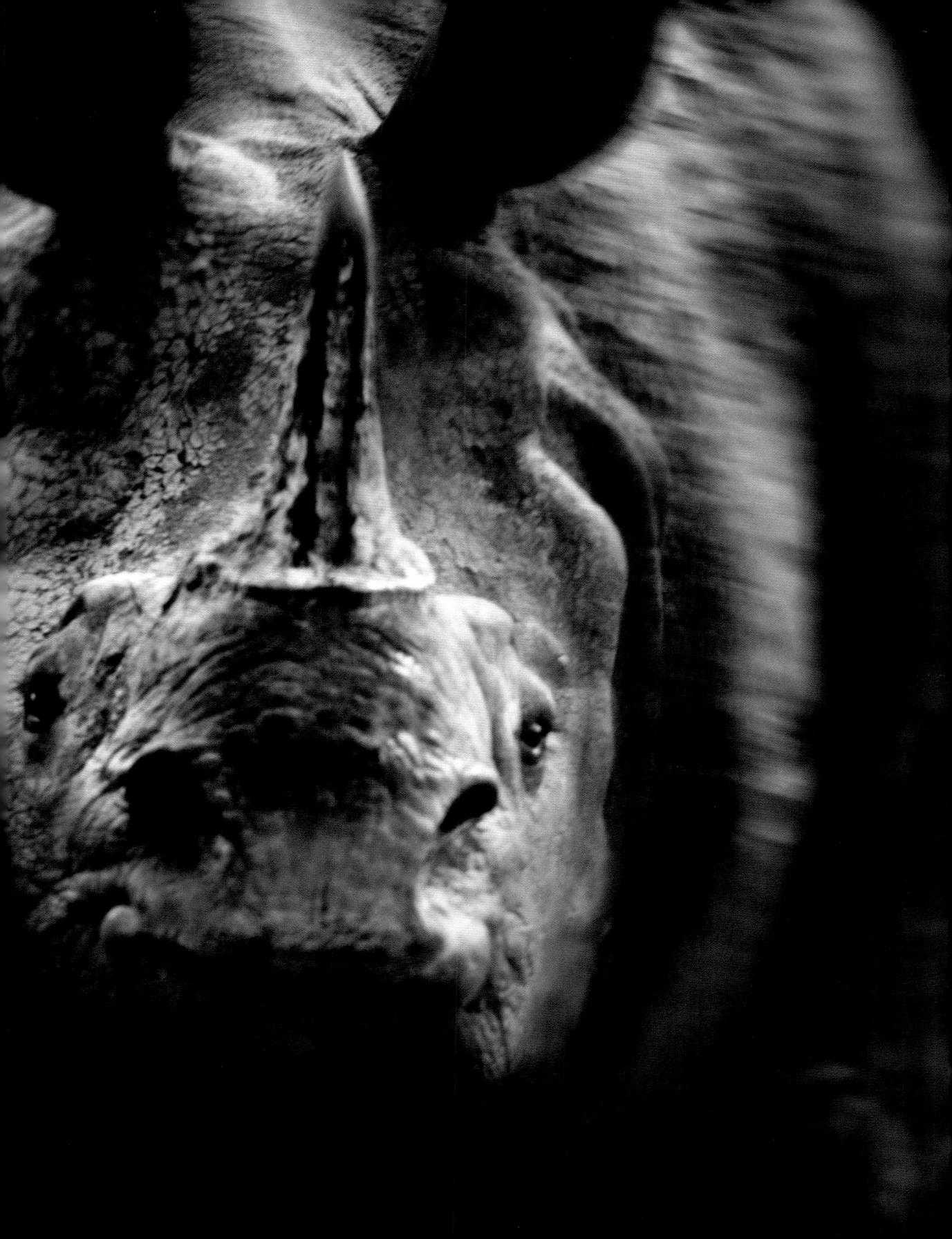

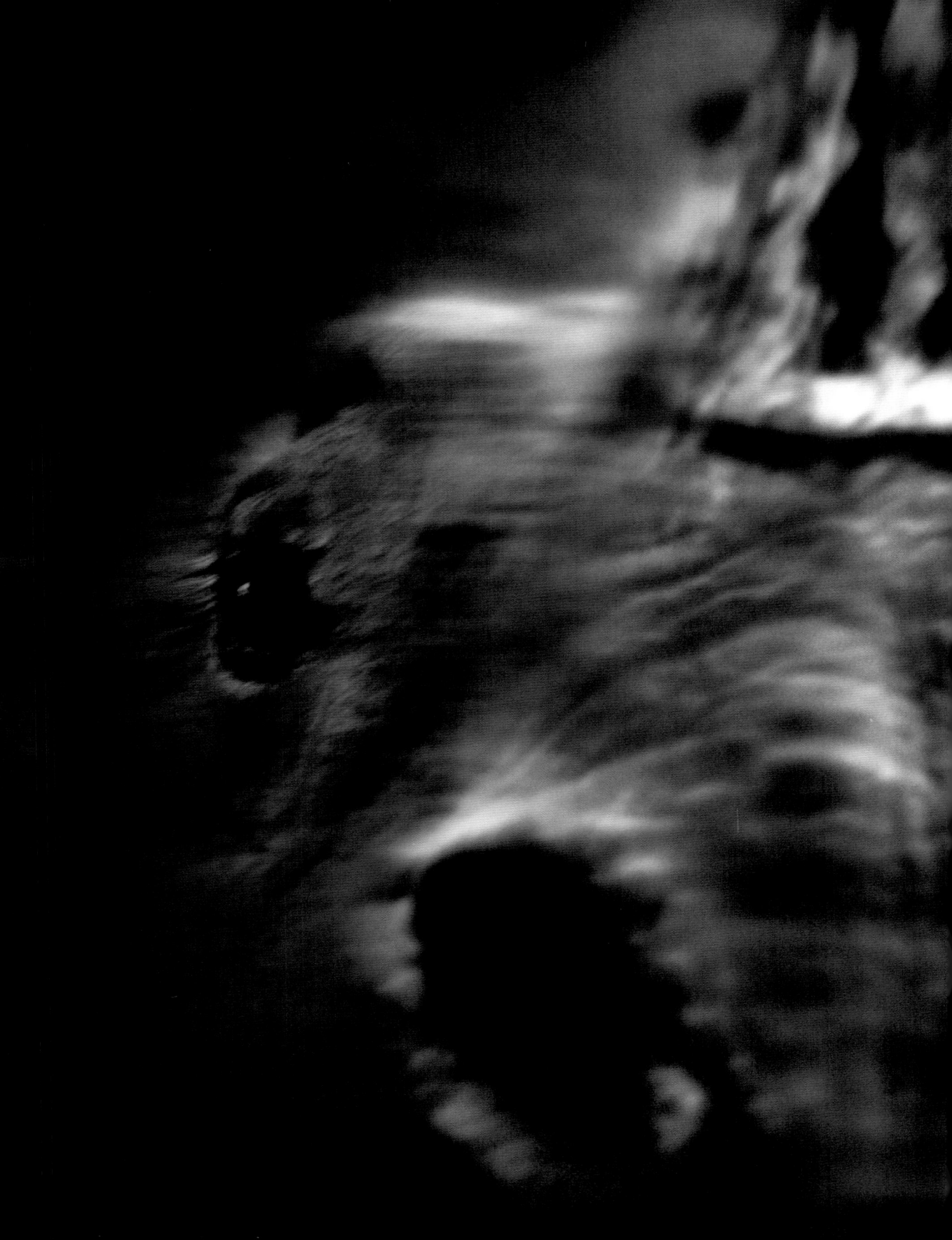

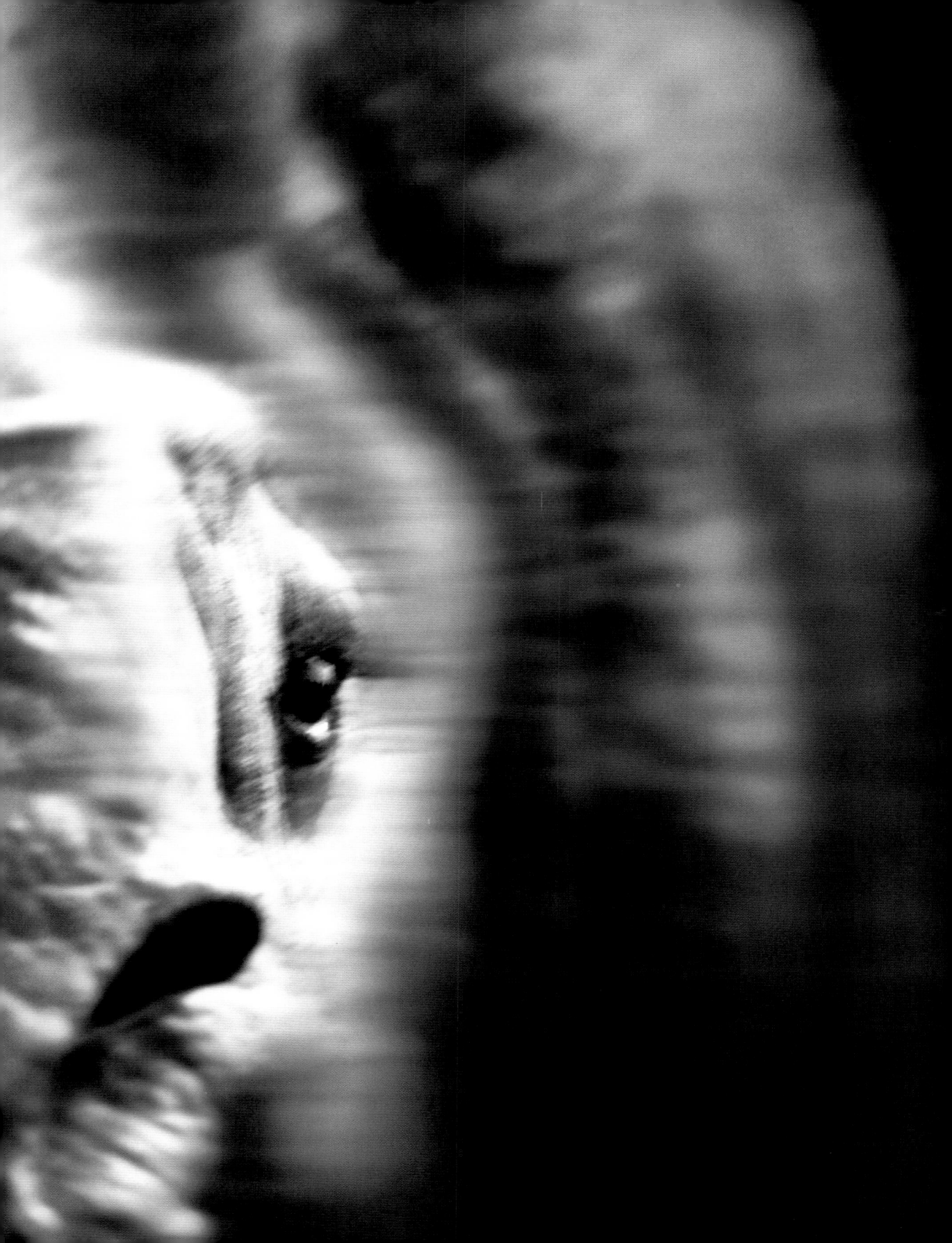

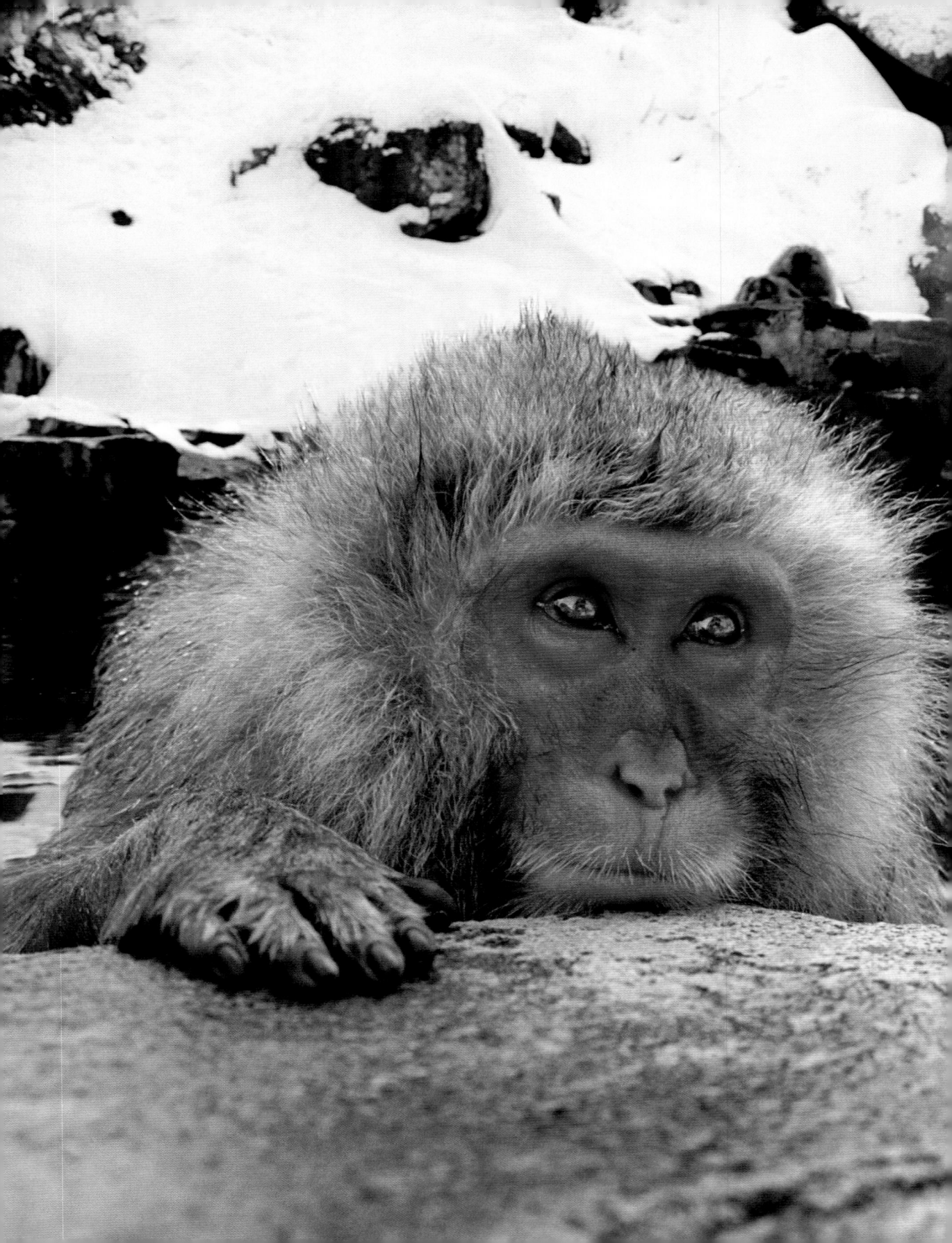

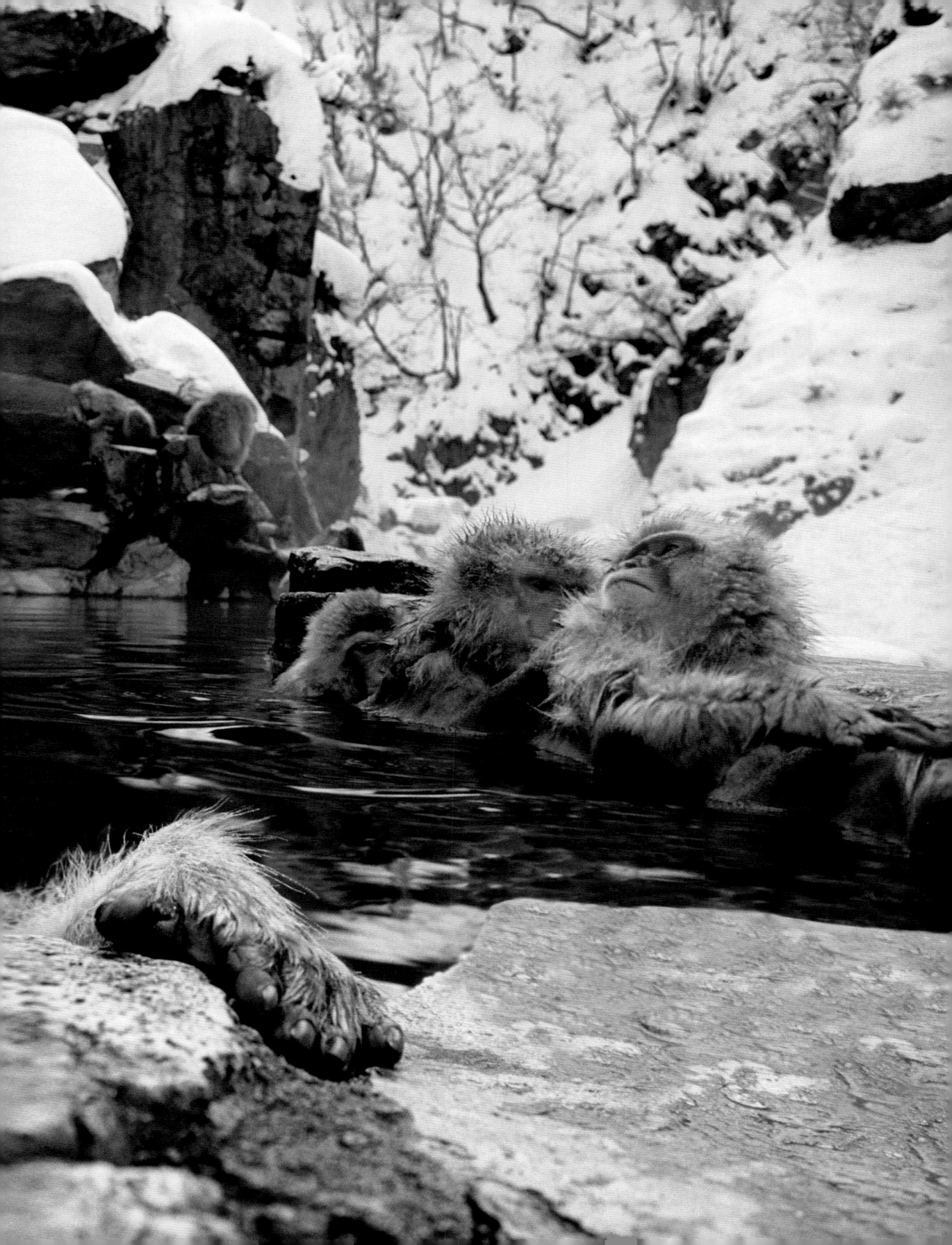

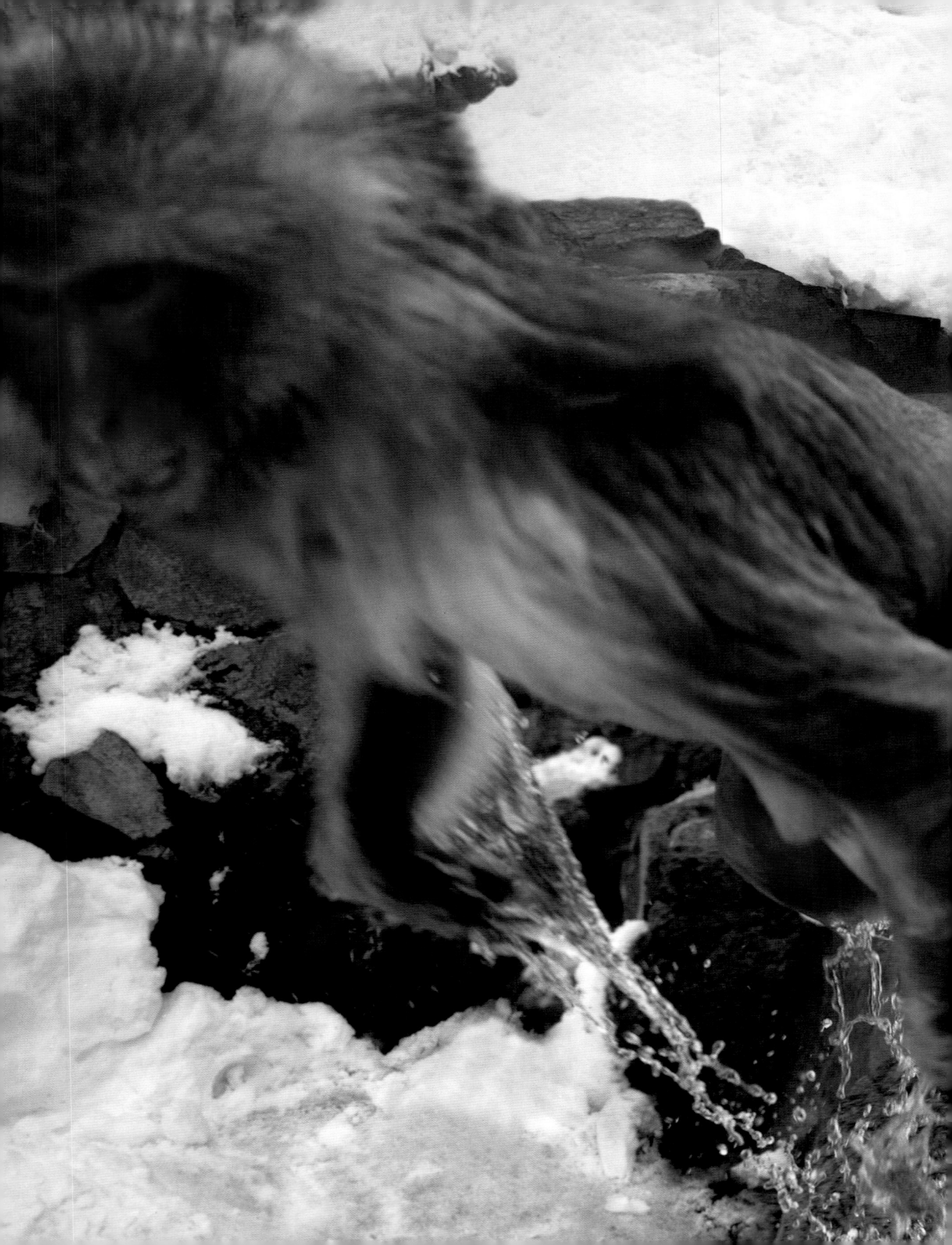

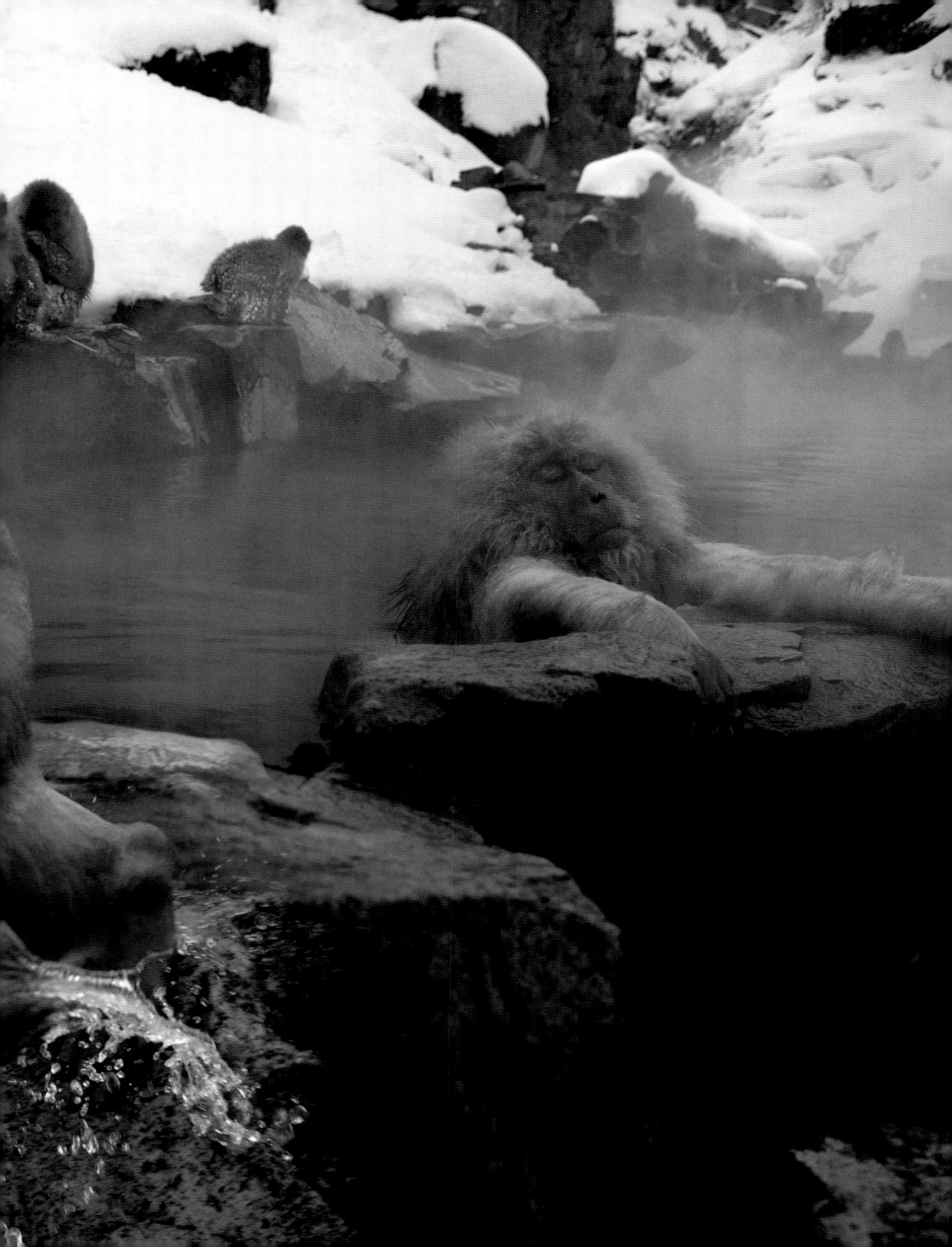

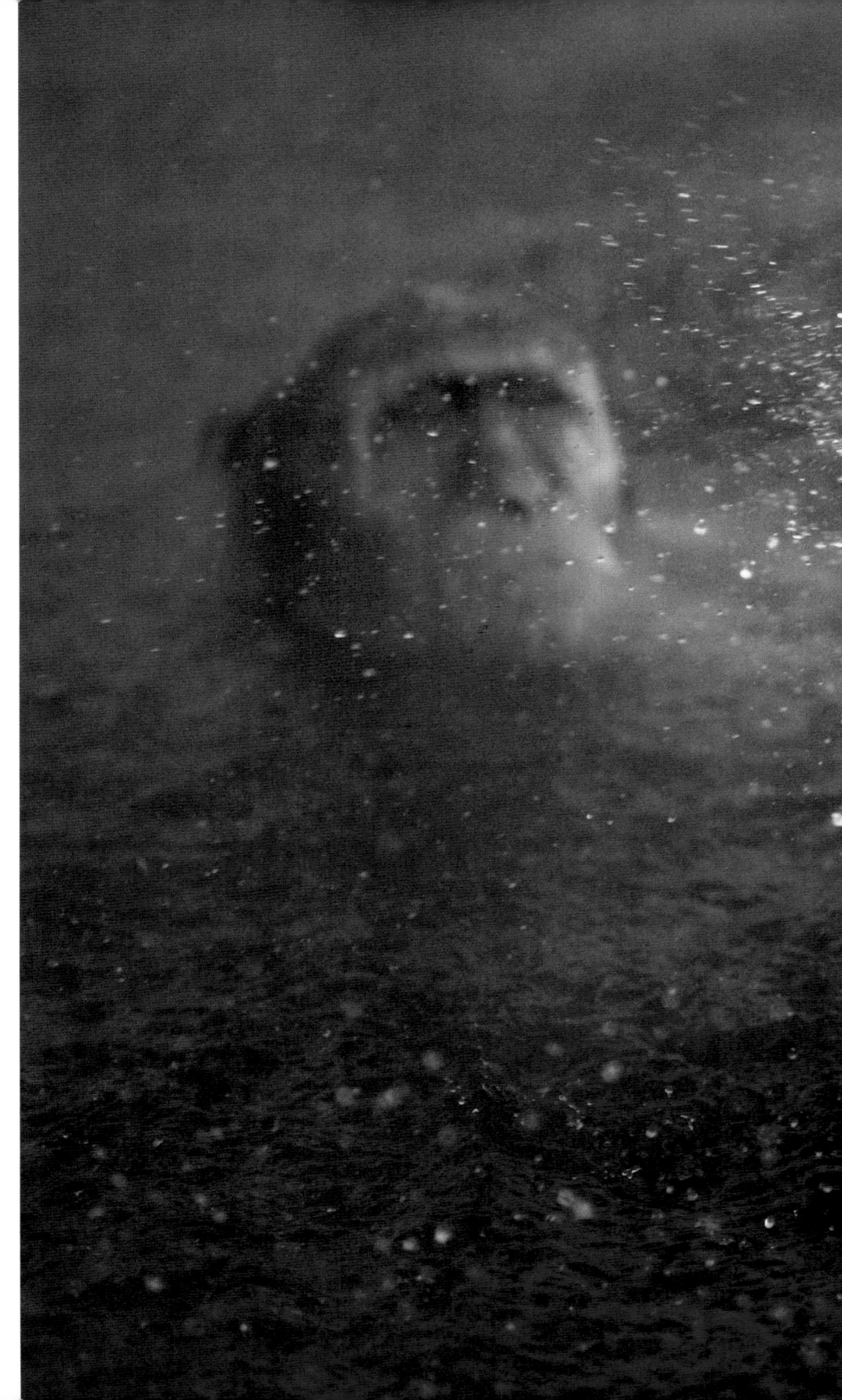

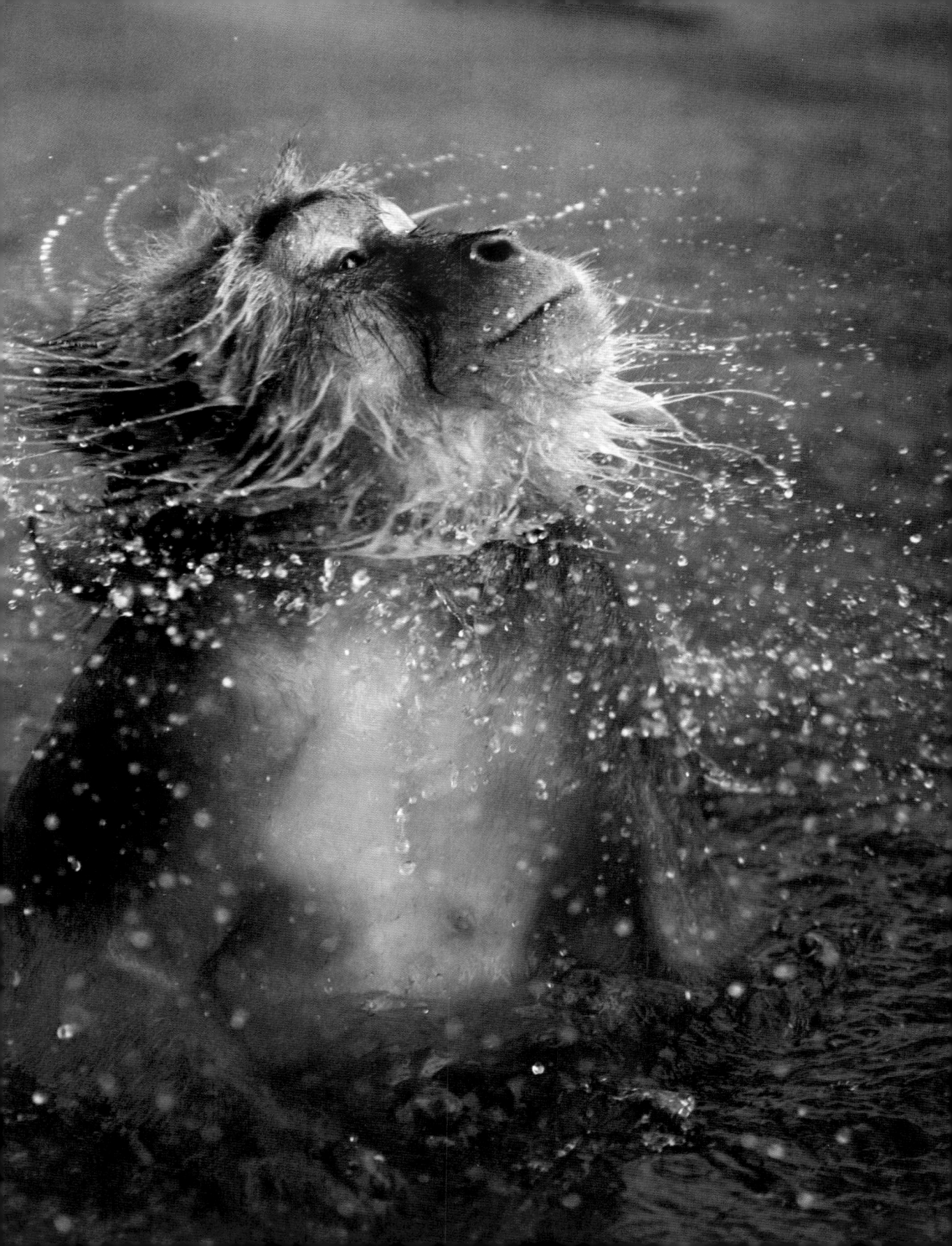

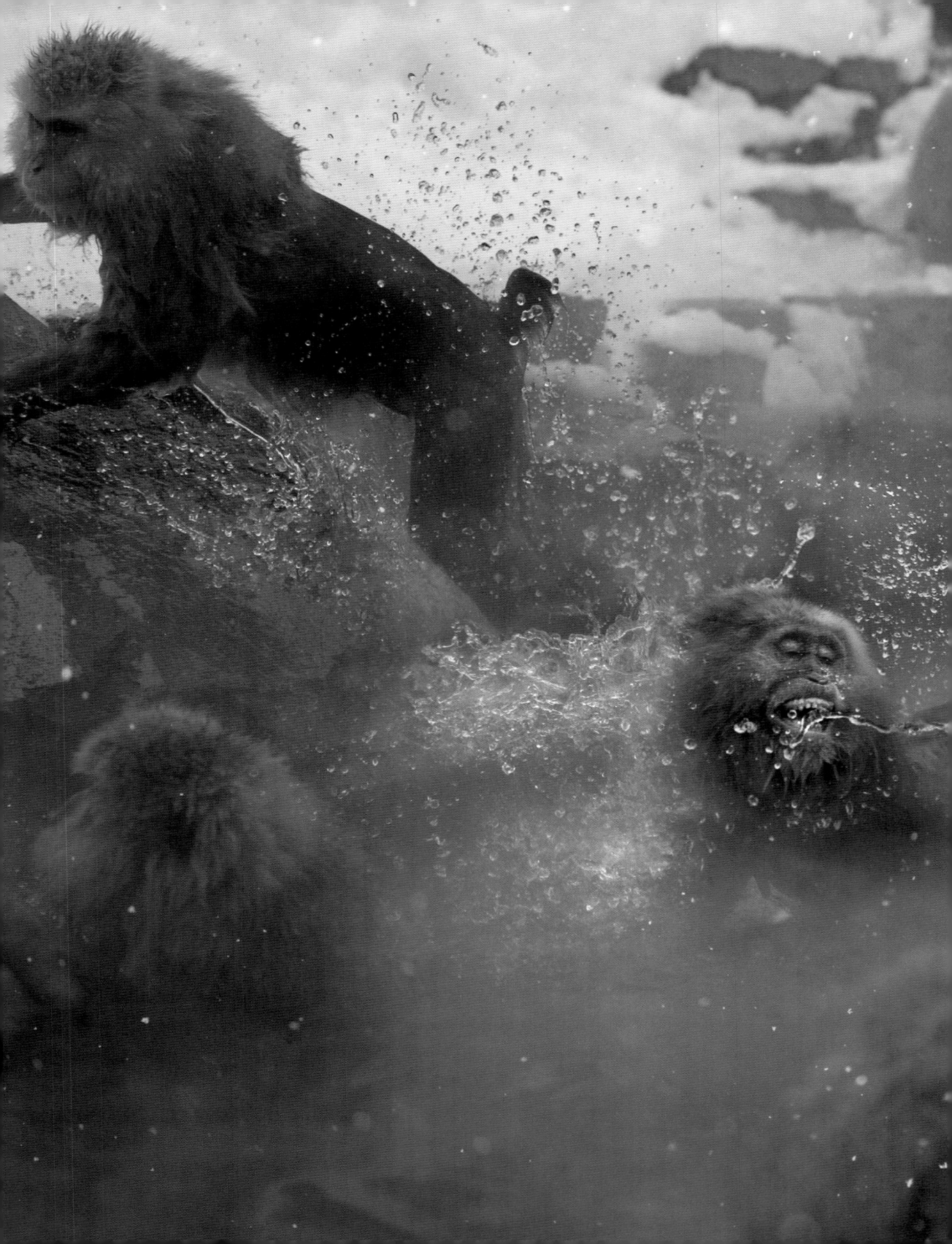

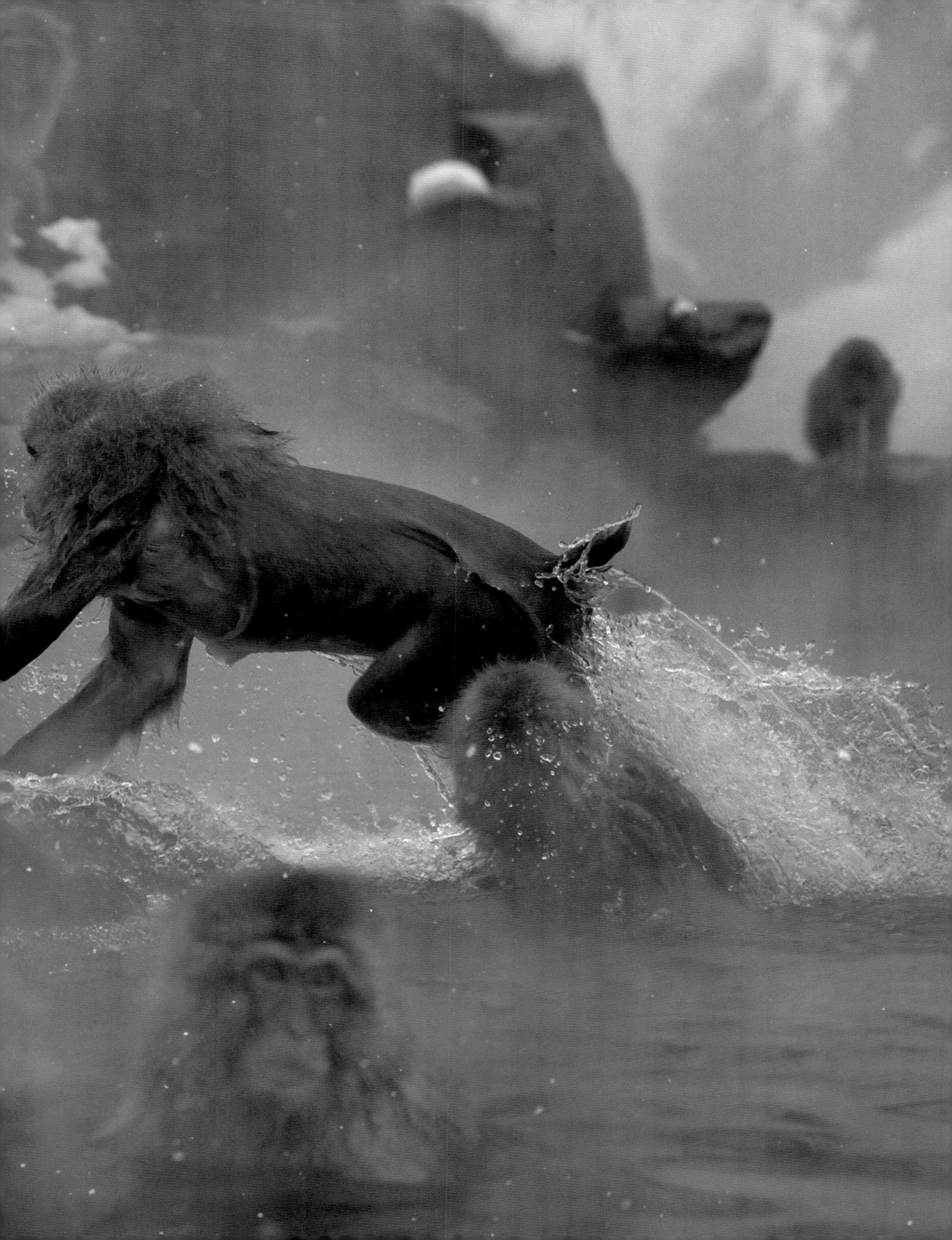

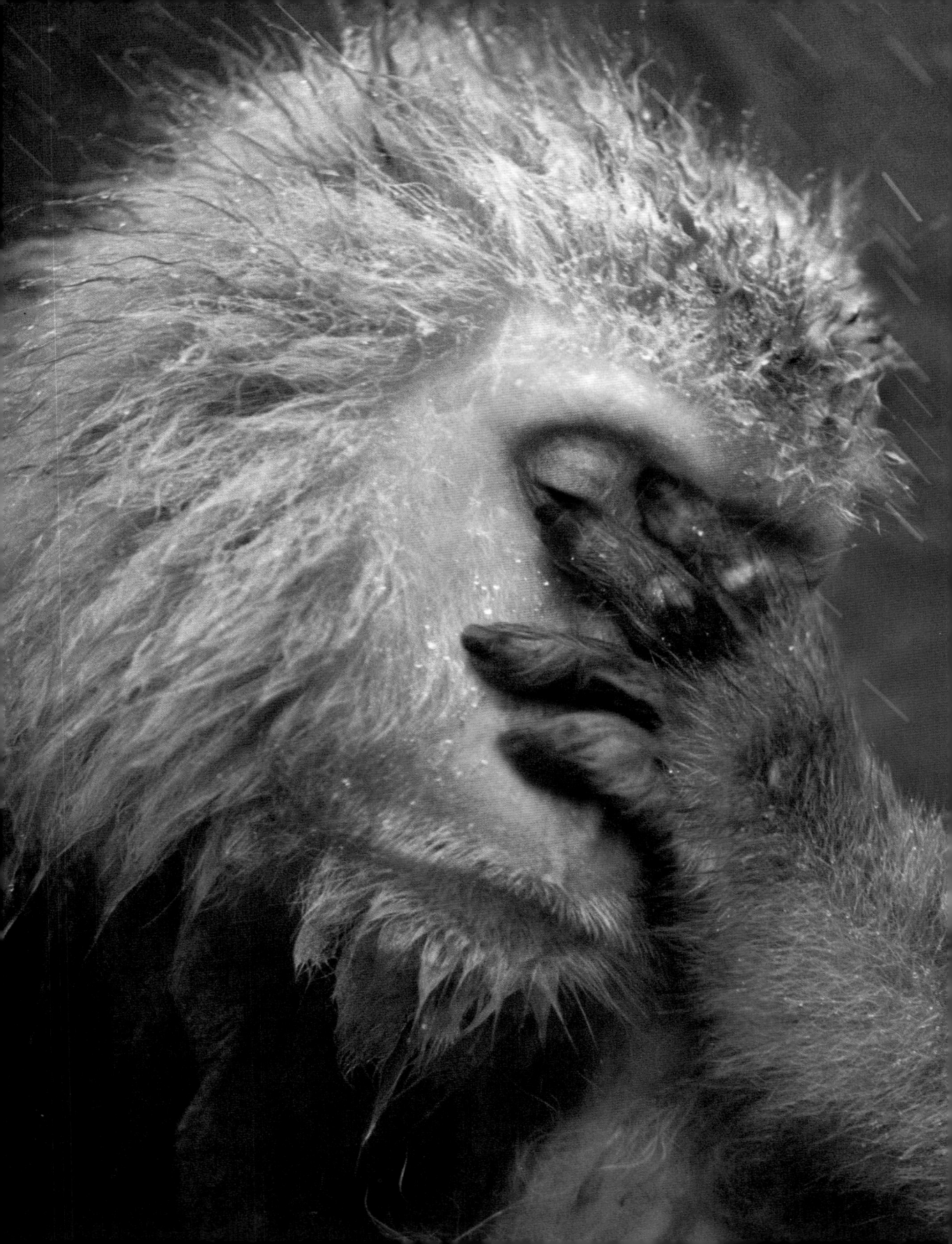

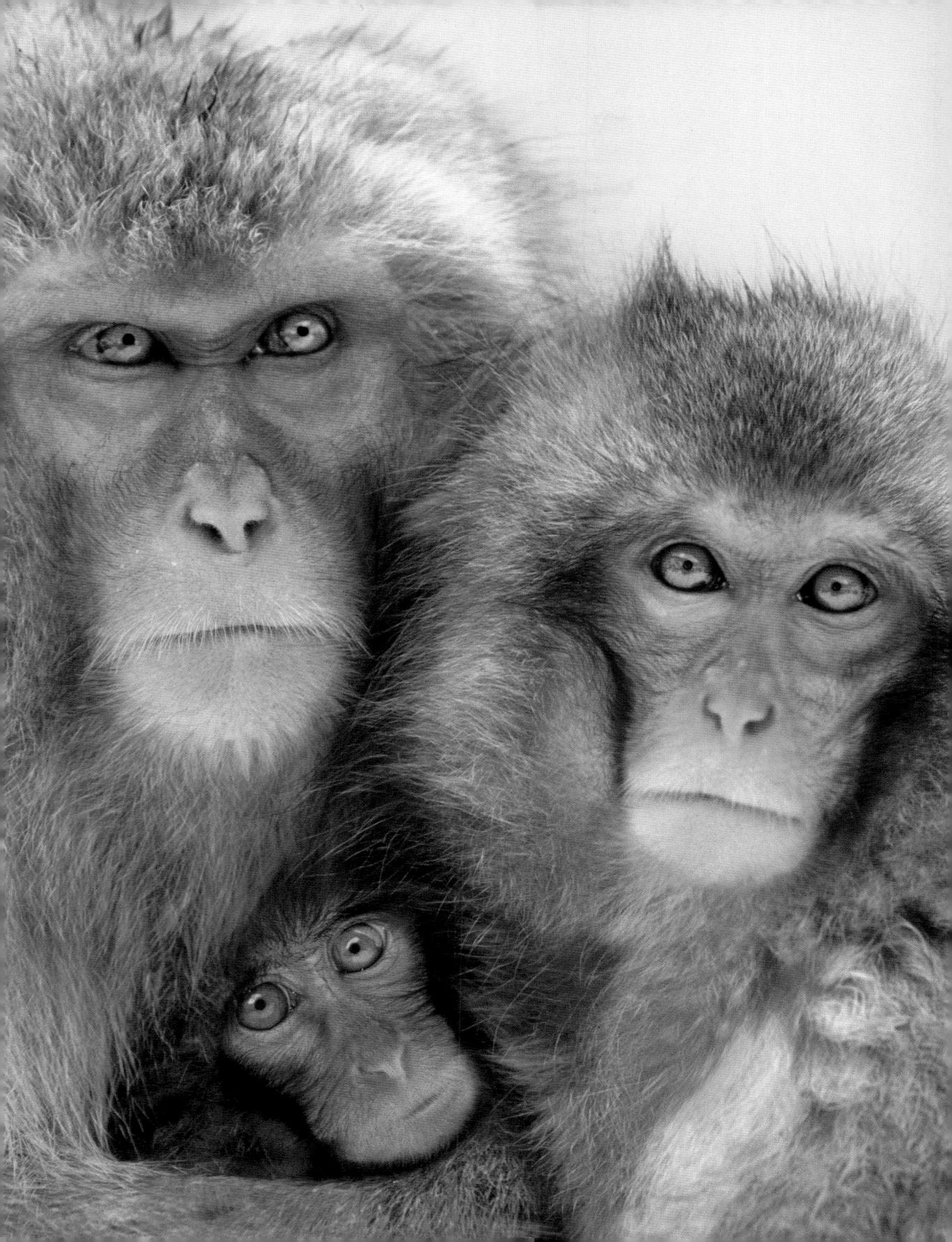

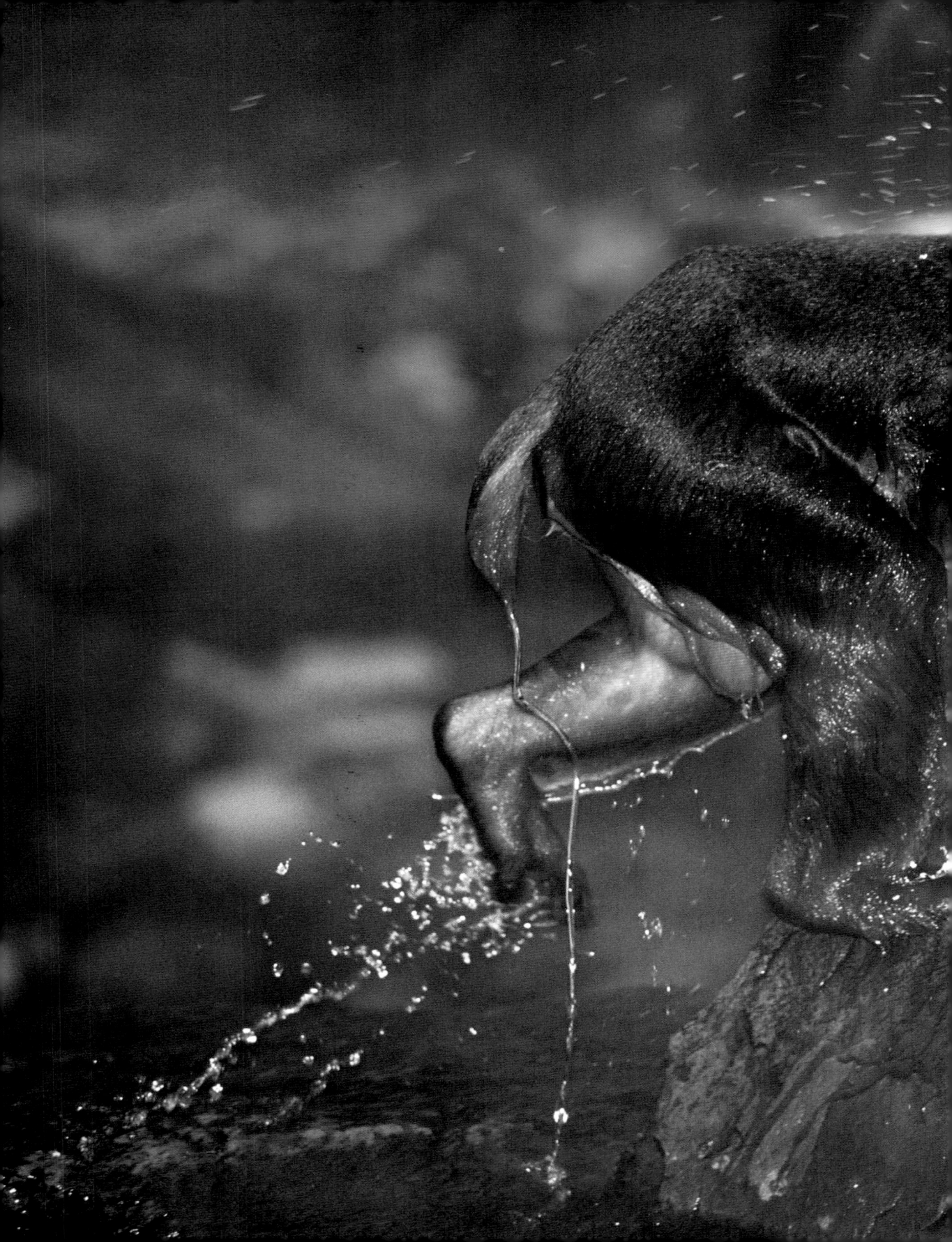

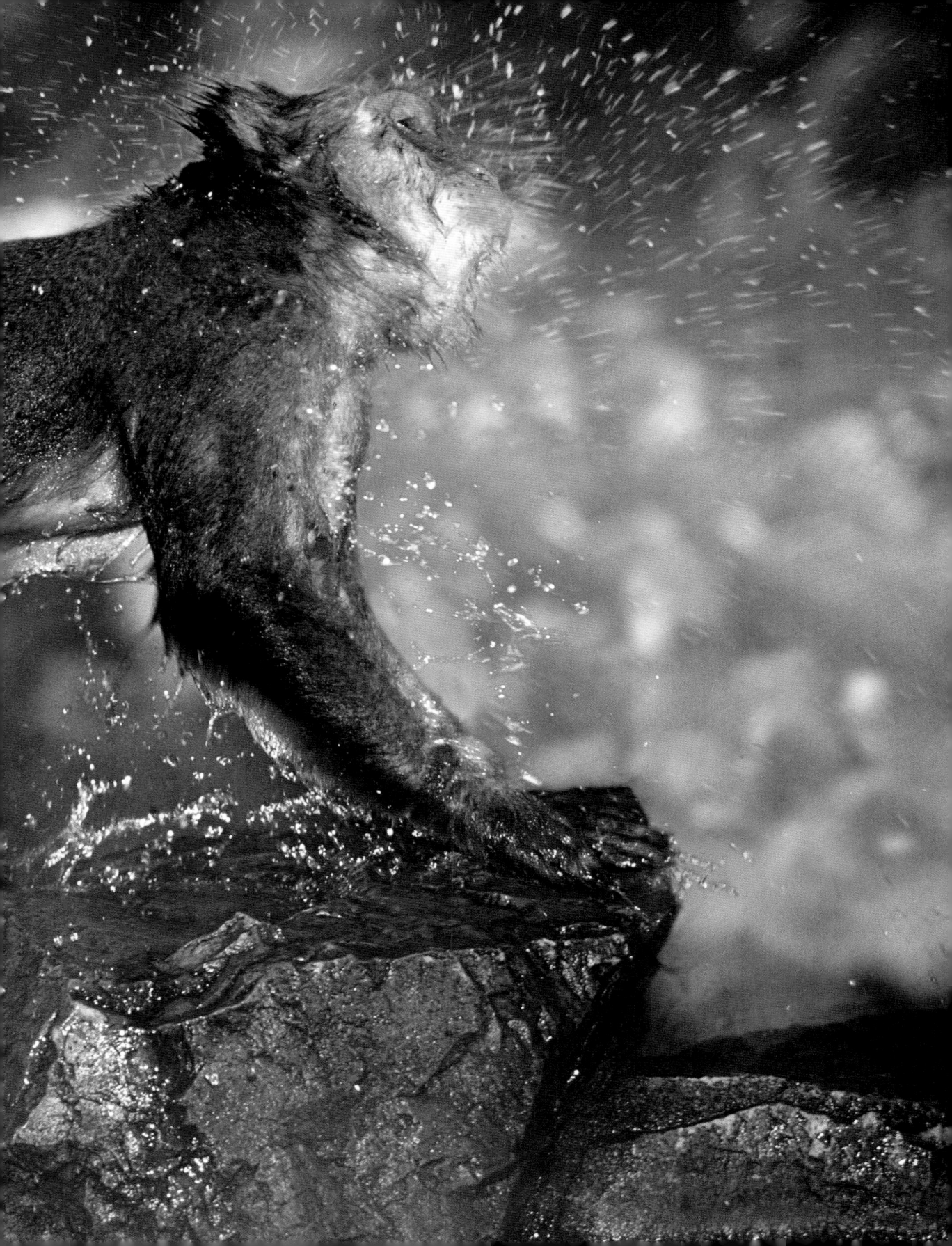

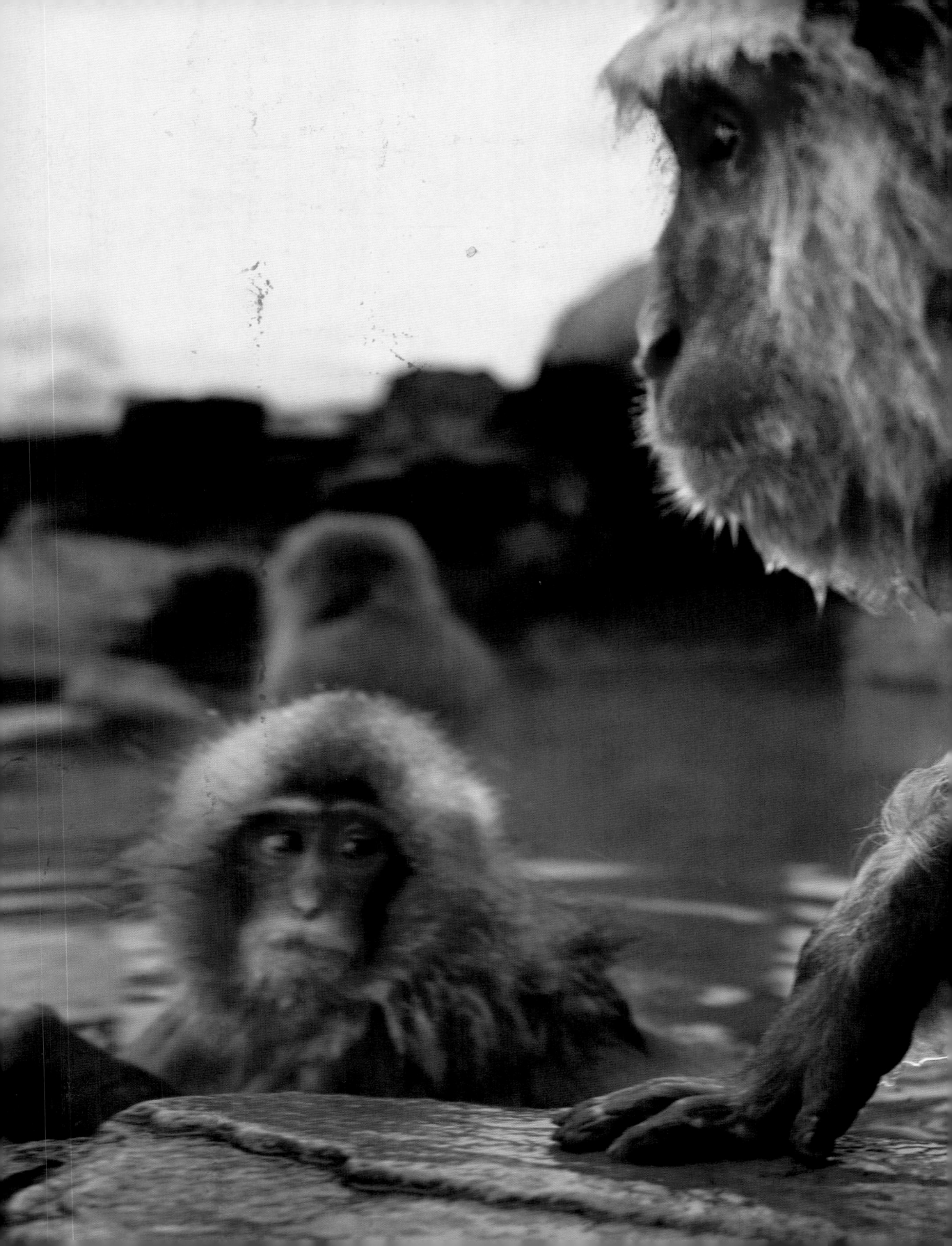

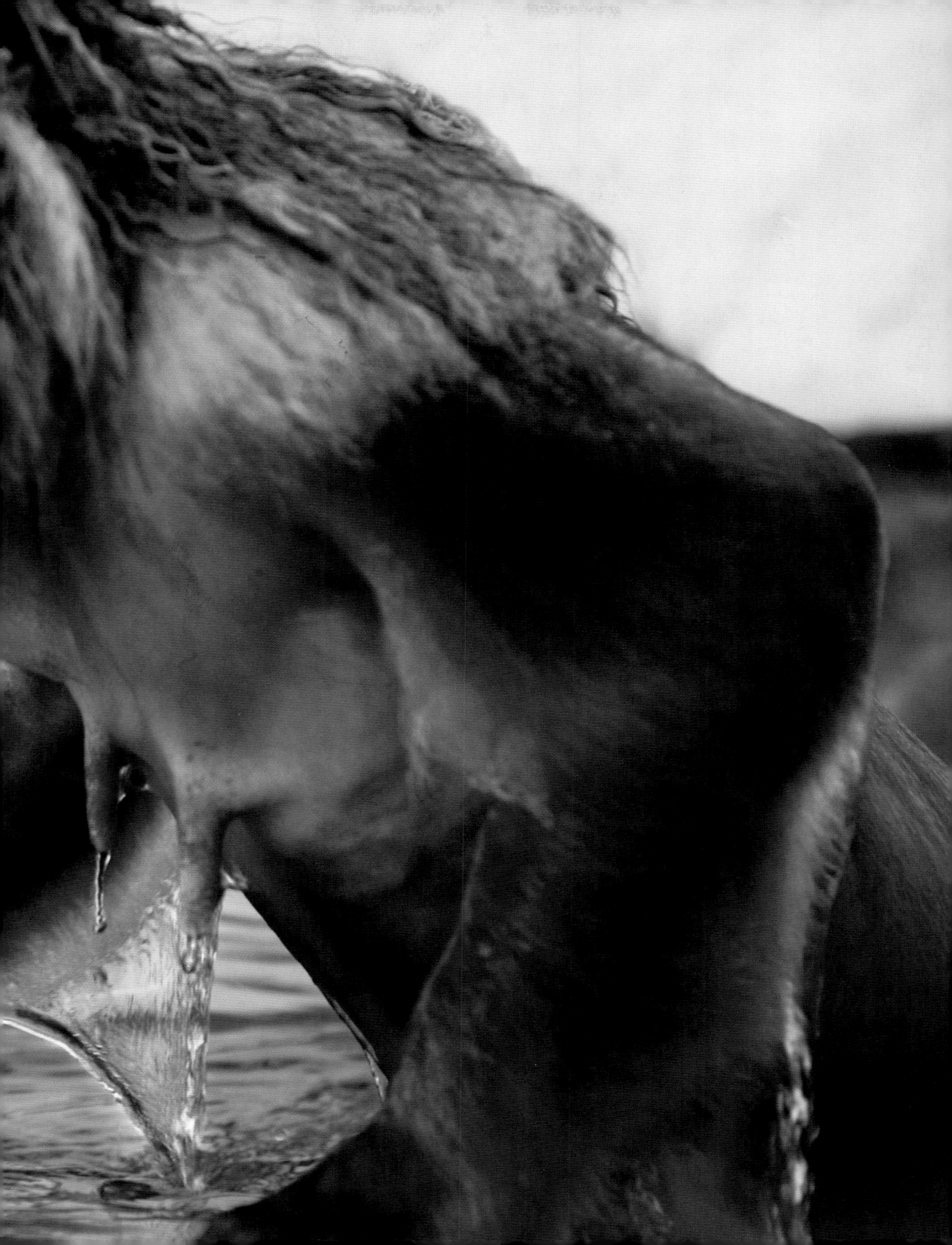

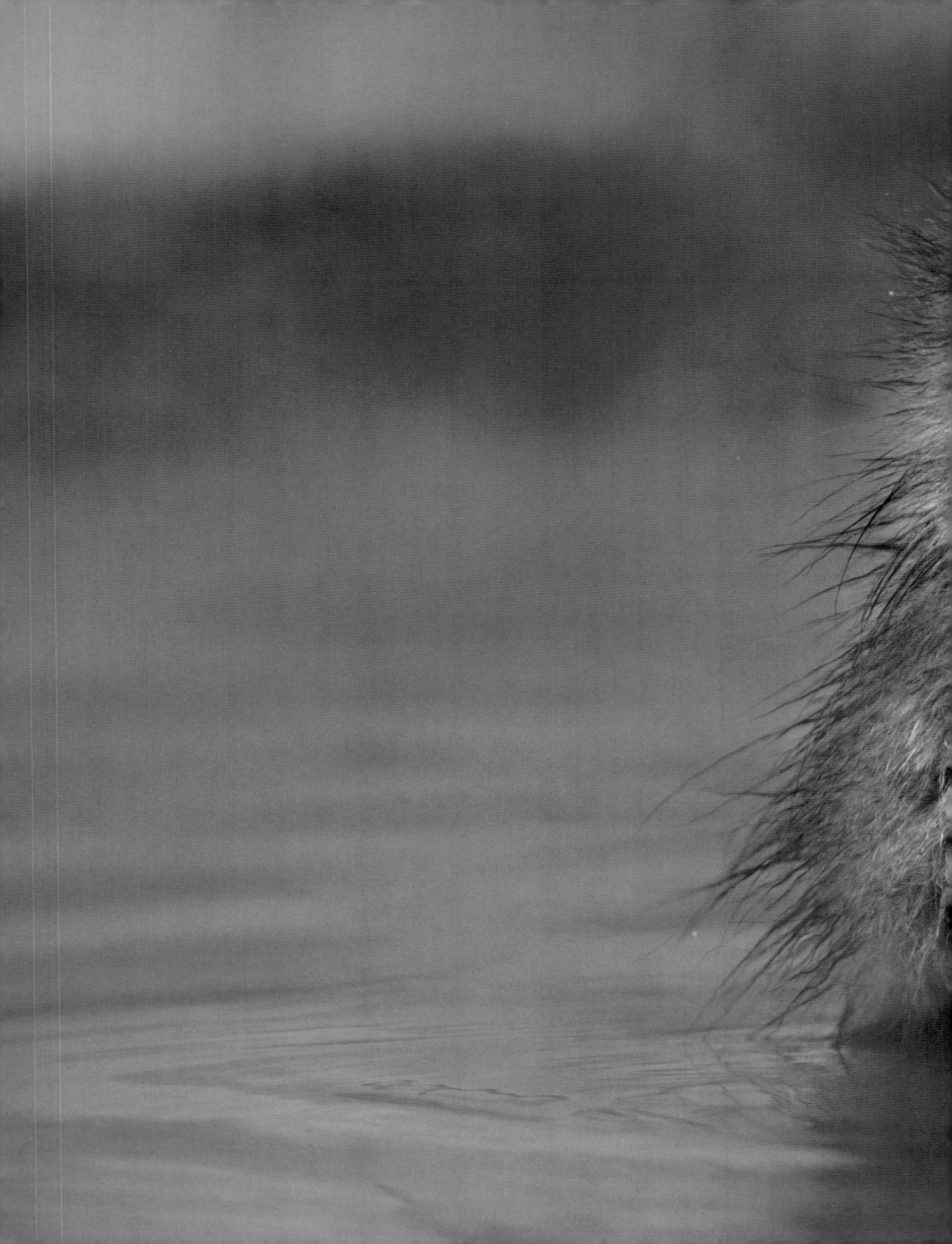

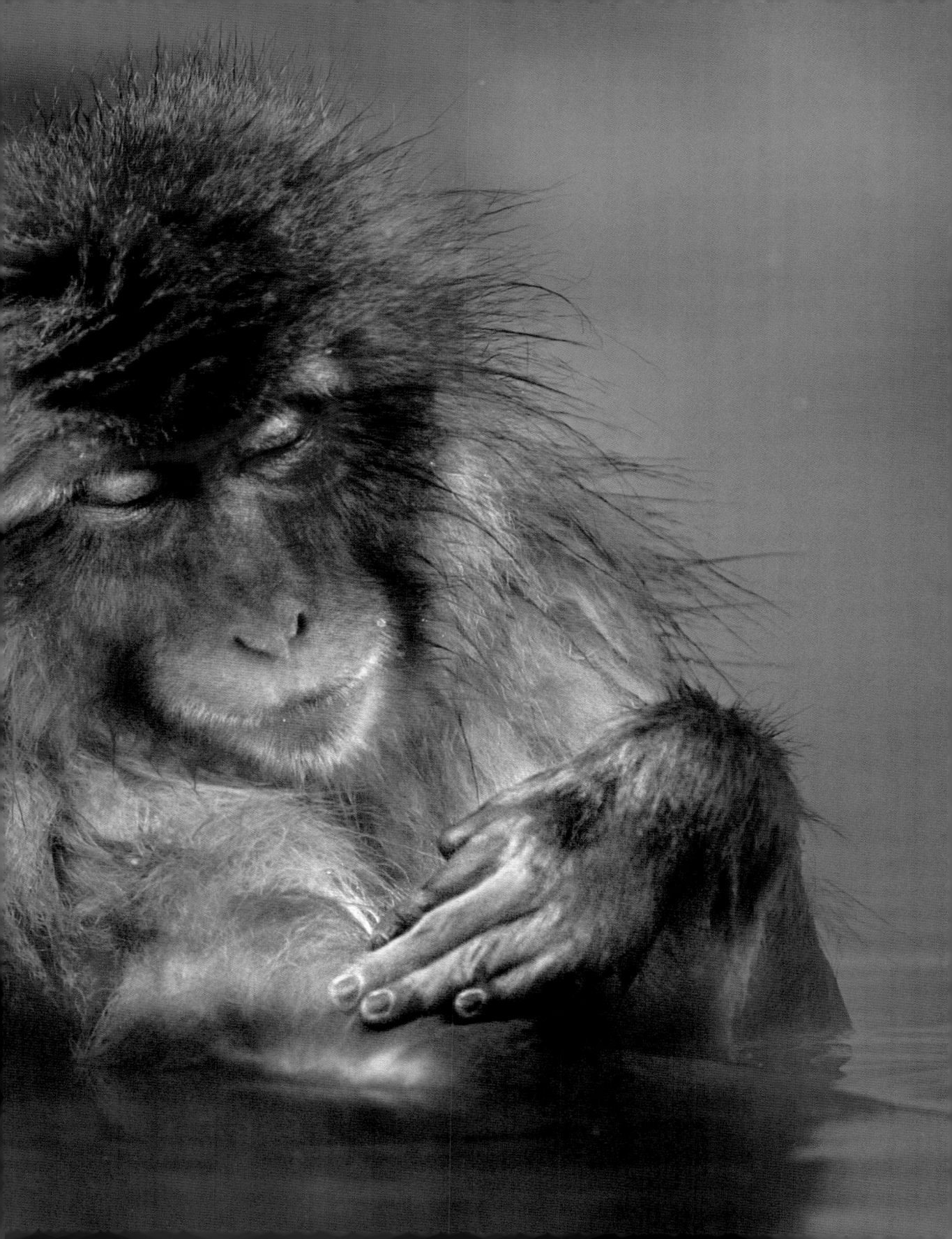

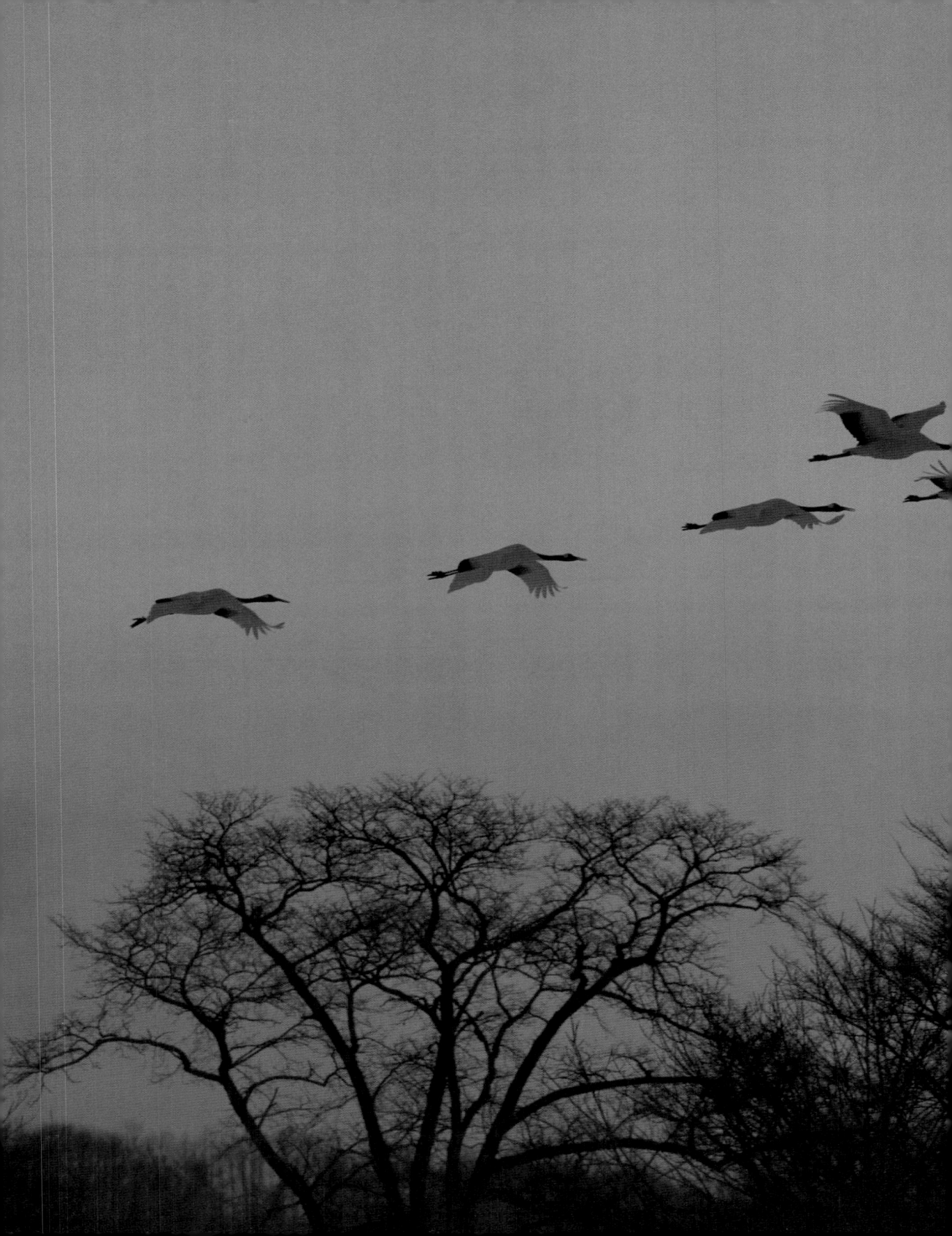

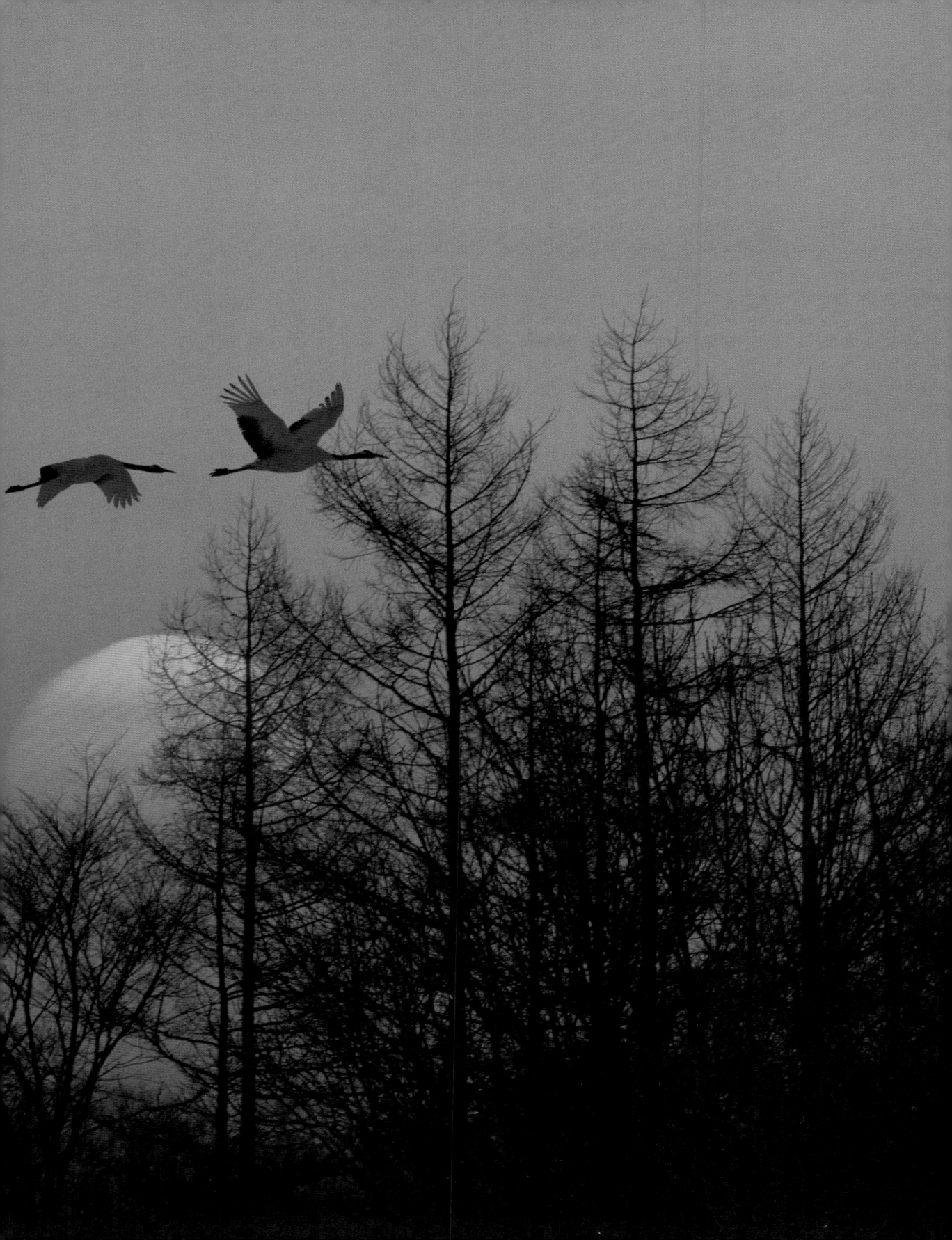

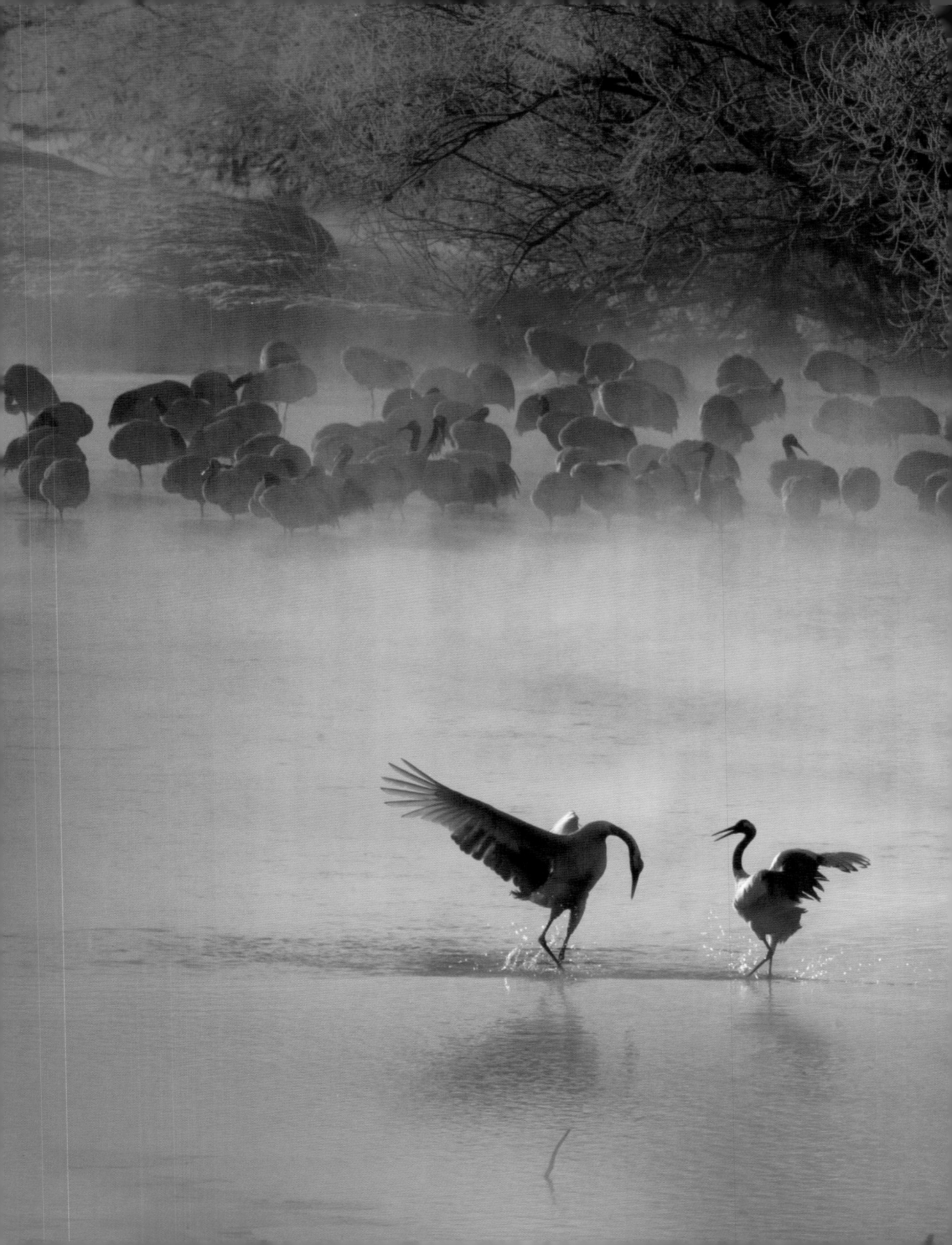

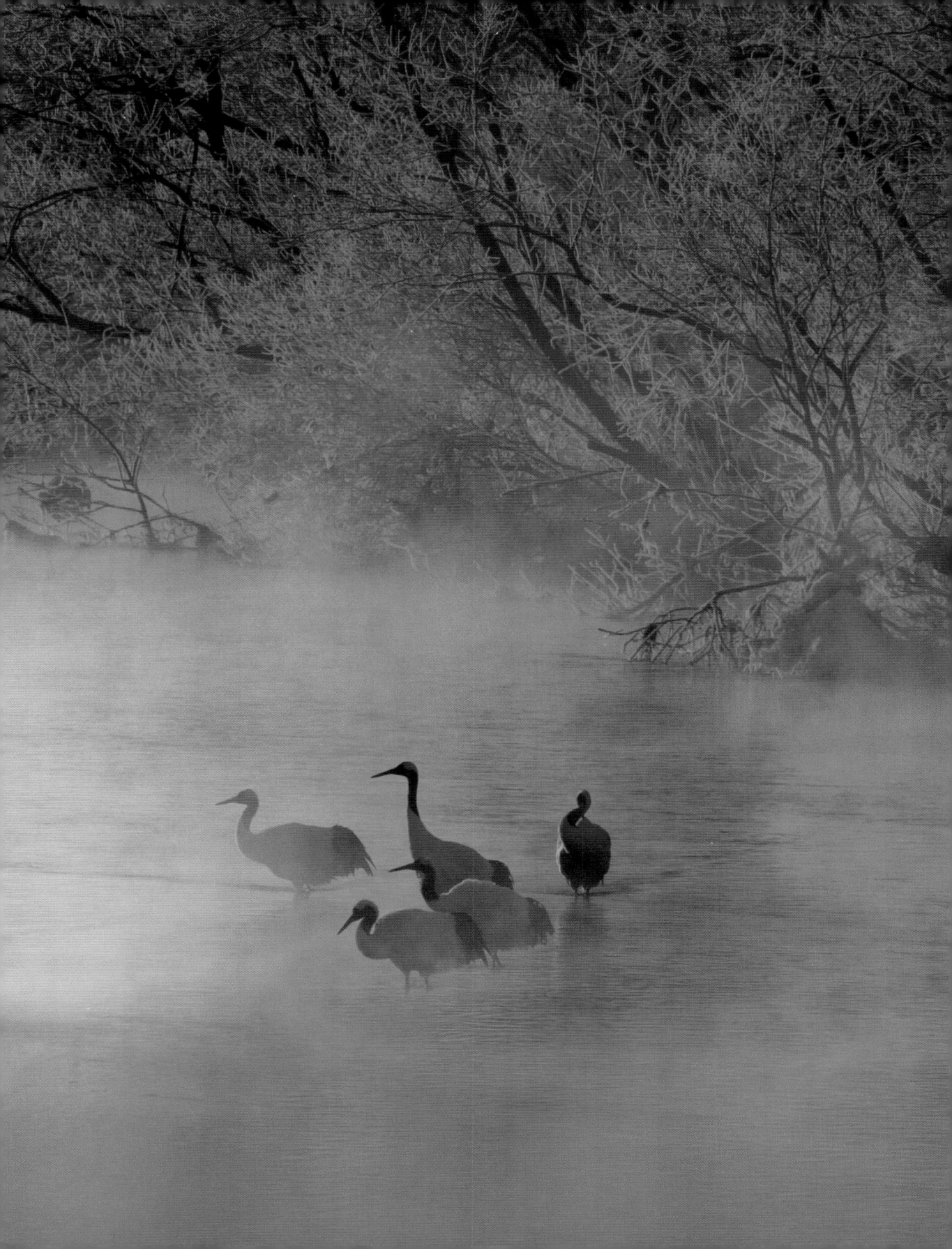

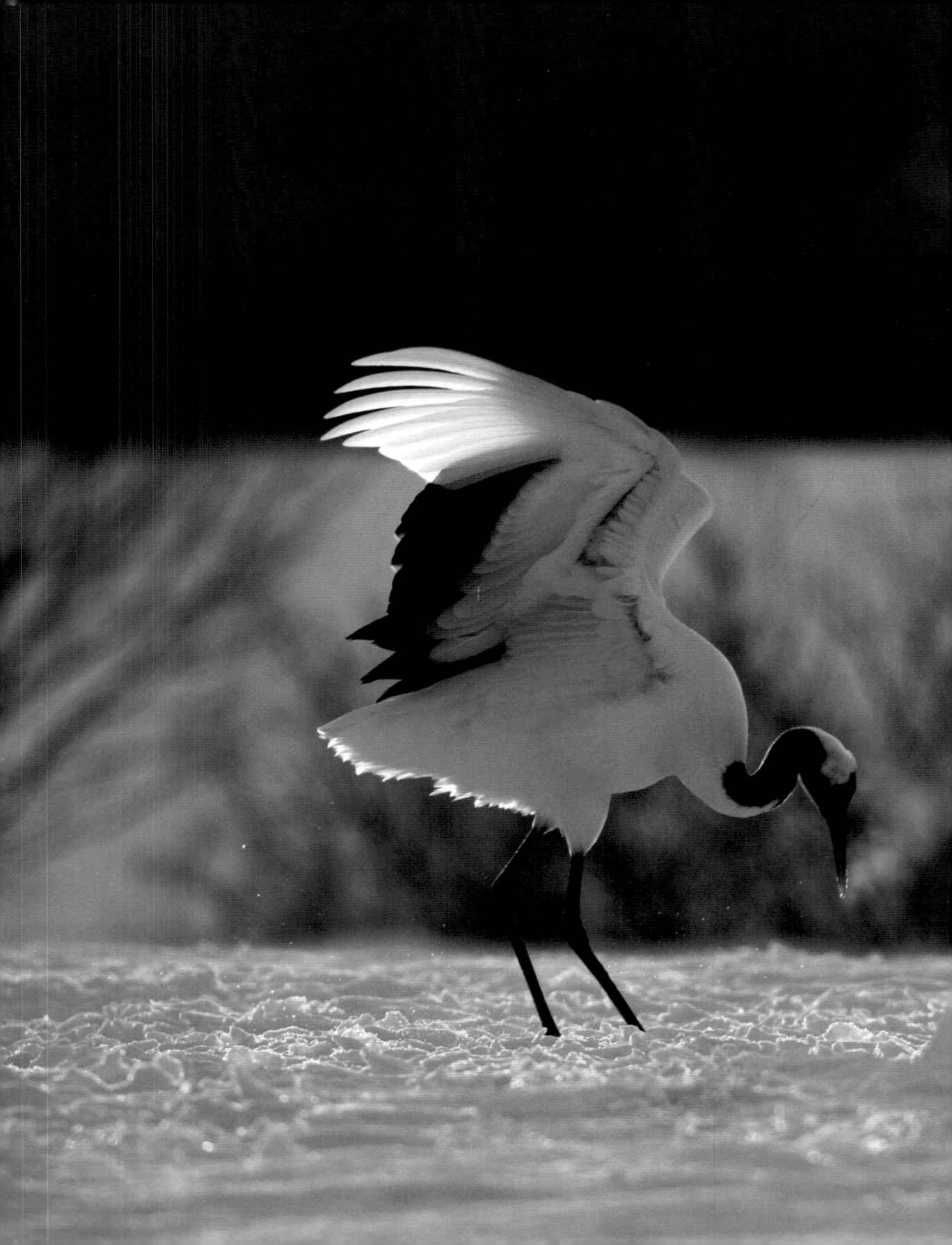

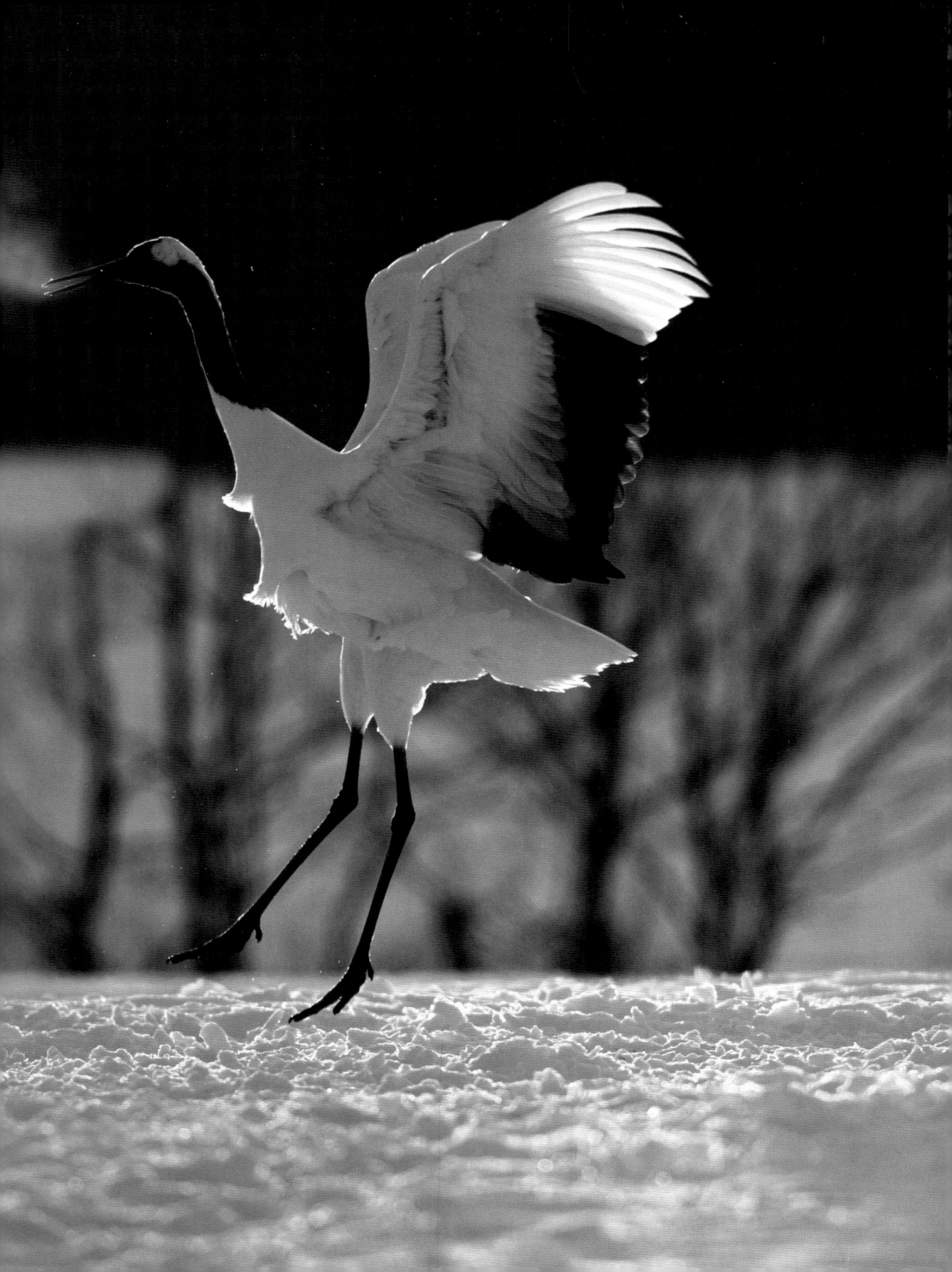

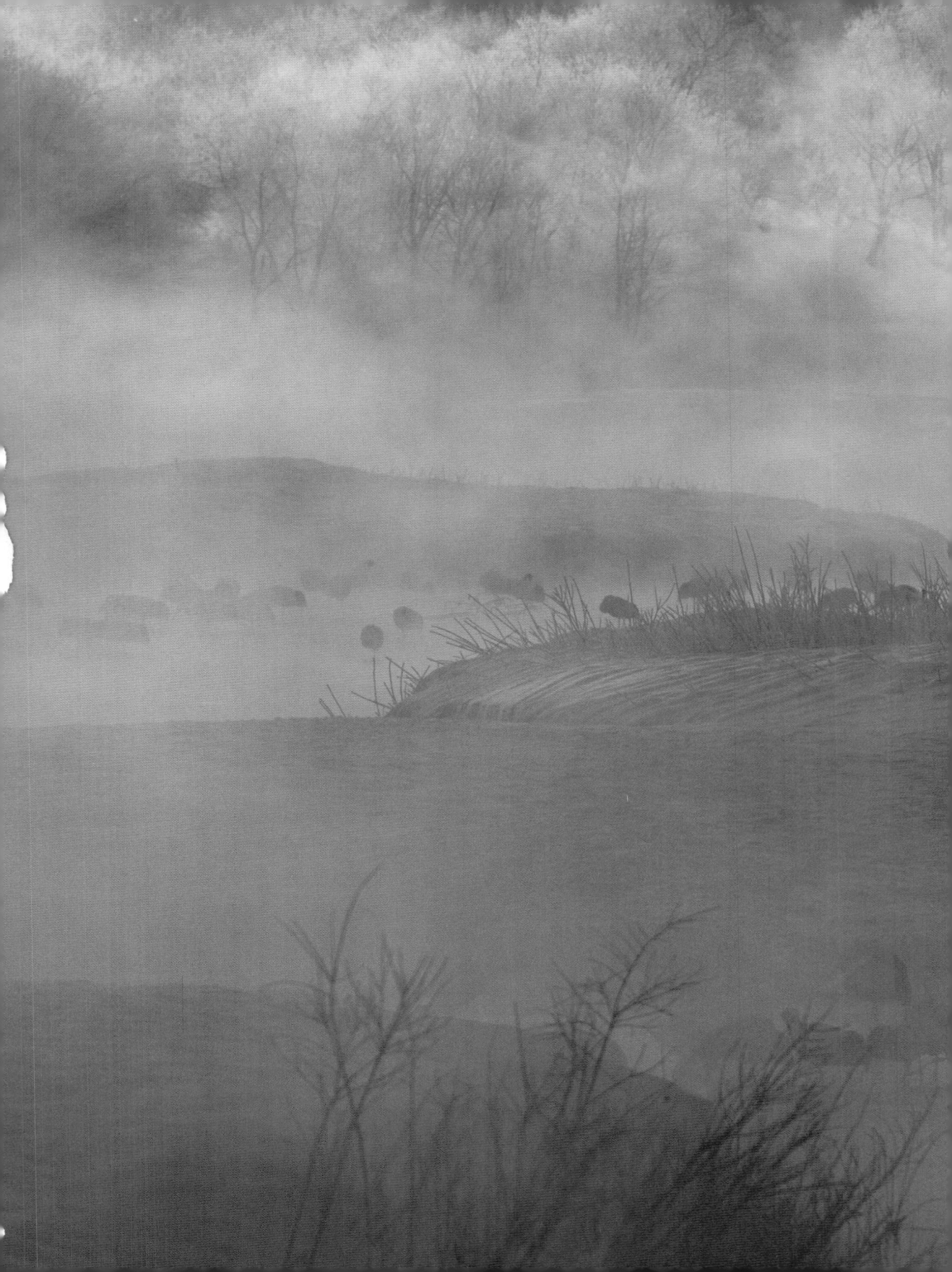

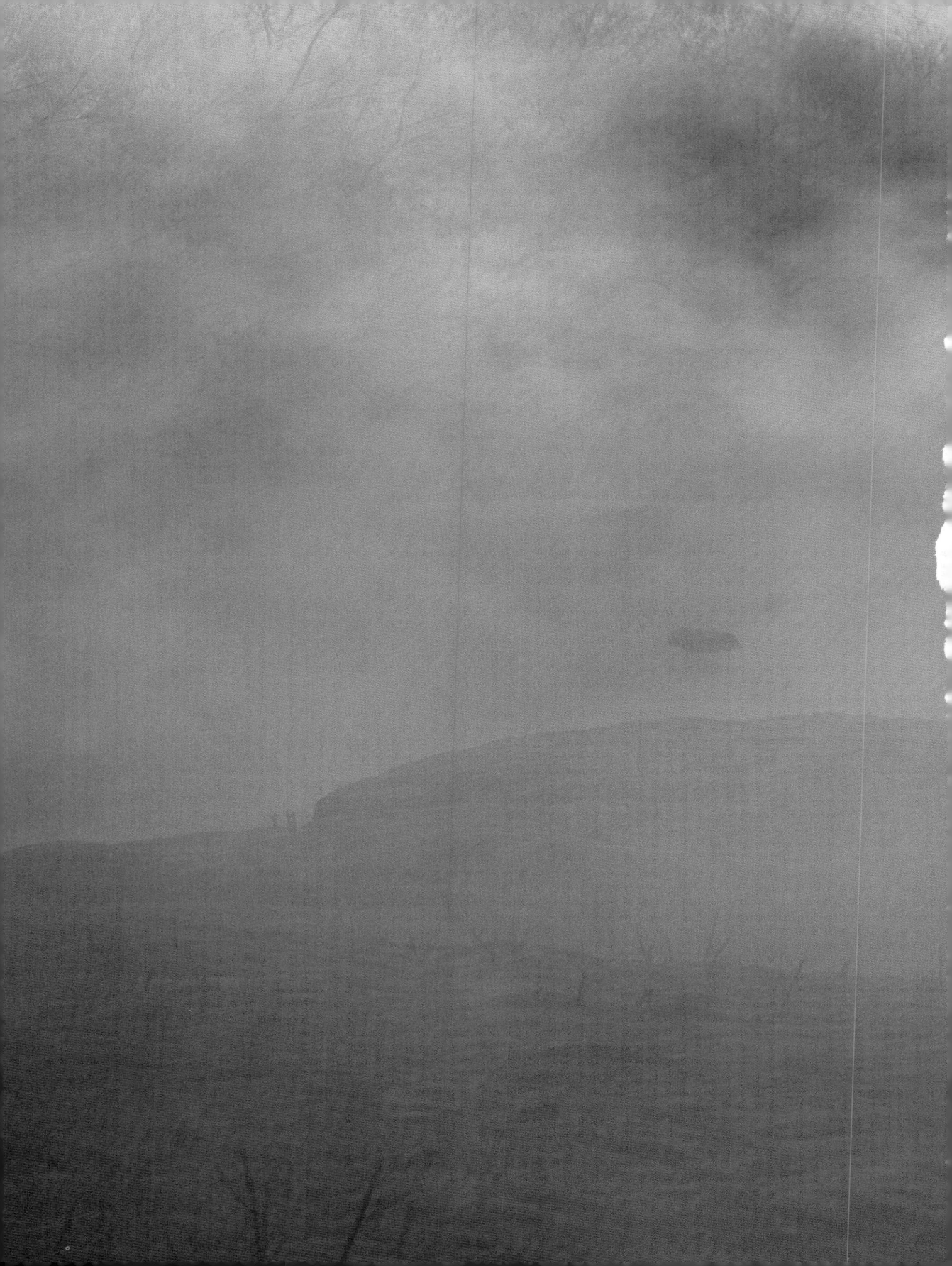

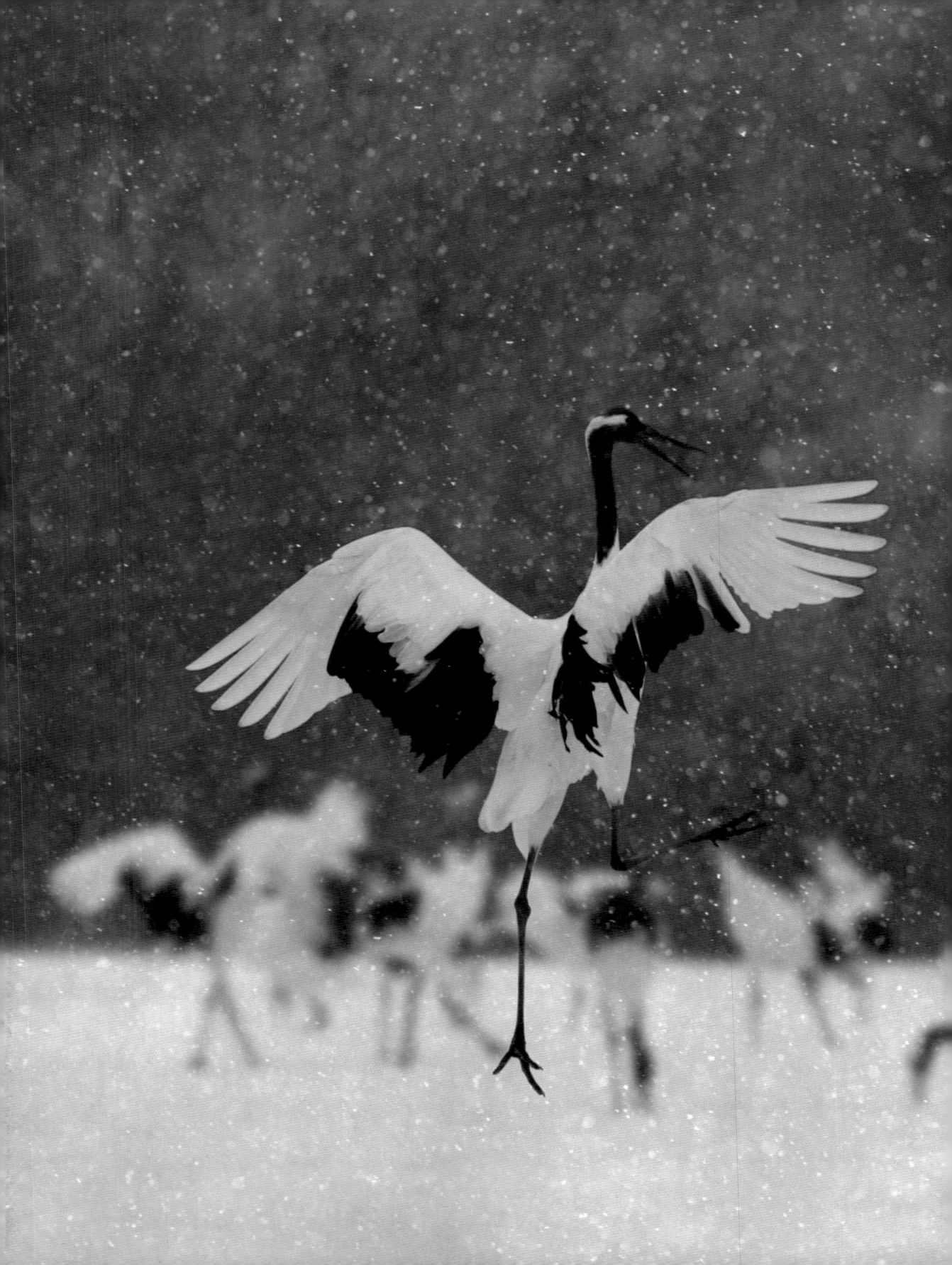

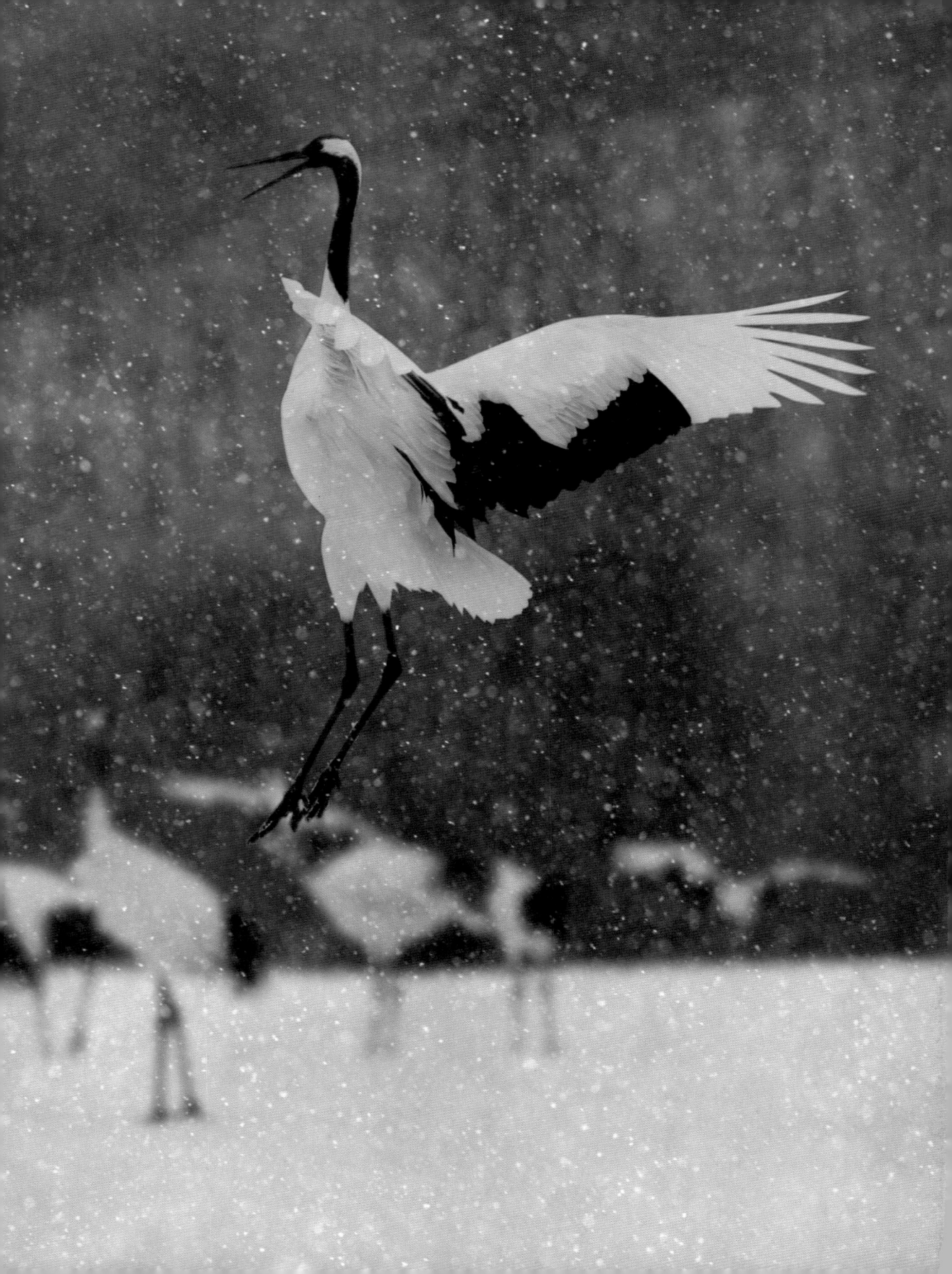

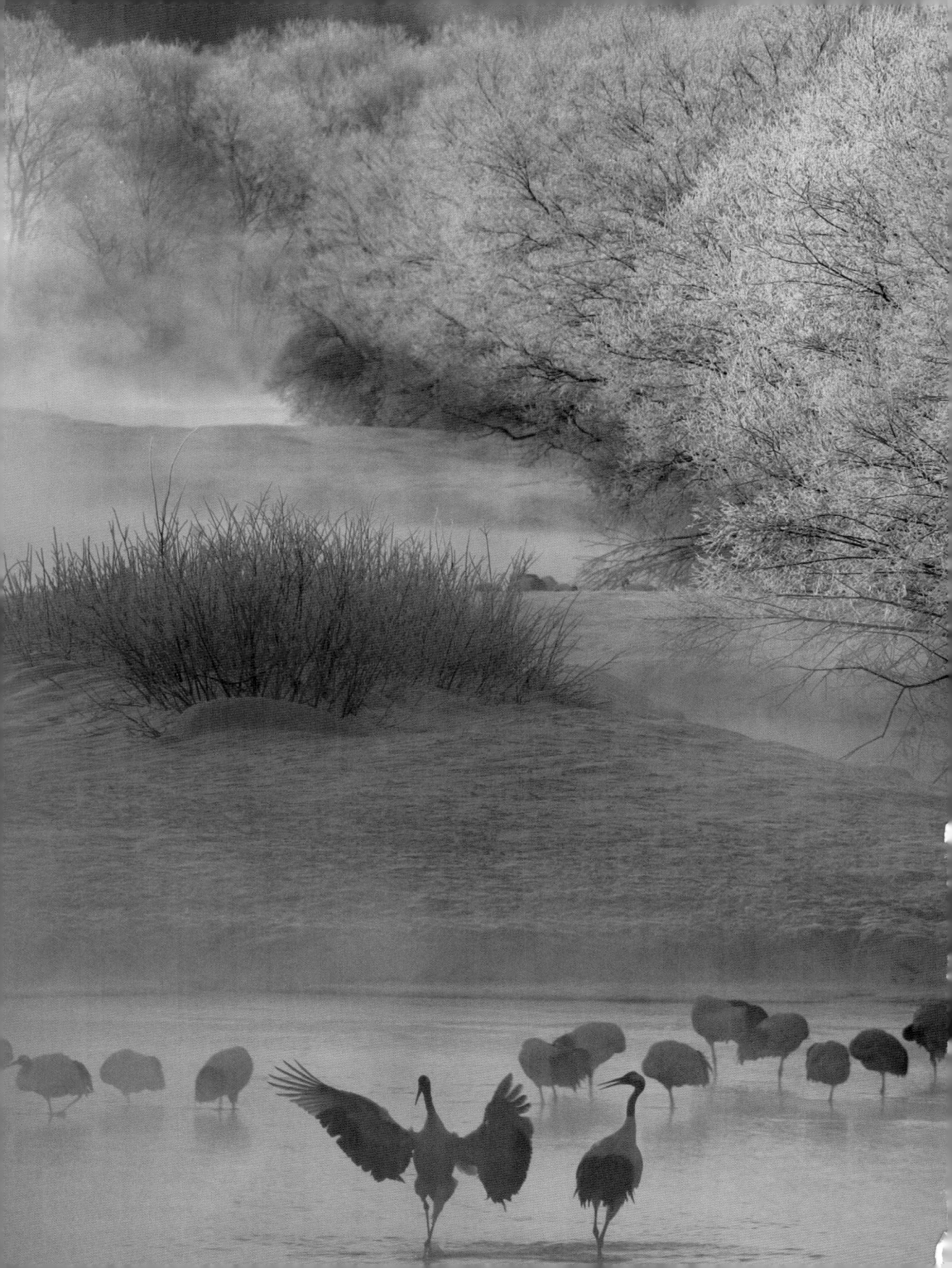

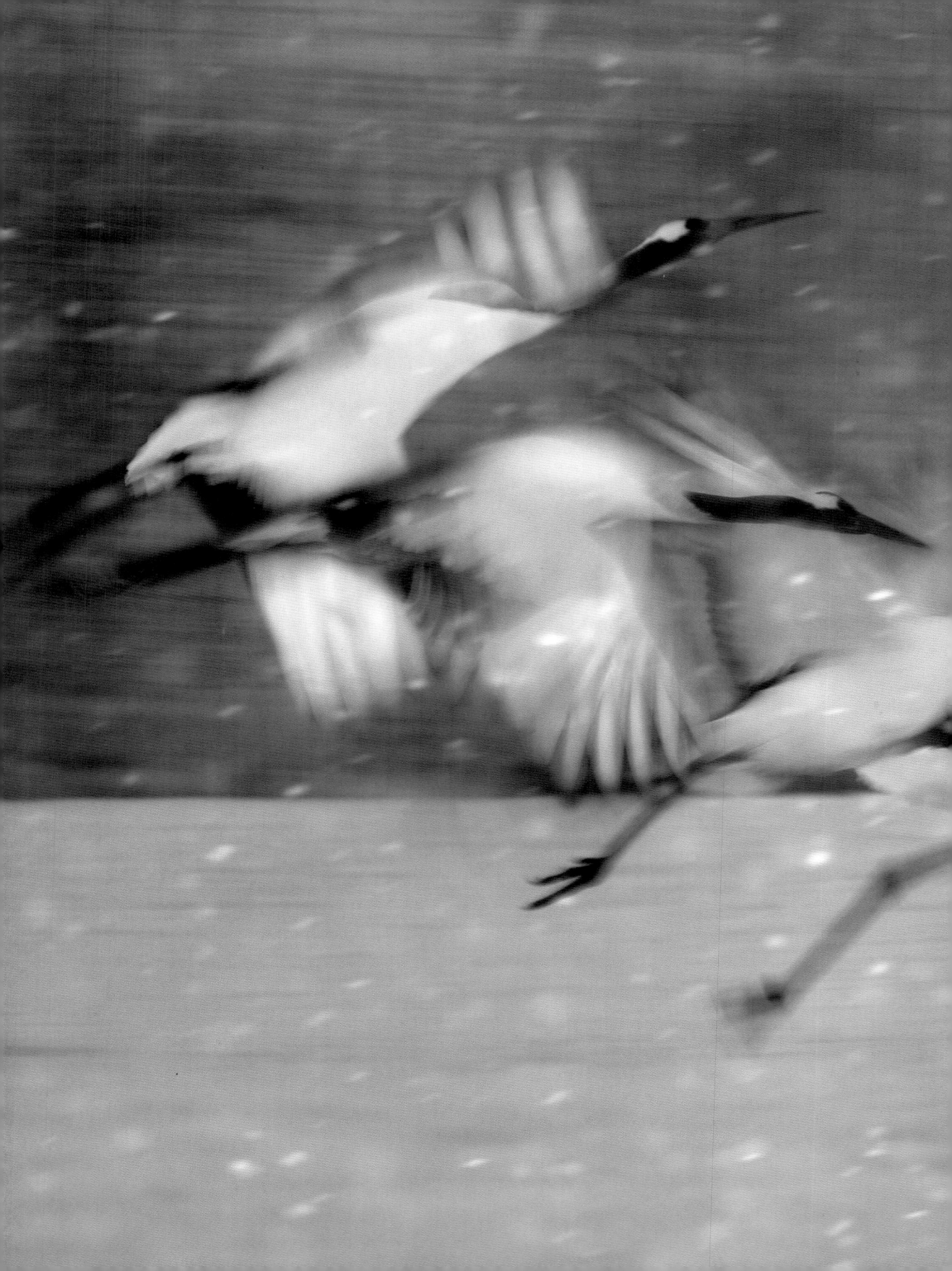

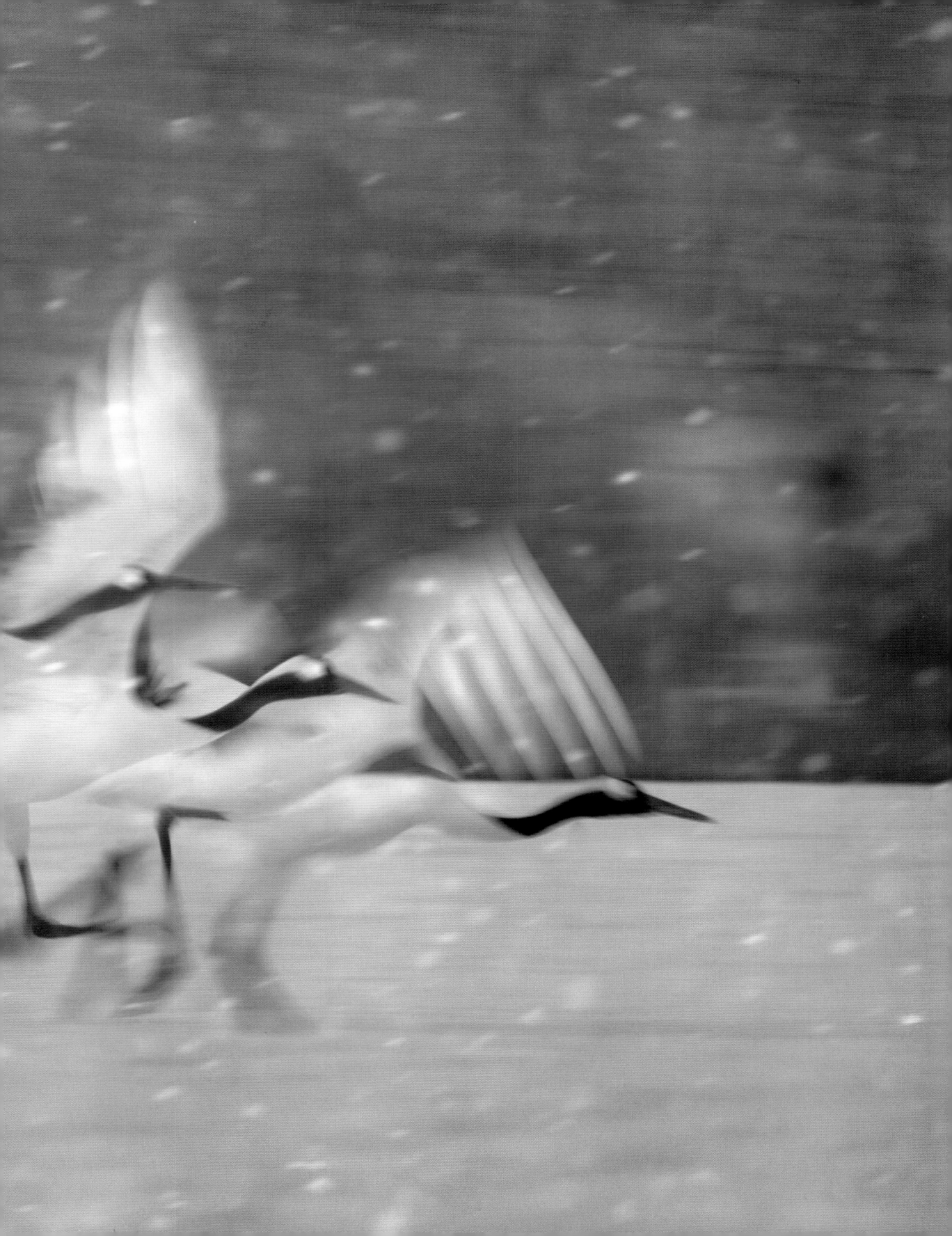

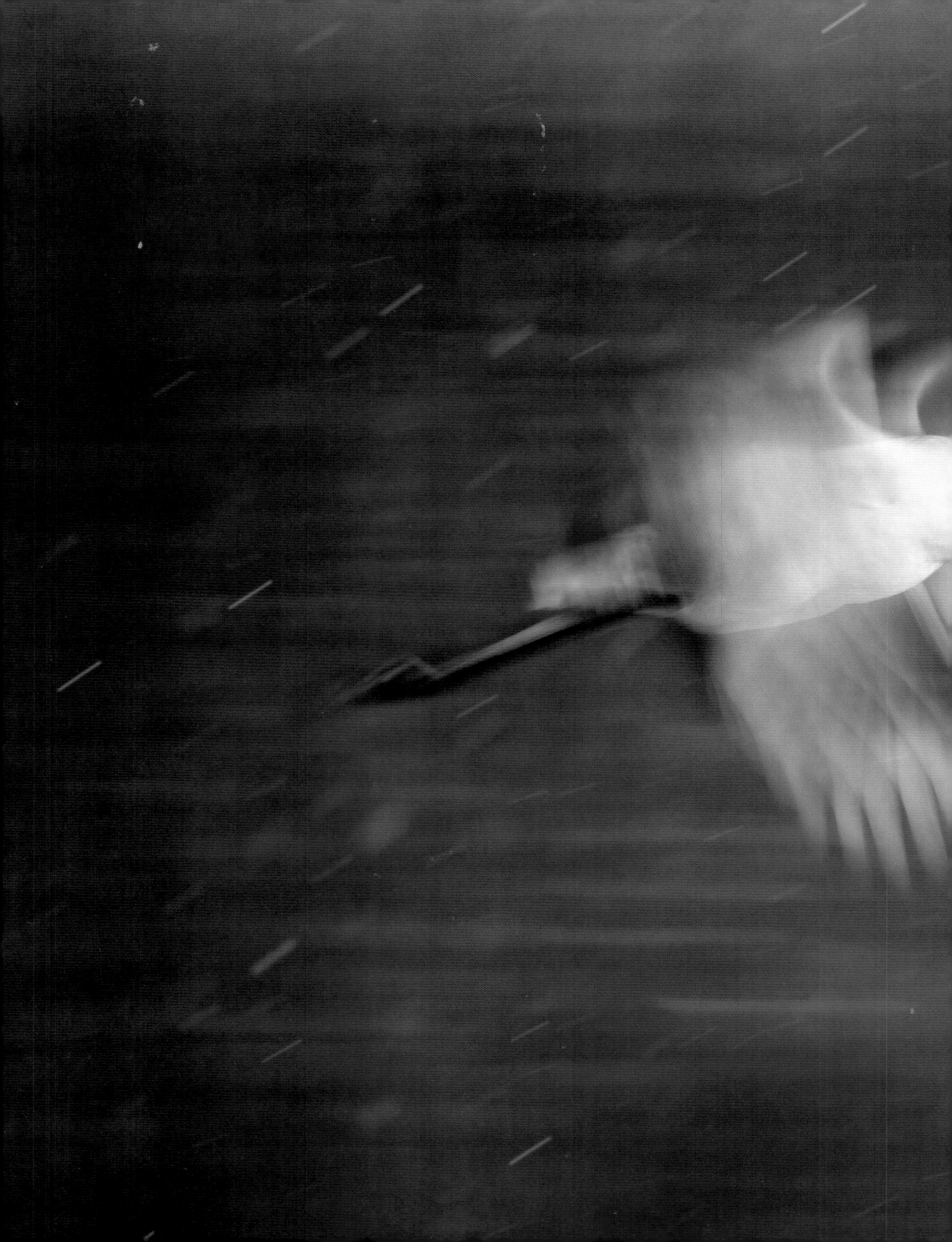

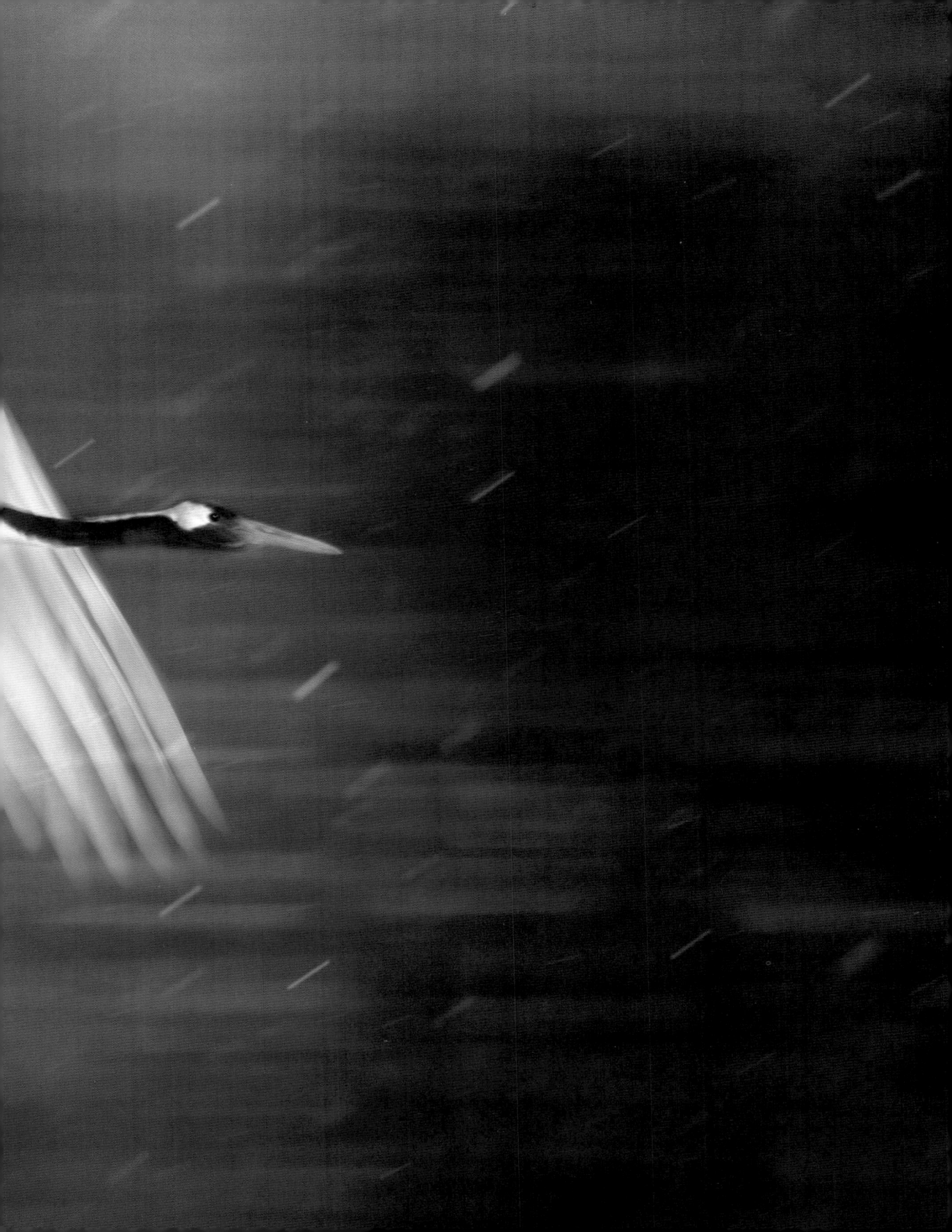

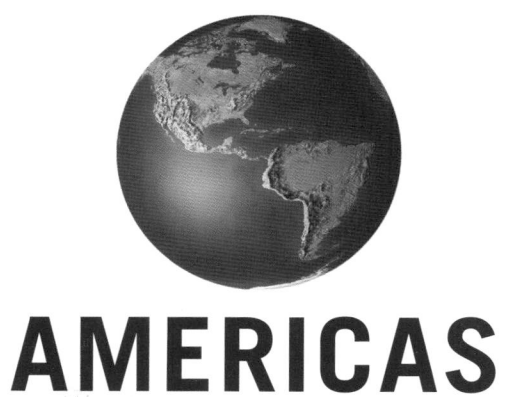

AMERICAS

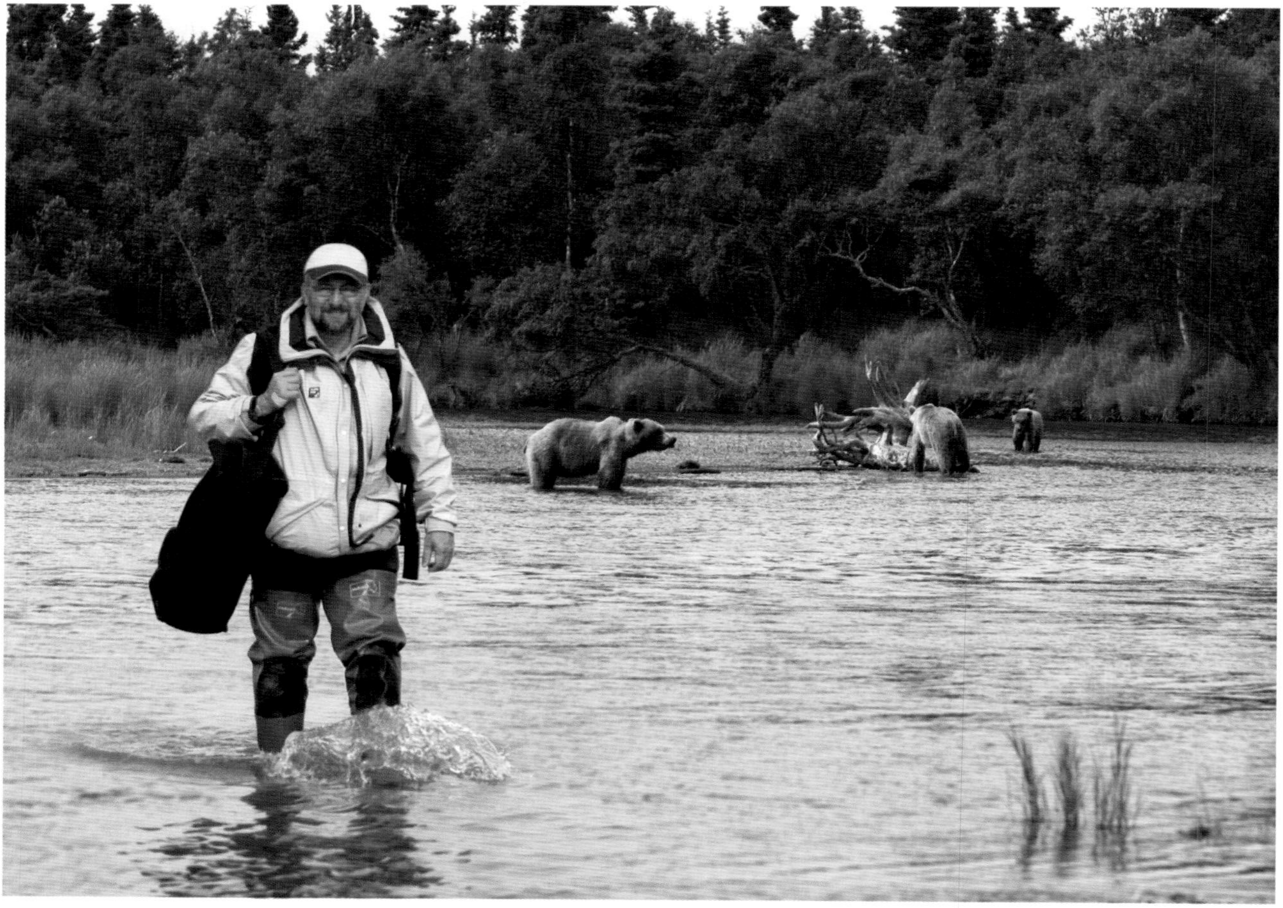

"THE HAUNTING, HOLLOW SOUND
OF HUMPBACK WHALES
TOUCHES THE BASE OF MY SPINE
AND SOOTHES MY SOUL."

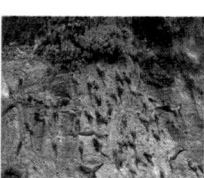

Deep in the Amazon jungle, wild macaws and parrots congregate at clay walls that rise up from the rivers. They eat the clay, which neutralizes the strong acids found in their fruit diets. The clay lick is also a great place for socializing. For two days I traveled along Peru's Tambapatha River with my son, Daniel. We camped near the riverbank, rose at five each morning, and were treated to a delightful spectacle as the morning light was briefly filled with hundreds of colorful birds.

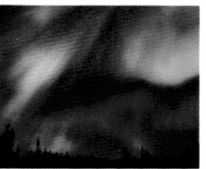

In the starlit arctic sky, a faint and delicate touch of pale green emerges. As if to defy the monochrome of night, it hangs for a while, a luminous streak. Other colors appear, expanding, surging, and finally erupting in a crescendo of crimson and scarlet and green. A ballet of quivering veils fills the sky, each unfolding to reveal its own unique dance. Slowly the light dissipates, fading away to let the darkness creep back in and the stars punch their way into the night.

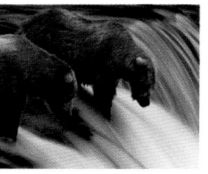

Grizzly bears are solitary by nature, so during the salmon run they jostle for position at waterfalls and in rivers to fish. An uneasy truce sets in as each bear finds his position on the watery conveyer belt and waits patiently for the imminent delivery of the next meal.

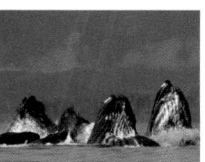

I have been enraptured by the sound of gibbons singing in the forest, by the morning chorus in an English meadow, and by the cacophony of thousands of king penguins all crying out at once. But nothing prepared me for the moment when I first hear humpback whales singing. The initial sound from an underwater mike, electronic and detached, gives way to an air filled with choral harmony when the whales surface and I am at last able to see and hear them directly. The haunting hollow sound touches the base of my spine and soothes my soul.

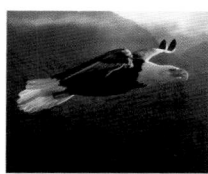

In Alaska, the winter sunrise floods the air with light and color. I see the early beams shine through the translucent beaks of bald eagles until they glow in the sun's spotlight. The morning light soon gives way to rain and snow, leaving a lingering afterimage of the illuminated birds as the day descends into the gloom of winter.

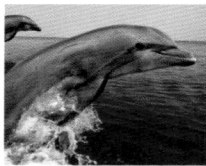

Dolphins evoke feelings of peace and freedom. These graceful mammals always bring pleasure as they swim alongside our ships. They share many of our characteristics, such as curiosity and bravery. Like us, they are pleasure seekers. Often trapped in fishing nets, they have suffered cruelly at the hands of humans. However, they have been known to act altruistically and guide distressed people to safety.

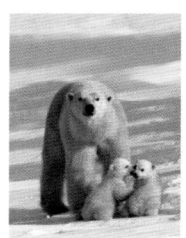

The temperature plummets in the arctic wind, the air painfully claws at the exposed flesh on my face. I blink, and my eyelids freeze shut. We scour the frozen fields in Canada to search for a polar bear emerging from her den with her young cubs. We endure blizzards and whiteouts while our mechanical equipment struggles to function. When we find the bears, relaxed and playful, I am acutely aware of my own fragile nature. Shivering in my high-tech clothing, I watch the infant cubs play in the snow, so well protected by their magnificent coats.

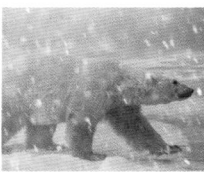

Each winter polar bears gather on the edge of Canada's Hudson Bay to wait for the sea to freeze before going onto the ice to hunt seals. Their presence is transitory. Photography depends on accurate timing, the right weather, and exceptional luck.

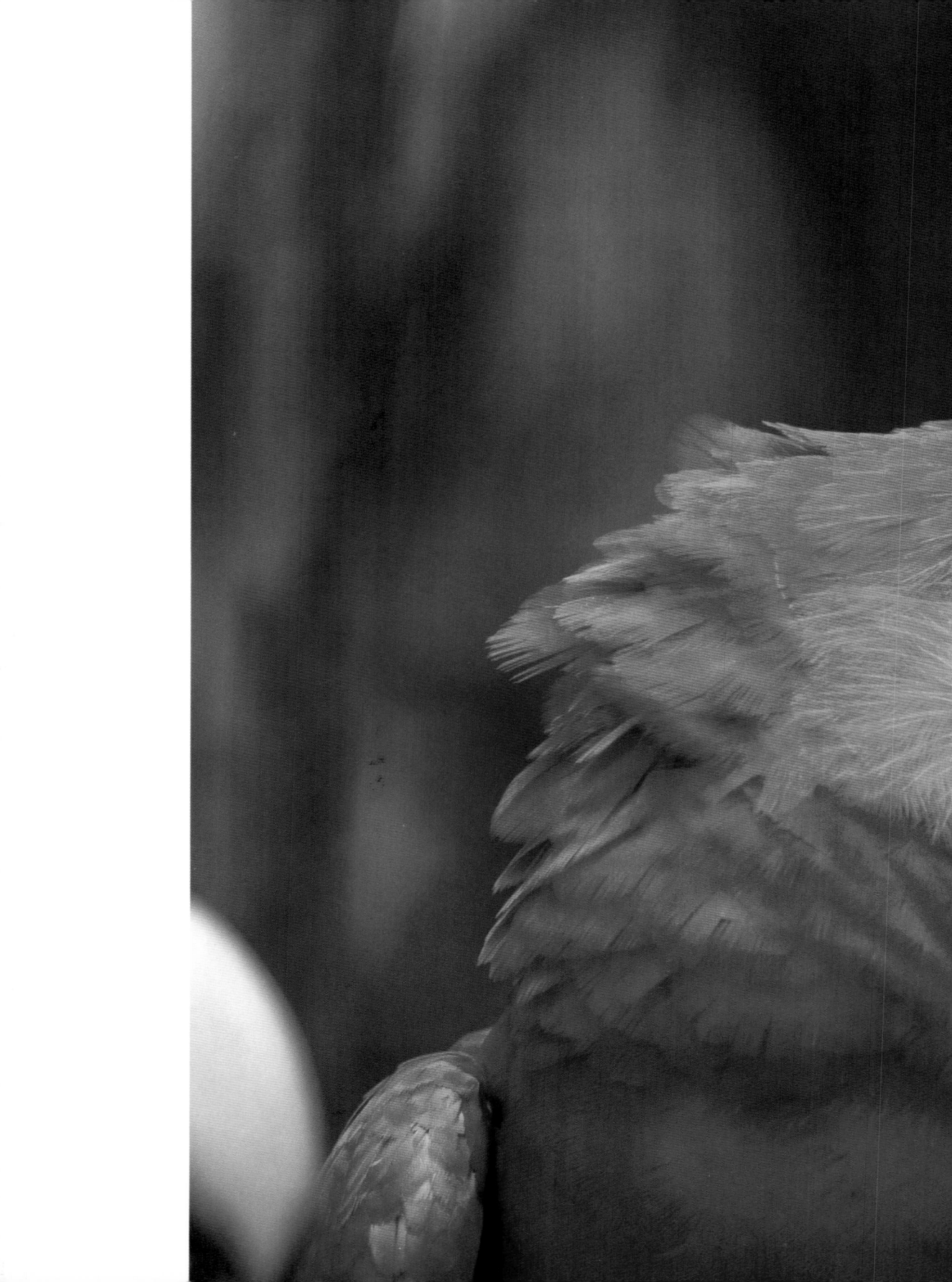

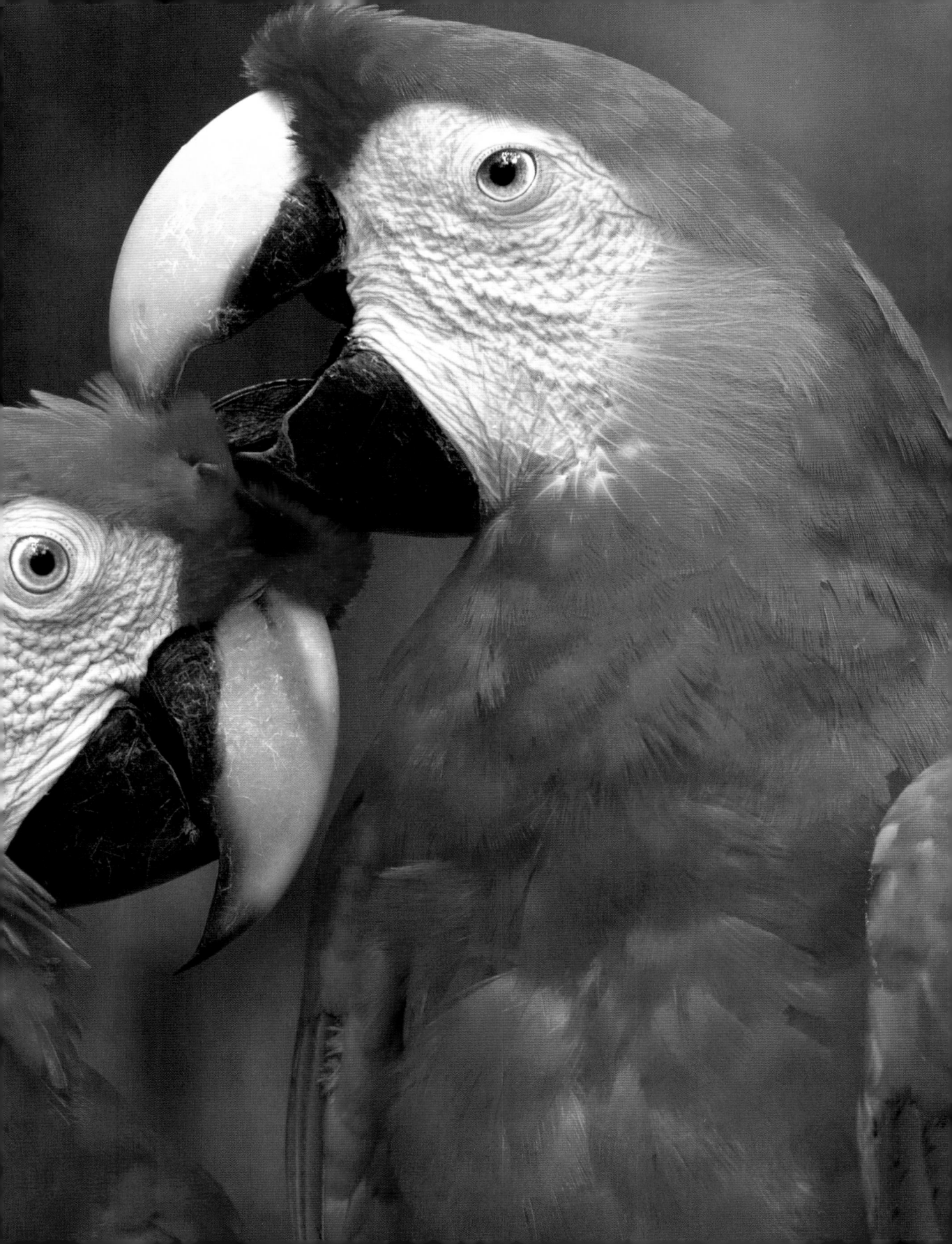

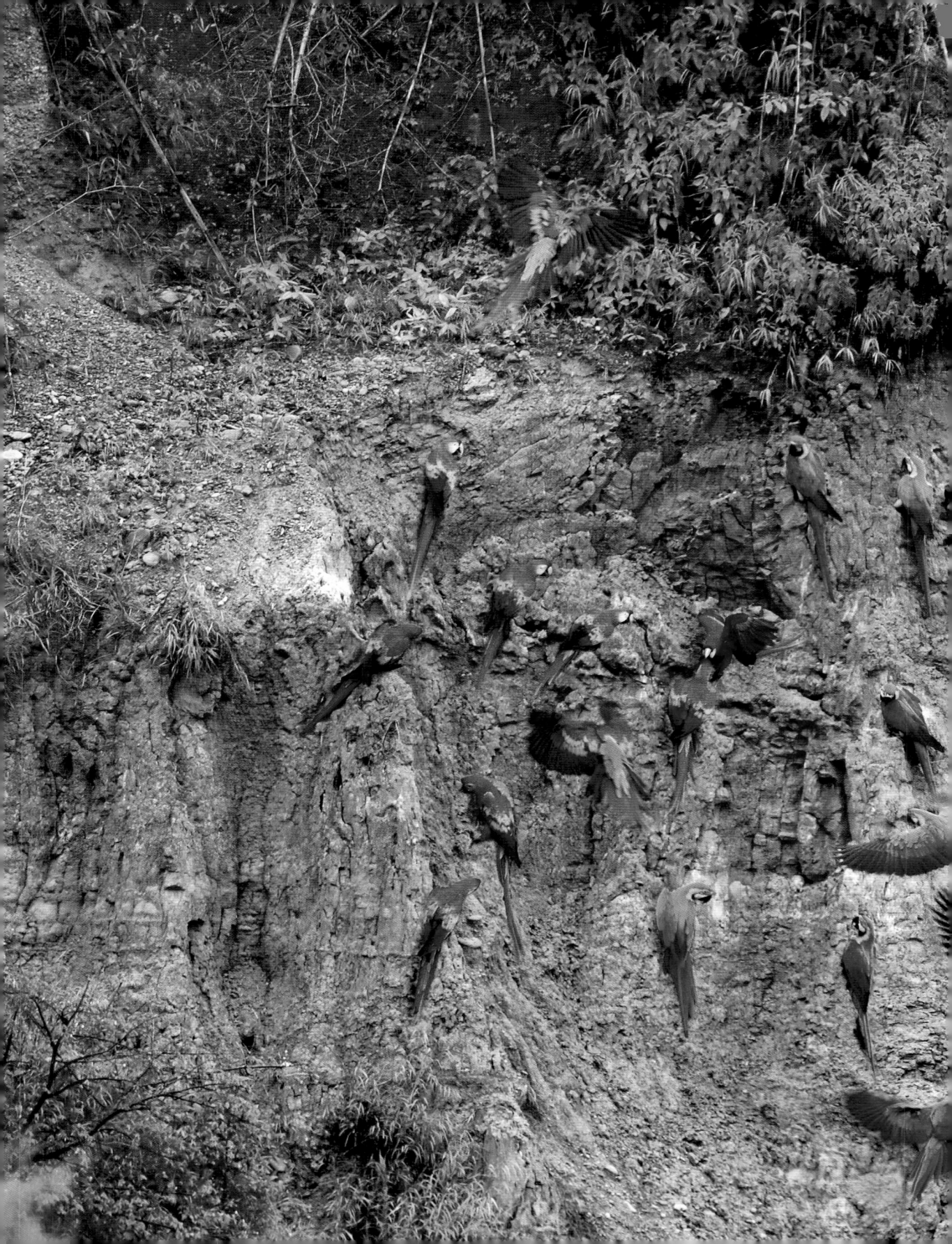

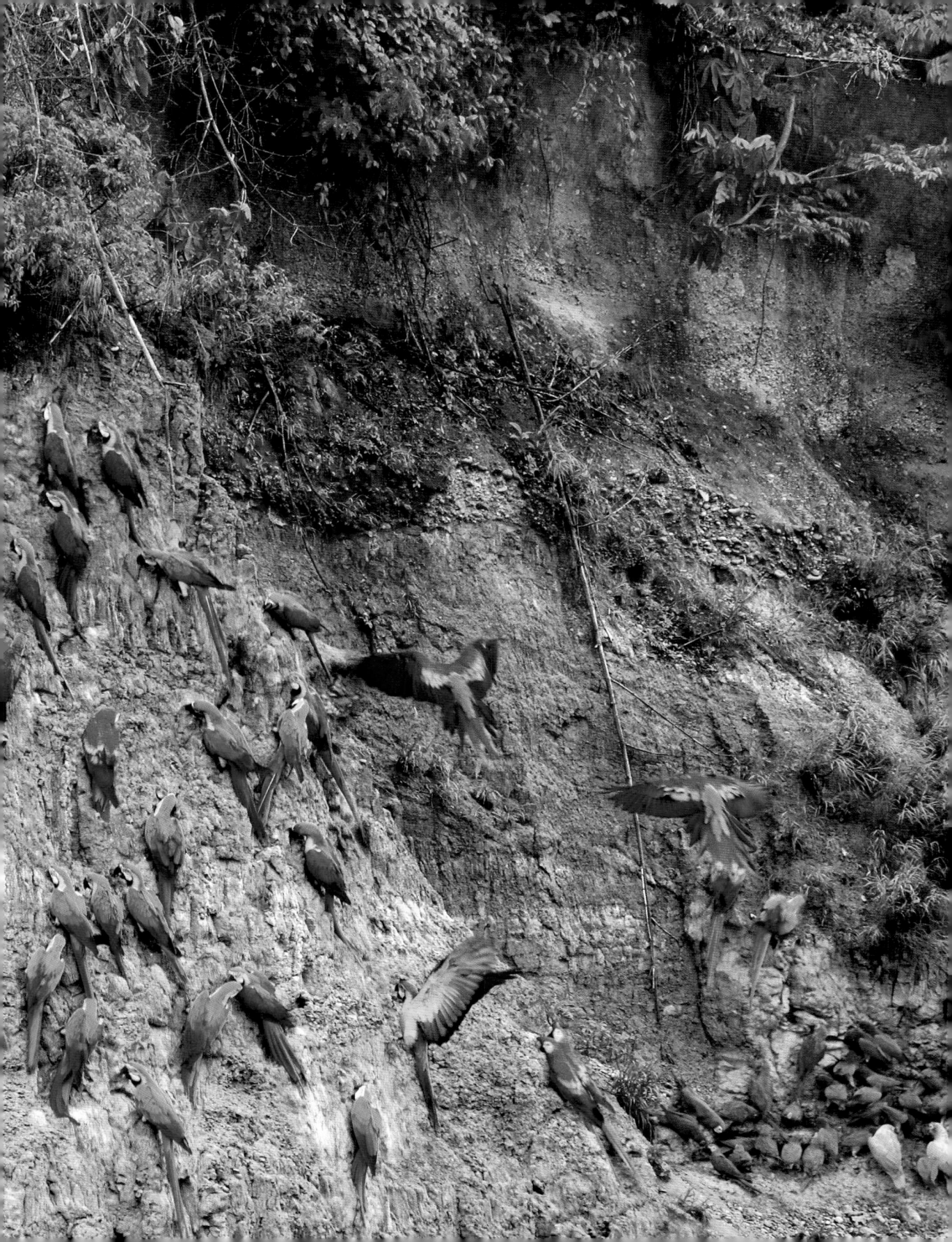

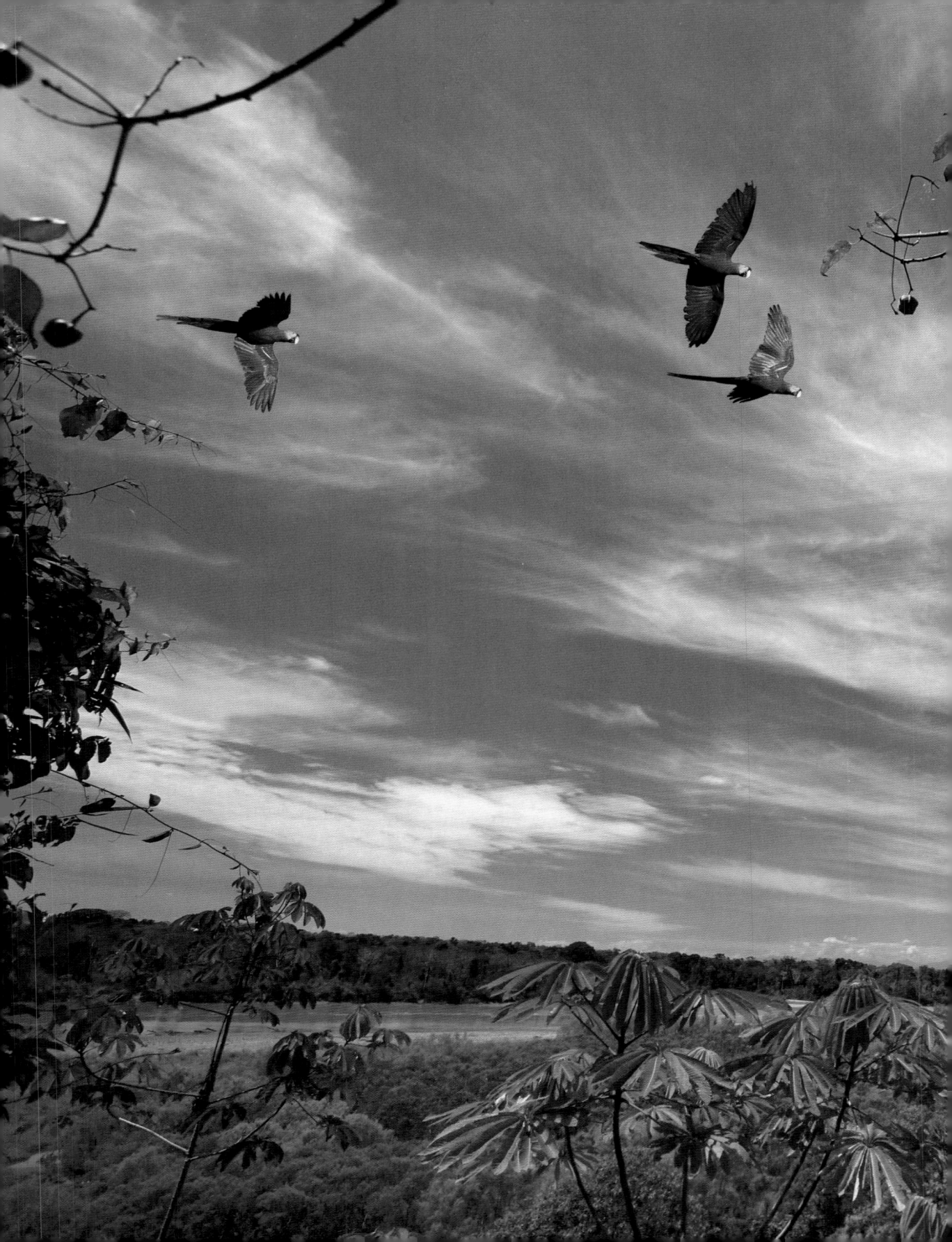

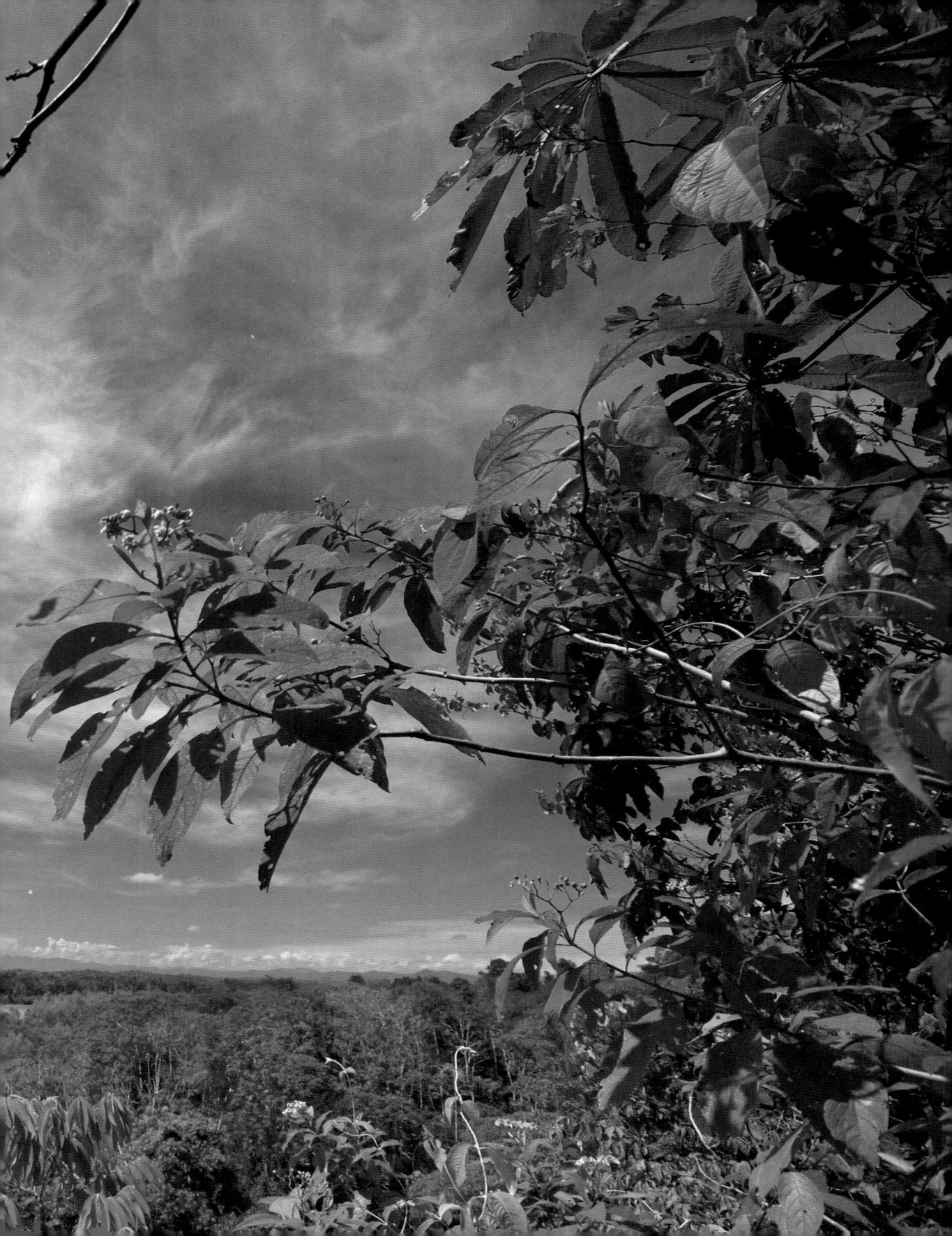

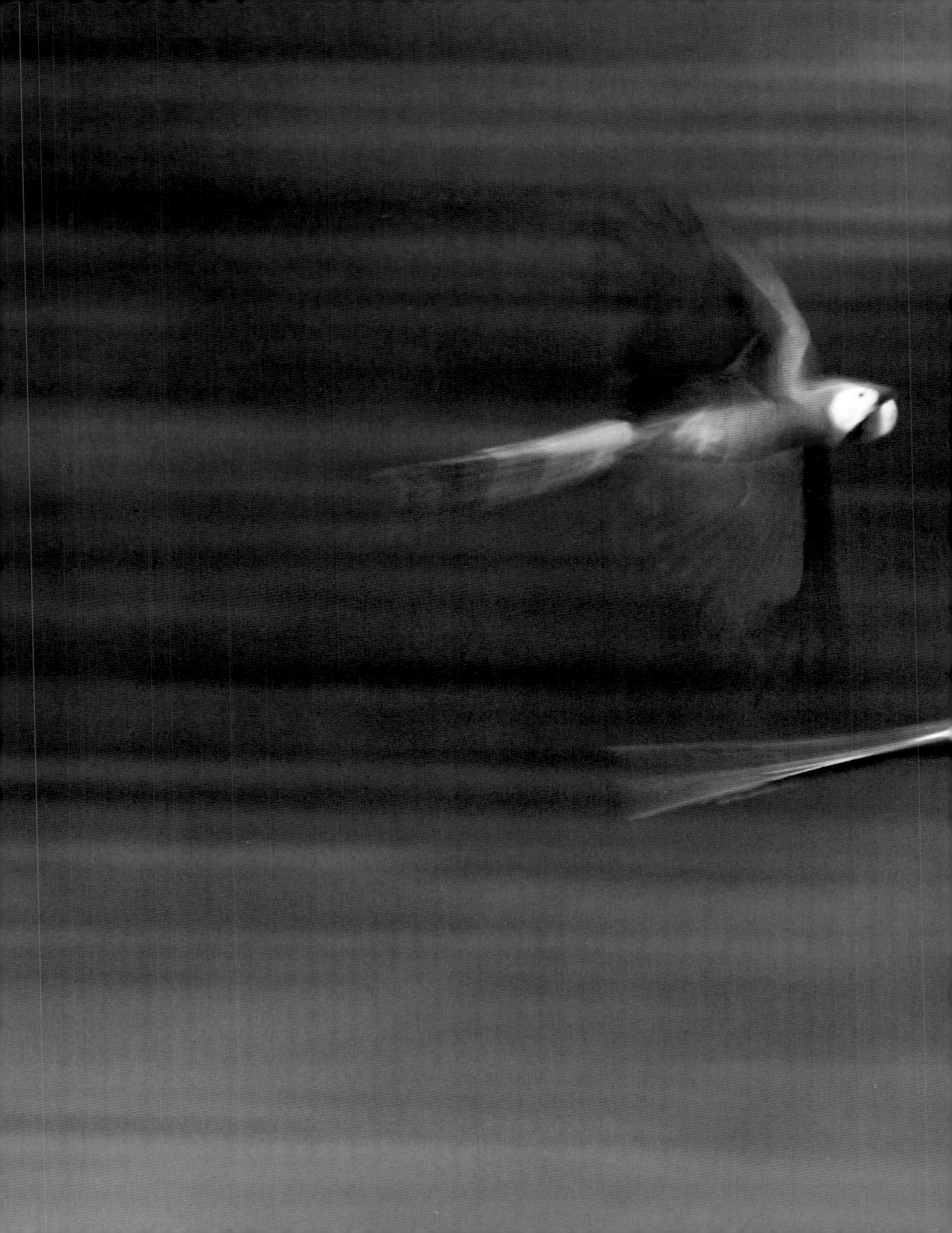

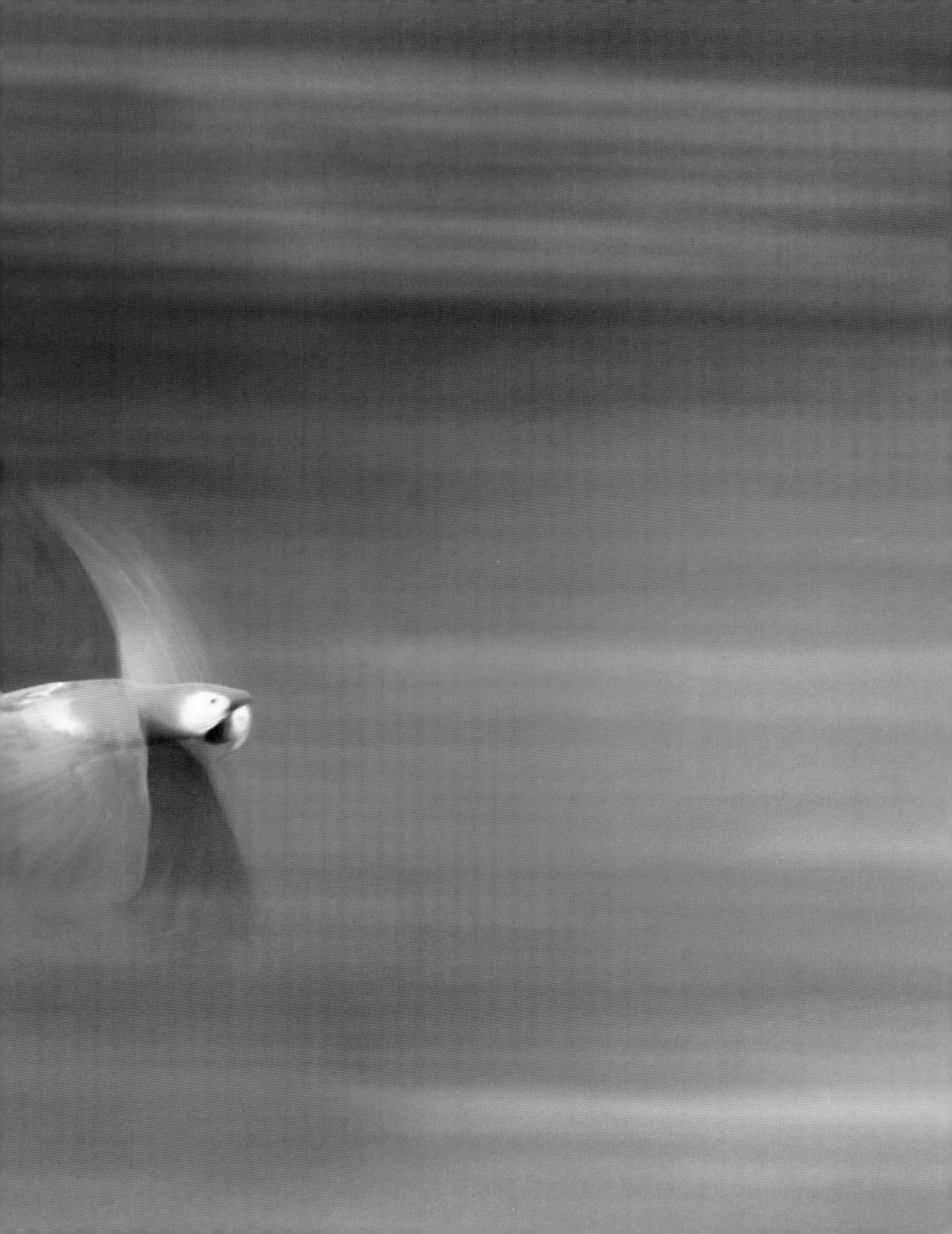

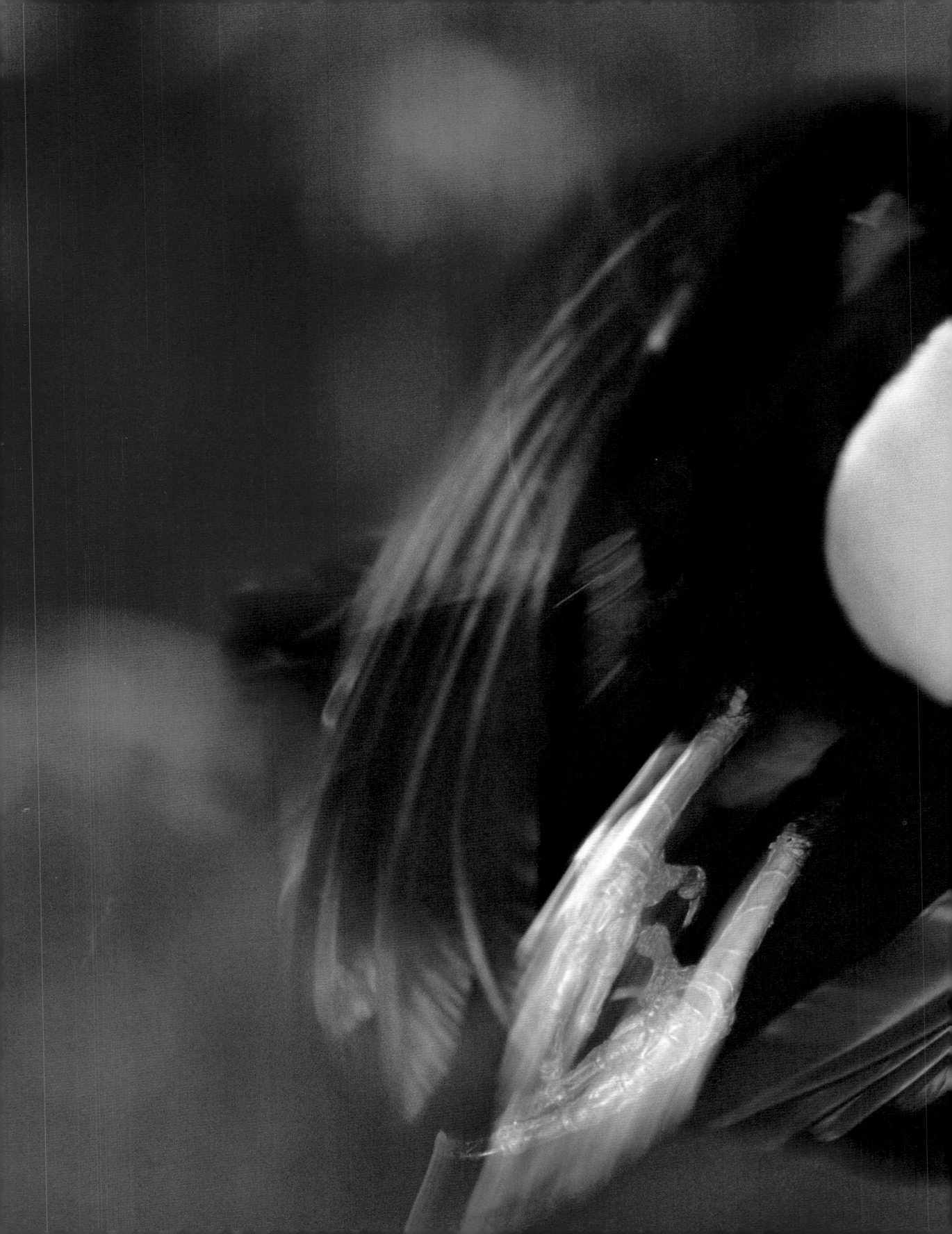

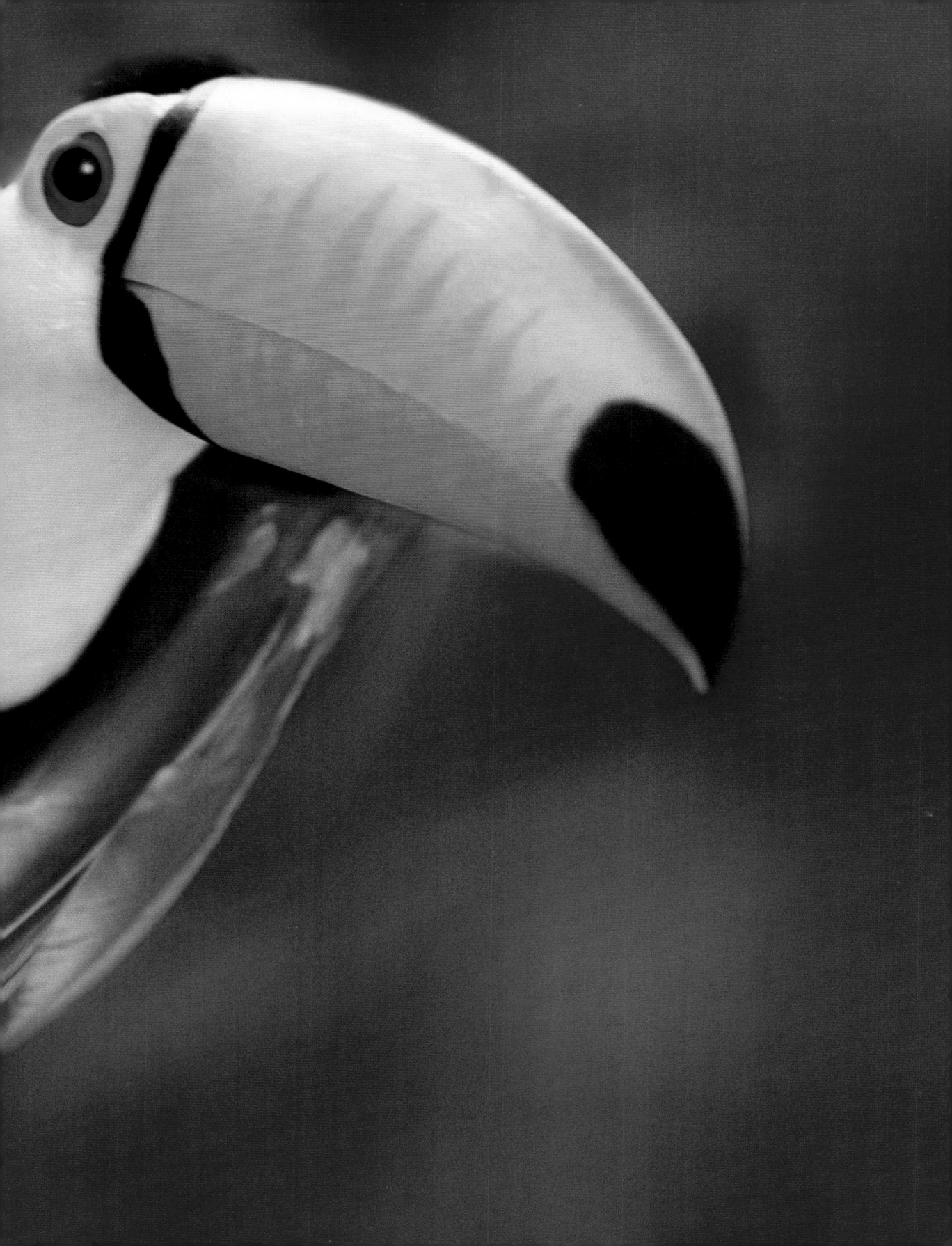

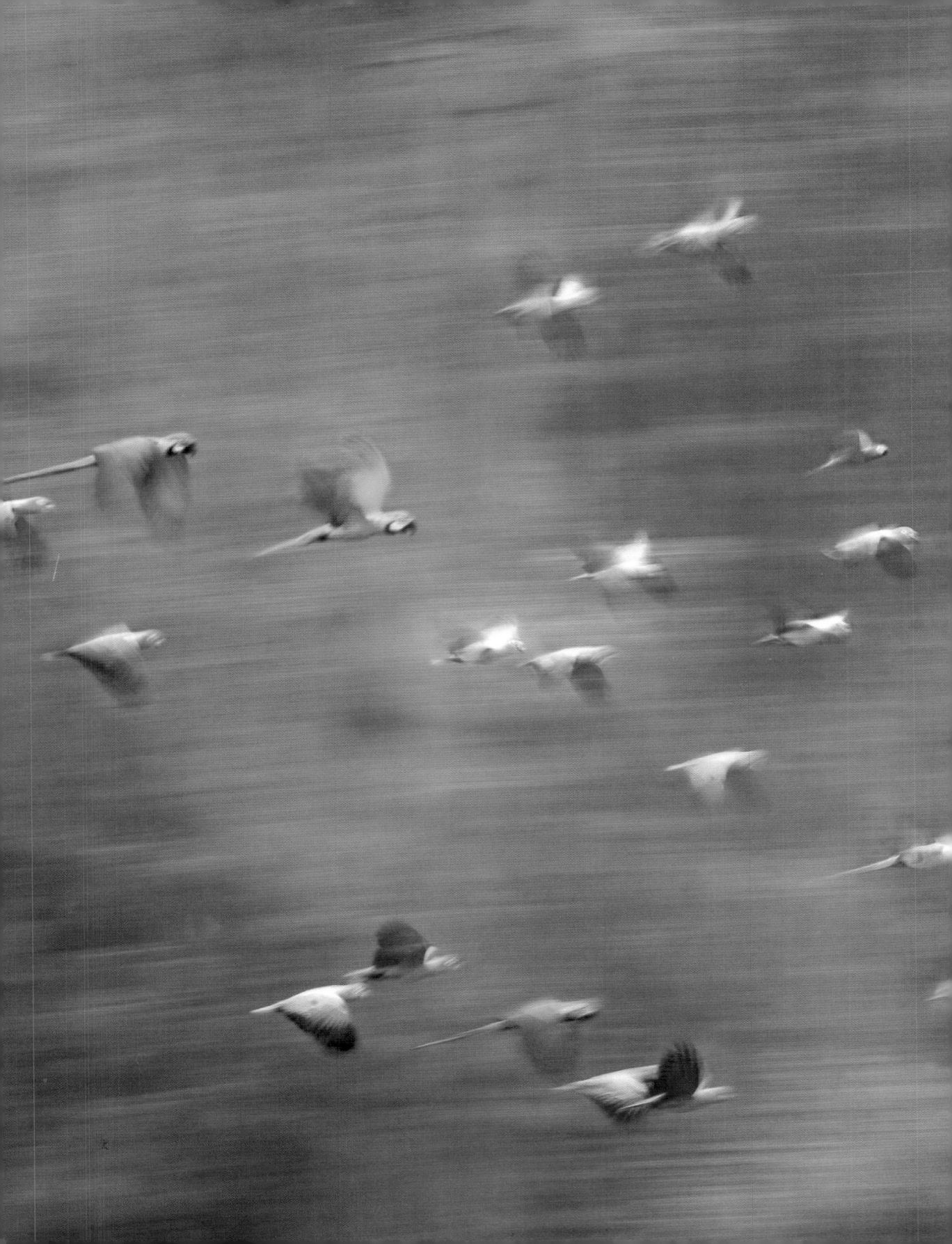

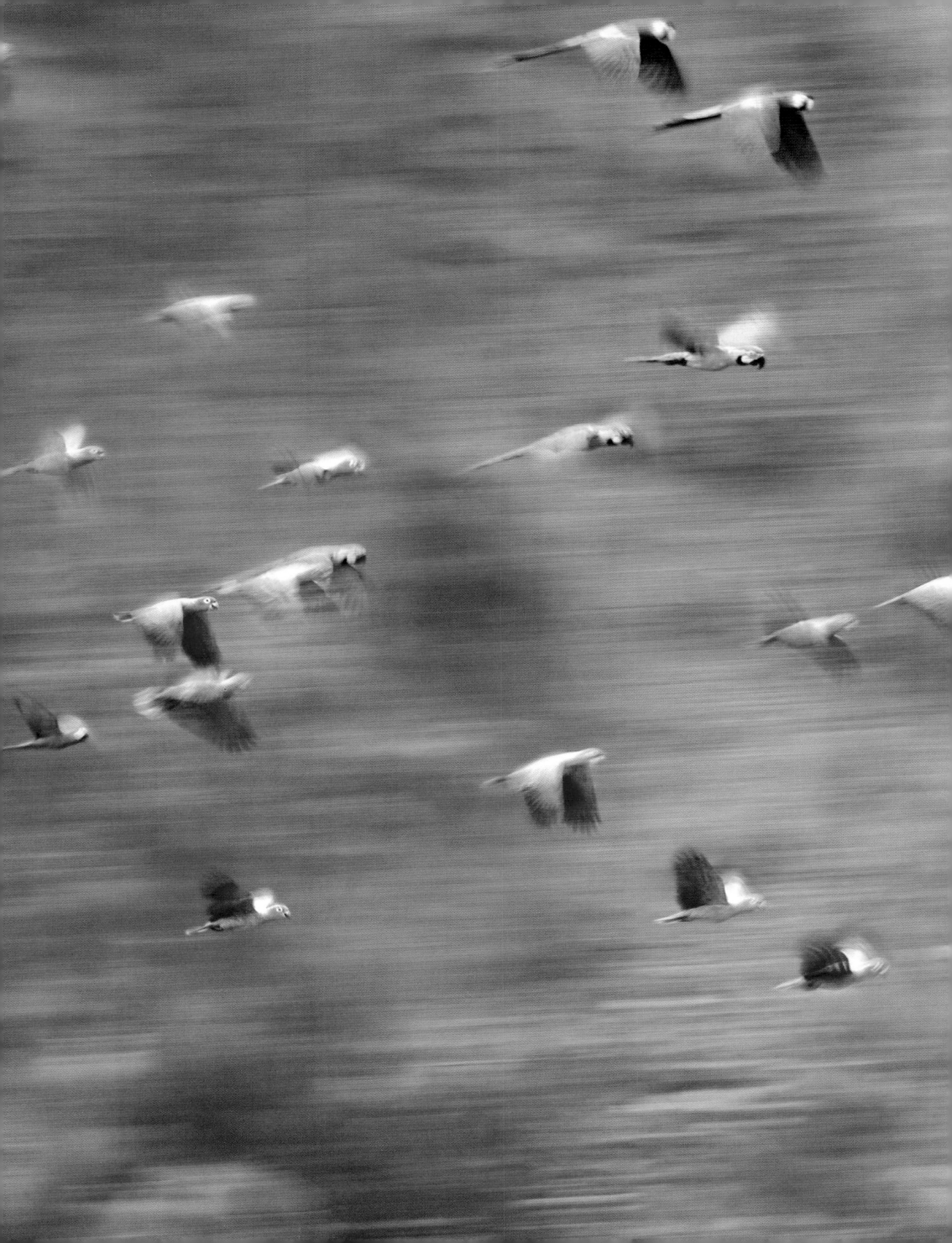

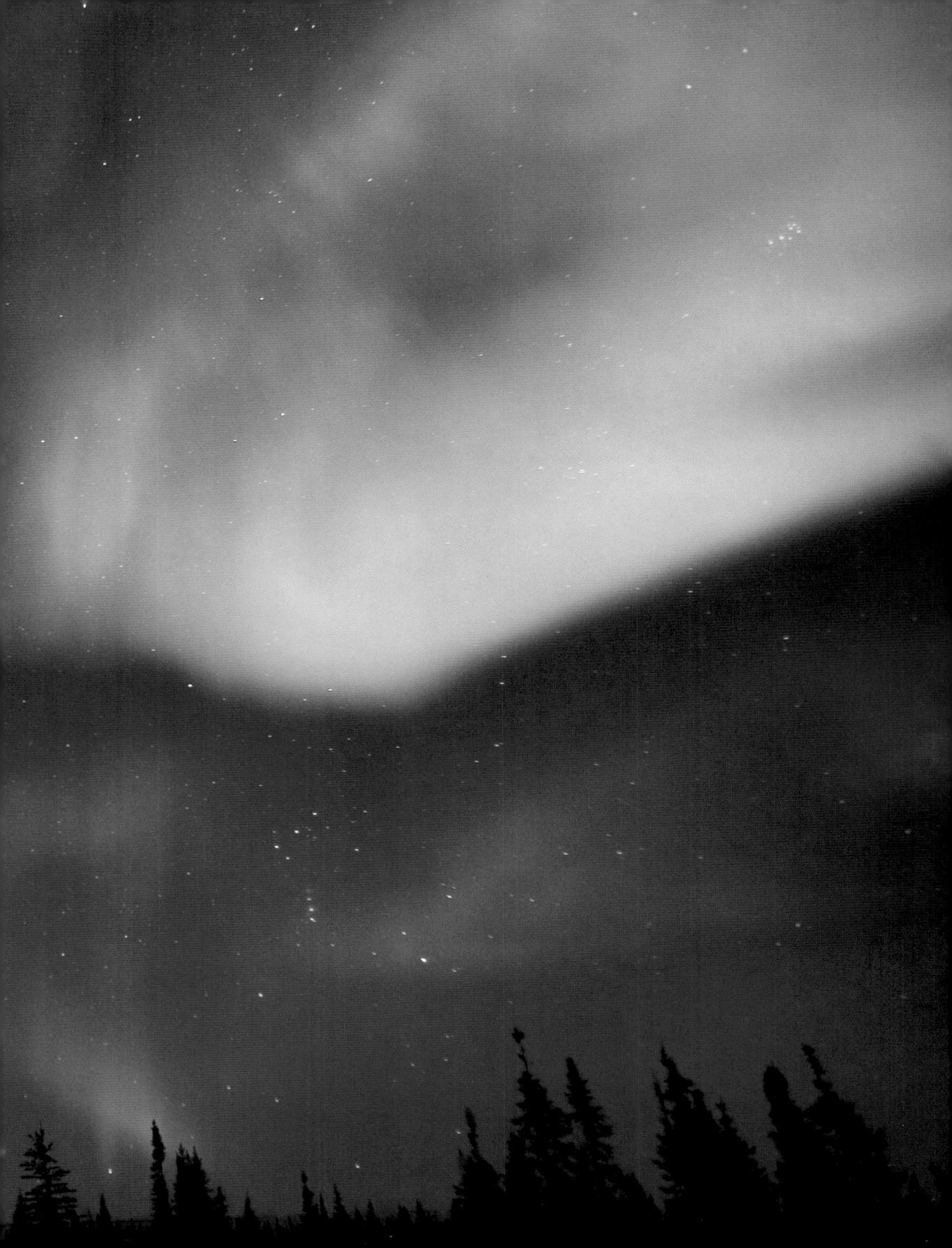

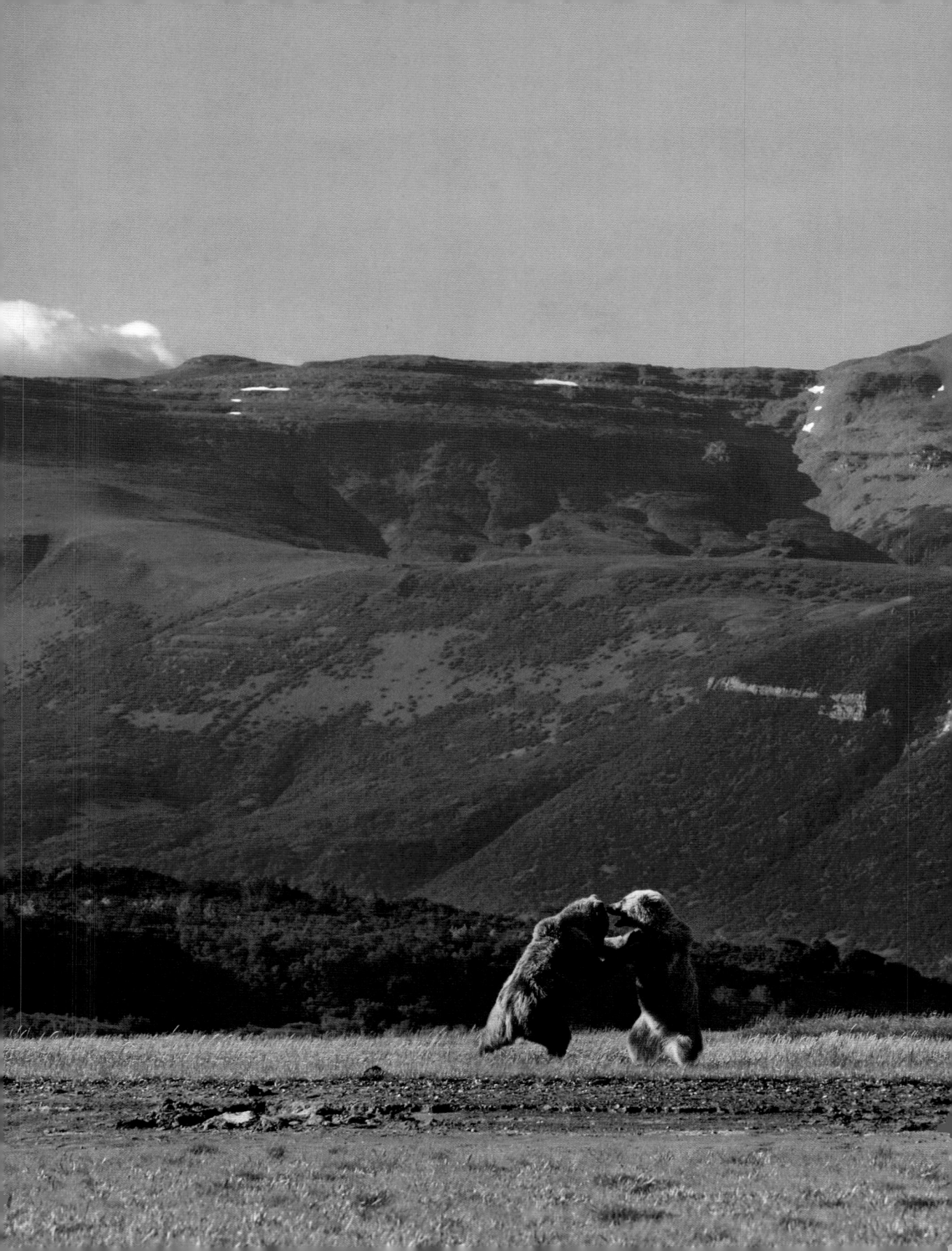

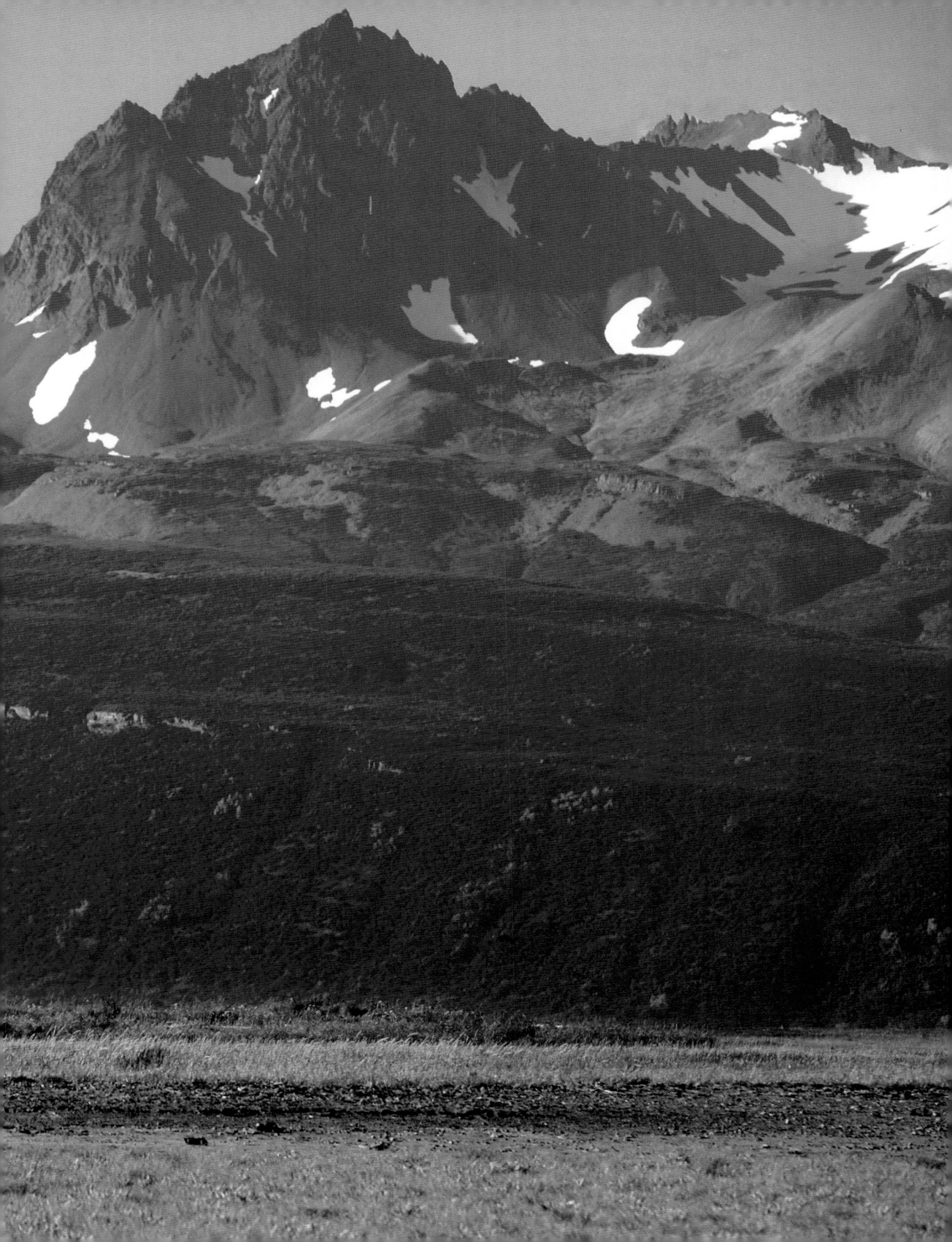

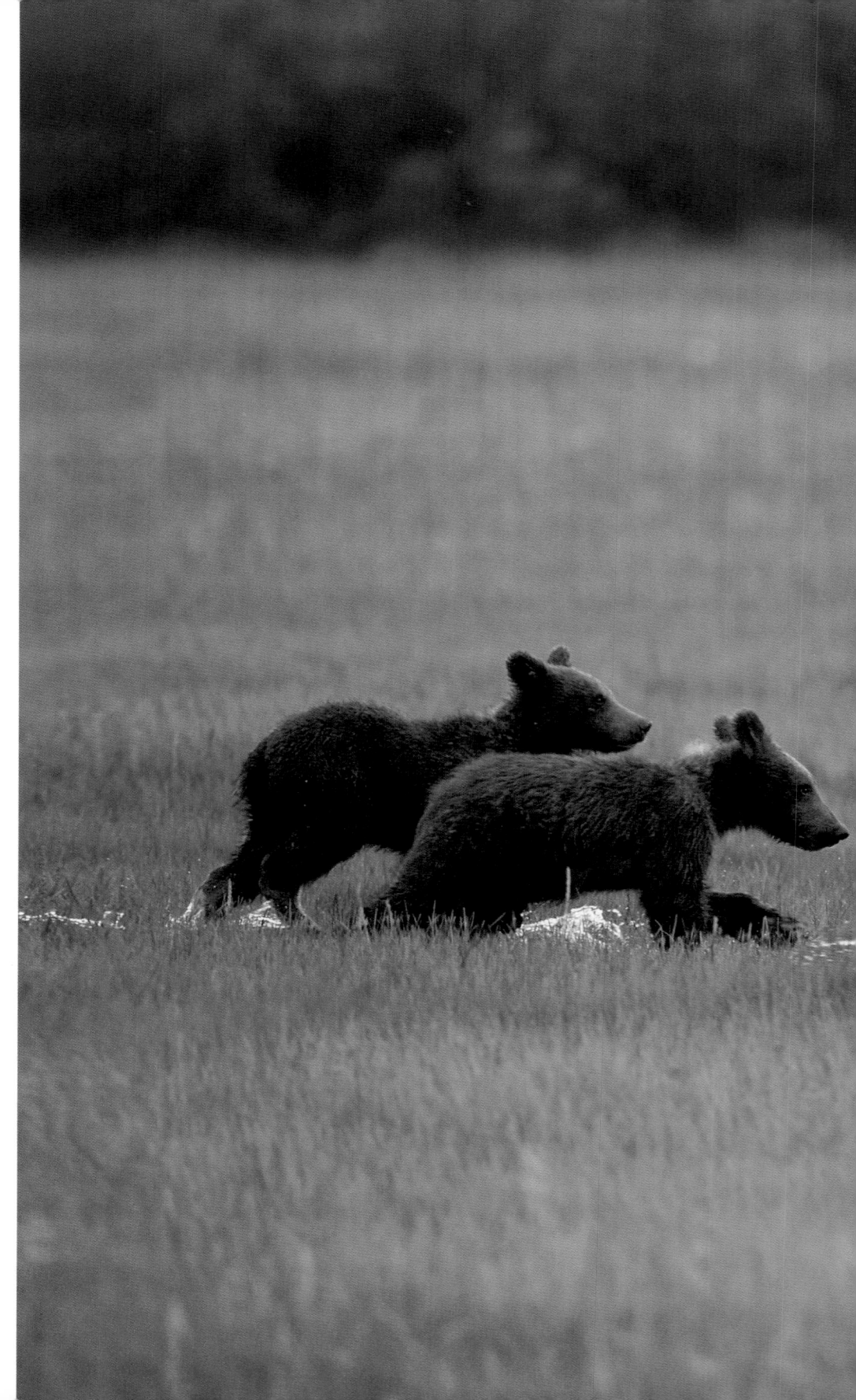

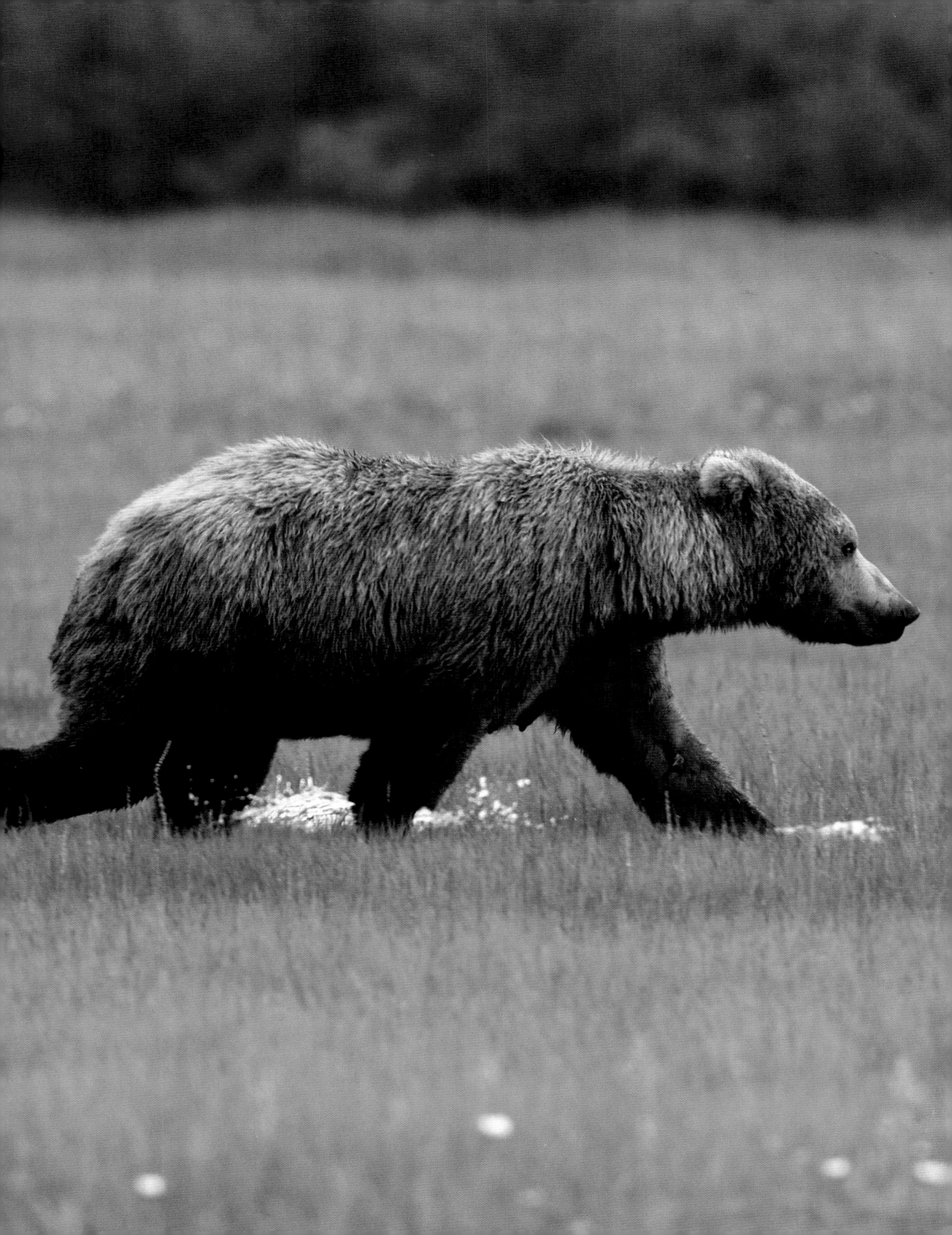

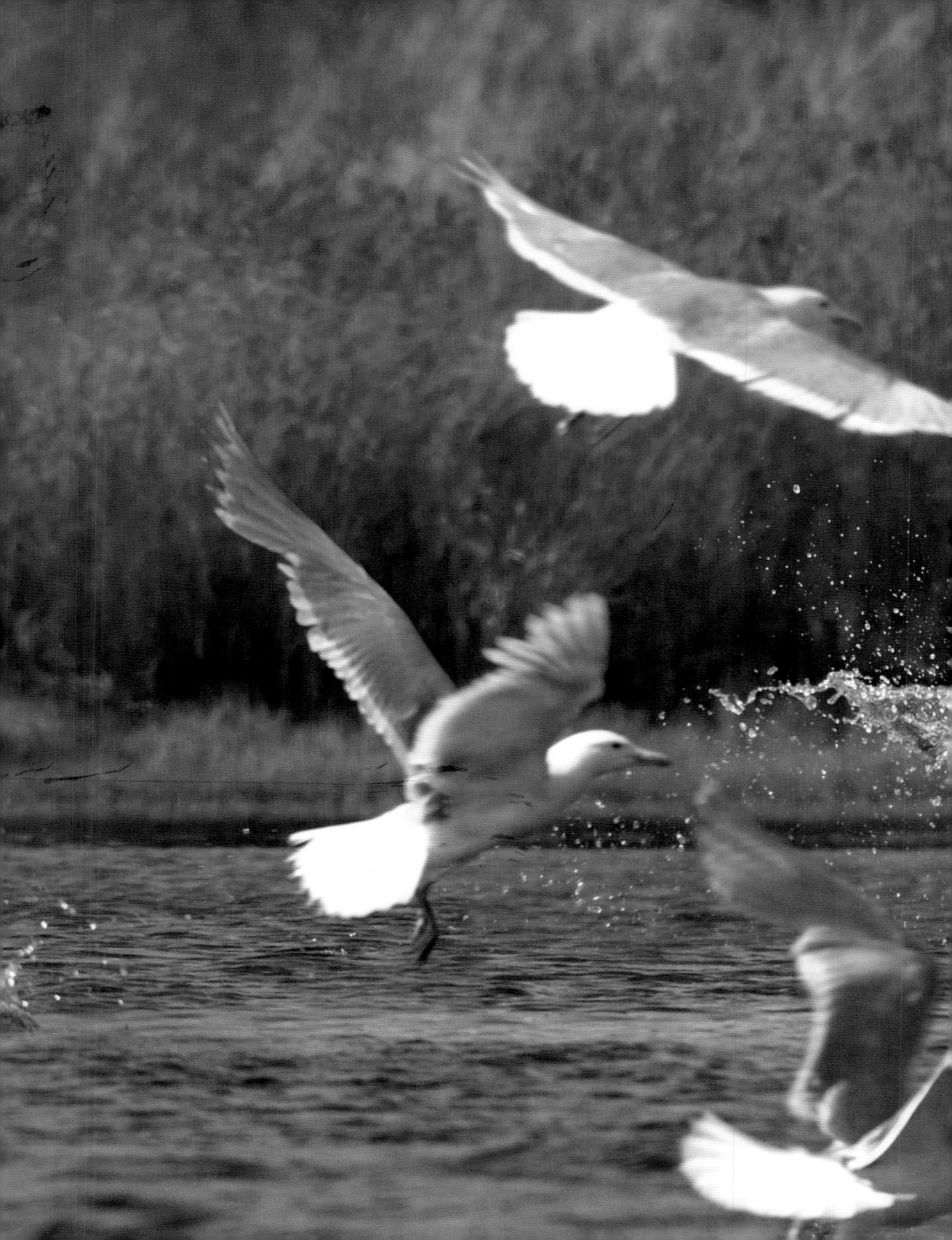

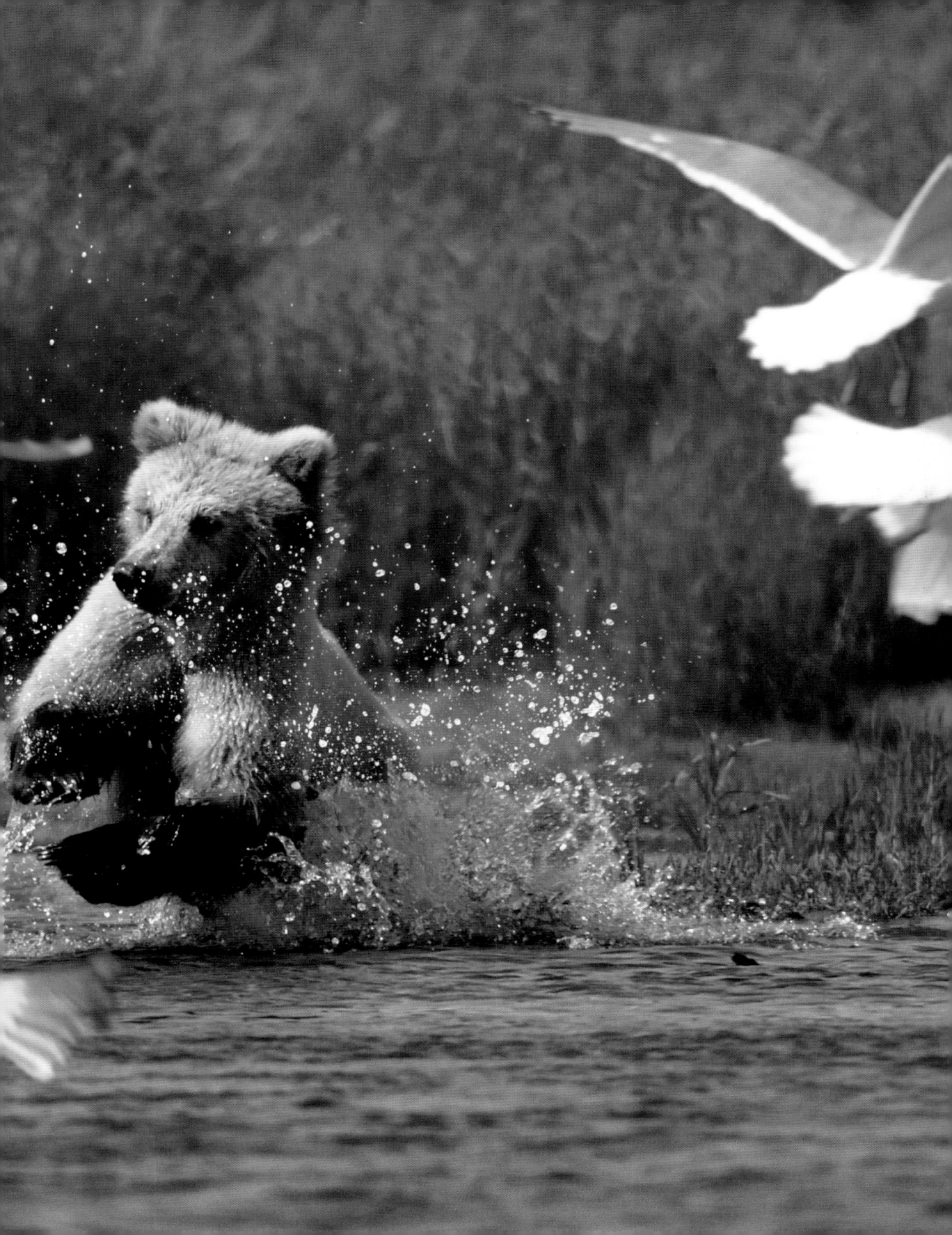

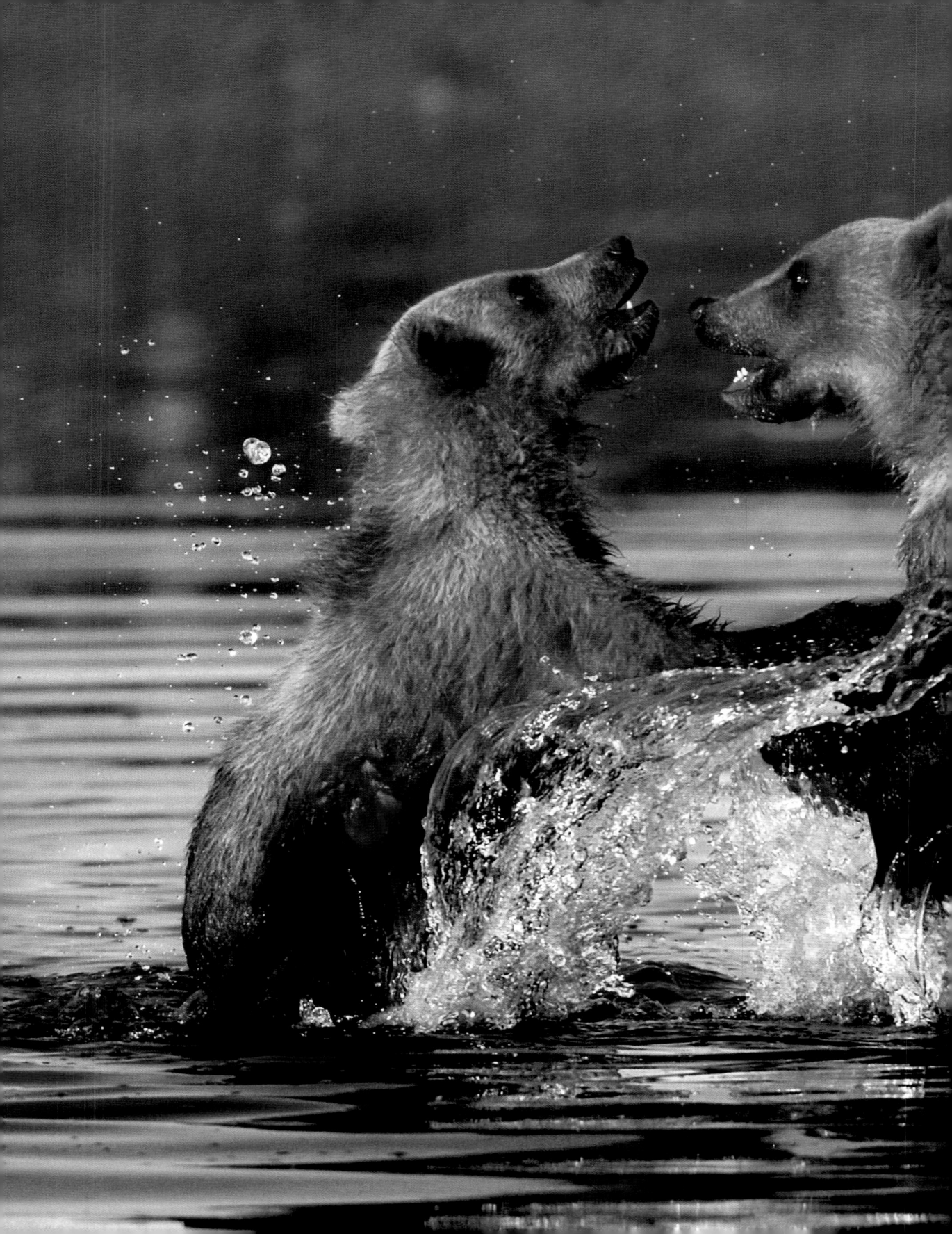

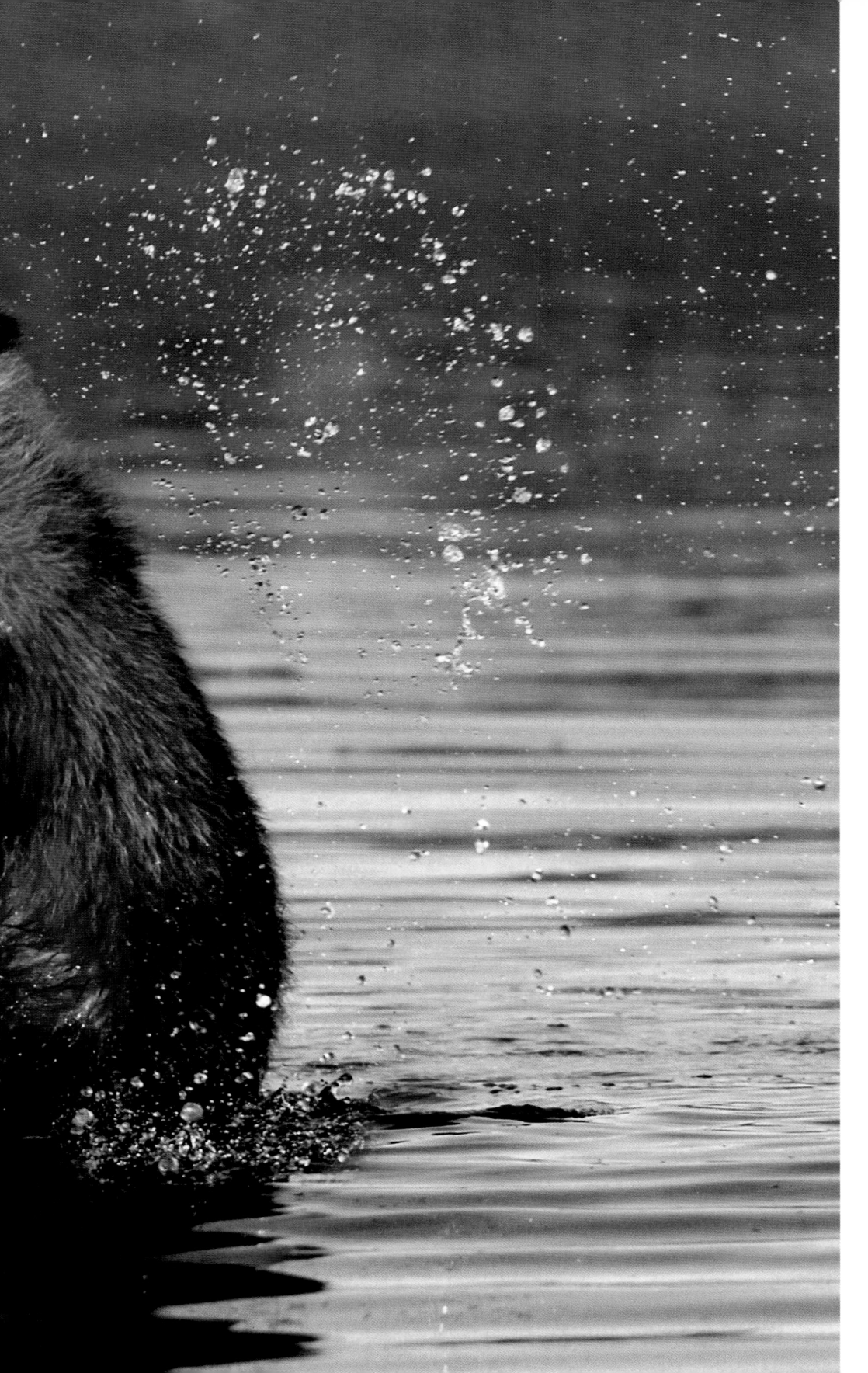

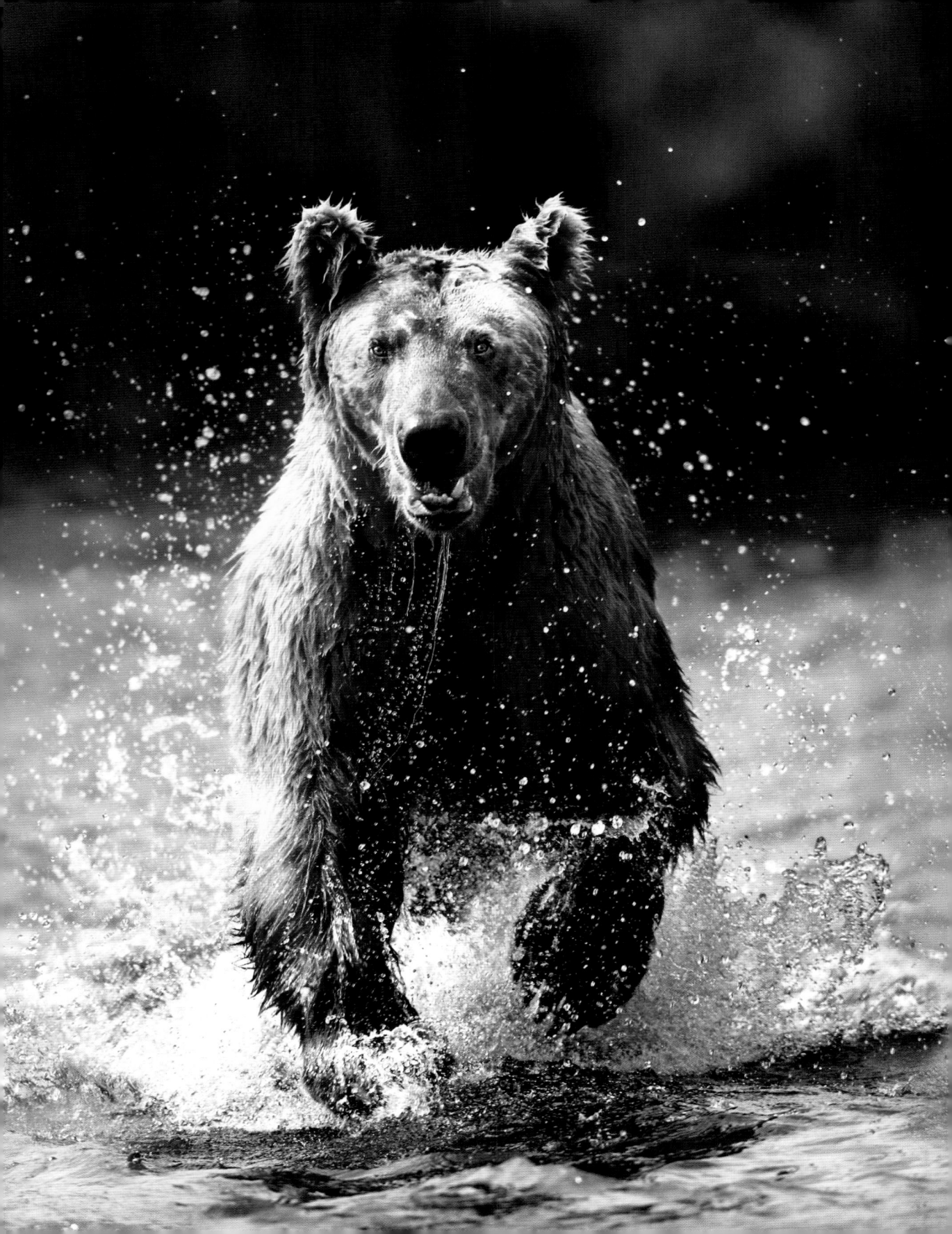

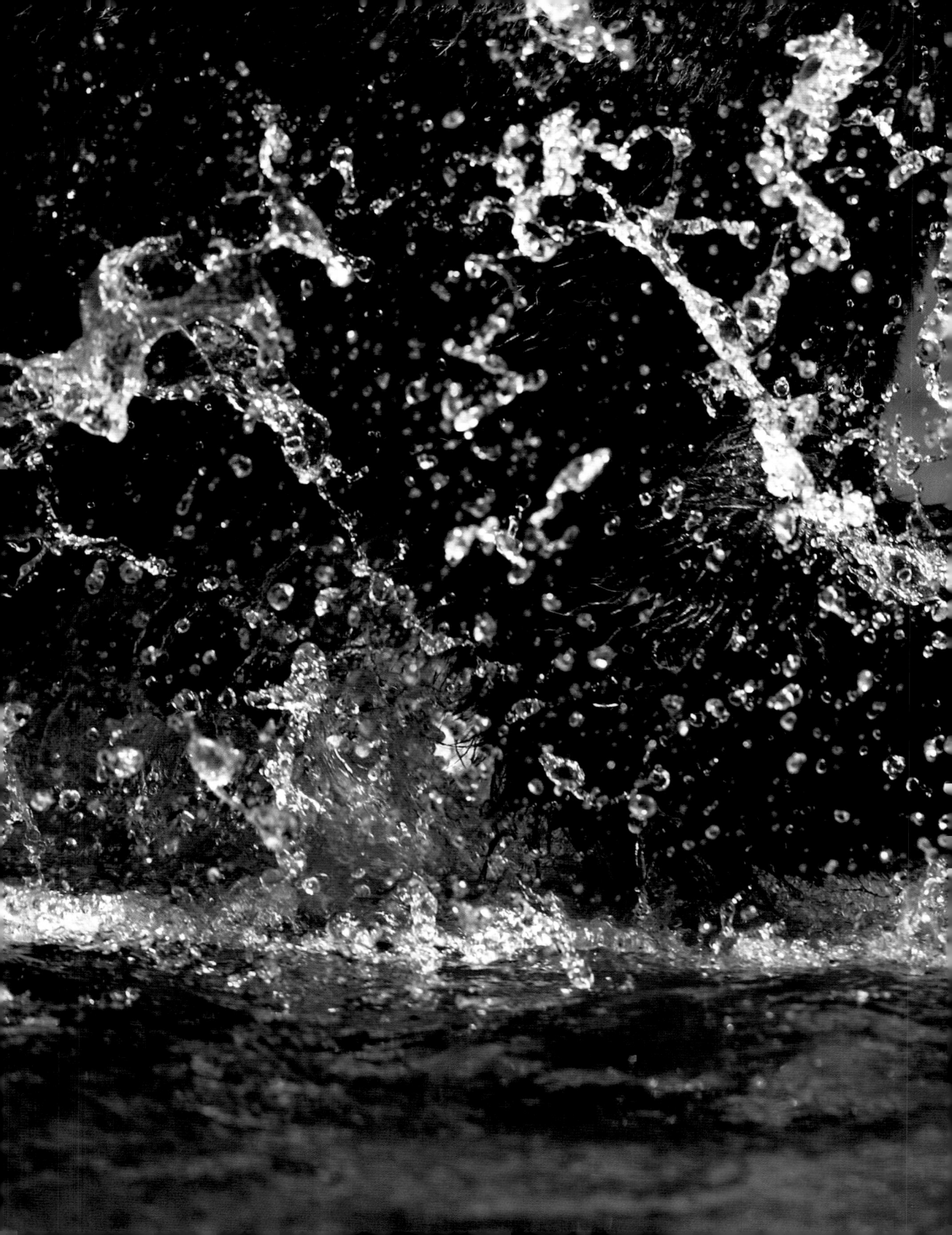

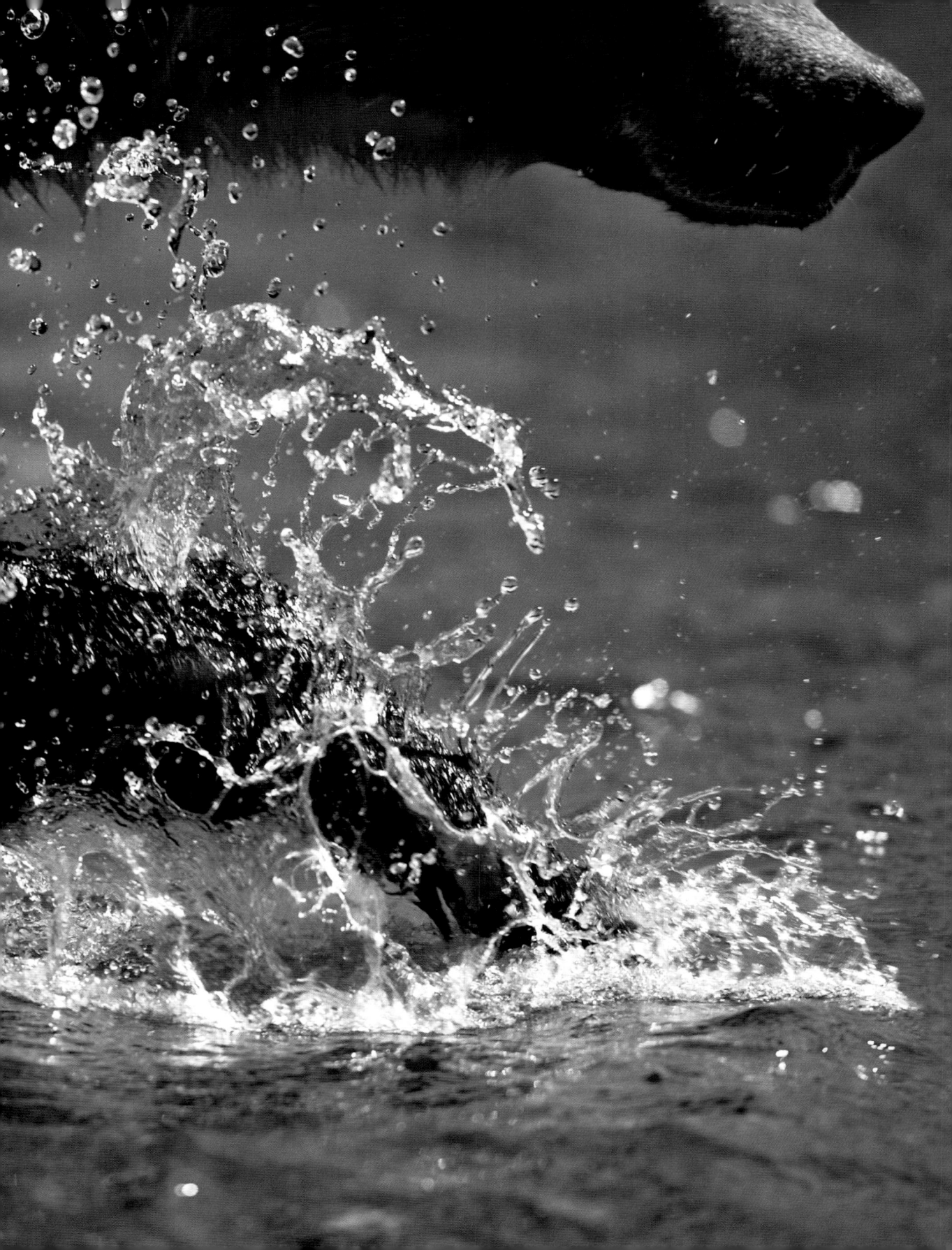

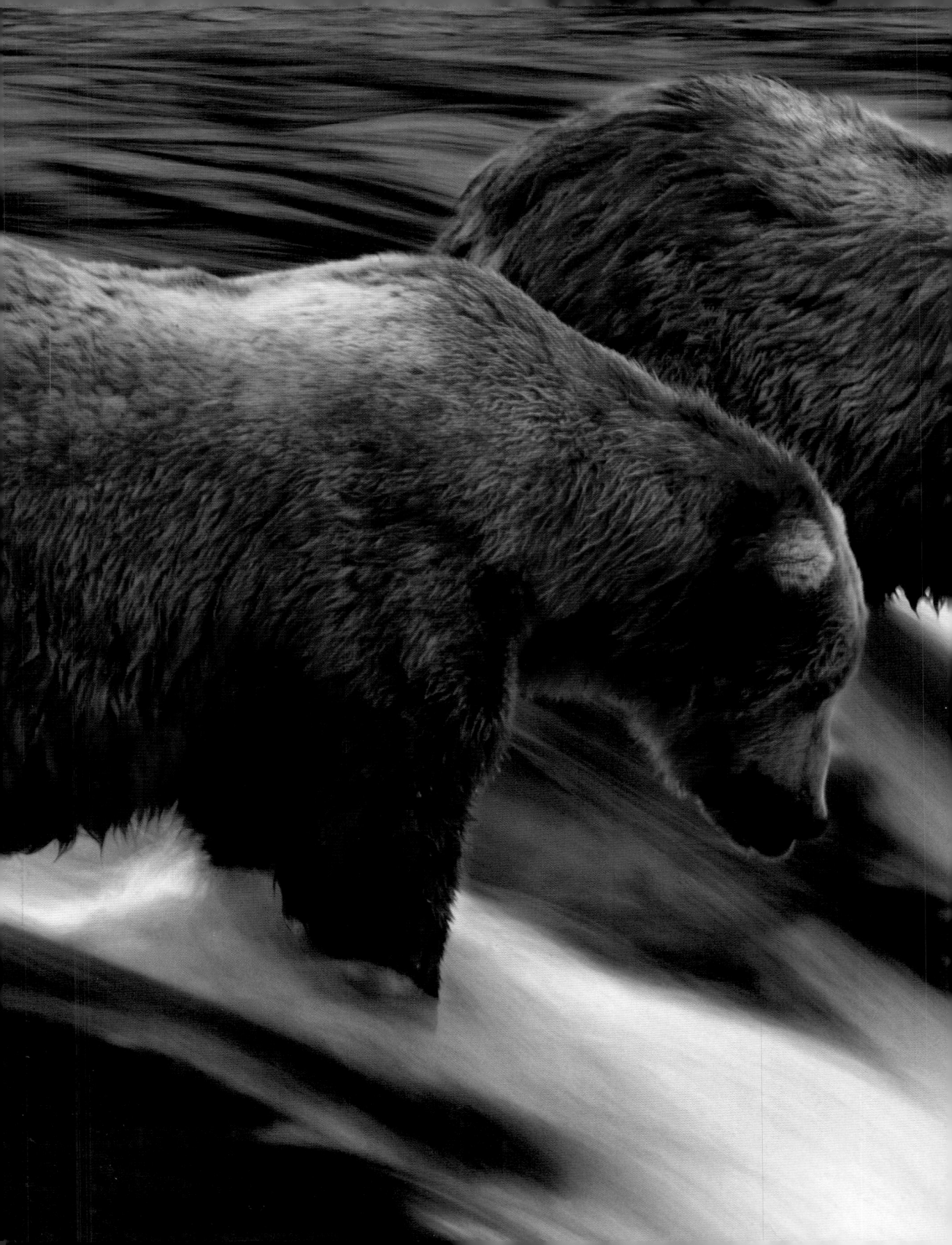

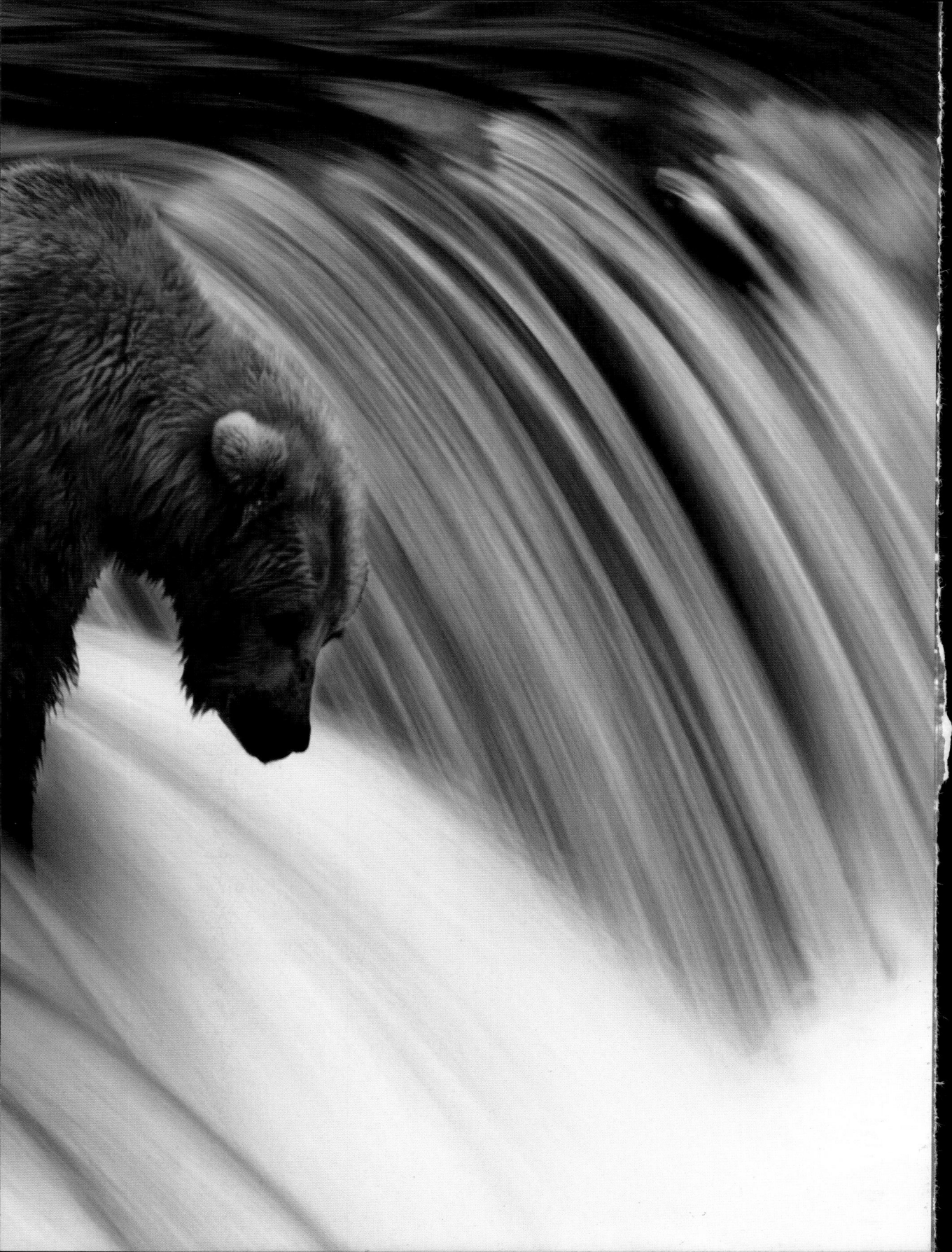

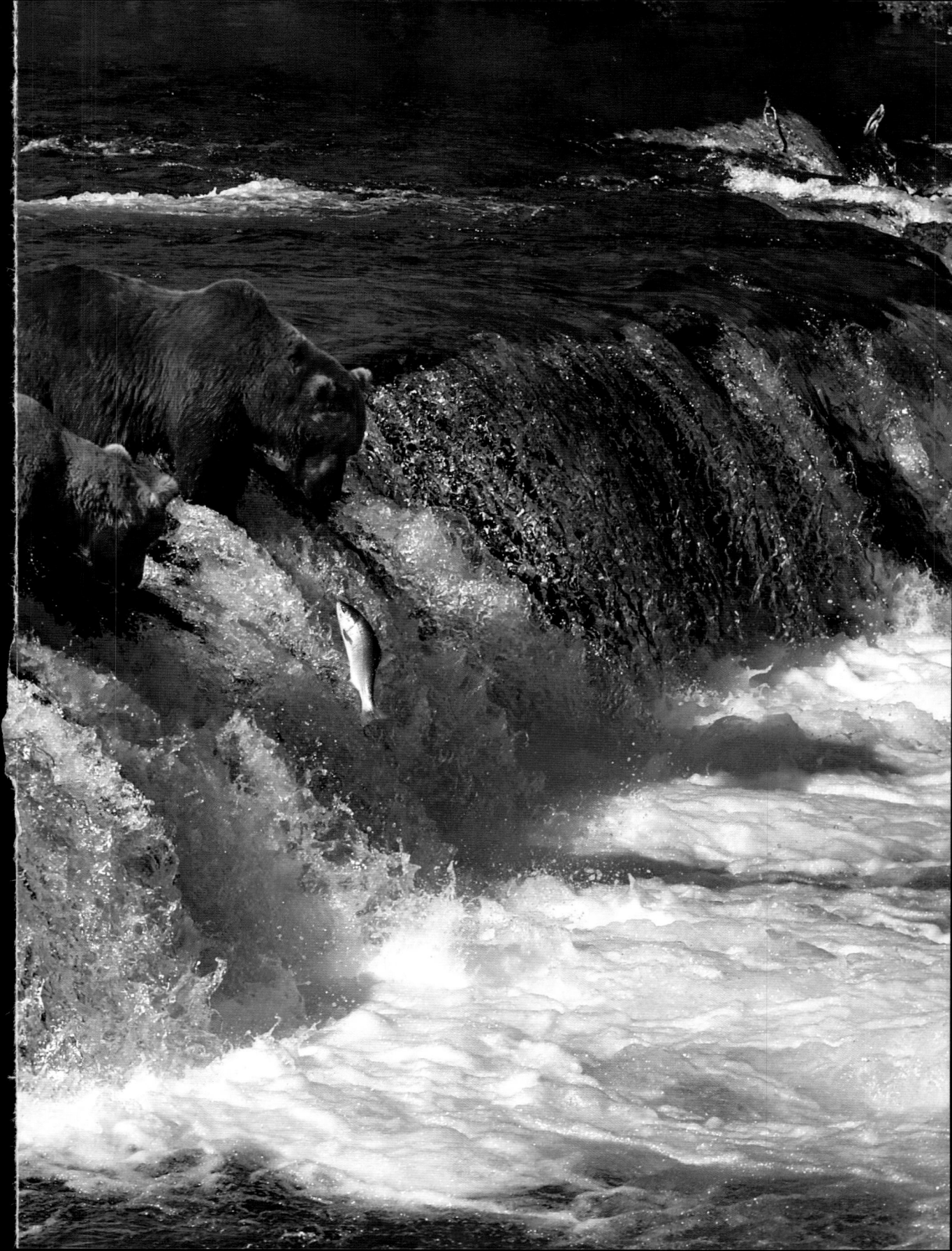

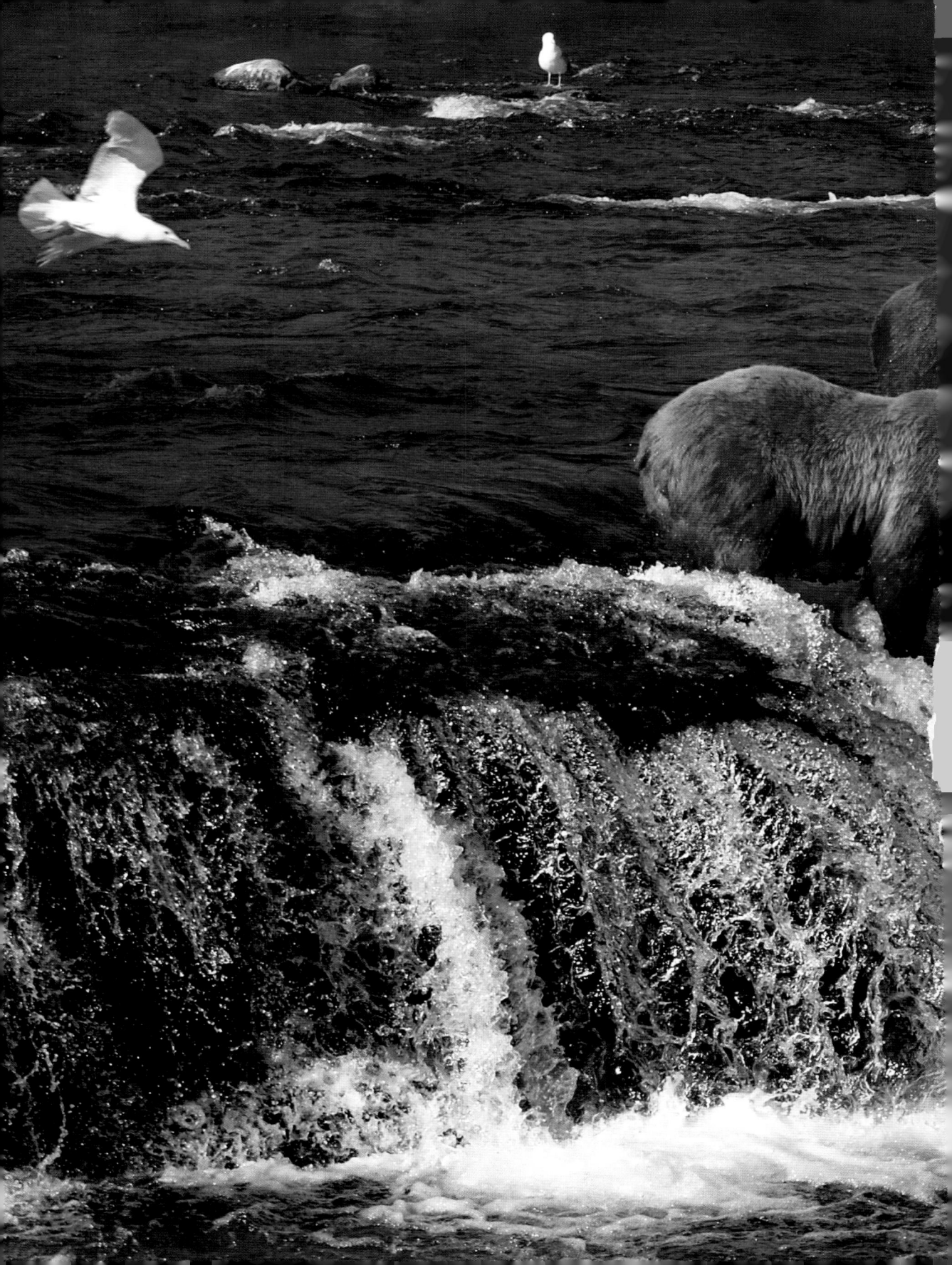

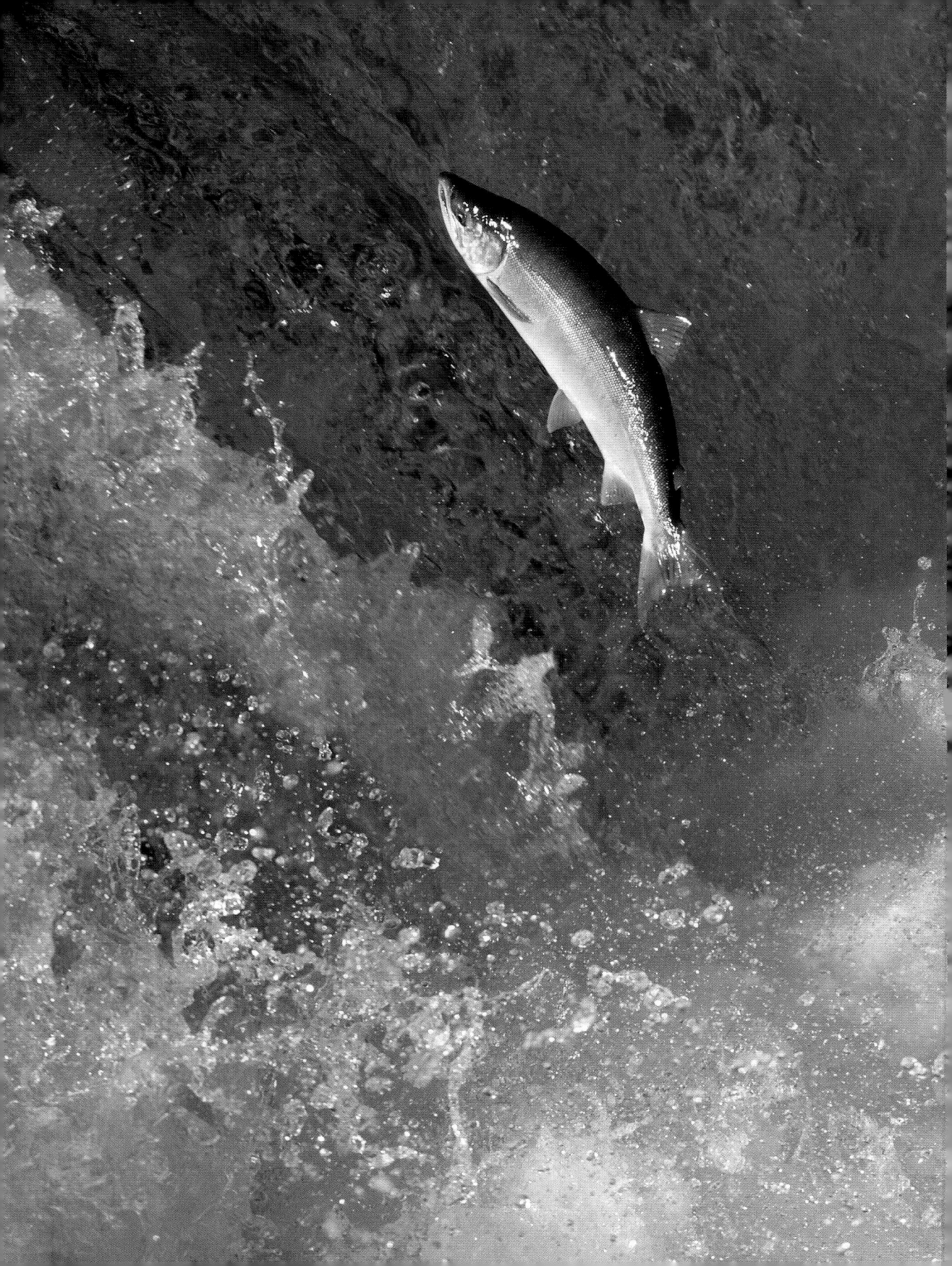

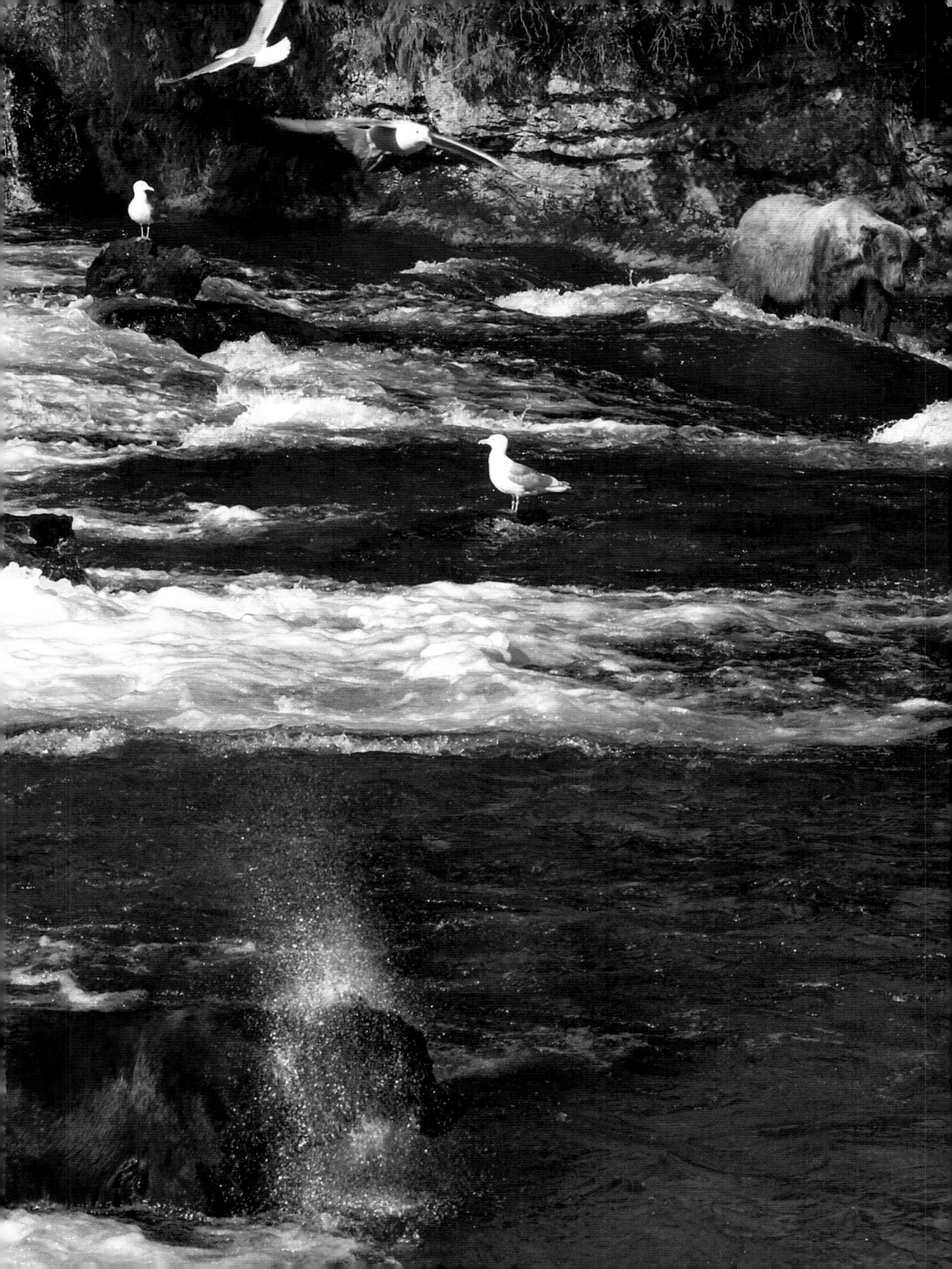

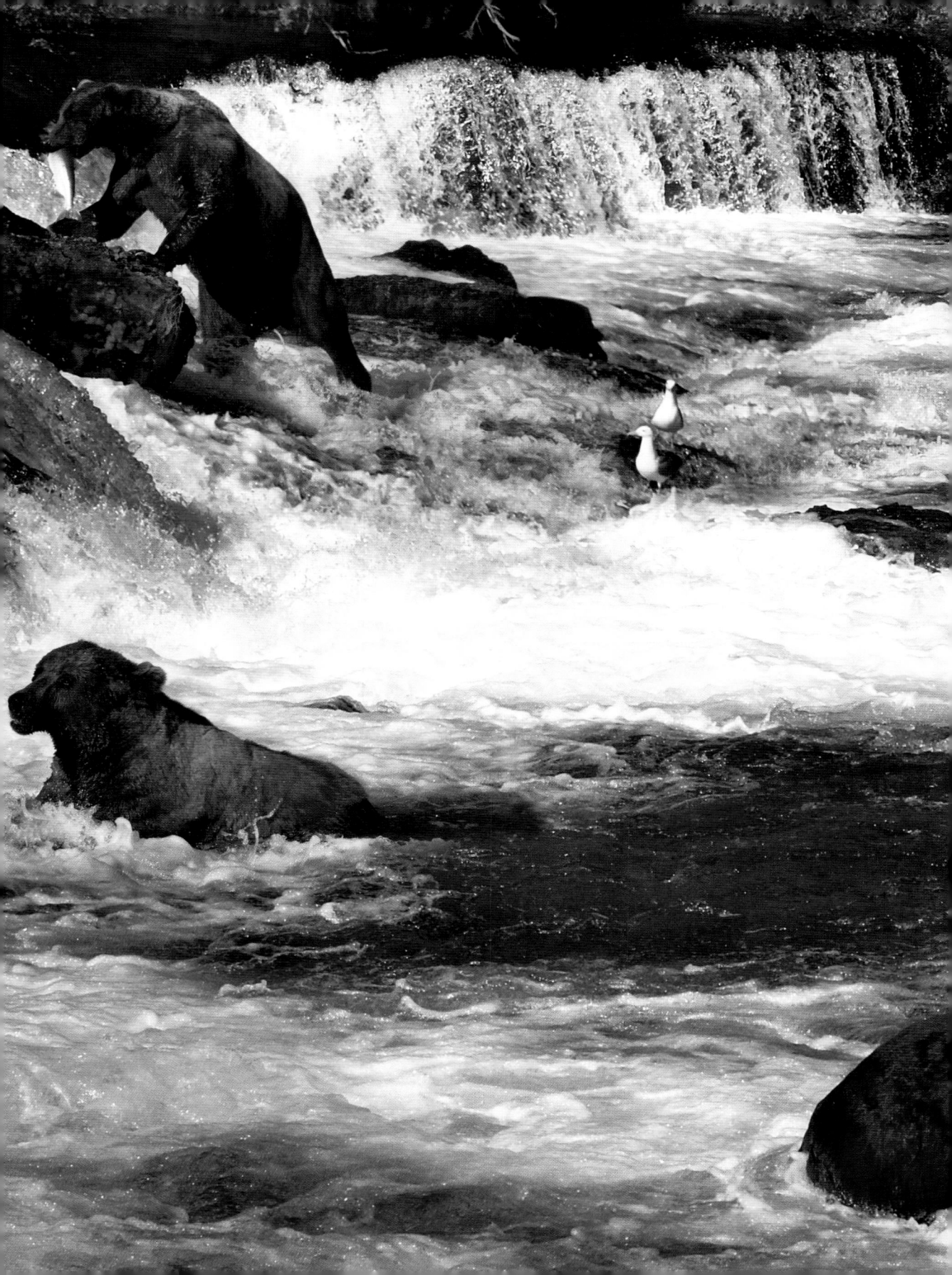

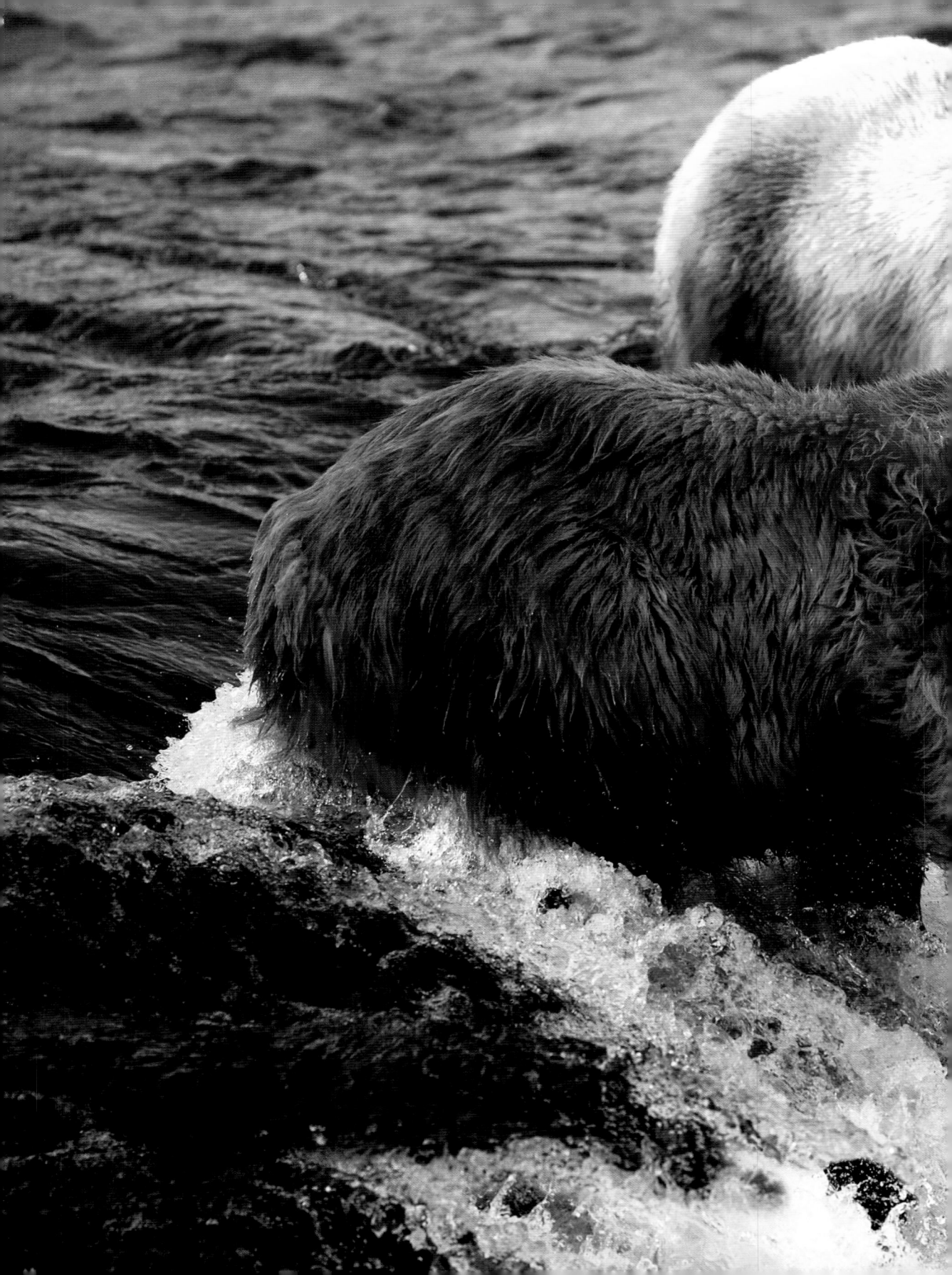

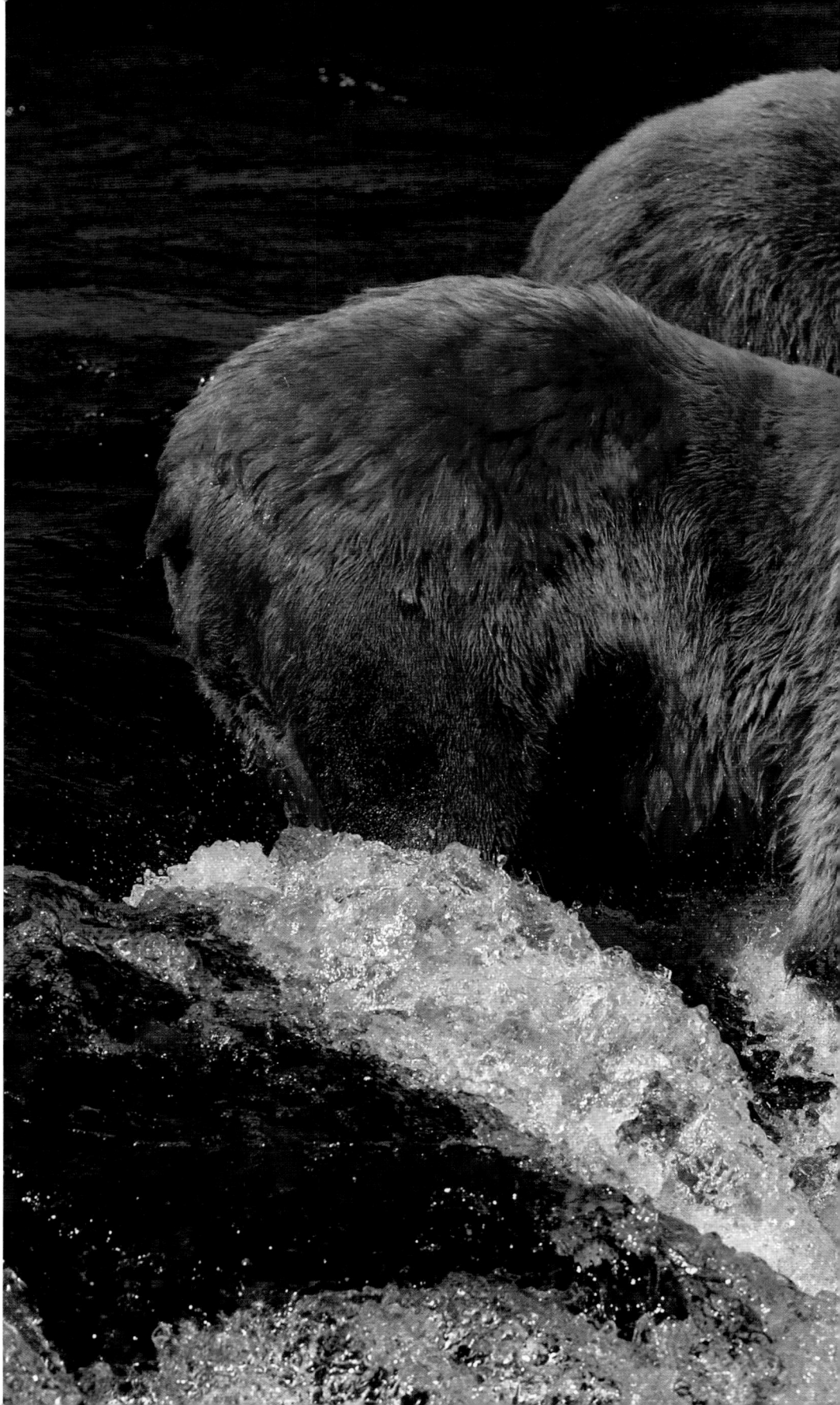

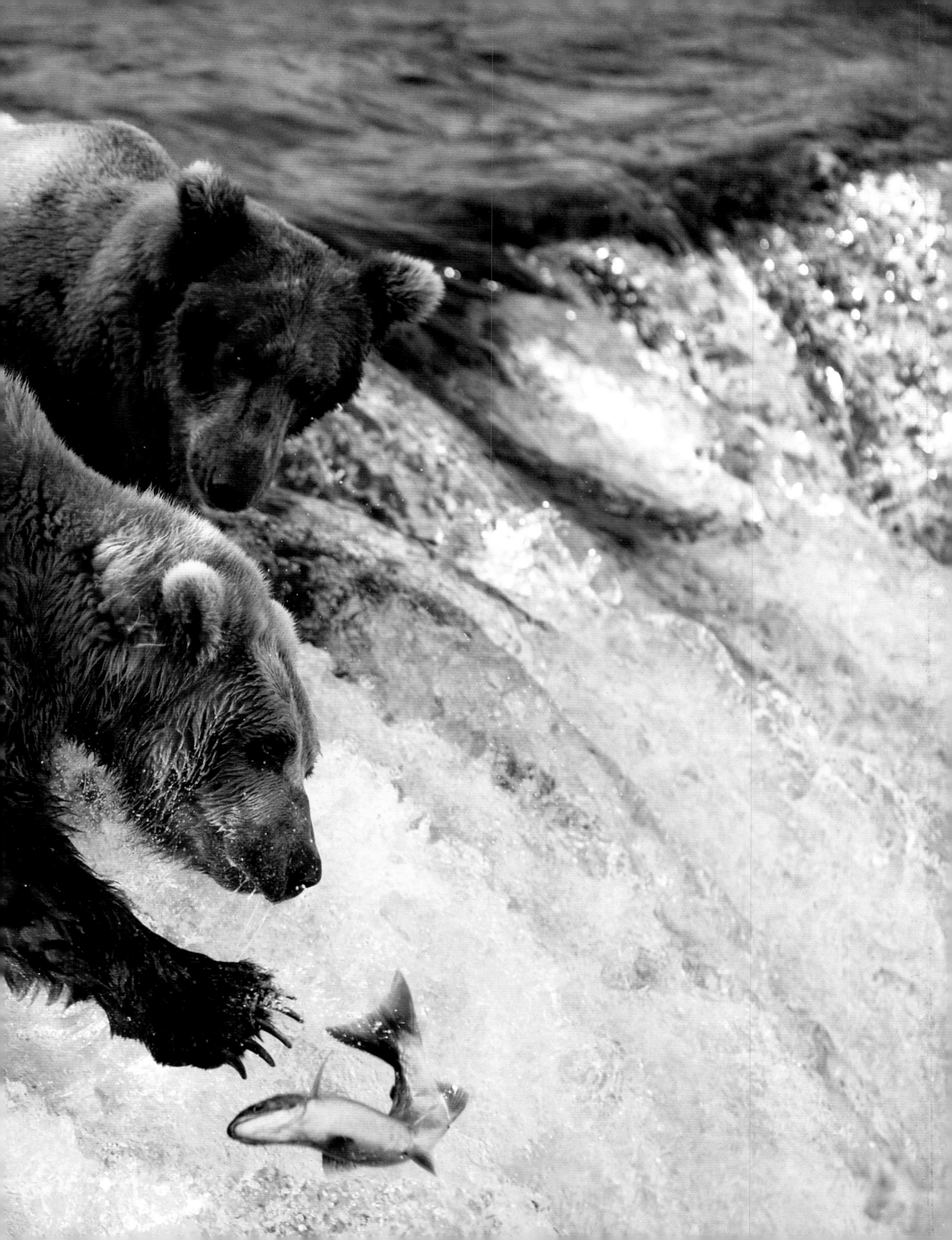

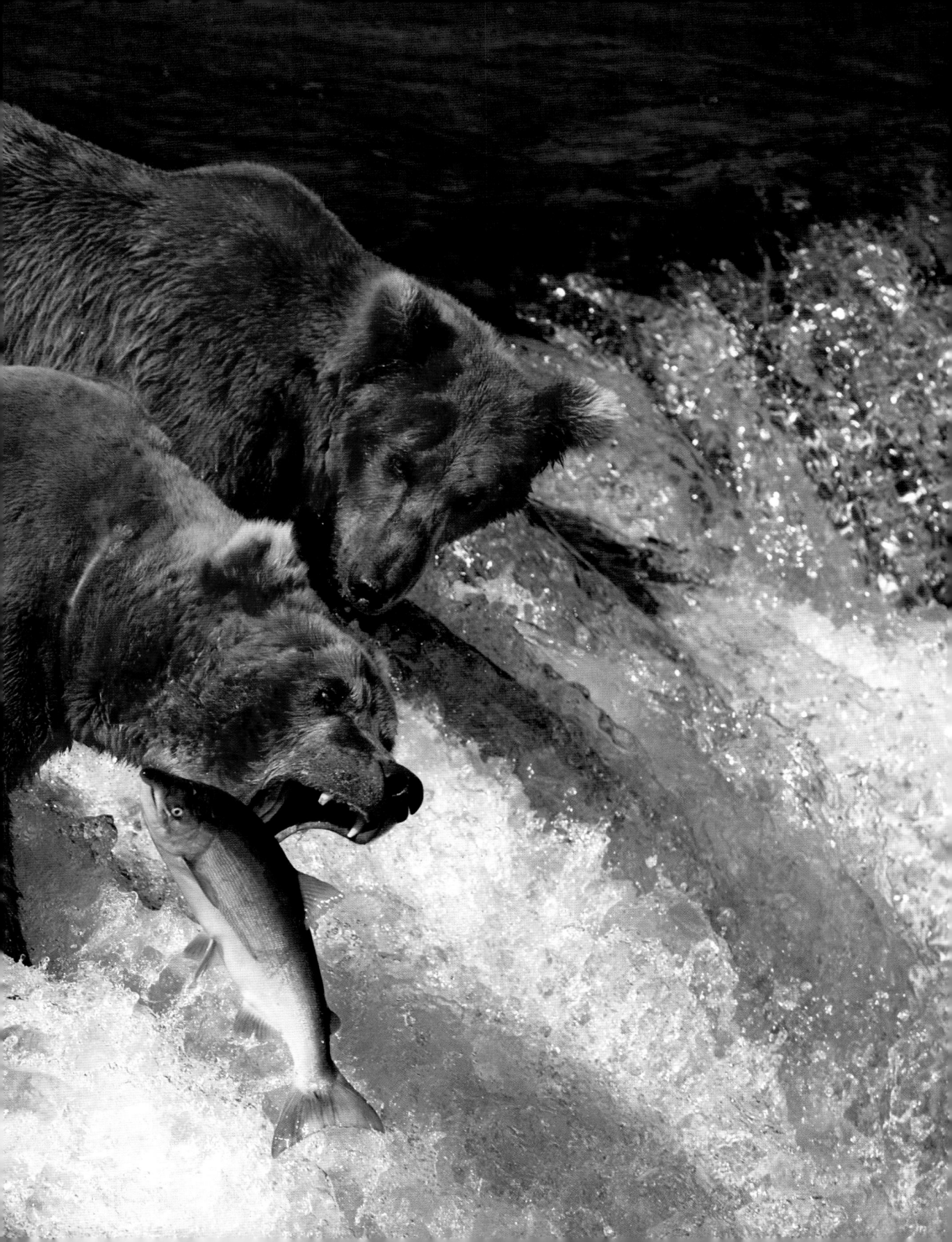

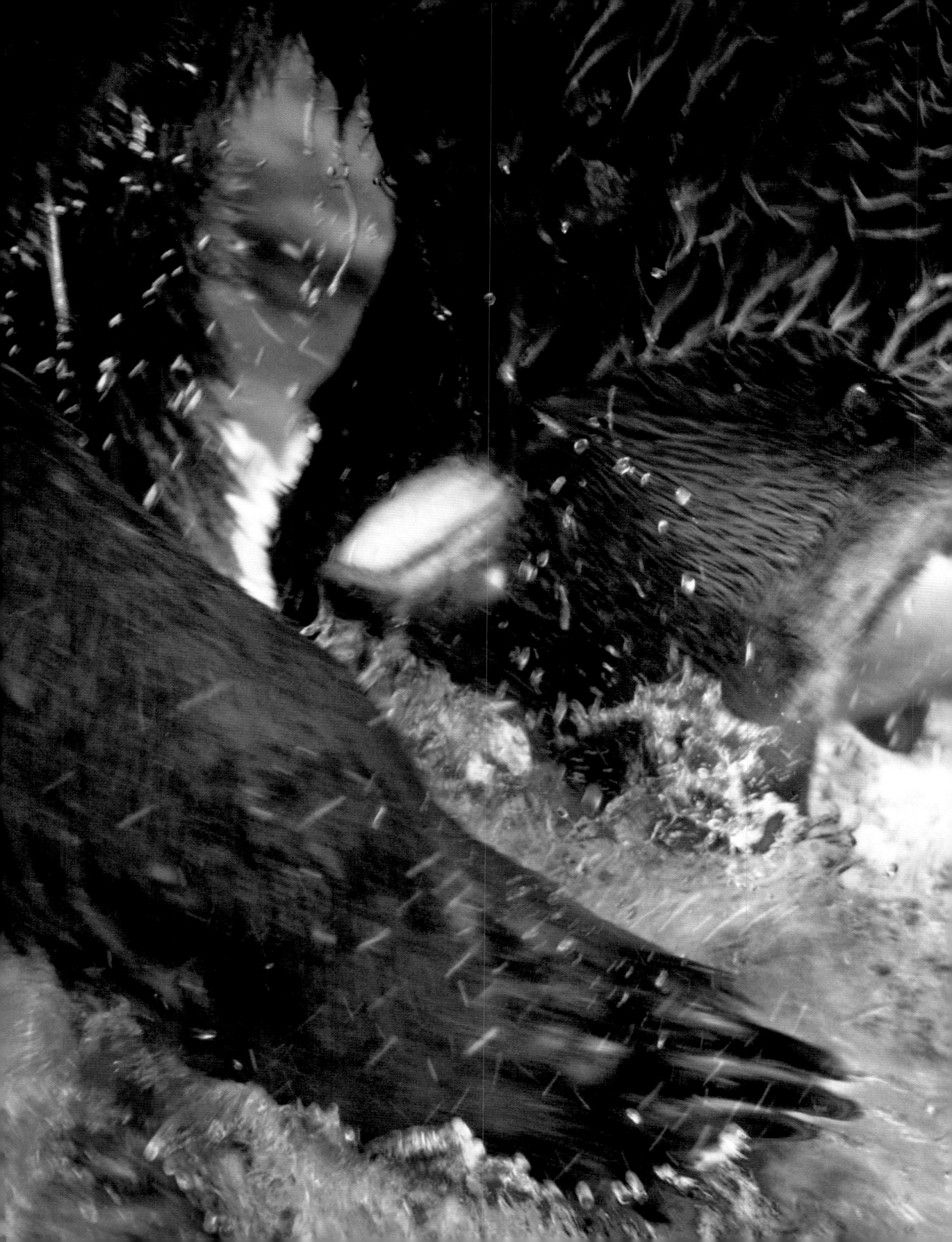

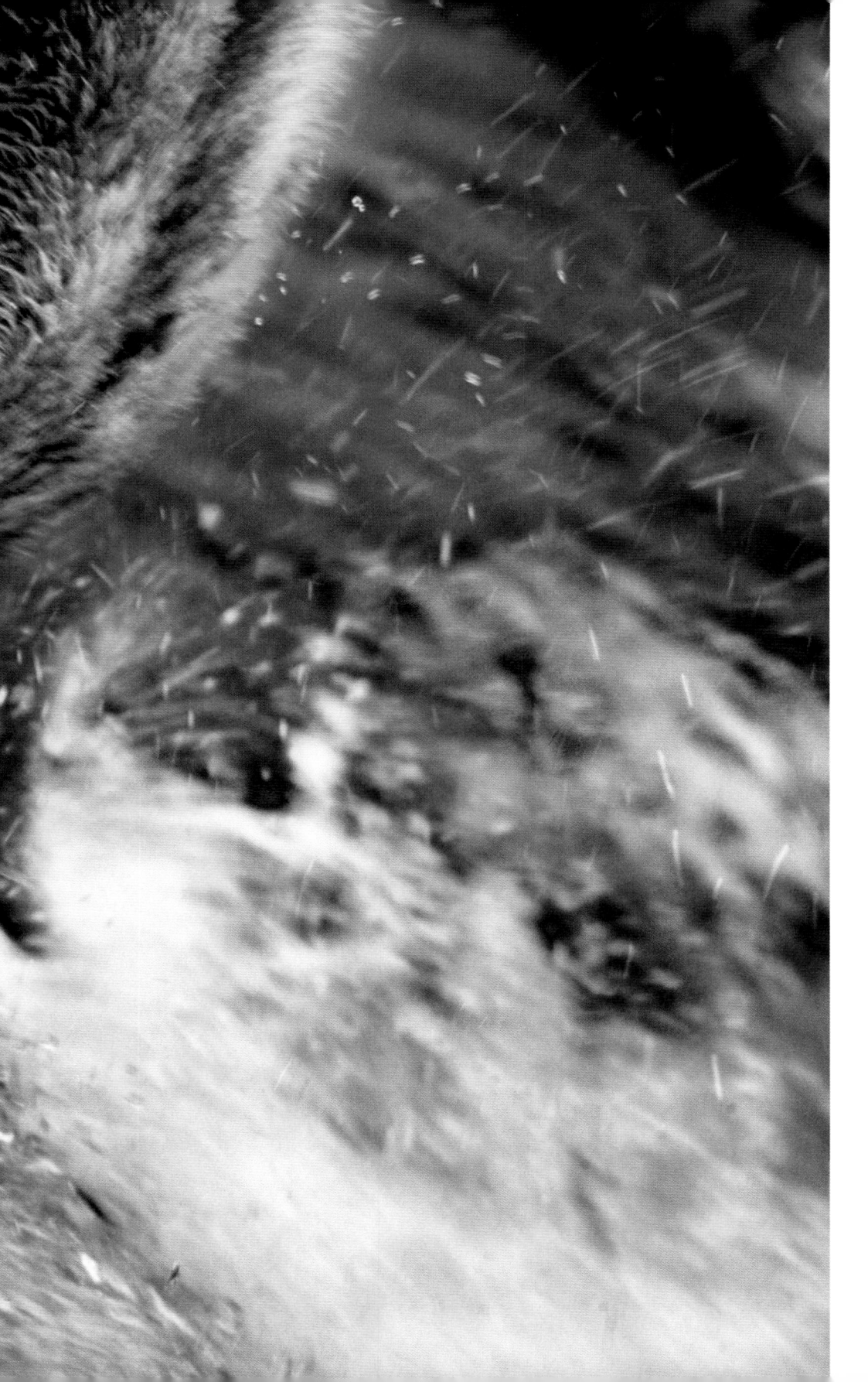

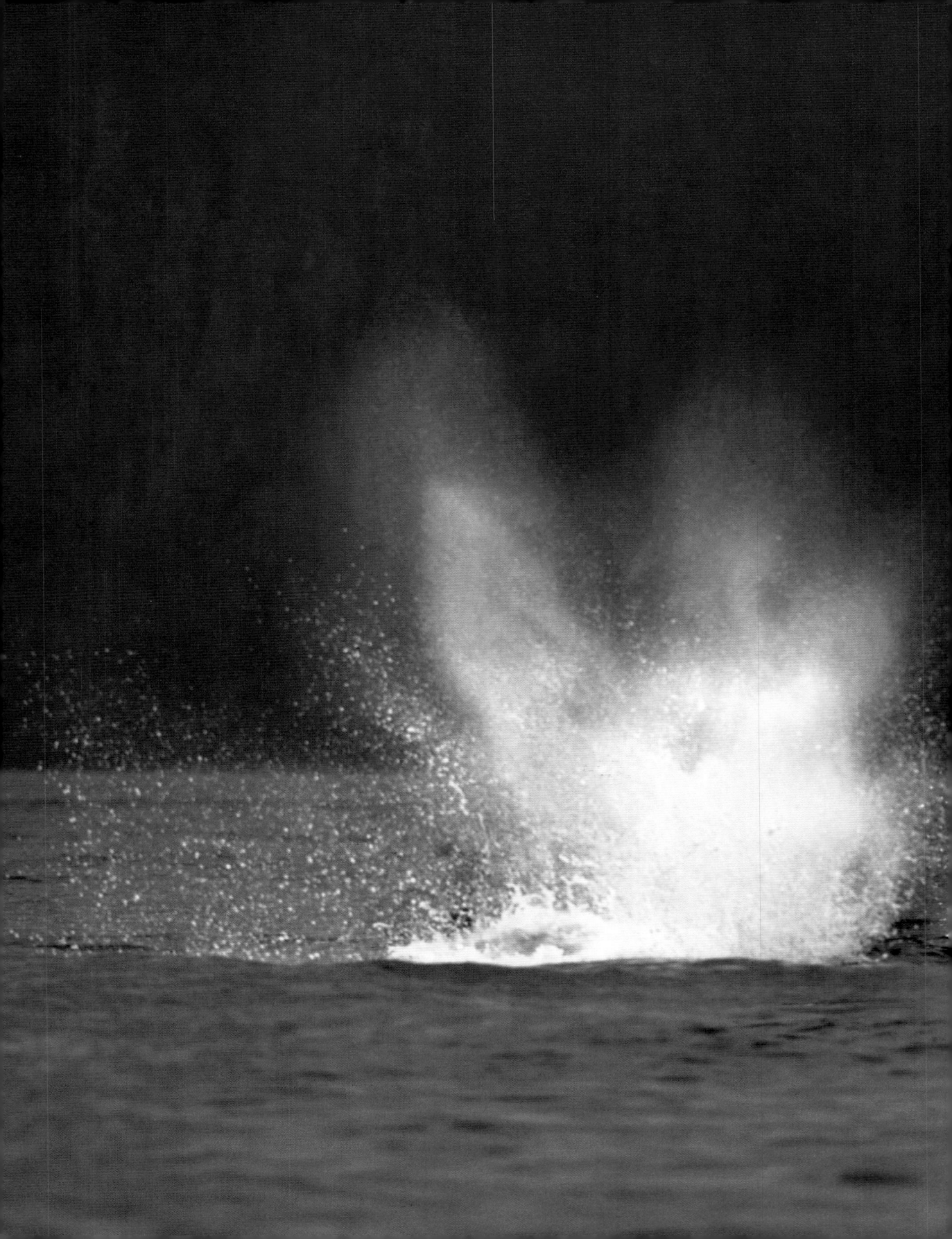

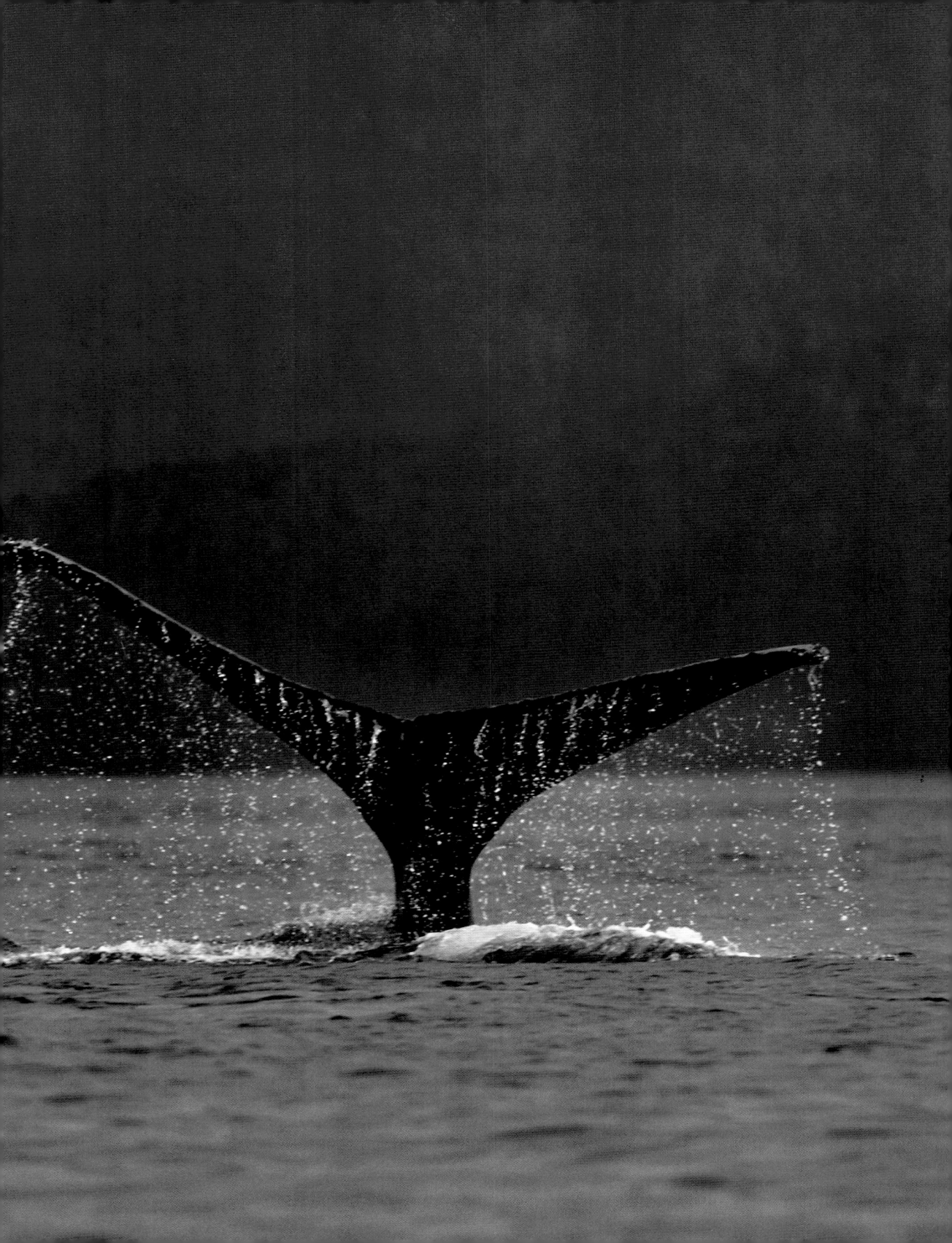

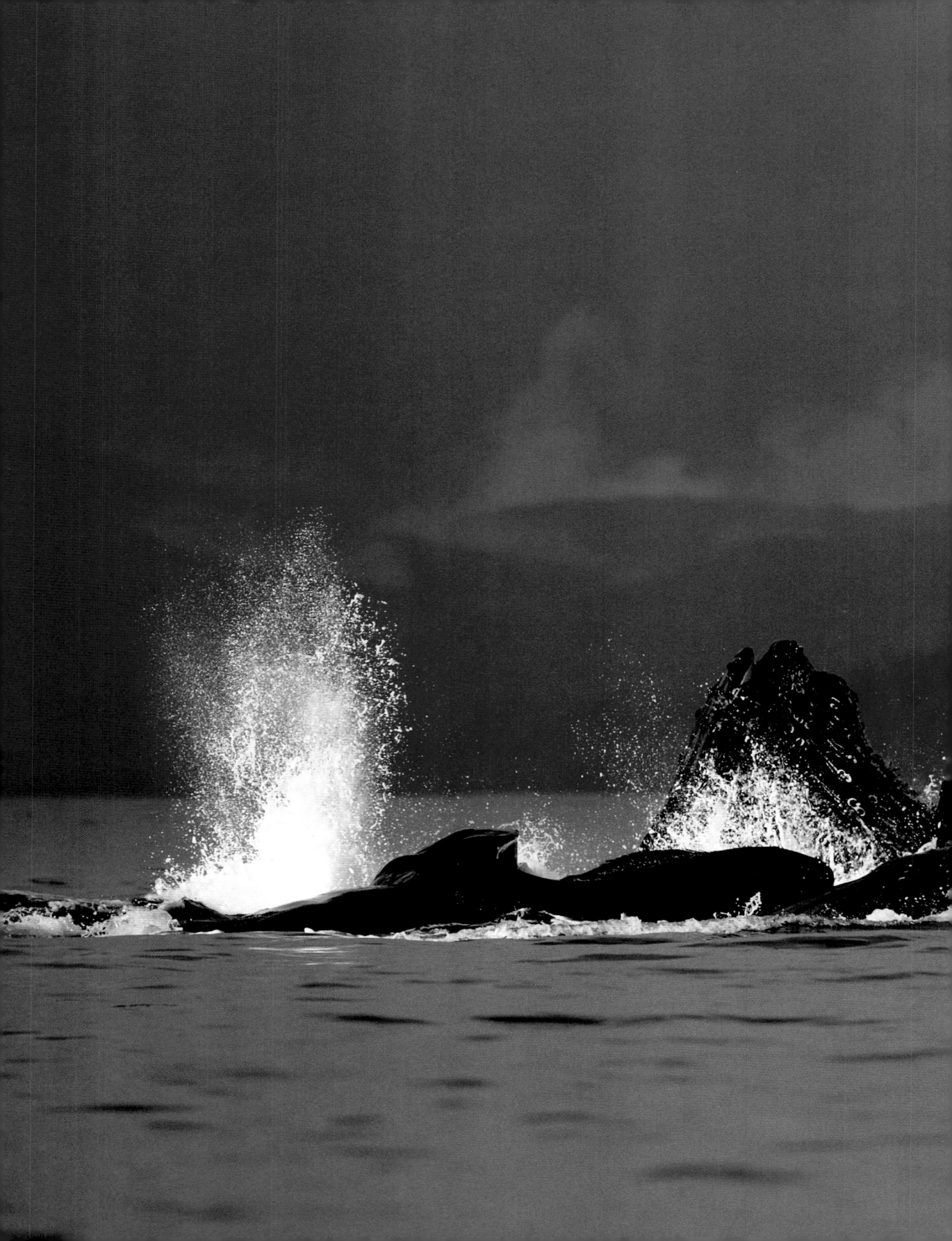

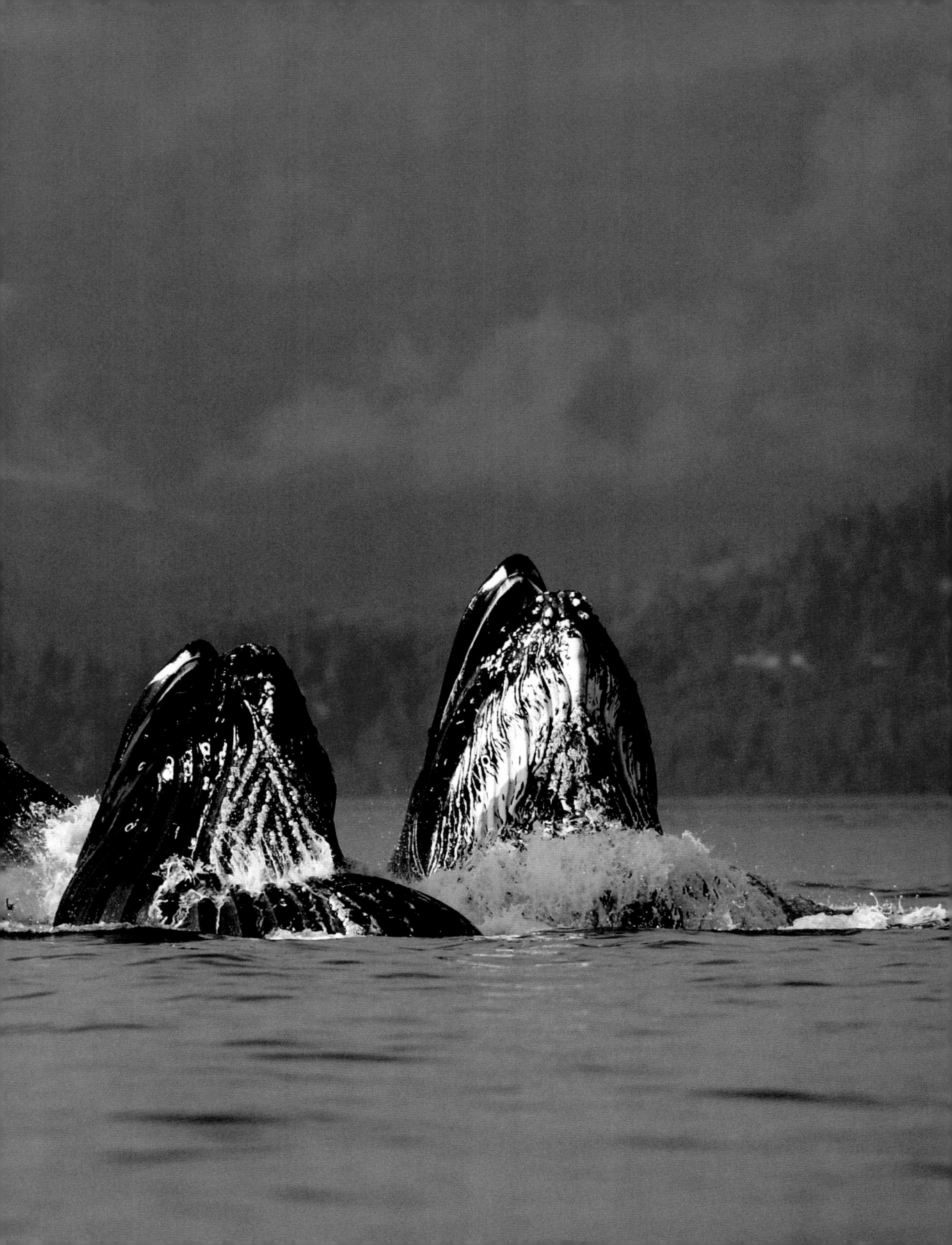

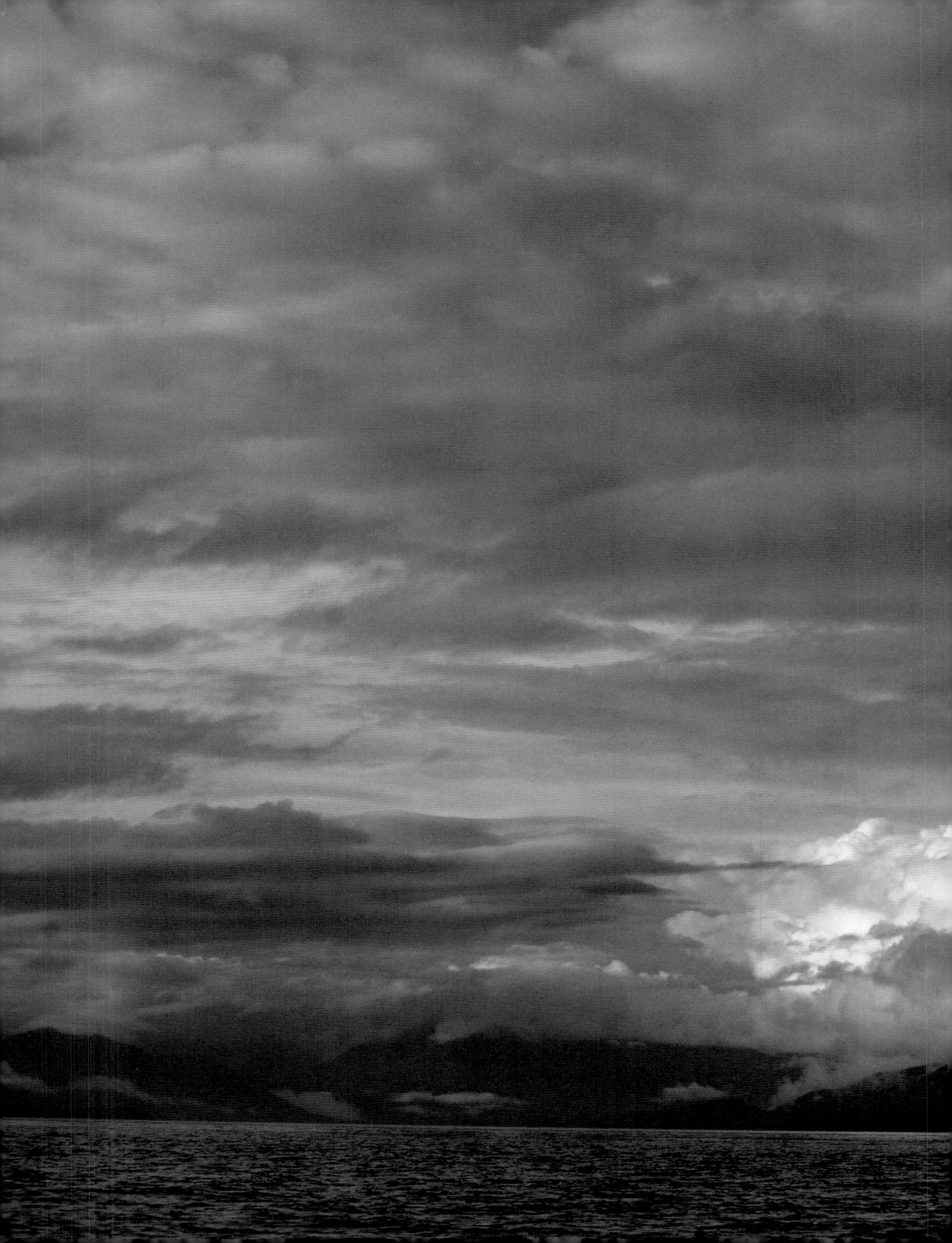

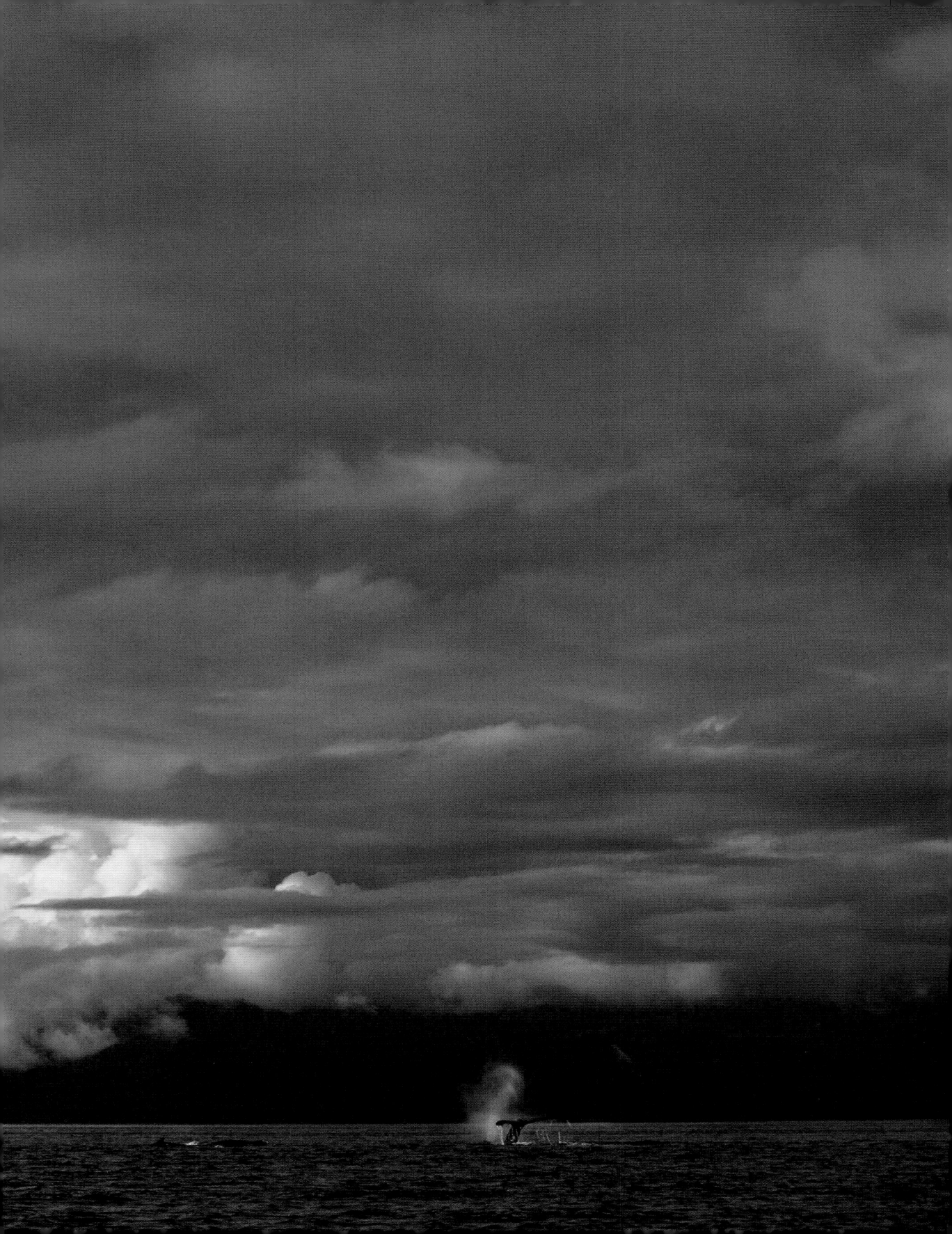

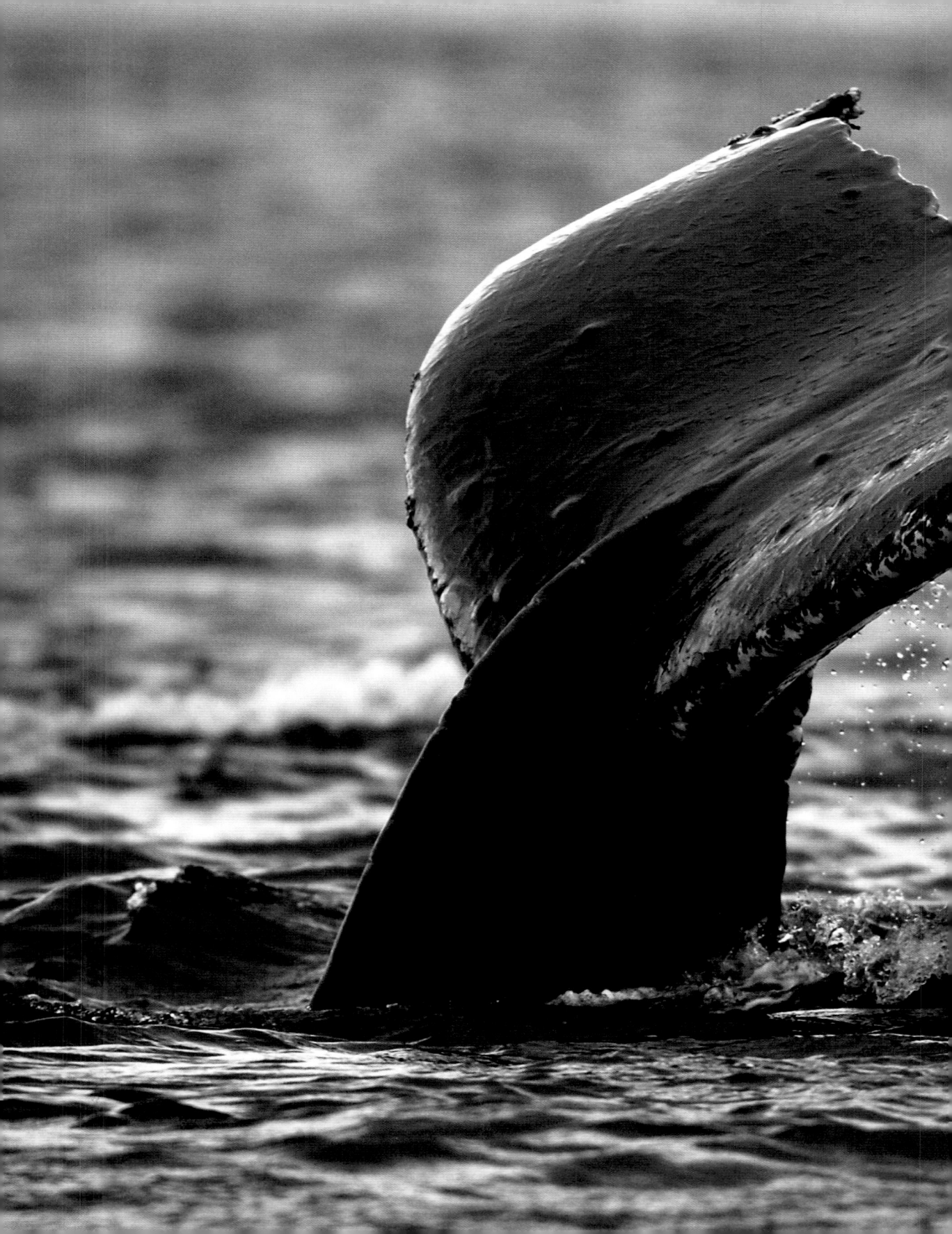

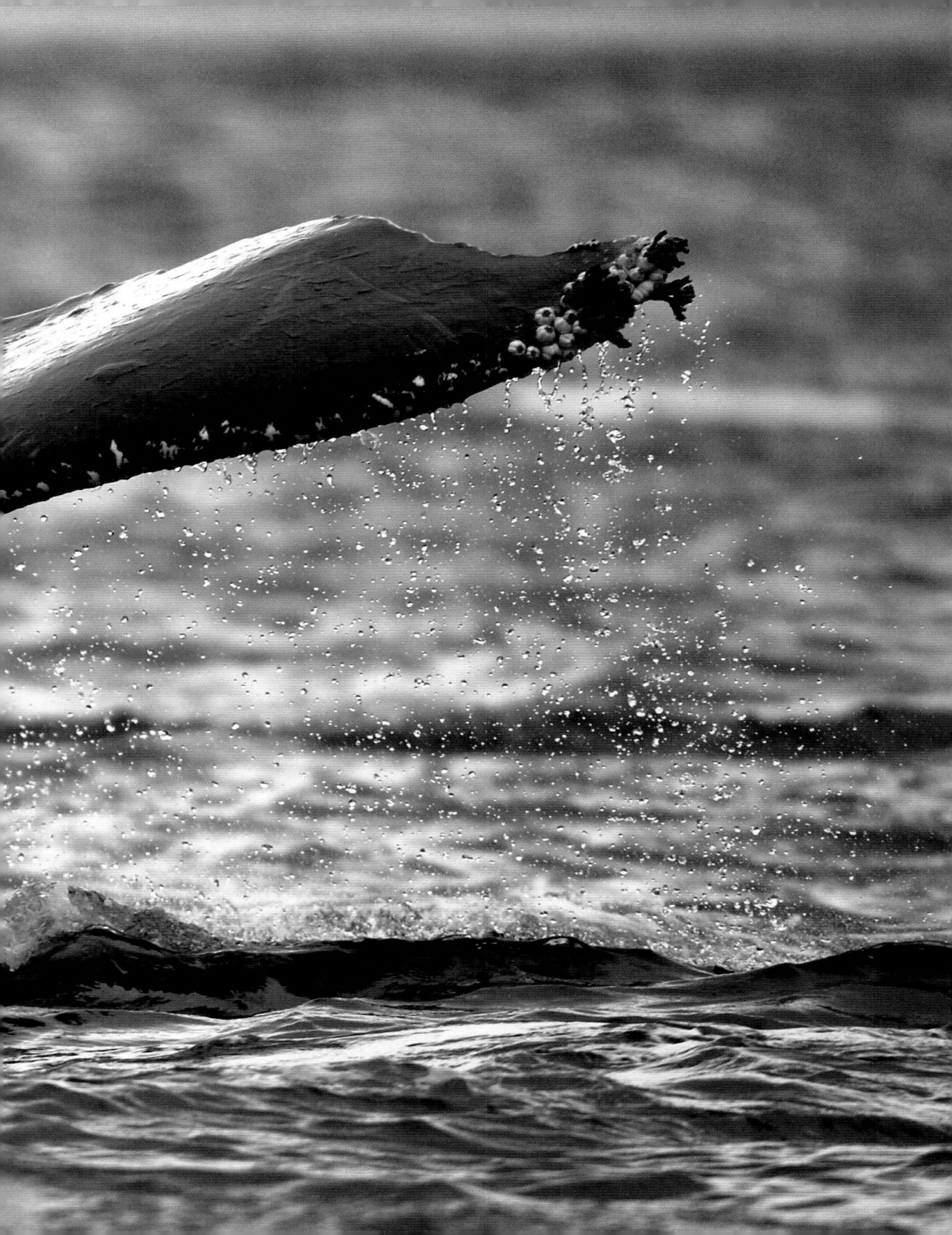

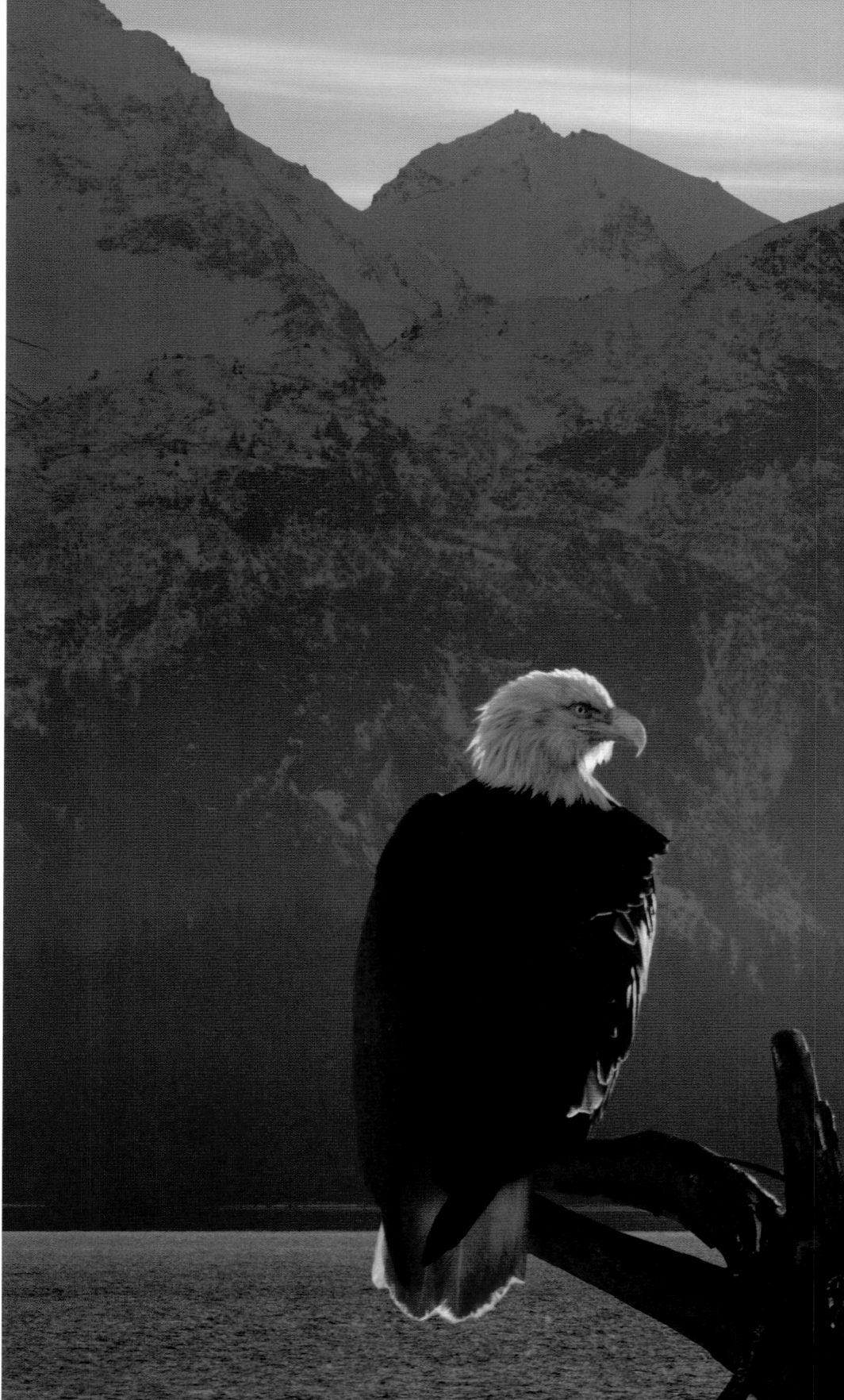

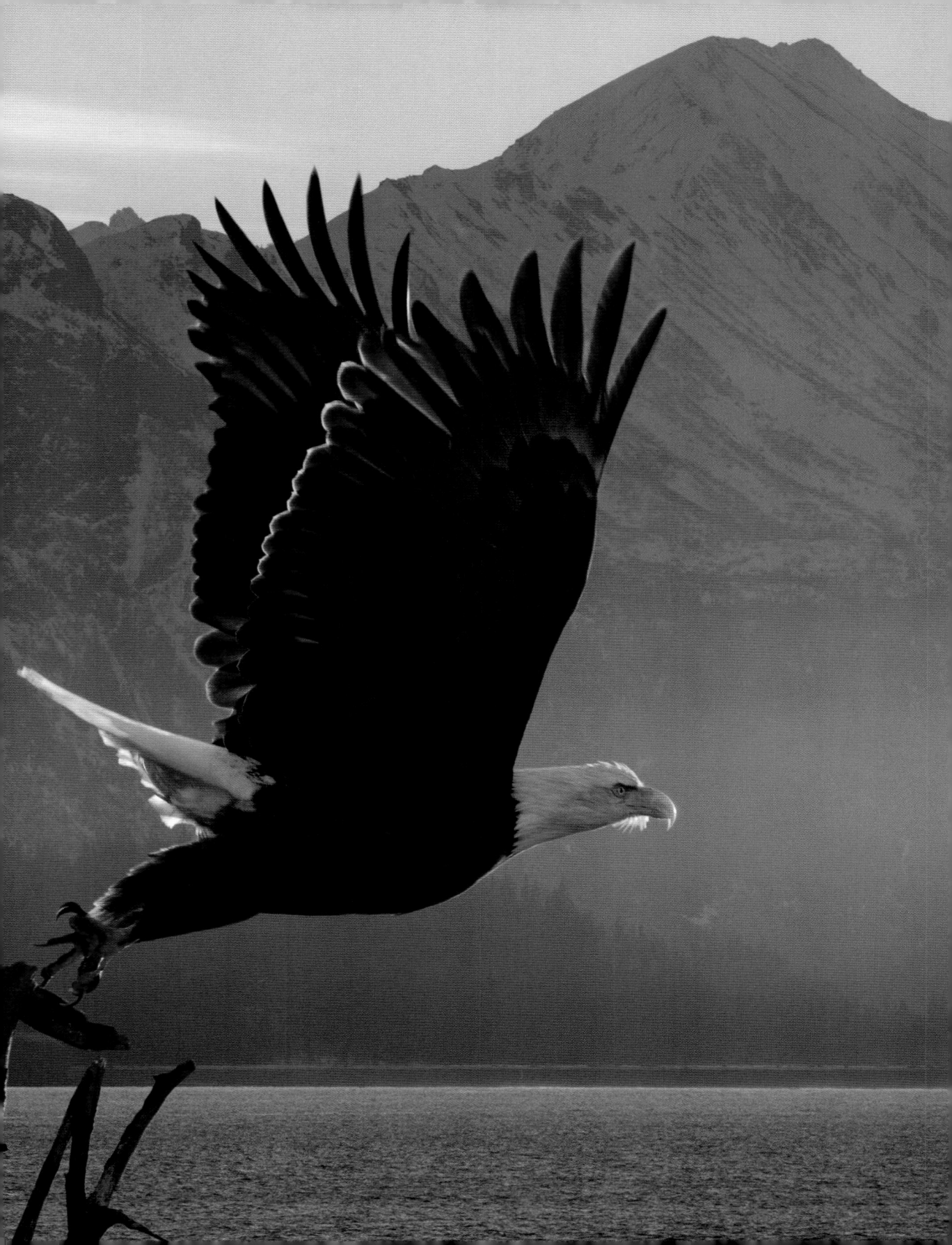

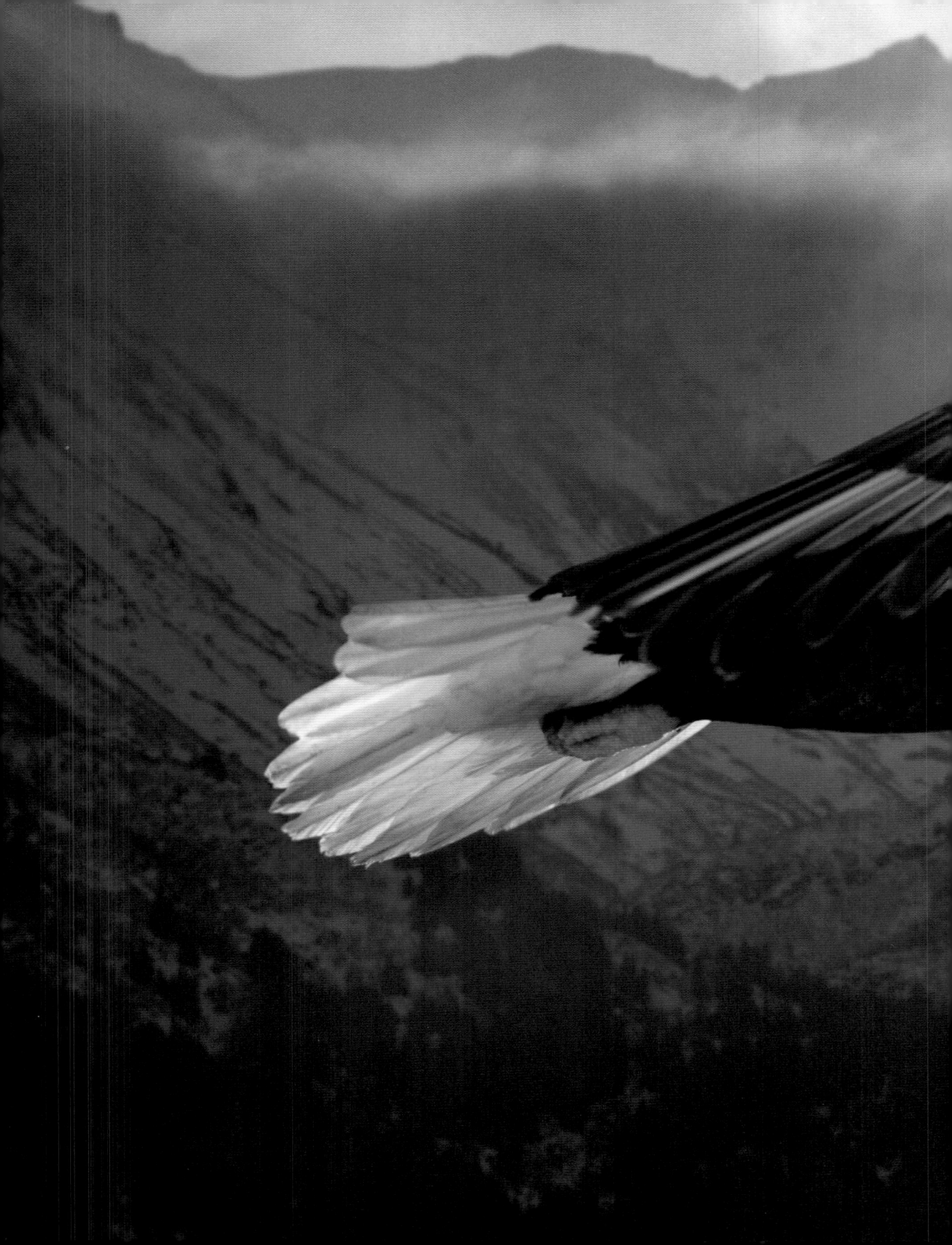

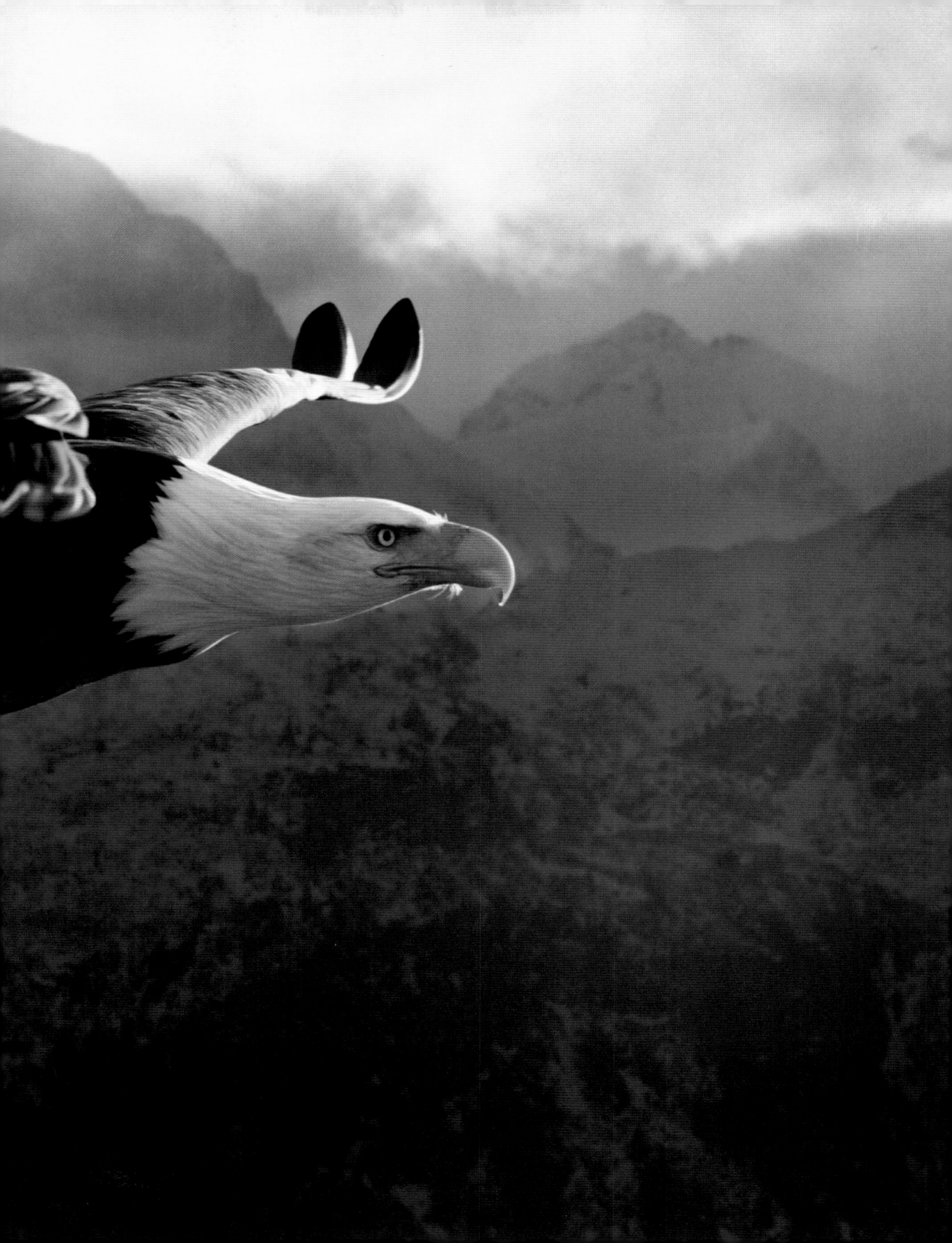

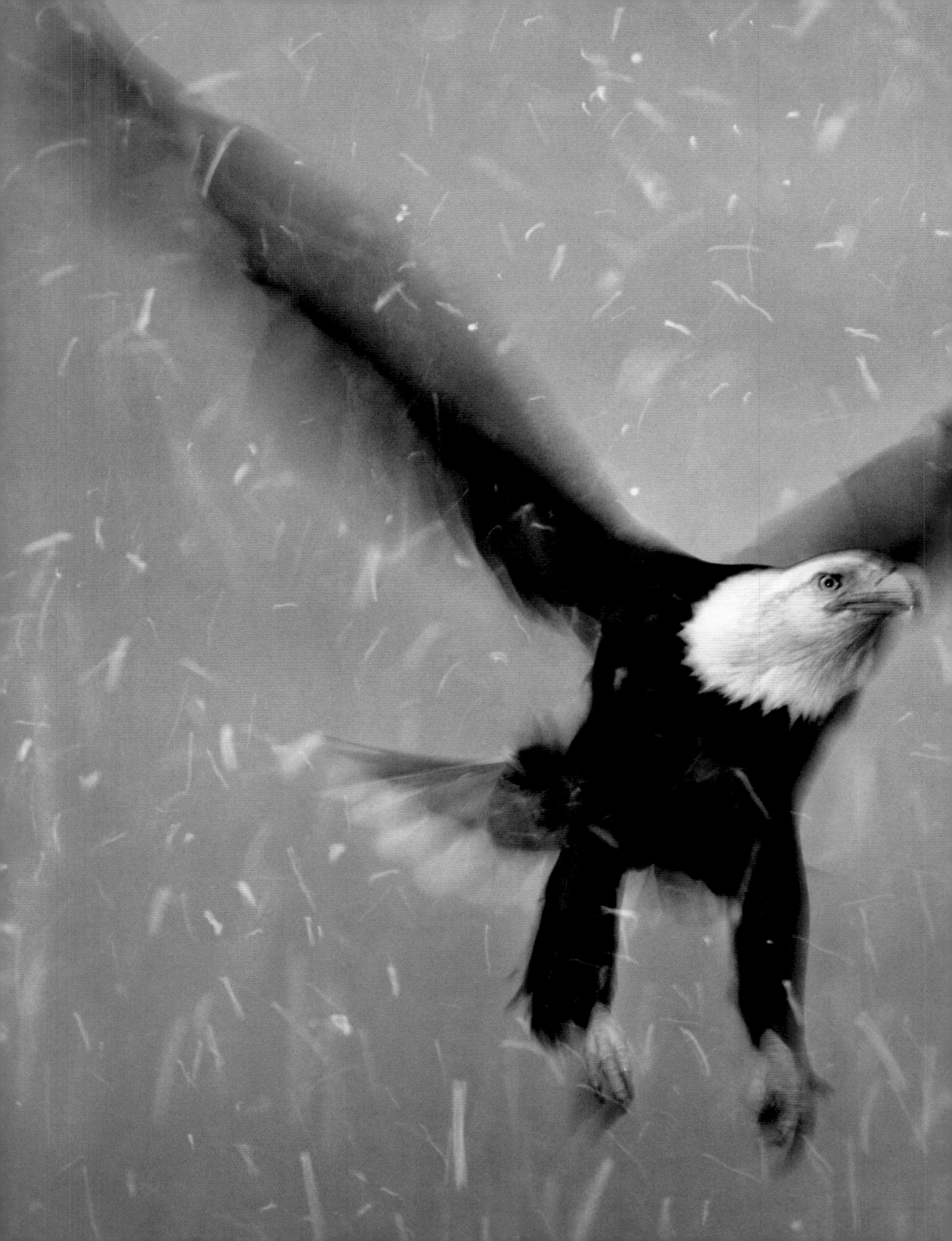

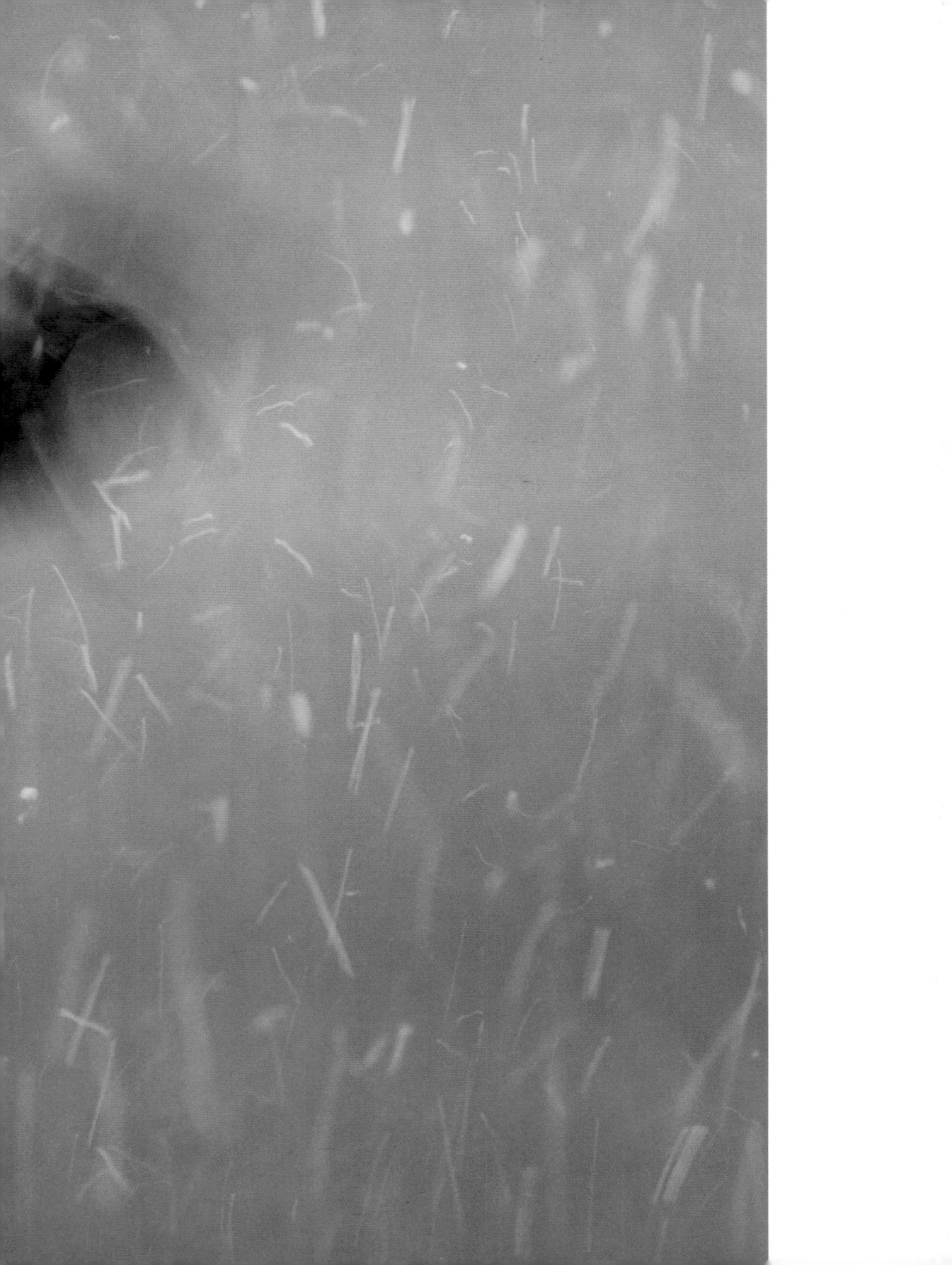

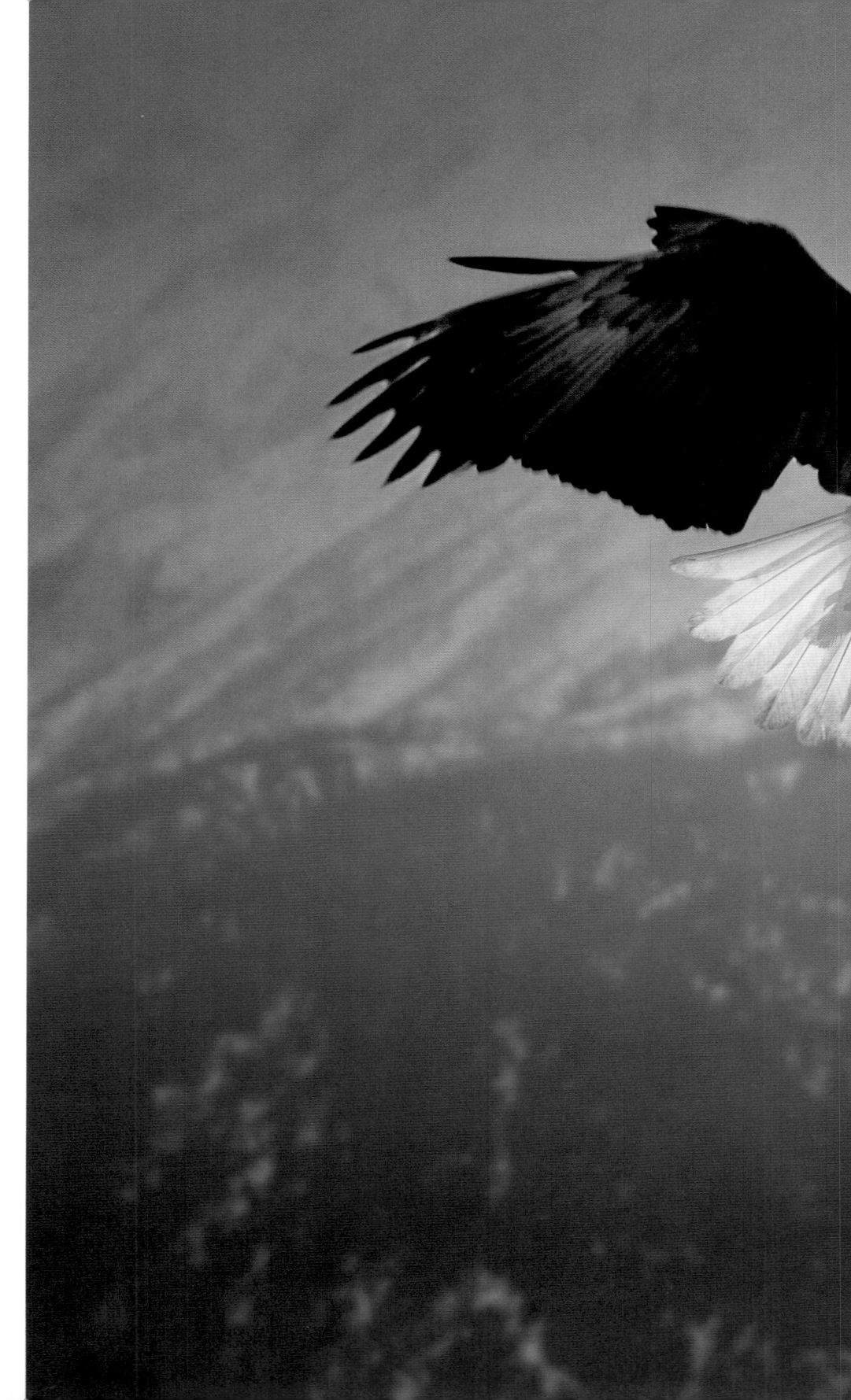

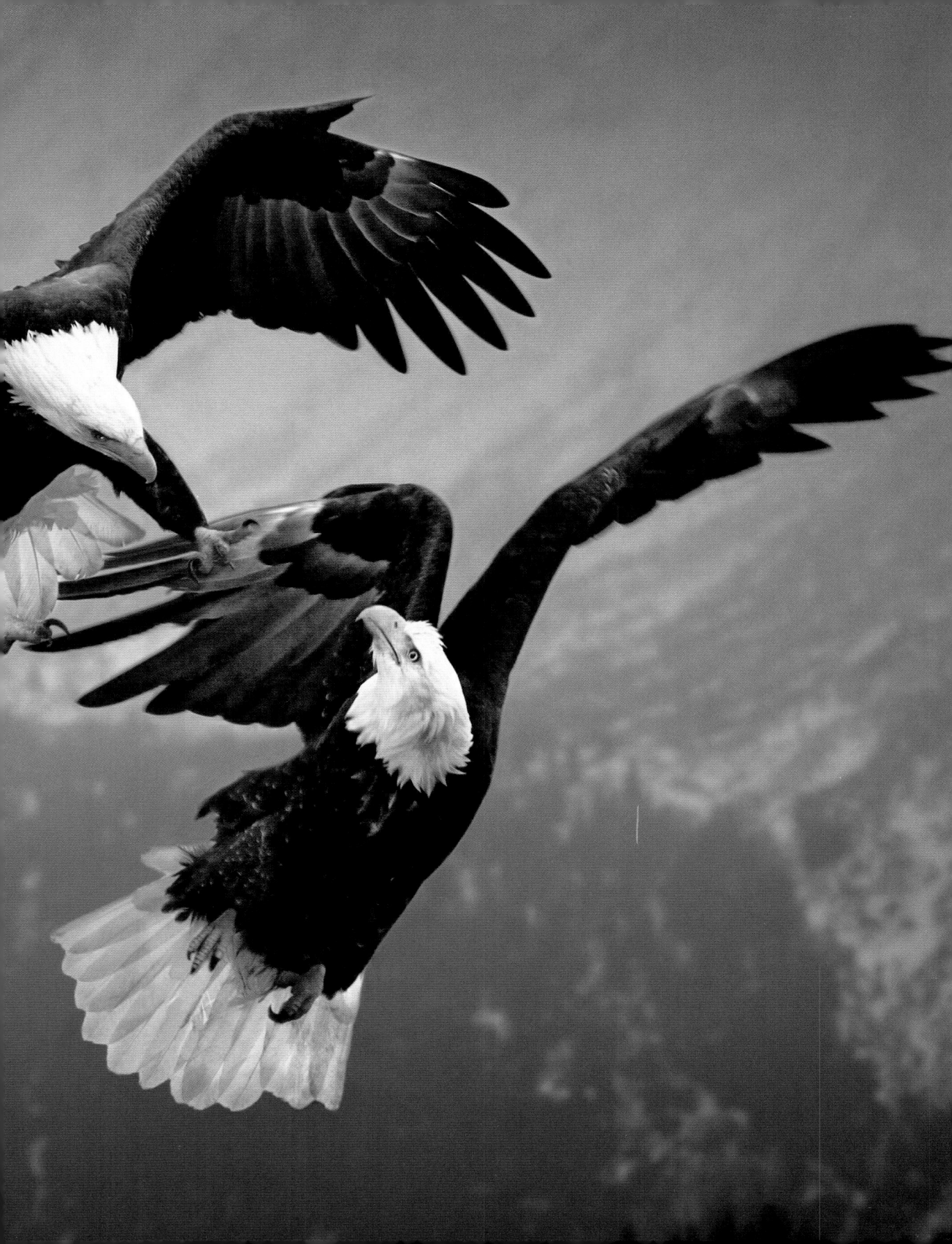

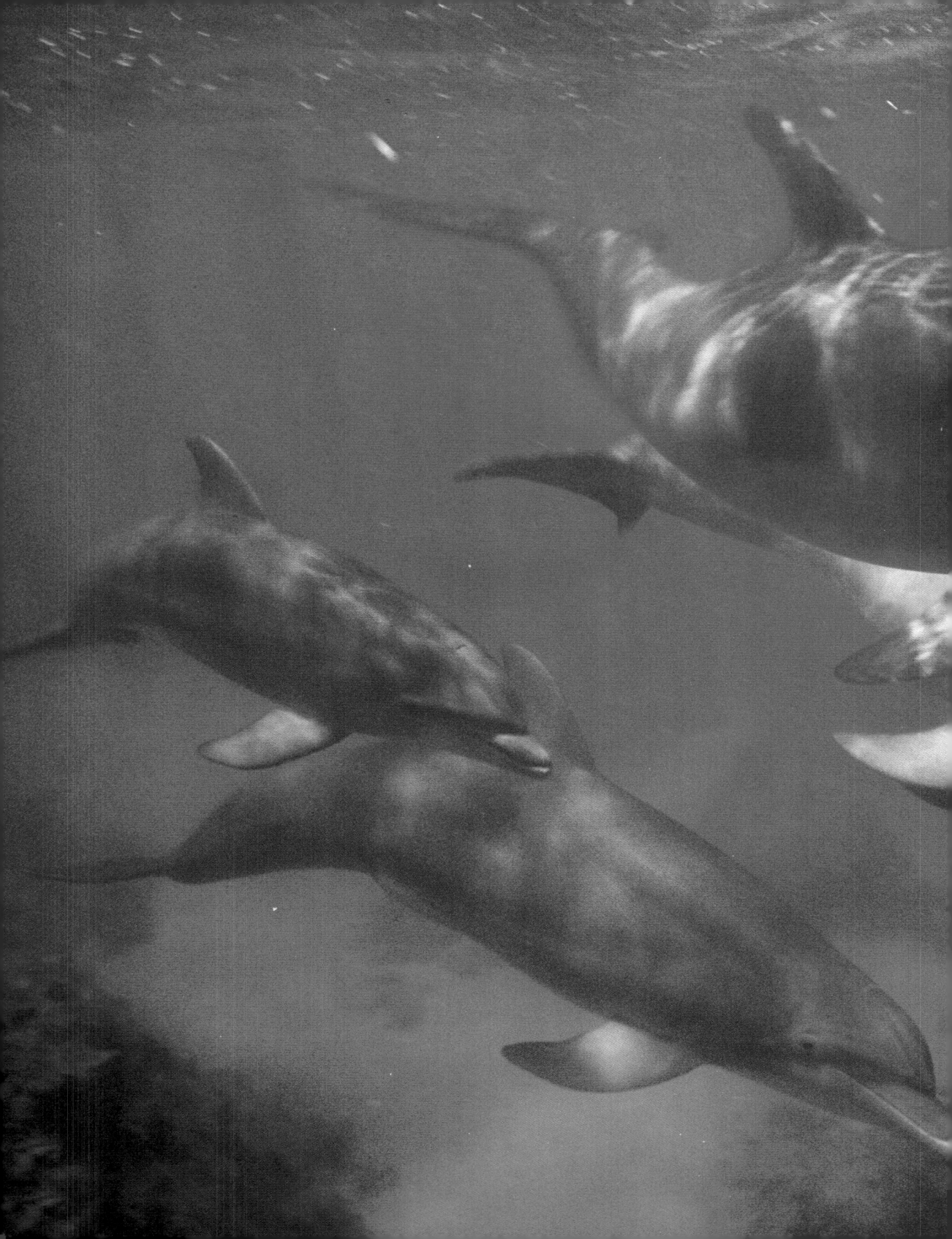

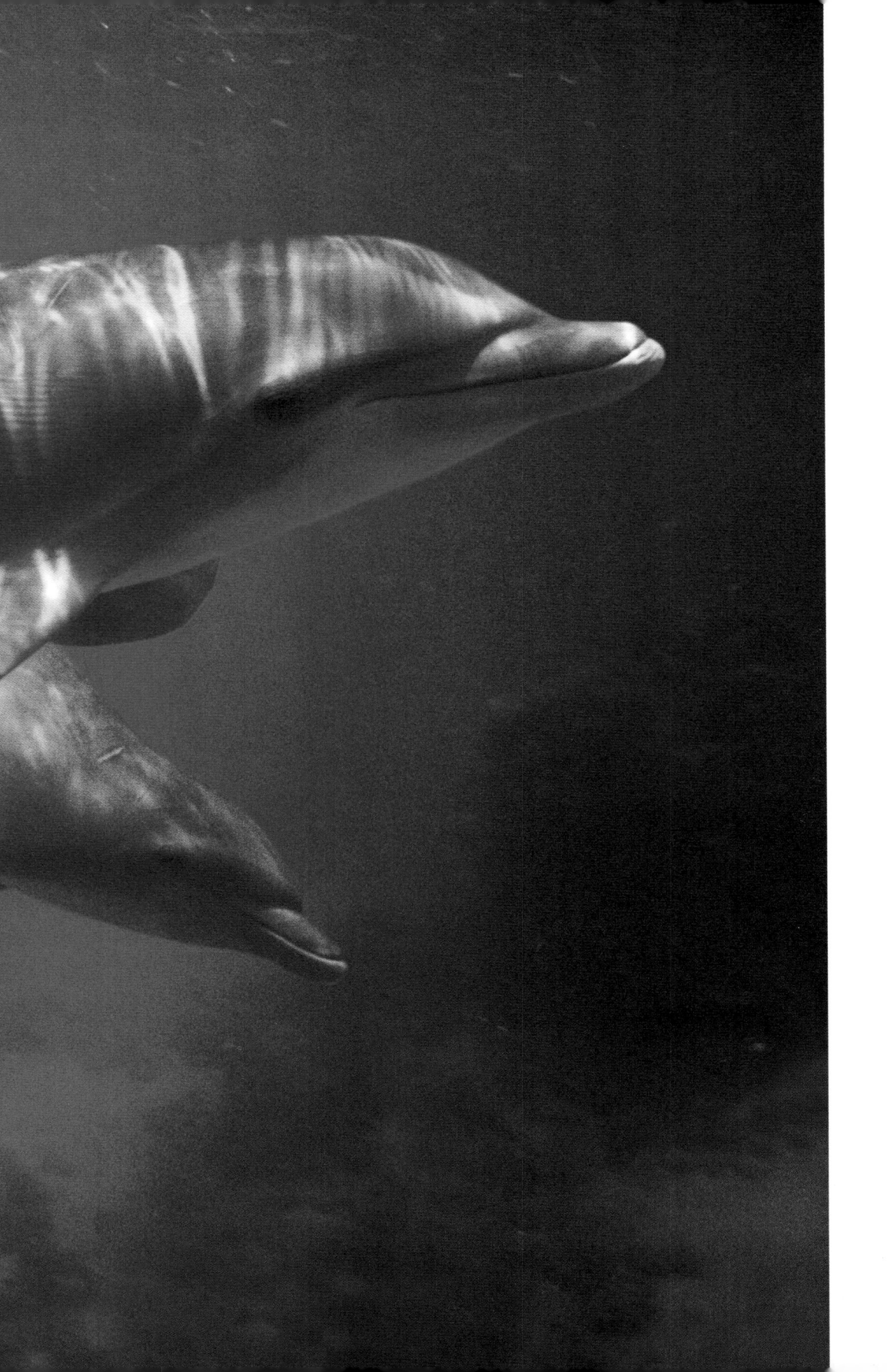

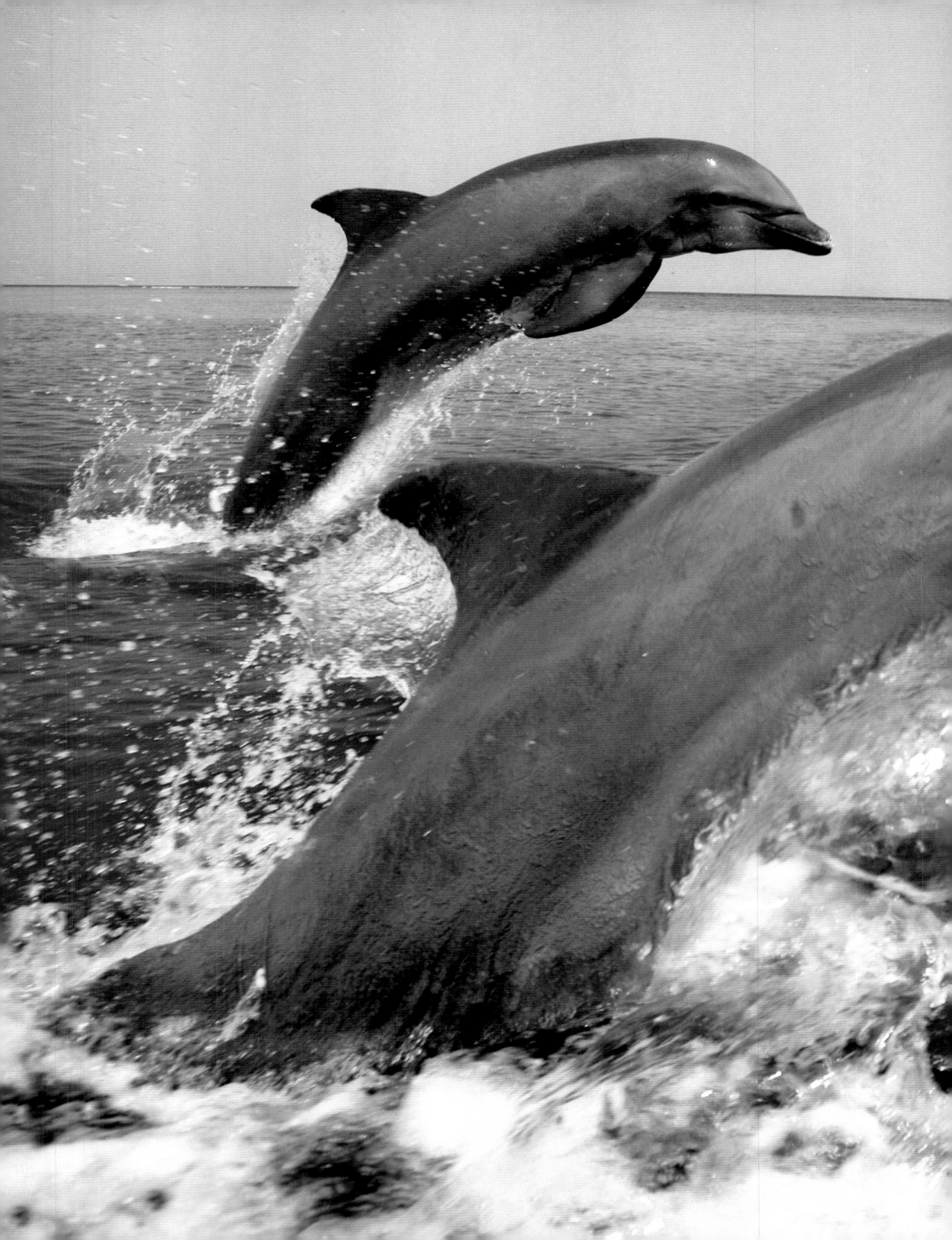

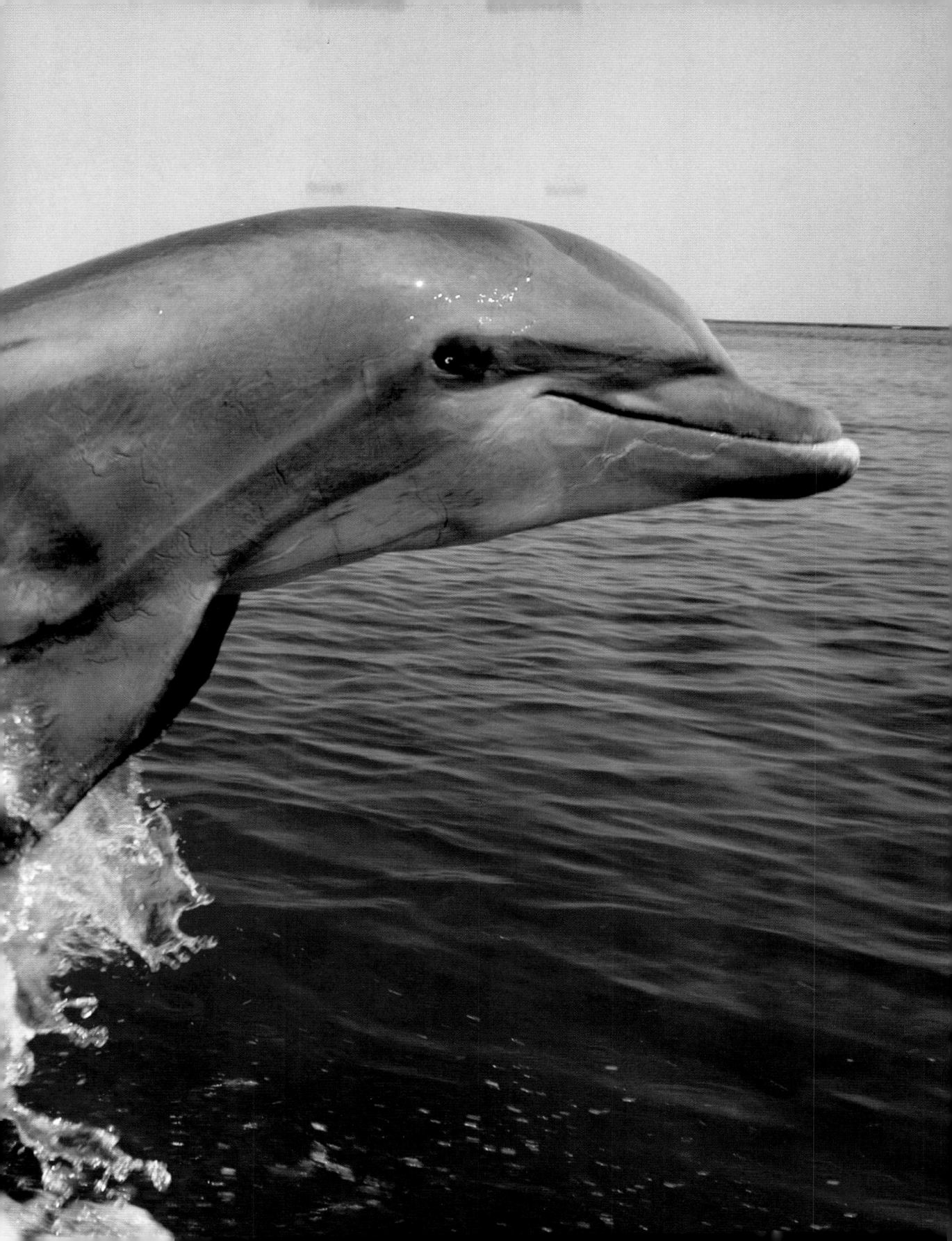

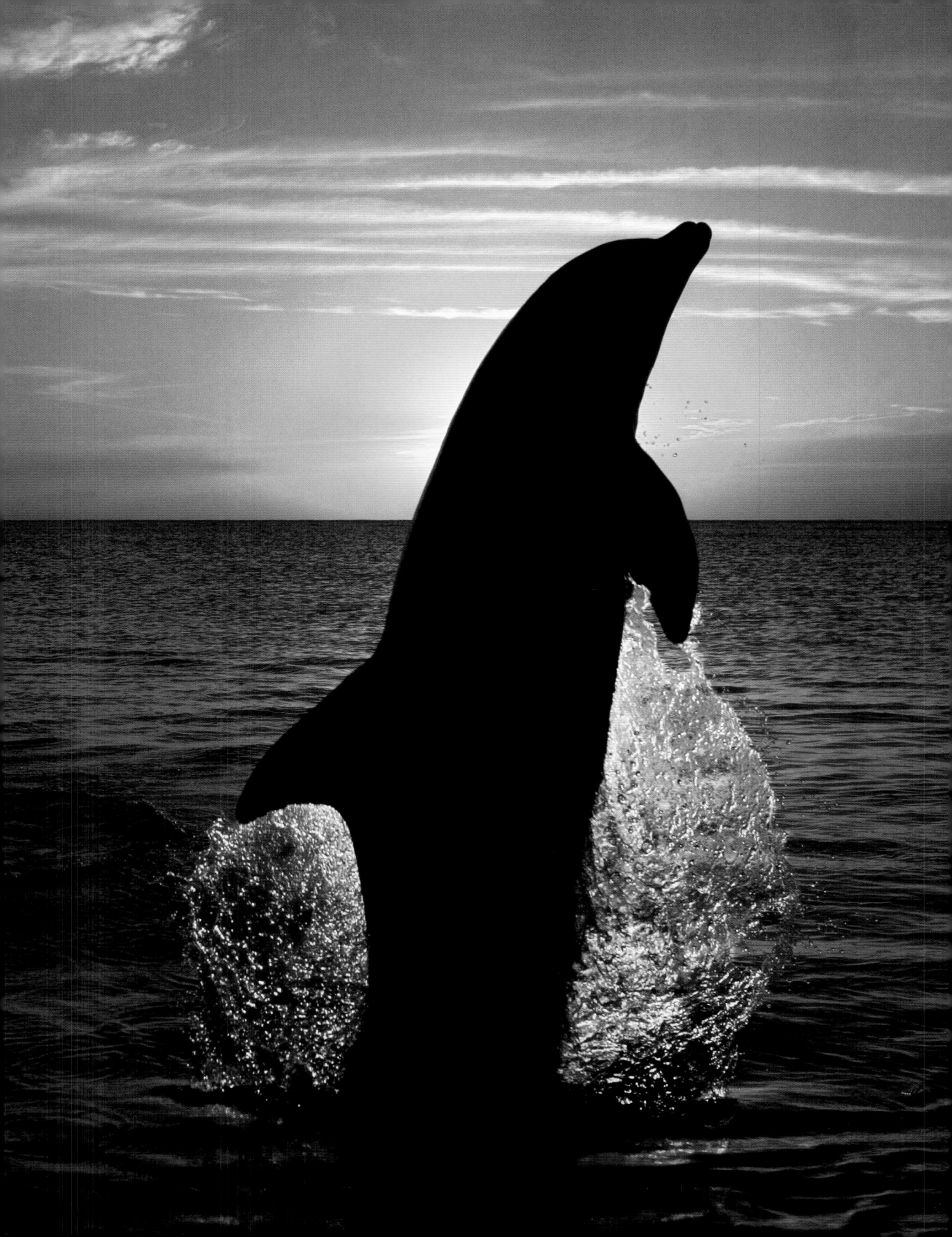

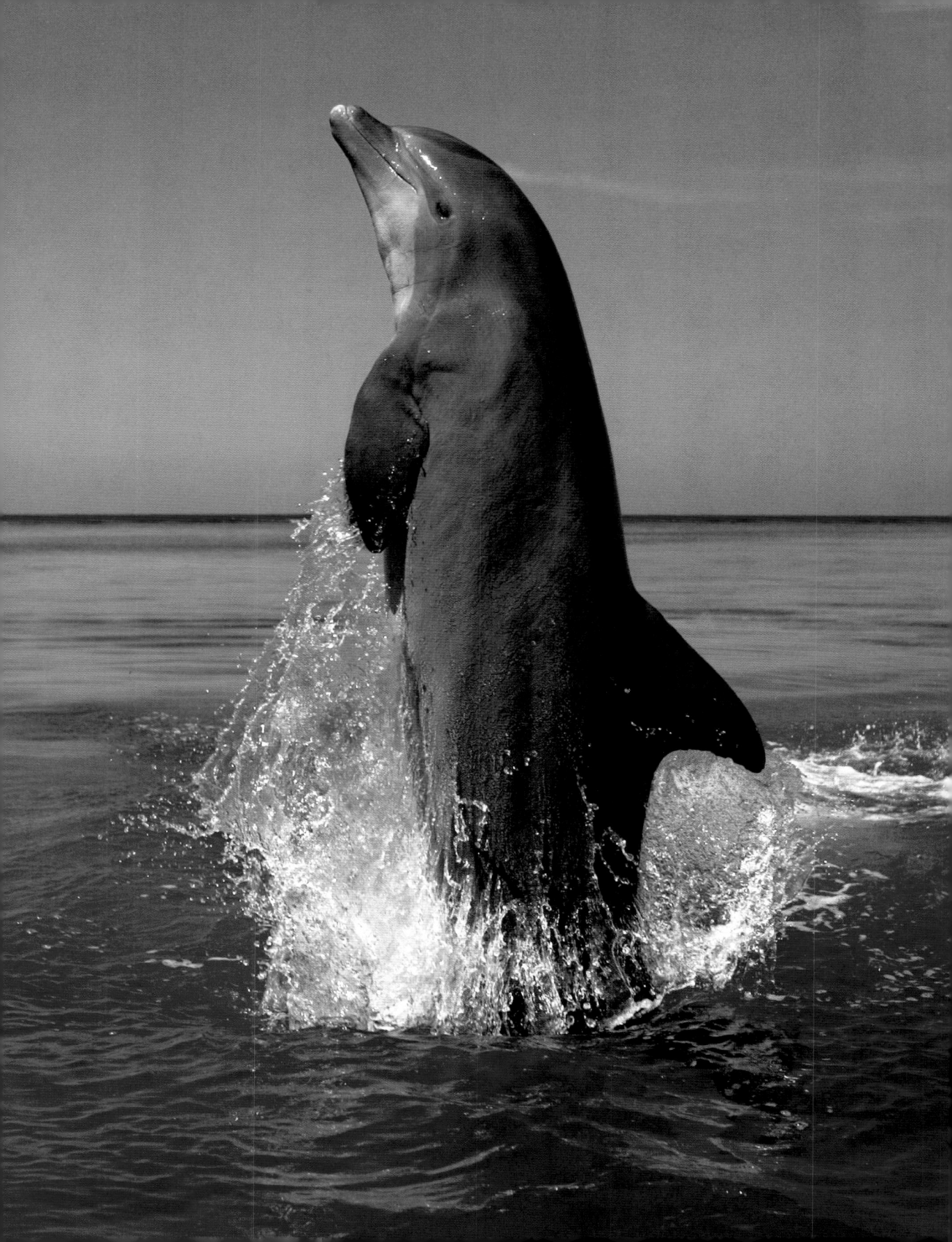

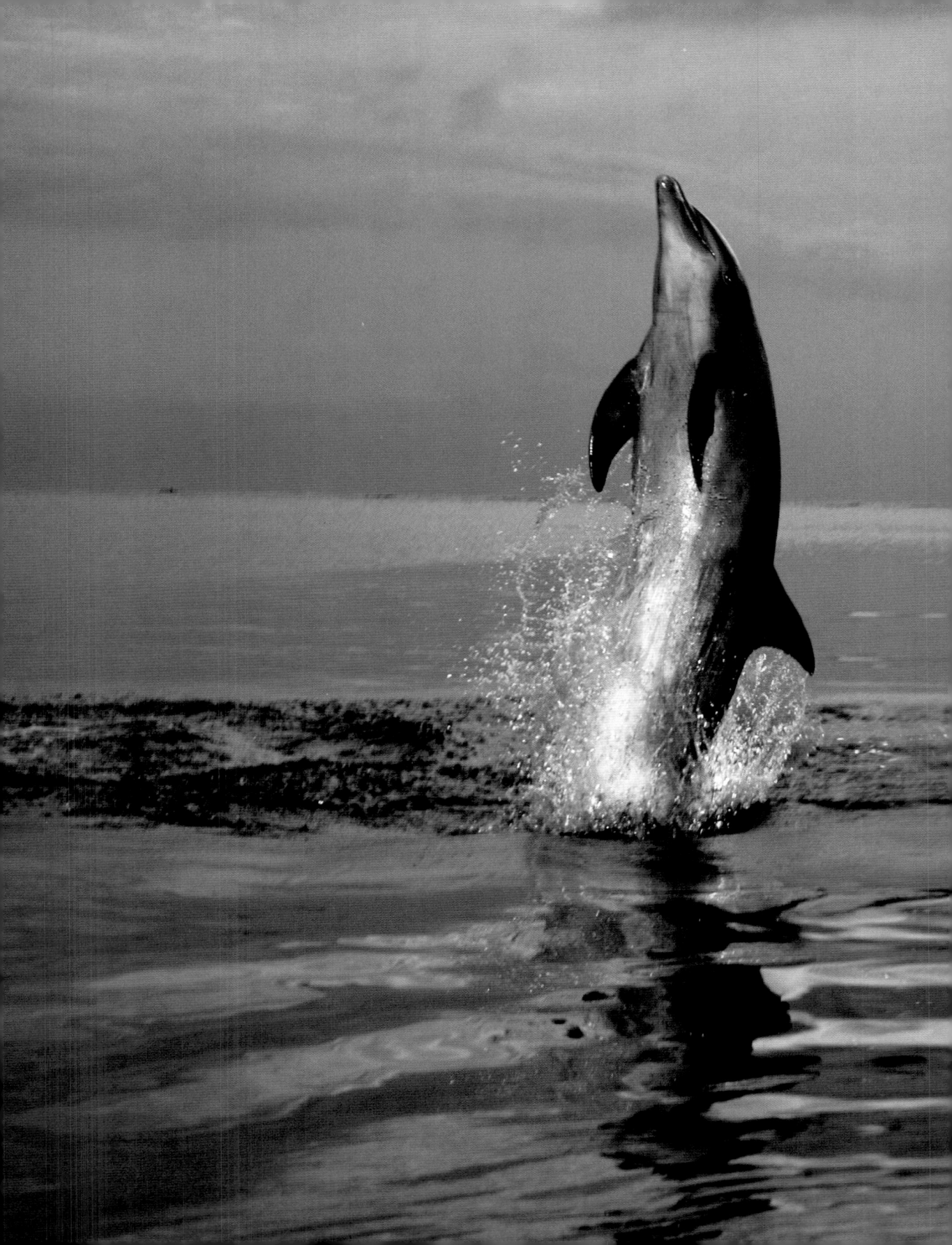

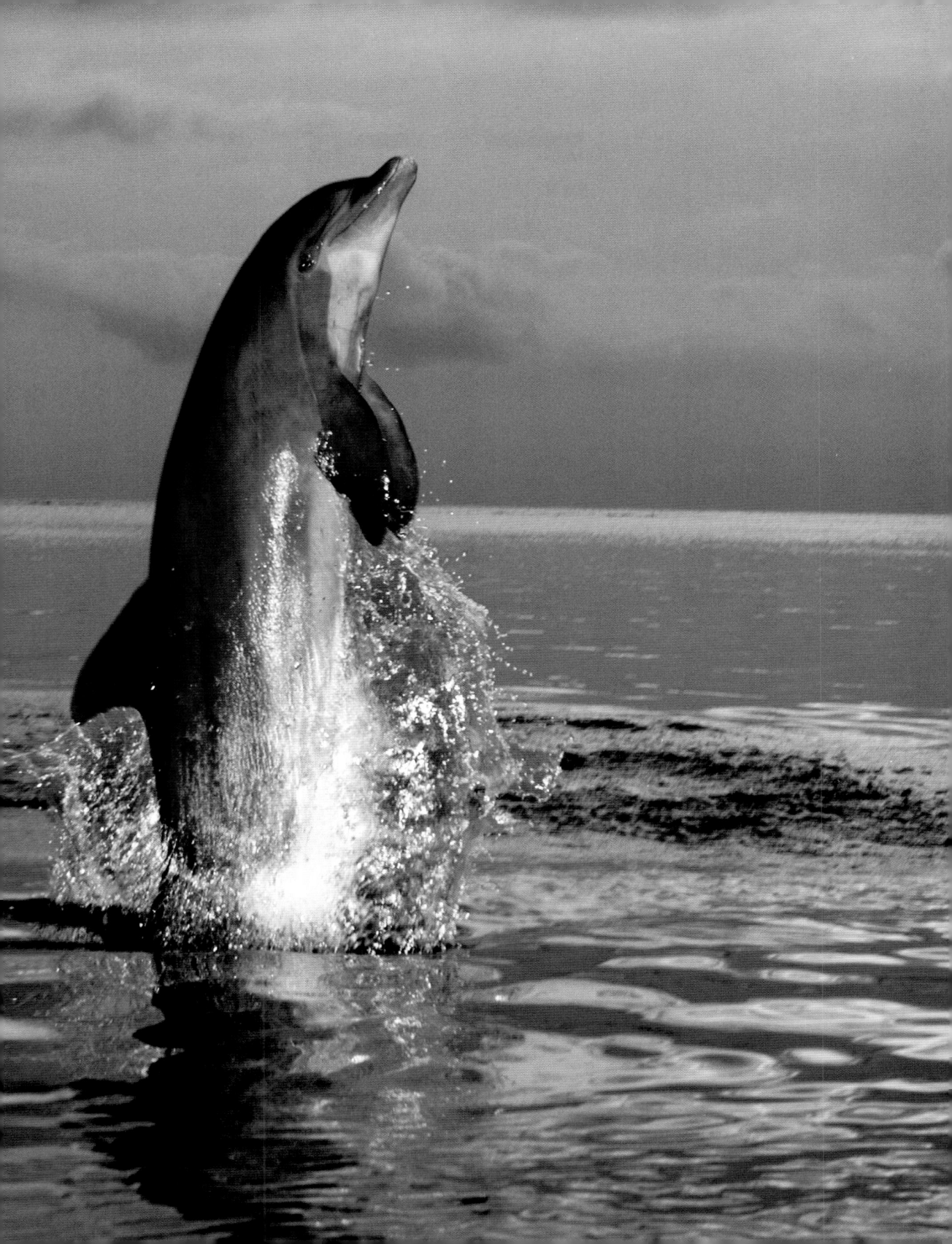

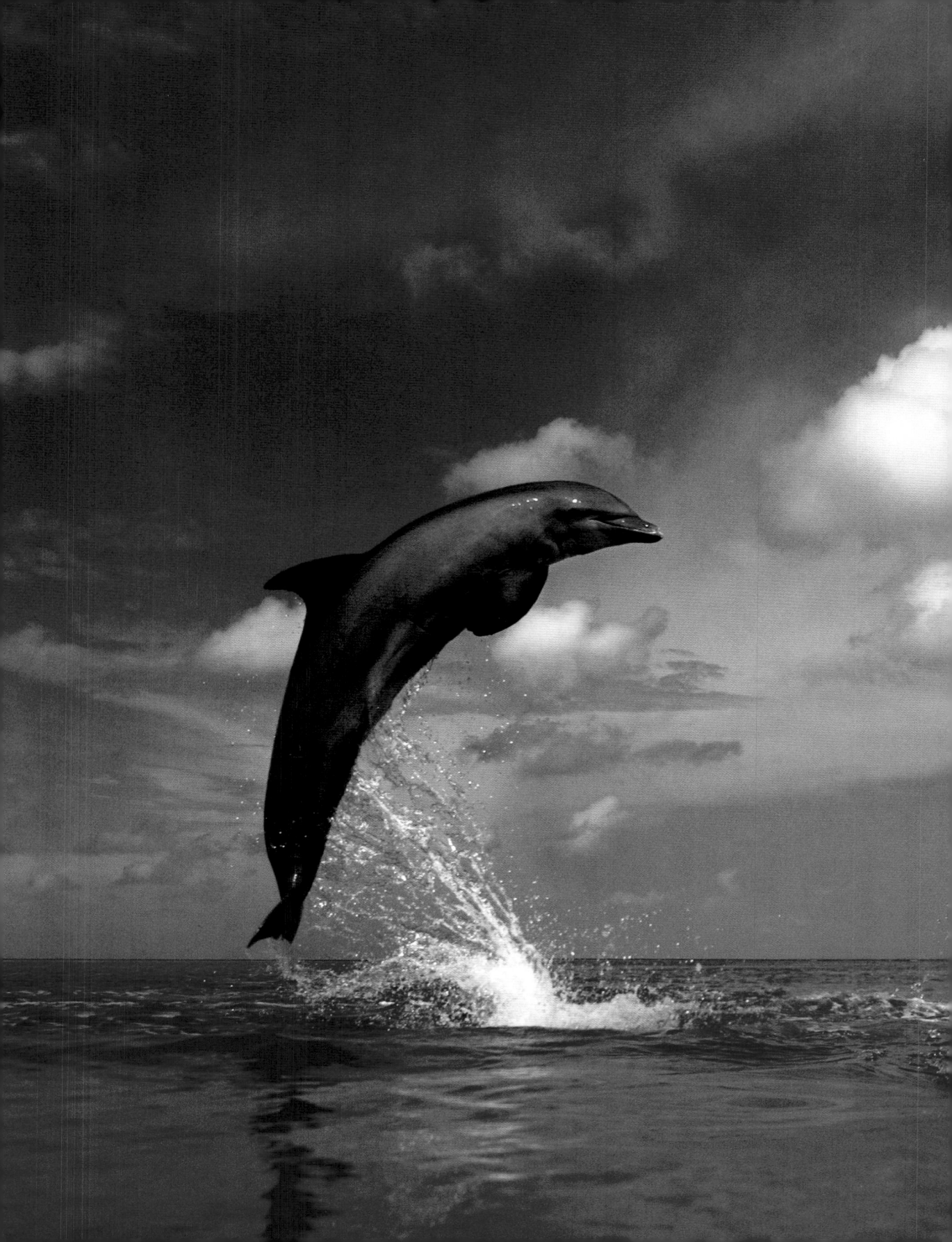

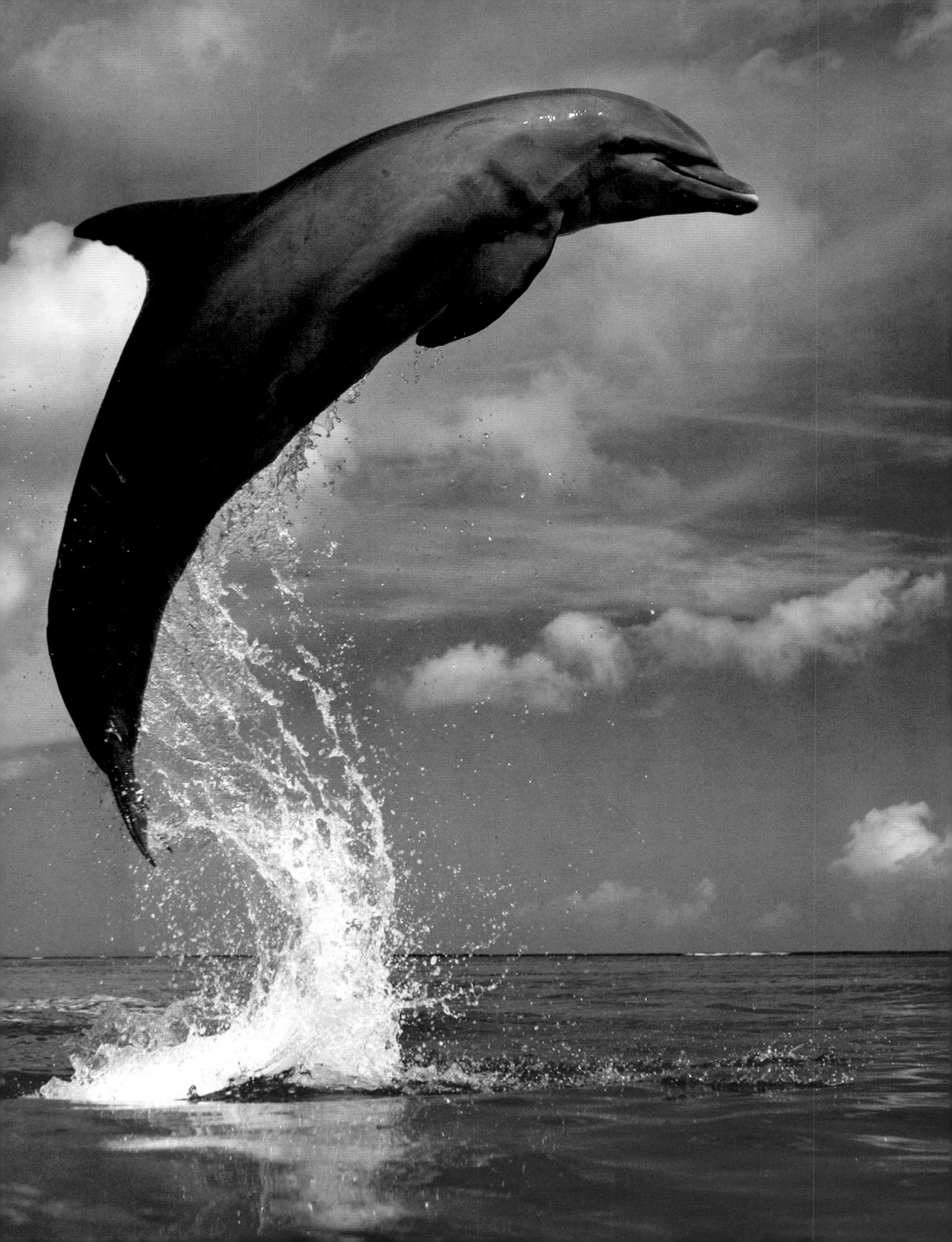

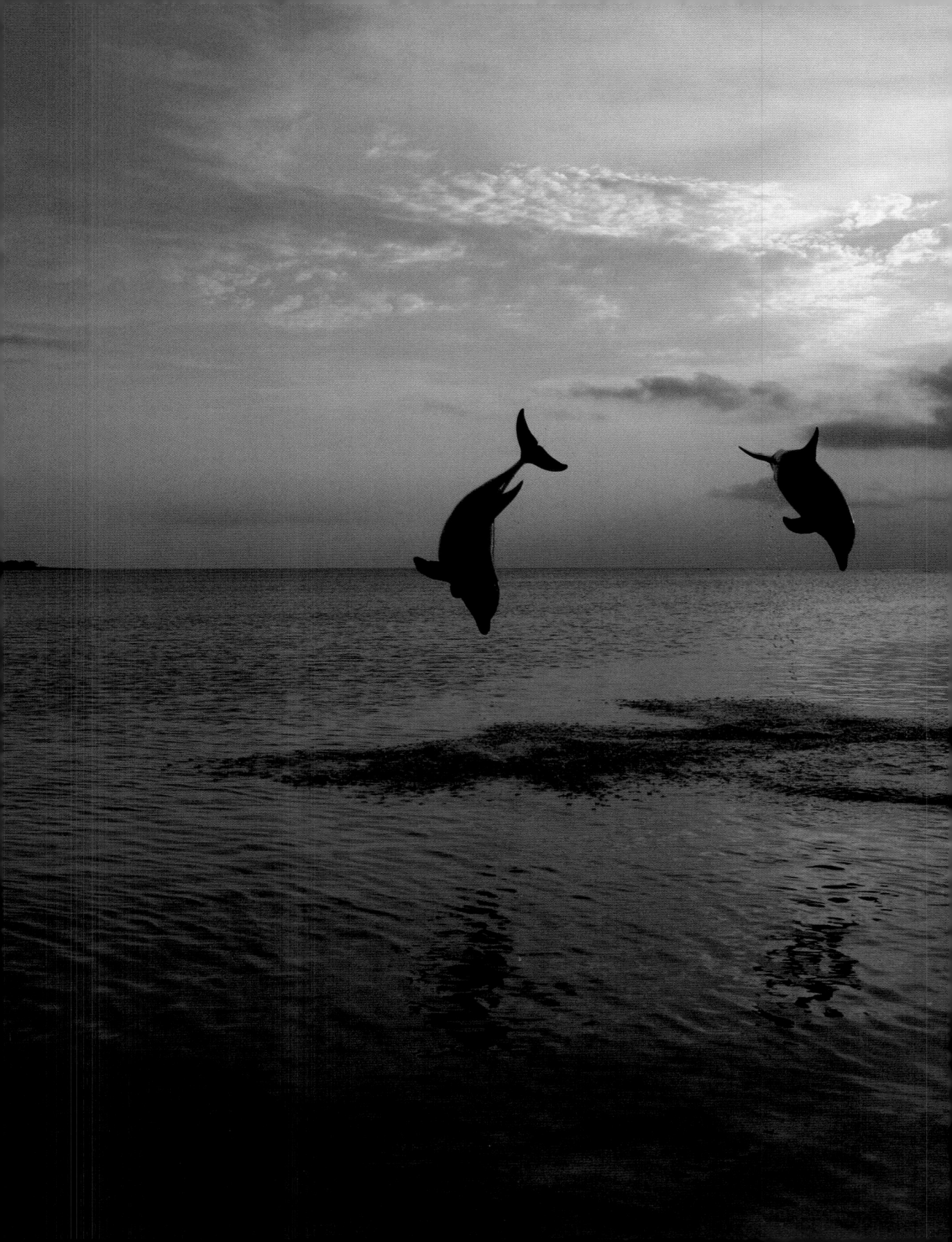

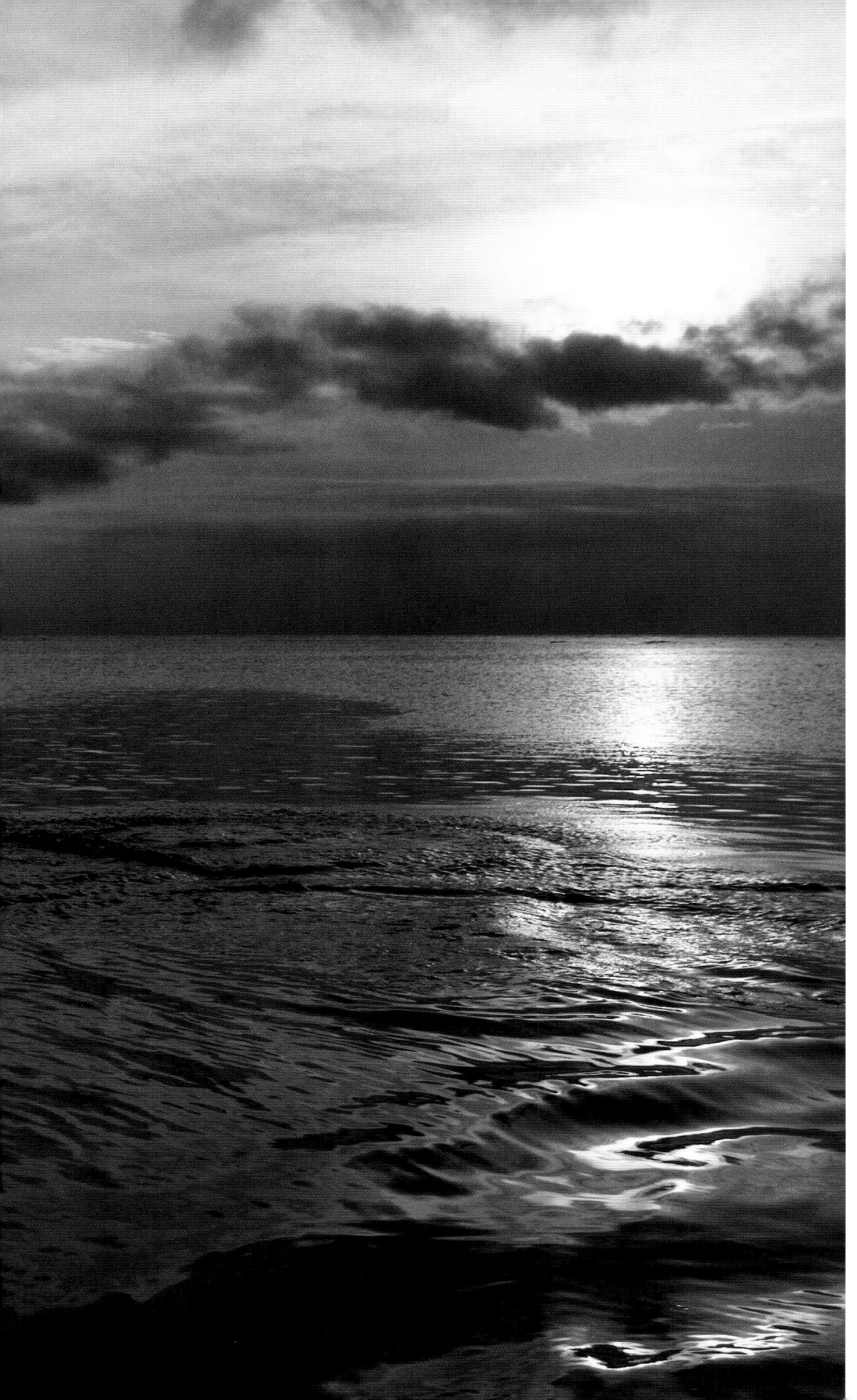

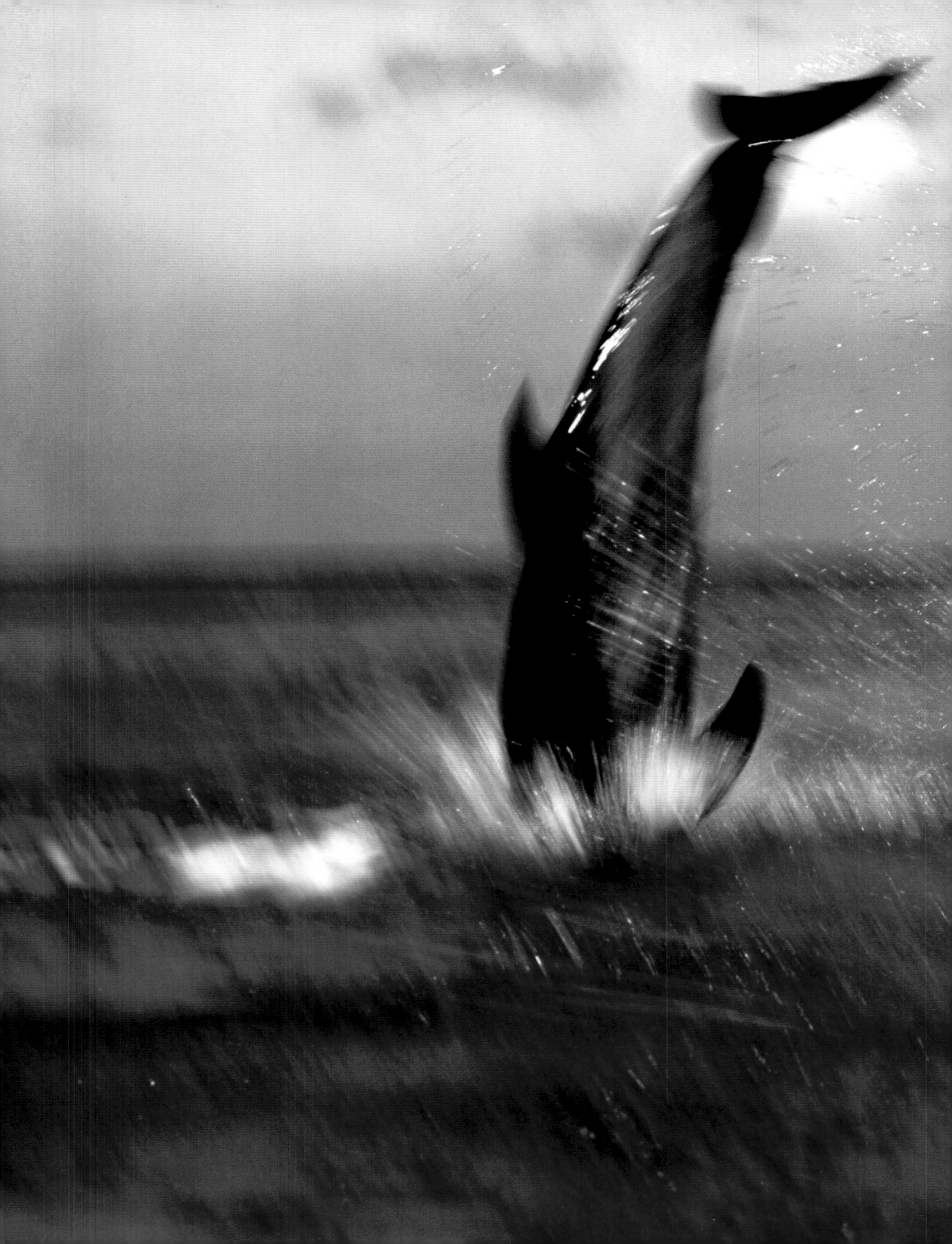

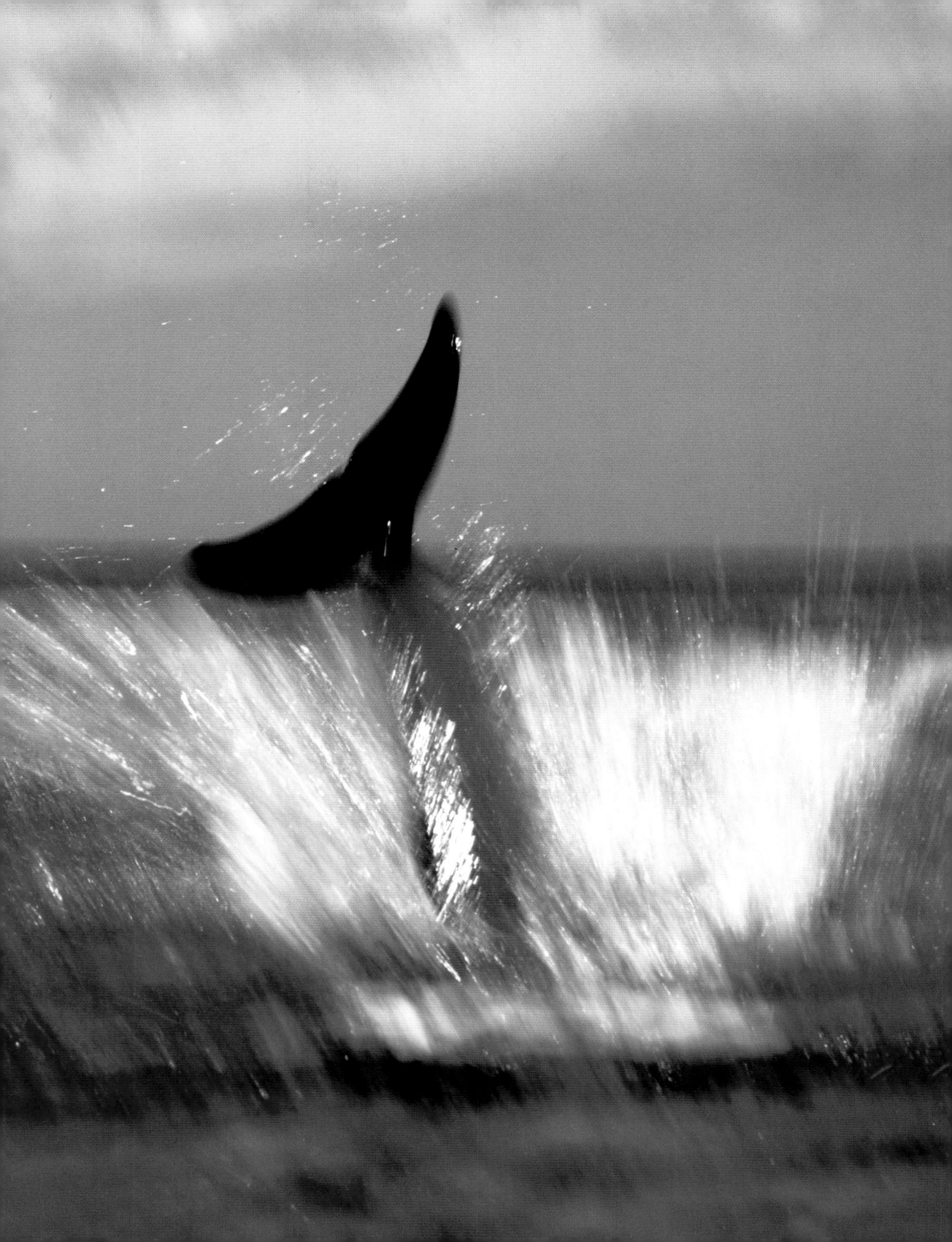

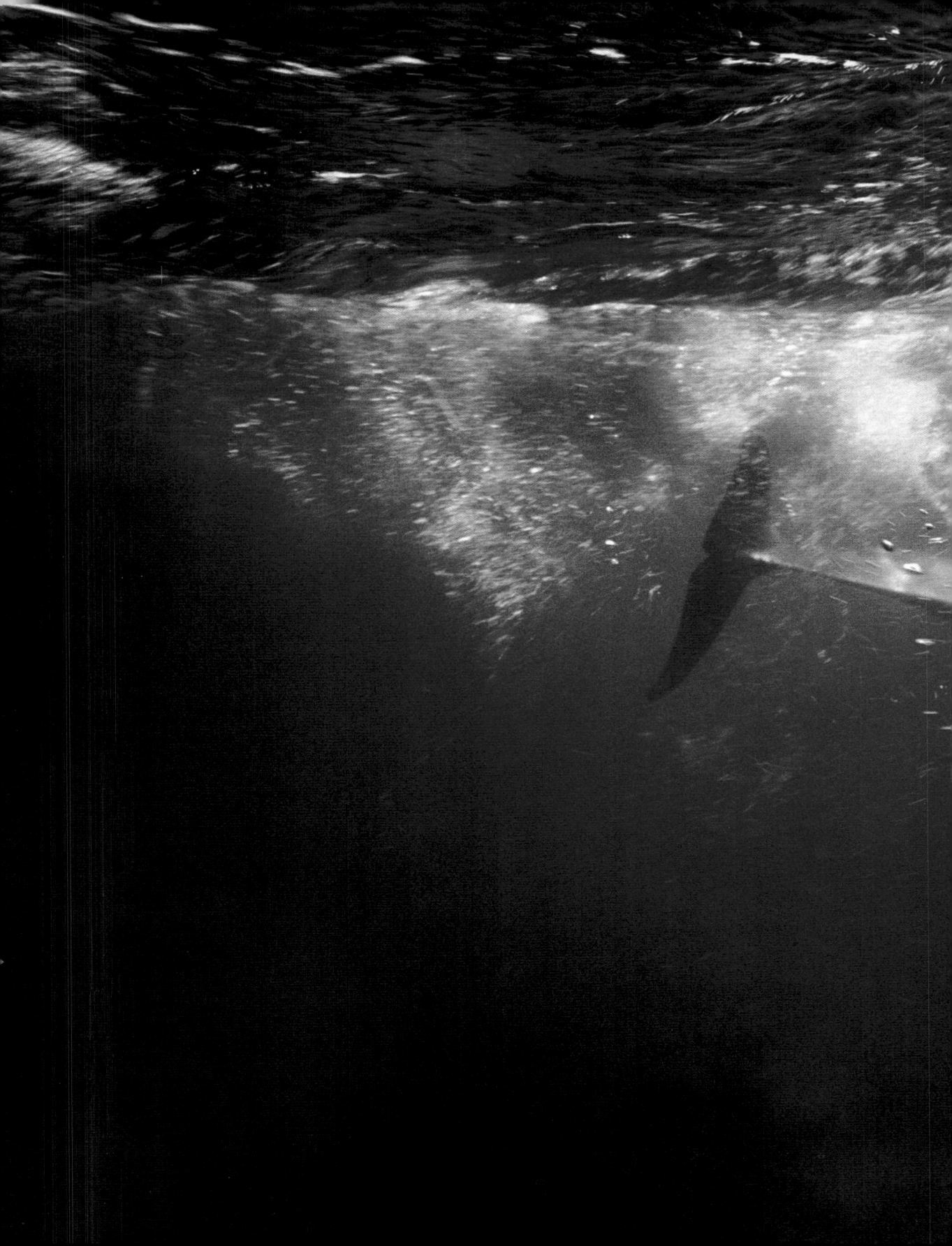

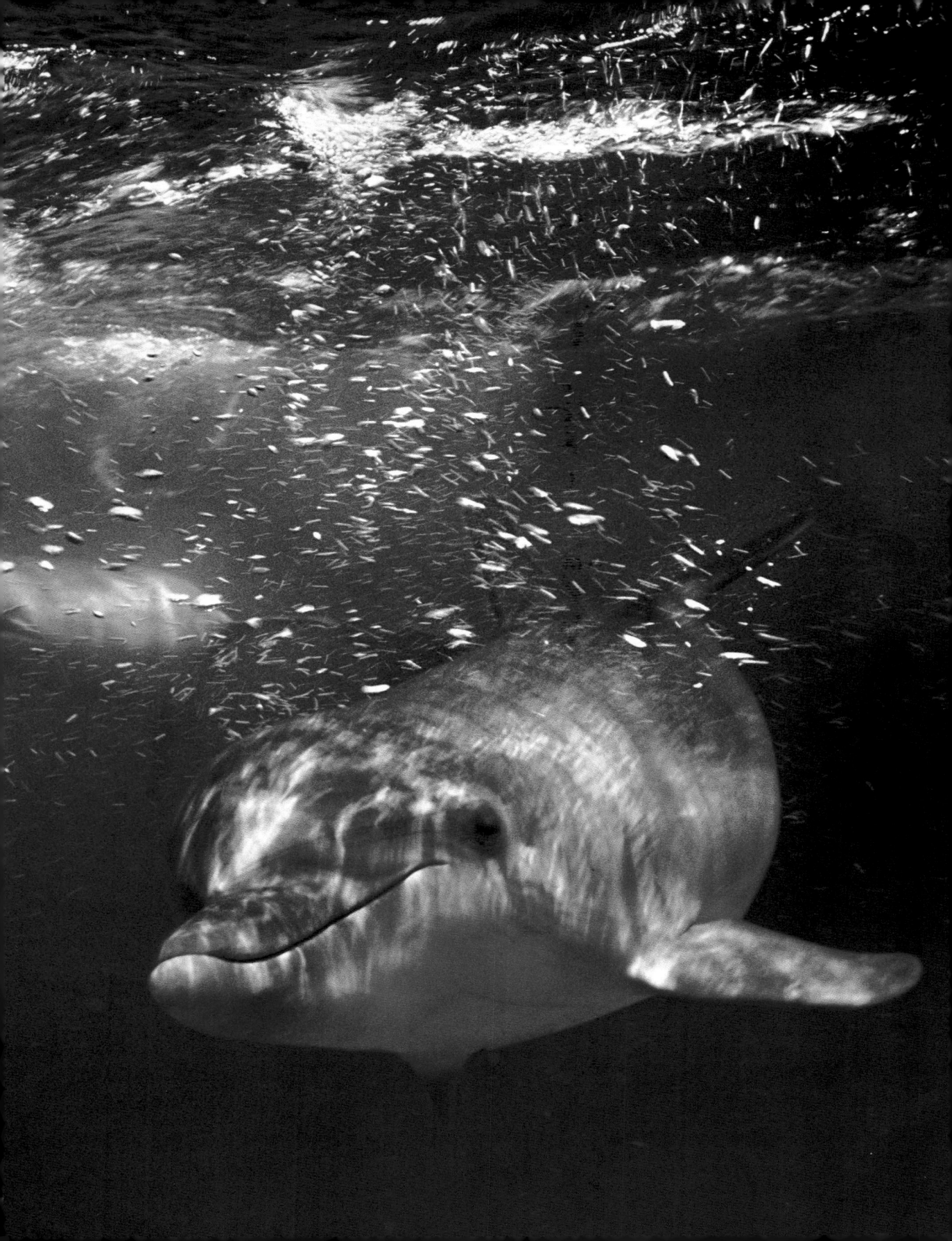

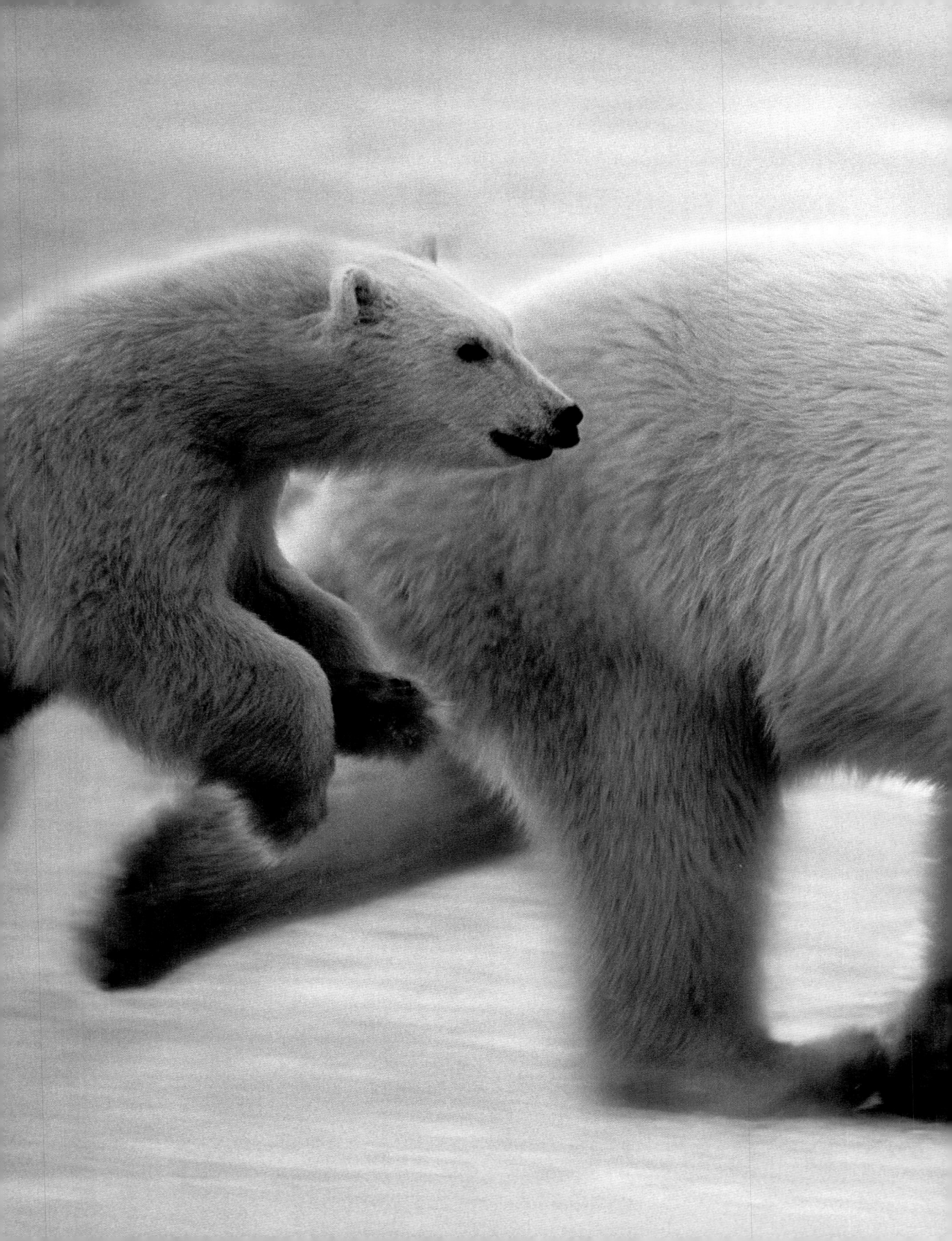

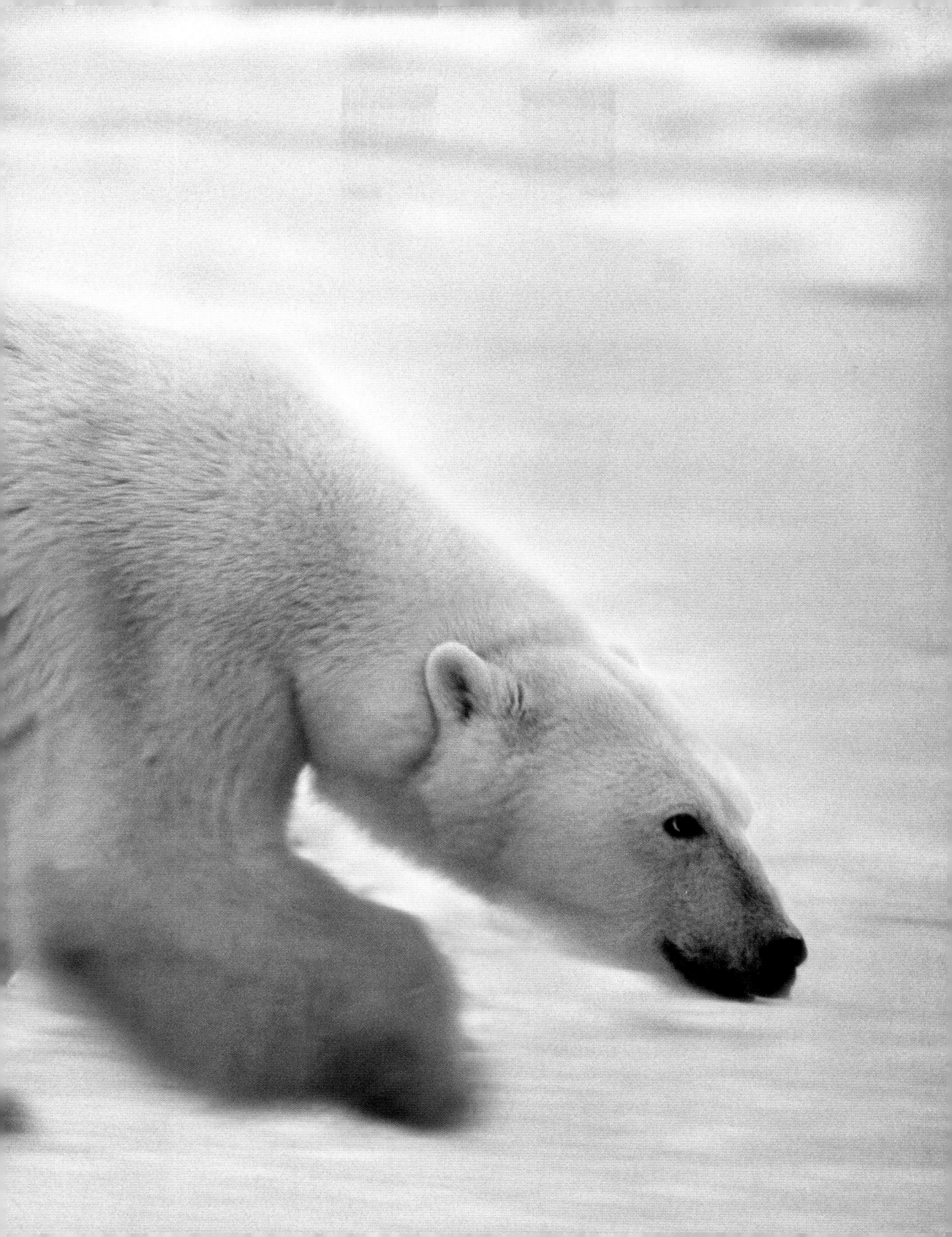

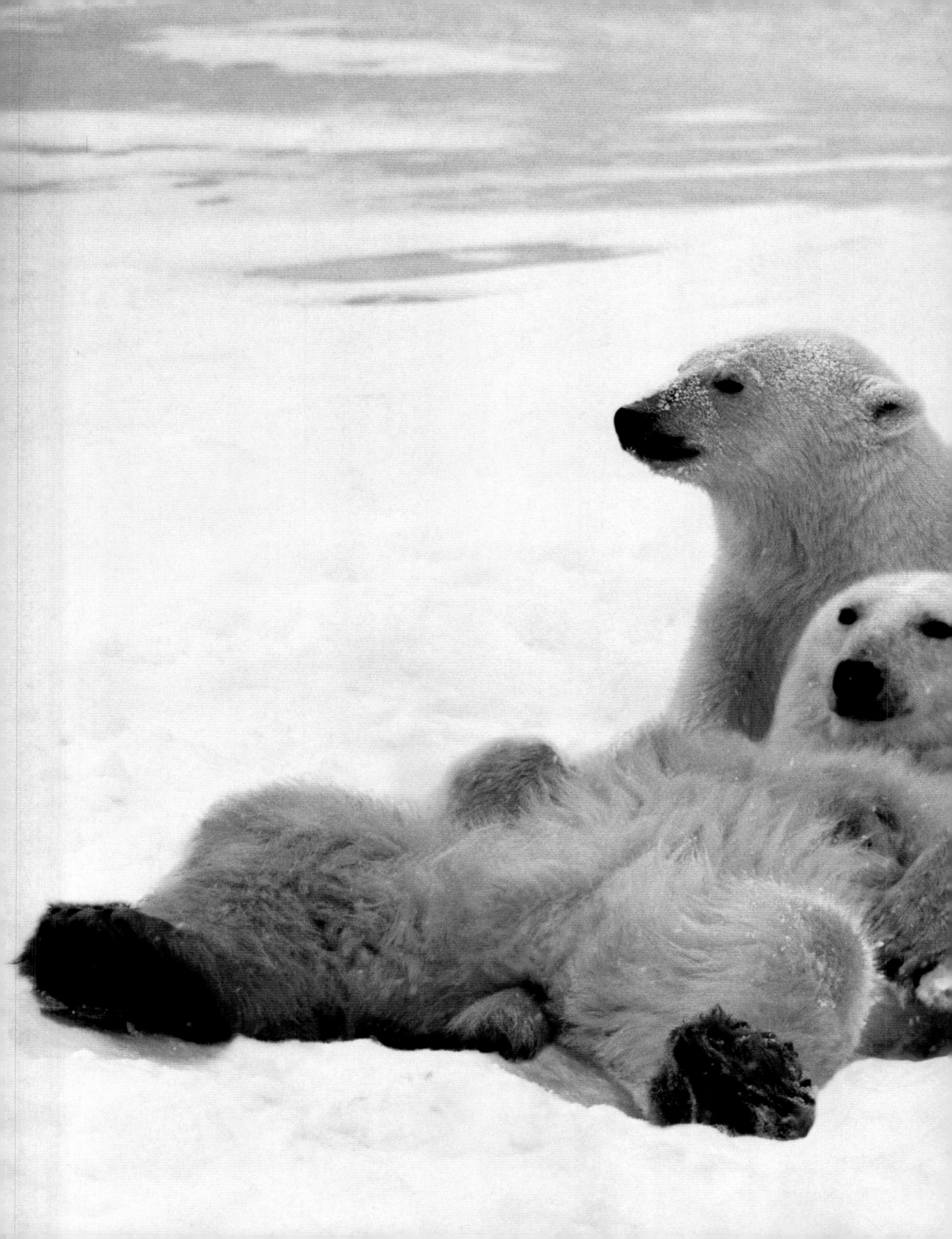

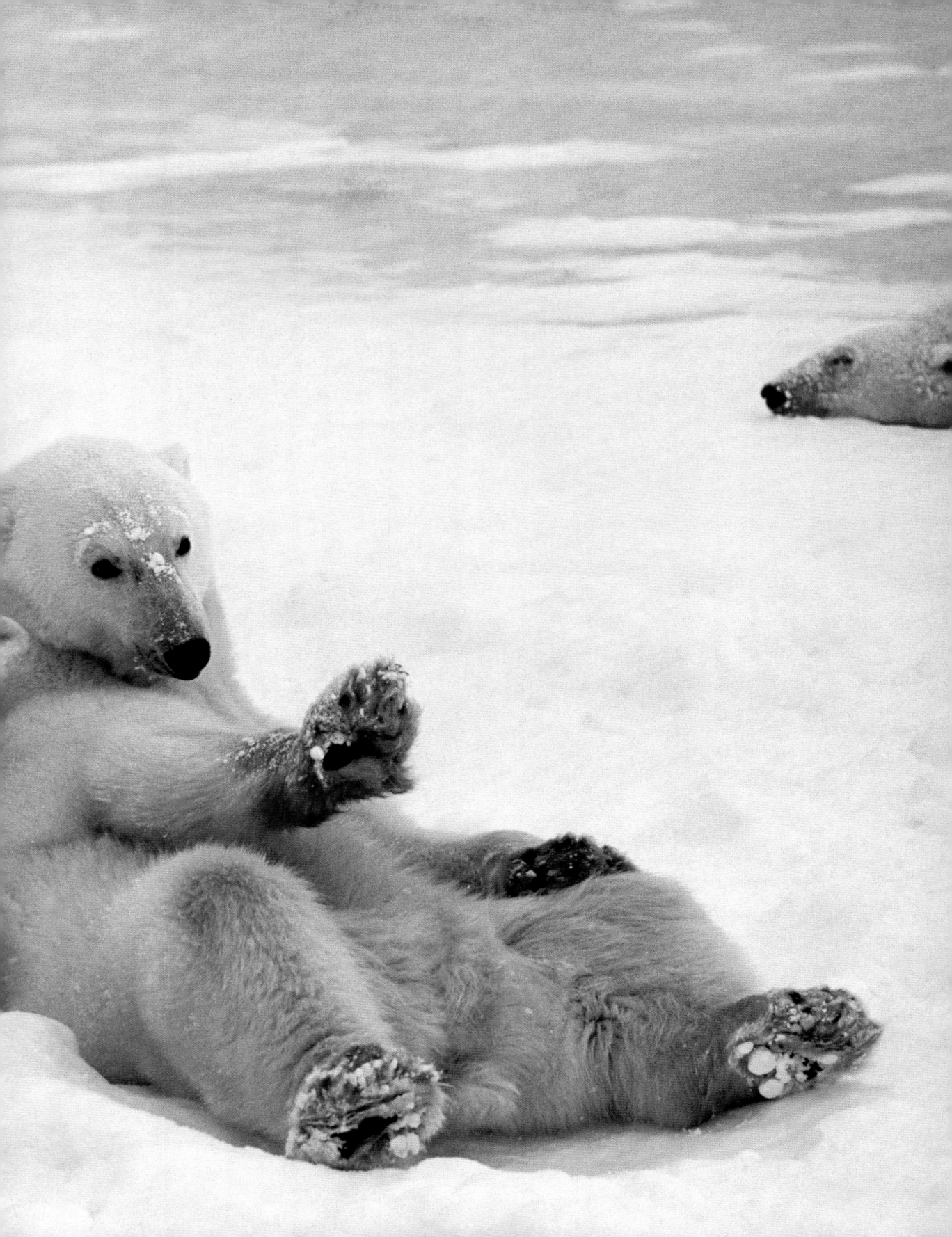

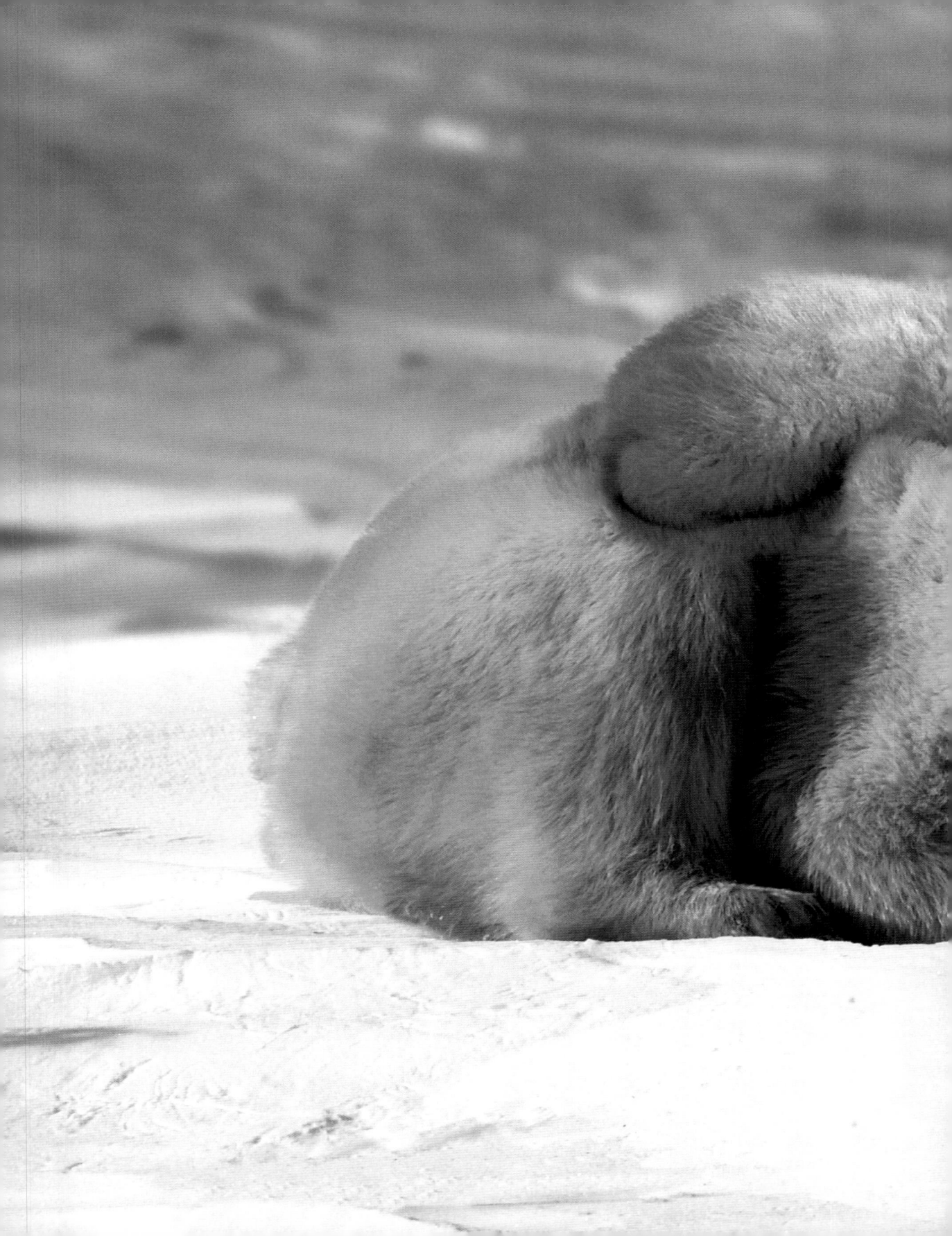

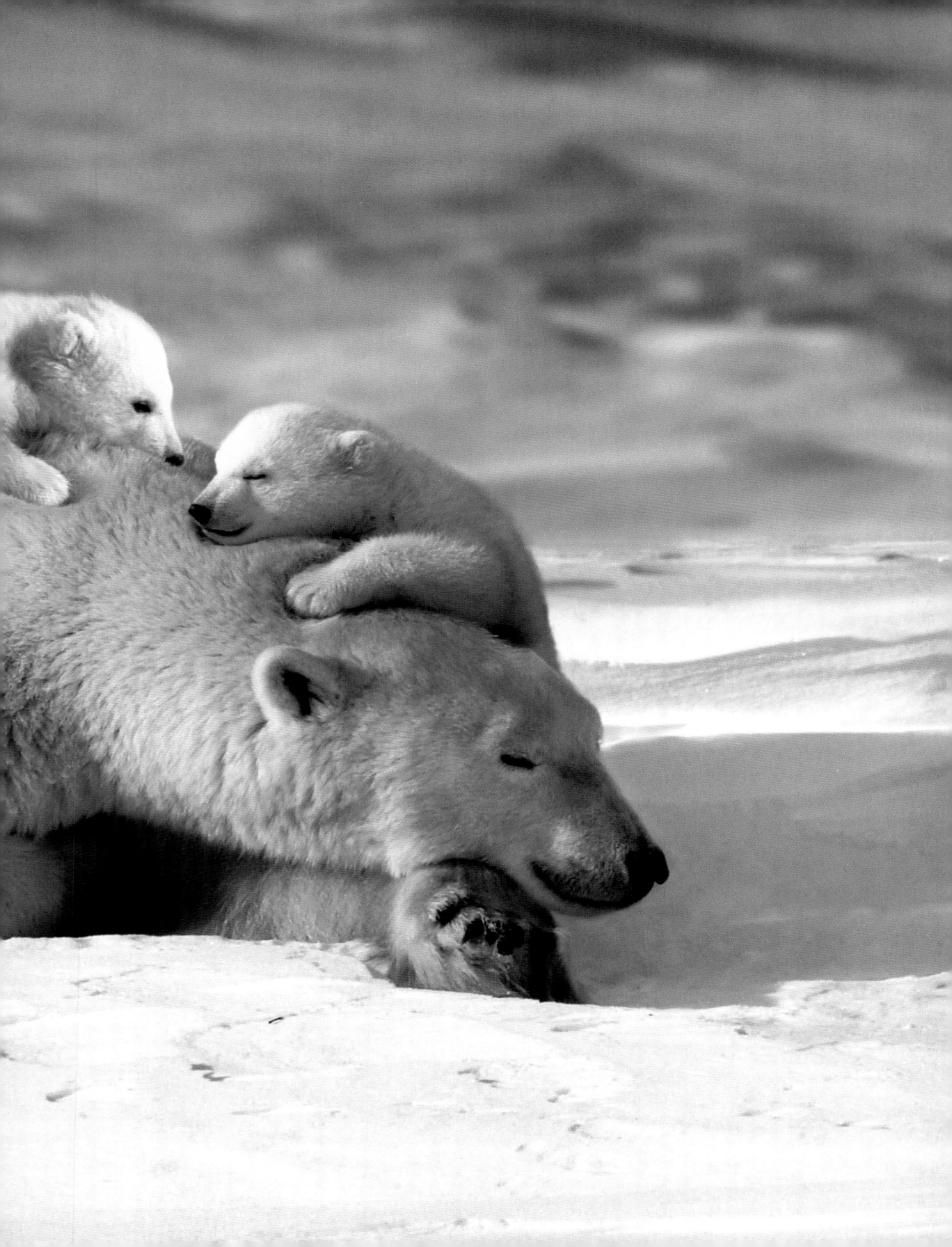

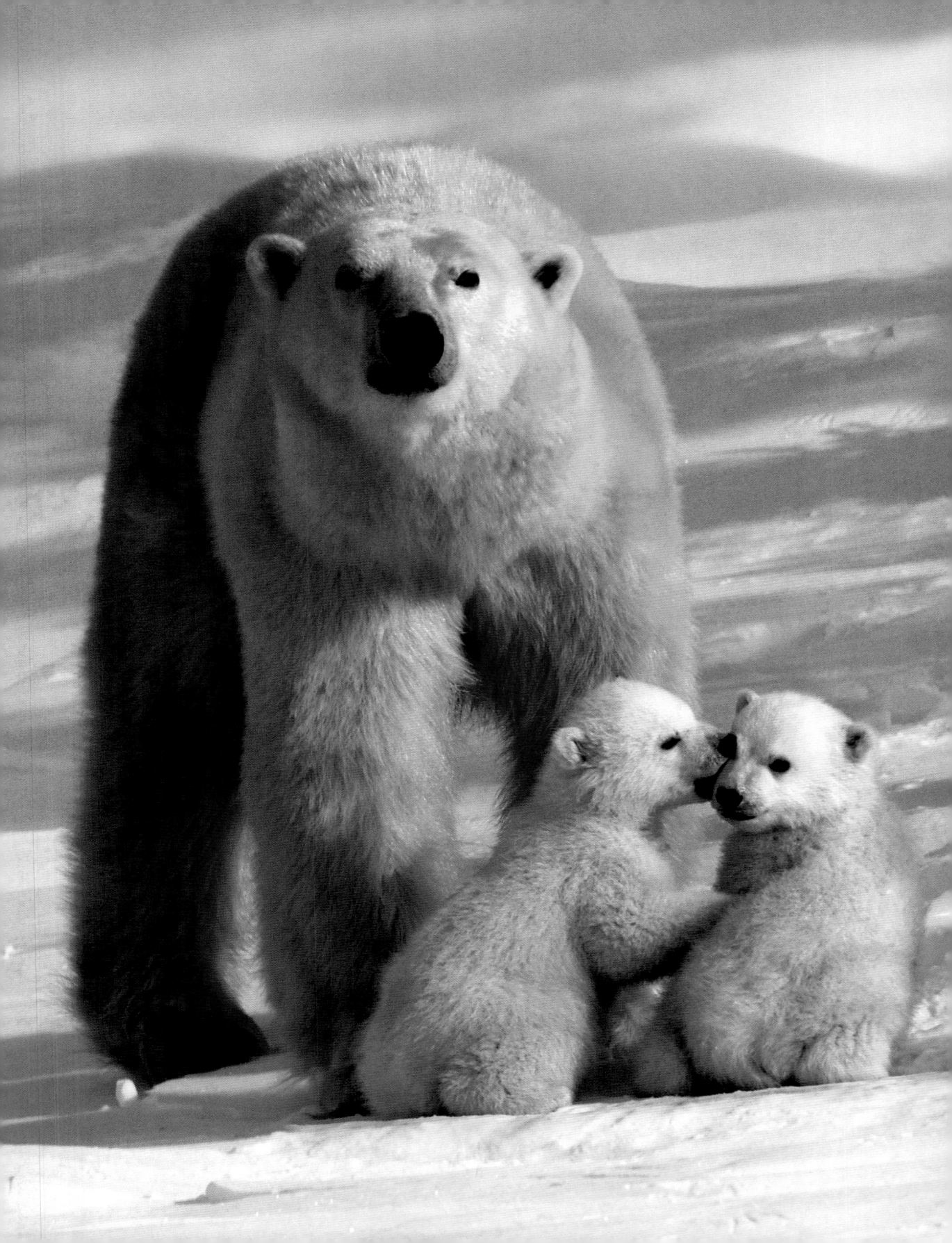

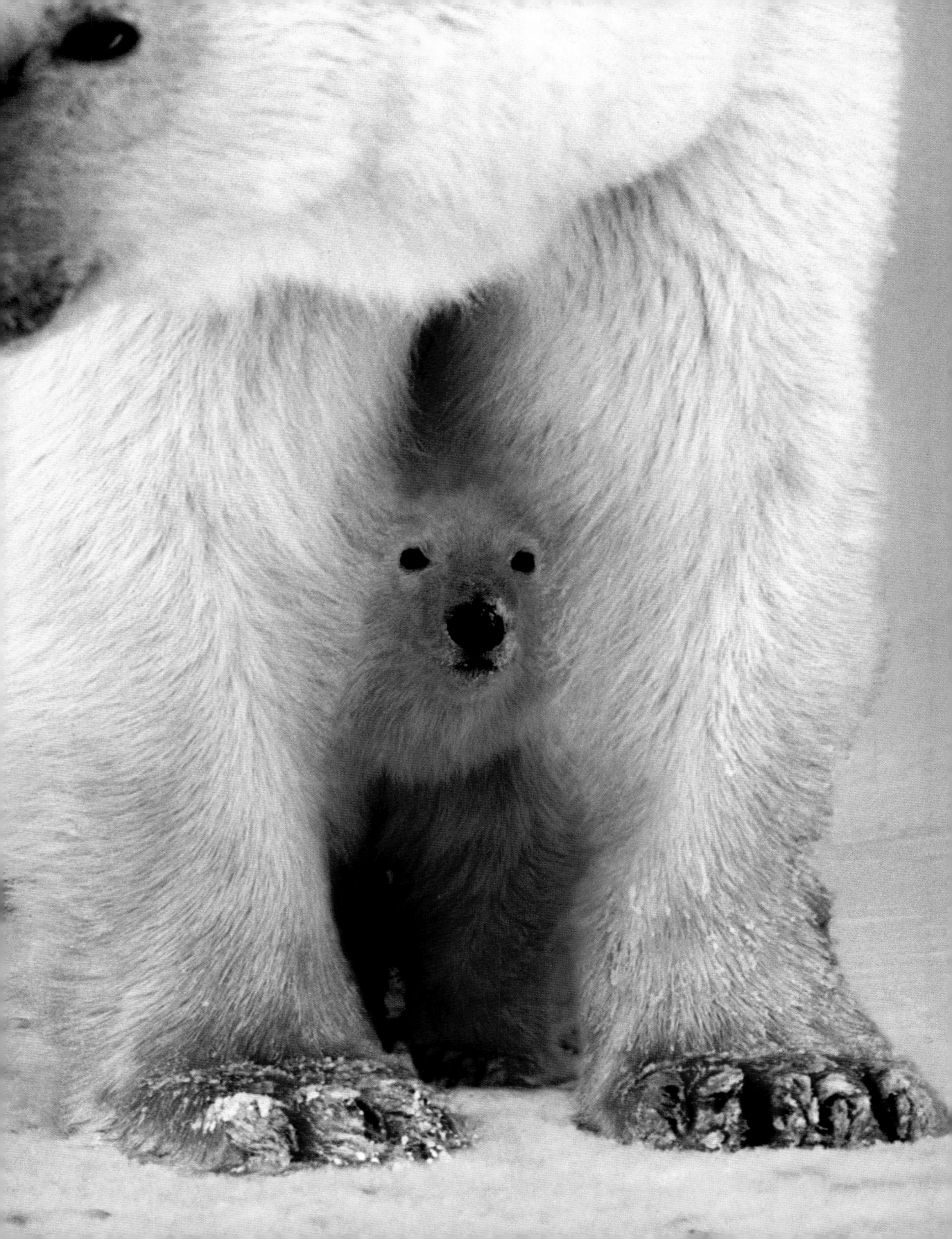

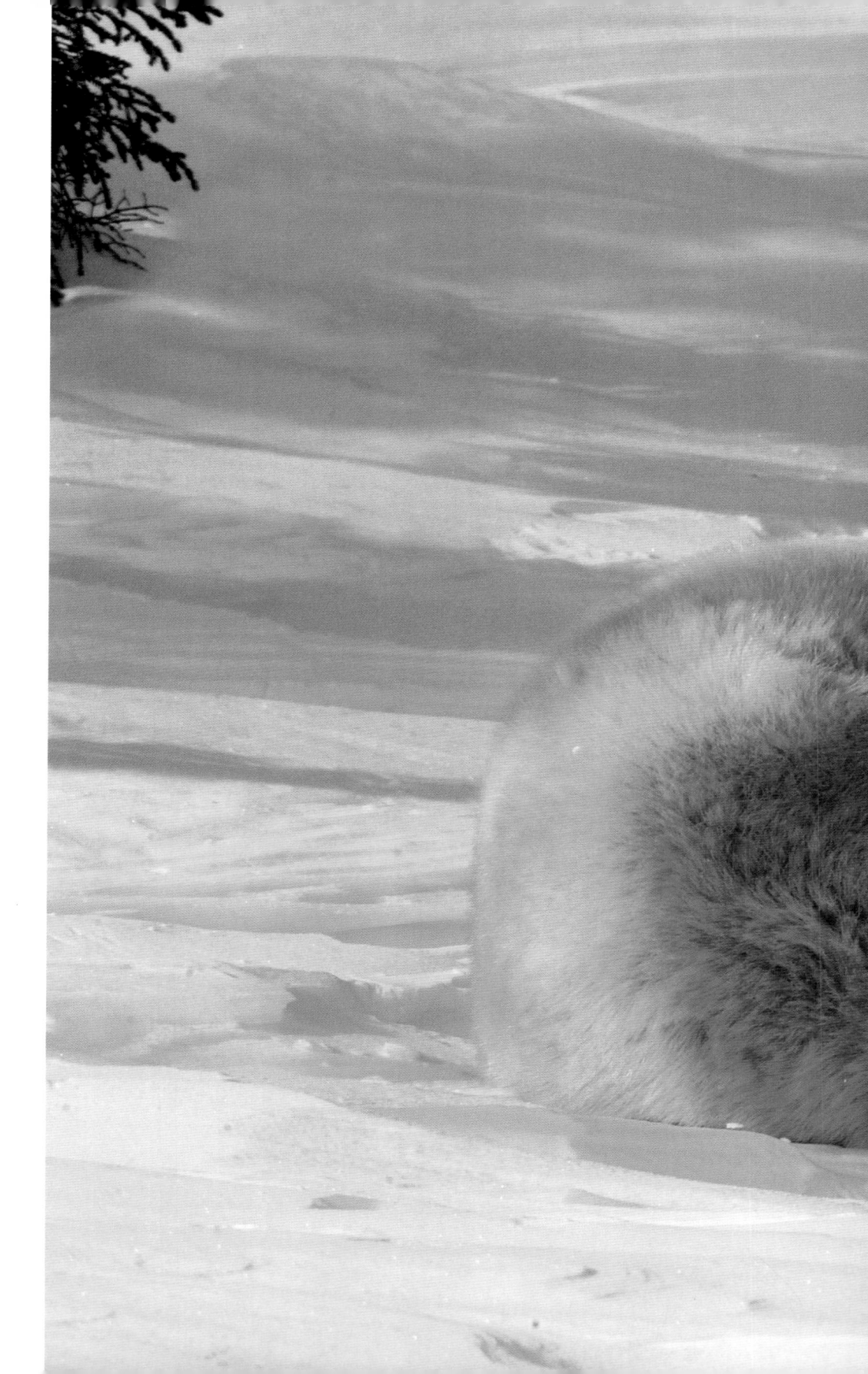

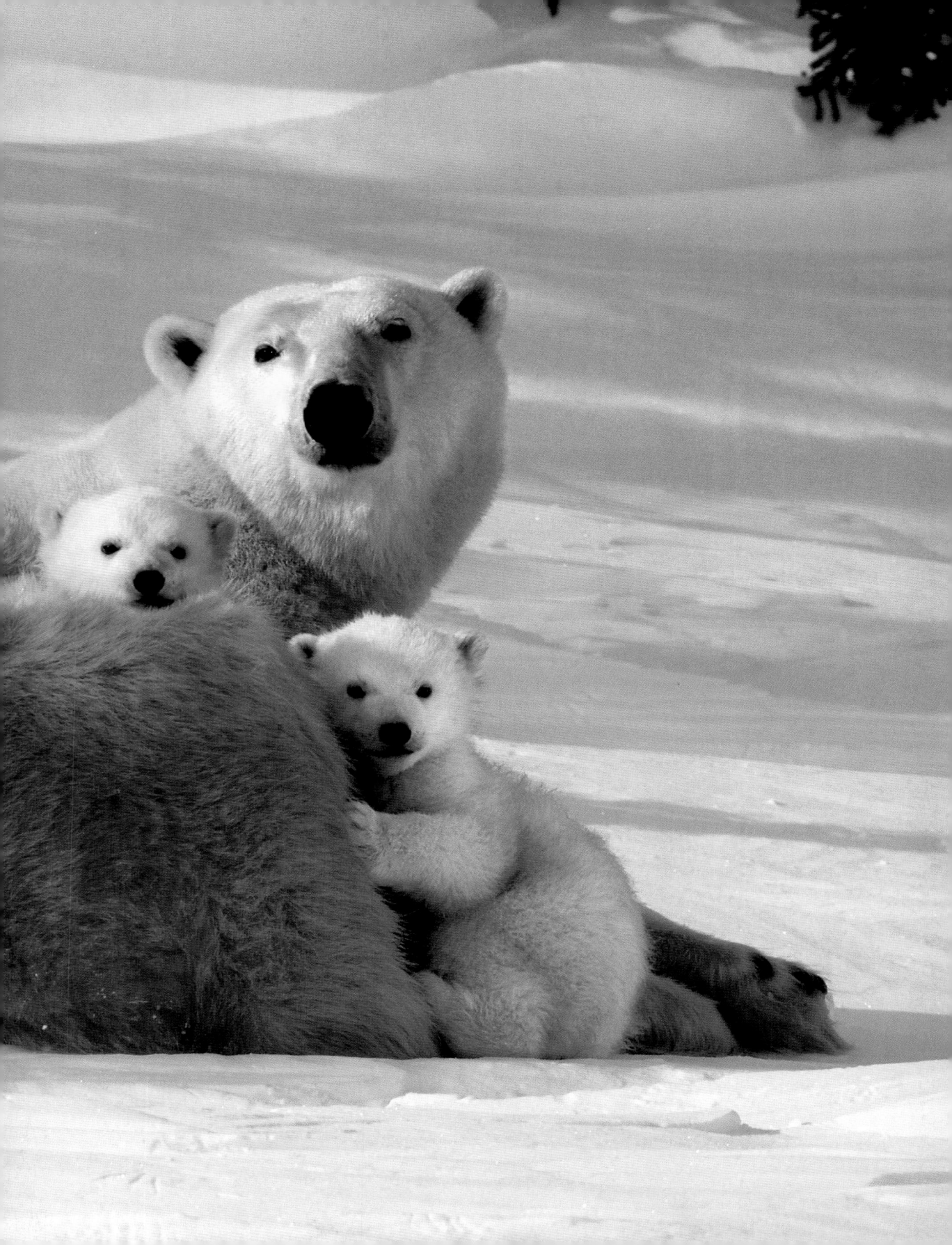

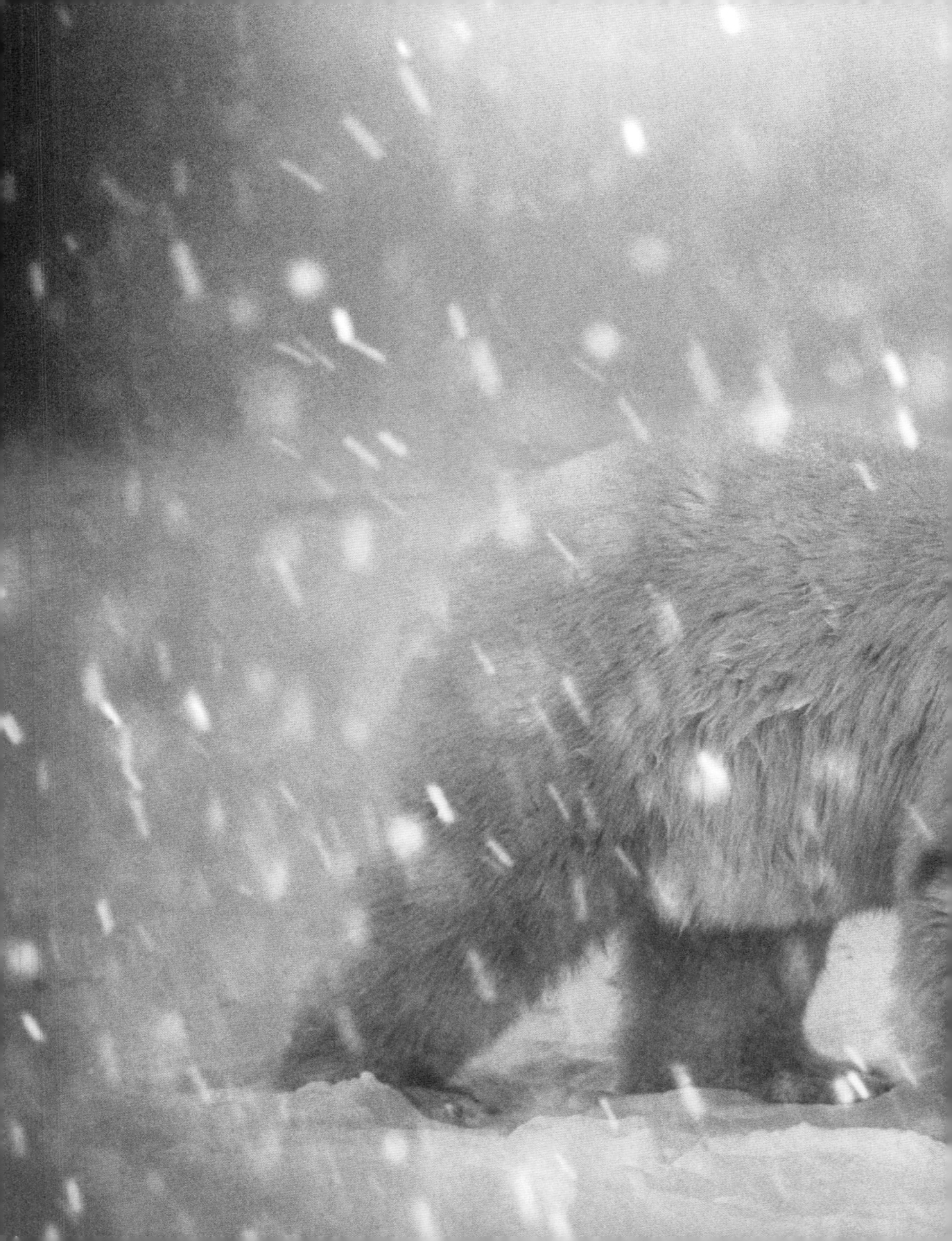

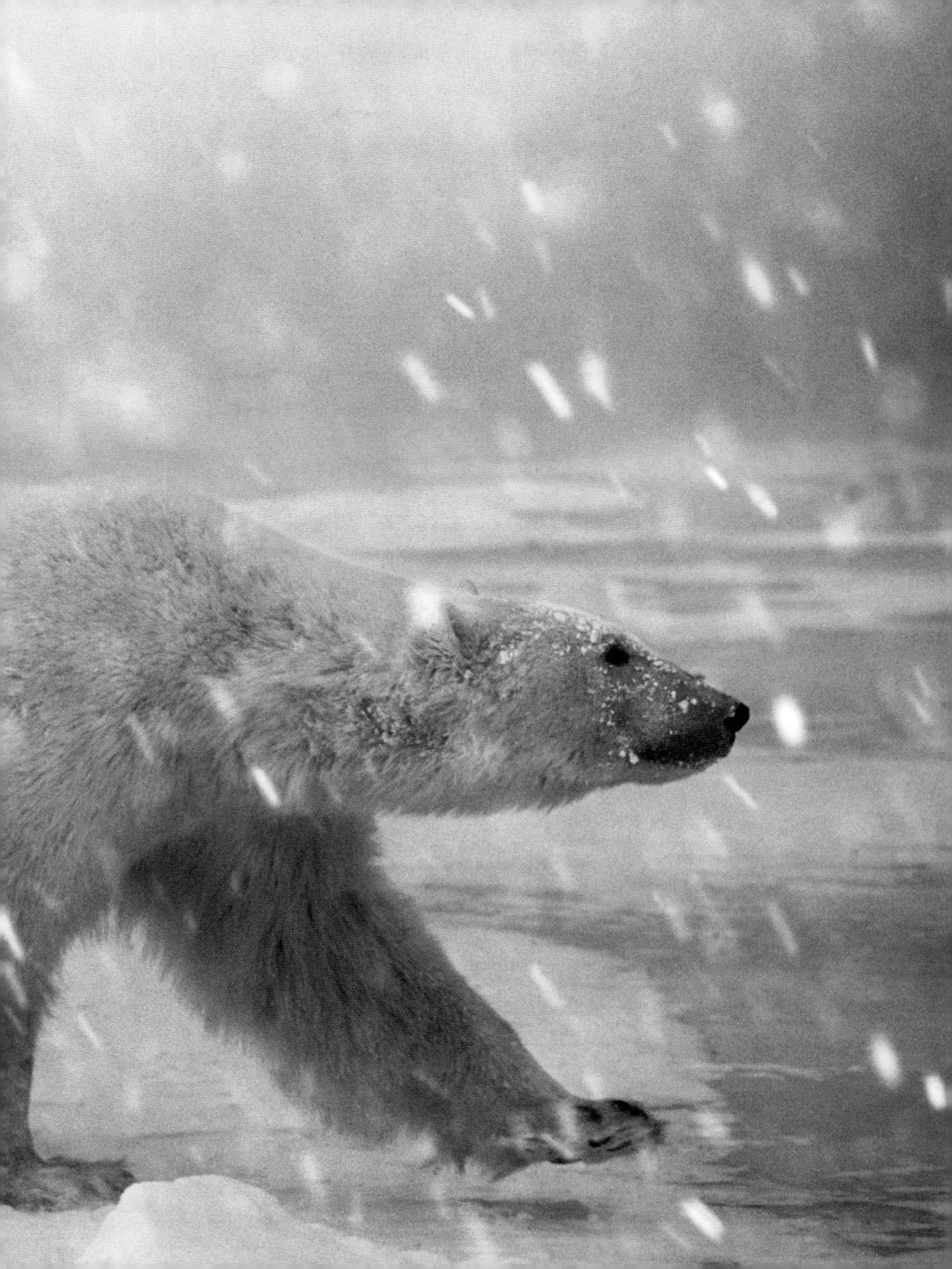

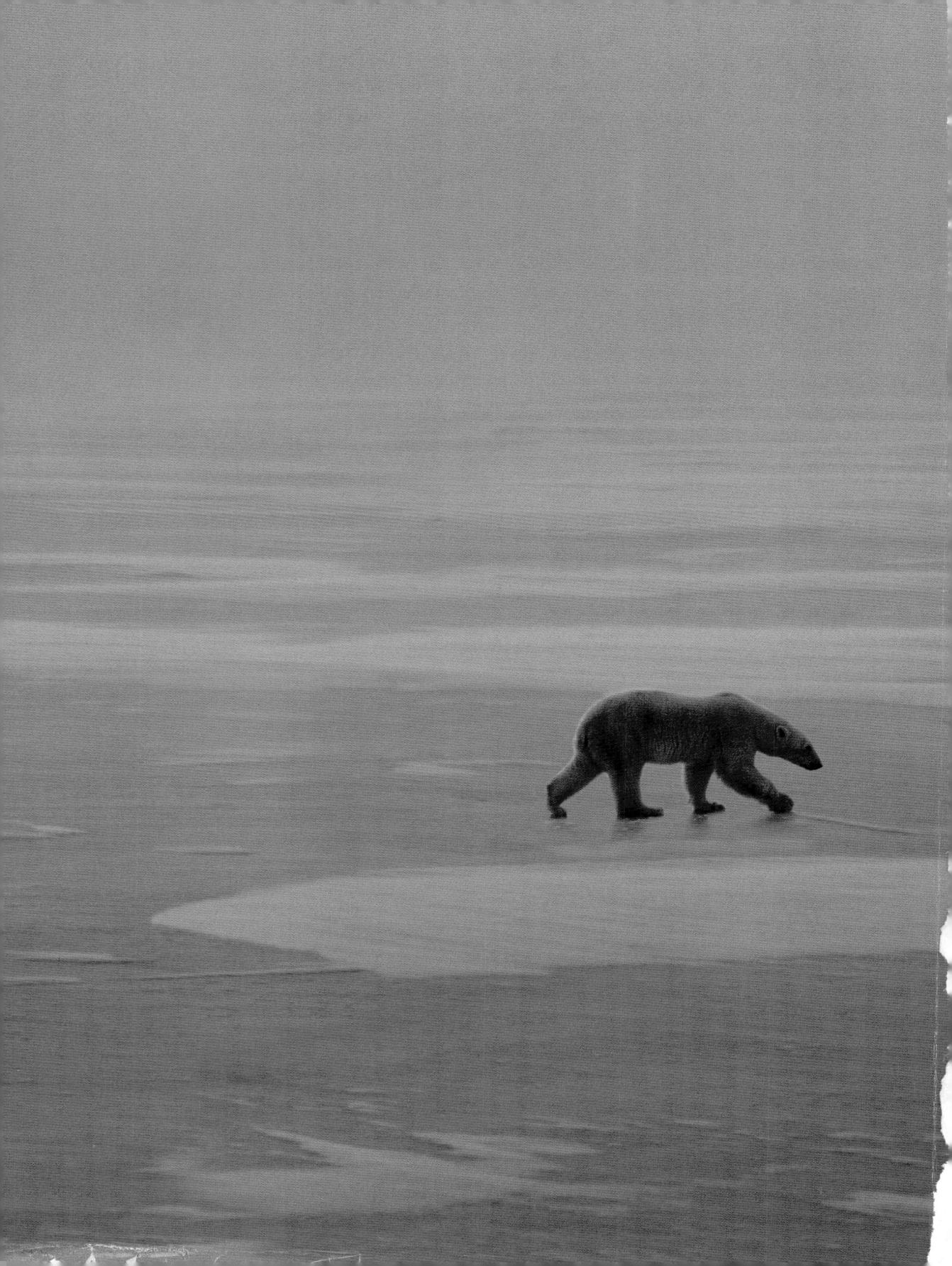

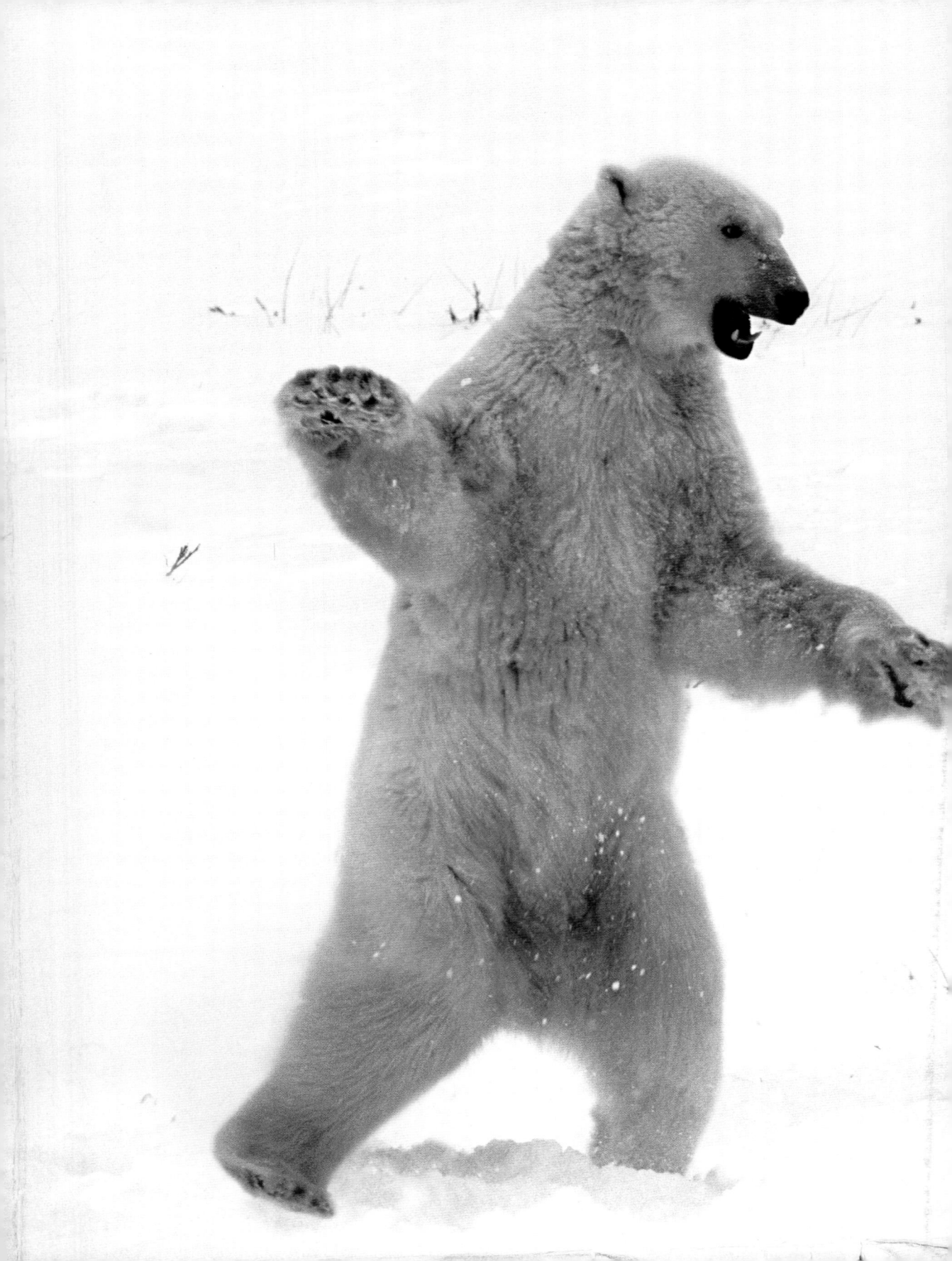

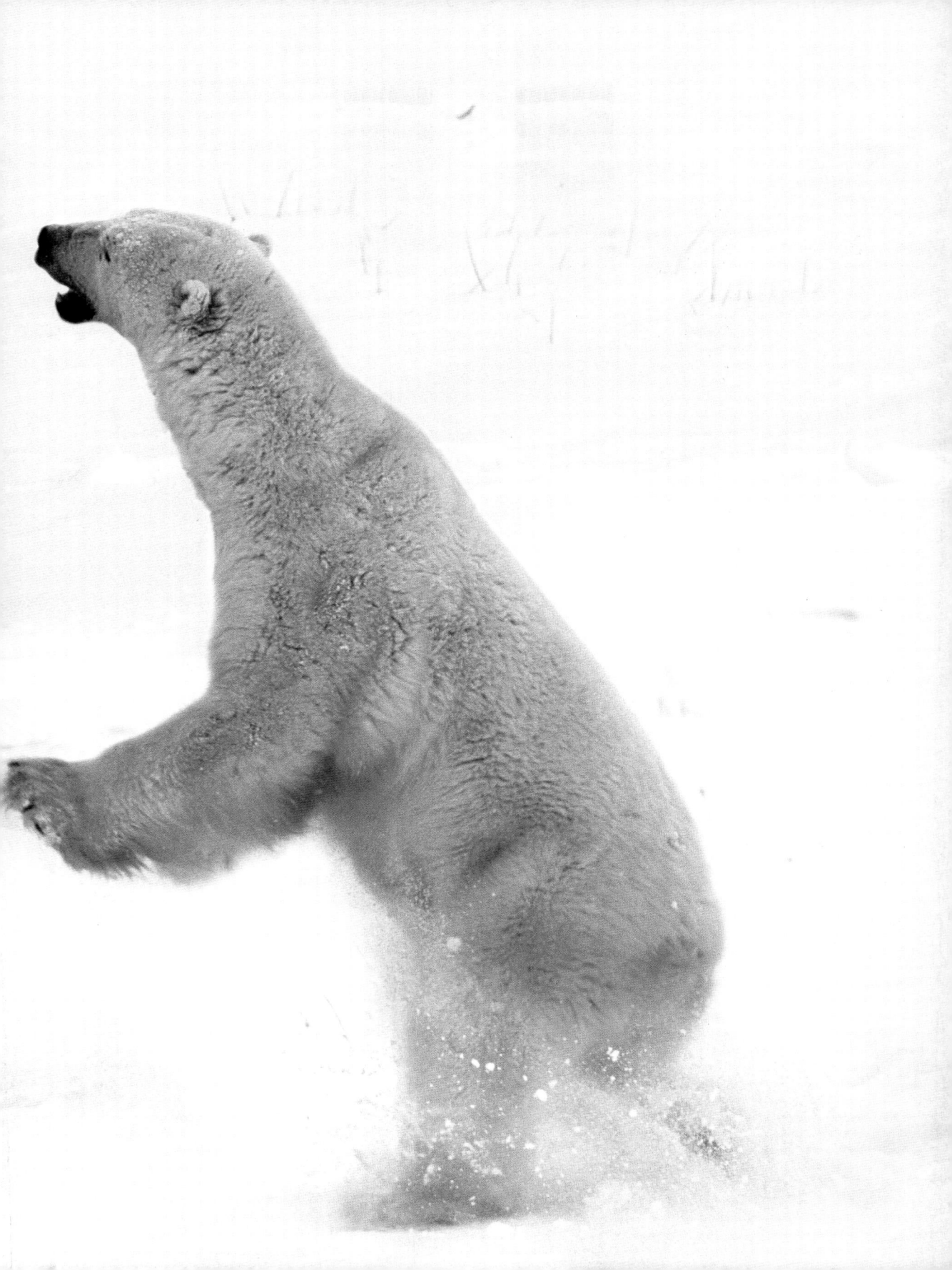

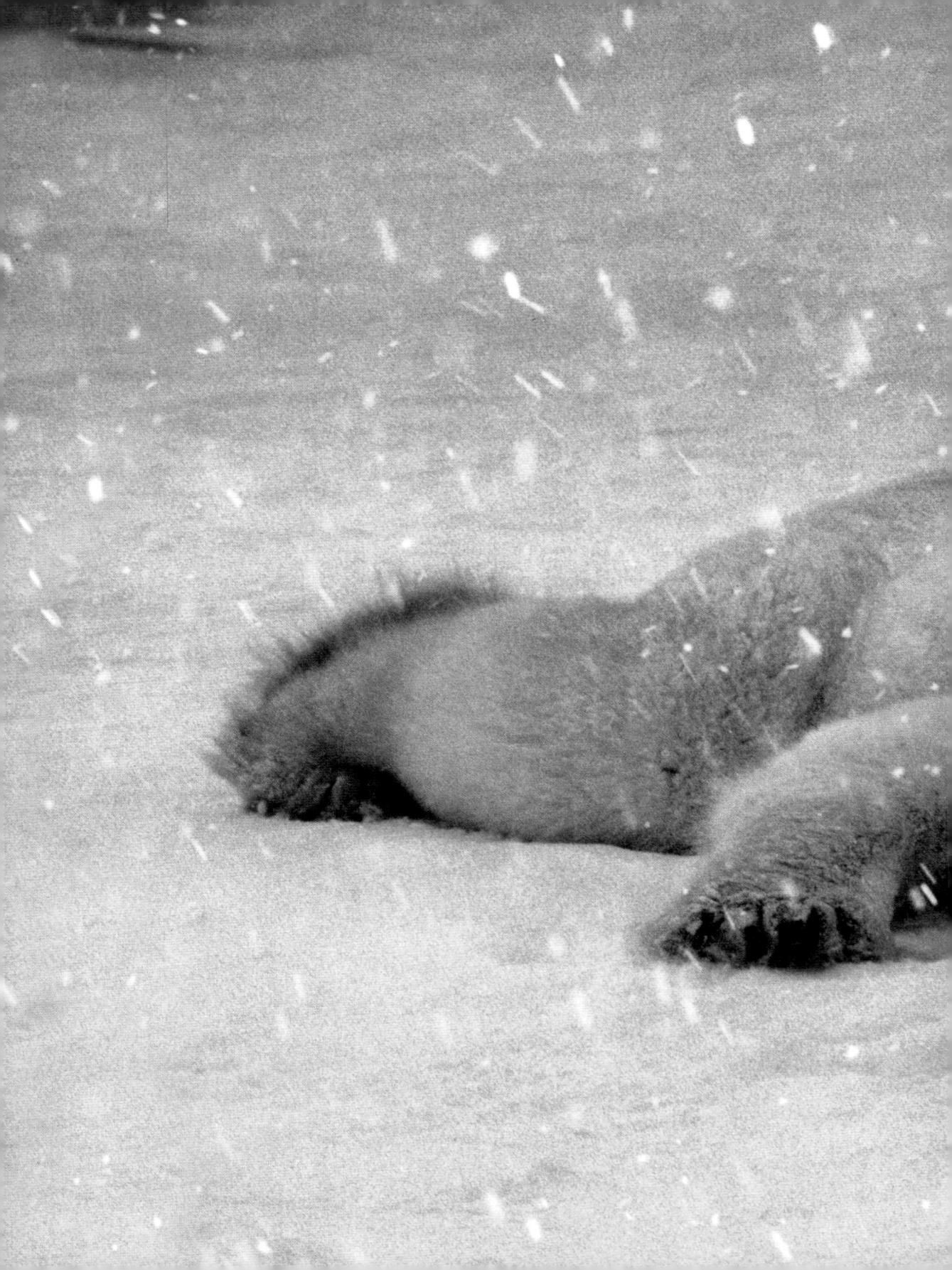

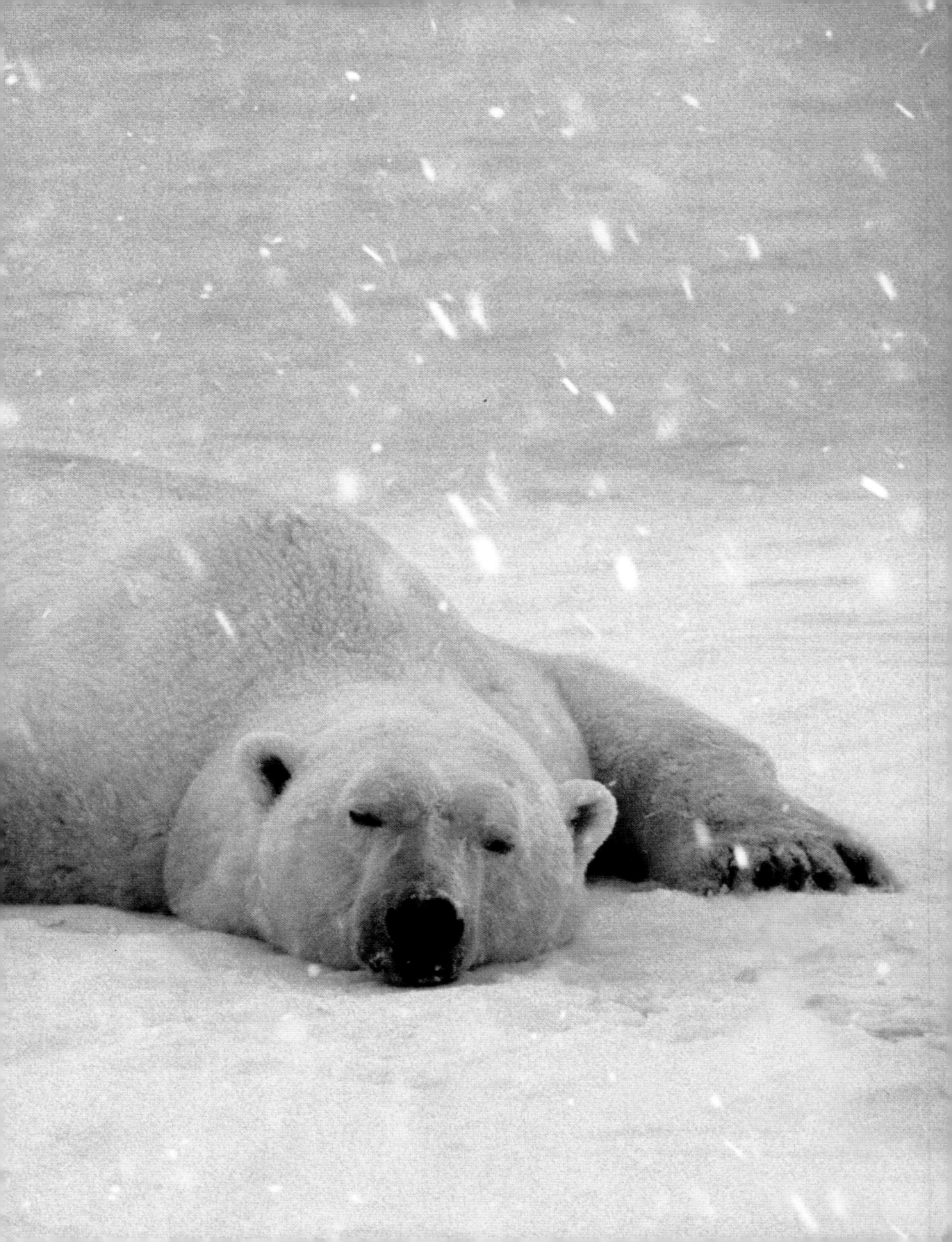

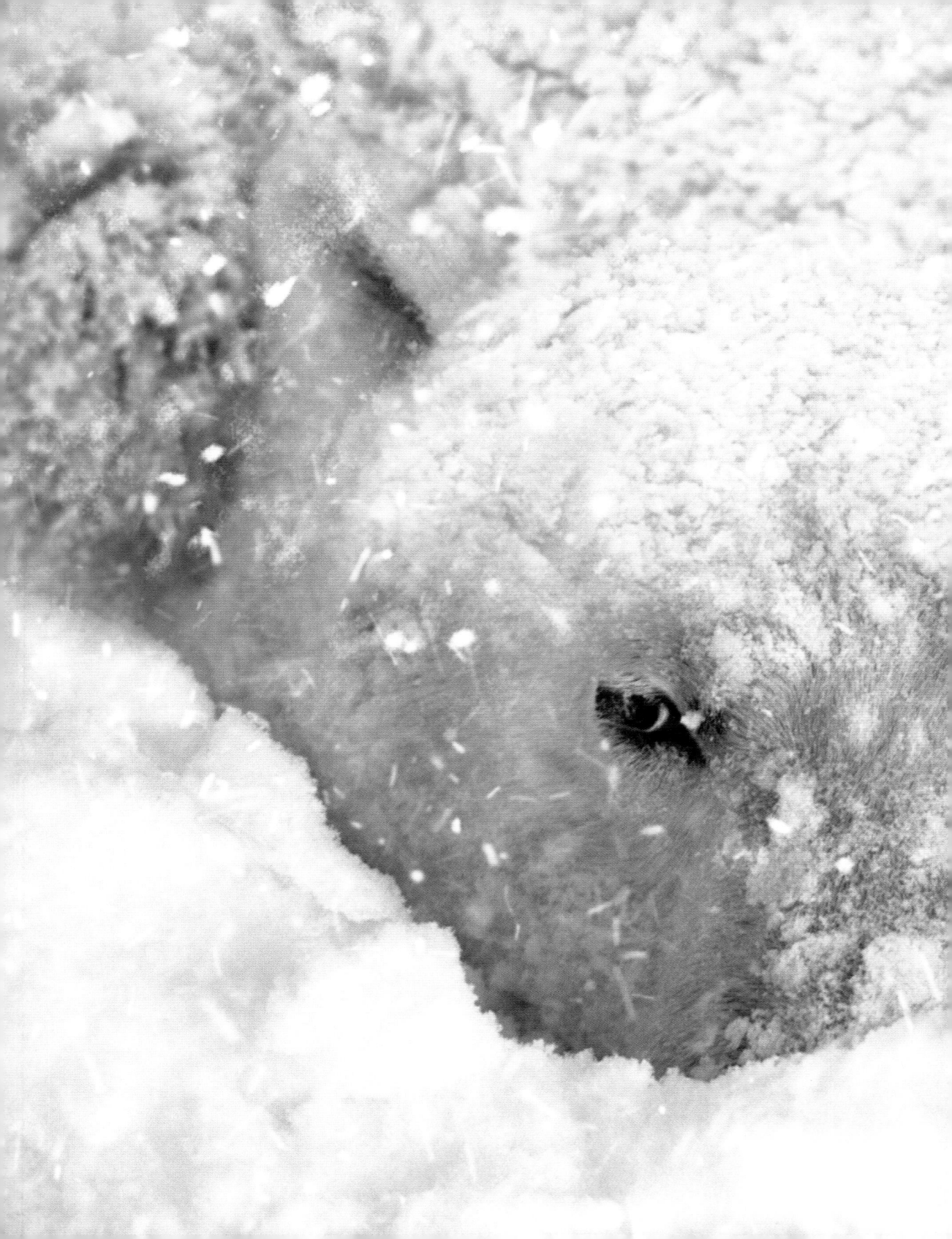

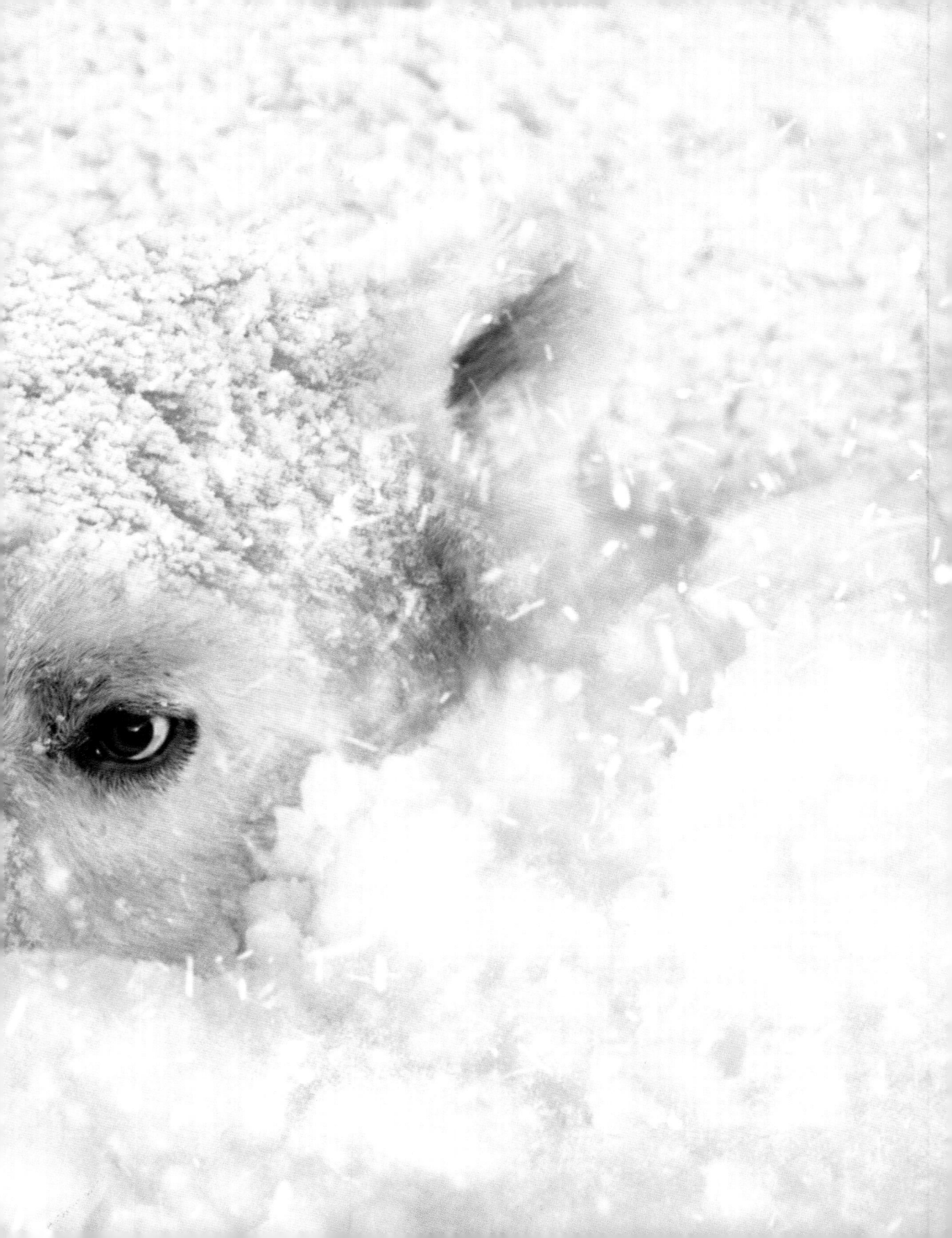

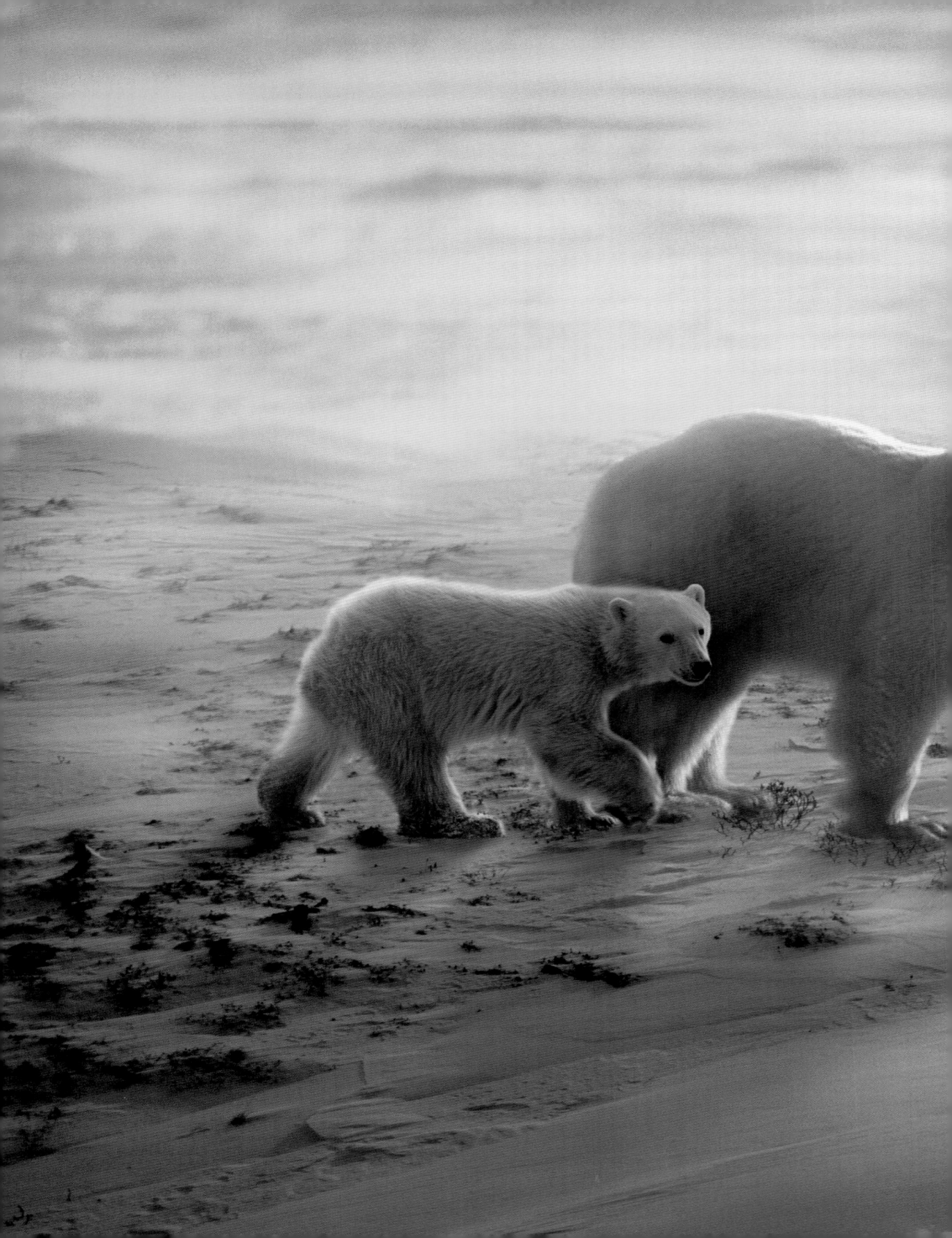

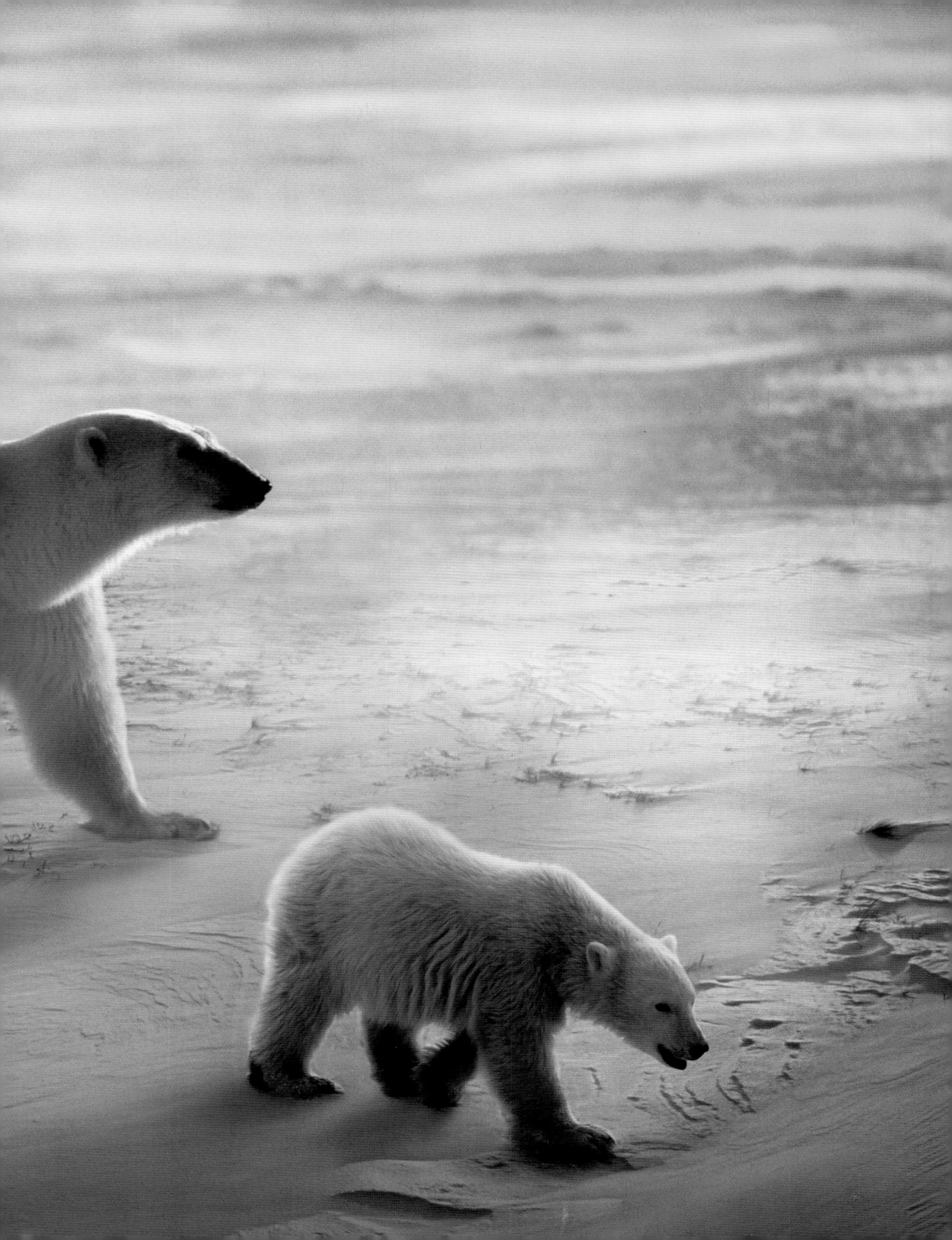

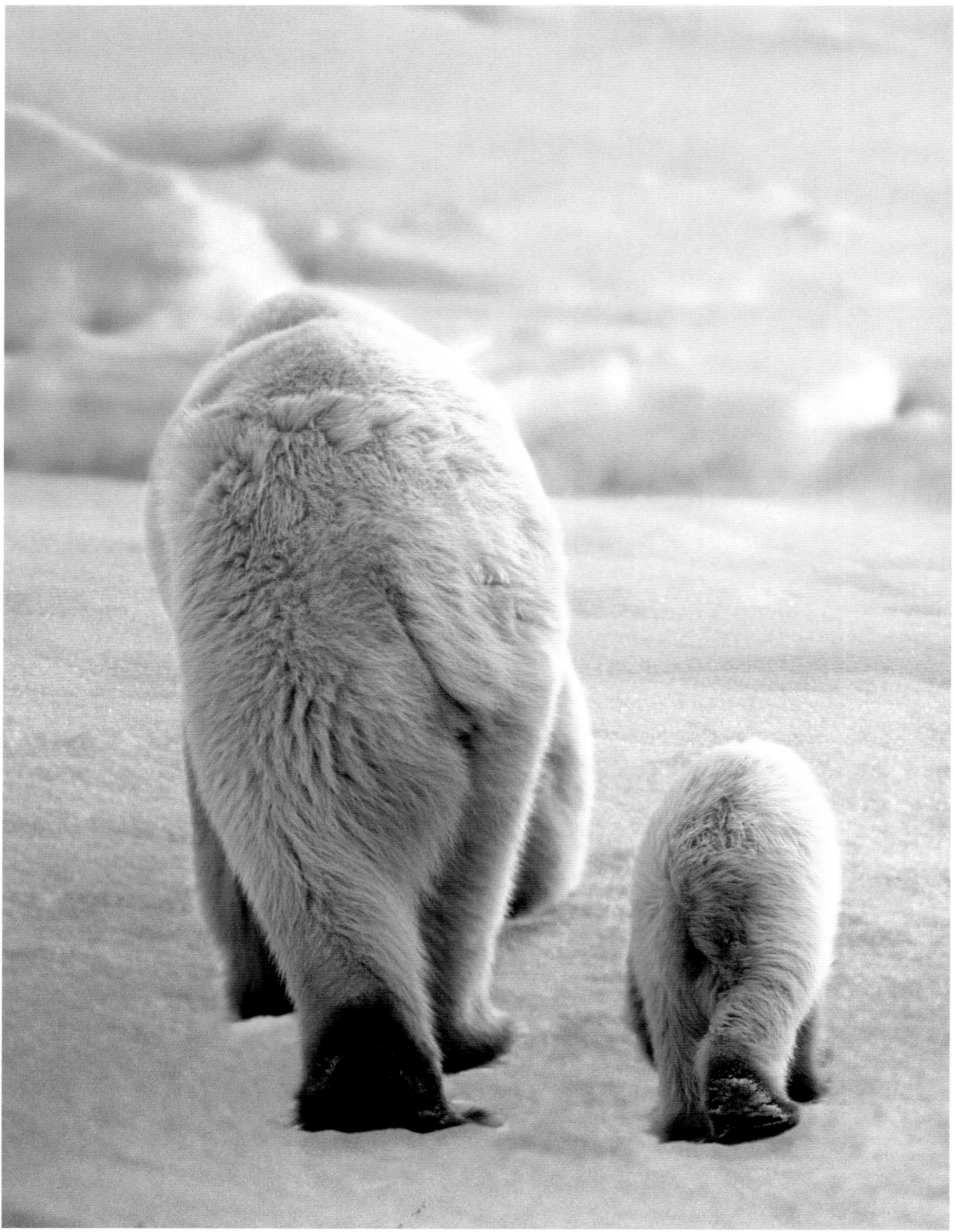

CAPTURING THE LIGHT

Work is the long journey to rediscover, through the practice of art,
those early impressions that first stirred the soul.

Sometimes our lives make unexpected turns that arise out of an accumulation of events not always of our own making. I started wildlife photography relatively late, just after my fortieth birthday. I traveled with my wife to South Africa on a safari holiday, where I took some photographs of animals. At that time I was directing a photographic post-production studio in London that served the needs of advertising agencies. My work entailed knowledge of the communicative power of images and their ability to evoke emotional reactions in people. On a whim, I wanted to see what I could do with animal photography.

My own personal photography had been dormant for a number of years, as the need to earn a living took precedence over creativity. The holiday in South Africa reawoke my early passion for taking photographs and released powerful driving forces. A new career, and journey, had begun. What particularly attracted me to wildlife photography was the realization that animals cannot be easily directed. Since nature provides the choreography, the photographer interacts with the elements of chaos to a greater extent than with other types of photography.

A couple of years later I traveled the world to photograph the great apes and other primates. I ended up thousands of miles from the city life to which I was accustomed, having swapped my office in London's Oxford Street for some of the remotest locations on earth. I recall traveling along Borneo's Sekonya River early one morning, watching proboscis monkeys in the mist. I felt immensely privileged, and grateful, to have taken the opportunity to work in such an uplifting place.

For two years I mostly photographed primates. Then I concentrated on Africa's wildlife and traveled to many places on the vast continent. The more I photograph and explore, the more I reaffirm that photographic possibilities are limitless, and there is a much wider world to be investigated. On such a premise the idea for this book was born, so I set out to photograph animals on all the world's continents. My objective is conceptually simple, yet extraordinarily difficult to carry out. I endeavour to convey, via photography, the raw energy of life itself and the common threads that link living beings together. I have not attempted to gather a comprehensive documentary record of species and behavior. I am drawn, instead, to subjects that look and feel dynamic.

The dramatic events portrayed in these pages can be seen as thin slices of momentary excitement. The atmosphere is sometimes magically filled with energy. I strive to assimilate that energy, and through the mechanics of photography, capture some of its essence and so form visual poetry.

The eye is led into a picture and taken on a journey. Balance of tone, color and composition are as important as the subject matter in order for an image to convey deep feelings. Ansel Adams likened the negative to a musical score and the print to the performance. Printmaking is a painstaking process of interpretation.

The science of photography is going through a fundamental change. Rapid technological advances have seen photography undergo transformations more profound than in any other period during its history. The ongoing shift in recording medium from silver to pixels opens up new opportunities for seeing and portraying the world around us. Gone forever are the limitations of the traditional camera and darkroom. Photographs can now be created intuitively, more in line with the way the human eye sees and the brain interprets experiences. Movements such as Impressionism and Cubism have demonstrated how it is possible for an artist both to reveal more fully the feelings evoked, and explore themes in fresh ways. I am encouraged by the ways in which it is now possible for me to handle images with greater skill, and so draw the observer more into the picture. While the tools for creativity are continually improving, it should never be forgotten that they remain mere tools and cannot replace the challenge of artistic vision.

The spectrum of photography is broad. Balance and harmony, and the relationship of color and shapes can instil feelings of tranquillity. It also encompasses turbulence and chaos, where various forces come together in a struggle for supremacy—explosive moments when significant changes occur. I continually search for the forces of nature that underpin the sense of being alive. Art and nature are inextricably linked, and photography is a way of crystallizing that art.

Photography is also about choice and interpretation. Photographers, like painters, see things differently from one another. If two photographers record the same event, they will most likely produce surprisingly different results. What a photographer chooses to reveal about a subject is as relevant as what he or she chooses to exclude. This is why photography can be accepted as an art form. Nature is dynamic, and the photographer, as part of nature, extracts and portrays those elements that are deemed to be important to the viewer.

Some pictures show turbulent moments that erupt briefly before dissipating. For example, the picture of the great white shark breaching the waves was extremely difficult to take, yet the sequence lasted less than a second. Photography's great strength is the ability to freeze transient events that would otherwise fade into distant memory. It perpetually reinforces their magnitude.

Water is a theme I return to again and again. All living things interact with water in order to survive, and I am drawn to the elements of chaos in patterns formed by droplets. Water plays a major role in all our lives and an animal's relationship with water captivates me as a photographer. Surely the shapes formed by moving water, so patently transient, reinforce the fleeting nature of all life?

The images in this collection are derived from ten years of ongoing work, the last eighteen months of which were shot with digital cameras. In recent times I have moved away from the machine-gun approach to photography, the practice of shooting as much film as possible in the hope of capturing the perfect moment. Paradoxically, I have discovered that decisive moments can still be captured while shooting individual frames, even with fast action sequences.

Shooting digitally has freed me from the anxieties of damaging airport x-rays, and the physical problems of carrying hundreds of rolls of film onto airplanes. It does however mean that I now worry about electricity supplies in remote locations, and carry bags full of electrical devices to store images. The ability to preview images in the field has been liberating, although it should never detract from the intense concentration required while watching the subject.

I travel as lightly as possible, but am often limited by the sheer weight of the equipment. The best professional cameras and lenses are sturdy, and consequently heavy. More often than not I work alone, single-handedly carrying my equipment over considerable distances in difficult terrain. If I capture a worthwhile photograph, exhaustion is accompanied by a sense of elation. Fatigue is the great enemy, overcome only by a sense of purpose.

On a typical shoot I will bring up to four camera bodies and an array of lenses, including spares. Many locations are extremely difficult and expensive to reach, so extra equipment is an insurance against technical failure or loss. My lenses range from 16mm to 600mm. Some are zooms, while others are prime lenses. I have used Canon 35mm SLR cameras and lenses from the very beginning. Film stock has predominantly been Fuji Velvia and Provia slide film. I carry a lightweight but strong carbon tripod, although I tend to use tripods far less than most other photographers in my field. Tripods are useful in eliminating camera shake, but they can be a hindrance when attempting to photograph action sequences, which arrive at extraordinary speed, and from any direction. The advent of image-stabilizing lenses in recent years has been immensely beneficial.

When working from vehicles in Africa's game reserves, I fill bags with beans and place them on the window openings. While photographing, the long lenses are placed on the bags. Although an ideal substitute for a tripod with static subjects, bags make it difficult to follow moving animals such as running cheetahs.

The equipment I use in the field is often subjected to enormous stresses. Cameras and lenses have been drenched in water and mud, frozen to -58°F (-50°C), endured high humidity, subjected to desert dust storms, and sprayed with seawater, yet they seldom let me down. In such circumstances it is essential to understand the effects of such conditions and take precautionary measures, shielding and protecting equipment wherever possible. For example, condensation and cracking of glass are serious problems in severe subzero weather. Taking a camera from a freezing environment into a warm room requires considerable care, and it should be sealed in a plastic bag before entering the warm environment.

Awareness of body language is of paramount importance when photographing animals. As far as I am able, I make sure I let them know I am no threat. A sudden or confrontational approach will result either in an attack or in the animal's retreat. Neither consequence is conducive to successful photography, as it places unwarranted stress on both photographer and subject. Individual animals can be approached to different degrees, and so it is important to know how far to go without intrusion. It is equally important to stay relaxed in their presence and treat the encounter with sensitivity.

It is also essential to understand how to behave if a situation becomes potentially dangerous. Grizzly bears do not like being surprised, so you should make your presence known without being threatening. There is no point in running away, since no human can outrun a bear, and that would send out the wrong signal. Be submissive with mountain gorillas, avoid direct eye contact and keep a bowed head. Just as we sometimes need to be more on our guard in certain human situations, the same rule applies to animals. For instance, in areas where animals are hunted, photography can be much more difficult and sometimes dangerous. Humans are, after all, the greatest threat to the world's wildlife. At all times conscious respect should be shown to animals.

Hopefully these pictures take you on an inspiring journey to the most wonderful places, and give you a flavor of both animals and the terrain in which they live. As a photographer, I am often torn between the desire to spend a long time in a particular place, and the wish to photograph as widely as possible. It is a difficult balance, but I try to allow quality to have priority over diversity. With the knowledge that photographic perfection is an unattainable goal, I accept the necessity to leave one location and move on to another.

—Steve Bloom

CAPTIONS

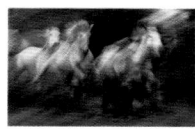

1 / Camargue Horse, France.
On a gray and drizzly day, a herd of Camargue horses paints a trail of ghostly light as they gallop across the fields of Provence. Young foals initially have dark coats, which soon lighten to become the characteristic white of the Camargue breed.

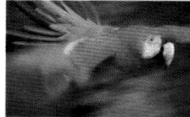

2 / Scarlet Macaw, Peru.
A riot of color in motion, a wild scarlet macaw darts through the Amazon. The largest of parrots, macaws use their strong beaks both to crack open very hard nutshells and to help climb among the branches.

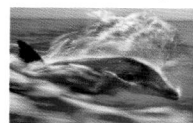

3 / Bottlenose Dolphin, Honduras.
Propelled like a torpedo, a bottlenose dolphin skims over the warm coastal waters of the Caribbean. Friction in air is lower than in water, so dolphins can achieve higher speeds alternating between the two.

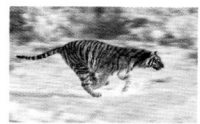

4 / Siberian Tiger, Northern China.
Sprinting through snow, a tiger shows his power and vigor. The world's largest cat, the Siberian tiger relies mainly on stealth when stalking prey, closing in with a final short burst of speed for the kill.

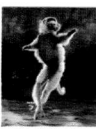

5 / Verreaux's Sifaka, Berenty, Madagascar.
Wide-eyed and riding high, a baby sifaka holds tightly as his mother leaps in the sunlight. Sifakas are a type of lemur that can hop upright for long distances on the ground or leap from tree to tree.

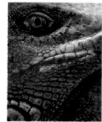

6 / Green Iguana, Honduras.
The reticulated face of an iguana forms a colorful mosaic. Living high in the forest canopy throughout tropical areas of the Americas, these robust reptiles survive falls of up to fifty feet (fifteen meters) without injury.

AFRICA

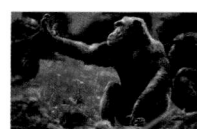

7 / Chimpanzee, Monkey World Rescue Centre, UK.
With outstretched arm and open fingers, a chimpanzee explores falling raindrops. Monkey World is an organization that rescues and rehabilitates primates into natural social groups.

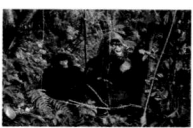

8 / Mountain Gorilla, Parc des Virungas, Democratic Republic of Congo.
A male and female mountain gorilla, alert to any strange sounds or movements, sit in the crater of an extinct volcano. This dense African rainforest is their natural habitat.

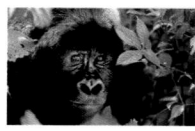

9 / Silverback Mountain Gorilla, Mgahinga National Park, Uganda.
A gorilla peers inquiringly through dense jungle vegetation. The silverback, the dominant male of the gorilla group, is ever watchful for intruders.

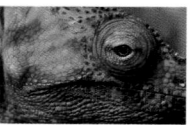

10 / Parson's Chameleon, Perinet, Madagascar.
A close-up of the head of a Parson's chameleon, its emerald color mimicking the green of the rainforest. As in all chameleons, the bulging eyes rotate independently to give a 360° view.

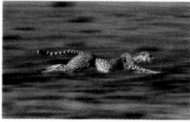

11 / Cheetah, Masai Mara, Kenya.
In a blur of speed, every leg off the ground, a hunting cheetah races through grassland. A combination of unique physical characteristics, including light bone structure and elongated body shape, enables the cheetah to achieve near-flying motion over short distances.

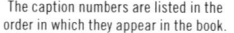

The caption numbers are listed in the order in which they appear in the book.

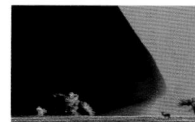

12 / Springbok, Namib-Naukluft National Park, Namibia.
Dwarfed by the curve of a towering red sand dune, a springbok antelope stands alone. Home to the highest sand dunes in the world, the Namib is also one of the world's most humid deserts.

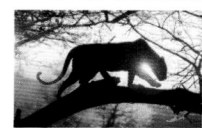

13 / African Leopard, Namibia.
A glowing African sunset silhouettes a leopard walking along a horizontal tree trunk. Leopards, typically solitary animals, rarely hunt by day but become active in the early evening and at night.

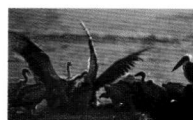

14 / Vulture and Marabou Stork, Masai Mara, Kenya.
Silhouetted by the golden light of dawn, a jostling flock of vultures and Marabou storks fight over the remnants of a lion kill. These carrion eaters perform a vital role in the ecology of the African plains by disposing of animal remains.

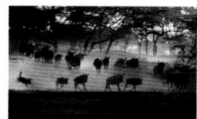

15 / Wildebeest, Masai Mara, Kenya.
Sunrise lights the dusty silhouette of a herd of wildebeest moving through scrubland. While young wildebeest frolic with energy at the start of the day, older members begin to lead the herd toward places to graze and drink.

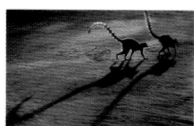

16 / Ring-tailed Lemur, Berenty, Madagascar.
Walking in the early morning, ring-tailed lemurs cast long shadows on the ground. These highly social animals use their long tails held upright as a signaling device.

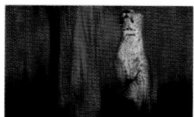

17 / Leopard, Namibia.
Eyes concentrated on the vertical jump, a leopard gathers strength in his hind legs before leaping into a tree. Leopards can scale impressive heights, and also haul prey heavier than themselves to high branches to protect it from scavengers.

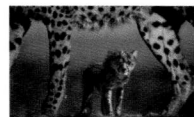

18 / Cheetah, Namibia.
With amber eyes and mane of the newborn, a baby
cheetah is framed by his mother's legs. Cheetah
cubs just one month old are expected to take solid
food from kills and to walk long distances.

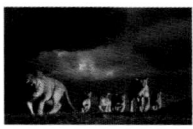

19 / Lion, Masai Mara, Kenya.
Against a darkening backdrop of heavy storm clouds, a
lion family with cubs roams through the savannah. These
dark rain clouds signal the end of the dry, hot summer.

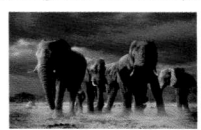

20 / African Elephant, Botswana.
Congregating on dusty ground, five elephants await an
impending thunderstorm. These heavy rain clouds are
forerunners of renewed growth across the parched land.

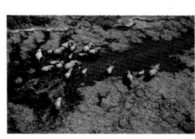

21 / African Elephant, Amboseli National Park, Kenya.
A herd of elephants wallow in Amboseli's abundant
swampland. Meltwater from snowcapped Mount
Kilimanjaro provides permanent springs, feeding marshy
waterways that remain lush throughout the year.

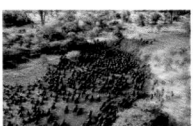

22 / Buffalo, Okavango Delta, Botswana.
An aerial view of a large herd of buffalo moving
from swampy grassland onto firmer ground. While
a buffalo herd has no actual leader, the animal most
familiar with the area at the time takes control.

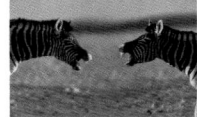

23 / Zebra, Etosha National Park, Namibia.
Face to face, teeth bared, two Burchell's
zebras confront each other. A strict hierarchy
dominates zebra groups at all levels, and they
fight fiercely to maintain their social rank.

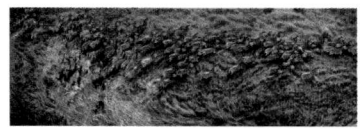

24 / Zebra, Okavango Delta, Botswana.
An aerial view of a running herd of zebras as
they wheel around watery grassland in the
Okavango. The strong herd instinct in zebras acts
to protect each individual against predators.

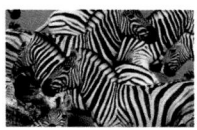

25 / Zebra, Etosha National Park, Namibia.
Easily startled, a group of zebras scrambles to escape from
the water's edge. The confusion of black and white stripes
makes it difficult for predators to target a specific animal.

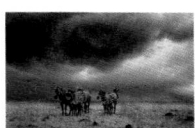

26 / Zebra, Masai Mara, Kenya.
A bedraggled group of zebras waits patiently in
a heavy downpour. The long-awaited rain will
rejuvenate the dry savannah and bring new life.

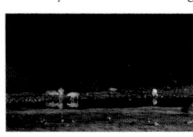

27 / Black Rhinoceros, Etosha National Park, Namibia.
Reflected in a water hole, four black rhinos drink
in the stillness of the African night; a fifth sleeps
nearby, and several ghostly giraffes appear in the
background. The black rhino is highly endangered,
mostly due to the illegal trade in rhino horn.

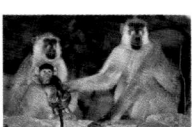

28 / Yellow Baboon, Amboseli National Park, Kenya.
Typical of their social nature, a baboon family
shows its strong bonds of attachment. The pink
flesh on the face, ears, and extremities of the
baby arouses care and attention from adults.

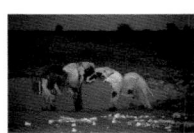

29 / African Elephant, Etosha National Park, Namibia.
In the receding evening light, two young elephants
spar by a water hole, trunks intertwined and small
tusks at the ready. Play between calf elephants is
important for learning social interactions in the herd.

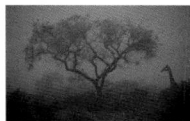

30 / Giraffe, South Africa.
In the blue mist of early morning, beside the silhouette
of a tree, a giraffe appears. This tallest animal on
earth prefers to spend the night hidden among
trees and bushes, venturing out during the day.

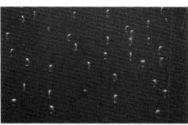

31 / Flamingo, Lake Magadi, Kenya.
Appearing from the air like bright commas against blue
water, flamingos feed. Spread out at regular intervals to
give each other space, these flamingos use their curved
beaks to filter the mud for small crustaceans and algae.

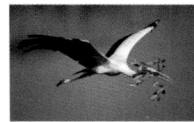

**32 / Yellow-billed Stork,
Okavango, Botswana.**
Flying low over water, a yellow-billed stork collects
nesting material in the Okavango wetlands. The
male chooses a site, usually in a tall tree near water,
and both parents work vigorously to build the
untidy platform on which they rear their chicks.

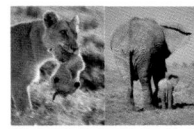

33 / Lion, Masai Mara, Kenya.
Hoisted by the scruff of his neck, a lion cub hangs
limply as his mother carries him to safety. Lionesses
display remarkably gentle maternal care, carrying
their young when the pride is on the move.

34 / African Elephant, Masai Mara, Kenya.
A rear view of an elephant cow walking intimately
with her week-old calf. Blood vessels at the
back of their large ears serve to expel heat and
cool the elephants in the African sun.

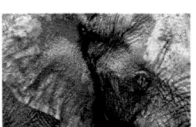

35 / African Elephant, Etosha National Park, Namibia.
A close-up of the lined face of an elephant, cooled
with water, then caked in dust to shield him from the
harsh sun. Elephants take great care of their sensitive
skin, which contains many sweat and sebaceous
glands such as the one seen between the eye and ear.

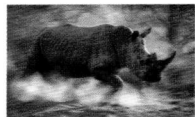

**36 / White Rhinoceros,
Kapama Game Reserve, South Africa.**
A cloud of dust rises under the trampling hooves
of a charging white rhinoceros. A charge by this
square-lipped animal, the largest living species
of rhinoceros, usually ends harmlessly.

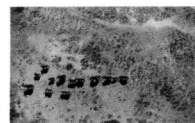

**37 / African Elephant,
Amboseli National Park, Kenya.**
A small band of elephants is dwarfed by the
vast, arid landscape. The dusty plain is formed
by ancient volcanic ash from early eruptions of
Mount Kilimanjaro, Africa's highest mountain.

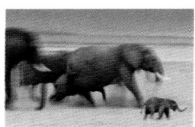

38 / African Elephant, Masai Mara, Kenya.
In a blur of rapid movement, an elephant family
advances across the savannah. Walking beside the
leading elephant cow are two calves, one just days
old yet well able to keep pace with the herd.

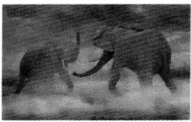

39 / African Elephant, Botswana.
Raising a cloud of dust in their excitement, two
elephants aggressively square up to each other
under gathering storm clouds. Serious fighting
between bull elephants, although a rare occurrence,
includes head ramming and tusk clashing.

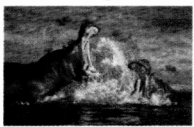

40 / Hippopotamus, Okavango, Botswana.
A quiet waterway erupts with raucous bellows of fighting
male hippos. Their gaping mouths reveal large tusks,
capable of inflicting serious, even fatal wounds. A noisy
display is often sufficient to deter the less dominant male.

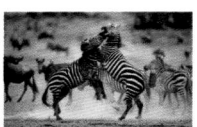

41 / Zebra, Masai Mara, Kenya.
Under the watchful eyes of background zebras
and wildebeests, two zebra stallions rear up, vying
for dominance. Adult zebras form hierarchies
and will fight to maintain their position.

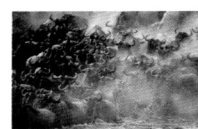

42 / Wildebeest, Masai Mara, Kenya.
Packed in a close stampede, massed wildebeests pour
down a riverbank and into the water to cross the Mara
River. Such concentrated numbers leave many wildebeests
injured or dead during the seasonal Great Migration.

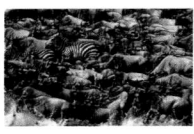

43 / Zebra and Wildebeest, Masai Mara, Kenya.
Hemmed in by a dense herd of wildebeest, two zebras
splash their way across the Mara River in Kenya. Mixed
herds of zebra and wildebeest are not unusual in the seasonal migration when both species search for new grazing.

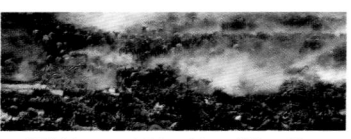

44 / Wildebeest and Zebra, Masaqi Mara, Kenya.
Reaching the Mara River in massed formation,
wildebeests and zebras plough through the waters to
make a crossing during the Great Migration. Large
herds congregate seasonally for this mass movement.

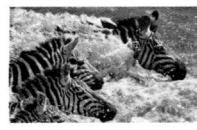

45 / Zebra, Masai Mara, Kenya.
Heads held above the churning water, zebras make a dash
across the Mara River. During this seasonal migration
towards greener pastures, these zebras are aware of the
dangers from crocodiles in watecourses along the way.

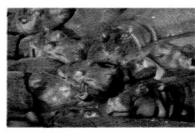

46 / Hippopotamus, Masai Mara, Kenya.
Lazily resting their heads on each other while
wallowing in a river, adult and baby hippos
doze in the hot sun. Known to cluster in large
social groups submerged in water, mothers form
nurseries and share in the care of their young.

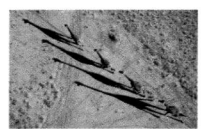

47 / Giraffe, Amboseli National Park, Kenya.
Casting long shadows in the early morning sunlight,
giraffes move swiftly across the arid scrubland. A large
area of Amboseli is comprised of an ancient lakebed that
becomes a barren and dusty plain in the dry season.

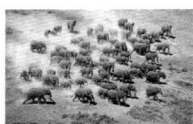

**48 / African Elephant,
Amboseli National Park, Kenya.**
An aerial view of a fast-moving herd of elephants. A large
herd of over fifty animals consists of "kindergartens"
overseen by cows, juvenile and subadult groups, and
bull elephants that usually lead the formation.

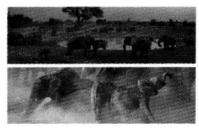

**49 / African Elephant,
Etosha National Park, Namibia.**
Encircling a water hole at dusk, a herd of elephants
drinks, then bathes in cool mud or protective dust.
This herd, replenished after the day's walking,
includes numerous cows with calves and subadults.

**50 / African Elephant,
Etosha National Park, Namibia.**
Dust engulfs the playful antics of young elephants as they
frolic on dry earth around a water hole. Much of elephants'
behaviors are learned rather than instinctive, so interac-
tion within the group teaches them vital survival skills.

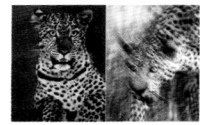

51 / Leopard, Masai Mara, Kenya.
Wide-eyed and alert, able to hunt in the dark, a leopard
peers over a rock at night. The fur of a leopard varies in
color from light to darker shades of brown, depending on
whether it lives on the high steppes or in the savannah.

52 / Leopard, Namibia.
Senses focused with concentration, a moving leopard,
camouflaged in tall grass, stalks his prey. The markings
on the fur break up the leopard's contours, and the
masking effect helps him to blend into the background.

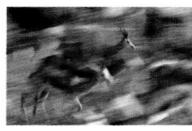

53 / Springbok, Etosha National Park, Namibia.
A herd of running springbok is blurred in motion
on the plains of Etosha. As their name implies, these
antelopes leap when running by arching their backs,
legs held together, displaying a flash of white hair. This
causes a frenzy of jumping throughout the herd.

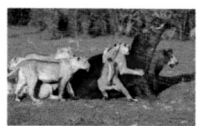

54 / Lion and Hippopotamus,
Masai Mara, Kenya.
Bloodied and distressed, a hippo raises his head above the deadly efforts of a group of lions attacking him. A formidable prey, he can, if caught off guard, be brought down successfully by lions acting together in a pride.

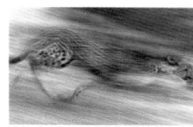

55 / Cheetah, Namibia.
The supple body and long legs of a cheetah create an impression of flowing motion as it moves. Naturally streamlined with a highly flexible spine, this athlete of the feline world can outsprint all other wild mammals.

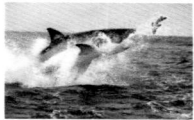

56 / Great White Shark,
South Africa.
Propelled into the air by the power of the attack, a great white shark seizes its prey. Despite its reputation as a man-eater, great whites favor seals as quarry.

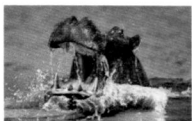

57 / Hippopotamus,
Okavango Delta, Botswana.
With its mouth wide open and jutting above the water, a hippo threatens any potential rival. A noisy and aggressive display is often sufficient to deter less dominant males.

ANTARCTICA

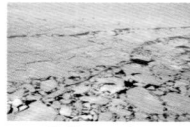

58 /Antarctica.
An aerial view of a white frozen seascape shows the tiny form of an icebreaker forging a laborious path through the ice. Twice as much pack ice forms in the Antarctic as in the Arctic, reaching a maximum area of some 13 million square miles (20 million square kilometers).

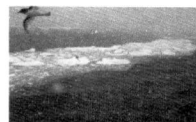

59 / Antarctic Petrel.
In the white fury of a blizzard, a flock of petrels gently wheels, glides in turning circles, and dives above choppy, icy, Antarctic seas, as if unencumbered by the relentless snow and harsh winds.

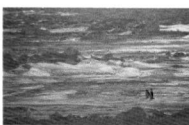

60 / Adélie Penguin, Cape Adare, Antarctica.
Penguins walk on a vast ice floe surrounded by natural ice sculptures. Adélie penguins are widespread in the Antarctic and are able to withstand a variety of harsh winter conditions including subzero blizzards.

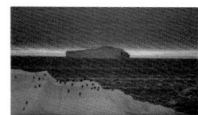

61 / Chinstrap Penguin, Antarctica.
Resting precariously, chinstrap penguins look out onto an icy seascape. A massive iceberg looms against the distant sunset. These penguins complete their fishing excursions in the open sea before returning to their colony.

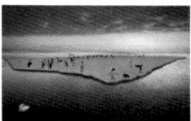

62 / Adélie Penguin, Cape Adare, Antarctica.
Riding a sheet of flat ice, Adélie penguins look out on a calm sea. Members of the same colony, they are resting between spells of deep-sea fishing before returning to the mainland to feed their hungry chicks.

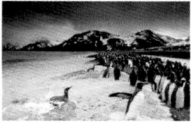

63 / King Penguin, St. Andrew's Bay, South Georgia.
Foamy seas wash ujp to the feet of a colony of king penguins. The impressive size of this breeding community is seen stretching into the distance.

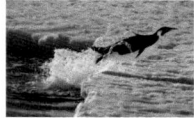

64 / Emperor Penguin,
Cape Washington, Antarctica.
Launching itself from the water, an emperor penguin dives onto the ice. The thickness of the ice shelf makes this mode of arrival on land a commonly used technique.

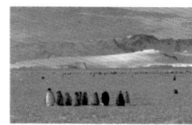

65 / Emperor Penguin, Cape Washington, Antarctica.
An isolated group within a larger scattered colony, two adult penguins stand by chicks on a landscape of ice. Still to acquire their adult feathers, these fluffy fast-growing youngsters wait to be fed by their returning parents.

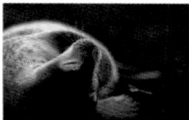

66 / Antarctic Fur Seal, Antarctica.
Lying peacefully on her back in dim light, an Antarctic fur seal sleeps undisturbed. These beautiful animals are named for their thick woolly coats, which once led to the mass killing of fur seal pups for their pelts.

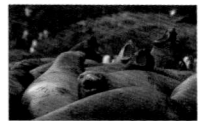

67 / Elephant Seal, Antarctica.
Elephant seals are extremely powerful swimmers, though on land their enormous bulk makes them clumsy and unwieldy. Normally solitary at sea, they come together in large shore-based colonies to breed. Even outside the breeding season they tend to lie together in smaller groups.

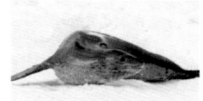

68 / Leopard Seal, Coulman Island, Antarctica.
A leopard seal rests in the midnight light of the Antarctic, where the summer sun doesn't set for months. Though heavy and cumbersome on the solid surface of the ice, his natural hunting ground is the water, where he becomes a formidable and vicious predator.

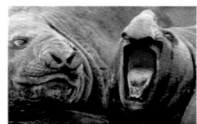

69 / Elephant Seal, Hannah Point, Antarctica.
With his trunklike nose inflated in excitement, a male elephant seal challenges another bull. These largest of seals protect a territory on the beach containing a harem of breeding females and will aggressively fight off other males.

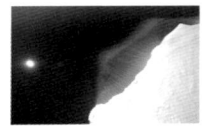

70 / Drygalski Ice Tongue, Ross Sea, Antarctica.
An aerial view of bright blue submerged ice. The
Drygalski Ice Tongue, still attached to the David
Glacier, protrudes into the Ross Sea. The Tongue
is an impressive 50 miles (80 km) long.

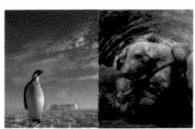

71 / Emperor Penguin, Cape Washington, Antarctica.
A lone emperor penguin keeps watch against an
Antarctic summer sky. The emperor is the largest of
all penguins, standing over three feet (one meter)
tall. A life span of twenty years is not uncommon.

72 / Elephant Seal, Hannah Point, Antarctica.
Showing face-to-face affection, a cow elephant seal
attracts the intimate attention of two seal pups.
Elephant seals give birth and rear their young
in breeding grounds located on beaches.

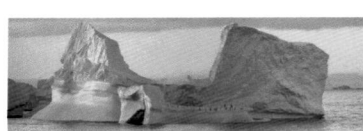

73 / Chinstrap Penguin, Antarctica.
Hitching a slow ride before nightfall, chinstrap
penguins perch on an iceberg in the calm sea. These
small penguins are dwarfed by the sheer scale of
the blue cliffs of the iceberg behind them.

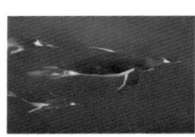

74 / Gentoo Penguin, South Georgia.
Elegant and streamlined in the blue water, gentoo penguins glide out toward the open sea. Unlike many other
species of penguin, gentoos often form lasting pair-bonds.

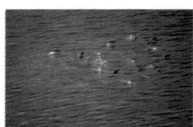

75 / Adélie Penguin, Southern Ocean.
Adélie penguins travel at high speed across the surface
of the water. Penguins are the only birds that "porpoise"
by launching themselves out of the water in regular
fluid arcs while continuing to swim forward.

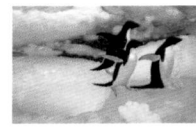

76 / Adélie Penguin, Antarctica.
Negotiating each slippery step on a moving ice floe, three
Adélie penguins hold their flippers wide for balance while
hopping towards the water's edge. Adélie penguins make
regular fishing trips from the ice shelf into the deep ocean.

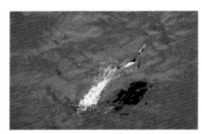

77 / Snares Crested Penguin, near Snares Island.
Viewed from the bow of an icebreaker, a Snares
crested penguin leaps high out of the water. This
species nests solely on the tiny Snares Islands, the
only New Zealand subantarctic islands that are
completely free of introduced land mammals.

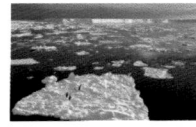

78 / B-15 and Adélie Penguin, Antarctica.
Four Adélie penguins linger on an ice floe. On the
horizon is B-15, the largest iceberg in the world. This
giant flat-topped iceberg broke away from the west coast of the
Ross Ice Shelf in March 2000, and originally measured
some 186 mi. (300 km) long by 25 mi. (40 km) wide.

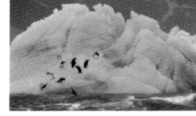

79 / Adélie Penguin, Antarctica.
Resting on a blue iceberg, Adélie penguins take a
break from fishing in the rough Antarctic sea. These
penguins live far south on the coast of the Antarctic
continent and on the barren islands that surround it.

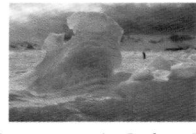

80 / Emperor penguin, Coulman Island.
Standing near a natural ice sculpture under stormy skies,
a single emperor penguin looks out across the frozen,
barren landscape. Emperor penguins are extraordinarily
tough and can survive the harshest winters.

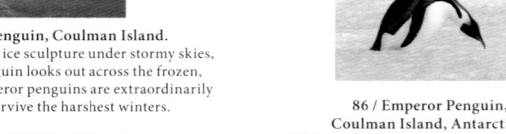

81 / King Penguin, Macquarie Island.
A dense king penguin colony, half a million strong,
occupies an area stretching from the shoreline
to high up the mountainside. It is a healthy sign
that such large colonies can still be found.

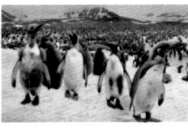

82 / King Penguin, St. Andrews Bay, South Georgia.
A vast colony of king penguins raises their chicks
beside cold subantarctic waters. Eggs are laid
from November to April, so at any one time chicks
of various ages are present in the colony.

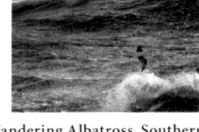

83 / Wandering Albatross, Southern Ocean.
Over the windy Southern Ocean, a wandering
albatross soars gracefully. These large birds ride the
thermals and are adept at staying aloft for long periods
of time, far from the land on which they nest.

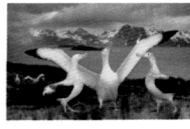

84 / Wandering Albatross, Southern Georgia.
Wings wide and head raised in a courtship display, a
wandering albatross advertises to attract a mate. Having
the largest wingspan of any seabird, they glide on air
currents for days over open sea, often following ships.

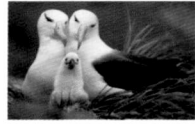

**85 / Black-browed Albatross,
Steeple Jason, Falkland Islands.**
Proud parents, two black-browed albatrosses sit with
their single chick. Both mother and father feed and guard
him until he is big enough to fend for himself. The adults
have an unmistakable yellow beak with a pink hook.

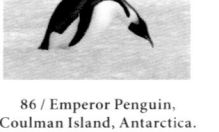

**86 / Emperor Penguin,
Coulman Island, Antarctica.**
With head dipping towards the ice, an adult
emperor penguin prepares to toboggan. These
penguins power themselves along with thrust-
ing feet, speeding up progress on land.

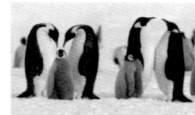

87 / Emperor Penguin, Coulman Island, Antarctica.
Two pairs of emperor penguins stand attentively over their chick. While it is the father who incubates the egg in appalling winter conditions, both parents feed and nurture their single chick.

88 / Emperor Penguin, Coulman Island, Antarctica.
A family group of emperor penguins is reunited as male and female reestablish their bonds. Chicks are frequently left alone while both adult birds forage for food.

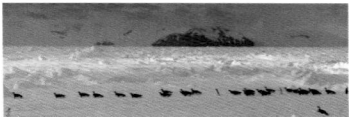

**89 / Emperor Penguin and
Adélie Penguin, Coulman Island.**
A line of emperor penguins, accompanied by several Adélies, moves steadily across the frozen landscape. These are the only two species of penguin that live south of the Antarctic convergence.

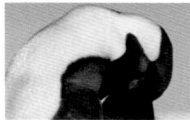

90 / Emperor Penguin, Cape Washington, Antarctica.
Beak tucked under his flipperlike wing, an adult emperor penguin sleeps with a bowed head. Although delicately colored, these penguins are extraordinarily tough at surviving harsh winter conditions.

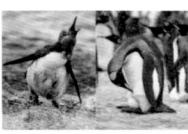

91 / King Penguin, South Georgia.
An ungainly young subadult penguin struggles for balance in the shallows. By about nine months old the chicks are sufficiently mature to join the adults at sea and hunt for their own food.

92 / Emperor Penguin, Cape Washington, Antarctica.
During a light snowfall, a colorful king penguin in a breeding colony bends over to check that an egg is firmly balanced on his feet. Keeping the egg off the ice is important for its incubation, a job shared by both father and mother.

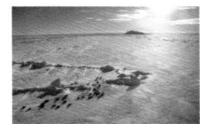

93 / Emperor Penguin, Cape Washington, Antarctica.
An aerial view of a group of emperor penguins traversing the ice on a clear sunny day, tobogganing as they return to their distant colony.

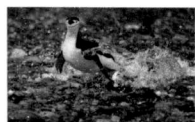

94 / Chinstrap Penguin, Antarctica.
Splashing across a pebbled beach, a penguin emerges from the sea at a run. Although not the largest of penguins, chinstraps are bold, energetic, and aggressive towards intruders.

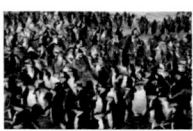

95 / Chinstrap Penguin, Antarctica.
A single penguin remains motionless amid a blur of activity. Chinstrap penguins can breed in very large communities, and a crowded colony such as this is an encouraging sign.

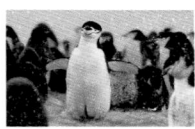

96 / Chinstrap Penguin, Antarctica.
In gently falling snow, a chinstrap penguin extends its flippers in a wide stretch. Behind this adult is a kindergarten of chicks covered with thick fluffy down.

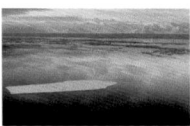

97 / Adélie Penguins, Cape Adare, Antarctica.
Set against a dramatic landscape of distant snowcapped volcanic mountains, Adélie penguins appear as tiny pinpricks on a sheet of floating ice in a calm sea.

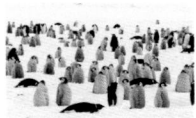

98 / Emperor Penguin, Coulman Island, Antarctica.
Chicks in emperor penguin colonies form large crèches, guarded by just a few adult birds. This allows the other adults to spend more time feeding at sea.

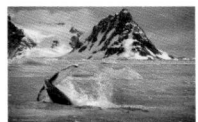

99 / Humpback Whale, Antarctica.
Against a panorama of snowy mountains and icebergs, a humpback whale slaps its tailfin on the surface of the water to communicate with other whales. Each summer humpback whales migrate to polar seas to feed on plankton.

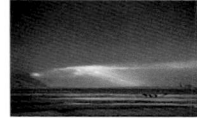

100 / Adélie Penguin, Cape Adare, Antarctica.
The sun's rays penetrate through the cloud, forming a dramatic backdrop. Adélie penguins leap high out of the water between ice floes in the immense Antarctic seascape.

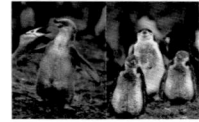

101 / Chinstrap Penguin, Antarctica.
A chinstrap penguin chick, soiled as a result of the cramped conditions in the overcrowded colony, is offered food by his parent. After foraging in the open sea, adults return to shore and regurgitate part of the catch for their young.

102 / Chinstrap Penguin, Antarctica.
An adult penguin overlooks two grubby chinstrap chicks, soiled from tobogganing on their bellies on muddy ground. As the chicks beg food from their parents, the adults, in turn, have their white chest feathers soiled.

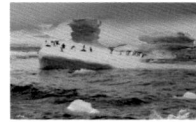

103 / Adélie Penguin, Antarctica.
In treacherous seas, Adélie penguins pause to rest on the flat surface of an iceberg. Like all penguins, they are powerful swimmers and travel great distances on feeding trips that can last for days.

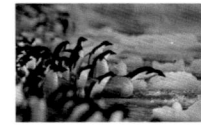

104 / Adélie Penguin, Antarctica.
Collecting in large numbers at the edge of an ice shelf, Adélie penguins begin their fishing expedition with an arcing dive into the icy waters. They fish in groups and will leap high out of the water back onto the ice when returning home to their colony.

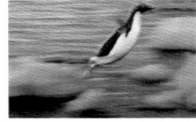

105 / Adélie Penguin, Paulet Island, Antarctica.
In a blur of motion, a bold penguin leaps from the sea onto the ice. The Adélie penguin is distinguished by a white ring around the eye and a short, partially feather-covered beak.

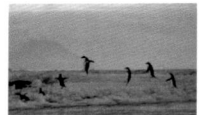

**106 / Adélie Penguin,
Cape Adare, Antarctica.**
A group of penguins launch themselves from the sea onto an ice shelf. They achieve this by transforming speed, built up while swimming underwater, into an upward thrust.

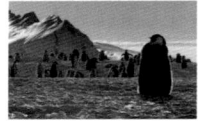

**107 / Emperor Penguin,
Cape Washington, Antarctica.**
Puffed out against the icy sunshine, an emperor penguin chick is insulated from the cold by his thick, downy coat.

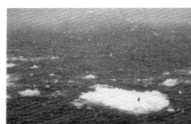

108 / Adélie Penguin, Antarctica.
Standing alone on an iceberg in a lashing storm, an Adélie penguin waits for the weather and winds to subside. When fishing in deep water, penguins use floating ice to rest on and ride out the choppy ocean waves.

**109 / Emperor Penguin and
Adélie Penguin, Antarctica.**
As if queuing to toboggan, a line of emperor penguins is watched by a single Adélie penguin. Ice formations tower behind them as they make their way toward the sea.

EURASIA

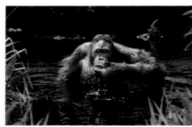

**110 / Orangutan, Tanjung Putting
National Park, Borneo.**
Standing chest deep in a river, an immature male orangutan scoops water into his mouth. Although large in size for an ape, this young male still lacks the beard, large cheek flanges, and fully developed throat sac that characterize the mature male.

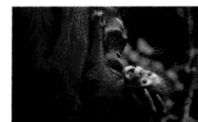

**111 / Orangutan,
Tanjung Putting National Park, Borneo.**
Relaxed in enveloping arms, a baby orangutan safely plays in his mother's affectionate embrace. This close bond serves to protect and shelter the infant while the mother teaches him self-reliance.

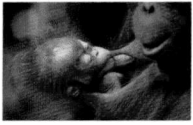

**112 / Orangutan,
Tanjung Putting National Park, Borneo.**
A baby orangutan eagerly suckles in the protective arms of his mother. He is largely dependent and will learn vital survival skills over a number of years.

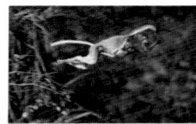

113 / Proboscis Monkey, Borneo.
A mother proboscis monkey, infant clinging tightly beneath her, leaps fearlessly through the trees of a mangrove swamp. Proboscis monkeys derive their name from the very large bulbous nose of the male; the female's nose is pointed and more aquiline.

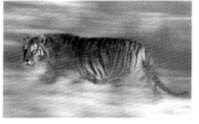

114 / Siberian Tiger, Northern China.
The largest of all cats, a Siberian tiger stalks through a wintry landscape. The pattern of stripes, common to all tigers, serves as an effective camouflage by breaking up the outline of the body in the dense forest undergrowth.

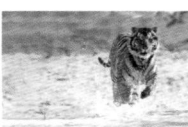

115 / Siberian Tiger, Northern China.
A charging Siberian tiger is a picture of unassailable power and strength. Yet, in reality, these magnificent animals have been hunted almost to extinction, retaining only a fragile hold on their very existence.

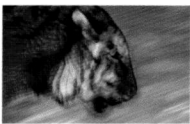

116 / Siberian Tiger, Northern China.
Dappled sunlight creates additional patterns on a Siberian tiger as he moves. The night vision of tigers, who hunt mostly nocturnally, is greatly enhanced due to an adaptation of the eye that reflects additional light back to the retina.

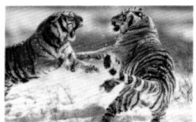

117 / Siberian Tiger, Northern China.
Conflict erupts as two male Siberian tigers rear up to challenge each other. Male tigers are territorial and solitary, continually marking the boundaries of their range and attacking other males who dare to intrude.

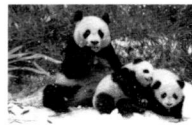

118 / Giant Panda, Sichuan Province, China.
With light snow falling, twin panda cubs play as their mother watches protectively. Usually bearing only a single cub, the birth of twins is a hopeful sign for a species on the brink of extinction.

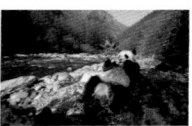

119 / Giant Panda, Sichuan Province, China.
Munching contentedly on his staple diet of bamboo shoots, a lone giant panda sits among rocks beside the river. Extremely rare in the wild, the giant panda has become a worldwide symbol for all endangered species.

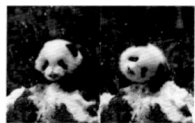

**120 / Giant Panda,
Sichuan Province, China.**
Playful and curious, a panda cub peers over a snow-covered mound. Initially white and very helpless at birth, cubs soon develop the distinctive markings of the adults.

**121 / Giant Panda,
Sichuan Province, China.**
With a jaunty whirl of the head, a young panda shakes off accumulating snow. A panda cub is weaned at about twelve months but stays with his mother for up to two years until she becomes pregnant again.

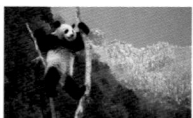

**122 / Giant Panda,
Sichuan Province, China.**
Against a backdrop of snowy mountain peaks, a giant panda balances precariously in the branches of a dead tree. Pandas, though slow and ponderous, are adept at climbing.

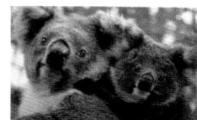

123 / Koala, Kangaroo Island, Australia.
By nature inquisitive and slow moving, a mother koala
and her young joey take a keen interest in the camera.
By six months, this furry silver gray cub is old enough to
leave the pouch and hitch a ride on his mother's back.

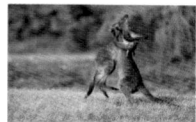

124 / Grey Kangaroo,
Kangaroo Island, Australia.
Two young male kangaroos playfully embrace with kicks
and punches. As they mature, such fights become more
vicious and assertive as they strive for family dominance.

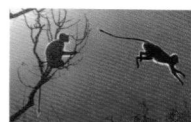

125 / Hanuman Langur,
Bandhavgarh, India.
Backlit against a golden sky, a pair of Hanuman langurs
leaps through the trees. Named after the Hindu god
Hanuman, these monkeys are considered sacred in India.

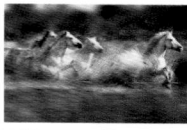

126 / Camargue Horse, France.
A band of white horses gallop through the marshy
waters of the Camargue. These compact and
sturdy animals are descended from a glacial wild
horse that was crossbred with Arabian horses.

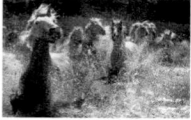

127 / Camargue Horse, France.
With wild splashing energy, a herd of Camargue
horses churn through the marshland. Groups are
usually comprised of mares led by a dominant stallion
and are confined to the area of the Rhône delta.

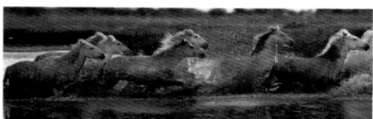

128 / Camargue Horse, France.
Running against the late afternoon sun, a herd of
Camargue horses surge through marshlands. This ancient
descendant of the glacial wild horse, though small like
a pony, compensates for its size in energy and speed.

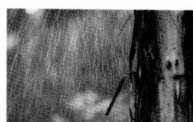

129 / Eucalyptus Tree,
Warrawong Earth Sanctuary, Australia.
Sunlight sparkles on water droplets as they fall in a
thirty-year-old replanted rainforest. The aromatic leaf of
the eucalyptus provides food for koalas and medicinal
oil for humans, and the bark exudes a sweet-smelling
gum as it peels away from the silvery tree trunk.

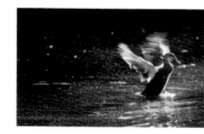

130 / Pacific Black Duck,
Warrawong Earth Sanctuary, Australia.
With a whir of sunlit wings, a Pacific black duck
rises out of a pond to shake its feathers dry. This
common duck with a boldly striped face is a surface
feeder or dabbler, eating water plants by dipping only
its head, neck, and upper body underwater.

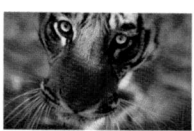

131 / Bengal Tiger, Bandhavgarh, India.
Startled from her sleep, the bright eyes of a Bengal
tiger stare up at the intruder. Bengal tigers were once
widespread throughout the jungles of the Indian sub-
continent. Due to hunting and habitat destruction, only
a few isolated pockets of these tigers remain in the wild.

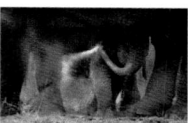

132 / Asian Elephant, Bandhavgarh, India.
Blowing dust from her tiny trunk, a baby elephant
shelters beneath the reassuring bulk of her mother.
An important national symbol that stirs the human
imagination, the elephant is intricately woven
into the fabric of Indian culture and folklore.

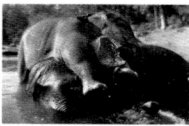

133 / Asian Elephant, Kanha, India.
A young elephant playfully climbs over his mother as they
bathe in the river. For 4,000 years, the Asian elephant has
been captured, tamed, and worked by man, but despite
this, significant numbers still survive in the wild.

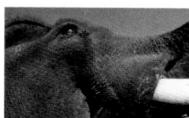

134 / Asian Elephant, Bandhavgarh, India.
A mature elephant bull, with mouth wide open, displays
his tusks; large, greatly extended teeth originate on
each side of the upper jaw. Elephants have been hunted
for their ivory since man first began using carving
tools and are still a target for poachers today.

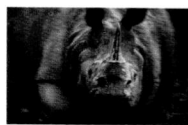

135 / Indian Rhinoceros,
Kaziranga National Park, India.
Heavy and threatening, a rhino charges menacingly,
defending his territory against intruders. Large,
horny plates studded with knoblike tubercles
cover his body, and huge folds of skin at the joints
and neck make him appear armor-plated.

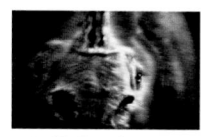

136 / Indian Rhinoceros,
Kaziranga National Park, India.
Blurred, moving fast, and almost too close to
avoid collision, a rhino thunders toward the
camera. Short-tempered and easily annoyed,
the rhino is handicapped by bad eyesight.

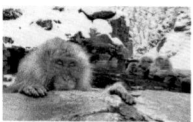

137 / Japanese Macaque,
Jigokudani National Park, Japan.
Chin resting on a rock, a pensive and content snow
monkey enjoys the warm water of a hot spring pool.
This most northerly species of monkey is capable
of surviving extremely cold, snowy winters.

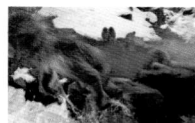

138 / Japanese Macaque,
Jigokudani National Park, Japan.
Fur streaming, a snow monkey leaps energetically
out of a pool. The double-layered structure of the
coat enables him to dry very quickly, thus avoiding
loss of precious body heat to the freezing air.

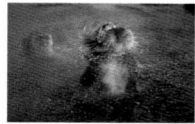

139 / Japanese Macaque,
Jigokudani National Park, Japan.
With a whirl of spray, a snow monkey shakes
excess water off his fur. These macaques are
the only nonhuman primates who regularly
bathe in the waters of natural hot springs.

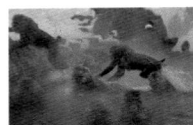

140 / Japanese Macaque, Jigokudani National Park, Japan.
Anticipating conflict, a snow monkey flinches as another member of the troop leaps toward him. Tempers can quickly flare in the overcrowded conditions of the pool.

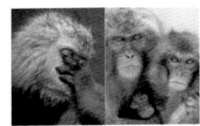

141 / Japanese Macaque, Jigokudani National Park, Japan.
Head in hand and seemingly deep in thought, a snow monkey rests at the edge of a hot pool. Snow monkeys are naturally red-faced, with the intensity of color increasing during the winter mating season.

142 / Japanese Macaque, Jigokudani National Park, Japan.
A family of Japanese macaques, also known as snow monkeys, huddles together on a winter's day. Snow monkeys are gentle creatures who live in troops, with both males and females sharing the task of nurturing the young.

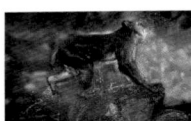

143 / Japanese Macaque, Jigokudani National Park, Japan.
In a shower of droplets, a macaque leaps out of the water and shakes himself dry. Despite the fact that the water reaches 176°F (80°C) and the air temperature can be as low as 5°F (-15°C), macaques are able to jump between the freezing air and scalding water without injury.

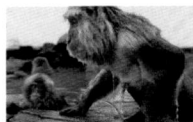

144 / Japanese Macaque, Jigokudani National Park, Japan.
A mature female macaque climbs ponderously out of the hot pool. Snow monkey society is matrilineal; although males tend to move from one group to another, the females remain in the same troop for life.

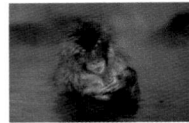

145 / Japanese Macaque, Jigokudani National Park, Japan.
Enveloped in steam, a solitary snow monkey examines her hand intently. These intelligent primates are capable of learning unusual skills such as washing their food, diving for shellfish, and bathing in geothermal springs. Consequently, a general social improvement can occur within the troop.

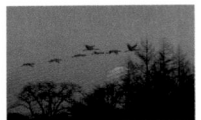

146 / Japanese Crane, Hokkaido Island, Japan.
Silhouetted against a soft pastel sunset, a group of cranes fly in formation. Once fairly widespread in Japan, only ten Japanese cranes remained in the Kushiro marshes by the 1920s. A concerted conservation effort over the years has resulted in a population of over 600.

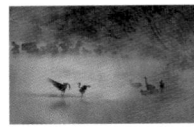

147 / Japanese Crane, Hokkaido Island, Japan.
Shadows against the golden mists of dawn, cranes begin a courtship display in which they bow, bob heads, leap high in the air, and perform an array of other beautifully choreographed dance elements.

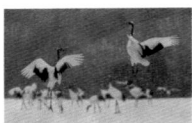

148 / Japanese Crane, Hokkaido Island, Japan.
With breath steaming, two rare Japanese cranes perform an elaborate courtship display. Mating pairs emit loud trumpetlike calls during their elegant, stylized dance, which establishes or further strengthens their lifelong bonds.

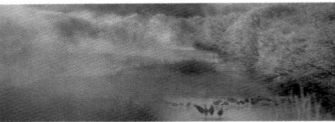

149 / Japanese Crane, Hokkaido Island, Japan.
Engrossed in their intricate courtship dance, a pair of cranes appears unaware of the falling snow. Standing about 5 feet (1.5 m) tall with a wingspan up to 8 ¼ feet (2.5 m), Japanese cranes are among the largest flying birds in the world.

150 / Japanese Crane, Hokkaido Island, Japan.
Pale sunlight of early morning glows on frost-covered branches of trees, which line the edges of the marsh. In the shallow waters, cranes collect to feed on the fish, amphibians, and plants that they gather with their spear-shaped bills.

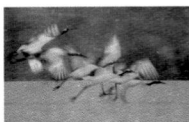

151 / Japanese Crane, Hokkaido Island, Japan.
Japanese cranes take flight in a snowfall. Known also as the Manchurian or red-crowned crane, this rare bird is an endangered species and was designated a special natural treasure of Japan in 1952.

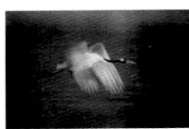

152 / Japanese Crane, Hokkaido Island, Japan.
A crane flies through a light snowfall. Excellent flyers in even the worst conditions, red-crowned cranes keep their feathers conditioned with a special oil secreted from the base of the tail.

AMERICAS

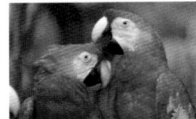

153 / Scarlet Macaw, Honduras.
Paired for life, scarlet macaws nuzzle each other affectionately. Prized in the pet trade for magnificent plumage and the ability to learn tricks, scarlet macaws are now endangered in the wild.

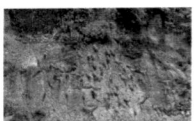

154 / Macaw and Green Parrot, Peru.
A rainbow of colors against the pale clay of a cliff face on the Tambopata River, scarlet macaws, blue and yellow macaws, and green parrots congregate at a clay lick. The medicinal properties of the clay help neutralize the strong acids in the fruit diet of these birds.

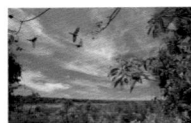

155 / Scarlet Macaw, Peru.
Three scarlet macaws glide over the Amazon jungle. The bright colors of these birds help them to locate one another in the thick foliage of the rainforest.

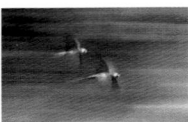

156 / Scarlet Macaw, Peru.
In a blur of vivid colors, two scarlet macaws flit overhead. The colors of these large parrots set against the dense rainforest canopy present an unforgettable spectacle.

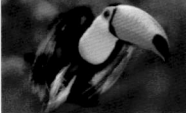

157 / Toco Toucan.
Indigenous to the South American rainforests, a Toco toucan is distinguished by its exceptionally large, colorful bill. Larger than the bird's body, the bill is used to pluck fruit and can also be used to duel with opponents.

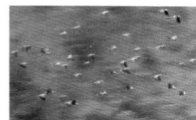

158 / Blue-Yellow Macaw and Green Parrot, Peru.
In a display of bright color, scarlet macaws, blue-yellow macaws, and green parrots pass by in flock. Green parrots, a smaller species of parrot than macaws, are hardier and more numerous.

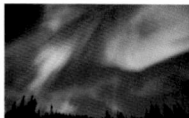

159 / Aurora Borealis, Manitoba, Canada.
The translucent glow of the northern lights (Aurora Borealis) shimmers in pale emerald green above the snow and forest firs. These luminous arcs and bands are caused by charged particles from the sun interacting with gas particles in the ionosphere. This effect is most noticeable near the poles where the earth's magnetic force is strongest.

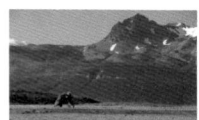

**160 / Brown Bear,
Katmai National Park, Alaska.**
Dwarfed by the landscape, two male brown bears struggle for supremacy. Once common across a vast range of habitats covering Europe, Asia, and North America, the brown bear is still the most widely distributed bear in the world.

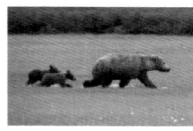

**161 / Brown Bear,
Katmai National Park, Alaska.**
A female bear splashes at a fast gait through grassy swampland with her twin cubs. Grizzlies usually give birth to two or three cubs. The mother is highly protective, defending them against any adversary.

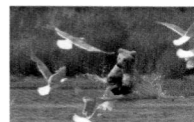

**162 / Brown Bear,
Katmai National Park, Alaska.**
Splashing through the water, a bear scatters a flock of gulls. The fur of brown bears varies in color from light cinnamon through brown to almost black.

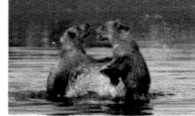

**163 / Brown Bear,
Katmai National Park, Alaska.**
Sparring in the sunshine, a pair of brown bear cubs plays in the shallows of the river. These young siblings, just months old, are unafraid of water and able to swim well.

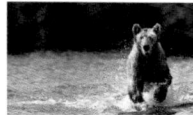

**164 / Brown Bear,
Katmai National Park, Alaska.**
Pounding through shallow water in pursuit of elusive salmon, a brown bear, also known as the grizzly bear, bounds toward the camera. Over short distances, this powerful animal can reach impressive speeds.

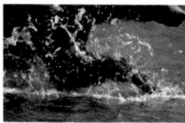

**165 / Brown Bear,
Katmai National Park, Alaska.**
Splashing through the water, a brown bear searches for fish. Although omnivorous, eating a varied diet of roots, berries, insects, and small animals, grizzlies make the most of the summer salmon run.

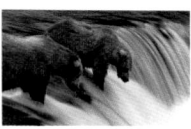

**166 / Brown Bear,
Katmai National Park, Alaska.**
Standing motionless in the rushing water, two brown bears fish for leaping salmon. The most dominant bears jealously seek the prime fishing spots on the waterfall and wait patiently for leaping salmon.

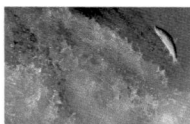

**167 / Sockeye Salmon,
Katmai National Park, Alaska.**
Leaping against an avalanche of water, a sockeye salmon battles upstream toward distant spawning grounds. Each year millions of salmon make this hazardous journey from the sea, running the gauntlet of hungry predators.

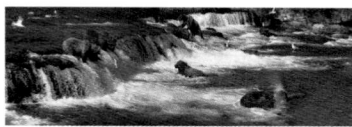

**168 / Brown Bear,
Katmai National Park, Alaska.**
Normally solitary, brown bears congregate around a waterfall to catch salmon as they swim upstream to spawn. This annual migration attracts the largest congregation of brown bears in the world.

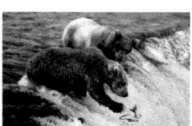

**169 / Brown Bear,
Katmai National Park, Alaska.**
A salmon twists wildly to escape the clawed paw of a determined hunter. Bears can either catch salmon directly in their jaws or swipe them out of the water and onto the riverbank.

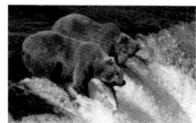

**170 / Brown Bear,
Katmai National Park, Alaska.**
With split-second timing, a brown bear lunges at a salmon as it leaps up a waterfall. This annual fish bonanza, which is high in protein, provides a welcome supplement to his normal diet.

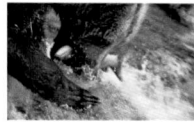

**171 / Brown Bear,
Katmai National Park, Alaska.**
Grappling with a wet, slippery fish, a brown bear endeavors to hold onto his meal. Although large and cumbersome, the grizzly is adept at fishing.

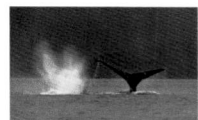

172 / Humpback Whale, Alaska.
Tail in the air, a humpback whale hits the water with a cascading splash. Whales communicate using haunting songlike sounds made up of complex vocal patterns.

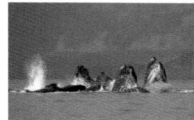

173 / Humpback Whale, Alaska.
Lunging to the surface, several humpback whales use bubble netting to catch fish. The whales encircle and entrap a school of fish with air bubbles, then rise up with mouths wide open to capture their prey.

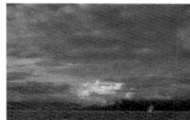

174 / Humpback Whale, Alaska.
Against a backdrop of wooded mountain slopes, a humpback whale surfaces in the bay. Known for their courtship displays, humpbacks, despite their huge size, can launch their bodies completely out of the water.

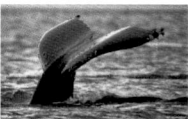

175 / Humpback Whale, Alaska.
Giant tail fin curved above the water, a humpback whale begins to dive. While other species of finback whale prefer the high seas, the humpback is a coastal inhabitant, swimming close to land and often entering harbors.

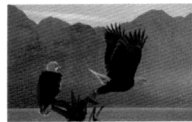

176 / Bald Eagle, Alaska.
Leaving his tree perch, a bald eagle launches majestically into the air. Pairs of bald eagles mate for life and return to the same nesting site year after year.

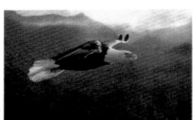

177 / Bald Eagle, Alaska.
Soaring effortlessly in the morning light, a bald eagle glides over mountainous terrain. The name "bald" refers to the white crown feathers. This large powerful raptor is the national emblem of the United States of America.

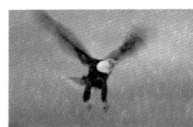

178 / Bald Eagle, Alaska.
Undaunted by falling snow, a bald eagle swoops down with a blur of wings. A type of sea eagle, the bald eagle is a large hunting bird who preys on fish and other birds, attacking them from above.

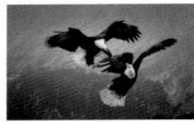

179 / Bald Eagle, Alaska.
With a show of midair acrobatics, two bald eagles fight aggressively. Their powerful talons and agility in flight enable them to ambush one another to steal prey such as fish.

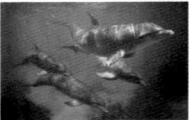

180 / Bottlenose Dolphin, Honduras.
Sun-speckled dolphins glide through clear tropical waters. A calf remains close to his mother for about three years and suckles for well over a year. The mother sometimes has assistance from another female dolphin who helps to protect the new baby.

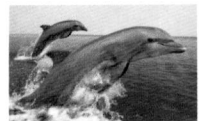

181 / Bottlenose Dolphin, Honduras.
Two dolphins porpoise effortlessly through shallow coastal seas. These highly intelligent creatures communicate with each other by using sounds (clicks and whistles), touch, and body postures.

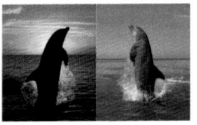

182 / Bottlenose Dolphin, Honduras.
Silhouetted against the setting sun, a dolphin leaps joyfully into the air. Frequently trapped in fishing nets and vulnerable to the effects of pollution, some dolphin populations are in serious decline.

183 / Bottlenose Dolphin, Honduras.
Bottlenose dolphins are among the most prevalent of the species and inhabit both temperate and tropical waters worldwide. More frequently found in small pods in shallow coastal waters, offshore populations tend to band together and can form groups as large as several hundred.

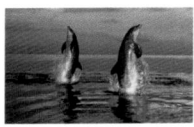

184 / Bottlenose Dolphin, Honduras.
Bursting through the still, reflective surface of the ocean, two dolphins leap in a synchronized ballet. A smooth, streamlined, and well-insulated body ensures that these marine mammals are superbly adapted to life in water.

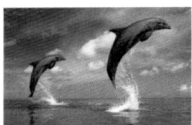

185 / Bottlenose Dolphin, Honduras.
With exuberant energy, two bottlenose dolphins leap high out of tropical waters. Though dolphins surface frequently to breathe through a blowhole located at the top of their heads, they can hold their breath for up to 10 minutes when diving deep underwater.

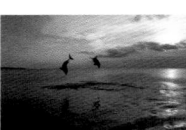

186 / Bottlenose Dolphin, Honduras.
Dolphins leap playfully in the early evening calm. Social creatures, they tend to live in groups or pods of fewer than twenty individuals and build a network of relationships with other community members.

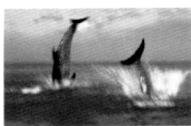

187 / Bottlenose Dolphin, Honduras.
Two dolphins crash down with an exuberance of wild abandon, leaving behind a blur of white spray as they disappear headfirst into the ocean. Dolphins are widely viewed as a symbol of joy and spiritual freedom.

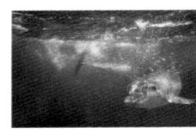

188 / Bottlenose Dolphin, Honduras.
Leaving a trail of shimmering bubbles in his wake, a dolphin reenters the water. Sensitive and intelligent, appearing always to smile, bottlenose dolphins are frequently held in captivity. Research has shown a dramatic reduction of life expectancy among captive populations.

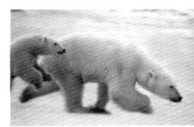

189 / Polar Bear, Cape Churchill, Canada.
Moving fast on icy ground, a polar bear mother and her cub forge ahead on their journey. Still dependent, a bear cub shows amazing endurance and can cover vast distances with his mother. At one year old he will begin to participate in his mother's hunting.

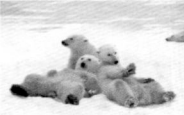

190 / Polar Bear, Cape Churchill, Canada.
Relaxing in the snow to conserve energy, three polar bears wait patiently for the sea to freeze at Hudson Bay. Seals, their principal food source, are hunted on the sea ice during the winter months.

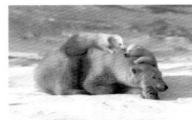

191 / Polar Bear, Manitoba, Canada.
Grouped together and resting intimately, two young cubs slumber on their mother's soft back. The cubs gain warmth from their mother's body and keep clear of the cold snow by resting on top of her.

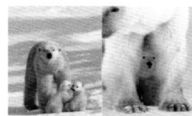

192 / Polar Bear, Manitoba, Canada.
Two carefree polar bear cubs, noticeably whiter than
their mother, play happily as she looms protectively
over them. Though prepared to defend them vigorously, she usually chooses to move away with them
rather than stand and confront any threat.

193 / Polar Bear, Cape Churchill, Canada.
Peering out from between strong and protective legs, a
young cub shelters beneath his mother's bulk. Mother
polar bears defend their cubs strenuously and ward
off much larger males who can attack the cubs.

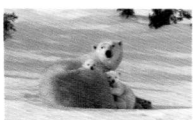

194 / Polar Bear, Manitoba, Canada.
Newly emerged from the den, a polar bear and her
two recently born cubs look out warily from a snowy
landscape. When first born, the cubs are tiny and
totally helpless, and remain in the den with their
mother until they are about four months old.

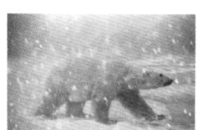

195 / Polar Bear, Cape Churchill, Canada.
A polar bear prowls purposefully beneath a heavy flurry
of snow. He is hungry and restless, eager to break his four-
month summer fast by hunting for seals on the sea ice.

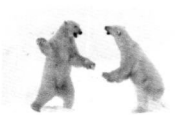

196 / Polar Bear, Cape Churchill, Canada.
Two male polar bears rise to challenge each other in the
snow. Normally solitary, these bears are forced together in
the autumn as they wait on the shore for the sea to freeze.

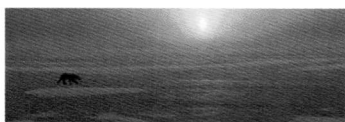

197 / Polar Bear, Cape Churchill, Canada.
Alone at sunset, a polar bear roams across a landscape
of ice. Polar bears conserve energy by taking long
steps, and their slow plodding gait enables them to
endure long migratory treks across the frozen wastes.

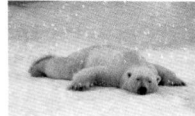

198 / Polar Bear, Cape Churchill, Canada.
Lying flat, a polar bear sleeps through a light fall of snow.
His white yellow fur is thick, warm, and waterproof,
enabling him to survive the most severe arctic conditions.

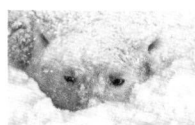

199 / Polar Bear, Cape Churchill, Canada.
Half buried, a polar bear waits for a snowstorm
to abate. Polar bears retreat to a day bed in the ice
of a ridge until a storm blows over and will often
awake covered with a thick blanket of snow.

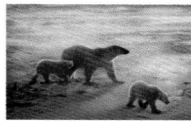

200 / Polar Bear, Cape Churchill, Canada.
A polar bear with her twin cubs moves through icy
wind and drifting snow at sunset. About a year old and
still dependent on their mother for survival, these cubs
continue to suckle but will soon begin to share in her kills.

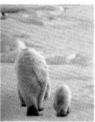

201 / Polar Bear, Cape Churchill, Canada.
A polar bear mother and her cub amble ponderously
through the arctic landscape. The word Arctic is
derived from "arktos," the Greek word for bear.

ACKNOWLEDGMENTS

The contribution my wife, Kathy, made to this book is immeasurable. She worked tirelessly, late into so many nights, researching and planning the trips. She also managed the image library, ensuring the economic viability of the project. And she was always there for our two children during my inevitable absences.

I am also indebted to so many assistants, guides, and friends, who made an invaluable contribution. Some gave much needed constructive criticism, while others advised me regarding travel and locations. There are those who offered hospitality in their homes, and those who gave constant encouragement. With every step on the path, I found warmth and friendship from people who were only too willing to give.

Susan Adie, Patrice Aguilar, Bryan and Cherry Alexander, Theo Allofs, Makoto and Shinobu Ando, Mr. Andreis and Aan, Christopher Angeloglou, Steve Baker, Miles Barton, D'amy Jean Benoit, Niall Benvie, Anne Blair, Andrew Boag, Tom Brakefield, Brandon Broll, Alson Brooks, John Bykerk, Doug and Gail Cheeseman, Alan Clark, Michel Contreras, Jim and Alison Cronin, Brent Dacomb, Nick Dibiasio, Chris Fallows, Keith and Christine Finnis, Biruté Galdikas, Nick Garbutt, Jane Goodall, Mr. T. Hagi, Joy Hanson, Sogo Hara, Nick Haywood, Julian Herrera Sara, Penny and John Hickey, Don and Susan Holmes, Jennifer Jeffrey, Alan Jones, Phil Jones, James Kateeba, Jeremy Keeling, Jean King, Charles Keim, Rob Lawrence, Michael Leach, Ashley Leiman, Jim Mahoney, Gillian Miller, Duncan Murrell, Fumie Naito, Chris and Gaye Nutbeam, Alexis Peltier, Peter Peristein, Russ Pinney, Bruce Plunkett, Des Pretorius, Jenny Quiggen, Ahmed Rajab, Michel Rawicki, Lente Rhoode, Tomanka Ole Selempo, Steve Shaw, Len Smith, Jill Sneesby, Tim Soper, Mike and Morris Spence, Keren Su, Tom and Rene Sucheck, Takafumi Suzuki, Roger Tabakin, David Tipling, Satyendra Tiwari, Steve Turner, Johann Vaatz, Stuart Westmorland, Janice Wickenden, Barrie and Helen Wilkins, Bill Yetz, and Hans Zwez.

Additional thanks go to Hervé de La Martinière, Audrey Demarre, and Benoit Nacci for their commitment to publishing this work.

There are so many omitted here, whose kind spirits contributed invaluably to the project, like the man who offered to lend me his spare boots after my feet froze in Canada. Many guides and assistants have been omitted to my regret, because of my own carelessness as a poor notetaker. My heartfelt apologies and thanks go out to you all.

—Steve Bloom

Captions: Kathy Bloom, Phil Jones, Brandon Broll
Scientific Advisor: Brandon Broll
The author has asserted his moral rights.

All photographs are by Steve Bloom, except:
Page 16: Des Pretorius
Page 118: Theo Allofs
Page 220: Keren Su
www.stevebloom.com

Project Manager, English-language edition: Céline Moulard and Magali Veillon
Editor, English-language edition: Erin Barnett
Jacket design, English-language edition: Michael Walsh and Shawn Dahl
Design Coordinator, English-language edition: Arlene Lee and Shawn Dahl
Production Coordinator, English-language edition: Kaija Markoe and Jules Thomson

Library of Congress Cataloging-in-Publication Data
Bloom, Steve, 1953–
Untamed / Steve Bloom.
p. cm.
Includes bibliographical references and index.
ISBN 978-0-8109-5611-7 (hardcover)
ISBN 978-0-8109-7237-7 (paperback)
1. Wildlife photography. 2. Bloom, Steve, 1953– I. Title.

TR729.W54B56 2004
779'.32'092—dc22
2004010029

Copyright © Steve Bloom (Text and Photographs)

Hardcover edition originally published in 2004 by La Martinière Groupe, Paris

Paperback edition published in 2008 by Abrams, an imprint of Harry N. Abrams, Inc.
All rights reserved. No portion of this book may be reproduced, stored in a retrieval system,
or transmitted in any form or by any means, mechanical, electronic, photocopying, recording,
or otherwise, without written permission from the publisher.

Printed and bound in China
10 9 8 7 6 5 4 3 2 1

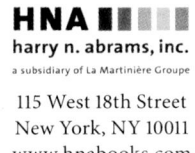

HNA
harry n. abrams, inc.
a subsidiary of La Martinière Groupe

115 West 18th Street
New York, NY 10011
www.hnabooks.com